More Praise for VIRGIL THO

D0498838

"A thorough, wise, and often witty book. . . . An impo..... , cultural history, well worth reading by those who lived through Thomson's era and, perhaps more so, by those who didn't."
—Gerald Walker, *Chicago Tribune Books*

"A masterly piece of work: exhaustive, penetrating, and eminently fair-minded." —*Publishers Weekly* (starred review)

"The discussions of Thomson's music [are] lucid and devoid of jargon. . . . The entire span of Thomson's life and work is covered here with scholarly diligence and a warm appreciation of a brilliant, perplexing, strangely vulnerable human being and original composer."
—Peter G. Davis, *New York*

"Indispensable to anyone concerned with American cultural history of the period." —Robert Craft, *New York Review of Books*

"[Tommasini] evokes the composer's critical ear and describes his music with words that bring us right into the concert hall."
—Nicholas Fox Weber, *New York Times Book Review*

"A clearheaded and fair-minded account of the life of a great American critic and a valuable composer. . . . Utterly convincing in its evaluation of Thomson's best work. . . . One of the most attentive biographies I have read in some years."
—Richard Howard, *Los Angeles Times Book Review*

"Writing with a contagious urgency, Anthony Tommasini valuably situates Virgil Thomson in time and place. His evocations of Kansas City in the teens, Paris in the twenties, Harlem in the thirties, the *Tribune* in the forties and fifties catch fire and themselves become history; and his sensitive, clear-eyed account of Thomson's sexuality amounts to a history of U.S. mores in the pre–gay liberation days."
—Ned Rorem

"Anthony Tommasini has written the story of one of the most fascinating composers and critics of the twentieth century—a musical biography that integrates life with music with unusual deftness, but also is itself musical in the flow of its prose. Besides all that, Tommasini's candor about Virgil Thomson's sex life makes his book a milestone in the maturation of gay musical politics."   —John Rockwell

"The best such work I have read on an American composer and his times. Anthony Tommasini has an innate understanding of Thomson's critical and compositional work, plus an ability to depict it (and the famous folk and exciting times that surround Thomson's life) with strong, vivid readability, yet with a judgmental accuracy that belies his close friendship (in Thomson's last years) with his subject."

—Patrick J. Smith, *Opera News*

"This compelling biography . . . explores the composer's career and milieu with a compassion and readability that earn the book a place on the shelf next to Thomson's own writings."

—Allan Ulrich, *The Advocate*

VIRGIL THOMSON
COMPOSER ON THE AISLE

VIRGIL THOMSON

COMPOSER ON THE AISLE

ANTHONY TOMMASINI

W. W. NORTON & COMPANY   NEW YORK LONDON

The text of this book is composed in Garamond Light
with the display set in Triset
Composition and manufacturing by The Haddon Craftsmen, Inc.
Book design by Jackie Schuman

Library of Congress Cataloging-in-Publication Data
Tommasini, Anthony, 1948–
   Virgil Thomson : composer on the aisle / by Anthony
Tommasini.
     p. cm.
  Includes bibliographical references and index.
  ISBN 0-393-04006-2
  1. Thomson, Virgil, 1896– . 2. Composers—United
States—Biography. I. Title.
ML410.T452T58 1997
780'.92
[B]—DC20   96-31695
                CIP

ISBN 0-393-31858-3 pbk.

W. W. Norton & Company, Inc.
500 Fifth Avenue,
New York, N.Y. 10110
http://www.wwnorton.com

W. W. Norton & Company Ltd.
10 Coptic Street,
London WC1A 1PU

1 2 3 4 5 6 7 8 9 0

Material from *Virgil Thomson* by and copyright © Virgil
Thomson is reprinted by permission of Alfred A. Knopf, Inc.
Material from the letters, unpublished writings, and other
published writings of Virgil Thomson is reprinted by permission of and is copyright © the Virgil Thomson Foundation,
Ltd. Material from the unpublished letters and excerpts from
the published works of Gertrude Stein are reprinted by permission of and are copyright © the Estate of Gertrude Stein,
Calman A. Levin, Director. Permission to reprint H. L.
Mencken's note to Virgil Thomson was granted by the Enoch
Pratt Free Library, Baltimore, in accordance with the terms of
the will of H. L. Mencken. *Peanuts* cartoon is reprinted by
permission of United Feature Syndicate, Inc. Frank O'Hara's
letter to Larry Rivers is reprinted by permission of and is
copyright © Maureen Granville-Smith. Material from the letters
of John Cage and the unpublished first draft of his Virgil
Thomson biography is reprinted by permission of the John
Cage Trust, Laura Kuhn, Executive Director. Material from the
letters of Briggs Buchanan is reprinted by permission of
Briggs Buchanan, Jr. Material from Betty Freeman's memoir is
reprinted by her permission. Material from the letters of and

the memoir by Alice Smith (Mrs. Frederick Madison Smith) is reprinted by permission of Dr. Paul M. Edwards. Material from the letters and unpublished writings of Jack Larson is reprinted by his permission. Material from the unpublished letters and writings of Kenneth Koch is reprinted by his permission. Material from the unpublished letters of Louis Rispoli is reprinted by his permission. Material from the unpublished letters and published writings of Ned Rorem is reprinted by his permission. Material from a letter by Roger Baker is reprinted by his permission. Excerpts from John Houseman's *Run-Through* and *Final Dress* are reprinted by permission of Joan Houseman.

All photographs used by permission. All photographs credit: the Virgil Thomson Papers, Yale School of Music Library, except as follows: Photographs between pages 144 and 145: insert page 3, credit: Dr. Paul Edwards; insert page 6, credit: Briggs Buchanan, Jr. Photographs between pages 304 and 305: insert page 1, top: copyright © 1977 Artists Rights Society (ARS), NY/ADAGP, Paris/the Man Ray trust; insert page 3, bottom, credit: Lee Miller, the Lee Miller Archive; insert page 5, bottom, credit: Kinsey Institute, courtesy George P. Lynes II. Photographs between pages 464 and 465: insert page 4, bottom, credit: Roger Baker; insert page 5, top, credit: Jack Larson; insert page 5, bottom, credit: Sam Falk/*New York Times;* insert page 6, top, credit: Beth Bergman, bottom, credit: Norma Flender; insert page 7, top, and insert page 8, credit: Betty Freeman.

CONTENTS

Acknowledgments   xi
Foreword   xiii

1 • The Saint Teresa Incident   *1*

2 • This Business of Being Baptists   *13*

3 • Virgil Acquires a Mentor   *28*

4 • The Pansophist   *39*

5 • A Lovely War   *55*

6 • I Didn't Want to Be Queer   *64*

7 • Loneliness in Pleasure at Harvard   *74*

8 • Virgy Thomson in Paris   *93*

9 • The Man Who Would Not Fight   *109*

10 • Sherry, George, Gertrude, Alice, and Susie   *121*

11 · Maurice   *139*

12 · Four Saints Are Never Three   *152*

13 · American Music Agitators   *173*

14 · The Flowers of Friendship   *196*

15 · Contacts and Contracts   *218*

16 · A Knockout and a Wow   *240*

17 · The Commando Squad   *267*

18 · Who Does What to Whom and Who Gets Paid   *296*

19 · The Trib   *319*

20 · 329 Pacific Street   *353*

21 · What Is the Question?   *378*

22 · Politics and Prizes   *401*

23 · Roger   *430*

24 · It's a Soft Egg, Baby!   *453*

25 · A Lord, a Genius, a Millionaire, and a Beauty   *476*

26 · Making Young Friends   *504*

27 · The Absence of the Presence   *524*

28 · All My Long Life   *546*

Notes   *573*
Index   *585*

ACKNOWLEDGMENTS

Although Virgil Thomson's papers are deposited in the Beinecke Rare Book and Manuscript Library at Yale University, it is the dedicated staffers of the Yale School of Music Library who maintain the collection. I am indebted to Kendall Crilly, the Mellon Director of the Music Library; to Ken's predecessor, Harold Samuel; and to Helen Bartlett, Suzanne Eggleston, and Kathryn Mansi. Many thanks to my former teacher Donald Currier, professor emeritus at the Yale School of Music; and his wife, Charlotte, for meals, a bed, and warm friendship during many days over the years of New Haven–based research.

Several other institutions with considerable holdings of Thomson materials were also invaluable: the Kansas City, Missouri, Public Library; the Music Library of the University of Missouri–Kansas City (Peter Munstedt, librarian); the Rare Book and Manuscript Library at Columbia University; and the Music Library at Harvard University.

Thomson kept a comprehensive collection of his papers at his Chelsea Hotel apartment, and without the help of the personal secretaries who worked with him during the last twelve years of his life, this book would have been impossible. Thanks to Victor Cardell, Louis Rispoli, Jay Sullivan, and Allan Stinson, my beloved friend who died in 1994.

My thanks to Ellis J. Freedman, Richard and Norma Flender, Charles Fussell, and James M. Kendrick, who through their association with the Thomson Foundation provided essential support.

Of the over sixty people I interviewed for this book, I was particularly privileged to meet with some great artists before they died: John Houseman, Lincoln Kirstein, John Cage, Otto Luening, and especially Maurice Grosser and his late-in-life partner Paul Sanfaçon.

Several of Thomson's friends became friends of mine during the course of this work. I am thinking in particular of Jack Larson and his late partner James Bridges, Morris Golde, Craig Rutenberg, Roger Baker, and Gerald Busby. I will always be grateful for the generous time and help given me by Kenneth Koch, Leonard De Paur, Betty Freeman, Lou Harrison, Donald Gallup, Betty Allen, and Jack Beeson. My thanks to Mr. Briggs Buchanan, Jr., for allowing me to use the unpublished letters of his father, and to Dr. Paul M. Edwards for entrusting me with the letters and unpublished memoir of his mother, Mrs. Alice M. Edwards.

I also wish to thank Steven Watson for kindly allowing me to read an early draft of his forthcoming book on the cultural history and genesis of *Four Saints in Three Acts*, which enriched my understanding of the surprisingly cohesive network of adventuresome people who worked in the arts in America between the world wars.

My thanks to the Estate of Gertrude Stein, which is directed by Calman A. Levin from the firm of Levin and Gann, for permission to use extensive materials, including unpublished letters by Gertrude Stein.

I am very grateful to another friend, Anne-Marie Soullière, who, while working for the development office at Yale, secured the support of two private foundations for my Yale-based research: the Goodwin Foundation in Connecticut, and the Jaffe Foundation in Rhode Island, run by my good friends Edwin and Lola Jaffe, who have always been there for me.

The first words of this book were written one wintry December at the MacDowell Colony in Peterborough, New Hampshire. I was grateful to win a coveted residency at that idyllic artists colony.

Several individuals read the final draft of this book and offered excellent suggestions, including Ned Rorem, Scott Wheeler, Tim Page, and, in particular, Vanessa Weeks Page.

I thank Hilary Hinzmann, my editor at Norton, for his belief in this book, his insightful reading of my manuscript, and his saintly patience with the slow pace of my work.

Many thanks to my partner, Ben McCommon, for helping me get through the rough times.

Finally, although perhaps I should say firstly since his contribution appears on the cover, I thank my colleague at the *New York Times* Bernard Holland, the chief music critic, for quickly coming up with an ideal title for this book when I had been stumped for weeks.

Anthony Tommasini
January 1997

FOREWORD

Virgil Thomson very much wanted this biography to be written. Yet it has not turned out the way he might have wished.

I met Thomson in 1979 through my colleague Scott Wheeler when I was living in Boston. Over the next few years I gave performances of his piano pieces, accompanied singers in his elegant songs, and was co–musical director for a college production of his vibrant opera *The Mother of Us All*.

In 1981, searching for a dissertation topic, I became interested in Thomson's musical portraits, which he composed just the way a painter might do a painted portrait: he made his subject "pose," so to speak, and started writing. In the course of my research, I contacted virtually every "sitter" who still existed, as Thomson put it, and the descendants of those who didn't. Since at one time or another, Thomson composed a portrait of almost all his colleagues and friends, when I was done I had in place a correspondence network of the most important people in Thomson's life. To move from there to a full-length biography seemed logical and interesting. Thomson, who liked my work that eventually became a book, thought so too.

When I found a publisher for the biography, Thomson signed an agreement granting me complete access to and use of his papers and materials, published and unpublished. We had already established a habit of doing long, taped interviews, and those, it was understood, would continue so long as he was available.

In general, the circumstances of my research with my subject could not have been more pleasant. I spent days at a time in his Chelsea Hotel apartment poring through his meticulously maintained files and storage boxes, while he poked around the place, dictating letters and handing out lists of errands to his personal secretaries. Often, when work was done, we cooked and ate together. I accompanied him to lectures and appearances, his "dates," as he called them. When in Boston he came to my place to meet my friends and eat my pasta.

Thomson was the most engaging conversationalist imaginable. You never knew what witty, insightful thing he might say next. Once, when I praised Wagner's *Tristan und Isolde,* which I had just heard at the Metropolitan Opera, Thomson said, quite straight-faced, "Yes, it's a remarkable piece. You can conduct it slow or fast, you can pull it or push it or do anything to it, and it always lasts exactly the same amount of time."

He was happy with my progress on the book, but not unworried. Thomson had worked hard to keep the spheres of his life separate, particularly concerning his homosexuality. In certain private company (never in front of ladies), he enjoyed boyfriend gossip and could be amusingly campy. But he did not talk of such things in public and essentially disapproved of those who did.

Naturally, there was some underlying tension in the initial stages of this project. "So what have you found out?" he would ask when he saw me going through a stack of old letters at his dining room table. Yet, from the beginning he talked on tape about his private life, his youthful folly, his crushes. "I say these things so you will understand the context," he would tell me. I'm sure he assumed that when the time came, he would be able to bully me into making any changes he wanted. And he was probably right.

As he declined over the years, Thomson realized that he would not be here when the book was done. Yet, he started talking even more freely, almost always adding, "Of course, these things are best spoken of when I am gone." I took this to be his tacit permission to tell the whole story. This is what I have done, concerning not only his private affairs but also his professional machinations. Thomson was a complex character, by turns generous, loyal, affectionate, inexplicably petty, and sometimes downright mean.

In the end, I think he felt that if the truth was to be told, it would best be told by a friend. In fact, the last time I saw him, two days before he died, though he was barely conscious, he wanted me to keep interviewing him. "Ask me questions," he said.

His deeply conflicted feelings about his private life were emblematic of what it meant to grow up "queer" (the only term he ever used) in the American heartland during the early 1900s. This aspect of his story is critical but, in a way, not central. The subject that engaged me for the ten years it took to complete this book was Thomson the creator who dared to compose straightforwardly at a time when maximum complexity was fashionable; Thomson the critic who used his post to skewer managers, promoters, and performers who catered to the status quo (and, when possible, unabashedly to promote himself and his allies); and Thomson the observer who uncannily predicted the current stagnation and crisis that would be the inevitable result of a situation where star performers who live off the standard repertory are valued more than living composers who enrich it. Indeed, Thomson had an aisle seat not just for the concerts he critiqued but also for the century he nearly lived through and reported on brilliantly.

Finally, a word on the unorthodox narrative shift that occurs in the final two chapters of this book. At the point in Thomson's life story where I entered the picture, I have allowed myself to enter the narrative. To write about events I witnessed in the all-knowing yet detached biographer's voice would have been contrived and false. So the last chapters take on the character of a first-person memoir.

For this I wish to thank the writer William Zinsser, who gave me five words of invaluable advice: "Write your own damn book." Virgil would have concurred. That's the way he always did things.

Anthony Tommasini
January 1997

THE SAINT TERESA INCIDENT

As soon as Lou Rispoli came back from lunch, he knew he was in for it.

In seven years as Virgil Thomson's personal secretary, Lou's daily routine had hardly varied. He would return around two-thirty, having taken a free hour for lunch and a paid half-hour or so for errands: mainly shopping for groceries, Xeroxing things at the downstairs copy shop, making bank deposits. When he got back, he might find Virgil puttering around the kitchen, a converted windowless closet in the Chelsea Hotel flat where he had lived since 1943. Or sometimes Virgil would be lingering over lunch at his all-purpose table in his all-purpose dining room, an Art Deco ebonized wood-and-chrome table that by day served as work space but at night could be cleared for Virgil's legendary dinner parties. Copland, Bernstein, Auden, Hellman, Lenya, and Loos had dined at that table; and Stravinsky had met the young John Cage there.

But most often Lou found Virgil in the parlor, asleep in his favorite armchair, his chin nestled on his chest, his hands holding a book propped open on his enormous tummy. Virgil could wake from his nap in an instant, bark instructions he had been saving and resume reading exactly where he had left off, or so it always seemed.

But on this day, Monday, November 10, 1986, Virgil was waiting for Lou, standing tensely near the ebony table, ready to pounce. He had found out about his birthday surprise and was not pleased.

1

In two days the Opera Ensemble of New York, a shoestring company that performed in the 449-seat auditorium of the Lillie Blake School (PS 6) on East Eighty-first Street, would open a nine-performance run of the Virgil Thomson–Gertrude Stein opera *Four Saints in Three Acts*. For Virgil 1986 had already been a year of festivals, concerts, and tributes in anticipation of his ninetieth birthday, on November 25. Radio stations had broadcast Thomson marathons, critics had published interviews and commemorative essays, and New York's Harvard Club had put on a fancy concert, exhibition, and party. A birthday bash for three hundred guests at the Plaza Hotel ballroom was coming up, a benefit for the American Composers Orchestra. John Houseman would preside, and an all-Thomson concert would be played, followed by a "Missouri dinner," the type of meal Virgil had grown up on: beaten biscuits with country ham, meat loaf with pan gravy, sautéed cucumbers, cornbread, Jeff Davis pie.

In terms of public performances, however, the production of *Four Saints,* the first in New York since 1973, was the main event of the birthday year. And as a surprise Lou had arranged for Saint Teresa to attend.

Saint Teresa was Mrs. Beatrice Wayne Godfrey, born Beatrice Robinson, who in 1934 had created the leading role of Saint Teresa I in the premiere production of *Four Saints* at the Wadsworth Atheneum in Hartford. To her delight, Virgil and his circle always called her Saint Teresa. As she surveyed her life from a small room at the Meadow Park Nursing Home in Flushing, Queens, a stout, eighty-two-year-old confined to a wheelchair but as alert and blunt as ever, Saint Teresa knew that heading the all-black cast of *Four Saints* fifty-two years back had been her grandest moment.

Saint Teresa had heard from Lou about the *Four Saints* revival and called regularly to check on the plans. "It would be wonderful to see it once more," she would say wistfully, assuming it was impossible. Lou decided to make it possible.

"I asked her if some way could be found to get her there, would she go?" Lou later said. "She of course was excited." Lou called the nursing home and obtained the name of a service that could provide a van with a lift. He called another friend from the VT circle, Peter McWilliams, a writer of wildly successful computer-instruction and self-improvement books who had taken a fancy to Saint Teresa. Peter agreed to split the costs with Lou. Transportation was arranged; the folks at the Opera Ensemble were alerted; Saint Teresa was to have an aisle seat; Peter would escort her.

Lou's main motivation was to grant the wish of a grand old lady. A skillful writer, a solid, gregarious gay man with the street smarts and jaded ways of a native New Yorker, Lou is a masterful facilitator. He thought that getting Saint Teresa to opening night would be a lovely surprise for Virgil and even more so for Maurice—Maurice Grosser, the painter and Virgil's oldest and closest friend, who had been part of the original creative team for *Four Saints*. Maurice was devoted to Saint Teresa. Unlike Virgil, Maurice visited her at the nursing home, especially after Peter McWilliams, who had a car, entered the picture in the early 1980s.

At the time of the revival Maurice was critically ill, close to death, it turned out. Yet he involved himself with the Opera Ensemble's preparations, deconstructing Stein's hermetic libretto for the cast, warning the director against lapsing into gimmickry, and getting everybody to trust the text, vaguely suggesting the discourse and daily lives of sixteenth-century Spanish saints, and the unperturbedly tonal music, a patchwork of hymnal harmonies, fanfares, anthems, oompahs, ditties, proclamatory tunes, and what Virgil used to call his "Missouri plainchant." Ill as he was, Maurice was determined to attend the opening and would surely be moved to see old Saint Teresa an honored guest there.

At Meadow Park Nursing Home everyone was excited. Few of the female residents on the third floor were as mentally sharp as Mrs. Godfrey, and fewer still had any idea of what her career had been. But they understood she was to be honored. "Our Mrs. Godfrey's going to the big city," the head of Meadow Lane said cheerily to Lou every time he called about it. Saint Teresa decided to buy a new dress. She asked Mrs. Carolan, the floor supervisor, to shop for her at Lane Bryant, a clothes store serving full-figured women, giving explicit instructions as to size, patterns, and cost—no more than sixty dollars. Mrs. Carolan returned with a forest green satin dress that was just right. For shoes, Saint Teresa's worn patent leather heels would have to do. She arranged to have her hair done up. The appointment from the visiting hairdresser was for Monday, the day Virgil got wind of the plans.

During Lou's lunch hour that day an administrative assistant from the home who had been in touch with the van people called for Lou but spoke with Virgil. When Lou walked in Virgil confronted him: "What's this about Saint Teresa coming to the show?" Lou was shaking. He said, "Well, Virgil, I'd wanted it to be a surprise, but guess what? Saint Teresa is coming to opening night. Everything is arranged." Virgil stiffened and said, point-blank, "No. I do not want her there!"

Lou was shocked. Some things could be undone, but not this. Speaking fast, he said it would be impossible, that a van had been hired, Peter was involved, Saint Teresa had bought a dress, all her friends were excited for her, it would break her heart. He tried to paint a cheerful picture and assured Virgil it would all work out.

Virgil snapped. "I do not want her there. I want you to call up and cancel these arrangements. I won't hear another word." He started gesticulating with his arms and shouted, "There's nothing more dramatic than an old fat black lady in a wheelchair making an entrance!"

Lou thought he knew all about Virgil's pigheadedness and ego. But stunned as Lou was, he was even more angry. "I can't do that," he said defiantly. "If this is going to happen, you are going to have to tell her yourself." Virgil stalked out of the room.

Lou immediately called Paul at work. Paul Sanfaçon had been since 1973 Maurice Grosser's lover. He maintained his own apartment on the Upper West Side within walking distance of the American Museum of Natural History, where he was a lecturer in Middle Eastern and comparative religions. But he basically lived with Maurice on West Fourteenth Street. Thirty-seven years Maurice's junior, Paul was steady and clearheaded and one of the few people who could talk back to Virgil when he got out of line. "Cut it out, Virgil!" "Oh just stop, will you!" Not even Maurice could say such things to Virgil.

Lou explained the whole situation to Paul. Then Paul called Virgil, and they had a long talk. Lou purposely shut the door to the parlor so that he couldn't hear them well. But Virgil wasn't doing much talking, it seemed. Nothing more was said about Saint Teresa for the rest of the day.

First thing Tuesday, however, Virgil demanded that Lou call Maurice and get him to tell Saint Teresa she couldn't come. To Lou this was utterly outrageous. It wasn't only that Virgil wanted somebody else to do his dirty work for him. It was that Maurice was so terribly ill. He had recently gotten out of the hospital and was home with a daytime nurse. Lou refused to call Maurice, so Virgil did. This time Lou eavesdropped, and this time Virgil did all the talking. "By that point Maurice was barely coherent," Lou later recalled. "I really don't think Maurice even understood what Virgil was asking him to do."

In the old days, when Maurice was healthy, he might have been able to handle it all. Virgil and he had met at Harvard in 1920, though their relationship wasn't really born until some years later in Paris. Virgil was capable of treating Maurice bullishly. Everyone had seen it. Yet if there was one person Virgil truly loved, one person he was truly loved by, it was Maurice. A courtly southern gentleman charged with a jolt of "Jewish nervousness," as Virgil put it, Maurice was guileless and, for all his physical jitteryness, unflappable. Like Saint Chavez, the character Maurice dreamed up to act as confidant to the imperious Saint Ignatius in *Four Saints,* Maurice had infinite tolerance for Virgil's fits and sputterings. Had he been well, Maurice might have settled Virgil down.

But he wasn't well. Even as Virgil spoke to Maurice, Lou called Paul from the desk phone. Furious, Paul called Maurice and told him to ignore Virgil, to do nothing. Then, seeing no way out, he dialed Saint Teresa.

Mrs. Godfrey could tell right away that Paul was not comfortable. He seemed to be "doing something he didn't want to do." He chatted about the opera. He said, "I hope the new Saint Teresa is as good as you."

"We'll see," Mrs. Godfrey said. "On opening night we'll just see."

"Well, oh, I meant to tell you," Paul continued, "we're not going to the opening night performance. We're going to go to a later performance. It's been rearranged."

"What?" she said.

Needing an explanation, Paul grabbed at the pathetic excuse Virgil had given him. "Well, the thing is, Virgil doesn't want you there on opening night. He says you're a celebrity. The new Saint Teresa is not, and she's nervous. If you come, she'll be intimidated. Her feelings will be hurt."

Lou remembers well Mrs. Godfrey's call later that afternoon. She was not crying when she called. But her pain was undisguised. "Through her talk, her hurt, I could hear the voice of an elegant lady with a tremendous amount of dignity trying to express her utter, utter disappointment. There was something grand in the way she talked, something which made me feel she didn't blame me."

She asked to speak to Virgil. Now that the news had been

broached by someone else, he agreed to talk with her. It was another call Lou shut the door on. But he overheard enough to know what was happening.

"One of Virgil's great accomplishments was his ability to charm, cajole, weasel people out of their bad moods, especially when their bads moods inconvenienced him. But I could tell he didn't get anywhere with Saint Teresa that day. My guess is she nailed him."

After the call Virgil told Lou to call the Opera Ensemble of New York and say Mrs. Godfrey would not be coming to opening night. Lou phoned them.

*   *   *

Why was Virgil Thomson so petty in the midst of so many honors? But then again, what did these honors amount to?

By most measures, Thomson was one of the fortunate few among contemporary American cultural figures. He was an early winner of the Pulitzer Prize for music, the only time the honor has been awarded to a film score (*Louisiana Story* in 1949). He was the preeminent American music critic of our time, not only during his fourteen-year tenure as chief critic of the *New York Herald Tribune* (1940–54), but throughout his whole life. His writing was not free of agendas and score settlings, but his incisive mind, salty tongue, and homespun style compelled attention. Virtually every word he ever wrote has been published and collected, recollected and republished several times over. Thomson was a distinctive American character: in Kansas City he was reared, at Harvard he was educated, in 1920s Paris he was formed, at the *Tribune* he reigned, and, later on, at the Chelsea he held court.

On the other hand, in comparison with composers of equal name recognition, Thomson's music has been ignored. "We all loved his music and rarely performed it," Leonard Bernstein declared to the press in his disingenuous Thomson postmortem. Thomson was convinced that the qualities he cultivated in his music—clarity, directness, textural simplicity—were the very things held against it by many composers and critics, and by the more cerebral academics who came to dominate the intellectual discourse about contemporary music after World War II. Ours has been an era that placed inordinate value on complexity and methodological rigor in new music.

Among his works are negligible pieces. Yet dozens of fresh, witty, poignant, and singable Virgil Thomson songs are forgotten about. His bumptious concertos, unsentimental choral works, and the *Symphony on a Hymn Tune,* which fractures the symphonic form and gleefully reassembles it with the broken pieces scrambled, seldom turn up on concert programs.

The fate of his operas was particularly frustrating for Thomson. Andrew Porter wrote in *The New Yorker* that every time he hears *The Mother of Us All* he is "tempted to consider it the best of all American operas" and, on calm reflection, would "hardly modify that beyond 'one of the three best.' "[1]

Yet how many operagoing Americans know it? Reviewing the Opera Ensemble production of *Four Saints,* the *New York Times* critic John Rockwell wrote, "It is a small but painful scandal that neither of the big New York opera companies has done a Thomson opera, since at least the two he wrote with Gertrude Stein . . . count as the finest American works in the form."[2]

Philip Glass has called Thomson "the godfather of experimental opera. Virgil was the maverick. He knew that the mode and style of operatic presentation, the content, the form—all these had to be renovated. When I started working with Bob Wilson, Virgil was the only person we had as a model."[3] Yet when Glass said this to a *Boston Globe* interviewer in 1988, he had never had a chance to see a staged production of *Four Saints.*

On a 1992 edition of the *Texaco Opera Quiz,* the popular intermission feature during the Metropolitan Opera's Saturday matinee broadcasts, three expert panelists were asked to name an opera with a saint in it. The panel was stumped at first. Then one person recalled Tchaikovsky's opera about Saint Joan. Another offered Messiaen's opera about Saint Francis. Finally, a panelist, straddling and stretching the question, suggested Liszt's oratorio on Saint Elizabeth and an obscure work about Saint Cecilia by a turn-of-the-century, Vatican-sanctioned hack, Licinio Refice. No one thought of *Four Saints.*

Thomson knew that his sphere of operations was a small place. "When I'm in a room where nobody knows me," he once said, "I know I'm in the real world." When recommending committees of artists prodded the cultural hierarchy to acknowledge him—as in 1983, when Thomson received the Kennedy Center Honors, during which ceremony he could be seen chatting amiably with his co-honoree Frank Sinatra, no less—Thomson was of course gratified. But what he really wanted was for his music to be played and respected.

For Thomson the issue was not whether his bottle was half empty or half full, rather that his bottle was not as full as Copland's. Or even Elliott Carter's. Let alone Philip Glass's brimming pitcher.

So a ninetieth-birthday production of *Four Saints* by a small New York opera outfit in an elementary school auditorium might not be glamorous, or what Thomson felt he deserved, or what he truly did deserve. But the little attention it was attracting he wasn't about to share. Especially with a long-forgotten and photogenic black diva in a wheelchair.

As if acknowledging some guilt, the New York cultural establishment really put out for the Opera Ensemble's production. Prior to the show, the Sunday *Times* "Arts and Leisure" section had a front-page spread: a five-column photo of Thomson and the stage director John Sheehan working with the cast and an insightful article by John Rockwell.

The opening-night audience was illustrious: Ned Rorem, Harold Prince, Lincoln Kirstein, Philip Johnson, critics from New York, Washington, Boston, Chicago, San Francisco. Snubbing the New York City Opera production of *Candide,* which was being broadcast on public television that night, Leonard Bernstein showed up.

Determined to attend, Maurice Grosser came. To avoid the crowds in the lobby, Paul had ushered the frail Maurice to his seat well before curtain time. Sadly, Maurice made it through just two scenes before Paul had to lead him down the aisle and home to bed.

But Saint Teresa was not there.

*   *   *

"I am the most fortunate woman to have had a friend like you for more than 30 years," Beatrice Wayne Godfrey wrote to Virgil Thomson in 1972. Seated in her nursing home room in 1988, still smarting from Virgil's slight of two years earlier, Mrs. Godfrey professed, "Virgil has always been my close, dear friend."

Before the premiere of *Four Saints,* Mrs. Godfrey's concert music career had been all a God-fearing black woman in the 1930s could realistically expect. A New York native educated at Virginia State College in Petersburg, the granddaughter of slaves, Beatrice Robinson spent three young adult years playing piano accompaniments for a touring evangelist, the Reverend J. E. Jeltzs. She sang in Harlem choirs and endured a seven-year marriage to Ivanhoe Wayne, a college graduate and a tall, handsome fellow who simply "wasn't husband material." In 1931 they parted for good "with a hug and a kiss in Penn Station."

But getting cast in *Four Saints* was "like a miracle." Instead of singing spirituals, ragtime tunes, and sentimental ballads, instead of playing an aproned maid in a pom-pom hat, as she had in a Radio City Music Hall production, she created the role of Saint Teresa de Avila, becoming a working colleague of Virgil Thomson, the producer John Houseman, choreographer Frederick Ashton, critic and *Four Saints* booster Carl Van Vechten—her dear "Carlo," who visited and sent birthday cards until he died.

She and Virgil, equally blunt and strong-willed, didn't get on at first. "Virgil didn't think I had any life, because I didn't fall over and have a fit every time I saw him." But Thomson recognized talent. His Saint Teresa had a robust, limpid, affecting voice, and her diction was natural and clear. In a later era, Beatrice Robinson might have become a Leontyne Price.

That same year, 1934, Beatrice Robinson did something to antagonize Virgil: she married Samuel A. Godfrey, a businessman of unsound health twenty years her senior with three children from a previous marriage. Virgil thought she was throwing away her chance at a career to become a live-in nurse, which is more or less what happened. After that, the Godfreys moved to Queens, where he struggled to run a home maintenance company, and she taught voice and piano and played the organ at her church. Every spring Mrs. Godfrey put on a student concert; every spring she asked Virgil to attend. He never did.

But he did help her financially, often: when Mr. Godfrey died in 1954; when she had an opportunity to sell her home and purchase a duplex so that she could rent half and finally have a steady income; when she had a stroke in 1978. When she entered the nursing home in 1981, Virgil and Maurice split the costs of her move. "You have never let me down when I sent up the distress signal," she wrote him in 1967.

He also made it to one Long Island affair, a 1977 testimonial banquet honoring Mrs. Godfrey, teacher of piano and voice and for thirty years the organist at Zion Baptist Church in Port Washington. Joining the guests at the head table in the banquet room of Manhasset's Lauraine Murphy Restaurant that day—Mrs. Godfrey, the pastor Reverend Watts and his wife, and Miss Helen Trow, a retired music teacher—was "Mr. Virgil Thomson, composer, world-wide lecturer of music in all facets," as the program book stated. After introductions and a speech by Mr. Thomson, the guests settled down to a baked chicken dinner and some uplifting songs, among them, "The Impossible Dream" and "I Want Jesus to Talk with Me."

Virgil seldom visited Saint Teresa. But he made sure she was invited to all his big New York events: concerts, ballets, his own testimonials, and every production of the operas. When she retired, he jostled the Association of Teachers of Singing into sending her the tiny pension she was entitled to. He regularly sent her Planters peanut bars—her favorite treat—whole boxes of them.

But this particular ninetieth-birthday *Four Saints* production was a sore point. There had been talk of a production at the Wadsworth Atheneum, where it was first presented. There had been talk of a production by the New York City Opera. Robert Wilson was eager to direct it somewhere. But Virgil had heard this talk before and knew better: "With the operas, I don't believe they're going to go on until I show up for opening night."

So here it was: the Opera Ensemble of New York would present the opera in the Lillie Blake School auditorium, and that would have to do. But Saint Teresa was not to come, and she understood why. "He didn't want to share the attention with me. It's stupid. It hurts. But what are you going to do? That's Virgil. He is so afraid somebody will take something from him."

Another composer might have considered that a picture in the paper of himself with his elderly, wheelchair-bound leading lady might have enhanced his public image. It might have informed today's audiences that Virgil Thomson had had the courage and imagination to cast his saints opera with black singers at a time when they could play only stereotyped colored characters.

Peter McWilliams and Lou Rispoli arranged for Saint Teresa to attend the Friday performance two days after opening night. The plans for the van having fallen through, Peter simply found a friend who had a car with a trunk that could accommodate the wheelchair. Maneuvering Saint Teresa was difficult. The stroke had incapacitated her, and she rarely left the home. But the four operagoers—Saint Teresa and her friend from the home, Miss Daisy, Peter and his friend Brendan Lemon—arrived at the school and got Saint Teresa to her seat. Before the performance, her presence was announced and the audience applauded generously.

Afterward an elderly man approached Saint Teresa to say he had seen her in the Broadway run of the original production. When the house was cleared, the cast came out to meet her, hug her, and ask for her autograph. Beatrice Robinson was again the great diva of *Four Saints,* surrounded by young black singers who saw her as a pioneer, and she was very moved.

For all the fuss and pain Virgil had caused by hogging the attention, the reviews of the production were poor. Discerning critics lavished praise on the piece. Of the designer Rouben Ter-Arutunian's contributions, the *Boston Globe* critic Richard Dyer wrote,

> His beautiful costumes and his fanciful sets—fashioned from rubber gloves, yogurt containers, soda bottles, plastic spoons, table-tennis balls, egg cartons, milk cartons, cigarette packaging and the cigarettes themselves—were not only an elegant tribute to the original designs of Florine Stettheimer, which were fashioned of cellophane, then a new commercial and technological invention, but also a tribute to Gertrude Stein's language and Virgil Thomson's musical style, which also takes things we think we know and somersaults them into something else by shifting the context.

But the choreography and dancing, he wrote, "were frankly embarrassing," and "only two of the singers were vocally outstanding." The conducting was "slack and there was insufficient precision and zest in the playing of the audibly under-rehearsed orchestra."[4]

The *New Yorker* critic Andrew Porter, whom Virgil respected immensely, wrote,

> The cast, directed by John Sheehan, conducted by Paul Dunkel, seemed to have no idea what Stein and Thomson were about. Simplicity, directness, candor, seriousness of utterance were missing. The Commère, Joy Blackett, distanced herself from the text with a non-stop grin. The audience sniggered at Stein's incantatory poetry, even during St. Ignatius' vision of the Holy Ghost descending. It was invited to enjoy a quaint, campy, all-black period entertainment when it should have been rapt in a wonderful vision of holiness, rendered—not without jokes, not without wit—in transfigured American speech and transfigured American song.[5]

Nevertheless, so great was the interest in the opera that the nine-performance run completely sold out. Virgil tried to talk up the show, telling all his friends to attend, congratulating everyone involved. But when Porter's review appeared his fortitude crumbled: "I agree with absolutely *everything* Andrew said!"

The director John Sheehan recalls that, true to form, Virgil had made a nuisance of himself. He insisted on auditioning the conductor, then selected a poor one. Sheehan had to promise Ter-Arutunian to keep Virgil away or else he'd quit the show. No one had anticipated the difficulty of recruiting an all-black cast of singers willing to work well under scale on an intricate ensemble piece. Without assured guidance the cast grew restive with the seemingly simple music and Stein's perplexing text. "It was pretty much a debacle," Sheehan admits.

Mrs. Godfrey, though unhappy, was tactful. "The show wasn't what I'd hoped it would be," was all Saint Teresa would reveal of her feelings. The whole experience wasn't what she had hoped it would be.

2 THIS BUSINESS OF BEING BAPTISTS

Y ou wouldn't have known from talking with Virgil Thomson that he had an ancestor who was knighted by Henry V on the battlefield of Agincourt. Virgil never brought it up. Perhaps he didn't believe it, since the ancestral name in question—his mother's maiden name, Gaines—kept changing, as Olde English names were wont to do: Gam, Games, Gaynes, and, finally, once the ancestral family settled in Wales, Gaines.

But a sixteenth-century pedigree, carefully maintained by his mother's family, states that a David Gam, having through his personal valor saved the life of King Henry, was knighted in 1415 and died some days later of battle wounds. Moreover, "there can be no doubt," the document reads, "that David Gam was the original of Shake-speare's character Fluellin in Henry V . . . as Llewelyn was the name by which he was known in the army."

A century later the Welsh Gaines family seems to have had a lock on the office of sheriff of Brecon County for nearly a century (1558–1657). The family embraced earls, knights, even a king of Wales. But Virgil never talked about his titled forebears.

There were American Revolutionary War heroes in his back-ground too. Virgil's great-great-grandfather Asa Thomson was wounded while serving under General Green in North Carolina. The Thomsons had come from Scotland, the first being Samuel Thomson, son of William Thomson, Gentleman, Blair Manor Ayreshire. Samuel settled in Virginia in 1717. But Thomson's roots in America go back even further on his mother's side. Thomas Graves, a London gentryman, found his way to Virginia in 1607, where he developed a tract of land he was awarded by the colonial government into a prosperous farm and became in 1619 a member of America's first legislative body, the Virginia House of Burgesses.

But landed gentrymen and ruling class Welsh were not the sort of ancestors an antiroyalist like Virgil Thomson cared to acknowledge.

It was his slaveholding, Southern Baptist forebears whom Virgil would tell tales of. "Farmers my people were, all of them," he wrote in his autobiography, "with an occasional offshoot into law, divinity, or medicine, rarely into storekeeping, never into banking. Baptists they were too, and staunch ones. I do not know when it got started in Virginia, this business of their being always Baptists. . . . In any case, all were Baptists, every forebear of mine known to me, and after the Civil War Southern Baptists."[1]

Virgil's portraying of himself in later life as an "unreconstructed Southerner" was, in part, a way of shocking his cultured New York friends. He was unabashedly proud of his slaveholding forebears. And the way he would matter-of-factly drop phrases like "the blacks" and "our blacks" into conversations was mischievous, as if he were daring those with liberal scruples to take offense.

Yet his people *were* Southern Baptist slave owners, and none did he talk about more eagerly than his great-grandfather Reuben Ellis McDaniel. In an oil portrait painted just months before his death on April 6, 1870, Reuben looks like an Old Testament prophet in a Missouri gentleman's wool suit—deep eyes, chiseled face, wiry hair, and a long white beard—a man of intimidating rectitude. Indeed he was a prophet, a Southern Baptist prophet, and a noted one.

Born in Prince William County, Virginia, in 1799, Reuben prospered as a farmer and storekeeper, eventually becoming the first postmaster of Sparta. But he grew restless with the increasingly congested, overtoiled countryside of eastern Virginia. Like all of Virgil's American forebears, Reuben got caught up in the westward migration that promised fertile lands and unbounded opportunity.

Leaving in the care of his pregnant second wife the five children from his first marriage, he traveled through Kentucky, Ohio, and Indiana. "Since I started out . . . I have nowhere seen a poorer country than the one I left," he wrote to Delia, his wife, in 1836. "When I get to St. Louis, I expect to buy a horse and travel through Illinois in such a way as I may be able to form a pretty correct judgment of what I see."[2]

Illinois turned out to be unacceptable, and it's not hard to guess why. During its territorial period, Illinois had legalized slavery in the form of long-term indenture. But by 1836 this arrangement was legally questionable, and the imminent end to slavery in the state seemed certain. Reuben McDaniel was steeped in the Southern Baptist conviction that God had created the Negro race to serve the white race and that, in turn, it was the white race's responsibility to convert, protect, and keep Negroes.

In the neighbor state to the southwest, slavery was legal, as a result of the Missouri Compromise. Reuben was somewhat perplexed by Missouri, officially and culturally a border state. In St. Louis he encountered a sight he had never seen before: a white woman waiting on a table in a hotel. But when he reached what Virgil Thomson used to call "Little Dixie," the central Missouri farming region that the Missouri River loops three-quarters around, he knew he had found the right place. Writing to Delia in 1839 from Holly Springs, he said,

> The town is situated in a country somewhat broken but the situation of the town is elevated and sufficiently level for health, abounding in as good spring water as I ever drank. I stopped at the largest hotel where there are about 50 borders, generally young men of all professions. I have not seen in the house or in the town one drop of spirit or wine of any kind. I have not heard a man mention that he wished a drink or proposed to any one to go to any house where it is kept for that purpose, though I understand it is kept in several houses here and sold by the drink. I have not seen a man who was drunk in the town. I have seen two who were under the influence of liquor but was told I was mistaken in one case and may have been in the other.[3]

Temperance was a family tradition well kept during Virgil Thomson's youth. Reuben's daughter Flora, Virgil's grandmother, decreed total abstinence. "No liquor crossed her threshold," Thomson wrote in his autobiography; "nor was it served in her children's houses. I have seen my Aunt Lonie's husband hide blackberry brandy in the carriage house and swallow aromatics after taking it rather than face her on the question."[4]

Reuben's ways were formal and stiff. But he loved his Delia

dearly. Everything he wrote to her, as in this 1835 letter from Baltimore, was tender and grandiloquent.

> Dear Delia,
>   At the approach of Saturday night when the bustle of business is over for a week and we stand on the threshold of another day of rest, we can but admire the wisdom of the goodness of God in giving that respite from toil without which labor would be past endurance, but we should feel a much livelier sense of gratitude when we contemplate that perfect and endless rest of which that is only a faint type. Saturday night by an association of ideas also crowd our mind with many pleasing images of home, of our firesides and those we love and whose society we are in the habit of enjoying for which enjoyment I would most cheerfully forgo this pleasure and gladly exchange this pen for a little chat with my Delia.[5]

This is exactly the kind of elaborate nineteenth-century speech that Thomson and Stein would pay operatic homage to, not without some parody, in *The Mother of Us All*.

Having found a desirable territory, Reuben packed up his household—fourteen family members and over sixty slaves—and traveled to Boonville, Cooper County, Missouri, a trip of 1,471 miles, 821 by land and 650 by river, in fifty-three days. Sometimes on river steamers, sometimes on rented horse-drawn carryalls, but often on foot, the McDaniel party—family, slaves, animals, wagons—traveled through central Virginia on rocky roads, over the Clinch Mountains in the southwest corner of the state and through the Cumberland Gap into Kentucky, northward to Louisville, where they boarded a steam ferry and followed the Ohio River west to the Mississippi, then headed north to St. Louis. Curiously, they did not take the winding Missouri River to Boonville, but traveled by land, in wagons, 157 miles, surviving nine days of rain, mud, fevers, and fleas.

Reuben's family prospered in Booneville. Through his mercantile business he sold staples to his neighbors. In 1844 he moved his family to Saline County, where his farm embraced five thousand acres. He opened stores in nearby Miami and Marshall. He helped found Baptist churches, then built one in 1851 on his own land in Bethel. He was one of five men who charted William Jewell College in Liberty. He became a Saline County judge and cofounded the *Marshall Democrat* newspaper. He died at seventy-one, leaving behind a thriving estate and twelve children, and unreconciled to the Confederate defeat.

One of the younger members of that migration from Virginia to Missouri was Reuben's eleven-year-old daughter, Flora Elizabeth, who would become Virgil Thomson's paternal grandmother. It was chiefly through Grandmother Flora, a "quietly wonderful storyteller," that tales of the McDaniel clan and the Civil War were passed down to Virgil.

In Bethel, Flora worked for ten years as a Sunday school teacher and assumed the duties of the eldest unmarried daughter in her father's house—until 1856, when she married Quincy Adams Thomson, a Baptist minister's son. "Quincy Adams Thomson, wiry and passionate, looks in photograph like a hothead," Virgil Thomson wrote.[6] When the war broke out, eleven of Quincy's brothers and brothers-in-law were serving in the Confederate army. He was already a thirty-four-year-old father of two. Though his wife was carrying her third child and he had pledged to maintain the family farm, he could no longer bear being out of the war. He enlisted in a makeshift regiment. Four months later he was dead, probably of typhoid, having been captured and transported in an open boxcar to a prison in St. Louis. His body was shipped to his widow and buried in the graveyard of their county church, where Virgil Thomson rests today.

Quincy, Jr., born on January 12, 1862, was only eighteen days old when his father died. At the funeral he "was lifted up for one long look at his male parent," Virgil Thomson wrote. "Later, from being so vividly told and retold the event, he almost remembered it."[7]

After Quincy left her a widow, Flora stubbornly refused to move back into her father's house, as Virgil Thomson recalled:

> She stayed on her farm, ran it with her own Negroes, not all of them available after Emancipation, and brought up her babies. If marauding troops came by, Blacklegs or Scalawags, she offered them food, which they would have taken anyway and beddings-down in the hay barn. She never locked her door, esteeming such precaution distrustful of God and futile against armies.[8]

Virgil was never sure how his grandmother managed to send her three children to college. The way his tight-lipped father explained it, after Quincy's death there was the equivalent of a bankruptcy sale.

Flora's farm, furniture, and belongings were bought by her father, Reuben, who after the war lost his large household of slaves, but still had dependable farming and mercantile businesses. Having bought it all, Reuben then simply gave everything back to his daughter. Why the public sale even took place, Virgil never understood.

Flora also inherited $4,000 from Quincy's father, Reuben Yancey Thomson, a liberal-minded Kentucky-born preacher and farmer who had resettled in Missouri. She must have been an able head of household. By the 1870s, with farm affairs under control, Flora was spending winters in the more up-to-date town of Liberty, north of Kansas City, so the children could be properly educated. Eventually, her oldest child, Virgil's uncle Reuben, attended William Jewell, the college his grandfather had helped found. The middle child, Virgil's aunt Leona, studied at a Baptist seminary for women in Columbia. Virgil's father, Quincy Alfred, the child most devoted to his mother, also graduated from William Jewell, where he studied Latin, English literature, and philosophy.

Flora had prayed for her youngest child to hear the call, but he "had early become resigned to not hearing it," Thomson wrote. Quincy loved working the soil, making and fixing things, all the "ingenuities done by hands with wood and stone, loved everything about life in the country from Monday's sunrise to Sunday's dinner with guests brought home from church." So when Quincy, at twenty-one, married Clara May Gaines, then eighteen, his mother, "respectful of his needs," divided her land and gave him his share. "Young Quincy thereupon built a frame cottage and moved into it with his bride."[9]

Clara May Gaines, born in Boone County, Kentucky, in 1865, had also made the westward trek with her entire family to a new life in Missouri. Her father, Benjamin Watts Gaines, born in 1832 and descended from a member of the Virginia House of Burgesses, was a type altogether different from the pioneering McDaniels men. When the war broke out, Benjamin offered himself to the Confederate troops, but was rejected for lacking two fingers. "He does not seem to have insisted on showing them how remarkable a shot he was with the other three," Virgil Thomson would write. In Slater, where he settled his family after the war, he bought a farm, sold it, built a house, retired at fifty, and never did a stroke of work again except for gardening. He died at a hundred.

When speaking of his father, Virgil Thomson barely digressed from the portrait he presented in his autobiography: Quincy, the man of the soil, forced by family necessities to relocate to the city, to become first a shopkeeper and then a civil servant; Quincy, the stolid Baptist and church deacon who loved his wife and accepted responsibilities uncomplainingly.

Quincy seldom left Missouri and died in 1943 before Virgil's New York circle could get to know him. But Virgil's mother, Clara May, known all her life as May, survived her husband by fourteen years and during that period visited New York almost annually. So Virgil's sweet accounts of his mother as a southern belle homemaker and hostess could later be challenged by firsthand observers.

"Gracious southern hostess? That was Virgil's fantasy!" said Minna Lederman, the pioneering writer on music and an early champion of Thomson the critic. Virgil considered her an insightful editor. She was insightful about people, too, and didn't mince words.

"May Thomson was dull, extremely ordinary and pouty," Lederman said flatly. And she knew her fairly well. When May visited New York, it was Minna whom Virgil often asked to escort his mother around town. "They'd do those ladies' things," Virgil said, "go to shops, have lunch out."

Others remember May as a somewhat stiff, well-meaning woman who was grappling with her son's lifestyle, which she couldn't possibly—and, in truth, didn't want to—understand. Virgil's great friend Maurice Grosser, himself a southern gentleman, recognized in May the southern hostess Virgil believed her to be. To be a southern hostess did not mean you never expressed displeasure. It meant you always spoke with tact. May Thomson had tact. "That's where Virgil learned it from," Maurice once said.

Quincy and May were married in 1883, and Ruby Richerson, their first child, came two years later. But during those years, as Thomson told it, his mother for the first time knew the solitude of farm life. Quincy was busy all day, every day out of the house. May went through her first pregnancy alone and unhappy. "What tactful softening up of my father's hard passion for the soil went on in the next few years one can only guess," Thomson wrote. "But he did decide eventually on selling the farm. And so they moved to a tiny village called Nelson, where with his newly realized capital he set up a hardware store and tin shop."

To his surprise, Quincy enjoyed the work: cutting tin and iron building materials, fitting stovepipes, stocking and selling tools. But he was a farmer, not a business man, as Thomson would later explain:

> He was a kind fellow and when people couldn't pay their bills, he wouldn't press them. So at the end of a year or so, he didn't have any money left. I later discovered that 1893 was the year of an enormous depression, so lots of people couldn't pay their bills. But I never heard him mention this situation, which was national. I'm sure he probably thought it was his fault.[10]

By 1894, six years after arriving in Nelson, they were broke. Like most hard-pressed small-town families, they thought their only recourse was a move to the city. Adding to their bad memories of Nelson and their desire for change was a family tragedy. In 1890 the couple's second child, Hazel Louise, was born. She died eighteen months later, as Thomson was to report:

> The child caught diphtheria, and in those days there was no serum for it. Either you got over it or you didn't. So the child was about to die and the doctor gave them an option of an operation which would put a hole in her throat so she could breathe. The child would never speak correctly, and the operation would be done without anesthesia—she would be in great pain. She was only two and, presumably, still innocent. If she died she'd go to heaven. If she lived she'd have a terrible life. So he made the decision not to have the operation. I was always very impressed, not with the decision, but with him for making it. When I was young, he spoke of this all the time. We lived with stories like that. Ruby was seven at the time. There was a large portrait of the child around the house.[11]

So the family went to the city, and Quincy Thomson found work as a conductor on the cable cars. For the first year the Thomsons shared an apartment with May's sister Lulu and her husband, Charlie Garnett, another former farm boy. Then Charlie helped Quincy locate an apartment on Tenth and Virginia. It was there on November 25, 1896, that the third and last Thomson child was born. And it was in honor of the baby's uncle, who had been such a support, that the boy was named Virgil Garnett.

"Thirty-five years old, with a wife and two children in his charge and with no money at all save a modest wage, [my father] did not look, to prosperous Saline County, exactly successful," Thomson would write. Steady work and a home of his own became Quincy's driving priorities. Within two years he achieved them. He passed the civil service exams and was appointed to the post office. With a bank mortgage and a loan of $3,000 from his sister's husband (Leona had married a prosperous man), Quincy purchased a lot on Wabash Avenue, at 2613, and had built under his supervision a two-story frame house of his own design. Back then the neighborhood was sparsely settled. The lots were roomy with large backyards for gardening. The streets were tree lined.

Today the area is a well-kept, predominantly black neighborhood. Many more houses have since been sandwiched between the homes of Virgil Thomson's memory. Trees have been lost to cement sidewalks and curbs. The house at 2613 Wabash still stands, occupied by a young black construction worker, who was startled but courteous when an inquisitive biographer knocked unannounced on his door. He had never heard of Virgil Thomson but was delighted to see his home described so lovingly in Thomson's book.

Virgil Thomson begins his autobiography by poking fun at Kansas City, Kansas, just the way "any Southern child" from Kansas City, Missouri, was taught to do by older friends.

> Kansas, the whole state, was dry. And moralistic about everything. . . . Though Kansas had always been a Free State and supported right in Kansas-City-Kansas a Negro college, most of our colored brethren preferred Missouri, where life was more fun. The truth is that Kansas was Yankee territory, windy and dry, with blue laws on its books; and the women from there wore unbecoming clothes and funny hats.[12]

Thomson always described his hometown as a bastion of southern customs and manners, with prominent businessmen from old Confederate families and, occasionally, a Yankee banker. This was a romanticized portrayal. Comparing Kansas City with nearby Independence, the hometown of Harry Truman, the biographer David McCullough writes, "Kansas City was a brassy Yankee town, 'moneywise' and full of 'new-people.' Independence was southern in both spirit and pace."[13]

What is indisputable, and what Thomson constantly pointed out to New Yorkers who had never been there, was that the Kansas City of his youth was a bustling metropolis of 200,000. Historically, its situation—at a confluence of rivers, the Missouri and Kansas, and wagon trails—had given it a pivotal role in the country's westward expansion. By the turn of the century it was second only to Chicago as a transportation center, the terminus of some twenty railroads, and boasted an extensive system of boulevards, the nation's third-largest municipal park, and a "political machine whose corruption was for nearly half a century an example to the nation," as Virgil later wrote.

Yet no visitor back then would have mistaken Kansas City—still part cow town, second also to Chicago in the size and smell of its stockyards—for Republican, eastward-looking, cosmopolitan St. Louis. Thomson remembered seeing "cowboys and Indians hanging around the railway station."

In 1900 Kansas City captured the Democratic National Convention, beating out Chicago. This was largely due to the Democratic partisanship of its populace and the existence of a huge downtown convention hall, built in the late 1870s and inaugurated with a band concert by young John Philip Sousa. But three months before the convention, the hall burned to the ground. Undaunted, the citizens simply set to work, constructing a new hall with modern electrical lighting. By the eve of the convention, the completed facility was festooned in bunting. That week the "Great Commoner," William Jennings Bryan, was renominated to run for a second time against President William McKinley. Among the 17,000 boisterous delegates was John Truman, a grain dealer from Independence, who brought his sixteen-year-old son, Harry. Bryan and his running mate, Adlai Stevenson of Illinois, lost the election to McKinley and Theodore Roosevelt.

If the "Union Depot, hotel life, banking, theaters, shopping—all the urbanities—were in Kansas City," as Thomson wrote, so "was open vice." He was not the only Kansas Citian to grow up enchanted by it. The writer Edward Dahlberg, who lived there during the 1910s with his single mother, a formidable woman who ran the Star Lady barbershop on East Eighth Street, later recalled,

> It was a wide-open town; there were more sporting houses and saloons than churches. The stews were as far out as Troost Avenue. When a bachelor or a stale codger was in sore need of easing himself, he looked about for a sign in the window which said: *Transient Rooms* or *Light Housekeeping*. A brakeman on the M-K-T knew where he could get a glass of beer for a nickel, which also entitled him to a free lunch of hard-boiled eggs with pretzels and

Heinz ketchup. There streets were cobblestoned hills, and their names were April songs of feelings: Walnut, Locust, Cherry, Maple, Spruce and Oak.[14]

Growing up there, Virgil Thomson loved the "neighborly jostling of culture, religion and low life," as he described it fifty years later: "The presence of visible vice, right alongside institutions of learning and studios of the arts, gave us all a higher sophistication, I think, and possibly a more realistic moral attitude than is available nowadays to young people who pursue their studies and their dreams in the seclusion of a garden suburb.[15]

Whether Virgil's parents thought the coziness of virtue and vice in Kansas City was beneficial to the moral education of their son is doubtful. To his father the city was the place you traveled to for work. At home, with Quincy's gardening and constant chores and May's cooking, canning and constant guests, the Thomsons might as well have been back on the farm in Slater.

But Virgil eagerly went downtown for everything: culture, school, mammoth spectacles, Wild West shows, burlesque. And, as David Mc-Cullough writes, "there was hardly a city in America where an observant youth could have a better day-to-day sense of the country's robust energy and confidence at the start of the new century."[16]

> Nobody remembers being a baby, but I remember being a child of two or three and growing from there to school age. Against the backdrop of my father's small but comely house and on a stage peopled by characters of all ages, I took my place quite early as a child performer. I was precocious, good-looking, and bright. My parents loved me for all these things and for being their manchild. My sister, eleven years older, looked on me almost as her own. My relations were pleased at my being able to read and sing songs and remember things. So with all this admiration around (and being, in spite of the praise, not wholly spoiled), I early seized the center of the stage and until six held it successfully.[17]

All babies are cute, and so was the infant Virgil Thomson. But those round-faced baby features stayed with him as he aged. His nose grew fleshy and his face puffed out, weighing down the sides of his mouth and giving him, when he was not laughing outright, a perpetual, crescent scowl. His eyes were large and penetrating. As an adult, he could look commanding when he wanted to; but few people would have called him handsome.

Thomson, however, always maintained that he was a beautiful child and an attractive man. His actions—always having hopeless crushes on handsome school chums, always arranging to have an attractive woman friend on his arm as the powerful critic headed out in public to a concert—suggest his true insecurity.

That he early on "seized the center of the stage" is unquestionable. He was a precocious and feisty youngster. Even as a tot, he balked at doing things he didn't want to do. Quincy tried to conscript his young son into helping with the chores, but Virgil hated it. "My father tried to get a little discipline into me by making me mow the grass once a week during the summertime. I had to do a bit of weeding, cut up the dandelions that were growing in the grass. But I never did any of that planting and farming in the backyard. I was strongly resistant."[18]

When Quincy was doing home maintenance jobs, Virgil would sometimes have to help. He'd be a gofer, fetching tools and holding buckets. But he was "not cooperative" and Quincy pretty much caved in. "I was not at war with my father. But I'm a city boy. I was always having piano lessons and practicing. I was a relatively good boy and bright, I did well in school, so I was allowed to do things my way. My mother was my ally in this."[19]

Quincy must have been too happy to pick a fight with his willful boy. Going on forty, he finally had a secure job and a home of his own with a yard he could practically farm in. The Thomsons ate fresh fruit and vegetables from the garden all summer, and during the winter there were canned peaches, tomatoes, cherries, peas, string beans, pickles, and jams. Within ten years Quincy was financially able to move the family to a slightly bigger house on the same block, a place with extra bedrooms for visitors and an even bigger yard.

He arranged his post office schedule so that he could spend half a day at home. "He either rose at five and gardened till noon or went to work at five and gardened all afternoon. He 'improved the place' also, building a stone cellar, putting in a furnace, wiring for electricity, painting, paper hanging, roofing, shingling. There was nothing about a house and yard he could not do with joy."[20]

As Thomson later recounted, his mother was also happy because she was a hostess again. Grandma Flora came with "sacks of chestnuts from . . . Uncle Will Field's trees and with a telescope valise full of quilt pieces." Uncle Charlie Garnett moved his family to Colorado, but Cousin Lela stayed behind during the school term to attend the superior Kansas City public schools. Lela, who was Ruby's age, became like a second big sister to Virgil. She brought an upright piano with her and gave Virgil his first lessons. Lela was still living with the Thomsons when she married and moved into her own home in Kansas City. Forty years later, her son, Lewis Blackburn, an electrical engineer, built for "Cousin Virgil" in the Chelsea Hotel apartment ceiling-high wooden cases in which to store his manuscripts and papers.

May's half sister Beulah Gaines, "a pretty girl who laughed and danced," came also for extended stays. And her half brother Cecil came fresh from high school in Slater to look for work in the city. "Handsome, full of jollities and jokes and card tricks, playing the banjo, knowing songs and darn-fool ditties, sophisticated about girls and adored by them, he filled the house with a young man's ease and laughter." Soon thereafter, Cecil's school chum joined him, and both, now working, boarded at the Thomson house, which helped with family finances. So every night's dinner "was now a company dinner, with steak or chops, hot breads, three vegetables, and dessert."[21]

May Thomson, a fine seamstress, made all the clothes for her family, except an occasional store-bought suit for Virgil. And Ruby, at fifteen, had instruction in china painting, becoming so adept that within two years she was taking on students and producing on order pieces that she fired in a basement kiln her father set up. With money she earned Ruby bought Virgil his first piano, after Cousin Lela moved away and took hers with her. Years later, when Virgil was chief critic at the *Herald Tribune* and Ruby was Mrs. Roy Gleason, Virgil returned the favor, paying for his sister's purchase of a professional kiln, which was installed in the basement of her Pittsburgh home. Virgil was always proud of Ruby's china work. Her teapots and serving trays were regularly used at his renowned dinner parties.

When Virgil Thomson's autobiography was released in 1966, the insightful British critic Wilfrid Mellers was perplexed. "Thomson writes like an angel, or at any rate like the slightly malicious cherub he now resembles, as he did (to judge from the fascinating photographs reproduced in this book) both as a small boy and a baby." Mellers praises Thomson's "wonderfully fresh and immediate" account of his youth; he commends to us Thomson's "dazzling sidelights on the palmy days of New York's cultural history." But for Mellers it remains a curiously incomplete story. During the account of the Paris years, Thomson "doesn't degenerate into name-dropping, but the great in artistic circles parade by among a plethora of countesses, and Thomson hardly makes us aware of them as human entities." Later he adds, "It is as though there's some defence mechanism in Thomson that makes him write more vividly of people with whom he is concerned remotely (whether topically or locally or both) than of those who have been closest and most meaningful to him."[22]

Mellers is not alone in his feelings. The book is an engaging narrative, cantankerous and sweetly nostalgic. It is alive with opinions and portraits, but the opinions are blunt, calculated to provoke, and the portraits are sketches. Even Maurice Grosser, who was the closest person Thomson had to a lifelong lover and companion, comes though indistinctly. It's as if Maurice was just a periodic stopover in the travelogue of Thomson's life.

Yet the book is a brilliant, fascinating work and an invaluable biographical resource. Moreover, sometimes, almost despite himself, Thomson is quite revealing, though those who don't know his secrets may miss the subtext.

One such moment is the story of his starting school, the Irving School on Prospect Avenue and Twenty-fourth Street, six city blocks from home.

> On my second day at school I got into a fight. That was a surprise to me, and so was the outcome. Physical brawling had not been part of our family life; nor had my father ever shown me, even in play, the stances of pugilism. Neither had I been taught to fear aggression. It simply had not occurred to me ever that I might be attacked, still less that I might be led on (for this may well have been what happened) to attack another boy. In any case, I did find myself, just off schoolyard limits, engaged in fisticuffs. I also found myself losing the match. Then somebody separated us. Neither bore any marks. But my surprise was definitive.
>
> It was definitive because it made clear to me, not yet six, that I was going to have to find other ways toward gaining respect than the head-on physical encounter. A boy named Maurice Baldwin, just as bright as I and just as small, early chose the athletic way. He could always out-wrestle or out-box a boy of his size and out-pitch at baseball many a taller one. But he spent all his out-of-school time keeping up that muscular command. My own choice was simply not to compete. This choice kept me mostly out of fights and always free from broken bones. It also left me time for music and reading. And if it often brought me the taunt of "sissy,"

it caused me to grow strong in other ways of defense and attack, psychological ways, and in the development of independence.[23]

This passage is the written recollection of a worldly author approaching seventy. But the portrait of the schoolchild—devising his own adult ways of defense and attack, exactly the techniques the score-settling *Herald Tribune* critic would deploy—is utterly convincing.

Already on his second day of elementary school, Virgil had confronted himself: he was bookish, clever, short, and preoccupied with secret longings that he felt acutely but couldn't identify. He would never be able to compete with the playground bullies. He would have to become, instead, an intellectual bully.

This remained true throughout his life. Whatever Virgil Thomson wanted—a romantic conquest, the friendship of a popular Harvard classmate, the praise of teachers, the support of patrons, the loyalty of performers, a powerful platform for his views—he would have to get through his stunning brilliance, his incontrovertible arguments, his beguiling charm, and his cutting wit. He learned these tactics early on. That he was also concealing insecurity and even shame, which those who loved him understood, accounted for the cutting wit, but didn't make it less sharp.

3 VIRGIL ACQUIRES A MENTOR

Virgil Thomson often said that he had complete respect for anyone who simply stated, "I do not have an ear for music." His father was such a person.

Quincy Thomson had absolutely no ear for music and never claimed otherwise. Doing his garden and house work, he was never overheard humming or whistling to himself. When music was playing, he could read or sleep right through it, and usually did.

And after Cousin Lela moved in with her upright piano, music was always being made in Quincy's house, even before his young son joined in. There was Cousin Cecil's banjo and "darn-fool ditties," which Virgil heard every day after Cecil started boarding with the Thomsons. There was his mother's half sister Beulah Gaines, an amateur pianist and capable sight reader who led family sing-alongs. When Beulah was in town, Ruby always threw a party. The rug would be rolled up, and the young folks would dance. Once, Ruby's acquaintance Harry Truman, who was working at a bank in Kansas City at the time, came to a dance party and wound up at the piano.

There was Virgil's mother's cousin Edward Gaines, who visited twice yearly. An amateur violinist, he would recruit Lela into accompanying him for hours. Virgil would later write of "rolling on the floor in ecstasy at hearing for the first time in real string sound the repeated high F's of the *Cavalleria Rusticana* Intermezzo."[1] Cousin Lela was a "city pianist" who had had proper lessons and favored classical music.

But Aunt Lillie Post, who was always visiting, was a "country pianist" who played a repertory of southern parlor pieces—"Old Black Joe" and variations on "Listen to the Mocking Bird" complete with pearly runs and oompah accompaniments.

May Thomson was delighted with the music making, although, except for the sing-alongs, she never participated. However, as a pre-payment for her son's taking a nap she used to sing to him "Darling Nelly Grey," which Virgil remembered as deeply sad, the souvenir "of an earlier Kentucky" with its "Arcadian landscapes," of a "father as a young man, and . . . [a] mother early dead." These musical souvenirs had over him "a power so intense that, as with my terror of the engines at the depot, I could almost not bear for it to either go on or to stop."[2]

All this music—parlor songs, ditties and dances, the hymn tunes he heard every Sunday at the Baptist church where his father was a deacon—lingered in Virgil's ears and turned up later in his compositions. And not just in the pieces one would expect them to—the film scores for *The Plow That Broke the Plains* and *Louisiana Story*—but as the raw musical materials for unprogrammatic formal works: the *Symphony on a Hymn Tune,* which uses as its main thematic idea "How Firm a Foundation," though bits of "Yes, Jesus Loves Me" and "For He's a Jolly Good Fellow" slip in as well; or the etude for piano, *Tenor Lead (Madrigal),* which, if the pianist carefully projects a buried inner voice, is revealed to be an arrangement of "Drink to Me Only with Thine Eyes."

Young Virgil demanded piano lessons, and Cousin Lela complied, teaching him correct scale fingerings and little pieces and discouraging him from playing by ear, thought to make one lazy about learning to read music. The lessons may have been provided as a corrective to Virgil's first musical experiment: an improvised portrait in sound, so its creator claimed, of the Chicago fire of 1871. Virgil never tired of stories about this fabled fire, which destroyed much of the city. Sitting at the piano, his feet dangling from the swivel stool, he would evoke the catastrophe by slapping the keys with flat fingers and pummeling them with his forearms.

Virgil must have been a quick student, because by the time he was ten he was being enlisted by his sister, then twenty-one, to play dance music for her get-togethers: waltzes, two-steps, German polkas. This was about the time that Cousin Lela married and moved out, taking her piano. Having purchased another, Ruby arranged lessons for her young brother from local teachers she assumed to be reputable. Though what did she know? It would be almost three years before Virgil realized how poor his initial teachers were: the first, a "well-born but ignorant woman" who forced him to concentrate on reading music, and her successor, a young man, an opera buff who taught him overture transcriptions, bits of Liszt, Mendelssohn, and Chopin, and had him read all the stories of the great operas.

Then, in 1909, Virgil met the person who became his musical mentor. His name was Robert Leigh Murray. They met at an outdoor concert.

Virgil loved band music. Ever year during the warm months, touring ensembles played free concerts in the band shells of Kansas City's public parks. John Philip Sousa's was then the most famous. But Virgil's favorite band was Arthur Pryor's. Formerly a trombone soloist and star attraction of Sousa's band (he was billed as the "Paganini of the trombone"), Pryor, a Missouri native, broke off from Sousa and formed his own band in 1903.

There were also touring Italian bands, military bands, and the so-called territory bands, regional ensembles that specialized in then emerging ragtime. Virgil's first exposure to opera came from these concerts: the "Sempre libera" from *La Traviata* arranged for trumpet solo and band; a brass version of the Prelude to Act Three of *Lohengrin*. During the summer season the weekly Wagner night was hugely popular and musically pathbreaking. Sousa was programming excerpts from *Parsifal* ten years before its American premiere at the Metropolitan Opera. The sounds of Verdi and Wagner arias played on the trumpet, the cornet, and the trombone lingered in Virgil's musical memory. "Oh, the euphonium was very effective indeed for the *Tannhäuser* 'Evening Star' air," he would say eight decades later.[3]

It was at one of these evening concerts during the fall of 1909, when Virgil turned thirteen, that he noticed a roly-poly, well-dressed gentleman watching him. Virgil recognized the man as Mr. Murray, the tenor soloist from the church he attended with his family, Calvary Baptist Church. Murray recognized Virgil as the precocious piano student he had heard about and noticed at services. He introduced himself and inquired after Virgil's musical studies. Soon they were at a nearby drugstore discussing over soda pops Virgil's musical pursuits.

Virgil believed that Mr. Murray was an Englishman and was never exactly sure why he had come to the United States. Many things about him were mysterious. One was his true age. When Virgil met him,

Murray was admitting to being over thirty. However, when America entered the war in 1917, Virgil was surprised that Mr. Murray was not called up. "That's when he told me he had been kidding about his age, that he was really older," Thomson recalled. "Besides which, he was a fat man, much overweight."[4]

Murray was actually born in Mooresville, Missouri, a small town some eighty miles northeast of Kansas City, in 1871, making him thirty-eight in 1909, twenty-five years Virgil's senior. His father, Francis Murray, was born in Baltimore of Scotch heritage. His mother, Jane James, was English-born. Robert Leigh Murray cultivated his Britishness. He had studied with a proper English vocal teacher. He nurtured the remnant of an English accent picked up from his mother. By the time Virgil met him, Mr. Murray was passing himself off as a native-born Englishman.

Murray was well-read and a professionally trained musician. As a young man, he had toured with male quartets, then very popular. For steady work, however, he was employed as a piano salesmen for the Olney Company, the local distributor of Knabe pianos. Yet he continued to perform every Sunday at church and, on occasion, in recital programs around town. Moreover, he cultivated associations with the most discerning musicians in Kansas City.

Murray arranged for Virgil to study piano and organ with the city's best teachers. As soon as Virgil's voice changed, Murray taught him how to place it, how to sing properly. And with Murray's background in English liturgical music (from his Anglican upbringing and British voice teacher), he was able to teach Virgil how to enunciate text. He hired Virgil to accompany him at least twice a week, paying him a dollar every session, virtually a professional wage. He took Virgil through the standard German art song repertory and introduced him to newer songs from France and England. Being on the complimentary lists of English publishers, Murray had an extensive and up-to-date collection of musical scores. When he sang a banquet date or, on occasion, an out-of-town recital, Virgil accompanied him, earning more money to help pay for music lessons. Sometimes Virgil would play a solo on these recitals: a Beethoven sonata, or shorter pieces of Schubert, MacDowell, Debussy.

Murray also saw to it that Virgil heard all the concert artists who passed through Kansas City. Through his piano company connections he could get free tickets to the touring Knabe artists. With Murray, Virgil heard the legendary opera singers Marcella Sembrich, John Mc-

Cormack, Johanna Gadski, the fabled pianists Vladimir de Pachman, Ignace Paderewski, Ferruccio Busoni. He heard the singer whose intelligence, searching musicality, and artistic dignity made her his idol, Mary Garden. Many years later they would become acquaintances and correspondents.

And during every winter break from school for the next six years, Virgil went with Murray to Chicago for a musical vacation. When they met, Virgil had still not heard live a string quartet, a symphony orchestra, or an opera. In Chicago they would attend the opera every night, go afternoons to art museums, to recitals, to plays.

Murray "profited as a singer from these excursions and took satisfaction from their benefit to me, for he had assumed the guidance of my musical development, being rewarded only by affection and by my delight in his adult companionship."[5] This was the official line as stated in the autobiography. In fact, the situation was more complicated.

Murray was a secretive homosexual. Even as a thirteen-year-old, Thomson understood this. "I was a little bit aware then, very much aware later, that he would have liked to do little things with me, but I wasn't interested at all, and he saw that. I always pretended with him as if I didn't know what he wanted, and he never told me literally what he did want."[6]

Murray carefully courted the good will of Virgil's parents, who, not unreasonably, were suspicious of this unmarried, foppish older gentleman who spent two evenings a week alone with their not-exactly-manly son and took him to Chicago, where they shared a hotel room. Recalling this, Thomson believed that his parents must have understood Murray's proclivity, although they never mentioned it, and perhaps never even acknowledged it to each other. To May and Quincy Thomson, Mr. Murray was conducting his life, so they assumed, the only proper way a homosexual could, by living celibately and concealing his nature. Murray's standing in the community and in the very church where Quincy was a deacon must have persuaded them to allow this relationship. Moreover, their son was grateful finally to have the professional advice neither they nor anyone else they knew could provide.

Even before Murray came into the picture, Quincy was reconciling himself to his son's musical pursuits. Once, when Virgil came home from sixth grade with a straight-A report card, his father gave him as a reward a ticket to an upcoming recital by Paderewski. It was a loving gesture from an uncomprehending father, and Virgil always spoke of it fondly. How could Quincy and May not let their son benefit from the solid professional guidance of a reputable neighbor? Mr. Murray was admitted into the family circle and became Virgil's musical mentor.

Kansas City was then home to some internationally trained music teachers and Murray knew most of them. Many were affiliated in some way with the small Conservatory of Music, founded in 1906. One was Moses Boguslawski, a dapper, Russian-Jewish pianist from Chicago, a brilliant virtuoso who gave all-Liszt recital programs, including the experimental late works, then hardly known or understood. Boguslawski assigned Bach's Two- and Three-Part Inventions in the then new and scholarly Busoni edition. These lessons continued through the following summer, until Virgil's father could no longer afford them.

The next summer Murray arranged for Virgil to study with his friend Gustav Schoettle, a cultivated musician from Stuttgart who "looked rather like Robert Schumann with his flowing hair." Schoettle taught Virgil piano but "threw in harmony lessons gratis"—keyboard harmony, harmonization of Bach chorales. Eventually Schoettle moved to Iowa City to head the music department at the university.

Then there were lessons from a Viennese émigré, Rudolf King, whose musical pedigree impressed Virgil immensely. King had studied with Leschetizky, who had studied with Czerny, who had studied with Beethoven. Technique building was King's main concern, however, and he put Virgil through a demanding series of technical studies and got him playing solos comfortably in public.

These lessons Virgil paid for himself from the musical jobs he was now starting to get. His "first receipt from any professional action" came during the summer he was thirteen. A silent movie house had opened in his neighborhood. "The program, changed nightly, consisted of an 'illustrated song,' sung to piano accompaniment and colored slides, and two short films—a drama and a comedy. I must have gone every night."

One night the regular pianist took sick, and someone actually came to Virgil's house asking if he would fill in. He did, earning a dollar.

Being unskilled in improvisation, I simply played pieces I knew while a trap drummer underlined the rhythm and added "effects" such as cowbells, horses' hooves, bass drum thuds, and cymbal crashes. . . . My first performance as a film accompanist could not have been brilliant. But I did substitute a few more times that month; and once, appearing in answer to a want ad, I was allowed by a none-too-confident manager to play through an evening at a tent show.[7]

Virgil would continue to earn fees from occasional theater gigs. There was steady money from accompanying Mr. Murray. But the primary musical means by which he earned his way for years to come, and right through Harvard, was from playing church organ jobs.

Mr. Murray introduced Virgil to Clarence Sears, the distinguished organist at the recently constructed Grace Episcopal Church downtown (which later became the Cathedral of Grace and Holy Trinity). Sears was no virtuoso. The virtuoso organists "all flocked to Paris to study with Widor," Virgil later explained, "But they were no good for anything but solo playing."[8] Sears, on the other hand, was a church organist who, Murray knew, could teach Virgil marketable skills. Sears took him on as a student, and so began Thomson's lifelong association with sacred music and the organ. His last completed organ works were three voluntaries commissioned by the American Guild of Organists in 1985. He was eighty-nine.

But now, at sixteen, he was a working professional. During the summers he started earning five dollars per Sunday substituting at Calvary Baptist Church for the regular organist, Mrs. Jennie Schultz. By the next summer Sears invited Virgil to assist him at the Episcopal church—a spacious, brown granite building with stained-glass windows, each dedicated by a prominent family from the congregation. At first he turned pages for Sears, learned the liturgy, and sang with the choir. Eventually he was allowed, when he had a piece ready, to play a solo prelude or postlude.

That Virgil was spending so much time in an Episcopal church was troubling to those relatives anxious for him to undergo adult baptism in the family religion. Aunt Leona, his father's sister, was the most outspoken. "Oh, I keep hoping and praying that our Virgil will someday become a Christian," she would say at family dinners. Virgil "put up" with such remarks and "kept a civil tongue," he recalled. "I didn't resist reasonable amounts of discipline or learning. I had a good disposition. But I just didn't take to salvation."

Quincy Thomson was a devoutly religious man, an elected church deacon. He was prepared to be supportive of Virgil's musical activities. But he would not allow his son to miss Baptist Sunday school in order to work at an Anglican church. They made a deal: Virgil agreed to attend Sunday school at 9 A.M. but was allowed to skip church in order to make the 11 A.M. service at the Grace Episcopal. It was one of the few times Quincy insisted on something from his headstrong son.

So Virgil's church work continued. After some time he started getting even better jobs, continuing lessons with Sears but working elsewhere on Sundays. Mostly he had success. But not always. At Westport Methodist Church a Mrs. Maclanahan was the choir director, soprano soloist, and minister's wife. One day she asked Virgil to transpose an accompaniment for one of her solos. He haughtily replied, "That is too much to expect from a five-dollar organist!" Mrs. Maclanahan had never been talked to like that. Virgil was promptly dismissed.[9]

The piano lessons continued. He practiced four hours a day during the summer and managed to get in at least two during the busy school year. Inevitably, the question of Virgil's future plans came up at home.

> I do not remember how the subject arose; but somehow, in conversation with my mother, father, and sister—a discussion of my studies and my future—I found myself declaring that there was no use their thinking I was not to be a musician, that I was one already, that music was my life and always would be.
>
> Now the family had never been in the least discouraging about music. I imagine that even then their chief aim was to find out my intuitions of destiny. Well, they found out; and so did I. The vehemence of my statement so surprised me, indeed, that before there was time for any reply I burst out crying and fled upstairs. From that day my musical vocation was never questioned.[10]

Yet, as Virgil's fledgling career prospered, he found that "thinking about music and reading about it" were becoming "no less an urgency than making it." Neither Sears, the church musician, nor Boguslawski, with his fancy technique, nor King, with his august musical lineage, was able to keep Virgil's interest for long. They were "too deeply embedded in pure music making," he said years later, "and I was reading books, I was intellectual."[11]

The teacher Murray eventually recommended who worked out best for Virgil was Miss Geneve Lichtenwalter. Born in 1867 in Cedar

County, Iowa, Lichtenwalter graduated in 1892 from the University of Kansas and taught there for some years. Virgil was impressed that she held a master of arts degree in music from Columbia and had studied in Berlin and Paris. She was a friend of the historian Will Durant. She "read non-fiction books. She also composed, and the texts she chose for her vocal works bore literary distinction."[12]

Lichtenwalter maintained a studio downtown on Ninth and Locust, near the massive, marbled courthouse. And in 1914—Virgil was nearly eighteen—he became her devoted pupil. Among her students, Virgil thrived in the role of class star and intellectual heavyweight, so excelling in his work that Miss Lichtenwalter arranged a solo recital at her studio. The program was covered by the local Kansas City paper, Virgil's first-ever review, headlined "Young Pianist in Recital." His last name is spelled incorrectly, with an inserted *p,* a mistake that would dog him for the rest of his life.

> One of the most promising young pianists presented by any instructor is Virgil Garnett Thompson, pupil of Geneve Lichtenwalter, who appeared in recital at Miss Lichtenwalter's studio last evening. The boy is not quite 18 years old, but in last night's exacting programme showed a broad musical understanding. His execution, while not faultless, is smooth, rhythmic and interesting.
>
> The first task was one that would make a professional wince, the playing of the four movements of Schubert's Sonata [probably the Sonata in G, D. 894]. To shade the monotony, especially of the andante movement, is in itself a test of temperament. A superb handling of the beautiful minuet and sharp rendering of the allegretto movement were worthy of any artist's method. The closing group were the MacDowell "Sea Pictures." "A Sentimental Song" was played in keeping with MacDowell's native nature and the young pianist got a great deal out of the elusive "Nautilus" bit.
>
> Robert Deigh [*sic*] Murray, tenor, sang a group of songs as assisting artist. The especially beautiful number was "Starry Woods" by Montague Phillips. Mr. Murray sang this number exceptionally well, his plaintive and resonant voice responding to the minor motif. Mr. Thompson accompanied him.

The biographer Kathleen Hoover reports that Virgil's "professional preliminaries at the keyboard" involved surveying the audience "De Pachman-fashion" and improvising a little "*à la Paderewski,* both gestures being tributes to his idols of the moment."[13] He almost never performed from memory. Yet there is no reason to doubt that in these years Virgil was a musicianly, technically efficient pianist.

Virgil paid for his weekly lessons with Lichtenwalter, which cost $2.50, by taking a $25-a-month job as a page at the public library. It was there he "came upon the absorbing narrative that is Richard Wagner's *My Life*," as he later recalled. "Although Miss Lichtenwalter, to whom I showed my discovery, knew it for not exactly the whole truth about this amazing genius, she merely remarked, 'You must also read his enemy Nietzsche.' So I went to the philosophy stacks, found the complete works there in English, began at the beginning."[14] During the next year, so he writes, Virgil read the whole set, in order of their composition.

With a fine piano teacher who was also an intellectual, a captivated class of fellow students, and jobs as a church organist and accompanist, Virgil felt established in the professional life. Significantly, all through his adolescence and young adulthood, the one musical activity Virgil Thomson did not pursue was composing. This he would not take up until 1920, at Harvard, when he was twenty-four.

For his musical growth and early education, he had Mr. Murray to thank. And in later years, Virgil always acknowledged his debt to this rather odd, lonely man—except for one time when it might have really mattered.

It was 1934, after *Four Saints in Three Acts* became the avant-garde succès de scandale of the day, garnering international curiosity, acclaim, and bewilderment. Now a somewhat famous man, living mostly in Paris, Virgil made a triumphant return to Kansas City, his way paid for by talks to ladies' clubs and musical organizations.

Virgil and Mr. Murray had not seen each other in over ten years. Though still living there, Murray was too sick to attend any of Virgil's Kansas City events, and, clearly, Virgil did not visit his old mentor. This pathetic, touching letter, addressed to Paris, where Virgil had returned after his trip home, is the only letter from Murray in the Virgil Thomson Collection at the Yale School of Music.

Kansas City, Missouri
July 9, 1934

Mr. Virgil Thomson
Paris, France

Dear Virgil,

I did think I had written you my last letter but here I am again. This is my last. Positively. I was sorry I did not see you for a minute when you were home in May. I know you were busy and that every moment was taken so I did not call you up—and I was so sick I could not go to your home—I am still sick—have an angina that confines me to my room and my bed. My doctor (Dr. S. Ayers) says I am al-right and will soon be out. I have no pain but have to be careful not to bring it back.

Life holds no further amusements for me and I shall be glad for the end—I've had four years of anguish—they have been pretty bad—and I kept going up to three months ago. God only knows how much longer.

I didn't mean to tell you so much of my woes—forgive me for bothering you with them. I only wanted to tell you that our friendship, on my part at least, is still alive and as strong as ever. In fact, it is a part of me—I would not part with it if I could. All I have ever done for you was done of this friendship. If any little part of it has ever been of the least help to you in any way I am more than repaid. If it was harmful, again I ask your forgiveness.

I do not need to say I benefitted from our association. I did, and in many ways. And I am glad our paths met and stayed together for ten years of happy friendship. It is past, but I can't forget our many happy congenial hours.

I am glad of your success. May it continue. I am sure it will. I know your ability for work and I know you will keep at it.

I am getting tired and there is no more to say.

Good bye my dear friend and may God ever bless and prosper you. This is my last letter, so again, Good bye, Good bye.

Sincerely your friend,
Robt. L. Murray

Discussing this letter in his later life, Virgil Thomson grew testy. Murray's fleeting apology suggests that, despite later denials, perhaps he did "do little things" to Virgil. If so, perhaps Virgil was not an unwilling object of Murray's attentions. Whatever the reason, Murray's letter made him uneasy.

Virgil Thomson never responded to this letter. Robert Leigh Murray died on December 12, 1936. He was sixty-five.

4 THE PANSOPHIST

No musician ever passes an average or normal infancy, with all that means of abundant physical exercise and a certain mental passivity. He must work very hard indeed to learn his musical matters and to train his hand, all in addition to his school work and his play-life. I do not think he is overworked. I think rather that he is just more elaborately educated than his neighbors. But he does have a different life from theirs, an extra life: and he grows up . . . to feel different from them on account of it.[1]

During his school years, Virgil Thomson worked hard learning his musical matters. There is no reason to doubt his account of his piano practice regimen: at least two hours a day during the school year, and four or more hours during the summers.

Yet this is the regimen of a serious student of music, not an aspiring concert pianist. When it came to being a kid in Kansas City, Virgil did not miss out on much. If he refrained from athletics, it was mostly by choice. And if he felt "different" from his other friends, there were reasons for this that had nothing to do with his musical pursuits.

As a youngster Virgil spent most Saturdays walking to the public library with his Irving Grammar School chums, pooling the streetcar fare given them by their parents to buy chocolate and chips. While downtown, he later wrote, "we changed our books, robbed the dime store, ate something sweet or salt, and as often as not walked home again." On Saturdays those with some extra allowance reported to the Gillis, a melodrama theater, for weekend matinees featuring *China-town Charley, No Mother to Guide Her,* and "similar classics."[2] During his teenage years at Central High School, a red sandstone building from the 1880s adjoining the business district, Virgil didn't exactly rush home to practice. Central High was temptingly convenient to the downtown stores and theaters, where Virgil usually lingered.

Central High offered a no-nonsense academic program. There was a chorus and band but no classroom courses in art or music. Virgil's transcript documents the work of an honors student who excelled at the verbal disciplines: English, advanced composition, public speaking, shorthand. He posted solid grades in Latin, algebra, solid geometry, chemistry, and psychology. His two lone P's (Poor) were for gym 1 and 2.

In his sophomore year Virgil took his one foray into acting, appearing as a drunken butler in the play *The Good Natured Man,* which starred an older student, William Powell, who would become the famous film star, though the best reviews went to the leading lady, Lola Eaton. Of Virgil's performance the school paper wrote, "Virgil Thomson entered into his role of butler with his customary alacrity and by its very naturalness made it a success."

Thomson always credited his solid early training as a writer to Miss Ellen Fox, an old schoolmarm, "cheerful and small with a face like a bulldog," he later wrote. "She was a New Englander but not a dour one, a lover of laughter whose own laugh was like a bark. And I never saw her show weakness. One day when from some fault of weather there were no streetcars, she merely got up earlier and walked the five miles to school."[3]

Miss Fox's method was to mark student papers in the left-hand margins with standard proofreader's signs. But the writers had to determine for themselves where the errors lay. "And not till every fault had been removed would she accept a piece of writing as work done."[4] Her texts were *Webster's* dictionary and George Crabb's *English Synonymes,* a book Thomson consulted all his life, and urged upon other writers, including this one.

Thomson's literary side flourished at Central High, but only after an initial disaster. Assigned to write a short story, he found himself barren of ideas. So he closely borrowed the plot and details of a comedy of errors he had read in a magazine.

[M]y English teacher proposed submitting it to the school paper. I
could not say no; I did not say no. It was offered with my consent; it was accepted; it was published. And then catastrophe fell.
Within the week I was denounced by a fellow student. The facts
were undeniable; I did not deny them; and an editor's apology
was printed the following month.[5]

Thomson's standing at the school, especially with the faculty, was
such that the incident was never mentioned again, his public humiliation deemed sufficient punishment. He continued to excel at English
and composition. In time he petitioned the department, successfully,
for an advanced course in writing, which turned out to be a short story
class. In his senior year a work of his again made it into the school
paper, the *Central Luminary,* this time without incident.

But Thomson learned a lesson from his hapless attempts at fiction:

The truth is . . . that I have no gift for imaginative writing. I can
describe things and persons, narrate facts. But I do not assemble
my pictures and my people into situations where they take on
memorability, which is what storytellers do. Nor can I make a language change its sound or words their meaning, which is the faculty of poets. Language, to me, is merely for telling the truth about
something; and it was during my high school years that I learned
to use it that way.[6]

From then on, Thomson wrote only nonfiction, except for a handful
of poems that eventually wound up in a green file box, also containing
some poems and recipes given him by friends, that he kept on a shelf
in his Chelsea Hotel bedroom.

Thomson graduated from Central High in June 1914. He had been
successful and was admired by his classmates. But that they were onto
him more than he may have liked is clear from the yearbook. Under
Thomson's picture is the peroration "O Shades of Oscar Wilde, Millet, and Paderewski"—linking him to the infamous Irish writer, the
grandiose French painter, and the flamboyant Polish pianist. Moreover, the senior ballot cites him as "Worst Girl Fusser." There is no
recorded explanation of this enigmatic phrase. Does it mean that Virgil fussed like the girls in school? More probably, it suggests a boy
who was the "worst" at paying attention to the girls in school. Whatever the case, the implication is that he was not exactly manly.

The logical next step for Thomson would have been college. The finances of his parents, with their toehold on the middle class, precluded this, he felt. Thomson was "ready, ever ready, for excitements and thrills and experiences and stimuli that the surroundings don't offer."[7] But as yet he saw no sure way out of those surroundings, and wound up taking an extra year of advanced classes at Central High, an option that few seniors exercised.

With his own classmates mostly scattered, he fell in with a small circle of friends. As a group, they were an unconventional lot. George Phillips was a bright young man popular with the girls and bound, he hoped, for medical school. But his plans were twice interrupted by stints in the military. He never got back on track, instead becoming a reporter for the city's third-rung newspaper, the *Journal.*

Eugene McCown was more of a soulmate, an aspiring painter, a charming, breezy fellow, and a fairly fancy jazz club pianist. Eugene would attend the University of Missouri in Columbia, then hang out with Virgil in Paris, stay there until the war broke out, and move to London, where he was launched as a painter by Nancy Cunard. He would also write two published books, "smart novels like the English write," Virgil called them. Eugene McCown at that time must also have been dealing with his homosexuality, though Virgil maintained that, for everyone in his circle, homosexual sex did not begin until they got to Paris in the 1920s.

Unlike his chums, Virgil was also cultivating friendships with adults or, as he put it, "capturing lions." There was Mrs. Hannah Cuthbertson, his sister's painting teacher, a "handsome woman of fifty whose toleration of me initiated a still unended series of friendships with painters that was later to furnish the ambiance and norm of my Paris life."[8] Mrs. Cuthbertson, or, "Cuffbutton," as Virgil was eventually allowed to call her, was a cultured woman. Her own works, some samples of which Virgil kept in his Chelsea Hotel storeroom until his death, were unremarkable, soft-hued still lifes of flowers and fruit.

Another lion was a portly English-born writer, James Gable, Cuffbutton's friend, also close to Robert Leigh Murray. Mr. Gable was Oxford educated and had studied painting at Académie Julien in Paris, "a generalized man of letters . . . but without original talent," as Thomson later wrote. Virgil was mightily impressed with Mr. Gable, who "had known as a young man everybody artistic and literary in London or Paris, including Wilde and Douglas and all the painters, and who had been everywhere, read everything."[9]

However, a mutual friend recalled that Mr. Gable was "something of a recluse, who lived alone and quite unconventionally in the matter of dress."[10] Once well-to-do, Mr. Gable was nearly impoverished by the time Virgil knew him, though he maintained a front of being comfortable and busy with literary matters. Like his friend Robert Murray, Gable was a homosexual who doted on Virgil, even dedicating sentimental poems to this bright young lad.

> *When Virgil plays,*
> *Ah, then the jealous winds grow strangely mute,*
> *And deem that Orpheus lives again,*
> *Or sylvan Pan plays on his reedy flute.*

Another poem, six stanzas long, sent to Virgil before he left for Harvard in 1919, suggests that Mr. Gable, like Mr. Murray, wished to be (or may have been) more than a mentor. It begins,

> *My path doth wind in the Westward way,*
> *Yours—I know not where.*
> *We part here at the river's edge,*
> *And parting I'd speak you fair.*

One stanza reads,

> *If I should stoop above your head,*
> *Pillowed on green moss pad,*
> *And clasp your hand as in other days.*
> *O friend, would you be glad?*

After Virgil left Kansas City, he and Mr. Gable seldom communicated.

At the time of his high school graduation, with sympathetic friends, the attentions of artistic traveled adults, and church organ jobs for money, Virgil was inclined to stay in Kansas City until he could figure out the next step. Then something happened to keep him there for sure. Central High School was relocated. In its old building on Locust Street, a junior college was opened, the Kansas City Polytechnic Institute. The school offered advanced high school and trade courses as well as college-level work in engineering, education, and liberal arts. The municipal junior college was then a new and intriguing idea; in its first year KC Polytech attracted about 150 students, most of them high school teachers seeking to further their education and motivated young people who otherwise might not have had the resources to attend a university.

By now, the fall of 1915, the war in Europe had commenced, vexing young Americans who feared that sooner of later the United States would be drawn in. Unlike the more affluent students who left for sequestered academic lives at better-known universities, the young adults who entered KC Polytech were pragmatic about their education. Many worried that their chosen career paths would be interrupted, and they wanted to learn all they could while they had the chance. They wanted their money's worth.

Virgil enrolled at the junior college for its inaugural fall term. There was no real campus, hence no campus life. So he continued to live with his family and took courses in English composition, French, Spanish, plane trigonometry, physics, chemistry, and astronomy.

There he met a young woman from Independence who would become his constant companion at school and a lifelong friend, Alice Smith. Alice was the great-granddaughter of the Mormon prophet and seer Joseph Smith, though Alice, self-effacing and determined to achieve her own identity, rarely talked of her famous forebear.

Joseph Smith founded the Church of Jesus Christ of Latter-day Saints in 1830 in Fayette, New York, moved the sect first to Ohio, then to Missouri, and eventually to Illinois. Smith was constantly persecuted, once arrested for treason, and, in 1844, murdered by a mob in Carthage, Illinois. A vacuum arose in the church's leadership, and the charismatic Brigham Young filled it, eventually directing a migration of his followers to Utah. Soon there was dissention over Young's leadership, particularly regarding the issue of polygamy. A reorganization was begun, and in 1860 Joseph Smith, Jr., became the president of this branch. Upon Joseph, Jr.'s death in 1914, his son, Alice's father, Dr. Frederick Madison Smith, became the president of the Reorganized Church of Jesus Christ of Latter-day Saints. These Missouri Mormons always considered themselves the sanctioned and true followers of their prophet and founder.

> Alice, monumentally proportioned and as a consequence lacking a little the experience of boys, was finding out, as I was, that unless one is destined to mate early, intellectual friendships are perfectly possible. She was pretty enough too, indeed not unlike those massive creatures that for a time after World War I Pablo Picasso drew and painted. Having always been a big girl, she was not imprisoned by her flesh; she moved with grace. As for the mind, it was quick like her mother's, tireless like that of her father. For me she was a mirror, also a pupil, someone to educate and to protect a little against being blighted by a virtually indigestible religious inheritance.[11]

Alice's account of their relationship does not dispute Virgil's. And her writing was every bit as blunt. They met, Alice recalls, in Minnie Perkins's freshman composition class. Alice, fulfilling a requirement for her last year of high school, was nurturing ambitions as a writer. Virgil, sensing a compliant audience that seems to have included Miss Perkins, quickly assumed the leadership of the class, as Alice would later tell it.

> [Virgil] had even then a faculty of pungent criticism, which he used freely on other class members, and I came in for some of the earliest examples. His criticism was sometimes a little harsh, and was always delivered with a combination of omniscience and patronage that was hard to take; but it was usually just and well-deserved, and no one ever hesitated to take it. Personally, he made me furious, but I always had to admit that he was right. And there was something about the friendly grin he threw in after taking off the hide and rubbing salt in the wound that took out the worst of the sting.[12]

Alice and Virgil became intellectual buddies. "I was the kind of girl that most boys treated like just another one of the fellows." At first her role was that of Virgil's protégée and, as he unabashedly put it, "mirror." But, as Alice would recall, "eventually we were friends because we could talk freely about a great range of things that concerned us deeply."

Alice died in 1973. But her reminiscences are contained in a remarkable unpublished memoir, the genesis of which is itself a tribute to their trusting friendship and Alice's keen perceptions.

In 1948 Kathleen O'Donnell Hoover, engaged in research for a proposed biography of Virgil Thomson, wrote to Alice Smith, then married to the Reverend Frank Edwards, a Mormon minister, asking her to write a memoir of her friendship with Virgil and to share his letters. Alice had once been burned badly by publicity. In 1915, when her grandfather died, she gave interviews to the press and was upset by their insensitive use of her personal recollections. Moreover, she thought the treatment given her family's history by some writers was "obnoxious and inaccurate." Suspicious of this biography project, she put Kathleen Hoover off and wrote to Virgil for advice.

> I'm of two minds about the notes [Hoover] wants. She says, make them as full and complete as possible. Now, Virgil. My memory is entirely too good, and my sense of humor too strong, to turn me loose with that kind of assignment. Besides, as I told her, if all I

can remember about the late boyhood and early youth is good publicity, I rather think I'd like to write it myself. And are you sure you can trust me? You know, you always accused me of being a bit "jeune fille" but have you any idea what a sweet young thing you were yourself? . . . Do you want me to tell them exactly what I think?[13]

Virgil wrote Alice back vouching for Mrs. Hoover's credentials ("a perfectly reputable music historian"), for the proposal ("don't imagine that the projected book is a publicity number"), basically telling Alice to cooperate or not, whatever she wanted:

Your letter seemed to me to reflect a question of conscience on your part, something you thought maybe I wouldn't want you to say. I know of no such item. My youth was no more foolish than most and less shameful than many. Besides, now that I am a public character of sorts, the facts are what anybody remembers them to be and I have no intention of changing anything, even were such a silliness possible.[14]

Alice decided to cooperate. She went through her correspondence from Virgil, preparing typed copies for Mrs. Hoover but omitting passages she deemed too personal, meaning something relating to her own life and family. A letter Virgil wrote in 1917 while stationed at Camp Doniphan illustrates Alice's criteria for censorship. In Alice's typed copy, Virgil's innocent, polite reference to Mrs. Smith's health is deleted: "I hope your mother's nerves and strength are improving. Give her my best wishes, please." But in the same letter Virgil's account of assisting an army psychiatrist who was weeding out malingerers from among the recruits, a passage that could be read as slightly anti-Semitic, is quoted in full:

I had an interesting experience some time ago in helping a psychiatrist, who was examining suspects for mental diseases, deficiency, and other abnormal states. He was a little Jew from Chicago named Hoffman, rather clever at his tricks, too. It was the most fun I have had since I have been here.[15]

After editing the letters, Alice sent the typed copies to Virgil for his inspection. She also wrote a memoir, eighteen typed pages. This she sent directly to Mrs. Hoover.

Apparently, Virgil was unconcerned about the memoir. When he wrote to Alice that there was no "item" from his youth he feared her talking about, he was completely confident that the unmentionable topic of his sexuality would remain unmentioned. He may have even convinced himself that Alice didn't suspect the truth, though that is unlikely. Alice might have been a proper Mormon minister's wife, but she was a perceptive woman with a Stanford education and half a lifetime of experience with the interpersonal machinations of the Mormon church.

In Alice's memoir there is not a hint of anything amiss in Virgil's relationships with his male friends and mentors. What emerges is a tactfully rendered portrait of a bossy, opinionated, intellectually intimidating young man. And there already in the person who took over Miss Perkins's freshman composition class we can recognize the curmudgeonly Virgil Thomson who in his eighties charmed and controlled a coterie of admirers, favor seekers, and patient friends.

Alice, three years Virgil's junior, understood and accepted the parameters of their friendship:

> Virgil told me what I did that was wrong (and there was plenty to tell about) and what I should do and not do, in about the same tone of voice, and I tried to take it in just about the same way. . . . He must certainly have enjoyed my companionship; but he enjoyed even more the role of teacher and preceptor, and I acted as audience for his monologues and a disciple to his constantly changing intellectual cults and fads, though I never went with him on such matters as vegetarianism, sun-bathing and Russian cigarettes.

She also acknowledged her debt to Virgil:

> Without to any extent disturbing my ethical outlook, though my religion came in for a little questioning under the lash of his criticism, he managed to introduce me to the twentieth century, in art and music as well as literature. Consequently, my adult tastes, culturally, owe a great deal to his deliberate tutoring.

Yet Alice found him exasperating and was troubled by his conceit:

> I believed in him unquestioningly. But his terrific assurance worried me. I always maintained that a fellow was at least safer when he assumed a becoming modesty. We used to talk about things like that for hours.

Alice recounts one incident when she and Virgil were sitting together on a windowsill at school, talking about his conceitedness. "What would you ever do," she asked him, "if you discovered a fault in yourself?"

He thought a minute, and then he reached up and pulled out quite a sizeable tuft of his silky, reddish-gold hair—I'll bet he'd give a lot for that tuft now—and holding it at arms length, he dropped it dramatically, just where a draft caught it and blew it down the hall. Then he wiped his fingers, daintily and with a air of utter finality. The gesture was typical and quite unforgettable.

Virgil became a frequent guest at Alice's home in suburban Independence. "He never asked if he might come," Alice wrote; "he just said, 'I can come to dinner Thursday,' or 'Saturday,' or whenever it was." When Virgil dined with the Smith family, he expected to have his vegetarian eating habits provided for, though this fad lasted only until he enlisted in the military in 1917. He also insisted on helping with the preparation of meals, to the consternation of the cook. But his kitchen skills, imparted by his mother, were impressive. Mrs. Smith complied, leaving to Virgil the making of mayonnaise, sauces, green salads with herbs, soufflés, and such.

After dinner Virgil usually, though not always, was willing to play the piano, including "half-formed compositions" of his own, as he described them, which were most likely quasi-improvisations. One night at Alice's house the electricity failed and Virgil played by candlelight, without music, for well over an hour, works by Schubert, Grieg, and MacDowell. MacDowell's *Sea Pieces,* then "quite unknown to the average listener," Alice writes, so struck her that she attempted a poem on the same subject. "The whole experience moved me very deeply."

Virgil charmed Alice's mother, who liked his "odd mixture of old-fashioned courtesy and modern frankness." Alice's father, on the other hand, was irritated by Virgil's "cock-sure attitude." Dr. Frederick Madison Smith, somber faced, balding, with a goatee and wire-rimmed glasses, was a savvy administrator and an unsanctimonious Mormon. A man of learning, he held degrees in science and liberal arts, a doctor of divinity from Graceland College and a Ph.D. in psychology from Clark University. He had been a professor of mathematics and had edited journals of history. He understood that this new generation, coming of age under the specter of a world-threatening war and pervasive technological change, was bound to be rambunctious. But he expected some deference from young people, and Virgil, though polite, acted as if they were equals. So it was ironic that what finally won Dr. Smith over to Virgil was an incident in which the adolescent agnostic confronted the learned Mormon minister over his personal values and family customs.

Dr. Smith's work brought to his home many scholarly, well-known people. Because of Alice's innate modesty and her father's innate belief in the subservience of women, a belief then shared by most non-Mormon males as well, Alice found it difficult "to venture a remark at the table." So did her younger sister, Lois. Alice's mother, long reconciled to this convention, never even tried to venture a remark of substance. When Alice did, she was summarily put in her place. Virgil resented this.

> Virgil once told my father very forcefully and pointedly that he was neither just nor kind in his refusal to recognize me as an intelligent human being. Dad was a very large man, physically, and was accustomed to dominating about any situation he found himself in. He was usually right, too; but whether he was right or not, he was not in the habit of taking a trimming in public and liking it. A completely effective telling off by one of his daughter's college friends was about the last thing he expected; and he was almost too surprised to be angry. In fact, Virgil's argument appealed to his really strong sense of justice, and he was even a little amused. From that time my father respected Virgil: and his liking for him grew steadily.

At the junior college Alice and Virgil were a curious pair. Fellow students nicknamed them "Mind and Matter," the foppish, brainy Virgil being mind, of course, the stout, substantial Alice being matter. Outside of their little group, Alice recalls, "Virgil was considered quite able, in a general way, very talented musically, extremely conceited and a little odd." She and her friends "accepted Virgil's leadership more or less without questioning."

Bored by the typical clubs and societies that were springing up even on this campusless junior college, Virgil decided to found an all-male club of his own, proclaim himself the president, and commence the publication of a club magazine. Eight other young men enlisted in the club, for which Virgil coined the grandiose and deliberately obscure name Pansophists. The first issue of their magazine, called *Pans,* appeared in May 1916. Virgil wrote virtually all of it, including the preamble:

> The Pansophists herewith make their official bow. We are a group of young men organized ostensibly for mutual benefit. We are interested in anything that can be known. Like Bacon, we take all knowledge to be our province; and like a good governor, we hope to get acquainted with our province. Not that we expect to ex-

haust the world in our sessions. Our universality means rather this, that any sincere point of view is just as interesting as any other. We do not even require sincerity provided the performer does not bore us. . . . We bind ourselves to no principles or convictions, and we exclude nothing from our horizon. This, in brief, is the personality of the Pansophists. What our character is, is another question. If you wish a distinction between character and personality, let us say that personality is the mask one wears in public; character is the mask one wears to oneself. It is then a mark of higher culture to have no character at all. We are striving toward this condition. Our ideal of a club personality, though, is a unified development of an infinite variety of viewpoints.[16]

Even before the premiere issue of *Pans,* the club had withstood the criticism of other students as being elitist and pointless. Virgil responded. The emulation of the Sophists of Greece, who "disputed for the sake of dispute, and who discussed merely for the pleasure of talking well," is, he wrote, "no more presumptive than the imitation of Christ." An anonymous letter to the school paper accused the Pansophists of being artificial, narrow, and undemocratic. Virgil pled guilty to all three charges: "Any attempt to unite distinct classes of minds is necessarily artificial. . . . Humanism itself is narrow." As to the charge of being undemocratic?

Of course we are! . . . Democracy is a device to insure the survival of the unfittest, a plan to reduce the world to uniformity, a synonym for mediocrity. All men are not equal; they should merely be given an equal chance to prove their superiority.

The premier issue describes a typical meeting of the Pansophists.

In our weekly sessions absolutely no dictation as to the nature of the program is given. Each member spends his hour in any way he likes, and the rest afford him an audience for the exploitation of his individual hobbies. . . . If the boys of the college haven't the good sense to see that it provides a chance for them to do what they want in their own way, let them organize one of their own sort or else pervert the present club to their purposes. If they want the narrow-scope society, full of traditions and other limitations, they can have it. Conventionality is its own punishment.

At the time, Virgil was lifting fragments of ideas from Schopenhauer (his view of the world as a constant conflict of individual wills resulting in frustration and pain) and Nietzsche (his contemptuous rejection of Christian "slave morality" in favor of a "will to power"). But his arguments have a facetious gloss that could come only from Oscar Wilde, whose works he devoured. Most of his solidly conventional classmates and professors would have considered such thinking morally devoid and rife with European decadence. But these currents were stirring in America. It was, after all, Virgil's well-read Kansas City piano teacher Miss Lichtenwalter, an ardent advocate of women's suffrage and equal rights, who first urged him to read Nietzsche.

But Virgil's tracts are mostly intellectual bluster. The actual issues his Pansophists advocated were pathetically standard small-college fare (calls for a college campus, a meeting place to "have class fights and hatch secret plots"), and more than normally vague (warnings that the college life was in danger of "dying of dry rot from lack of opposition").

Years later, Virgil acknowledged as much when he wrote of *Pans,* "I am not impressed today by its college-boy brilliance, but I remember much sport being had at its making."[17] Debating for the sake of debating was something Virgil Thomson did throughout his life.

The Pansophists did manage to find some controversy, however. And it almost got Virgil thrown out of school.

Alice, feeling miffed by her exclusion from the club, formed in response, with Virgil's encouragement, a women's club. She called hers the Anons because the members, all aspiring writers, would submit manuscripts anonymously for discussion at their weekly meetings. The two clubs often held joint meetings—social affairs, but "on a highbrow level," Alice recalls. "We considered ourselves very intelligent, quite bohemian and even a little naughty."

One day Virgil proposed reading at a joint meeting some poems from a new collection that had stunned him, Edgar Lee Masters's *Spoon River Anthology*. Published first as a series in a magazine, *Reedy's Mirror,* the entire work, 243 poems, appeared in one volume in 1915. The poems are the monologues of the dead citizens of Spoon River, a fictitious midwestern town, speaking from their graves. Gritty, gothic, and shocking, the poems created a sensation. Everyone in the cemetery speaks—sanctimonious civic leaders, drunks, deviates, and ordinary folks who may have lived forthrightly but rest in their graves embittered or remorseful.

There is Minerva Jones, the village poetess, "hooted at, jeered at by the Yahoos of the street / For my heavy body, cock-eye and rolling walk,"[18] who tells of being raped by Butch Weldy and then left to her fate with good Doc Meyers, who tried to help her but wound up killing her. There is Margaret Fulton Slack, the aspiring writer, who faced the choice of "celibacy, matrimony, or unchastity." She is lured by a rich dentist with promises of leisure for her novel. Instead she bears him eight children. "Hear me, ambitious souls, Sex is the curse of life!" she cries.[19]

Abortion, lust, lesbian relationships, the hypocrisy of small-town neighborliness, the corruption of civic officials—this was heady stuff for Kansas City Polytechnic Institute. Virgil Thomson, itching to test its provincialism, decided to read from the book at the next meeting of the Pansophists and the Anons. The meeting occurred. The women attended. And when the school authorities found out, Virgil was hauled before a disciplinary committee and threatened with expulsion. These were exactly the kinds of self-righteous people Masters was skewering, as Virgil knew. Before them he was deferential but defiant. Alice saved him.

He had warned her ahead of time what he was planning to do, she explained, so that she could "tell the girls to stay away if they wanted to." It was her insistence about this that reassured the authorities. Alice convinced them that Virgil's actions were a plea for artistic freedom. The inquiry was dropped.

Alice considered the whole incident an example of "semi-official literary censorship, . . . quite the deadliest kind." Years later she recalled the episode with delight. "Probably my attendance at that meeting was my first public revolt against the Victorianism of antique ruff and bonnet."

Long before the *Spoon River* affair, on that second day of grammar school when the playground bully beat him up, Virgil had determined that he would have to find an intellectual way to fight. He had fought the college and won. He was now notorious, and he loved it.

But it was an isolating victory. Alice left no written speculations about Virgil's private life. Another student, Donald Bush, a member of the Pansophists, was not so reticent, though his reminiscence is striking for its lack of understanding about the real issue:

> Virgil was disdainful of the popularity of the average fellow or girl. He showed none of the average or normal interest in "dates" and parties. A girl seemed most interesting to him as another agile mind to test his mental agility. But most of the time he just passed them up as not worth much of his time. . . . I remember thinking at the

time that Virgil was at times probably a little lonesome, but I may be wrong. Being an individualist he did not so far as I know form many friendships. There were not many at school that he considered worth the effort and of course this attitude was apparent to all.[20]

Bush's letter was sent to Kathleen Hoover for her research. Yet she did not use it. Neither did many of Alice's more pointed personal recollections make it into Hoover's 1959 book. Of course, Virgil had steered the biographer clear of his private life. He did not prevent her from using remembrances that portrayed him as stubborn, superior, and intellectually intimidating. Even in his own book he quotes Alice's reminiscence of him as being "harsh" in his criticisms, and he recounts with pride the tale of "manipulating the Doctor" into allowing Alice to participate as an equal in family dinner conversations. Yet all his life Virgil distorted his public image by censoring most references to his softness, his needs, his folly.

He and Alice remained good friends and frequent correspondents. Alice eventually married and raised four children, two of whom also went into the Mormon ministry. All of her later literary pursuits—a never finished novel in verse, a memoir of life as the descendant of a Mormon prophet, a literary column for a suburban weekly (this lasted sixteen weeks), and poetry that she feared was either old-fashioned, sentimental, or didactic—were more or less ignored by her Reverend Father and Reverend Husband. But Virgil was unfailingly supportive, tactful, and honest. Responding to Alice's self-bound manuscript of poems in 1968, Virgil wrote,

> I read your poetry with absorption. It is marked from the beginning by skill in choice of words and to the end by self-centered subject matter. And I suppose that for a preacher's daughter and a preacher's wife, there is not much other escape from the monolith. . . . I must say I like the vein you consider modernistic. The value of stylizations is that they tend to hinder banalities of sentiment by showing them up as just another convention. Anyway, there is a lifetime reflected and a good one and I enjoyed reading about it.

Once, upon hearing from Alice that she had commenced writing a literary column, and accepted a commission from a composer to write a text for a worship service, and had even painted some abstracts that had actually sold (paintings her husband "religiously failed to comment on"), Virgil wrote back an enchanting postcard.

NY, December 22, 1965

Dear Alice,

Letter lovely. Greetings good to have. Mine to you. And to Frank. Welcome to journalism and to the sacred music racket. As for painting, if it sells it's good.

Yours, VT

And as Alice battled failing eyesight, nervous exhaustion, and the mild stroke that eventually ended her life in 1973, Virgil kept up over five years a steady stream of advice about dealing with illness.

Me sorry you sick. But a good way to keep well, after all, is to have a disease and domesticate it.[21]

Please keep me informed of your progress. They say in France that health is a precarious state promising no good.[22]

I gather it is no fun being sick a long time, but that there are ways of sort of installing oneself in the situation, as one does in a drought or a war or a general strike.[23]

One final insight gained from reading Alice's memoir concerns Virgil's musical ambitions. For all his musical activities at the time, Virgil had still not taken up composing. In fact, Alice describes writing as his first love.

Virgil wasn't at all reticent about the fact that he expected to be a great man someday, though when I first knew him he had not decided whether to follow his first love, writing, as a vocation, and keep music for a hobby, or to pursue music and keep writing for a hobby. But that he was a genius, he himself and several others of us were entirely convinced.

So Virgil Thomson was secure in the roles of writer, critic, commentator, and polemicist before he even started his career as a composer. Perhaps he was waiting, as Alice thought, working tirelessly to "acquire the skills necessary for the expression of that genius." Perhaps he felt still in need of personal development and was anxious for a challenge. He found that challenge in World War I.

5 A LOVELY WAR

Virgil's Thomson's sixteen-month military career was messy, aimless, and homebound.

Though he first enlisted in a mounted artillery division of the National Guard of Missouri, he never rode an army horse. Later on, enrolled in the School of Military Aeronautics in Austin, he scored a 95 on his final exam in gunnery. But he never fired a shot except at clay pigeons. Though he was taught to analyze, repair, and maintain every component of an internal-combustion engine, he never drove a van or jeep or ambulance. Though he maneuvered to get himself into action overseas, he never got farther from home than Columbia University, in New York. After the armistice, he was honorably discharged as a second lieutenant in the Air Services Aeronautics Corps, the highest rank achieved by any male student from his Kansas City junior college. Yet he had never piloted an airplane.

This was not an atypical experience. For two years Americans had resisted involvement in the overseas war. By the spring of 1917 American participation seemed inevitable, but it took the sinking by German submarines of some American merchant vessels, supply ships to the Allies, for Congress to be provoked by President Wilson into declaring war. Even then a propaganda campaign, with which the national press fully cooperated, had to be waged before the country came around.

America was unprepared. A million men were needed. Only

73,000 volunteered during the first month after the declaration of war. Congress instituted a draft. Orders came from Washington for the training and mobilization of artillery units, air squadrons, and supply services, but the orders changed weekly. Over 50,000 U.S. military personnel would eventually die in the war. But tens of thousands more would never leave the camps where they were being trained, the bases where they were awaiting orders.

Many soldiers didn't mind this at all. But Virgil Thomson seems truly to have wanted to join the fight. Early on, tempted by the possibility of receiving expert instruction in band conducting, he nearly joined a navy bandmaster training program in New York. But except for this one sidestep, all his actions should have, he believed, and certainly could have led to his being shipped overseas for combat duty. His desire to get involved was motivated by a "yearning toward novel experience," as he later wrote, a yearning common among young men of his day, although Virgil was driven more by adventure than by idealism:

> Neither then nor later did I have much interest in whether any country involved in the war, including my own, was right or wrong. . . . After eighteen volumes of Nietzsche and ten of *The Golden Bough* I could only think of it as myth-in-action; and acting out myths was a mystery that I had as much right as any other man to get involved in.[1]

This apolitical stand was no bluff. Only once in his life did Thomson ever vote in an election: in 1948 for President Harry Truman. And that vote was motivated not by political principle but by Missouri pride.

His desire to get into the fighting, recalled with pumped-up bluster in later accounts, was nevertheless urgent.

> All those millions being killed, the sinkings at sea, the filth and the vermin of trench life, the pictures of bayonetted guts and burst Belgian babies, everything about it made it seem, to a boy just going twenty, a lovely war. You wanted to be a part of what so many were experiencing, to try yourself out, to prove your endurance. You certainly did not want the war to end without your having been through something.[2]

To try himself out. To prove his endurance. To assure himself that he was not, as he felt inside, some different kind of man. These were the self-imposed tests he simply had to pass. In the same month Virgil enlisted, former President Theodore Roosevelt, speaking to the

Harvard Club in New York, called all those Socialists, IWWs, and others who wanted peace "a whole raft of sexless creatures."[3] Virgil could not possibly let himself be one of them.

A relevant incident in his autobiography is telling. Before his second and final enlistment, Virgil went to seek the consent of his father, who was on the job at the post office. Virgil wanted to speak with him away from home. Quincy Thomson's father and every male family member of his father's generation had fought—and many died—in the Civil War. But the only uniform Quincy had ever worn was his civil service work clothes. War drew young men into the military, and war had managed to skip Quincy's generation.

As Virgil informed his father of his desire to enlist, Quincy listened carefully to his only son, then told him that the old house on Wabash Avenue, the one the Thomson family had moved from but still owned and rented, had been set aside for Virgil to sell, if he so chose. With that money he could go away to college.

> I answered that though going away to college had formerly been what I wanted most of anything, just now I was asking permission to join the army. His reply to that was that on any decision so important to myself he would neither urge me nor stand in my way.
>
> I was to know later that he approved.[4]

Virgil decided to enlist.

He later preserved every document of his military career, even a pilot's book from the Aviation Section, Signal Corp, U.S. Army, with not one flight recorded in it; and a nomination certificate inviting him to enroll as a veteran in the American Officers of the Great War organization, an invitation he never accepted.

On March 5, 1917, Virgil joined the Missouri National Guard field artillery regiment in Independence. At five feet five he was on the short side, but was deemed fit and mentally sharp. A month later the United States entered the war. Having signed up, Virgil then went back to Kansas City to finish the term at junior college. That summer, still waiting for orders, he went to Ann Arbor with his school chum Ross Rainsburg. Thinking he might eventually apply to aviation school, Virgil took some courses at the university in math and gas engines. To support himself he played piano and pipe organ for silent films at a downtown movie palace where Ross was working.

Hearing that the American Ambulance Service, a private agency taken over by the U.S. Army, needed drivers and was prepared to rush recruits overseas, Virgil took one lesson in driving on a Model T Ford and went to the service's main camp in Allentown, Pennsylvania, to enlist. He was misdiagnosed with flat feet and turned down.

Returning to his National Guard regiment in Missouri, he heard from his friend George Phillips, then a premed student, that an Army Medical Corps Detachment, renumbered the 129th Artillery and with Captain Harry Truman in command of one battery, was accepting recruits. Virgil requested and was granted a discharge from the National Guard and, along with George, enlisted in the army on August 6. This was a month after General Pershing led the American Expeditionary Forces to a landing at Château-Thierry.

At first, there was little to do. He lived at home, where George and his other hometown friend Eugene McCown were also temporarily boarding. During the daytime Virgil worked with an army medical team at the downtown convention hall, mostly tending to sore feet and giving vaccinations. One week during two afternoons over 1,100 men were vaccinated.

Eventually Virgil's unit was sent to Fort Sill, Oklahoma. Camp Doniphan was "a desert paradise of sun and dust, high winds, and hard ground. So hard was the ground that for setting up the square tents in which, by eights, we were to pass the winter each peg had to be driven into a hole dug out with a pickax and for thirty minutes softened up with water."[5]

Here Private Thomson was shaped up, drilled, and disciplined. He worked inspecting quarantine tents, tending to flu patients, vaccinating doughboys, and assisting an army doctor trained in the fledgling science of psychiatry. In his many letters from Fort Sill, he described army life vividly, as in this one written in December to Alice Smith:

> Lawton is a flat, ugly town four miles from here. It is utterly stupid. When we get tired here, we go to town in a jitney and buy a hot bath and some real food. We have to stand or sit in line two hours for the bath; and we have to crowd past colonels and generals to get a seat in a restaurant.
>
> . . . Living in such intimacy with fellows is bound to be an experience. There is the matter of privacy. And then there is the matter of judging how far it may be advantageous to fall into the general type, and where it may be better to resist the tendency.

. . . George and I often amuse ourselves by reading poetry aloud to each other, and it sometimes annoys the others extremely. Sometimes they like it, too. One pastime for vacant minds that I haven't learned to enjoy, tho I do my part dutifully, is to sit around the stove and sing bad songs in bad voices with badly faked harmony.[6]

By the end of the month, Virgil was stationed in the nearby isolation camp tending to soldiers with communicable diseases.

We have over 900 contact cases of measles, meningitis, mumps, diphtheria carriers, scarlet fever, and one tent of pox (chicken or small, it isn't known yet). There are five men in a tent; and each tent is a separate quarantine, nobody approaching within five feet of a man from another tent. So you can see there is a lot of work to be done for them. They must be fed, their mail must be delivered; and they must be inspected for disease twice a day.[7]

While at Camp Doniphan, Virgil applied for and was accepted by the flying service, the Aviation Section, Signal Corps. He had grown fearful that he would never leave Camp Doniphan and was eager to see action overseas, or so he wrote in his letters. The School of Military Aeronautics was in Austin. He was transferred there on January 21, 1918.

The two-month training at the ground school was rigorous—drill and study and lectures and tests and more drill, from five-thirty in the morning until ten at night. Virgil studied "machine guns, radio operation, the organization of foreign armies, airplane theory, rigging, military law, military hygiene, army paper work, engines, types of airplanes, maps, night and cross-country flying, photography and artillery observation, camouflage, meteorology, bombs and bombing, reconnaissance and contact patrol, care of the teeth and repair of wings."[8]

Every soldier had to pass a weekly test or else be busted back a week. More than one bust, and you were out of the school. Virgil wrote that of nearly 1,500 men in his school, "I was really proud of myself to have made the best grades in my class."[9]

Despite the rigors, he finally felt enough a participant in the war to brag about it to Alice, left at home to knit clothes and send care packages to her "dear cadet," as she called him: "Alice, I can't help a feeling of depression when I think of your situation, condemned to emotional patriotism. I should feel dreadfully if I couldn't get into things somewhere. At least, you can knit me the wash rag. I should be very pleased."[10]

Virgil's maneuver to get himself quickly into action didn't work. The military decided that there was a glut of pilots just then. But a radio-telephony detachment was looking for recruits and promising deployment overseas. Virgil applied and was accepted to the air service school for radio officers at Columbia University. He arrived in New York April 22, 1918, a month after the new Soviet government signed a treaty with the Germans.

The plan was that he would receive three months of instruction, be commissioned as a second lieutenant, be sent to Fort Sill for five weeks of flying, and then go overseas. "I am very glad I chose this course," he wrote to Alice, "as the fellows I graduated from ground school with may not be sent over for two years."[11]

The fellows from ground school were not sent over. But, ironically, Virgil's old 129th Artillery Division from Missouri was. In June it saw action in the Argonne offensive.

Meanwhile, flying school at Columbia, though intense and demanding, left him free on the weekends to "do the town," as he wrote, telling Alice of every cultural event he took in.

> I saw Mrs. [Minnie Maddern] Fiske in a beautiful play called *Service,* which failed, and Ethel Barrymore in a delicious nothing called *Belinda,* which is lovely. The real thrill was the Washington Square Players in Wilde's *Salome.* Mme. Yorska did the vamp role and Louis Calvert did the Herod in a corking, Henry VIII fashion, while Jokanaan, as they call the prophet, uttered scathing and beautiful speeches and a couple of handsome young men without clothes (much) talked about the moon. I have never sat thru such a fascinating hour and a half, such intensity and tragic horror and beauty and disgust.[12]

He also climbed "stairs like an Alpine" to reach his fifty-cent seat for a New York Philharmonic concert directed by the Czech conductor Josef Stransky, Mahler's successor at the Philharmonic, and heard operas at the Metropolitan. It was during this period that Virgil picked up a nickname he would favor until he settled in Paris in the mid 1920s.

> Alice, I absolutely forbid that in the future you should address me as "my dear cadet." Anything else you please. It is worth noting in my new character that I am no longer called Virgil, I am Tommy! It is much more human, don't you think?[13]

George Phillips, still with the 129th, wrote to say that he would soon be sent to Long Island, where his detachment would prepare to sail for France.

> I may be in New York and I am counting on you to show me the vagaries of that city which we of the middle-west idealize as wicked. Oh, I do hope that in this land of the brave there is still remaining some spot brave and free enough to harbor a little remnant of ostentatious wickedness.
> . . . I long to wallow in the sin of sins. . . . She need not be beautiful but she must have a quiet voice and know how to dress. It is most important that she be a fornicatory certainty.[14]

George could make it to the city for only one Thursday evening. Virgil took him to a French restaurant for an early dinner, then returned to his dormitory alone at seven-fifteen to study under guard.

Part of Virgil's requirements for graduation from radio school and final commissioning as an officer were three character recommendations. For one he turned to Alice's father, Frederick Madison Smith. "I can not but wish," Dr. Smith replied, "that in all cases where recommendations are asked I could write as hearty an endorsement as I can in yours."[15] Dr. Smith's previous reservations about Virgil were past. "Virgil Garnett Thomson," he wrote to the adjutant general in Washington, "is a man of sterling qualities, most excellent character and possessed of ability which holds promise of an efficient officer."

On July 13 Virgil completed his course, was commissioned a second lieutenant, Air Services Aeronautics, and directed to report to Fort Sill, in Oklahoma, which, since Virgil's earlier stay there, had "lost Camp Doniphan and acquired a flying field."

Virgil later described this training program as "bunk fatigue." They rose for drill at 4:30 A.M., did desultory flight training, and spent most afternoons lying on their "bunks and cussing." Mostly what they cussed was the heat, which hit "120 in the shade without any shade."[16]

From here he was transferred to Gerstner Field, in Lake Charles, Louisiana, a "soft aqueous jungle where giant mosquitoes that could bite through any blanket flew in V-shaped squadron formation." Here he was supposed to receive intensive flight training. Virgil's scant air time consisted of sitting in the back cockpit "playing in the air with wireless telephones."[17]

Here too he was stricken by the flu, which got him out of "some disgusting work" and gave him a week's adventure in the hospital, where he was "starved and sweated and purged and rubbed and examined and bathed by a nurse," he wrote to Alice.[18] Ten pounds lighter, he returned to the barracks, where a diet of chocolates and ten days of not moving from the bridge table restored him to his 130-pound weight.

Yet, however unprepared he felt, on October 26, 1918, his orders for overseas duty finally came. He was to report immediately to Hoboken, New Jersey, from where he would be sent to France for duty as a radio telephone operator under the chief of air service. During Virgil's aimless weeks of training in Oklahoma and Louisiana, his friend George Phillips had written to him from France, detailing his exploits and sending his condolences. "I commiserate with your banishment to Fort Sill. Here's hoping you are gone from there by now."[19] Finally, Virgil too would see real action.

He returned home on leave, where Geneve Lichtenwalter gave him a party. Mr. Murray photographed him in uniform. Best of all, Second Lieutenant Virgil Thomson attended Sunday church services with his proud father.

Yet Virgil never made it overseas. He never made it to Hoboken. He spent seven weeks in New York, waiting, fully equipped with his camel's hair sleeping bag and trench boots purchased from Abercrombie & Fitch, and anxious. But the final orders never came. What did come was the armistice. The Germans surrendered to the Allies on November 11. The war was over. George wrote from France, taunting Virgil somewhat.

> I hope very much that your orders will not be rescinded, though I fear that due to the sudden crumbling of the enemy, the government may have ceased sending any more Americans overseas. Of course, at this time, even if you should be fortunate enough to get across, you will have no opportunity to swim in the blood of battle. But in reality, actual conflict is only a part of what is to be experienced over here in France.[20]

Virgil Thomson requested and received an honorable discharge. He had joined the army to prove himself in combat overseas. No one could say he had not tried to get there.

Returning to Kansas City, he moved back under his father's roof and decided to enroll in more classes at the junior college. There he settled on two courses of action: to pursue a career as a musician, ideally, as a church organist in a well-off parish; and to attend an eastern university, Harvard being his first choice.

But another realization—furtive and powerful—was becoming undeniable. "I have become awfully fond of a fellow from California who goes to the theater and the restaurants with me," he had written to Alice from New York. "Saturday we are going up to the country at Newburgh on the Hudson and the people who invited us have promised to take us over to West Point and several other places I should love to go to. I think we are going to have a great time."

That fellow was Leland Poole. And if Virgil Thomson's army career had boosted his sense of manliness, his feelings for Leland just as surely dismantled it.

6 I DIDN'T WANT TO BE QUEER

W hen Oscar Wilde, not yet twenty-eight, came to America in 1882 for his extensive lecture tour, he was already an international celebrity, dubbed the "Apostle of Aesthetics," the "Long-Haired Divinity," and famously caricatured in cartoons by George du Maurier as Drawit Milde with flowing locks and handfuls of lilies.

Wilde gave over two hundred lectures in over 140 cities in American and Canada, from Boston to San Francisco, from Toronto to Fort Worth. On April 17, on the way to a date in Topeka, Wilde stopped in Kansas City for an appearance at the Coates Opera House. Reporters from the *Kansas City Star* and the *Kansas City Times* waited at Union Depot to cover his arrival at dawn. Young women from proper families and curious chambermaids stationed themselves outside Wilde's hotel room hoping to glimpse him. The opera house was nearly sold out. The papers were filled with anticipatory stories.

To Americans Wilde's "invocations of beauty managed to sound faintly subversive, faintly unhealthy," his biographer Richard Ellmann wrote. "His tour was a series of more or less successful confrontations in which his flagrant and unconventional charm was pitted against conventional maleness and resultant suspicion."[1] By the time Wilde arrived in Kansas City, his trademark turns of phrase ("too utterly too") had entered the local lexicon. In an article titled "Quite Too Too," a *Star* reporter wrote of Wilde's "aesthetically poetical language" and "effeminate, too utterly too smile," which the "damsels of New York and Boston went crazy over."

The reception Wilde received in Kansas City involved a precarious dance of wits. It would have been too utterly too easy to simply dismiss Wilde as a fop, a dandy. He was too confident, massive (over six feet, three inches and broad shouldered), and brilliant for that. Wilde was pushing the boundaries and inviting the ridicule.

Absent from the coverage of Wilde was even a suggestion that he actually might be a homosexual. This was not only because Wilde had a wife and two sons for cover but also because such a possibility was simply unthinkable—to Wilde's readers, to the women who flocked to his dressing rooms, even to the hard-nosed reporters who covered him—and therefore unmentionable. Naturally, it was assumed that if any man harbored such shameful desires, he would put all his energy into quashing them. The fact that Wilde could play at being a dandy proved that he was not worried about such speculations, much the way that, more recently, Liberace made his gender-blurring extravagance safe by maintaining—until the sad end of his life—an absolutely asexual public persona.

Even more telling about attitudes toward homosexuality in Kansas City at the turn of the century was the coverage of Wilde's infamous trial in 1895, the year before Virgil Thomson's birth. "Oscar Wilde Disgraced" ran the front-page headline of the *Kansas City Star* on April 5. The next day's account in the *Kansas City Times,* filed from London but reedited in Kansas City, described at length the chaos in the Old Bailey courtroom, "filled with spectators who were armed with newspapers and packages of sandwiches," and hinted at the relationship between Wilde and Alfred Taylor, called his "procurer." Intimations of immorality between Wilde and young Lord Alfred Douglas filled the copy: "It is no wonder that the Marquis of Queensberry protested against the intimacy between his son and Wilde. The wonder is, counsel said, that this man has been so long tolerated in London society."[2]

In courtroom transcripts Wilde was accused of "indecent practices" and "the grave offence." Yet even these veiled phrases were expunged from the Kansas City newspapers. This squeamishness was not confined to middle America. Even the *New York Times* would refer to the crime that landed Wilde in prison only as a "heinous charge."[3]

Virgil Thomson must have been flustered in the spring of 1914 when in the high school yearbook his graduation photograph was captioned, "O Shades of Oscar Wilde, Millet, and Paderewski." This may have amused the student editors, but the barb could have been no laughing matter to Thomson.

Yet he liked to brag about the open vice in the Kansas City of his youth. "Indeed, as recently as the 1920s," he wrote on the first page of his autobiography, "H. L. Mencken boasted for us that within the half mile around Twelfth and Main there were two thousand second-story hotels."[4] There was also a homosexual network in Kansas City. But it was deep underground, and no one talked, let alone boasted, about it.

Thomson's senior year, 1913–14, was a landmark period in Kansas City's confronting of vice. The city was dominated by the Democratic political machine run by James Pendergast, "Alderman Jim," a beefy Irish Catholic, and, when Jim died in 1911, by his younger brother Tom. The Pendergasts considered themselves champions of the downtrodden: immigrants, blacks, and laborers; none of their "friends" ever went hungry or stayed jobless. Liquor, prostitution, and gambling oiled the machine, and the Democrats were not about to dismantle it.

But there was another side to Kansas City: proper, Protestant, puritanical. The reformers and the machine loyalists were headed for battle when Thomson was a boy. What finally caused an open war was the shocking murder in early October 1913 of a teenage female prostitute.

A new chapter of the Anti-Vice Society was formed, and the local press provided daily front-page coverage. The reformers published newsletters that were distributed in churches and from street stands. One, called "Kansas City's Shame," reported the grim details.

> According to the last enumeration there were 544 public prostitutes in Kansas City. The Board of Public Welfare reports that the average number of visitors to prostitutes per day is four-and-seven-tenths. The amount expended with prostitutes in one year is nearly a million and a half dollars, or considerably more than the salaries of all the public school teachers in the city. . . . Recent startling exposures of immorality among boys and girls on the South Side are fresh in memory. . . . An estimated 61% of men and boys in Kansas City have or have had a venereal disease; 20% of

Kansas City men over 21 have an infectious venereal disease. About one in five Kansas City women will marry an infected man.[5]

The frenzied antivice crusade was not free of absurd excess. In one *Kansas City Times* article a local antivice leader cited the "vicious popular song" as a major contributor to the problem: "The great portion of popular music constitutes a text in vicious sexuality."[6] It took four efforts, but in 1921 the antivice activists finally got passed a law that defined prostitution as a public nuisance, negating a previous ruling from the state supreme court, stacked with Pendergast's appointees.

Yet virtually missing from the literature of this crusade is any open mention of homosexuality. Combatting this unspeakable offense was part of the agenda, but one must read between the lines to discern it. For example, in September 1922 the Law Enforcement Association released the statistics of teens who had appeared before the juvenile court during a recent crackdown. Of 157 citations to minors, most involved charges of stealing, lying, incorrigible behavior, or truancy. There were 12 arrests for sex delinquency, which surely meant teenage prostitution. There were also 6 arrests of males for "sex perversion."

Virgil Thomson, already an avid newspaper reader, would have followed the front-page coverage of the antivice campaign. In most other ways the fall of 1913, the fall he began his senior year in high school, was unremarkable. Much-needed September rains brought relief from a punishing, but not atypical, summer drought. The Midwest was caught up in a fad for plant juice, and the local papers carried almost daily testimonials from area citizens to its beneficial effects on health and well-being. It was reported that the number of motor cars in Kansas City had climbed to 5,311. Ty Cobb's signing of a contract with the Detroit Tigers for the highest-ever salary in baseball ($40,000) made headlines.

Respectful feature articles and adulatory reviews in the *Star* and the *Times* accompanied the appearance at the convention hall of the Chicago Opera with Mary Garden in Massenet's *Le Jongleur de Notre Dame,* and Tito Ruffo in Verdi's *Rigoletto,* and the recitals by Geraldine Farrar, Louise Homer, and the charismatic Paderewski—all of which Thomson attended.

On November 25 Thomson turned seventeen. For his birthday he received a present from Robert Leigh Murray—a hard-to-find book, the second edition (1909) of *De Profundis,* Oscar Wilde's anguished, bitter, rambling journal written from Reading prison. The main body of the work consists of letters written to Lord Alfred Douglas. The G. P. Putnam edition includes four letters written to the editor, Wilde's friend Robert Ross, as well as a sensitive preface by Ross.

At the time of this gift, Murray, the outwardly hearty, inwardly tortured church tenor and piano salesman, was providing Thomson with much-needed professional guidance and introductions to Kansas City's best teachers. The book is inscribed, "To a lad whose friendship is a very pleasant thing to me." This was a touching and sad gesture and an unspoken confession. "This is who I am," Murray would seem to have been saying. "And I think this may be who you are too." He was inviting Thomson to a secret sect. Thomson would have recoiled at the idea.

Yet the handsomely bound volume with inlaid gold lettering on the cover spoke deeply to Thomson. He kept it all his life. In it passages from the text are underlined and bracketed in pencil. Sometimes there are commentaries in the margins written in Thomson's distinctive handscript. When these emendations were written is unknown. But the unabashed seriousness of tone suggests they date from his youth.

> No man of my position can fall into the mire of life without getting a great deal of pity from his inferiors.[7]

This is bracketed by Thomson with the word "inferiors" underscored. Where Wilde writes,

> I may say candidly that I am getting gradually to a state of mind when I think that everything that happens is for the best. This may be philosophy or a broken heart,[8]

Thomson underlines the final sentence and notes in the margins, "It is truly." Other pencil-marked passages include these:

> Do write clearly. Otherwise it looks as if you had something to conceal.[9]

> Where there is sorrow there is holy ground.[10]

> I must be far more of an individualist than I ever was. I must get far more out of myself than I ever got, and ask far less of the world

than I ever asked. Indeed, my ruin came not from too great individualism of life but from too little. The one disgraceful, unpardonable, and to all time contemptible action of my life was to allow myself to appeal to society for help and protection.[11]

Society, as we have constituted it, will have no place for me, has none to offer; but Nature, whose sweet rains fall on unjust and just alike, will have clefts in the rocks where I may hide, and secret valleys in whose silence I may weep undisturbed. She will hang the night with stars so that I may walk abroad in the darkness without stumbling, and send the wind over my footprints so that none may trick me in great waters, and with bitter herbs make me whole.[12]

One spring day at his Chelsea Hotel apartment, Virgil Thomson, then ninety-one, got to talking with uncommon candor about this time in his youth and his homosexuality.

I didn't want to be queer. No! No! No! That was another hurdle I didn't want to have to jump over. Nowadays it's much easier. But in those days if you got caught around Harvard you got kicked out. And the same way with the instructors.

. . . Kansas City was a center not only of culture but of vice. I knew all about it by the time I was ten or twelve. But I wasn't doing anything.

. . . You didn't mention it. You didn't say everything, but you understood everything. After the war, you could do what you wanted, as long as you didn't tell anything. You see, now they tell people and talk about it, and they use the terms in books! Of course everybody knew about the Oscar Wilde case.[13]

Nowadays, in most ways, it is much easier, as Thomson acknowledged. He lived to see that ease come to be. Yet during Thomson's youth, the homosexual world was so hidden that, ironically, it was often overlooked by the antivice activists. The 1990s have seen the emergence of fundamentalist avengers calling for the eradication of homosexuality. They not only speak of it; they are obsessed with it. Former Surgeon General C. Everett Koop, a conservative Republican uncomfortable with homosexuality, has said that homophobia is too mild a term for what he witnessed during his watch. It wasn't fear but hate, he said, that consumed the antihomosexual crusaders.

Still, in Thomson's youth, the subject was simply not mentioned in proper company. Not even acknowledged. If a homosexual person was carelessly open, or flagrantly defiant, he could be ostracized at best, imprisoned at worst. But the blackout on discussion of the matter actually allowed it to exist in private enclaves with what may have been less surrounding hysteria than what many homosexuals have faced in the 1990s.

Thomson didn't want to be queer. He would eventually have to concede that he was. But he learned well the lessons of his youth. All his life he was loath to talk about himself, and was critical of those who did. Even during his Paris days, and certainly after he returned to New York in 1940, Thomson maintained two circles of friends. He had many gay friends with whom he loved being catty, outrageous, and affectionate. He was eager for gay gossip and full of advice (mostly outmoded) for coping.

But he also had a circle of "proper" friends, mostly heterosexual, with whom he never talked about "being queer." He would rarely mix his proper friends with his more outspoken gay friends. Of course, those gay male friends who knew how to be polite in mixed company— deferential to women, discreet—were welcomed into mixed gatherings.

Thomson maintained this separation scrupulously. During thirty-seven years of close friendship and collegial work with the mezzo-soprano Betty Allen, a grand woman, a superb artist, and an insightful person, he never once mentioned being homosexual. She knew this was a subject not to be broached, and she never did. She was one who "didn't say everything, but understood everything." Almost all of his other women friends report the same experience.

In public—for going to concerts, dinners, testimonials—Thomson always preferred to have a female companion. During his life he had a whole series of women friends, mostly younger, often married, who were suited to this role and happy to oblige.

Thomson would not allow his sexuality to be referred to in print, though he couldn't keep it from the underground gay press and didn't really care, thinking no one who really mattered would see it. In his 420-page autobiography there is no mention of it, though there are veiled, mostly contrived stories of youthful attachments to women. Even Ned Rorem was cautious about writing of Thomson's sexuality. Thomson is a recurring figure in Rorem's extensive and popular diaries. Rorem relates many anecdotes of Thomson's being flirtatious with men, remarking with approval on someone's handsomeness, or displaying a campy wit. But not once in those four volumes do you read the flat-out statement that Virgil Thomson was homosexual. And Thomson used to say—not directly to Rorem—that he would have sued had Rorem done so. In this Thomson was conducting himself like Oscar Wilde, who went to his grave publicly denying that he was homosexual.

When the gay liberation movement emerged, Thomson was largely opposed. He wished no one persecution and was pleased to think that this movement might lessen it; but he was against the new openness, which he considered misguided, not understanding that it was a precondition to change. He always counseled keeping homosexuality absolutely private. When his younger openly gay friends told him of their ostracizing parents, his reaction was to ask, "What did you expect? They didn't want to know!" He disliked the term "gay" and never used it. His word was "queer," which he preferred for its shock value and its connotation of manliness rather than effeminacy. Thomson lived to see the word "queer" gain politically correct currency, which miffed him.

In his life Virgil Thomson had his share of involvements with men. He knew unrequited love, powerful attraction, anonymous passion, and long-term devotion. But at the age of seventeen he "didn't want to be queer." That feeling and its attendant humiliation would never really leave him.

There is no reason to doubt his story that he didn't "start being queer" until he went to Paris as a Harvard student. But in the army he met a man who tempted him.

Leland Stanford Poole was born in Michigan two years before Virgil Thomson. When they met in 1918 in New York, they were both in the service. Virgil was taking courses at Columbia to obtain a commission as a squadron radio officer. Leland's family had moved to California. An affable, well-read young man with his Irish mother's fair skin and sandy hair, Leland became Virgil's regular companion at theaters and restaurants. Virgil was clearly taken with his new friend, whom he nicknamed "Prim," and also, "D.O.T." (Dear Old Thing). Eventually their lives split in direction, and they seldom saw each other. But the friendship survived the distance and is documented in some revealing letters.

In November 1918, while awaiting his official discharge, Virgil wrote to Leland in Rich Field, Texas, "Dear Prim, What on earth is the matter? I thought you might have been busy or blue and didn't want to write to me. So I have begun to worry as mothers do when their children don't come home."[14] And nine days later: "Really and honestly Leland. I miss you a lot in New York. There are so many things and thrills that I feel you really ought to share with me. The opera and the concerts and the theater and the places to lunch and especially the Newburgh [Hotel] doesn't seem the Newburgh without you under the pink comforter."[15]

By the spring of 1919, having decided to attend Harvard, Virgil wanted Leland, now living in San Francisco, to come live with him, though he was cautious in suggesting it.

> O Leland, it would be great if you would come East next year. And whether we lived together or not (I think we would get on, don't you?) your being there would be a moral support. I am afraid bachelor's apartments are expensive and garrets exorbitant in price. But doesn't a hall bedroom in Cambridge with an electric stove and a grand piano, eight minutes from Boston on the subway, sound romantic? It does to me. Write me soon. Toujours. Votre ami devote, Tommy[16]

By July something had happened to make Virgil, back home in Kansas City for the summer, boost his effort to bring Leland East. Leland wrote with two ideas. One concerned his finding work in New York. The other raised the possibility of his getting married to a young woman from San Francisco. It took all Virgil's powers of persuasion to knock down the latter. Through the pumped-up bluster of Virgil's prose and his invention of a love affair, one senses his true hurt and fear.

> Certainly, if such "practicality" is the alternative to Boston, by all means, go East young man. Go East anyway, Lee, and if Boston is really as good for your object as New York, then my arms and my garret are open.
>   . . . Marrying on $100 a month!! God!! Should think you *would* rip your vest buttons. Certainly the prospect would never make me rip my breast buttons. Marriage is all very well if the girl is charming and has a million dollars. Also if she is ugly and has a million dollars.
>   But remember, as the Smart Set says, that mere money ($100 a month, for instance) can't buy happiness, it takes a whole lot of money. I utter these blasphemies in spite of the fact that I've been deep in silly calf love all summer. But I just wish you could view Heine Hoffman's domestic bliss. And some more too. You see them—soldiers come home to a wife and a damn baby and a before-the-war salary! Two months kills all the "esprit de la vie" they ever had. "Esprit du corps" in its literal sense is all they have

and that becomes just habit in six months. Far be it from me to disparage "true love." But it's like any other project. It takes money to develop it. Let the future go to hell. Come East and we'll build a past that no female can resist.[17]

By the end of August, Virgil was at Harvard in the "city of culture, beans and salt cod," as he described it to Leland, and resigned to Leland's staying in San Francisco, though he did not give up his campaign.

I'd love to be with you, old slut, charming, sentimental, puritanical, emotional bohemian. But Boston is no place for the investment business. What do you say to New York year after next, two years from date?
Affectionately yours, Tommy[18]

Leland would never make it to Cambridge, or to New York, for anything more than a short visit. Nor would Leland ever marry. As Virgil commenced his Harvard career, he was outwardly cocky. But throughout this period he voiced his insecurities and heartache in letters to Leland.

In his nineties, Virgil Thomson claimed that he had known Leland for ten years before realizing that he was "queer." ("We didn't talk about these things, and I wasn't doing it.") Their letters suggest otherwise. But only suggest. One simply didn't talk about these things.

7 | LONELINESS IN PLEASURE AT HARVARD

Virgil Thomson used to say that he decided to go to Harvard because "that's where all the money was." And he did wind up winning awards and fellowships for each year of his academic career, though not enough to support himself.

But there was more to this decision. Harvard meant prestige. Harvard was the best. Thomson was still uncertain about his professional path. He wanted to study music, for sure. But he was reluctant to enter a conservatory. His musical skills were still too undeveloped and his intellectual curiosity too expansive for that. Boston could provide access to conservatory training in organ and piano. And being an organist and choir director at a well-heeled suburban church was beginning to seem like a secure and not unpalatable choice. For this the pedigree of Harvard would clearly help. Thomson later wrote that he also intended to pursue a composer's career. But if this was so, he didn't act upon it until the summer after his first year at Harvard, when he composed his first acknowledged works.

Thomson also chose Harvard because he wanted to get far away from Kansas City. He would not let himself become like Archibald Higbie, the artistic-minded resident of Edgar Lee Masters's poetical town Spoon River who tried life on the Continent but returned home a failure and died embittered.

And there in Rome, among the artists,
Speaking Italian, speaking French,
I seemed to myself at times to be free
Of every trace of my origin.
I seemed to be reaching the heights of art
And to breathe the air that the masters breathed,
And to see the world with their eyes.
But still they'd pass my work and say:
"What are you driving at, my friend?
Sometimes the face looks like Apollo's,
At others it has a trace of Lincoln's."[1]

Thomson echoed these sentiments in his July 21 letter to Leland Poole, explaining his decision to attend Harvard and trying one last time to persuade Poole to join him: "You can make more money East. You can get better experience there. And no young man has any business living at home. The more comfortable the home, the more dangerous its influence."[2]

Virgil Thomson would later write with nostalgia of his Missouri roots and say that he went to Paris to tell everybody there, through his life and works, about Kansas City. But this was only after he had escaped. The pattern of leaving home, of going to the big city, the old continent, the new frontier, only to realize how much you are bound to your "nativity," as Masters put it, only to extoll it from afar: this is a recurring theme in American culture. In Thomson's case, the sense of being stuck had an added sexual element. Maybe by his going away his sexual confusions would go away too. He'd grow out of them. Or, alternatively, far from home he would feel free to resolve them, to act upon them.

But starting this East Coast adventure would require some seed money. For this his turned to his friends the Smiths. Alice had told him of a Mormon scholarship fund for prospective teachers. The award could be paid back either through service or in installments. Virgil had no intention of teaching in a church school, but Mrs. Smith, thinking this idea an excellent solution to Virgil's dilemma, was convinced the teaching obligation could be fudged.

One night Virgil asked for an audience with Dr. Smith in his study. Impressed by Virgil's self-confidence, Dr. Smith agreed to provide $2,000 from the church's scholarship fund. At the time Virgil was unconcerned about repaying the loan, thinking that later on he could finesse it. It took twenty years and a series of acrimonious letters from the trustees of the Mormon church before Virgil caved in and settled the debt.

Before he left for Harvard, Virgil was to receive one more bequest: $100 from his grandmother. Flora Thomson had been spending the winter, as usual, with her son's family. She had long ago distributed what remained of her lands and spent what money she had left. Yet she wished to leave a legacy to Virgil. "I was her only male grandchild," Virgil later wrote, "and I had been a soldier like her husband." She changed her will, then took to bed.

> Shortly afterward she ceased to be aware. Her speech, however, kept following familiar patterns. She would pray aloud: "Forgive us our sins and come to see us soon." When she died asleep, late in March, we took her to Saline County for burial beside her Confederate soldier, waiting since 1862 in the graveyard of their county church, called Rehoboth. On the morning of the funeral there arrived by train, for paying her last call on "Miss Flora," a Negro woman of near Miss Flora's age who had in early years belonged to her.[3]

As this exaggeratedly nostalgic account from Thomson's autobiography suggests, another thing he inherited from his grandmother was a plantation attitude toward black people. Moreover, writing to Leland Poole while pumped up with manly bluster, Thomson portrayed the incident as a big brother: "My grandmother died last Monday," he mentions in passing. "I am back from the country where I met great aunts and cousins indefinitely and even some niggers who had belonged to her."[4]

Virgil arrived at Harvard in mid-August 1919. On his first day there, he found a large, comfortable room in a college-owned boardinghouse run by a massive British widow. The three-story, frame house was located on Oxford Street, a block from Harvard Yard. When, during his second year there, the lighting was converted from gas to electric, Virgil was relieved to be rid of the gas fume smells.

Not wanting to rely for practice on the overutilized college pianos, Virgil decided he must have an instrument in his room. He found one at the downtown Boston store of the piano manufacturer Charles Stieff, a new mahogany grand priced at $785. Writing to Dr. Smith of his arrival at college, Virgil boasted of his savvy purchase: "The manager took a fancy to my playing, and thinking perhaps he was getting in on the ground floor with a rising genius, or something like that, offered to sell me a piano at wholesale price, paying $20 a month and $100 down. . . . So I have secured a perfect piano as cheaply as I could rent a bad one, and one which I can clear from four to seven hundred dollars at any time I want to sell it."[5]

Virgil's landlady, Mrs. Brown, was delighted at the prospect of her new boarder's music making, as he told Leland in a letter: "I have a gorgeous piano. My landlady comes in and stands with hands folded, just to gaze on the great shiny red thing. She gave me a silk cloth to dust it with. She was afraid to touch it."[6]

Virgil and Mrs. Brown got on splendidly. Before long they were cooking together, even making illegal brews, Prohibition having been decreed earlier that year. Using recipes from the woman's seventeenth-century English cookbook, they produced meads of fermented honey and water, and other alcoholic concoctions even less effective.

Mrs. Brown's wholesome meals cost eight dollars a week. The house was busy all the time and filled with "swell chaps" from school, including one who owned a motorcycle and sidecar who took Virgil for jaunts to towns as far away as Plymouth. There were "only a few interesting older people," including a Japanese naturalist and a doctor whom the students suspected of doing secret service work.

Virgil immediately secured a French tutor, a former officer of the Foreign Legion who promised to impart a proper Parisian accent. Every Harvard undergraduate was required to pass oral examinations in French and German. Virgil was determined to pass French without enrolling in any course, and eight weeks into his first semester he did. He also found a job playing organ for occasional evening meetings of the Tremont Street Methodist Church, near Boston Common.

Since Harvard gave no credit for studying musical instruments, Virgil arranged for private lessons in piano or organ. Heinrich Gebhard was a German-born pianist and composer who had studied with Theodor Leschetizky. An advocate of contemporary music, he had given the first American performances of Strauss's *Burlesque* for piano and orchestra. He later taught Leonard Bernstein. Thomson paid him a steep ten dollars per lesson, which meant that he could afford only weekly half-hour organ lessons at four dollars from Wallace Goodrich, organist of the Boston Symphony Orchestra and dean of the faculty at the New England Conservatory. For organ practice Virgil had to rent time at twenty-five cents an hour at Appleton Chapel, near the north brick wall of Harvard Yard.

Because Virgil had completed nearly two years at the junior college in Kansas City, he was registered at Harvard as an "unclassified student," his year of graduation to be determined. He was given credit for the science and mathematics courses he had taken, but placed in entry-level history, philosophy, and German courses.

He was miffed about being assigned to Music I, the beginning harmony class. This was the ruling of the professor with whom he would have a chilly four-year relationship, Walter R. Spalding, chairman of the Division of Music and a Teutonic traditionalist. (Another former student, Elliott Carter, remembers Spalding as "stubborn, uncompromising and pedantic.")[7] Virgil disdained Spalding's courses and advice, and Spalding, Virgil later wrote, "correct[ed] me without cease for my uppishness."[8] In truth, Virgil's knowledge of harmony was spotty, his awareness of this being one reason he had avoided a conservatory.

There was another conservative on the music faculty, however, whom Virgil respected immediately, Dr. Archibald T. Davison, known as "Doc," at the time "thirty-four, smallish, sandy-haired, and balding" and "a Scottish disciplinarian of relentless mission."[9] Born in Boston, educated at Harvard, and, except for one year of organ study with Widor in Paris, associated with Harvard throughout his career, Davison was a pioneer in the rediscovery of early music: Gregorian chant, medieval organum, Renaissance polyphony, a repertory that had been almost totally forgotten. In 1946 he would coedit (with Willi Apel) the *Historical Anthology of Music,* comprehensive volumes still assigned to most university music students.

But it was as conductor of the Harvard Glee Club for twenty-five years that Davison decisively shaped Virgil and generations of other musicians. When he took over the singing group in 1912, his colleagues couldn't understand what this sober scholar would do with an ensemble that sang mostly football fight songs and breezy ballads accompanied by mandolins. But Davison intended to transform the club into an choir for the performance of serious European classical music. In his manifesto "A New Standard for Glee Clubs," published in 1915 by the *Harvard Musical Review,* Davison wrote that initially his plan was met with "absolutely unbroken opposition," particularly from alumni who felt there was "something a bit unearthly about young men really taking a delight in performing works of the early church composers."

But within three years, Davison wrote, the young choristers took pride in the "approbation of professional musicians and the respect of the public." As they prepared their programs, the singers found themselves "increasingly enthusiastic over the *music* rather than the *concert.*"

In his article Davison's disdain for popular music was tactfully broached: "Much of it is good in its class, and more of it is worthy because of the memories it awakens." However, he did not object to the blunt assessment of his conservative colleague Daniel Gregory Mason, who, in his preface to Davison's 1922 *Harvard University Glee Club Collection,* wrote "that nature abhors a vacuum, and that it is only empty minds that harbor jazz."[10] Mason applauded the edifying choices Davison published in this groundbreaking volume, works by Josquin, Allegri, Lassus, and Bach, among them. He even vouched for a few "modern and more ambitious pieces" by Gounod, Dvořák, and Rubinstein.

Virgil joined the choir's tenor section that first semester. By then, the fall of 1919, the men were giving concert tours during vacations and appearing regularly in Boston's Symphony Hall. Their importance to the musical life of the city grew steadily. A Symphony Hall advertisement in the *Boston Evening Transcript* one spring week in 1922 gives equal billing to upcoming concerts by the violinist Jascha Heifetz, the soprano Rosa Ponselle, the Handel and Haydn Society, the Boston Symphony Orchestra under Pierre Monteux, and the Harvard Glee Club with a guest soloist, the cellist Pablo Casals.

This was heady music making, and Virgil took to it. "The choir is wonderful," he wrote to his sister, Ruby. "We sing medieval things in Latin without accompaniment, and sing them beautifully."[11] Virgil also joined the University Choir, a joint ensemble of men from Harvard and women from Radcliffe who sang for Appleton Chapel services and ceremonial college occasions. Participation in the glee club meant that Virgil needed formal clothes. He found them—a dress suit, a tuxedo coat, and a white dress vest—downtown at J. C. Littlefield, outfitter to the Boston Brahmin set. The clothes cost $100, exactly the amount of his grandmother's bequest.

Virgil remembered Doc Davison as a man of tremendous personal reserve, who "lived with a widowed mother and did not marry till she died."[12] Their association did not survive Virgil's years at Harvard.

However, with his faculty adviser, the Cambridge-born, Harvard-educated Edward Burlingame Hill, Virgil established a collegial friendship, exchanging letters until just before Hill's death in 1960. Hill was a fellow Francophile, and Virgil signed up that first semester for Hill's course called "Modern French Music: D'Indy, Fauré and Debussy," a subject tolerated by Spalding, the conservative chairman, because Hill was a tenured senior colleague.

Hill was a prolific composer whose works were suffused with the harmonies and colors of the French impressionists he adored, particularly Ravel. Given the tradition-bound thinking of his colleagues, Hill was a refreshing mentor who was alert to new music and wrote with excitement about Stravinsky and respect for Schoenberg. On the other hand, when Virgil arrived, Davison was still talking with outrage of a 1914 performance the conductor Karl Muck had done with the Boston Symphony of Schoenberg's *Five Orchestra Pieces.*

Hill encouraged his students to investigate the indigenous music of this country—folk music, gospel—as possible source materials for truly American concert works. He flirted with jazz in his own works during the early 1930s: a propulsive Piano Concertino and his *Jazz Studies* for two pianos. However, he knew the risk of this flirtation and was unhappy with Copland's jazz-inspired *Music for the Theater* when he heard it performed in 1925. "Close to rotten," he called it in a letter to Virgil. "The usual clever Hebraic assimilation of the worst features of polytonality, and little of expressive interest except the jazz burlesque."[13] It would seem from his language that, for all his sympathy for young composers, including Copland, Hill was tainted with a touch of anti-Semitism, as were many of his colleagues at pre–World War II Harvard.

Hill decried the cold shoulder American composers got from American orchestras, identifying a problem that persists today: "Since American orchestras are with few exceptions led by foreign conductors, we find that their tendency as a rule is to accept frequently second or third rate works by foreigners of their countrymen, in preference to giving Americans a chance."[14] His students would include Ross Lee Finney, Randall Thompson, Walter Piston, Elliott Carter, and Leonard Bernstein. Carter remembered that during the late 1920s, when Serge Koussevitzky at the Boston Symphony Orchestra was commissioning new works, particularly American works (a legacy that is the glory of the orchestra), only Hill among the Harvard faculty was supportive. Davison, Spalding, Ballantine—"they hated it," Carter said; "they thought Koussevitzky was crazy, that most of modern music was hopeless. The Harvard music department at that time was primarily interested in producing organists for churches."[15]

Thomson later credited Hill with being his only valued teacher of orchestration. In addition, Hill encouraged Thomson to write about music, encouragement that turned out to be pivotal. When Hill died, Thomson wrote to the professor's son, "Of all my teachers he was the one from whom I learned the most and for whose teaching I remained most grateful. Grateful too for kindness and for the adult courtesy so few of our teachers in those days offered."[16]

There was another faculty member at Harvard, not a music professor and never formally Thomson's teacher, who nevertheless changed Virgil's life. S. Foster Damon, a "slender, pale poet with a blond mustache,"[17] was at that time an instructor in freshman English. Born in nearby Newton, he had graduated from Harvard in 1914 and, in the fall of 1919 when Thomson met him, was pursuing a master's degree at Harvard that it would take him until 1927 to complete. But Damon was uninterested in studying the approved canon of writers and poets certified by Harvard as suitable subjects for academic theses. Damon was an intellectual adventurer, a composer and musical scholar as well as a poet drawn to modernists and visionaries. Another of Damon's younger student friends, e. e. cummings, later told his biographer that "practically everything I know about painting and poetry came to me through Damon."[18]

At the time Damon was "preparing privately, since Harvard would have none of it," as Thomson later wrote, a pathbreaking book, *William Blake: His Philosophy and Symbols*. Damon hadn't even bothered to submit it as a master's thesis to the conservative Harvard English department. Yet, as Malcolm Cowley, another student from that time, later wrote, Damon's book, eventually published in 1924, "was to inspire many doctoral dissertations."

Damon was modest about his musical compositions, but proud of being a founder and editor of and contributor to the *Harvard Musical Review*. Undaunted by the certain disapproval of his colleagues, he wrote insightful articles defending popular music and called attention to the music of Erik Satie, then dismissed by cerebral Harvard composers as a negligible eccentric. Damon predicted in this 1914 article that Satie might become the "leader of a return-to-simplicity school, which is bound to come, considering the tremendously complicated work of the Germans and the Russians." With the advent in 1920s Paris of the band of composers dubbed Les Six, this prediction came to pass.

For a scholar working in academia, Damon's writings were unconventional: articles on Schoenberg, Strindberg, Sibelius, and the Chinese poet Li Po; a 1931 article on Mickey Mouse; a history of square dancing in America. He revered and befriended the poet Amy Lowell, brought students to her home in Brookline, and became her first biographer.

Given that Damon found little sympathy from his faculty colleagues for his unorthodox interests, and that even most Harvard students were resistant, it's not surprising that he sought impressionable, unjaded undergraduates as intellectual soulmates. At twenty-three, Thomson was only three years younger than Damon when they met. So their friendship was particularly easy. There was not a tinge of sexual tension in this relationship. Though shy with women, Damon was securely heterosexual. Thomson found it a relief to be with someone so psychologically solid and intellectual interesting. And he was flattered by Damon's attentions.

Thomson remembers once being taken by Damon to the big family house in Newton. But usually he visited him in his room above the Western Club in Harvard Square. There they talked music and poetry. Some of the works Damon introduced Thomson to were "merely informative or charming": the critical writings of T. S. Eliot, the poetry of Stephen Crane and Herman Melville. "Others changed my life," he wrote: "the piano works of Erik Satie, a pile of them four inches high, and a thin small volume called *Tender Buttons,* by Gertrude Stein."[19] Satie would become for Thomson a musical idol, a composer whose simplicity and directness of statement, whose beautifully deliberate inconsequence, fortified Thomson's own tendencies in that direction and allowed him to resist the complexity and "one hundred percent dissonant saturation" that within a decade would be demanded of all composers who expected to be taken seriously. And *Tender Buttons* not only led to a meeting with his most important collaborator but gave him a vision for an entirely fresh way to write music.

Damon was an "opener of doors," Thomson wrote. But there was one door that Damon had never tried. It was Thomson who opened it for him, when he introduced him to the pleasures of peyote.

Virgil had tried peyote during his junior college days in Kansas City—just once. The person who introduced him to it was, of all people, Alice's father, Dr. Frederick Madison Smith. The Mormons had well-publicized prohibitions against alcohol and drugs. As head of the church, Dr. Smith did not believe he could exempt himself from its rules. But he did not believe that peyote was, technically, a drug. To him it was a natural substance, an ancient means to tap one's inner powers derived from hallucinogenic cactus "neither injurious nor habit-forming."[20] As a psychologist, Dr. Smith was drawn to the study of parapsychology. While pursuing his Ph.D., he had read in Have-lock Ellis of the rituals and powers of peyote. One winter, the year before Virgil met him, Dr. Smith had taken his wife, who was recuperating from an illness, for a rest visit to Texas. There he observed Native American Indians who ate the drug in pellet form and others, Catholic converts, who made from it a tea for communion.

Dr. Smith was a believer in man's powers of prophecy and vision. His grandfather's accounts of his own visions were the bedrock of the Mormon religion. Dr. Smith wanted to understand the process. His dissertation, subsequently a book, *The Higher Powers of Man,* published in 1918, was an examination of ecstatic states, a phenomenon that men glimpsed, he thought, only occasionally: in the experience of getting a "second wind" of energy after a hard physical workout; in emergencies (shipwrecks, mine disasters) when man was able to "tap the deeper lying layers of energy and keep up his own courage and that of his fellow unfortunates."[21]

Dr. Smith believed that Jesus Christ may have been the "One who, more than any other throughout His public ministry, maintained this higher and more exalted state." In the book he discusses three states of ecstasy—ecstasies of inclination (such as sexual love, sacrifice, religious ecstasy); aesthetic ecstasy; intellectual ecstasy—and devotes a whole chapter to the wonders of peyote religions. Naturally his research involved interviews with Indians from the Texas reservations and reflections on his own experiences with peyote, though these he did not dare to chronicle.

One night in his study after dinner, Dr. Smith described to Virgil his peyote "highs," with their "characteristic excitation to feats of endurance and to colored visions." Virgil asked if he might try it. Dr. Smith obliged him, for he believed that musical ecstasy was particularly powerful. ("It ravishes with a bliss equal to love cramps. . . .")[22] His one condition was that Virgil promise to write of his experience for use in Dr. Smith's studies. He gave Virgil "five bumpy little buttons, less than an inch across and hard as wood," and suggested he chew them up before he went to bed.

I did exactly that, though the taste was so horrid, especially where tough crumbs stuck in my teeth, that eventually I vomited. This clearing of the stomach relieved the nausea without interfering with the drug. The effects, full visions each as complete in color and texture as a stage set, began slowly to appear before my closed or open eyes, then came more rapidly till two hours later they were flashing at least twice every second, with no delay involved in their complete perception. Each one, moreover, had a meaning, could have been published with a title; and their assembled symbolisms or subjects, though not always sequentially related, constituted a view of life not only picturesque and vast, but just as clearly all mine and all true.[23]

This experience lasted from ten in the evening, after he had vomited and when the full effects of the peyote took hold, until eight the next morning. Virgil did not sleep at all. But he emerged from his bedroom feeling no fatigue, his family unaware that anything unusual had happened.

All this he later described to Damon, who was intensely interested and wanted to try it. Virgil wrote to Dr. Smith, who was still obtaining peyote from those Texas Indians. The Mormon president became Virgil's supplier. He and Damon, and sometimes also the young poet Robert Hillyer, would take peyote together—about ten times over the next few years.

The effect on Damon was profound, judging by the turn his writing took. He started reading the *Occult Review* and published articles in it: "The Symbols of Alchemy" and "The Evidence for Literal Transmutation." For Virgil these peyote adventures with Damon were always surprising and visually sumptuous. "But in none did the heavens so definitely open as they had for me that first time, alone in my room."[24]

In 1927, frustrated with his colleagues' indifference to the poetry and modern art that excited him, Damon left Harvard for a position in the English department at Brown University, where he taught for forty years, respected by his peers and beloved by his students. He married Louise Wheelwright, the sensitive sister of the poet John Wheelwright, to whom Damon had been a mentor at Harvard. Later, Louise suffered bouts with mental illness—delusions, paranoia—that required periodic stays in psychiatric hospitals. At home in Providence little children in the neighborhood started making fun of her. Instead of chasing them away, Damon built a playroom in his basement, invited them in, and got them to face up to their fears of people who were different. The Damons never had children. Foster and Louise eventually settled together into a nearby nursing home.

Virgil should have been happy at Harvard, what with intellectual mentors, music making, practice regimens, and a pleasant rooming house. It was an epoch of "formal informality," he later wrote, for "ankle-length coonskin overcoats, if you could afford one, and for soft brown hats crushed shapeless."[25]

In the first flush of his college enthusiasm, his letters to Leland in San Francisco reflect his confidence: "I am doing wonders at the piano, building up the weak places in my technique very methodically. I am not allowed to play yet but I am thumping out Chopin Etudes as five finger exercises in the nerve-racking tempo of only 30 notes per minute."[26]

Before long, however, dissatisfaction, doubt, confusion, and longing for Leland set in.

> Dear old Prim,
>   You have been sending me the most delightful letters and cards of all those places I would so like to go, and feeling a bit lonesome for me, I know. And today your letter from the warm, blue room in Seattle came so wistful, so fragrant of the Leland I miss. . . .
>   O, Lee, I miss things! Must one always love the working of fate and of circumstance? I suppose poise demands it and that anything else is a bit shameful. But I can't help wishing that you were in Boston or that I was on the Pacific. I have spells of feeling that I sort of need to have you around. At any rate, sadness seems to wrap itself about me like a fog and to color all the sunsets brown. . . .
>   I have moments, precious ones, from time to time, when I am conscious of growth, but in general I am concerned with the very practical matter of practicing this or that trick at the organ, reading this or that book, or attending this or that lecture, or discussing this or that matter with somebody. It is pleasant to work alone. But sheer enjoyment by oneself is a contradiction, isn't it? That loneliness in pleasure comes pretty often these days, because there is so much that would be fine if you were here that isn't anything without you. See what I mean when I say I need you?[27]

Two months later Virgil received in the mail a Christmas package from Leland, souvenirs from San Francisco's Chinatown—a little green Buddha, four kinds of incense, candles, pictures, exotic teas, a stuffed cat. "Really Lee, I haven't had such a Santa Claus ecstasy since I was a very small child," Virgil, now twenty-three, wrote in thanks. "But most of all I was touched. It takes a good deal to get down to my sentimental skin, through all the callous layers of my deliberate and temperamental egotism."

But despite Leland's gifts and encouragement, Virgil's dark mood remained.

> You are a dear to have faith in me and say I've captured the great idea and all that, but I am sure I haven't captured anything very brilliant and sometimes I am even losing faith in myself. Every day I play the piano worse; my organ technique is going to hell; my tastes in music have changed so much I don't like anything except what outrages and violates my ear. Musically, philosophically, artistically, I am almost completely adrift. Of course, Harvard is not a very good place to find oneself, either. No academic atmosphere is.
>
> . . . O Leland, keep writing to me all the time and put up with my ingratitude and my carelessness. I have wished and grown lonesome for you time and time again, but I have forgotten you sometimes too.[28]

Virgil had hoped that college life and well-directed work in music would snap him out of his slump. But it didn't. He was still tormented with confusion and shame about his sexual urgings, which he poured out, always in code, in letters to Leland, but kept secret from his Harvard friends and almost certainly, it appears, did not act upon. Moreover, if he had hoped to find student friends who would support his professional work, all he found were ambitious music majors who threatened him. There was Randall Thompson, a star of the glee club and already composing: chamber works, incidental music for the professional stage, and, by 1922, a piece for full orchestra. There was Leopold Mannes, of the distinguished musical family, an exceptional pianist who had studied with the legendary Alfred Cortot. And there was Walter Piston, three years older than Virgil, who arrived with considerable professional experience (having played the violin in orchestras and the saxophone in dance bands), with confidence backed up by talent (he "was by gift the best musician of us all"), and with something Virgil must have also envied, a pretty young wife. Before long Piston was conducting the student orchestra. Virgil found Piston to be "grim, without free play." The feeling was mutual.

("Piston hated my guts!")[29] Their enmity was to last for five decades.

Of the aspiring Harvard composers from Virgil's time there, the only one he felt compatible with was affable Melville Smith, the first American musician to discover Nadia Boulanger in Paris, a teacher who would mold three generations of American composers.

In March 1920, the midterm of Virgil's second semester, he met Leland for a weekend in New York. The visit was obviously troubled. From Virgil's confused, apologetic subsequent letter, it appears that he may have tried to act upon his feelings, or at least raised the topic in some indirect way, and that Leland's response was harsh.

> I have been trying to get my ideas into orderly shape to take up our discussion where we left it in New York, but I don't seem to be able to state, in any sort of intelligible language, either your view or my own. So that it is impossible for me to compare them logically and so see wherein they differ or whether. The only thing that is certain, whatever its cause or justification, is that your disapproval has produced a definite reaction and made me stop and take account of a good many things.[30]

By the end of the spring term, several things had happened to boost his spirits. Virgil, now a mainstay of the glee club, was formally elected a member by its officers. He also secured a position as organist and choir director at a family-endowed church in North Easton, about twenty-five miles south of Boston. The job involved some commuting and the loss of a free weekend night for socializing. Virgil would take the train there on Saturday afternoon, "rehearse, sleep, play one service, eat, come back." But the work with the mostly young, thirty-voice choir was satisfying and it paid well—$600 a year, with two months off for summer vacation. He would keep the position until he left for Paris in June of 1921.

He was also cheered by news from his sister that she was pregnant. Six years earlier Ruby had married, at twenty-eight, a fellow she had known from grammar school, Roy Gleason, exactly her age. When they married, Roy was a buyer of ribbons and lace for a dry goods store in Kansas City. Eventually Roy worked in the food wholesale business, becoming a district representative for a canned milk company. Roy was a hardy, talkative man who loved his wife and enjoyed his work. But he and Virgil never got along particularly well, Virgil being rather jealous of his sister's attentions to another man. But the idea of a child in the family gave him a kick, though his letter of congratulations reads more like a grim lecture on the relative rewards and risks of child rearing.

> Of course it's difficult and expensive and dangerous, but we mustn't be afraid of things like that. A family that doesn't go through them and risk things is decayed. There is no way of protecting ourselves from life that isn't stupid, and the only way to be somebody is to do all the important things and do them with gusto. To get married without having children is rather begging the question, I think, side-stepping the main issue. I am glad the family isn't delaying, and I hope when you can afford it there will be one or two more. I hope it is a squalling lusty boy with dark red hair and freckles.[31]

Actually the baby was a girl, Margaret Elizabeth "Betty" Gleason, born December 8, 1920—the only child of Virgil's only sibling.

The best news of the spring term was that Virgil was awarded two academic scholarships for the coming year, including the Price Greenleaf Aid ($200). Despite his chronic unhappiness, he was doing strong classroom work and impressing the two teachers who mattered most to him: Doc Davison and Professor Hill. Both offered Virgil teaching assistantships for the coming year. On top of this, there came in June from the office of Harvard's President Lowell the news that Virgil had been nominated for a Rhodes Scholarship from the state of Missouri—one of fourteen Harvard candidates that year. The next month brought the news that Leland had landed a good job at a San Francisco financial management company. "In the mutual congratulation party I am completely swamped by your superior honours. To have one-fourteenth of a chance at a Rhodes Scholarship is positively juvenile in comparison with having trapped alive and skinned and dressed a real position of responsibility."[32]

Virgil was excited by the prestige of his nomination, but surprised. Rhodes Scholarships were traditionally for scholar-athletes, and Virgil was no athlete. Short, stocky, soft, and not particularly agile, he was in basically good condition and had physical endurance. For exercise he took long walks, played tennis now and then, and rowed sculls on the Charles River, a popular Harvard pastime.

Still, walks and recreational rowing did not amount to real college athletics. So in writing the essay for his Rhodes application, Virgil slipped in some inflated accounts of his physical activities. The essay is typical of the application essay genre, filled with strategic exaggerations. (Virgil claims, for example, to have been thrice elected president of the Pansophists at KC Polytech, but neglects to mention that this "fraternity" was something he started himself that did not survive his departure.) Virgil was already adept at projecting a command of subjects he in truth knew little about, a skill he would cultivate for the rest of his life. Given this, the tone of the Rhodes essay is surprisingly timid. But it is an endearing document.

> While I was at the Polytechnic Institute I studied the piano and played in public a good deal. I was also organist for the Troost Avenue Methodist Church. I played tennis and practiced track athletics, especially the dashes, but I didn't enter any important meets. I was thrice president of the Pansophist fraternity there, and edited the magazine published by them in 1916.
>
> From August, 1917, till December, 1918, I served in the army and was discharged Second Lieutenant of the Air Service. My special duty was that of radio-telephone officer. I studied at Austin, Texas and Columbia University and served at various flying fields.
>
> At Harvard I have spent most of my time on music. I am a member of the Harvard Musical Club, the Appleton Chapel Choir, and the University Glee Club. I have continued to study the organ, and I am organist and choir director for the Unity Church, North Easton. I have been appointed for next year as assistant to Professors E. B. Hill and Dr. A. T. Davison in three courses: Musical History; Modern French Music; and Choral Music. I row daily on the Charles River, except when it is frozen.
>
> In general, my interests are in literature, music, and philosophy, rather than in the sciences. I spend a great deal of time out-of-doors at a good many different kinds of sports—rowing, swimming, tennis, walking, fishing, riding, but I have neglected the highly organized games, and I have never entered any collegiate competition, because there wasn't time for regular training and my musical interests also. I have decided to join a Greek letter fraternity here.
>
> I am spending the summer at organ practice, musical composition, and outdoor sports. At Oxford I should like to concentrate on musical theory and philosophy.

Another scholar-athlete, not from Harvard, was selected as the 1920–21 Rhodes scholar from Missouri, though Virgil believed that his rejection was due not to his athletic insufficiencies but to a bad interview.

> When those in charge of the Missouri selection asked for an interview in St. Louis, I decided to risk the fare. It was the president of our state university who received me; and like my examining

officer for aviation school he asked just one question, "Where are the Virgin Islands?" (just acquired by the United States and in the news). When I replied, "I've no idea," he thanked me and rose, later selecting someone from his own university.[33]

When he returned to Cambridge from his short trip home that summer, Virgil finally faced up to his fears, plucked up his ambition, and composed his first formal works. He had written composition exercises in theory class. But these new pieces were the first he acknowledged in later life.

Two were short songs, the texts of which—Amy Lowell's "Vernal Equinox" and William Blake's "Sun Flower"—were certainly inspired by his association with Damon. The date on "Vernal Equinox" is July 1920, and only during summer vacation could Virgil have written this song, for any of his composition teachers would have slammed it. The vocal line moves from a one-note chant to disjunctive wildness; the harmonic language ineffectively combines Renaissance parallelisms, unhinged impressionistic harmonies and careless dissonance. "Sun Flower," written that September, though more cautious, is more successful—a simple, singable tune with an undulant accompaniment. Only its episode of chromatic intensity seems a melodramatic miscalculation.

But that summer he also wrote a striking choral work. For his text he chose an English translation of the Latin liturgical prayer "De profundis" (Out of the deep I called unto thee, O Lord)—a text that must have touched him the way it did Oscar Wilde. In Davison's choir and classes Virgil had encountered Renaissance counterpoint, and in this ruminative choral piece he deftly utilizes the idiom, spiked here and there with modern harmonies, some of them way out of keeping with the ancient style. Interestingly, in a 1951 revision for publication, Thomson altered the moments of dissonance, making the piece tamer, but stronger.

There is no record of Hill's or Davison's reactions to these works. But Virgil's composing career had finally begun.

That fall of 1920 when Virgil's classes started, his duties as teaching assistant to Davison and Hill turned out to be more demanding than he had assumed. Hill expected him to learn thoroughly a stackful of orchestral scores that they would play, in four-hand arrangements, as classroom illustrations for the "Modern French Music" course. In fact, this work was decisively influential, introducing Virgil to all the newest scores from France, including those of Stravinsky. Virgil also played examples for Davison's "History of Choral Music." And Davison started using him as an assistant conductor with the glee club, giving Virgil a star status with his mostly younger choir chums that he was careful not to gloat about.

"For two years time stopped," Virgil later wrote. "I am enjoying Harvard and music and even a little of life in general," he told Leland. "I work like a grind, exercise like a horse and loaf like a gentleman. I am earning $1,400 this year and not doing anything unpleasant either."[34]

Virgil later reported that during this period his thoughts turned decisively to Paris. The virulent anti-German sentiments that had fueled America's participation in World War I were still flaring in intellectual circles. However, Virgil's French orientation had started with his Kansas City piano teacher Geneve Lichtenwalter, who had introduced him to the repertory of Ravel and Debussy, and with Mr. Murray, who had turned him into an acolyte of Mary Garden, the American soprano of Scottish birth who championed French repertory and created the role of Debussy's Mélisande.

Yet the events that ultimately brought Virgil to France happened without any planning on his part. That winter it was decided that the glee club would accept an invitation from the French government to make a summer concert tour of France. The plans were finalized by February 18, for on that day the *Boston Evening Transcript* announced the tour and ran a half-page photograph of the choristers in formal concert dress. At the same time, two traveling fellowships named after John Knowles Paine, the founder of the Harvard music program, became available. The stipend ($1,400) would support one-year's study abroad "at such places and in such manner as shall be approved by the faculty." Virgil's friend Melville Smith, recipient of the first Paine Fellowship, was already studying with Nadia Boulanger in Paris. Professor Hill, who, fortunately for Virgil, was chairman that year while Spalding was on sabbatical, urged Virgil to apply for the fellowship and to follow Smith to Paris. Davison concurred. Virgil applied. In June he received news of his appointment.

The plan was to go with the glee club for its late-summer tour, then stay in Paris for the academic year. In anticipation of their son's absence, Virgil's parents took their first train trip East to visit him.

Virgil's landlady found them a nice room, temporarily empty, in her boardinghouse. They went to restaurants—his father loved the fresh lobster—and visited with the family of Oliver Payne, Virgil's friend from the glee club. Oliver's mother, a widow, could not afford to put her sons through school. Instead, she simply moved to Cambridge, rented a house, took in roomers, and in that way put two sons through Harvard. She was a gracious southern lady, the type of woman Virgil's courtly southern father was comfortable with.

The Thomsons took in the sights, including a boat trip to Cape Cod, where they passed at sunset through the canal and slept aboard. Virgil also took his parents to New York, where they stayed at a "perfectly reputable second-class hotel near Times Square," and visited Virgil's "really grand New York friends,"[35] whom he had met while in the army. They were two ladies, sisters, from the Stuyvesant family, who lived in a private brownstone on Fifty-seventh Street. There was also a dinner with Virgil's friend Emily Sherman, descended from Roger Sherman, a signer of the Declaration of Independence.

The Thomsons went back to Kansas City by way of Kentucky, which May Thomson had not seen since she was a little girl, visiting relatives and boasting of their visit with their son. Meanwhile, Virgil went back to Cambridge to practice, to earn his last weeks' salary from the North Easton Church, to pack up his music and books for advance shipment to Paris, and to prepare for the glee club tour.

8

VIRGY THOMSON IN PARIS

When the Harvard Glee Club entourage arrived in New York on June 11, 1921—sixty male choristers, the student manager, Avery Claflin, Doc Davison and the university chaperons, Professor Edward C. Moore of the Department of Theology and his wife, the only woman on the trip—the final exam period was still under way at Harvard. Some of the men would wind up taking exams on board. "Exams were given in the *salon d'ecriture* right over the engine room," one glee club member recorded in a diary. "The perspiring exam candidates heard furnaces being cleaned as they worked. When it was over, the sufferers marched thrice around the deck and threw books and notes into the sea with a great shout."[1]

However, as the glee club party assembled at Pier 57 to board the ship, *La Touraine,* the weather was clear and balmy, the young men were boisterous, and no one was thinking about exams. The boat, with 346 cabin passengers and 45 steerage, was "small and dirty," the unidentified diarist records. They left at 3 P.M. and would dock at Le Havre ten days later. The first night at dinner, the ship's captain toasted the young Harvard men as representing "the best of America in a mission to express to France the deep feeling of camaraderie both as allies in war and as brothers in peace." Our diarist was mostly unimpressed: "We sang on board informally and gave one regular concert. Poor food. Poor room. Poor singing. One night we tried to have

a dance, but there was no room. Playing cards was our chief amusement. Liquor flowed freely."

Virgil, thrilled to be finally getting to Europe, was easier to please.
"The servants on this boat and most of the passengers speak only
French," he wrote to his sister; "excellent practice for us."

> One can have plenty of exercise and the food is quite good.
> Everybody has an enormous appetite. . . . Fine air, lazy deck-chairs,
> conversation, reading, long and elaborate dinners, sometimes a lit-
> tle concert or a dance in the evening. . . . Always the sea to watch,
> different every day with moonlight and clouds and blue sky and
> sunset afterglow.[2]

The idea of the tour had been opposed by some Harvard alumni,
who thought it frivolous; the effort spent raising the necessary $50,000
would be better put to European relief, they argued. However, the
two governments saw in this tour the opportunity for a symbolic gesture of solidarity between victorious allies. Savings effected by the
French Foreign Office had cut the required budget in half. Newspapers on both sides of the Atlantic seized on this saga of good will.

In Europe the choristers were treated like triumphant heroes.
When they docked on June 20 at 10 P.M., they were greeted on board
by the mayor of Le Havre, and Colonel Azan of the French army, who
held an honorary degree from Harvard for the work he had done there
during the war as a military affairs instructor. The American visitors
slept on ship that first night, but were up the next day at 6 A.M. for
breakfast and a tour through town. Later, arriving at the Hôtel de Ville
for a reception, the Harvard men were greeted by cheering crowds
of townspeople, who had to be restrained by ropes and gendarmes.
"There is not a man in the club who is not profoundly touched and
who does not feel the serious mission of the trip," reports the diarist.
"In Le Havre alone, 12,000 soldiers were killed. The papers are full
of our visit." Virgil, who also kept a diary for part of the trip, was more
impressed by the food. "Grand reception at the Hotel de Ville. Many
flags and flowers, a band, speeches, toasts and champagne. We sang
some pieces and the national anthem. More champagne, pastry and
candies. Never seen such pastries!"[3]

That night they took the evening train for Paris, arriving at eleven,
where they checked into a hotel on the rue de Vaugirard in the Latin
Quarter. Virgil was glad to see Melville Smith, his Harvard friend in
Paris on a Paine Fellowship, who stopped by the hotel. The men were

treated to more receptions and banquets, and performances at the Opéra Comique of Offenbach's *Barbe-bleue,* and Debussy's *Pelléas et Mélisande.* ("Singing not too good. Orchestra fine," Virgil, already the blunt critic, reported of the Debussy.) One night they were guests for a dress ball, to which they impishly wore straw hats. As they left at 1 A.M. in taxis, a dissenting crowd in the Place de la Concorde, mostly socialists, beat against the sides of the vehicles in protest of such luxuries.

On June 26 they took an early bus to the suburb of Fontainebleau for the official opening of the American Conservatory in Salle Henri II, where American composers for the next six decades would come to study with Nadia Boulanger. The school was commencing its first summer course for Americans, and among the participants was a young composer from Brooklyn, an awkward fellow with a toothy grin named Aaron Copland. The distinguished speakers that day included Widor, Saint-Saëns, and Ravel.

Back in Paris that night, the evening prior to their first concert, a rehearsal went badly. Pitch was off, several section leaders had head colds, diction was poor. The next morning's rehearsal, the final one, was even worse. Disaster was anticipated. Doc Davison ordered everyone to rest in his room for the remainder of the afternoon.

Somehow the men revived. The concert, their first official program, was one of their best ever. The reviews were ecstatic. The Harvard Glee Club "is unsurpassed by any similar organization we know"—*Petit Parisien.* "Their attack is comparable to that of the famous first violins of the Colonne Orchestra"—*Action Française.* After the glee club's "triumphant" second concert, the *Petit Parisien* critic issued this challenge to his countrymen: "The day when not only in Paris but also in our other great cities all the schools can realize such a program, France will be ready to become a 'singing France' and truly artistic."

And so the tour proceeded for the next eight weeks. The programs began typically with the American and French national anthems. Then there would be music from the Renaissance (Palestrina, Praetorius, Hassler); sometimes Gregorian chant; English part-songs by Morley, Dowland; folk song arrangements by Brahms and Dvořák; more recent works by Borodin, Sibelius; and sometimes—as when over five thousand students turned out for a concert at the Trocadéro amphitheater, just outside Paris—Doc Davison would relent and let his men sing some Harvard and Yale fight songs.

The itinerary took them through Dijon, Nancy, Strasbourg, Mulhouse; then into Germany—Wiesbaden; then to Italy—Milan, Rome, Naples, Venice, Pesaro, Ravenna. The students saw the landmarks, the cathedrals, the salt mines, the beer factories. They swam in the thermal baths at Nancy; they visited the battlefields at Verdun, finding forests bereft of trees and villages where not a standing stone wall remained.

There were mishaps, of course, one near-catastrophe. In Italy, on the way to a concert at Pesaro, a tour bus lent by the nearby agricultural school where the men were staying broke down. The concert started forty-five minutes late. Moreover, Doc Davison, during a heat spell, was bedridden with something the *Boston Transcript* reporter described as "Italian fever."[4] Unable to conduct, he turned over the duty to Virgil, who enjoyed, according to our anonymous diarist, a triumph: "Virgy Thomson did the job and very well too. The best a concert has ever gone without Doc and better than some with him. Audience was large and enthusiastic in spite of the troubles."

Doc had to be left behind in Pesaro when the glee club traveled to Ravenna to sing as part of the commemorative ceremonies marking the 600th anniversary of Dante's death. Virgil conducted that program as well. The men were supposed to participate in a service at the cathedral, but at the last minute Pope Benedict XV forbade it. The club diarist offered one possible explanation: "He wasn't going to have a bunch of Protestants singing in one of his churches." The concert was shifted to a municipal theater.

Getting back to Pesaro proved difficult because the student who had hired the buses was jailed for breach of contract, which certainly soured our diarist on Italy. "The arrest was a hoax to get our money. We paid the judge. In France the bus would have been given us. For the most part, we found the Italians a backward, dirty, ignorant, dishonest, rotten bunch of people."

Whereas this student's diary records every place they sang and every sight they saw, Virgil's incomplete diary recounts everything he heard and everything he ate. At Notre Dame, Poulenc played the organ for the Americans, and some French students played a string quartet of Milhaud. At Strasbourg, "Dr. Albert Schweitzer played Bach to us on an organ of 1740 in the Thomas Kirche—in the dark." In Koblenz, Virgil tried his first authentic German wurst.

When the men gathered in Paris for the return trip home, they were loaded down with mementos, the most elaborate being a Sèvres porcelain statuette of the child Mozart holding his violin, a gift of the government of France. Today the child Mozart stands atop a dusty doorway in the cluttered offices of the Harvard Glee Club in Holden Chapel.

As planned, Virgil did not travel back to Paris with his glee club chums. There was some time left him before he was to take up his fellowship studies for the academic year in Paris. So he remained in Geneva, where the glee club had stopped overnight, for two weeks, then spent "four delicious weeks in England, two of them at Oxford."[5] He bought an English bicycle with handbrakes and set off for ten days of touring the countryside. And when he returned to Paris in mid-September, he felt he had come home.

> In later years I used to say that I lived in Paris because it reminded me of Kansas City. And Paris can present to anyone, of course, since it contains all possible elements, an image of his origins. In my case, I now learned, not only was Paris to be my new home town, but all France, so little did I feel alien there, was to be like another Missouri—a cosmopolitan crossroads, frank and friendly and actually not far from the same geographic size.[6]

In his letters from the glee club tour and from his solo post-tour excursions, Thomson is already many things he would later be noted for—a vivid chronicler, an eager traveler, an insightful (and sweeping) social observer, and a beguiling writer on almost any topic. On Oxford:

> Oxford is very pleasant and I can imagine loafing here for several years with good profit. But as for me, give me an American college every time. Our rich may be vulgar, but they are seldom idle.[7]

On French sunsets:

> You can understand the French devotion to pink and blue when you see their hills and their sunsets. French sunsets are invariably Louis XV, delicate, slightly grayed, graceful in line, and always pink and blue.[8]

On Switzerland:

> Perfect country! They speak French, they can cook, they charge as little as possible for anything, they are amiable, there are no profiteers or thieves, the police are incorruptible, there is no graft in the government or smoke in the cities, they have beauty both

of art and nature and every modern improvement for efficiency and comfort, and the only pressure of public opinion is in the direction of tolerance and freedom.[9]

On Italians, whom Thomson clearly liked more than the glee club diarist did:

> Italians [are] well-educated, great linguists . . . , sportsmen—learned, versatile, and charming. Peasantry has every opportunity for education and they always take what they need, ambitious and capable people. A man has to speak four languages to get a waiter's job in Venice.[10]

Back in Paris by late September, Thomson had arranged, through the intercession of Melville Smith, to study with Nadia Boulanger, then thirty-four and already teaching counterpoint, harmony, and analysis to Smith and Copland. Thomson's relationship with Boulanger, who would become one of the century's most influential pedagogues, was mixed. He always boasted about being one of the first Americans to discover her, and recalled her lovingly in his autobiography:

> A tall, soft-haired brunette still luscious to the eye, she had already resigned womanly fulfillment and vowed her life to the memory of her sister (a gifted composer early dead), to the care of her long-widowed mother (who had married her elderly voice teacher at eighteen), and to musically bringing up the young. A certain maternal warmth was part of her charm for all young men; but what endeared her most to Americans was her conviction that American music was about to "take off," just as Russian music had done eighty years before.[11]

In later interviews he pointed to Boulanger's unspoken ability to put students at ease in front of the music paper. In contrast, German pedagogues "made it seem a little daring of the student to write a piece of music at all."

When Boulanger was asked for her memories of Thomson for use in Kathleen Hoover's biography, she replied graciously, excusing her poor written English. Yet her focus on Thomson as a thinker and writer ("intensely intelligent . . . a right words finder . . . his conversation one of the brightest one can dream of") may have been her tactful way of avoiding comment upon his music.[12] When Boulanger wrote these words in 1949, Thomson was ensconced on his powerful platform at the *New York Herald Tribune;* she did not want to alienate him.

Elliott Carter, who studied with Boulanger during the 1930s, reports that she was mystified by Thomson from the start. "I once asked her what she thought of Virgil. She said he came to her with some tangos he had written. She told him, 'You know, there are people out here on the Boulevard Clichy who can teach you how to write tangos better than I can.'"[13]

Subsequent documents revealed the depth of Thomson's disaffection with Boulanger. When a book of his selected letters was published in 1988, nine years after her death, Thomson was pleased to have "let out of the house" a particular letter that "debunked a bit the Boulanger cult." The letter concerned young Paul Bowles, then an aspiring composer, who had come to Thomson in 1931 asking advice about whether to take lessons with Boulanger. Thomson recommended Paul Dukas and suggested that Bowles write Aaron Copland for additional advice. Copland had been the young composer's mentor, and Bowles revered him. Knowing this, Thomson sent a feisty letter to Copland stating his case against Boulanger.

My story is this:

If [Paul] wants Nadia's particular and special merchandise, namely, a motherly guidance to overcome American timidity about self-expression, then he had better go and get it and take the trimmings with it. Otherwise he had better buy his trimmings where they are cheaper and better.

Nadia is not the same as when we were there. The flattery and guidance was precious to us and inspiring and the counterpoint lessons were competent enough and that's all there was.

When I went back in 1926 I discovered that the counterpoint was still fair (though expensive, because we talked all the time about things in general and seldom got through the work I had done) but that the main thing was all changed. The guidance wasn't worth a damn. On the contrary, quite troublesome. Once the habit of composition was established, she used every art of sympathy and generosity to make it grow in her own pet channels. I refused and stopped my lessons and she has never forgiven me.

. . . Her tastes are sentimental and *démodé*. Her lack of comprehension of everything is complete. She lives in a temple of adulation and knee-bending that is disgusting and her aged parent scents any heresy a mile off and begins putting the screws on to make you feel ashamed of eating her cakes and tea while you are secretly questioning the divine oracle.[14]

Thomson's disenchantment may have been affected by Boulanger's advocacy of Copland, who by this time had had four major premieres with the Boston Symphony Orchestra under Koussevitzky. The conductor from Russia listened to his old friend Nadia in these matters. In any event, Bowles did study with Boulanger, briefly and, for the most part, unprofitably.

Settling into Paris for his fellowship year, Virgil Thomson found a room at 20 rue de Berne, "chiefly inhabited, like all that street, by daughters of joy."

> I valued its freedom to make music at night, when my neighbors were out, dining late or dancing, love-time for kept girls being afternoon. And there was a hideous, kindly chambermaid, who washed my socks and all day long on vericosed legs climbed the five flights of circular stairs, bringing hot water at any time, a tray if I were ill.[15]

In his room he kept a rented grand piano mounted on blocks and fitted with organ pedals, on which he wrote his counterpoint exercises for Boulanger while standing up.

He had some American friends there, including his old Kansas City companion Eugene McCown, who had been bumming around the French countryside. During the early months of 1922, Gene lived with Virgil. Like authentic Paris bohemians, they spent each other's money, wore each other's clothes, shared meals and—it would appear, since the room was so small—a bed. Virgil lived meagerly off his quarterly fellowship payments. But Eugene was "quite prosperous," as Virgil wrote to Leland Poole:

> He plays jazz on the piano nights (10 till 2) at Le Boeuf, which is the rendez-vous of Jean Cocteau, Les Six, and les snobs intellectuels—a not unamusing place frequented by English upper-class bohemians, wealthy Americans, French aristocrats, lesbian novelists from Romania, Spanish princes, fashionable pederasts, modern literary & musical figures, pale and precious young men, and distinguished diplomats towing bright-eyed youths. He plays remarkably well and is the talk as well as the toast of Paris. He paints afternoons and has recently had a sudden access of financial success.
>
> . . . I take my social life vicariously now. Thru Eugene. I almost never go out. I practice the organ, do counterpoint and write music. I mostly eat alone and seldom see Gene except mornings.[16]

Virgil also became friendly with Bernard Faÿ, the young, Harvard-trained history professor who had made all the arrangements from the French government's side for the glee club tour. Bernard was from a family of bankers and lawyers, "ultra-bourgeois by financial position and ultra-Catholic through their mother," two of whose brothers were important bishops.[17] At the Faÿ afternoon teas Virgil met Bernard's younger brother Emmanuel, a painter and a rather haunted young man: "He was strong in mind, weak in body, intense from withheld emotion, in manners sweetly reserved, as if smiling over pain. He loathed the Catholicism of his family."[18]

At the Faÿ teas Virgil encountered France's newest wave in music and letters: the poet Cocteau; and the unorthodox composers the journalist Henri Collet had dubbed, rather arbitrarily, Les Six—Darius Milhaud, Francis Poulenc, Georges Auric, Arthur Honegger, Louis Durey, Germaine Tailleferre. There Virgil also met his beloved Erik Satie, then fifty-six, not in good health, drinking heavily, composing less and less music, increasingly secretive and eccentric. Satie had lived for thirty years in an unheated flat five miles from Paris, a flat absolutely no one saw. When, after his death in 1925, some friends went to Satie's flat, they found it almost bare: a bed, a chair, a table, a cupboard with twelve identical velvet suits folded and piled on top, and a useless old piano whose pedals were controlled by strings.

In later life Thomson was uncomfortable when asked about his personal relationship with Satie. When they met in 1922, Thomson revered Satie's music. Yet Satie's personal quirkiness, his prolonged silences, the devotion of the young composers who almost always accompanied him—all this made Thomson hesitant to pursue a friendship. Moreover, he wanted to "get inside" Satie's music first, then "make my homage later through performance," so that they might begin their relationship as professionals.[19] But Thomson never had another chance to cultivate a companionship with Satie, for when he returned to Paris in 1925 Satie was dead.

In letters from his year in Paris, Thomson mentions all the music he was then writing: "three or four choruses, a few piano pieces, half a dozen organ pieces and some stray opuses of one sort or another. I am doing now a long business in three movements for organ and orchestra."[20] However, of these works only a striking and severe Prelude for Piano, two tongue-in-cheek tangos, and four short choral works made it into his later catalog of sanctioned works. The "long business" for organ and orchestra turned out to be ideas for an abandoned symphony. However, for someone who had come late to composition, Thomson, then twenty-five, was at last developing the daily habit of writing music, and finding it essential.

At this time he was also producing his first professional works in another discipline that for long spans of his life would become a daily habit as well: musical criticism. Before Thomson left Cambridge with the glee club, he had won over the confidence of the respected Boston journalist and critic Henry Taylor Parker, or "H.T.P.," as he often signed his articles. Born in Boston, educated at Harvard, Parker worked for some years as a London and then a New York correspondent, before settling into the job he held the last thirty-nine years of his life: music and drama editor of the *Boston Evening Transcript*. With its special Genealogical, Patriotic-Historic, and Society sections, the *Transcript* courted Brahmin Boston. Its coverage of the arts was intelligent and extensive. And H. T. Parker was mostly responsible for the informed tone and reach of that coverage. He was interested in all the latest music. When in early 1922 Stravinsky's Concertino was to be presented for the first time in Boston, Parker prepared his readers with an advance article on the piece and a photograph of the score's opening pages.

When Parker, then fifty-four, met Thomson, he was impressed by the young man's clearheaded thinking and crisp writing style. So he invited Thomson to cover occasional events for the *Transcript* while he was in Paris.

This credential allowed Thomson free admittance to almost any musical and operatic event in Paris. Many of Thomson's items in the paper that year were folded into Parker's weekly columns. Reporting on a new Paris production of Mussorgsky's *Boris Godunov,* Parker writes, "All agree that music, action and illusion gain much by Louis Laloy's new and altogether admirable translation of the text"—information clearly fed him by Thomson.[21]

But soon Thomson was writing his first lengthy newspaper reviews with a byline, and earning his first receipts in journalism. One droll and vivid article reported on a newsworthy performance he attended in Paris with his glee club colleagues during their summer tour: the Swedish Ballet's productions of *L'Homme et son désir,* music by Darius Milhaud, and choreography by Jean Borlin, and *Les Mariés de la Tour Eiffel,* a burlesque with scenario and spectacle by Jean Cocteau and music by five of Les Six.

The piece of Thomson's "that changed history," as he would put it in his autobiography, was the review that ran on February 8, 1922, of Serge Koussevitzky's Paris concerts. Titled (using one of the then acceptable English alphabet transliterations of his name) "Kusevitsky, Conductor—The Risen Russian Suggested for Boston," the piece was influential in securing for Koussevitzky in 1924, at fifty, his post as conductor of the Boston Symphony Orchestra, from which for the next twenty-five years he would transform and tirelessly promote contemporary music in America. Thomson's article may well have "set in motion a train of events," as he later wrote, that resulted in the Russian's appointment. "I owe to you the only available pictures of Koussevitzky," H. T. Parker told Thomson a year after the article ran; "and the trustees of the Boston Orchestra have meditated on your article about him."[22]

However, Thomson in no way "discovered" Koussevitzky, as he tended to suggest in later years. Koussevitzky was already internationally known for his "Concerts Kusevitsky" in Moscow and Petrograd, begun in 1910, and by 1921 presented in London and Paris. In fact, six days before Thomson's piece ran, H. T. Parker in his weekly *Transcript* column mentioned Koussevitzky as a possible successor to the Boston Symphony's retiring conductor, Pierre Monteux. Clearly, Parker had asked Thomson to check out the much-talked-about Russian.

That said, Thomson's enthusiasm at least stoked the movement to bring the conductor to Boston. The concerts, a series of six, presented an orchestra of musicians specially selected by the conductor from the established orchestras of Paris in wide-ranging and provocative programs, including new French works and an evening of unknown Russian compositions. The performances, Thomson wrote, were "unequalled anywhere in Paris for balance, precision and commanding force."

> One would like to dwell on the aliveness of the old pieces as Kusevitsky played them—pieces, many of them that we have grown to loathe, as children loathe the Bible through much clerical mouthing of it, and some of them pieces so lacking in romantic sensationalism that few conductors dare to play them at all nowadays. Bach's Brandenburg Concerto in G for string orchestra, as played by Kusevitsky, was so clear in outline and so lively in rhythm that the orchestral embellishments of modern music seemed effeminate and silly. The Symphony in E minor of Karl

Philip Emmanuel Bach was even more moving, particularly the second movement with long lines of melancholy, a restrained and tender sadness. . . . Beethoven's Overture to "Egmont" seemed more symphonic in sweep than many of his symphonies, and the great Fifth became a sheer contrast in forces—the repeated chords at the end falling like blows from a pugilistic Prometheus, who cries to Fate, "Take that! And that! And that!"

Thomson would one day poke fun at critics who described works like Beethoven's Fifth with this kind of Promethean imagery. For all the influence of this article, Thomson may have been embarrassed by its effusions, which may explain why he kept no copies of his *Transcript* articles in his personal files, nor did he ever uncover and reprint them in his published collections.

Later in the article, however, Thomson takes on a new work of Arthur Honegger, *Horace Victorieux,* a "mimed symphony," performed as a concert piece, a work Thomson found impressive as "sheer music."

[Honegger's *Horace Victorieux*] is sheer counterpoint from beginning to end, without any harmonic implications whatever. It is ponderous and learned. Obviously, coloristic or decorative orchestration is out of place with such architecture. Consequently, there is almost incessant use of strings, subdivided ad infinitum to carry the many voices in equal power. Is it beautiful or affecting? It seems so. The love scene was such, and so was some of the battle music. There is rather an excess of pompous fugal writing, though setting and action might moisten the dryness.

Here is the Thomson style—incisive in analysis, audacious in description—that twenty years later composers would fear (or cheer, as the case may be) and *Herald Tribune* readers would devour.

Virgil grew to enjoy the routine of his year abroad—arduous lessons with Boulanger, much time spent alone in his flat composing and practicing, a small circle of friends, and associations with older composers and writers. His letters home mostly spill over with optimism and even vanity, as in this one to his sister:

I have just recently had an experience. I took the hair off my legs. Eugene told me I was ugly with such a growth on me. So to amuse myself I put some of this depilatory paste on, and now I am white and clean as a baby. I am really quite infatuated with my looks as I take my morning exercises in front of the mirror.[23]

Virgil put great faith in his ability to vamp his way through life, relying on his brilliance and youthfulness to court patrons and employers. But now, approaching twenty-six, he had to devise an elaborate technique for achieving the desired rosy-cheeked look, as is clear from this advice to Leland:

> Pull your maturity pose all you like, if it satisfies your conscience and theirs, but don't neglect to use your smile and your complexion for all they are worth. Take it from one who has lived for some years by just such vamping of one influential or official source or other. Whenever I go to call on a middle-aged or elderly person of either sex, but particularly men, I do my complexion with cold cream and hot water, I run all the way up the stairs, and then I slap myself as I ring the bell. Talk well, of course; put over your line, or whatever the cue is. But look your most adolescent.[24]

That spring from Harvard came the expected news that Virgil's traveling fellowship would not be renewed, though a reapplication would be considered favorably if he first finished his degree in Cambridge. With the offer of a teaching fellowship from the music department and a job offer as organist and choir director at Boston's historic King's Chapel, the prospects for earning a living income looked good. A year in France had firmed forever Virgil's Francophile inclinations. "I had not yet begun on the French classics, nor had I set foot in the Louvre," he later wrote; "but I felt at home with France, its music, its food, its people, its reading and writing."[25]

When, in late August, Virgil boarded a ten-day, New York–bound ship, he knew he would be back.

During his last year at Harvard, 1922–23, installed in his old room on Oxford Street, Virgil took courses in fugue, advanced orchestration, composition, Italian, French literature; he assisted Doc Davison and Professor Hill in their classes, playing as examples for analysis four-hand piano arrangements of Renaissance choral works, French modern music, and Stravinsky ballets. He rejoined the glee club, which, in the year following its European triumph, had become a mainstay of Boston musical life. The *Transcript* covered all its concerts and ran advance articles when a new work, such as Milhaud's setting of Psalm 121, was to be performed.

King's Chapel, just down the slope of Boston Common from the state house, looked like a granite Greek temple. The land had been granted in the 1680s by King William and Queen Mary to be "used in perpetuity for services in the Church of England." But the Revolution brought a break with the English bishops and a rededication of the chapel as New England's first Unitarian church, though Anglican customs and clerical dress were retained.

The chapel had a renowned four-manual organ. Virgil's contract paid over $1,000 for a work period from September to March. This was good money, but a lot of work. Virgil had to provide organ and choir music for some sixty-five Sunday and church holy day services a year. In addition, he played a daily half-hour service—organ only— at noon from November through Easter, and a weekly organ recital at noon on Saturdays. The twenty-three men in the choir, each paid $3.00 a week, were skilled singers. "We follow Dr. Davison in the character of our music," the chairman of the chapel's music committee wrote to Virgil in his letter of appointment.[26] But within those parameters, Virgil had "carte-blanche on choice of music."[27]

"I am up to my ears in work and enjoying it all enormously," Virgil wrote to Leland that September. "I am taking organ lessons from Mr. Wallace Goodrich at the Conservatory, my former teacher. I am playing kettle drums in the orchestra at the Conservatory. I am practicing the piano, a little mechanisme every day. I commence my rowing on Monday. Doesn't that all sound amusing?"[28]

That year Virgil also joined a club. The Liberal Club, located in a pleasant, old, frame, three-story house just off Mt. Auburn Street in Harvard Square. On the middle floor a large reading room stocked all the advanced periodicals of the time such as the *Dial,* which published Marianne Moore, and *Broom,* which published Hart Crane and Gertrude Stein.[29] The Liberal Club had been started right after the war when leftist politics were fashionable. Yet it "remained small and, in spite of aspirations to a world-wide view, parochial."[30] By the time Virgil joined in 1922, it had devolved into an eating club—a cheery, stimulating hangout for afternoon bridge and tea, discussions of culture, and contentious intellectual dinner conversations. It wasn't particularly "liberal," and certainly not activist. But it was a tolerant and free-spirited hangout. And, in contrast with other Harvard clubs, it welcomed Jewish students and men from modest families.

At its dinner table Virgil met some impressive young men: the historians Garrett Mattingly and Allen Evans; John Knedler (later dean of the college at New York University). Some club members would become lifelong friends: the crystallographer Alan Holden; the historian of architecture Henry-Russell Hitchcock; the editor, writer, and ballet impresario Lincoln Kirstein. One young man there, an aspiring painter, Maurice Grosser, would change Virgil's life, though their intimacy did not begin until both were later in France.

But by January, Virgil was feeling stifled, overworked, and lonesome for Paris, as he told Eugene in a letter. Gene was not entirely sympathetic: "Poor dear. I can quite understand what with prohibition and the Ku Klux Klan and the blizzards and the coal strike, America seems from this perspective altogether hazardous. But now for that well-known practice of counseling wisdom: if you were here you would pine for Cambridge. You are built that way."[31]

Still, Virgil managed to excel at his King's Chapel job and complete his studies successfully, though, to his chagrin, he stumbled badly on his comprehensive exams—the "generals," they were called then—which one had to pass with distinction in order to graduate with honors. "What proved to Walter Spalding that I should have taken his course in Appreciation was my referring, wrongly of course, to an Introduction in Beethoven's Fifth Symphony."[32] In his official letter of report, the grim, conservative Spalding, never well disposed to this upstart older student, was unsparing but conciliatory.

May 31, 1923

My dear Thomson,
    I wish to inform you in the name of the Department of Music, and I expect you to believe the statement, that my colleagues and I were very keenly disappointed that your work in the examinations was of not sufficient merit so that you could be recommended for the degree with distinction, although you passed the examination. But your work was so mediocre in harmony, counterpoint and fugue that on the evidence submitted no other verdict was possible. We all wish you to know, however, that we have a high opinion of your general musical ability, especially as a conductor, as a pianist and as a student of musical literature, but we regret that your grammatical knowledge of the subject is so deficient that a distinct deficiency is apparent in your writing of music and I hope you will set to work at once to remedy this deficiency because I am sure it will *handicap your career*. I hope at your early convenience you will arrange an interview with me, as I should like to go over your work with you and I think I can make some helpful suggestions to you.
                    With cordial regards,
                    W.R. Spalding (for the Division of Music)[33]

Virgil chose not to make that appointment, thinking advice from Spalding, who had never approved of his learning counterpoint from a woman, was the last thing he needed. Worst of all, Virgil's poor exams meant he would have no additional traveling fellowship.

However, for all this exasperation, Spalding must have felt badly about Virgil's predicament. Because when a $1,500 fellowship from the Juilliard Trust became available—the recipient could use it for any educational purpose—Spalding offered it to Virgil, who accepted it, intending to go to France.

But he did not go overseas. He was tempted instead by an opportunity to study conducting with a training orchestra in New York. He was also tempted by something else: a young man he had met at the Liberal Club, Briggs Buchanan.

In accounting for his poor showing in the generals, Virgil would later write that he had that spring semester been "deep in unrequited love, with all love's classic symptoms of distraction. My passion, like all my intensely conceived ones, came to nothing."[34]

He does not reveal the source of that unrequited love. It was Briggs. And what came of it was not exactly "nothing."

THE MAN WHO WOULD NOT FIGHT

enry Lush Buchanan was a self-made financier, and there was never any question but that his son, Briggs Wheeler Buchanan, would go into the family business. The senior Buchanan had started his career with a "curb" exchange for outdoor trading, the Wild West of Wall Street wheeling and dealing. Eventually he bought a seat on the American Stock Exchange and started his own firm, H. L. Buchanan Securities.

However, Briggs, born in 1904, turned out to be something of a dreamer. He was a pensive, handsome, rather frail young man who wrote fiction and showed a talent for drawing. Briggs was loath to let himself be prodded into the family firm. Yet he lacked the confidence and clarity to form an alternative plan. Even his admission to Harvard was a fluke. On a lark Briggs traveled to Cambridge with an older high school friend who was scheduled to take entrance examinations. With nothing else to do in an unfamiliar city, Briggs took the exams as well. He passed. His friend didn't. Not having completed high school, Briggs showed up at Harvard for his freshman year in 1920. He was just sixteen.

His father was not entirely pleased. He worried that Briggs would stray into the wrong circles, which is what happened, for Briggs befriended aspiring writers and majored in fine arts. Still, Mr. Buchanan supported his son's decision, although Briggs's tuition was provided mostly by his uncle George Briggs Buchanan, of Brown Brothers &

Co. The father was wealthy; Uncle George was super wealthy.

It wasn't until the fall of 1922 that Virgil, back from his year abroad, met Briggs at the Liberal Club. Briggs was eighteen and impressionable. Virgil was twenty-six and opinionated. Briggs was confused about everything. Virgil appeared to be confused about nothing. Briggs was looking for a mentor. Here was Virgil: brilliant, up on the latest artistic trends of Paris, fluent in French, talented, a fascinating conversationalist. Briggs loved music and welcomed Virgil's taking him to concerts and telling him what to think. Virgil gave Briggs walking tours of the Boston museums and the architecture on Commonwealth Avenue. Briggs had vague aspirations to be a writer. Virgil was a working journalist. Naturally, Briggs was flattered that Virgil took such an interest in him.

Virgil's interest had a strong sexual underpinning, although he had to finesse this with Briggs, couching it in terms of male bonding, free expression, and Nietzschean willpower. Briggs didn't know what to think, as he admitted to Virgil: "That end, the light I seek, is in sight. The necessity for a natural means of expression I clearly see, and am willing and ready to strive for. The equally pressing need for sex expression is not yet clear, however, nor the means. I wonder—, but there is nothing I can say. I must wait, but wait with open eyes, my desires in view."[1] Virgil was relentless and dazzling in his determination.

That summer of 1923, for all the confusion that Virgil's attentions had caused him, Briggs, writing from his family's summer place on Cedar Lake, in Denville, New Jersey, missed him badly.

> Dear Tommie,
>   . . . When are you coming east? Yes! I admit it, I am bored. I miss your company. I sleep and eat—Yes! and neglect my work—living after a fashion. How we longed to get away from Cambridge. Now what a heaven all our life there seems. . . . I have no place to eat, no Atlas Cafe to go to, no Liberal Club, no movies, only a damned monotonous lake to look at in the suburbs with suburban people and their cabin'd, crib'ed, confined suburban minds. . . . I am insufferable—my temper unspeakable. I grouch and growl; I long to escape. All this I say to you. You must have expected it—to hear that my infirmities are all emphasized—headaches, my stomach and all are with me stronger than ever.[2]

Yet, in terms of the relationship he coveted with Briggs, Virgil had so far gotten nowhere. Briggs seems to have been curious about exploring a physical dimension in his relationships with men, which would have been a not uncommon curiosity for Harvard men of the 1920s. But his interests, such as they were, seem to have been directed at men younger than Virgil. Briggs wanted Virgil to be his mentor, not his lover. He often signed his letters, "Your friend and brother" or "Your son." And once, "Your illegitimate son."

Virgil was frustrated and angry. He might have chosen to give up and, using his no-strings-attached fellowship, return to Paris. But when some professional opportunities presented themselves in New York, he decided to take them.

Chalmers Clifton, an associate of Professor Hill's from Harvard, had taken over the directorship of the American Orchestral Association in New York, a training ensemble. That fall of 1923, Virgil accepted Clifton's invitation to enroll in his conducting class. There he learned how to digest an orchestral score, to conduct a Beethoven symphony, and to play all the percussion instruments in the orchestra. He also took private composition lessons from Rosario Scalero, the Italian composer, then the chairmen of the theory department at the Mannes College of Music. Scalero later taught Samuel Barber, Gian Carlo Menotti, and Lukas Foss. Suspicious of the conservative Italian, Virgil did not show Scalero his compositions. But he later admitted to having profited from Scalero's insistence on practicing the "normal" harmonization of a chorale—"though I resisted it at the time," he would write, "Paris having taught me that no such harmonization exists save in the German academic mind."[3]

He also struck up associations with the cellist Luigi Silva, the violist Lillian Fuchs, and her violinist brother, Joseph. Virgil questioned them constantly about their instruments. And this would remain his preferred way to learn matters of instrumentation—directly from performers.

However, what made him decide to remain in America was his unabated longing for Briggs. In later years he would emphatically state that "nothing ever happened" between them. Most likely, nothing much did, physically. But the centrality of Briggs Buchanan to Thomson's life during this period, even when they were apart, is made clear in a series of revealing and, in most cases, previously unpublished letters.

The correspondence begins in September 1923, when Virgil moved into a flat at 55 East Thirty-fourth Street in New York and Briggs was

a senior at Harvard. The incidents related are confusing to follow because they describe their struggles with euphemisms and metaphors.
Virgil seldom stated his desires explicitly. Sometimes they taunt each
other with accounts of indiscretions with other men, indiscretions that,
particularly in Briggs's case, may not have amounted to much more
than collegiate "experimenting." But the taunts stung.

That September, Briggs wrote with news of his arrival back at
Harvard, gossip about friends, complaints of his poor health, and intimations of other men's attentions. "Archie came in last night, and
oh my, how affectionate. And though I protested, who could mind?
If Hugh had been there how he would have envied me. Healthy, rosy,
buxom; all cheer and sweetness; bosomy, billowy; he has the peaches
and cream complexion no one can resist."[4] This elicits a sharp response from Virgil: "On the Saturday of your departure Lewis went
home with me to share my bed and bath. Don't forgive me. It would
alleviate the offense. And after all, I suppose it does even up for
Archie."[5]

This squabble, like most of theirs, did not last. But just as Virgil
was resigning himself to a life of work without Briggs in New York,
a tragic incident occurred that shook him and, ironically, reinvigorated
his resolve over Briggs—the death of Emmanuel Faÿ, his friend from
Paris.

The Faÿ family of ultra-Catholic bankers and solicitors had befriended
Virgil in Paris, particularly the urbane older brother, Bernard, and the
mercurial Emmanuel, who had taken up painting. That fall, as Virgil
was settling into his New York flat, the Faÿ brothers came for a visit.
Virgil repaid their hospitality by showing them Boston and New York.
Bernard then returned to France. Emmanuel took a room in Manhattan. There, in mid-October, he died. And Virgil felt partly responsible.

> Though in New York myself, I had neglected him that week; and
> so had others. It was cold weather. And a lady of means who had
> commissioned him to paint a room had changed her mind when
> she learned that paint and canvas alone (the best was all he had
> thought to use) would cost more than she cared to spend. So one
> evening in his Stuyvesant Place lodging he took some sleeping pills
> and lay down by an open window. Found unconscious in the
> morning, he was removed to a public hospital, where still un-
> conscious, he died of pneumonia. And in the short time between
> his being carried away and the sealing of his room, his pictures

disappeared. Avery Claflin, his brother's closest friend, and Roy Larson, then a young newspaper man, instigated a police inquiry and carried out on their own some questionings in the house. Not a scrap of actionable information, or of painting either, ever turned up. A small sheaf of drawings is all that remains today from this gifted artist and ever-so-touching young man.[6]

Virgil sent word to Eugene McCown, still in Paris and Emmanuel's intimate friend. Eugene was dissatisfied with Virgil's account. Avery Claflin had also written, and his version differed in key details. Whereas Virgil had written that Emmanuel was "last seen on Sunday by Avery, well and cheerful," Avery had reported that Emmanuel on that day looked "exhausted, miserable and obviously feeble." Virgil said that Emmanuel was found by his landlady and removed to St. Luke's public hospital. Avery wrote that he and another lodger from the building had him checked into Bellevue.

Eugene was angry with them both. He wanted the full story. None that resolved the differences was ever provided. Moreover, Eugene was appalled at a plan, mostly Bernard's, to exhibit Emmanuel's paintings in a permanent room at Harvard. Emmanuel had always been fiercely protective of his work. "Really, the blithe way people rush in after his death and try to do for him what he most avoided during his life is . . . fantastic and vulgar. It would have revolted Emmanuel."[7]

Eugene had his own reason for feeling culpable. Part of Emmanuel's distress may have been due to his unrequited love for Eugene. But this tragic episode haunted Virgil for years. Writing to Briggs, he romanticized Emmanuel's death, in part, because of lingering guilt over it.

> There is only one thing to say of Emmanuel's death. That it was a triumph. And for the last months as he moved eagerly toward it, he had about him an air of achievement. He became more beautiful and calm and lucid the last weeks. His conversation was positively luminous. (Ceux qui atteignent un salut dans ce monde n'y restent pas longtemps.)* He had all the essential experiences and found them bitter. To live longer would only be a repetition which he didn't care to face. He was too intelligent to compromise or to forgive the universe for its essential tragedy. And he saw very well that the only way to triumph in tragedy is to will it.[8]

More immediately, Emmanuel's death swept Virgil into a fit over Briggs. He lost patience with Briggs's chronic fretting about his poor

---

*Those who achieve salvation in this world don't stay here long.

health, his timidity, his failure to engage. Virgil tried to use Emmanuel's tragedy as a stick with which to beat Briggs into action. Letters seem to indicate that they met in New York that October and that
Virgil was more insistent than ever. Virgil must have written an apology, for, back in Cambridge, Briggs sent his reply:

> Well, My dear Tommie, it is late and tired as I am I cannot main-
> tain my anger long. Therefore let things take their course. You have
> apologized; I have registered my expected anger; my analysis is
> in, my impatience with cracked hardness hardening again is also
> registered. May we not now act? less like gentlemen, as I re-
> quested, and more like ourselves—friendly, badly-brought-up
> Americans, etc.—you, the right-minded, faintly insistent; I, the
> weak-willed, always acting my part perfectly with you.[9]

In November there was another visit, an encounter that drew
from Virgil an elaborate letter, at once confused and perceptive,
oblique and revealing.

> My dear Briggs,
>   Of your tragic little visit there remains simply this: that it is not
> your physical state which terrifies me. But your mental. The res-
> ignation. You won't fight! And with the example of Emmanuel so
> recently in my mind, and your letters—well, you see the nature
> of my concern. You are apparently dying of prolonged spiritual
> constipation. Your body-ailments are of no importance, they can
> be arranged. If you do not establish a function of expression you
> will not last out the winter. The only means necessary to that func-
> tioning being the English language.[10]

The correspondence continues in mostly undated letters with
scant references to outside events. They reveal Virgil to be still groping for a way to engage Briggs, still exasperated with Briggs's ailments,
still seizing on Briggs's aspiration to write as a means to make himself essential.

> I woke up this morning again in stark terror. Have you any idea
> of the vision of yourself you vouchsafed me on Friday night? I will
> not allow this state to continue. I will fight it. I will nurse you
> against it. I will hold you with my body. I will communicate to
> you some of the energy which is a burden to us if I can't share it.
> I will not allow you to canonize me. I will not allow you to "sit at
> the feet," etc. My intellectual habits are of me and I will not per-
> mit you to ruin your own by worshipping or imitating them. I will
> tear off of you every wrap which is only mine and not yours. If I

don't receive some sort of satisfying response to this letter, I shall come to Boston at the end of the week. Or before.

I see dire results from a failure to attack the problem immediately. I can't accept suicide from you as from Emmanuel. If you had been thru what he has, I might forgive your fatigue. Tho there is this difference in your problems. Emmanuel died because he was not needed by those who were necessary to him. Frankly, you are necessary to me. I have reduced my life to two things—you and music. I can't throw away either, because each gives me the strength which I spend on the other. Nor throw over both, because they are both unfinished essentials. Anything else can go out of the windows without a quiver. My profoundest intuition is that I am necessary for you, if only as the avenue to a more essential need. I therefore make this request. It is the first I have ever made of you. I have only suggested before. I ask that you come to me (or that I may come to you if that is simpler) and that you accept my help in this matter of writing. It is about the only thing I can really do for you. I have no desire to meddle with your inner life. I want to realize as humbly as possible the unfathomable and indescribable differences between us. . . . You may find this letter brutal, or sentimental, or insulting. But if there is any fight in you you will accept the challenge. Love, Tommie[11]

Briggs was intrigued, touched, yet always overwhelmed by Virgil's confusing and extravagant passion. He did not accept the offer of help with his writing. As the end of his senior year approached, he was pressured by the other patriarchal man in his life, his father. A job was waiting for him at his uncle's firm; Briggs could see no alternative to taking it.

For the 1924–25 academic year, Briggs and Virgil switched cities. Briggs worked on Wall Street; Virgil returned to Cambridge as a teaching assistant to Davison and Hill. By spring, conceding that his fantasy of a relationship with Briggs was just that, Virgil decided to move to Paris. While spending the summer in Kansas City, he wrote a letter that essentially announced a severing of his emotional tie.

Dear Buch,

I haven't written you, because I haven't wanted to. Same reason I didn't come to the country with you. I was afraid. You've no idea the weight that was lifted when I announced that I wasn't going to do it. You appreciate my difficulty, no doubt. The summer passes. I've been here a month. It's been very hot. I've been enormously bored. Most of the days I spend either in sleep or in a bored kind of reading or in an equally bored sort of meditation.

If being amused counts for anything, I am afraid the summer counts for a total loss.[12]

Replying from New York, Briggs is lonely, increasingly resigned to his stultifying work, and eager for letters from Virgil to "lighten the barren weeks which begin each summer." Clearly wishing Virgil to remain in America, he adds, "Despite the sentiment aroused by innumerable cards from abroad, I still think Paris—necessary yes!—but bunk."[13]

Virgil's reply, in which he refers to sketches for what would become his shocking *Sonata da chiesa* and to his first musical experiments with texts (unspecified) of Gertrude Stein, is chatty, detached, and cynical.

My plan is to go abroad and stay awhile. I shall go to Paris, because that is where people are, especially Nadia Boulanger. I like to have her handy. I've no plan or intuition for the future. I shall practice my trade. If I practice it competently, I shall make money. Some, at least. That's all there is to the story. I could do the same anywhere. Except that it's too easy in America. And too uncomfortable. By easy, I mean there's no competition, only rivalry. By uncomfortable, I mean I'm a misfit. I'm not a vegetable, a salesman, or a joiner. Paris, as such, is bunk. But, my God! So is America. Besides, I want to go to Paris. And there is no reason why I shouldn't. Can't one choose one's bunk? *Ubi bene ibi patria,* says Erasmus; that's the story.

Various activities keep me mostly occupied here. The local prints have published my face and history. The Little Symphony will play the damn Tangos next season. I've rescored them for their combination. My Synthetic Waltzes have progressed to a conclusion. They would orchestrate nicely. Perhaps I shall later. The C. T. and F. [Chorale, Tango, and Fugue] unfolds slowly but surely. I fancy it is for wind instruments, perhaps four saxophones and banjo. That is vague yet. There isn't any description I can give till I see the finished piece. The Stein things also mature slowly, because they are a knotty problem. Wrote an article last night. Will do another soon. Satie died. I've lost my faith in Stravinsky. And jazz (high-brow or low-brow) is a dead art already. The world is blank and lovely like a clean blackboard. My love-sores grow less painful everyday. I feel 21 again. Competent and not afraid of anybody. In such a mood, Paris is inevitable.

I am writing a philosophic work. Maxims of a Modernist. Begun in conversation with G. Phillips about the lovely tomfoolery in Tennessee [the Scopes trial]. It was evident that first day that [William Jennings] Bryan, though a wicked man, had a program, and the foolish defense [Clarence Darrow], though right, had none. I am consequently engaged in producing a statement of radical agnosticism—to include work, sex, pleasure, art, war, theory of the state, ethics, and so forth. Be a nice boy and write me another letter soon. I reply to yours same day. And say when you'll be in New York, Love, Tommie[14]

The philosophic work referred to was never published. What remains of it is a manifesto of principles, written in pencil. The document is remarkable for a man of almost twenty-nine—audacious, pervasively cynical, filled with bluster. It would be easy to read it as the outcry of an embittered man nursing love sores from an unrequited relationship. Viewed differently, it gives us Thomson at his most outrageous, like Oscar Wilde, promoting his sexual desires and program for action without a trace of morally uplifting justification.

Maxims of a Modernist

The Three Duties of Man:
1. To sustain life
2. To enjoy sexual activity
3. To assist the ego

These duties are superior to any moral scruple.

All motivations derive from these duties and are equally praiseworthy and all desires equally valid.

There is no duty which does not accomplish some pleasurable end.

The past is an illusion; the present does not exist; all living is anticipation and preparation for the future.

Happiness exists in regarding the immediate future with confidence.

Satisfactory living consists in activity and the preparation for it.

The consolations of philosophy and religion are illusory and precarious. The contemplative life is only satisfactory as a preparation for activity.

The aim of will or desire is action. The purpose of thought is to clarify desires and devise the means of their achievement.

Thought is a means. The gratification of desire is an end in itself.

Crime is the illegal gratification of desire. It is wrong when its consequence frustrates the performance of man's three duties.

A successful marriage is one which assists the performance of man's three duties. An unsuccessful marriage is one which hinders it.

Love is the anticipation of a successful marriage.

Affection is the feeling we entertain toward persons who are useful to us in a more limited way.

If I habitually chose turnips to asparagus, that taste is largely a matter of indifference to my neighbors. With exactly equal indifference do I regard the varieties of sexual habit manifested by my friends.

I can not love properly whom I do not know or be interested in those who are of no use to me.

The function of government is to govern as little as possible. The function of the governed is to be intimidated (*governed*) by government as little as possible.[15]

Shortly after writing this, Virgil moved to Paris. While he lived the life of an expatriate, Briggs worked unhappily for his uncle George. ("You, bright in Paris, the brilliant; I, what would you?—in the soft coal smoke.")[16] His letters, handwritten on Brown Brothers & Co. stationery, are bleak with resignation and longing for the vitality that his friendship with Virgil, for all its confusions, had sparked.

Of myself! The story depends on the materials selected. According to one version, I have laid the foundation for great success in the brokerage business. I look healthier than for several seasons. Rumor has it that I love my cousin and she me. We make a splendid couple, my aunt said. Father suggests that I join the Masons. Shortly I shall begin to study accounting. Then I will collect art. And finally, Amen! Unfortunately the other version in synthesis amounts so far to this: an unspoken disaffection, exploding occasionally in epithet. I am waiting, my friend, waiting. And more, I want to wait. My mind has not ossified; my body is stronger, my complexion better. I am but little constipated. I have acquired no opinions. Lastly, it can be said to my credit that no seduction has got me to attend the family church this winter. What would you? More correspondence? With spring and summer, yes! But even though my letters never reach you, know that, more than ever, I am yours. Love, Briggs.[17]

By April, Briggs's letters were filled with tortured apologies for his inadequacy as a correspondent, best-face efforts to accept his situation, and fantasies of escape.

By going to work I exchanged my whole routine of thinking and living for discipline in mechanical precision. . . . But there is a red dawn in sight, a revolution of attitude toward my job. I will accept it completely, seriously, or quit it.[18]

But the revolution never came. And any idea that Briggs could muster the will to change his status crashed along with the stock market in 1929. His father suffered devastating losses and basically retired from the business. Briggs now had to support a grandmother, his sister, her husband and child—and he never retreated from his responsibility. He bought a seat on the New York Stock Exchange when they were going for Depression prices. He bought a town house on Park Avenue and moved his family there, though in later years he lived in the family place in Denville, New Jersey, and commuted to Manhattan on the Lackawanna railroad.

In 1936 he met and married Florence Reynaud, who was born Catholic in a mixed-income neighborhood in Roxbury. Though not from a proper Bostonian family, Florence had learned the piano, attended Radcliffe, and studied chemistry. As an adult, however, she tended to be private about her past accomplishments. She married young, separated, met Briggs, and agreed to marry him. With the assistance of Briggs's Harvard friend Henwar Rodakiewicz, a documentary film maker, Florence traveled with Briggs to Reno for a divorce, then went on to Hollywood, to the director John Ford's house, no less, for an elaborate private wedding ceremony. Henwar had arranged everything.

Florence loved the Park Avenue social set, the parties, and the culture. Briggs didn't, but he was happy for his wife's pleasure. Two boys came along in the 1930s—Briggs, Jr., and David George—and the family routine seemed complete.

However, Briggs had taken some courses at Columbia, systematically studying archaeology, which utterly fascinated him. When he reached the subject of Near Eastern seals, he was hooked. These seals had been excavated and collected, but only scant analysis and cataloging of them had been done. This was something that Briggs, with his methodical ways, his eye for design, and his discipline, thought he could do. He applied for a Fulbright Fellowship to go to the Ashmolean Museum at Oxford and begin a project to catalog the Sumerian seals in their collection. He was awarded the fellowship.

This began a period when every summer Briggs and the family would go to England. Florence was distressed by Briggs's emerging passion for research and his resulting lack of interest in the firm. But Briggs never looked back. To continue his work, Briggs needed an academic affiliation. The art history department at Yale provided one in 1953, appointing him a research associate with an on-campus office. That same year he retired from the firm and moved his family to Guilford, Connecticut. At Yale he prepared a massive, three-volume catalog of Babylonian seals, sketching the illustrations himself.

Briggs was a devoted father who wrote adventure stories for his boys and read to them in German, French, and Spanish. He became a deacon of the Episcopal church in Guilford and, breaking with the conservative Republican politics of his father, worked as an adviser to Governor Abraham Ribicoff, a liberal Democrat. The Buchanan family lived comfortably and securely, but not lavishly.

And at all their homes—in New York, in Denville, and in Guilford—Virgil was a welcome guest who often brought his friends along: Maurice Grosser, who used to paint on the rooftop of the New Jersey house, from which you could view the valley, and young musicians Virgil thought Briggs and Florence would enjoy: Leonard Bernstein, Ned Rorem. That Virgil was homosexual was perfectly understood, but never discussed, which was the way he wanted it.

Florence had been intimidated by Virgil at first. But they cooked together, played piano duets, and soon grew close. And if his intimacy with the family had come only after an initial period of distancing, this was a process Virgil accepted. Briggs had taken a path to married respectability that Virgil could not follow.

"Florence understood perfectly well about Briggs and me," Thomson said in later life. "But she set herself out to make a friend of me. You see, when my friends marry I usually disappear until I'm summoned. I was in Europe a good deal during this period. Eventually, Briggs started asking me to the house. I became a member of the family. I'm godfather to one of the boys. But I must disappear until I am summoned."[19]

SHERRY, GEORGE, GERTRUDE, ALICE, AND SUSIE

10

In 1973 Virgil Thomson received a letter from a woman at the University of Tulsa who was the newly appointed music editor of a fledgling quarterly called the *Lost Generation Journal*. Wishing to do an article about Thomson, she had a long list of questions about his early years in Paris. Thomson dismissed her with one of his trademark postcard replies:

> I wish you well regarding the Lost Generation Journal.
>
> I am sorry I have not the leisure at present for answering your many questions, though I am grateful for your interest.
>
> I may add that I have never really liked the term "lost generation." Nobody involved was any more "lost" than young people are at any other time. And anyway, the term was from the beginning without much in its favor save as personal publicity for Ernest Hemingway.[1]

Thomson devotes two pages of his autobiography to unraveling the evolution, as he understood it, of the term "lost generation"—from an offhand comment by Gertrude Stein's *hôtelier* that so many young returning French soldiers were "lost" to their chosen professions, to Stein's application of it to American war veterans, to Hemingway's misquoting of her, in Thomson's opinion, to suggest that the experience of the war had left many young Americans permanently rootless. Of course, in later life Thomson discovered that debunking the whole notion that the expatriate American artists who lived in Paris during the 1920s constituted a "lost generation" was helpful to his own personal publicity. It made him provocative and quotable.

Thomson's stated reason for returning to Paris in September of 1925 was to get away from a professional life that was starting to stifle him. During his previous year as a teaching assistant at Harvard, he was offered a job directing the music department at the University of South Carolina. While visiting his family that summer, he was offered the organ post at the Episcopal cathedral where he had once worked as a substitute. He declined both.

Thomson's return to Europe, as he would write, was at once "a coming to and a going from."

> I was coming to the place where music bloomed. I was leaving a career that was beginning to enclose me. I was leaving also an America that was beginning to enclose us all, at least those among us who needed to ripen unpushed. America was impatient with us, trying always to take us in hand and make us a success, or else squeezing us dry for exhibiting in an institution. . . . As Gertrude Stein was to observe, "It was not so much what France gave you as what she did not take away."[2]

At Harvard, Thomson had been discouraged, he felt, from trusting his home-bred experiences as a source for inspiration. His professors found fault with his exercises in composition. This shook his confidence. But he didn't altogether trust the critique. He had to get away to find himself. Ironically, the only place safe from America's cultural inferiority complex about Europe was in Europe.

Moreover, Paris suited him. You could live cheaply, sharing rooms, clothes, and money with your artist friends. Asked later why he left for France, Thomson usually replied with two standard quips. One was that he went to Paris so that he could write about Kansas City, then came back home later to tell everybody about Paris. The other, often quoted, was "I figured that if I were going to starve, I might as well starve in a place where the food was good." Both quips were essentially true.

But there were other feelings closing in on Thomson. If his music didn't belong, didn't fit in at home, perhaps neither did he. Or so he started to feel. He was almost twenty-nine and had never had a successful romantic relationship. That summer, in a somewhat veiled letter to Briggs Buchanan, he seems to acknowledge his isolation, his need to break away, and also his fear of doing so.

. . . I am conscious from day to day of a certain very personal and private sentience, which is subject to no right of search by any instructor and which involves no obligation to mountebankery for the education of my contemporaries, for indeed the dears have no need of education, being genuinely consecrated to their businesses and their wives and to the happy process of begetting upon them incomes and babies. And this private existence of mine represents a small but growing deposit in a sort of intellectual savings bank, against the rainy days of the mind which December in Paris is likely to bring, or against the next "winter of my discontent" in Cambridge.[3]

Paris in the 1920s was not some wanton Bohemia. "Back then, if you wanted sex you went to Berlin!" Thomson used to say. In Paris people explored everything—art, opium, and sex, too. But they did not impose their discoveries on anyone else. "Everybody knew what everybody else was up to. But you did not talk about it," Thomson said. In company, even with your artist friends, you were courteous and respectful. You may have had one suit to your name, but you kept it clean and wore it when you went calling. You could be any kind of eccentric artist, thinker, radical, or character you wanted to be. But so long as you were polite and did not tire people with your propaganda, you could have a circle of friends and a pleasant life. These customs perfectly suited Virgil Thomson, who claimed the right to live by his modernist maxims but didn't want to talk about them, who wanted friends and affection, but needed them, in the words of Stein, "to leave him inside of himself completely to himself."[4]

The first time Virgil sailed for Paris he had traveled with the entire Harvard Glee Club. This time, departing on September 1, 1925, he traveled with one friend, Sherry Mangan, a comrade from the Liberal Club.

John Joseph Sherry Mangan was the son of Dr. John Joseph Mangan, an Irish-born pediatrician of wide renown who was also a classical scholar. Sherry was born and raised in Lynn, Massachusetts. An only child, he was adored by his parents. Eight years Virgil's junior, Sherry all his life looked older than he was. As an adolescent, he had accompanied his father to Europe for research on his father's exhaustive, two-volume biography of Erasmus. Following his father's example, Sherry became a student of the classics and also, later on, a poet, calligrapher, book designer, and editor.

Just eighteen when Virgil met him, Sherry was a big-drinking, fleshy, Irish charmer with thick red-blond hair and a disarming smile, a ladies' man who was comfortably affectionate and open with male friends. Rebellious and insubordinate with his professors, he once created a scandal by sucking suggestively on a pickle in an advanced writing class. Expelled as a junior, he was conditionally readmitted, and managed to graduate cum laude in classics.

Being from a devout Catholic family, Sherry was "High Tory" in his politics, according to his first wife.[5] The catastrophe of the Great Depression changed all that. By the 1930s he was an ardent Marxist active in the Trotskyist Fourth International. He would become a correspondent for *Life, Time,* and *Fortune,* the flagship magazines of the Henry Luce empire. In the 1950s he investigated firsthand the struggles of the tin miners in Bolivia with the idea of writing a historical novel. The physical exertion of the work drove his second wife to a premature death from a heart attack and permanently shattered Sherry's health.

At Harvard, Sherry thought Virgil brilliant, amusing, and headed for greatness. Virgil was flattered by the devotion of a handsome younger man so comfortable with his masculinity. Sherry would bring over his girlfriends for evaluation by Virgil, who was dazzled by Sherry's nonchalant reports of his sexual adventures. "I seriously begin to think, Tommy," Sherry once wrote, "that all this gadding about with the not so very fair sex has been merely an attempt to live up to the reputation which usually attaches to young Irishmen. Recently while embracing a young lady with supposed rapture I found myself tenderly stroking my own hand by mistake."[6]

Writing to Virgil from Massachusetts, Sherry once began a letter with this epitaph:

> "And having composed his soul and scratched his balls, great Virgil slept"
> Thus thought I the other night of you, while engaged myself in that soul-satisfying operation. How do you think it would go on your tombstone?[7]

There were not many popular, heterosexual young men in Virgil's life who were at ease talking sex with him—and Virgil found it a great relief. Sherry understood Virgil's nature, but knew not to broach the subject openly. By 1928 Sherry would have to return home to tend to his ailing father. Thus commenced an epic correspondence. Nearly three hundred letters from Sherry survive in the Thomson archives, multipage typed letters filled with political argument, personal ruminations, and poetry, and handwritten letters in Sherry's elegant calligraphic script. Sherry would eventually come back to Paris in the late 1930s. Virgil sometimes found Sherry exhausting—always needing to talk deeply, to confide, to boast, to carry on. But during those first two years, they were constant and affectionate companions.

Thomson's first month in Paris was terrible. He confided the sorry details—including his account of getting mixed up with an "apache," a street hustler—in a heartsick letter to Briggs. Yet he was not so sunk that he couldn't also deliver an incisive analysis of cultural affairs. This ruminative, revealing letter, which Thomson edited heavily before allowing its publication in 1988, is quoted in full:

> November 2, 1925
> Provins
>
> Dear Briggs,
>   I've wanted very badly in these last weeks to write you, but I haven't because I wanted you too badly. There was nothing really to say except that I was miserable. A dozen reasons for it. Lost my baggage. Cold in the chest ever since I arrived. Couldn't work. Missed two articles. Sherry a great trial. Paris cold and damp. Rain rain. No heat till November 1st. No satisfactory dwelling. No piano. And besides, after three years of America, I had to get a certain amount of vice off my system—never a cheerful procedure. Came down here to spend a few quiet days in a warm provincial hotel. First thing I did was to get mixed up with an apache. From which I came home with a nice black eye. Since then I've been industrious and cheerful. Rainy weather and heated room, sore throat and weary nerves, sleep, work, and country meals are more pleasant indoors than local sight-seeing out. Spite of tenth century towns and twelfth century churches. I have soiled great quantities of music paper, written letters, eaten food, and reposed in solitude. Tomorrow I go back to Paris. My cold is some better. Also the eye. My house will be heated. (November 1st is past.) The ancient actress will have departed and I can have my old room. My piano will arrive from Pleyel. Baggage and money are still short, but my depression is so much lifted that perhaps I shall eventually write an article or so. In any case, I rather plan to spend my last hundred dollars (if it arrives) on a trip to Vienna in December. The lost trunk contained dress clothes, suit and a half of day clothes, 2 over coats, raincoat, shoes, manuscript. I shall probably never see them. Steamship company's fault, however, mostly. Work under construction. The last few days have started the well

to flowing again. Feel infinitely better, as always when I can work. Think I shall go away somewhere every week for a few days. Costs no more than eating in Paris. (Here a heated room is 10 francs, eight-course meals with wine, nine francs. 1 franc = 4 1/2 cents.) Now that my crisis is over and I can see my way clear, everything is all right. Nothing matters but to sit quiet and work. And for the moment I don't want to do anything else. If I get all involved again and unhappy and everything, I may not have the sense to keep still. Anytime you get a tragedy letter from me like the one I recently wrote last week, just send me a cable saying to shut my damn mouth and quit belly-aching. The cable will be a certain consolation (to know someone would go to the trouble), and the message should have its effect.

Write of your state and doings. Are you working? What at? How do you like it? Any time you want to visit me I'll house and feed you for the pleasure of your company. Buy you clothes if necessary. Get you a job if you want it.

Paris is pretty dull. I think it's going to be an awful season. If anything happens in America, write me of it. It's a dull winter everywhere, I presume. 1920 is finally démodé and there is nothing to take its place. *Surrealism* has not been as fecund as one hoped. Everyone has gone out hunting for an idea. Gide has gone to Africa, Etienne de Beaumont to America, Stravinsky (at last) to Russia. I, for one, welcome a dull season. I shall probably work from *ennui*. Nadia and I are engaged in a search for my character. With usual clairvoyance she comes right to the point at the second interview. "In spite of the fact," she says, "that I am acquainted with you as a talented musician, a charming person, and an incredibly intelligent young man, I have the feeling of not knowing you at all inside." Imagine the effect of that on an already turbulent and unhappy mind. Well, the black eye was just the shock, moral and nervous, that I wanted. I thanked the young man, gave him all the money I had, and shook hands. I came home and wrote fugues for three hours, and today I started a symphony. If I only had your clarifying presence, I should likely write an article.

Love, Virgil

The "old room" being vacated by the "ancient actress" was the flat at the student hotel on the rue de Berne that Thomson had rented during his fellowship year. He moved back on November 3. Some, but not all, of his baggage was eventually returned. His plans for weekly trips to the country and a winter vacation in Vienna never materialized. He had arrived with just $500 and only hazy prospects for work.

However, Thomson had an open invitation from the editors at

Vanity Fair to submit story ideas. During his last months in Cambridge and his summer visit to Missouri, he had written several longer pieces for *Vanity Fair* that had attracted attention and earned him a healthy fee—$100 each. The editors liked his peppery style and sweeping analyses, all in the context of pieces that purported to be primers for the layman on sophisticated musical matters. In "How Modern Music Gets That Way" (April 1925), Thomson answers distressed concert subscribers (" 'If composers want to say something new,' they ask, 'why can't they say it with the old language that we can understand?' ") with this blunt, almost exasperated, and perfectly sensible reply:

> They can't for the same reason Beethoven couldn't. Music is made of sounds, not ideas; and the only way to make new music is with new sounds. Much of this music is pretty poor stuff. Much of music always has been. But the people who make stupid modern pieces would certainly make just as stupid ones if they wrote in the style of Schumann.

This article, though filled with insights on the French/German aesthetic divide, the purely coloristic and rhythmic functions of harmony, and such, is not free of Thomson's biases—his positioning of Satie as a leader of modern music, stated here as an indisputable truth:

> Of the three major influences, the representative figures in modern music, Schoenberg, Stravinsky and Satie, not one of them, probably, would have been intelligible to Brahms; and Brahms has been dead less than thirty years.

There were articles entitled "The Cult of Jazz," "The Satirical Tendency in Modern Music," "The Profession of Orchestral Conducting," "The Future of American Music"—all of them scintillating, ardent on behalf of new American musical developments, and outrageous.

> Ravel has admitted the sterility of his well-known manner by attempting (and not too successfully) to make himself a new one.

> [T]he enthusiastic nationalists of Hungary and England—Kodaly, Bartok, Williams, Holst—are too deeply occupied with the problems of their racial idiom to be of more than exemplary value to us.

To earn a living, Thomson also gave some private piano lessons. But his first year in Paris was a period of scant money, uncertainty, borrowing from friends, asking $100 of his father (only once, and reluctantly, though it was quickly provided), and frequent relocations.

In one of his first forays from his room on the rue de Berne, Virgil headed to Shakespeare and Company, the hospitable Left Bank bookstore on the rue de l'Odéon near the Luxembourg Gardens. The wood-fronted shop with overcrowded shelves, which stocked mostly English-language literature, was operated by the New Jersey–born bibliophile Sylvia Beach, a small-framed, cheerful, chain-smoking woman who had been an ambulance driver during the war. Sandwiched between a corset maker and a nose-spray supplier, the shop was a haven for writers, particularly Americans. Shakespeare and Company was already renowned in literary circles for having dared to publish in 1922 under its own name—and at Sylvia Beach's personal expense—the first edition of James Joyce's *Ulysses,* at a time when no established publisher would touch it. Against one wall a large stove placed before the hearth warmed Beach's visitors. American writers with shifting addresses could collect messages and mail there.[8]

After some initial wariness, Sylvia invited Virgil into the Shakespeare and Company circle, meaning he had free borrowing privileges and was welcome at readings. There Virgil met James Joyce, Ernest Hemingway, e. e. cummings, Ford Madox Ford, and the poet Ezra Pound, who was also, Virgil believed, a composer and musical thinker of surprising accomplishment. In the spring of 1926 Virgil would hear a private performance at the Salle Pleyel, where Chopin and Liszt once played, of Pound's opera to a text by François Villon—a minimally accompanied and carefully prosodized setting of Old French, "not quite a musician's music," Virgil later wrote of it, "though . . . its sound has remained in my memory."[9]

There also Virgil met the young American composer George Antheil who lived with his Hungarian-born wife Boski Markus in two small rooms above the shop. The son of a shoe store keeper and, like Sylvia, a New Jersey native, Antheil had been taken up as a cause by the writers who gathered at Shakespeare and Company. Above the hearth on one of the few bookless patches of wall was a photo gallery, a Shakespeare and Company Hall of Fame of literary luminaries. Only one composer ever dominated the display: George Antheil. There were pictures of George as a youngster with his hair in bangs, of George as a pugnacious-looking young man posing acrobatically, dangling from a balcony, and generally displaying the swagger of the self-proclaimed "Bad Boy of Music," as he later titled his autobiography. Upstairs, George kept an upright piano. Every day at four-thirty patrons were invited to tea and music there, a gesture toward Sylvia, who had objected to placing a piano in the tiny upstairs flat.

Antheil, Virgil later wrote, was "the literary mind's idea of a musical genius—bold, bumptious, and self-confident; he was also diverting."[10] Born in 1900, Antheil started his career as a virtuosic pianist. Before moving to Paris in 1923, he had befriended Stravinsky in Berlin and was powerfully influenced by the Russian's anti-Romantic, rhythmically propulsive compositions. Antheil took the machinelike rhythms one step further, turning out abrasive and outrageous works titled *Airplane Sonata, Sonata Savage, Death of Machines.* His harmonic language favored the use of cluster chords, and block harmonies spiked with dissonances that, rather than demanding resolution, were used like mallets to pound out the pulse.

In his music Antheil's literary friends discerned, or so they believed, a reflection of the mechanized modern times. Antheil's career was being guided primarily by Ezra Pound, who had written articles and a book, *Antheil and the Treatise on Harmony,* which compared the composer's technique of juxtaposing disparate blocks of sound over a propulsive time span to cubism, which juxtaposed painted shapes and objects on a canvas.

Virgil had heard about the riotous reception that greeted a concert of Antheil's piano pieces at the Théâtre des Champs-Elysées on October 4, 1923. Sensing in George a fellow iconoclast and flattered by his attentions, Virgil was easily won over. "I envied George his freedom from academic involvements, the bravado of his music and its brutal charm. He envied me my elaborate education, encouraged me to sit out patiently the sterile time it seemed to have brought."[11]

Virgil and George became allies. For working space, George had rented a small room with a piano around the corner from Sylvia's shop. When Virgil dallied on the Left Bank past the time for streetcars, he was welcome to stay there. For all his self-promotional savvy, George was indebted to Virgil for arranging a concert that won him some welcome respect in musical circles, a concert made possible by Nadia Boulanger.

Despite Virgil's distrust of the critique he had taken from his Harvard professors, he was determined to address their concerns. So, reluctantly, he had returned to Boulanger for lessons soon after arriving in Paris. Their working relationship this time was as troubled as before. Boulanger "insists I have greater possibilities than I give myself credit for, that I am a real composer," Virgil wrote to Briggs. "But frankly she doesn't understand me. She only recognizes, which after all is a lot."[12] Still, Virgil persevered.

Boulanger was then a member of the program committee for the Société Musicale Indépendante, an organization founded in 1909 by Fauré to present new music in subscription concerts. Its board included, among others, Stravinsky, Bartók, Ravel, and Schoenberg. Boulanger had conceived the idea of a special concert outside the regular series by top-notch performers devoted to the music of young Americans. There would be piano pieces by Herbert Elwell, several chamber works by Aaron Copland, a piano sonata by Walter Piston, and a sonata for violin and piano by Theodore Chanler—all current or former students of Boulanger's. Virgil suggested, and Boulanger agreed, that Antheil's string quartet be included.

Thomson was represented by his *Sonata da chiesa,* his "bang-up graduation piece in the dissonant neo-Baroque style of the period."[13] Grafting modern harmonies and materials onto solid baroque forms, Thomson scored the piece for five seemingly disparate instruments: E-flat clarinet, D trumpet, viola, F horn, and trombone—Thomson's idea being to show off his ability to blend them in striking and satirical ways. However, for all its conceptual audacity, this sixteen-minute piece is no prank. The first movement, a chorale, with its ruminative solo statements and its concerted group responses, evokes a Negro church service Thomson had heard in Kansas City. Following this is a lurching, profane, faux-tango. The finale is a "fugue to end fugues," as John Cage called it, spiked with rude dissonances. This was the last piece Virgil would write for Boulanger, making it, as he defined the term, a "masterpiece," a piece to please your master—in other words, a work you wrote to get your teacher off your back.

The concert, held at the Salle Gaveau, attracted leading French composers (Florent Schmitt, Albert Roussel), critics, potential patrons, the American military attaché ("tone-deaf but serious in the performance of his assignment"),[14] James Joyce, and a contingent of American composers (including George Foote, Walter Damrosch, and young Roger Sessions). A Paris-based reviewer for the *New York Times* (not identified with a byline) covered the event with gleeful irreverence. Thomson's work "started off the show on the road to uproar," he wrote. The fugue "works into a collection of squeaks, grunts and whistles that sound something like the Gare Saint-Lazare when the boat trains come in."

Not content with his inaugural review in Paris, Virgil wrote his own in a letter to Briggs Buchanan, a beguiling mix of irrepressible confidence and astute critical analysis.

> The most impressive work (by number of players engaged, novelty of form, and strangeness of noises produced) was the "Sonate d'Eglise" [French title] by V. Thomson. . . . In general one may say that, leaving out about two ill-advised experiments, the instrumentation is unquestionably a knockout. The chorale is a genuine new idea, the other movements decently satisfactory. The faults are a dangerous rigidity of rhythmic texture (especially in the chorale), an excessively contrapuntal style in the fugue, and an immature comprehension of the profundities of classic form. The work manifests, however, a mind of great strength and originality. The public awaits (or ought to) with eagerness Mr. Thomson's next work, a symphony in the form of variations on an American hymn tune.[15]

This event would solidify the bond between Virgil and George "Let me say what I said last night," George wrote in a note to Virgil after the concert, "that I believe in you more than I believe in certainly any other American, and perhaps even a lot more of other nationalities." And Virgil wrote of a new ally in a letter to Briggs.

> For the first time in history, another musician liked my music. For the first time since I left your society, somebody said hello. Somebody recognized what I was all about. Or recognized that I was about something worth looking at.
>
> Imagine my gratitude.
>
> More particularly since this support and admiration came from the finest composer of our generation (of this there isn't any doubt) and was supported by deeds. I must admit that the encouragement has been mutual, the contact has bucked up George just as much as me, perhaps more. . . . Antheil is the chief event of my winter. He has admired me, he has quarreled with me about theories, he has criticized my pieces, he has consulted me about his, he has defended me to my enemies, to his enemies, to my friends, to his friends. He has forced my acceptance by people who intuitively feared me, notably Mrs. Antheil and Sylvia Beach. He has talked, wined, and drunk me by the hour. He has lodged me and fed me and given me money. At this very moment he is trying to persuade a rich lady to give money to me instead of to him, although he is perfectly poor himself.[16]

Nothing ever came of Antheil's efforts with the "rich lady." Virgil never even learned her name. However, Virgil managed to meet his own rich lady, Mrs. Christian Gross, a sugar millionaire whose husband was then the first secretary of the American embassy, whom he was introduced to through a mutual friend, Alice Woodfin Branlière, an amateur musician from Vermont, long resident in Paris, well connected in society.

At that time Parisian musical circles were not exactly incorruptible. Bribes to critics, funding of claques, and payoffs to newspaper editors were standard practice. The judgments that mattered were formed mostly from concerts presented in private salons attended by the cultural elite, to which an aspiring artist or potential patron had to be invited. As the wife of a diplomat, Mrs. Gross, convent reared, intelligent, and not yet forty, had no natural entry into this artistic and intellectual network. Nor did she have the patience for the "rung-by-rung technique," as Kathleen Hoover put it. Virgil suggested a more rapid course—namely, that in her palatial suite on the Champ-de-Mars Mrs. Gross present concerts of new music to which he would invite the intelligentsia of Paris. Basically, his idea was that Mrs. Gross set up her own salon.

She was willing to try it, leaving all the programming and arrangements to Virgil, who immediately brought George into the bargain as chief manager. Three Friday afternoons following the Grand Prix week were selected; the services of the rising conductor Vladimir Golschmann and first-class assisting performers were engaged; George and Virgil invited every presentable artist, composer, and author they knew and requested that they bring their patrons, if they had any. Virgil also made it clear to Mrs. Gross's chef and majordomo that they must "surpass themselves."[17]

The concerts were preceded by a champagne buffet; the programs consisted exclusively of Thomson and Antheil. At one, Virgil's *Five Phrases from the Song of Solomon* had its premiere—a haunting work, really just five elongated melodic phrases of plaintive, Semitic character, accompanied only by percussion, alternately a tom-tom, a small drum, a gong, a cymbal, and a wood block. At another, Virgil's *Sonata da chiesa* had a repeat performance, this time conducted by Golschmann and enthusiastically received.

And at a final gala on June 19, 1926, this one presented at the Théâtre des Champs-Elysées, Antheil's *Ballet mécanique,* an audacious work originally scored for sixteen player pianos and a battery of percussion instruments, received its belated premiere. The score had been intended to accompany a Dada-inspired film by the painter Fernand

Léger, but the problems of coordinating a film with such a sprawling ensemble proved insurmountable. Instead it was presented in a reduced orchestration, basically all that could be fit into the space: one player piano with amplifier, two pianos, three xylophones, a metal propeller, four bass drums, and siren. The piece created a sensation. A vogue among socialites for new American music was launched. So was Mrs. Gross.

However, Mrs. Gross's celebrity in salon circles was short-lived. At first, pleased by her success, she presented Virgil with a check for $500, a commission for a new work. By that fall she had left her palatial suite, her diplomat husband, and her children and eloped with a Mexican. "As innocent at musical patronage as at social climbing, she did not again, to my knowledge, essay either," Thomson wrote; "rumor had it she remained content with love."[18]

Virgil did not attend the final gala concert, in part, because no work of his was on the program. But his absence was the first evidence of the chill that was settling between him and George. He had not been happy when George insisted that Ezra Pound be brought into the planning.

> Ezra did say to me, on a bench in the Luxembourg Gardens: "If you stick around with me, you'll be famous." But in view of how domineering he was, I was not very interested in being made famous by him, nor in sticking too close; and he must have felt this. In any case, our brief association soon ended. A decade later Ford Madox Ford recounted that at one of Mrs. Gross's musicales Ezra had pointed me out: "You see that little man there? That's the enemy."[19]

Thomson was the enemy, no doubt, because he began to believe that George's music, for all its innovative uses of sound and rhythm, was increasingly beholden to literary ideas. To him, Antheil's works were the prototypes of what today are sometimes called "program-note pieces," pieces whose rationales can be explained neatly in a program note, not pieces that resonate musically in ways that can be articulated only feebly. Antheil had in him no power of musical growth, Thomson later wrote. This " 'bad boy of music' . . . merely grew up to be a good boy."[20]

The *Ballet mécanique* was heard in New York on April 10, 1927, and received disastrously. Antheil moved to Germany to try his hand at avant-garde opera, with little sustained success. By the 1940s he was making his living composing film scores in Hollywood, writing a syndicated newspaper column for the lovelorn and prophetic analyses of the war for the *Los Angeles Daily News,* and making radio broadcasts. During this period he continued to compose and assiduously courted the good will of his onetime friend, now the most influential critic in America, this despite the fact that, back in the Paris days, Antheil had strongly urged Thomson to give up musical criticism altogether.

Though he would later write somewhat defensively of his falling under Antheil's spell, Thomson remained grateful to him for one collegial gesture that completely changed his life: through Antheil he finally met Gertrude Stein.

During the winter of 1925–26, Stein had heard Antheil acclaimed as "that year's genius." So "she thought she really ought to look him over."[21] Through Sylvia Beach she issued an invitation. George, knowing of Virgil's regard for Stein's work, invited him to come along. Virgil had wanted his first meeting with Stein to come about informally. This was his opportunity.

Everything about the house at 27 rue de Fleurus, near the Luxembourg Gardens, already renowned in literary circles, was just as Virgil had expected. This being the evening, the maid had gone home. Virgil and George were greeted at the door by Alice B. Toklas, Gertrude's selflessly devoted companion since 1907, also her stenographer, personal secretary, cook, gardener, and part-time veterinarian to the pet poodle Basket and, later on, his successor, Basket II. Walking through the narrow hallway with its book-lined walls, they would have noticed the quite small dining room off to the right. On the left was the closed door to Alice's room, which she had moved into permanently in 1913 after Leo Stein, Gertrude's brother, moved out. Gertrude and Leo lived on an inheritance—about $150 a month each—that had come from the sale of the family business, a cable car line in San Francisco, and some other properties. They had quarreled incessantly over money, over the merits of the modern paintings they collected (Gertrude championed Picasso, Leo thought cubism was utter rubbish), and over Gertrude's writing, which Leo detested.

Upstairs at the house were two bedrooms and a bath, but few guests ever saw these quarters. Walking through the hallway, Virgil and George would have entered the pavilion, and from here, through a passageway cut through the wall, into the atelier, the famous salon where Gertrude worked by day (and sometimes into the early morning hours) and held court by night. The furniture was mostly dark oak and walnut—Louis XIII, Spanish, Italian Renaissance. Placed about were baroque-style nicknacks of an ecclesiastical nature—candlesticks and statuettes of saints. In the center of the room was a solid-oak table, Gertrude's desk, with an inkstand, personal stationery, a ceramic jar for pencils, and stacks of the blue-covered, lined French school composition notebooks that Gertrude used for writing, always in long-hand and always in pencil. The puce-colored walls, which stretched high on all sides, were covered, every inch of them up to the ceiling, with paintings by Picasso (almost all of them pre-cubist, from his Blue, Rose, and early Negro periods), Matisse, Cézanne, Renoir, Gauguin, Toulouse-Lautrec.

Alice presided from the tea table (though sometimes, with more familiar guests, she would occupy herself with her petit point). Seated in a roomy, throne-like, wood-framed chair was Gertrude, then fifty-three, and that night wearing one of her trademark long brown skirts and an embroidered vest, much like the one embroidered by Alice and given by her as a memento to Virgil after Gertrude's death, a gift he treasured—though he kept it in his closet and seldom showed it to anyone—for the rest of his life.

Gertrude and Alice made an odd couple. Alice was small and thin, with a penetrating gaze, a shadow of a mustache, and a large mole on her lower forehead that she tried to cover by trimming her straight black bangs to just above her eyebrows. Gertrude was short but monumental, a brusque, self-assured, hardy woman with a deep belly laugh. At that time she still wore her hair long, bundled up in a bun. When that spring she cropped it short, she "looked a great deal like a Roman emperor," Virgil later recalled. "Before that, she looked like a chunky, intelligent and possibly friendly woman."[22]

Alice was definitely unfriendly. Fiercely protective of Gertrude and quick to be jealous, she was troubled by Virgil's premature familiarity. But Gertrude and Virgil had much in common. "We had both enjoyed Harvard. We had both enjoyed World War I, which, many people don't understand, was a very popular war. We got on like a couple of Harvard boys."[23]

Neither Gertrude nor Alice found George to be anyone worth bothering about. Moreover, he was too cozy with the enemy camp, the crowd at Shakespeare and Company that was promoting James Joyce, Gertrude's rival in the experimental writing business. Gertrude had been an early patron of the shop. And Sylvia Beach stocked Gertrude's books, the few that had been printed. But when Sylvia published *Ulysses,* their friendship, ostensibly still intact, became very strained.

Unlike George, who hadn't a clue, Virgil talked with sympathy and excitement about Gertrude's writing. He had been addicted since college to *Tender Buttons* and *Geography and Plays.* His keen interest pleased Gertrude immensely. When the young men left, Gertrude said a curt good-bye to George. To Virgil, she said, "We'll be seeing each other."

Yet they did not see each other or even communicate until the summertime, when Virgil sent Gertrude a postcard from the country. That fall and winter he visited them several times, attending a Christmas Eve party with a tree and carol singing and a cake made by Alice decorated with a real ribbon and candles. But it was not until New Year's Day, 1927, when Virgil dropped off as a present his musical setting of Gertrude's short poem "Susie Asado," that the friendship was cemented and Alice was completely won over.

Virgil had spent considerable time composing this ninety-second song, his first Stein setting. He knew he was onto something. The poem, taken from *Geography and Plays,* would seem to be hermetic. (The second line reads, "Susie Asado which is a told tray sure.") The vocal line is by turns declamatory, lyrical, and eerie, projecting with utter clarity every nuance of Stein's abstract text. The functional piano part consists merely of a broken-triad pattern, some scales in parallel sevenths and ninths, and a concluding passage with solemn chords of open fifths. The result is spare yet strong, playful yet haunting, funny yet oddly moving.

The meanings in "Susie Asado" are certainly abstract, though, activated by Thomson's setting, they don't seem to be absent. As the first line implies, Miss Asado is clearly a gracious hostess who serves "Sweet sweet sweet sweet sweet tea." She's also, as the wordplay suggests, a sweetie. And a "tray sure" (a treasure). Even more, a *"told* tray sure," which may mean she is fabled among the circle of women who drink her sweet tea. Sometimes Stein seems to be spelling out her meaning, as with "A lean on the shoe this means slips slips hers," which, as projected by Thomson's deft word groupings, indicates that Miss Asado wears slippers ("slips hers"). And so on.

At the climax of the song, the vocal line builds in intensity and direction to a resounding high G, and the singer sings, almost ominously, "Trees tremble, the old vats are in bobbles, bobbles which shade and shove and render clean, render clear must." These words, Thomson felt, "explode off the page at you." And when his setting of them is sung with conviction, this moment has gripping resonance.

Thomson later explained his discovery:

> My hope in putting Gertrude Stein to music had been to break, crack open, and solve for all time anything still waiting to be solved, which was almost everything, about English musical declamation. My theory was that if a text is set correctly for the sound of it, the meaning will take care of itself. And the Stein texts, for prosodizing in this way, were manna. With meanings already abstracted, or absent, or so multiplied that choice among them was impossible, there was no temptation toward tonal illustration, say, of birdie babbling by the brook or heavy heavy hangs the heart. You could make a setting for sound and syntax only, then add, if needed, an accompaniment equally functional. I had no sooner put to music after this recipe one short Stein text than I knew I had opened a door.[24]

"Susie Asado" was finally published in 1935, along with nine songs by other American composer-agitators. The publisher was Cos Cob Press, an operation funded by a generous patron, Mrs. Alma Wertheim, but run by the composers themselves, with Aaron Copland leader of the pack. In this collection are early songs, one each, by Roger Sessions, Aaron Copland, Israel Citkowitz, and Theodore Chanler, a Paul Bowles setting of a French text and a Marc Blitzstein setting of "Jimmie's got a goil," e. e. cummings's impish evocation of Brooklynese. Each of these songs is distinctive; but none is more daring and, in its way, more modern than "Susie Asado." Thomson had indeed opened a door.

Before Virgil, composers had balked at setting Gertrude Stein. So Gertrude was thrilled with "her Susie." She could not read music, could not really carry a tune, and needed Alice, who had once been a trained pianist, to decipher the piece. In thanks, and by way of explaining why they were not able to receive the gift in person when he had dropped by, Gertrude wrote to Virgil:

> . . . I like its looks immensely and want to frame it and Miss Toklas who knows more than looks says the things in it please her a lot and when can I know a little other than its looks but I am completely satisfied with its looks, the sad part was that we were at

home but we were denying ourselves to everyone having been
xhausted by the week's activities but you would have been the
xception you and the Susie, you or the Susie, do come in soon
we will certainly be in Thursday afternoon any other time it is luck
but may luck always be with you and a happy New Year to you

always

Gertrude Stein[25]

By the beginning of 1927 Thomson had found his compositional
voice and a promising new direction. His music had been presented
in elite musical circles, reviewed in the press, whistled and hooted at,
and admired. He still had much of Mrs. Gross's $500 commission to
get him through the winter, and no Mrs. Gross demanding to see what
she had paid for. He had made friends, discovered inexpensive restaurants, found excitement and contentment. Reflecting on his state in a
letter to Briggs, he wrote, "Great progress in tranquility. Consequently
in expression. Great satisfaction (spite of weather, poverty, and
mishaps) with Paris as a place of residence. For the present I shall remain. I do well here. Elsewhere in Europe I should feel lonely. In
America I should go mad."[26]

11 MAURICE

As he got older, Virgil Thomson lost patience with visitors who viewed him primarily as a repository of information about Paris in the 1920s. Scholars, journalists, writers—they would arrive for an interview at the Chelsea Hotel, only to ask about all the famous people he had known. But these were not necessarily the people Thomson had been closest to, and he had little interest in discussing them.

Usually, he would answer with standardized anecdotes. Asked about Picasso, say, he would call up his Picasso stories, most often the one about going to Picasso's studio to compose his musical portrait, a story Thomson could deliver without thinking. James Joyce? Without fail the interrogator would get the story of the Paris Opéra commission. After the success of *Four Saints in Three Acts,* Joyce asked Thomson to compose a score for a ballet to be presented at the Paris Opéra with choreography by Leonide Massine based on the children's games chapter of *Finnegans Wake.* Thomson demurred, not wanting to wound his "good friend Gertrude," who thought Joyce a rival.

When Thomson found the questioners tiresome or uninformed, he dispatched them testily. "Did you know Duchamp?" he was once asked. "Yes!" was the blunt reply, followed by a stony silence that did not invite a follow-up. Another time, asked whether he knew Sartre, he answered wearily, "Yes, yes. Nice fellow. Didn't like his girlfriend."

Thomson was seldom asked about the people he had been closest to in Paris. But whenever he was, particularly if the questioner had done some homework by reading what Thomson already had written, he could be effusive in his answers.

One such friend was Henry-Russell Hitchcock, whom Thomson knew from the Liberal Club at Harvard. The Boston-born Hitchcock never achieved the celebrity of a Hemingway, but he would become the preeminent architectural historian in the United States and the author of over twenty groundbreaking books. Thomson always appreciated people who understand Hitchcock's importance without being told.

Even as a young man, Russell, as friends called him, looked professorial. Red-bearded, tall, stocky, with an imposing voice and expansive midriff, he would take Virgil on long, winding walks through Paris explaining the architecture to him. Russell was homosexual, but relatively untroubled by it. He was one of the first people with whom Virgil felt comfortable talking "queer talk"—gossip, catty put-downs.

There was also the group of painters who for a while during the 1920s were dubbed the "Neo-Romantics," a term they didn't disavow. Thomson championed their cause, which was to express, in full reaction against cubism, "tenderness, mystery, and compassion."[1] He especially enjoyed the brothers Eugene and Leonid Berman from St. Petersburg. Eugene, "Genia," the more original talent, was then doing dark landscapes and nocturnal scenes of mysterious quays with sleeping beggars and pyramid-shaped piles of vaguely unidentifiable stuff (freight, shipping cartons, trash?). He later became a stage designer, working at the Metropolitan Opera and the New York City Ballet, creating sets for works by his longtime friend Igor Stravinsky.

There was also the handsome Dutchman Kristians Tonny, a child prodigy who came to Paris at age ten and had paintings exhibited at twelve. All his life Thomson kept several works by Tonny, whom he recalled as "blond, muscular, and Dutch, with the sea at the back of his eyes."[2] Tonny was much younger, only nineteen, when the Neo-Romantics had their group exhibit in 1926, which Stein, at Thomson's urging, attended. She owned and admired a portrait Tonny had done of her poodle Basket.

Pavel Tchelitcheff was from an aristocratic Russian family. Like Genia Berman, he became a successful stage designer, attracting attention in Paris with designs for Diaghilev. For a while Stein was intrigued by Tchelitcheff's work. "The young Russian was painting colour that was no colour," she wrote; "he was painting blue pictures and he was painting three heads in one."[3]

But of this group, it was the sullen Christian Bérard, nicknamed Bébé because of his fleshiness and boyish face, whom Thomson grew devoted to. Bébé was forever disheveled. "He seemed to live dressed only in a soiled white terry-cloth bathrobe," Maurice Grosser recalled.[4] Later on, Bérard would sport an unkempt beard to counter his babyish look. When Thomson met him, Bérard was already an addicted opium smoker—two or three pipes in the morning, more in the afternoon, and seven or eight with friends in the evening—a regimen strictly adhered to. It was difficult not to feel protective of Bérard. And difficult not to be entranced by the fantasy and sometimes bleak power of his work, which eventually included stage and film designs, notably for Jean Cocteau's film *Beauty and the Beast.*

With the exception of Tchelitcheff, all these young men were introduced to Stein by Thomson. They wound up squabbling with each other over her attention and patronage. At first, Stein was curious about their work, particularly that of Bérard, whose paintings she found "are almost something and then they are just not."[5] Eventually, their pictures began to disappear into the walls, she told them. "They go out the door naturally."[6] But Thomson would later keep work by all of them, particularly Bérard, at his Chelsea Hotel flat.

Two women held close but quite different positions in Thomson's inner circle, though neither was as close as he claimed. With the $500 from his short-term patron Mrs. Christian Gross in hand, Thomson took a vacation in the summer of 1926 at Thonon-les-Bains, near Lake Geneva. There, in a hotel lobby, he met and apparently charmed Madame Louise Langlois, over forty years his senior, a grand, gray-haired, slender, chain-smoking woman from the educated upper class. Madame Langlois was the favorite sibling of her older brother, a naval admiral, who doted on her, remained unmarried (partly to protect her), and wrote every day he was not with her. Her husband, married late, was a professor of physiology, also a man of culture, accepting of his wife's independent ways. Thomson and Madame Langlois (and he never called her anything else) fell easily into a routine of taking walks, playing bridge, swapping books, and sharing sympathetic views on art, ethics, families, friendships.

Thomson's accounts of Madame Langlois are rich with examples of her character and breeding. Out of gratitude to a manservant who had been devoted to her husband during his final illness, Madame Langlois kept him employed, even though he was stealing from her. Rather than confront him, "she gave up her apartment, pensioned him off, and went to live for the rest of her life, ten years, in a hotel."[7]

However, the paucity of correspondence between Thomson and Langlois suggests that this association was motivated mainly by his fancy for friendships with upper-class women. Throughout his life he continued to court wealthy friends, particularly women. He enjoyed the gracious lifestyle, dinner parties, and, often times, patronage that his wealthy friends could offer. They, in turn, basked in his artistic pedigree. In such circles he was always on his best behavior—familiar, full of tales, and delightfully wicked.

The other woman in his Paris circle was Mary Butts, one of the few women Thomson professed to have been romantically involved with. Seven years his senior, Butts was from a respectable, but rather dull, middle-class family in Dorset, though she cultivated (and Thomson believed) a story of her coming from landed gentry, with servants, fox hunts, and vested squires. She had been educated at the University of London and showed early promise as a writer of intensely personal fiction. But her development was stymied by a ruptured marriage to a poet, a daughter from that marriage (whom she neglected), and an intemperate love affair with a Scot who introduced her to opium and rituals of magic. Ostracized by the Bloomsbury set and by an unforgiving and convention-bound mother, Butts escaped to Paris with her Scot, who subsequently died.

Butts was lovely, with white skin and carrot-gold hair, Thomson recalled. When they met, she was living in a flat near the Eiffel Tower, cluttered with papers, books, and dishware. Her life was similarly chaotic.

> I used to call her "the storm goddess," because she was at her best surrounded by cataclysm. She could stir up others with drink and drugs and magic incantations, and then when the cyclone was at its most intense, sit down at calm center and glow. All her stories are of moments when the persons observed are caught up by something, inner or outer, so irresistible that their highest powers and all their lowest conditionings are exposed.[8]

Mary waged war against Virgil's "youthful reserves" and "middle-class hypochrondrias." He was flattered by the attentions of so striking a woman. All his life, and in his autobiography, Virgil spoke of Mary as his great female passion. The account of their relationship in his biographer Kathleen Hoover's book, an account sanctioned and heavily edited by Thomson, is inflated with drama.

> Until then, a woman's attraction had lain for him in her cerebral sparring powers. It assumed new dimensions with his discovery of the siren that thrives in some specimens of the sex. But after embarking on this intellectualized love affair, he came to perceive that Mary Butts had a feminine weakness for marriage.[9]

In fact, Thomson was one of a series of homosexual men whom Butts pursued. Robert H. Byington, her biographer, suggests that Butts idealized male homosexuals as spiritually higher beings stunted in their sexuality, a disorder that only she with her special powers (in bed, with drugs, through magic) could cure, a belief she held tenaciously despite a long record of failure.[10]

Thomson was happy to leave the impression with his friends and in his book that he and Butts enjoyed a great romance. But the journals Butts left behind, Byington reports, suggest otherwise. She was chronically in debt, fearful of being alone, and desperate to escape. She may have seen in Thomson the promise of security, and perhaps a ticket to America. But her constant requests for loans, her demands for affection, and her quixotic lifestyle all proved too much for Thomson. By 1928 they seldom saw each other, though during the 1930s he arranged for some of her stories to be published in Sherry Mangan's literary journal *Pagany.*

Butts was bitter over what she felt was Thomson's abandonment of her. When Byington interviewed him for the biography, Thomson was startled to hear of the private journals. The interview grew tense. He was desperate to learn what Butts had written of him. Byington knew it would be unwise to reveal too much. Not getting his way, Thomson threatened a lawsuit if Byington published anything compromising.

In 1937 Mary Butts, living in England again, took ill while staying in her hometown of Dorset. A local physician, apparently misdiagnosing her condition as indigestion, left without treating her. She died of a ruptured appendix.

Virgil Thomson allowed Kathleen Hoover to conclude in her book that Butts represented "the one emotional involvement of his life that was focal rather than peripheral, the one woman who almost succeeded in holding the entire man."[11] She was nothing of the sort.

One day during the autumn of 1925, with the soft September sunlight overhead, Virgil was sipping a café crème on the terrace of the Deux Magots when he noticed someone at the next table with his face buried in a copy of the Paris *Chicago Tribune*. To his surprise it turned out to be Maurice Grosser, the young man he had known casually from the Liberal Club at Harvard. Pleased to see each other, they started spending time together. And when, in December, Virgil, who had been staying in a furnished room at the Gare St. Lazare, was offered the use of a two-room flat in Saint-Cloud, he asked Maurice to come live with him and share expenses. Thus commenced the primary relationship of Virgil Thomson's life, though you would not gather this from reading his autobiography. It was a curious match; in background and temperament, Grosser and Thomson could hardly have been more different.

When Maurice Grosser was born there in 1903, Huntsville, Alabama, was a town of some seven thousand inhabitants—mostly cotton farmers and merchants—with handsome colonial architecture and a celebrated source of fresh water, later discovered to be contaminated with the typhoid virus. His family on both sides were German Jewish immigrants. Maurice's father, handsome, affable, and always well dressed, ran a successful men's clothing store. His mother was largely responsible for shifting the family's religious loyalty from Judaism, which they had never practiced very strictly, to Christian Science. Maurice never took to either.

His parents worried about Maurice, who daydreamed and was secretive. They were indifferent to his passion for books and uncomprehending of his affinity for math, which he wound up majoring in at Harvard. Only Maurice's maternal grandfather, "Papa Oscar," understood him, defended him, and protected him from his parent's admonitions and their "Christian Science nonsense." Papa Oscar did not object, however, when Maurice's parents decided to ship him off to the Webb School, a regimented institution for troublesome boys in Bell Buckle, Tennessee, lest, as they all feared, he turn out to be a sissy.

Maurice sensed early on the direction of his sexual interests. He was naive about sex and personally insecure. But, remarkably for a

ABOVE: Quincy Alfred Thomson
and Clara May Gaines on their
wedding day, 1883. He was
twenty-one; she was eighteen.
RIGHT: Virgil Thomson at twelve,
in 1909.

ABOVE: Virgil Thomson, high school graduation photo in 1913. RIGHT: Ruby Thomson at sixteen, in 1901. Virgil Thomson's sister, who made hand-painted china and sold it to pay for her little brother's piano lessons.

ABOVE LEFT: Alice Smith, at her high school graduation in 1916. The great-granddaughter of the founder of the Mormon church, Alice was Virgil Thomson's intellectual comrade in junior college. ABOVE RIGHT: Dr. Frederick Madison Smith about 1930. The father of Thomson's friend Alice, Dr. Smith was the president of the Missouri branch of the Mormon church.

ABOVE: Virgil Thomson in uniform, 1917, home in Kansas City for a visit during his sixteen-month stint in the military. OPPOSITE, TOP: Leland Poole while in army aviation training school in New York, 1918. Leland was an early attachment of Virgil Thomson, who called him "Prim." RIGHT: The Harvard Glee Club at Milan cathedral during its summer tour in 1921. Virgil Thomson is in front-row center, holding a hat.

Briggs Buchanan in his mid-forties, when he was working successfully but unhappily on Wall Street. At Harvard, Virgil Thomson fell hard for Briggs, who was eight years younger.

Maurice Grosser at nineteen, in 1922, while a student at Harvard. A native of Huntsville, Alabama, Maurice was the closest Virgil Thomson had to a lifelong companion.

Christian Bérard in Paris, about
1926. "Bebe" was Thomson's
devoted painter friend.

man of his generation, he was never particularly tormented or guilt ridden. In a charming memoir left incomplete at his death and, but for two excerpted chapters, never published, he wrote about the sexual play among Webb School boys with a disarming nonchalance.

> My first roommate, a tall, dark, sharp, sallow-skinned boy from New Orleans, declared to me passionately as we lay in bed that love was the most wonderful thing in the world. I told him roughly to turn over and go to sleep. His approach was probably wrong. He had used the Intellectual, which is easily countered, more so than the Physical Direct. If he had tried the Comradely Affectionate, I might not have been so impervious. However, I was what is now called a "late bloomer"—I did not learn to masturbate until I was past sixteen—and consequently I had no idea what he was talking about.[12]

The Webb School curriculum was restricted to Greek and Latin grammar, English prose, history, and mathematics. Discipline was severe. Speaking out of turn or missing a Latin verb resulted in a whipping: a "certain number of licks with a birch switch on the palm of the held-out hand, which left painful welts." Many boys dropped out or were expelled. When Maurice graduated, his class, numbering seventy his first year, had been whittled down to eleven. But when he took his entrance examinations for Harvard, he passed brilliantly.

At Harvard, Maurice basked in the freedom. He attended the Old Howard burlesque in Scollay Square and ate in Italian restaurants on Washington Street near the Boston Common. Not knowing how to use a library or to handle the permissiveness, his grades plummeted to C's and D's. A trivial encounter with a friend of a friend who came one night to dinner at the dining hall changed Maurice's life. This fellow had been to a life drawing class in the basement of the Boston School of Architecture, where, for only a quarter, he got to inspect a naked woman for two hours. Intrigued, Maurice accepted the fellow's invitation to come along. The model that night turned out to be a chubby young man in a jock strap. But Maurice stayed, and sketched, and was astonished at the results—as good as anybody's in the class.

> I had never suspected that I possessed this talent. I was the literary member of the family. It was my brother Edward, not I, who copied comic strip characters and drew pretty girls from magazine covers. From that moment on I was hooked. The Architectural School's life class took place on Tuesday and Thursday nights. Another life class was held in the South Boston School of Art on the

nights of Monday, Wednesday and Friday. Life class drawing had
become my passion and I attended them all.[13]

Maurice enrolled in art courses at Harvard, held in the Fogg Museum. But these, geared for students intending to become museum
curators, did little more than acquaint you with various painting techniques. To become an artist, he would have to study after Harvard,
preferably in Europe, though how this was to be accomplished he
could not imagine.

It was not a student or teacher but a writer from Virginia who
helped to shape Maurice's plans. James Mahoney, then about twenty-
six, was publishing short stories in *Cosmopolitan* and the *Saturday
Evening Post*. Maurice was taken with Mahoney's worldly know-how.
A handsome man with straight black hair and a striking profile, Mahoney had served in Europe in the American Ambulance Corps,
stayed on to study art in Paris, but abandoned this and returned to
Boston.

> He was delighted to be able to give aid and affection to someone
> who possessed the eye and hand he lacked. He took me in charge,
> criticizing my drawings, directing my morals, scolding me for my
> shortcomings, and in general telling me what to do, just as an older
> lover should, all following a quite classical pattern and I am sure
> very good for me.[14]

Not once in print or in public did Virgil Thomson recount a comparable homosexual relationship with such uncloseted gratitude.

Coming back from Christmas break in his freshman year, Maurice was invited into the Liberal Club. There, in 1922, he met Virgil,
just back from his year abroad. Virgil "was enormously entertaining
and enormously self-possessed, up on all the latest in Paris fashions
such as the then-new Dada, had associated with Satie and already had
his eye on the writings of Gertrude Stein."[15] Virgil, who had learned
from the painters he befriended in Paris, took Maurice gallery hopping on Newbury Street and explained modern art to him. It was in
Virgil's company that Maurice saw his first Cézanne. But no real
friendship was stuck up at that time.

At Harvard, Maurice worked on his painting with increasing determination and hatched plans for his summers that would keep him
away from his parents, now living in Chattanooga. The summer of
his junior year he agreed to go on a merchant marine adventure with
a friend from the Liberal Club, Henwar Rodakiewicz, a "tough and

sturdy young man with a jutting chin and a triangular face" who "seldom ever spoke." Henwar insisted that prior to their sea trip they meet at the Cape Cod commune run by the young Harvard graduate Charles Garland, the notorious "Love Farm," as the newspapers called it, supported by Garland's million-dollar inheritance, where anyone was welcomed, love was free, and all goods were held in common. Garland was a "tall, dark, sad, beautiful and inarticulate young man" who, despite his "high Tolstoyian ethics, was lost and somewhat unhappy." The commune turned out to have only five sullen, aimless members of all ages. Maurice was sought out by a plump, forlorn young woman. "We walked in the moonlight holding hands and she told me about her abortion, how she had managed it by drinking turpentine and falling down stairs."[16] Nothing came of this friendship. Then Garland's mother, Marie, a marvelously handsome women in her early fifties, showed up and immediately bedded Maurice, who had no choice but to comply.

> She was so much more experienced than I that our love making took on something of the aspect of a guided tour. I do not quite remember how I managed, but when Henwar turned up for our merchant marine adventure, I moved out and installed him in my place. It suited him perfectly, better even than going to sea.[17]

It suited Marie perfectly too. She wound up taking Henwar and Maurice to her estate at Buzzard's Bay, where they spent the summer wandering through the woods. Marie cooked. Henwar swam. Maurice took sunbaths and painted. When Henwar and Maurice returned to Harvard, Marie came too, took an apartment in Cambridge, and married Henwar in an elaborate ceremony to which none of his college friends were invited.

After graduation, having been turned down for a travel fellowship, Maurice became an apprentice to Charles Connick, then the best-known designer of stained glass in America. Determined to continue his painting, he applied again for a two-year Holden Fellowship from Harvard, which would provide an annual stipend of $1,200, a lordly sum, for travel and study abroad. This time he was accepted. Papa Oscar was so pleased with his grandson's success that he paid his fare to Paris: third-class passage on the *Ile de France*.

The Paris apartment that Virgil Thomson invited Maurice Grosser to share with him in the fall of 1925 belonged to an aspiring composer from a moneyed family in New York, Theodore Chanler. In his book, Virgil describes Chanler as "then eighteen" and an "experiment in upper-class male education," who had opted to become a composer without taking time out for college, but going directly to Nadia Boulanger.[18] In fact, Chanler was twenty-three and had spent three years at Oxford before coming to Paris. But for the months from December until April, Teddy was going to be visiting his mother in Rome. Hence the offer of his tiny flat. On Christmas Eve, 1925, Virgil and Maurice moved in. Maurice wrote lovingly about their life together.

> The flat occupied the upper floor of a small villa on the heights of St. Cloud. It overlooked the Seine and had a splendid view of the Eiffel Tower....It had a living room containing an upright piano, a small bedroom, some kitchen facilities, some toilet facilities—not enough, I seem to remember, to include a bath. The quiet domesticity we enjoyed was a delight to both of us. It was a clear, mild winter. We walked in the nearby forest of St. Cloud, sometimes as far as Fontainebleau, visited friends in Paris. We never had money enough, I am sorry to say, to dine in one of Paul Poiret's three river barges fitted up as restaurants for the exposition and named after the three French words which are masculine in the singular but feminine in the plural, Amour, Délice, et Orgue, but our landlady brought us beautifully cooked dishes to supply our table.[19]

The above passage from Maurice's incomplete memoir was slightly different in its first draft. Describing the kitchen facilities and the contents of the apartment, Maurice originally had written that in one corner of the flat was a small double bed, "where Virgil and I shared many passionate moments together." When in 1985 Virgil read this passage—Maurice had asked Virgil for his comments—Virgil became enraged. He absolutely forbade Maurice to refer to the sexual component of their relationship, no matter how tactfully and tenderly. Maurice protested and hoped that Virgil's stubbornness would subside in a few days. It didn't. If Maurice hoped to publish his book, then it had to be changed. It was; to this colorless substitute: "The quiet domesticity we enjoyed was a delight to both of us." Maurice was hurt. But he couldn't fight Virgil. Maurice was already suffering from the ailments that would take his life the next year.

Theirs was a complicated and strangely devoted relationship. Even as a young man, Maurice was fidgety. "I was possessed of a nervous energy which often forced me to bore my friends with an excess of verbal turns and funny stories. I was easily swayed in most things but silently and unmovably stubborn about the things that really mattered, like work or love."[20] But to those who knew him, Maurice's physical anxiety, his outward insecurity, did not mask his solidity and strength of character. Maurice was gentle, dependable, wise, nonjudgmental—in many ways a courtly southern gentleman.

Virgil was Maurice's opposite. He "could charm the birds off the trees," as Ned Rorem once put it, but could sputter and shout hysterically when things did not go his way. Though not impervious to Virgil's bluster, Maurice mostly let it roll off his back. With his outburst so neutralized, Virgil quieted down and behaved. For all of Maurice's jitteryness, Virgil found him to be a calming presence.

They disagreed on issues of sexuality. Maurice enjoyed sexual adventures, encounters with strangers. For Virgil such encounters, though he engaged in them (more often than he admitted), were heavy with guilt and humiliation. Maurice cheered the emergence of gay liberation; Virgil thought it essentially misguided. Yet in truth, Virgil marveled at Maurice's lack of guilt and inhibition regarding sex.

Virgil loved Maurice—this muscular, vigorous, small, stocky man seven years his junior—for his passion. He also loved him for his devotion, though this never meant monogamy. Throughout their lives, which included other affairs, lovers, and, in Maurice's case, a final thirteen-year partnership with a younger man, they remained devoted. In essential ways, they were each other's most important person.

From the beginning Maurice was in awe of Virgil's brilliance. From Virgil he learned about music, about how the world of culture operates. And if at times Virgil could be an intellectual and emotional bully, well, that was something Maurice knew how to handle—by defusing him, by letting it pass, but, if these failed, by caving in, which was easier than fighting.

For two years in Paris, Maurice studied in the studios of artists and shared in Virgil's friendships. He credited Virgil with helping him to realize that he was an "academic painter," much more interested in connecting himself "with the traditions of painting than in joining with Modern Art to explore the eccentricities of the Cezanne style."

When Maurice's fellowship ended, he returned, heartsick, to America, taking a room at the Chelsea Hotel in New York, working first for a glass designer and then a painter of murals, and trying, unsuccessfully, to arrange a gallery exhibit of his work. Then came a windfall. A doctor friend of his former mentor James Mahoney, who was also living in New York, bought one of Maurice's paintings, a "ratty little picture, a smoothed-out Cezannesque still-life," for the extravagant sum of $450 dollars. Maurice went on a joyous spending spree, quit his job, and bought a ticket back to Paris. Once there, he sent a challenging letter to his parents, who still opposed his pursuit of painting: "Here I am and what are you going to do about it?"[21] Impressed by Maurice's determination, Papa Oscar persuaded the family to support him. From then on, he sent his grandson $100 a month.

With such a sum in the Paris of 1929 Maurice could eat well, live comfortably in small flats, even travel and buy clothes. He took a room in a student hotel around the corner from Virgil's place, and settled in, basically residing in Paris—like Virgil, with occasional trips back and forth—until the Second World War forced them both back to America.

That fall, when Maurice's painting routine floundered badly, Virgil took charge.

> Virgil had some very practical rules for setting the process of artistic creation into motion. Most effective, according to him, were the two cures, the "rest cure" and the "unrest cure." The "unrest cure" demanded irregular hours, new people, excitement, rich food and drink, and so on. It was the routine by which one got ideas. The "rest cure," its exact opposite—regular hours and no excitement whatsoever—was necessary when carrying them out. Virgil's idea was that I should forget about painting and pretend to be a gentleman of leisure, with no thought in mind except to keep my nails clean and my shoes polished, being careful about my clothes and nice to everybody. This was essentially a form of the "rest cure," and according to his strict theory, would seem in my particular case to be counter-indicated. But it worked. In a very short time I was sick to death of the idleness and limits of a gentleman's life. In greatest secrecy, I set up a small still life in my hotel room, and began to paint. It turned out to be easy enough—I had plenty of ideas and had reacquired the habit of work, a habit which I have never since lost.[22]

Virgil introduced Maurice to his painter friends—the Bermans, Bébé Bérard, Tonny, Tchelitcheff—and brought him to Gertrude and Alice, who disliked Maurice at first.

Gertrude had a special way of dealing with couples. She would take over the artist or writer, leaving Alice to deal with the friend or wife. Alice would eventually get tired of the friend or wife and she would enlist Gertrude's help and try to make the pair break up. There is a typical example of this in *The Autobiography of Alice B. Toklas* where Alice begins taking French lessons from Fernande [Olivier], at that time Picasso's mistress, so that Fernande would have enough money to leave him. At one point, I believe, Alice attempted to separate Virgil and me. One evening when Virgil was alone with them, his relations with me were vigorously attacked. Virgil stood up for me and the matter was not mentioned again.[23]

Eventually, Gertrude and Alice grew fond of Maurice, in part because he devised the scenarios that enabled Gertrude and Virgil's two operas, with their almost hermetic texts, to be put on the stage.

The lifelong pattern of the Thomson/Grosser relationship—Virgil was bossy and brilliant; Maurice was obliging and tolerant—was established early. Reporting in 1926 to Briggs Buchanan about his first winter and new friends in Paris, Virgil wrote, "Maurice has been pleasant in domestic affection. Mental intimacy impossible, however."

Perhaps this patronizing statement was intended to reassure Briggs. But by then—Virgil was thirty—he must have known how few people in his life were willing to provide the unconditional affection that Maurice genuinely felt.

It is striking that Virgil ordered Maurice to excise from his memoirs the tender reference to their sexual relationship. Yet when this letter to Buchanan was published in a 1988 collection of letters whose contents Thomson completely controlled, he allowed the euphemistic reference to Maurice's "domestic affection" to stand. What made it acceptable for publication, it would appear, was the accompanying jab about "mental intimacy" being impossible. But Thomson was not bothered at making public this put-down of his beloved friend's intellect.

12 FOUR SAINTS ARE NEVER THREE

uring the exceptionally mild Paris winter and typically rainy spring of 1927, Virgil Thomson's life was personally stressful. He was living again in his cramped student apartment on the rue de Berne, Teddy Chanler having moved back into the sunny apartment near the Eiffel Tower he had let to Thomson while away in Italy. His only income was from infrequent articles for the *Boston Evening Transcript* and loans from hard-pressed friends. His bond with Antheil had deteriorated. He fought endlessly with Mary Butts. Aaron Copland, his sometime friend from the early days with Boulanger, came from New York for a visit that summer with news of performances of his works by the Boston Symphony Orchestra under the conductor Serge Koussevitzky, who would become a pivotal Copland booster. At last Thomson had someone in his life, Maurice Grosser. But the reality of a relationship was not as rich as the fantasy had been when he was without one. And being viewed, even by his friends, as linked with another man made Thomson testy and defensive. Besides, that summer, sadly, Grosser went back to America. Thomson missed Briggs Buchanan terribly. Without Briggs around to spoil things by being Briggs, Thomson could nurture his fantasy of a relationship that he knew could never be.

Yet, during this period Thomson was positive in public, often quite chipper, and remarkably productive. Almost thirty-one, he was finally finding his voice as a composer and growing confident that he had something to say. Thomson would later realize that during this year he was grappling with two issues that became distinctive features of his compositional style. The result was a series of striking works, some of the most significant of his career.

One issue concerned the question of how to allow free rein to your imagination without sabotaging compositional continuity. Musical continuity of a linear or quasi-narrative kind is not such a problem when a composition speaks in one style. But many styles of music were competing for the attention of Thomson's inner ear. There was the remembered music of his youth: hymns, dances, parlor songs, Negro church music, gospel, sacred organ works; the waltzes and two-steps his cousin Lela played on the family piano for his big sister's dance parties. There was the music he had performed and studied at Harvard: medieval chant and Renaissance sacred works; glee club anthems and football fight songs; the latest works by Satie, Stravinsky, Debussy. In France he had been drilled by Boulanger in traditional counterpoint and harmony, charmed by the intentionally inconsequential music of Les Six, and impressed by the propulsive, misbehaved music of George Antheil. With the *Sonata de chiesa,* Thomson had proven to himself that he could write an audacious piece that was saturated with dissonance, yet structured according to tried-and-true forms. But that work was essentially a brilliant satire. Although he enjoyed skewering sacred cows, and knew he was good at it, Thomson now wanted to peek from behind the protective cover of humor. How could he recall the music that he loved in his youth without slipping into sentimentality? How could he fashion all the disparate music that spoke *to* him into an authentic voice that spoke *for* him?

The answer to this he found, in part, from Dada. Dismissed as a hoax in intellectual circles, the Dada movement was born in seriousness during the darkest year of World War I. Refugee artists from all over Europe had taken "their pacifist convictions to neutral Zurich," in the words of the biographer Kathleen Hoover (words that were scrupulously edited by Thomson himself). There the artistic refugees worked in a local cabaret, putting on entertainments and forging a credo to reject a civilization that had degenerated into a "tragic farce."

> If the world wanted to destroy itself with bombs and poison gas, they would speed its extinction with ridicule. A gaily blasphemous manifesto proclaimed their intention to live by non-reason: sources of inspiration hitherto inhibited must be opened; primary mental processes—that part of the self in which the individual remains a

child or a savage—must be utilized; the creative process must become pure psychic automatism, art a compilation of the accidental.[1]

The Dadaists felt an irresistible urge, in Hoover's exalted but apt
description, "to go back beyond the horses of the Parthenon to the
rocking horses of their childhood." For the very name of their movement, she points out, they choose the "infant prattle term" for that
childhood toy.

Thomson was not interested in any manifesto. He found the Dada
propagandists as grandiose as the establishment protectors they pil-
loried. But he too wanted to draw from the music of his rocking-horse
days, to unleash his inhibited sources of inspiration. Dada provided
the encouragement he needed. "Much as the use by free impulse of
incongruous material clashed with his whole academic training,"
Hoover writes, "it suggested a new and vital mode of extending
music's vocabulary, a way of saying fresh things by fresh means."[2]

The liberating example of Dada seeped into his work, culminat-
ing with the *Symphony on a Hymn Tune.* The germinal ideas for a
symphony that would use Protestant hymns as thematic source materials came to Thomson at Harvard, though he was wise enough to
shield his preliminary sketches from his professors. In Paris in 1926
he worked on the piece in earnest. It did not come easily. He struggled for over two years, completing the first three movements by the
spring of 1927. Then he laid it aside, daunted by the prospect of the
final movement. In this he was not unlike most of his symphonist pre-
decessors who found the last movement the hardest to pull off. It is
easier to expound, develop, and divert than to conclude. Not until
July of 1928, after he had completed the vocal score of *Four Saints
in Three Acts,* did Thomson return to his symphony and finish it.

Thomson had ambivalent feelings about his background in
church music. As if to exorcise some lingering resentment, he simultaneously wrote during 1927 four sets of organ works, eventually collected and titled *Variations on Sunday School Tunes.* "Taking the
form of a gadfly," in John Cage's phrase, Thomson "proceeds to torment the noble and heroic pipe-organ."[3] The pieces are variations only
in that the music is various. Familiar tunes become fodder for works
that riotously go haywire with wrong-note harmonies, out-of-sync part
writing, musical non sequiturs, tone clusters, absurdly pompous and
meandering fugues—music that no proper church organist could ac-

tually perform. During college Thomson himself had been a professional church organist. The *Variations on Sunday School Tunes* represent his door-slamming on even the possibility of becoming one again. In fact, with the exception of two 60-second miniatures, Thomson would write no additional organ works until thirty-five years later, when a handsome commission proved impossible to refuse.

But having purged some lingering hostility to his church music past, Thomson was now able to write an ambitious symphonic work that would pay homage, though not without high spirits, to the Protestant hymns he grew up with. Two hymns were used for thematic source material: the serene "How Firm a Foundation" and, one of his favorites, the rousing "Yes, Jesus Loves Me." ("Southern Baptists used to raise the roof with 'Yes, Jesus Loves Me.'") From time to time in this work, the hymn tunes sound forth unaltered; but mostly they are milked for motivic ideas. In its overall layout, the symphony draws from diverse styles. Thomson's achievement was in finding a way to fashion these disparate sources into a solid symphonic fabric.

The piece begins with a theme stated in bare parallel fifths, like the medieval sacred music Thomson once sang in Doc Davison's chorus. As the parallelisms diverge, some fluttering, distant dissonance intrudes, played quietly, but ominously, by two trumpets. An odd, unsettled line in the solo trombone marked "espressivo" then begins. Is it sacred chant or some rude interruption? Suddenly, the strings state with dignity in proper four-part church harmony the tune of "How Firm a Foundation." The second phrase of the tune is taken up by the woodwinds and horns, with slightly astringent dissonance tucked amid the harmonies. Then the music segues into a quiet, curious waltz, with the oompah-pahs in the lower strings and the hymn tune, gone a bit tipsy, sung by the oboes. This music builds in intensity and strangeness; the snare drum rustles below the textures, the horns fill out the harmonies. The strings sing bits of "Yes, Jesus Loves Me," until the flutes and oboes burst into a rhythmically jerky send-up of this hymn tune that sounds suspiciously similar to "For He's a Jolly Good Fellow." But the mood is not silly; it's joyous, like that of a revival meeting.

The miracle of this music is that Thomson found a way to connect the material, to make each new event sound as if it were evolving compellingly, if not logically, from the previous event. To achieve this continuity, he let himself be guided by intuition until the music seemed true to his own sense of inner narrative. For listeners willing to make the intuitive leap with him, it works. The shifts and segues startle you, confuse you, amuse you, disturb you. But you are hooked.

He continues this through the other three movements. The second movement is undulant, like a lyrical barcarole. The third uses a phrase from "How Firm as Foundation" as an insistent bass pattern, like some rustic dance, or perhaps a baroque passacaglia. The finale is a grand synthesis of everything that's gone before. But throughout the movement the music is interrupted, shaken up, poked at, and distracted. Like Thomson's wall sculpture by the Dada pioneer Jean Arp—a sculpture built of oddly shaped, variously colored, painted wood pieces mischievously fitted together, a sculpture that hung prominently for almost fifty years in Thomson's Chelsea Hotel apartment—this symphony places odd musical shapes next to each other and invites us to find delight and beauty in the contrasts. As a *Boston Globe* critic, Richard Buell, writing in 1986, put it in a review Thomson was pleased with, the symphony's "peculiar procedures somehow suggest that Thomson has given both a kit for a symphony and the improbable assembled thing itself. There's nothing extraneous, it's strong as hell and the parts fit, but you could swear that some of them have deliberately been put in upside down."[4]

It took almost seventeen years for this symphony to have its first professional performance: in New York in 1945, by the Philharmonic-Symphony Society, with Thomson conducting, this at a time when he was the country's most prominent music critic. But shortly after its composition, the symphony was arranged for piano, four hands, by the American pianist John Kirkpatrick, and in that version it was performed on occasion and had a lasting influence on many composers, including Copland. But it influenced Thomson most of all, liberating him, giving him a confidence that was about to come in handy.

The other major issue Thomson was grappling with during this period was prosody, which for him meant the art of setting texts to music in distinctively American, as opposed to imitatively European, ways. Having cracked open Gertrude Stein for musical treatment with his setting of "Susie Asado," he kept at it, setting in late 1926 a thoroughly hermetic text, "Preciosilla." Here he lost his footing somewhat. He couldn't figure out what to do with the poem. (It begins: "Cousin to Clare washing. In the win all the band beagles which have cousin lime sign and arrange a weeding match to presume a certain point to exstate to exstate . . .") He fashioned a neo-baroque recitative and aria that is rather too tame for the text.

In 1927, however, Thomson took on Stein's 1923 work "Capital Capitals." This turned out brilliantly, and Thomson knew it. The text, almost three thousand words (and he set every one), evokes, as he has written, "Provence, its landscape, food, and people, as a conversation among the cities Aix, Arles, Avignon, and Les Baux, here called Capitals One, Two, Three, and Four. It also reflects the poet's attachment to that sunny region, which she had first known as an ambulance driver in World War I."[5] The evocations are obscure, to say the least. Much of the text is devoted to typical Steinian verbal theme-and-variations games. ("If in regard to climates if we regard the climates, if we are acclimated to the climate of the third capital.") Stein also plays on the British colloquial use of the word "capital," as in a "capital" fellow.

Thomson's music plays the Steinian word games ingeniously. The musical setting, which takes a good eighteen minutes, is for four male singers and piano. Whole passages of the text are intoned on one-note chant. The accompaniment is often minimal, sometimes even absent for extended periods. Not once do any of the singers sing at the same time. Thomson turned the text into a true musical conversation, a rather competitive one, in fact, a verbal joust employing Steinian statistics and demographic field reports as weapons. Some of the statistics are delightfully fanciful. ("The first capital is one in which there are many more earrings.") Others seem completely sensible. ("The third capital. They have read about the third capital. It has in it many distinguished inventors of electrical conveniences.")

The music segues seamlessly through various styles: Thomson's Missouri plainchant; C majorish ditties; ominous perorations sung over undulant Spanish rhythms; sweetly lyrical flights by turns satirical and tender. In the piano part are church harmonies, fanfares, pealing bells, bass tremolos suggesting timpani, treble tremolos suggesting xylophones, passages of parallel scales at practice room tempos. But beneath the surface whimsy is a sturdy structure. To compensate for the minimalism of the harmonies, Thomson presents a virtual compendium of verbal rhythmic variety: lines freely intoned on one note; lines rhythmically notated but sung on one note; chantlike lines that explode with the jerky natural rhythms of American speech; and lyrical, supple melodies. The music is so direct and elemental it's shocking. What else written in 1927 continues to sound so radical? That it has spawned no progeny from other composers is a confirmation of its daring.

It sounded insurrectionist to the first audience that heard it. This was in June of 1927, a costume ball given by Elizabeth de Gramont, duchesse de Clermont-Tonnerre, a friend of Stein's and a grand lady with feminist ideals and literary aspirations. The duchesse's residence was an eighteenth-century gatehouse on the Right Bank's rue Ray-nouard, a street of exclusive private homes across the Seine from the Eiffel Tower. Benjamin Franklin once lived here. The duchesse's house was exquisitely furnished, but the rooms were not large. So the party drifted on to the garden where blue-cupped candles lit the walkways and a quartet of horn players hidden behind bushes played divertimentos and dances.

At Stein's suggestion, a performance of *Capital Capitals* with Thomson at the piano had been arranged as the midnight entertainment. At the last minute one of the singers took ill, so Thomson had to sing the bass part from the keyboard. No matter. The performance was a smashing success. Thomson reported to Briggs Buchanan that the piece seemed "to remind everyone of what he heard in childhood."[6] Mary Butts heard Greek chant; Jean Cocteau heard the Catholic liturgy. Edward Ashcroft, the English poet, heard Gilbert and Sullivan patter. Miguel Covarrubias, a Mexican painter and folklorist, heard Mexican sacred music. Fania Marinoff, an actress, and the wife of the critic Carl Van Vechten, one of Stein's closest friends, heard the music of a Jewish synagogue.

> Since its performance there has been a stream of visitors to my door . . . for purposes of hearing said work and others. All French people at the duchesse's. More dukes than you could see for all the ambassadors. Not the Princesse crowd. Cocteau came to see me more or less as their representative, I presume. His comment on my music was "At last a table that stands on four legs, a door that really opens and shuts." The French who know no English all exclaim "What an extraordinary sense of English prosody!" I suppose what they mean is that it is English that sounds like English.[7]

Earlier in April, soon after completing it, Virgil had performed *Capital Capitals* privately for Gertrude and Alice, singing all four vocal parts and playing the piano. Gertrude enjoyed Virgil's one-man performances. Shortly after they met, he had invited Gertrude and Alice to his flat to play for them his beloved *Socrate* by Satie. Not being musical, Gertrude was only somewhat interested in the piece. But she was touched by Virgil's music making, by his reverential attitude toward this subdued, indrawing composition. After the visit, driving

Alice home in "Godiva," their private name for their Ford, a country-touring model with a collapsible roof and no back seat, she commented that Virgil was "singularly pure *vis-à-vis* his art," that to him art appeared to mean "discipline, humility, and loyalties rather than egocentric experience."[8]

Gertrude and Alice were terribly excited by Virgil's one-man rendition of *Capital Capitals*. He revealed a genuine affinity for Gertrude's works, later attested to by Stein in *The Autobiography of Alice B. Toklas*.

> He had understood Satie undoubtedly and he had a comprehension quite his own of prosody. He understood a great deal of Gertrude Stein's work, he used to dream at night that there was something there that he did not understand, but on the whole he was very well content with that which he did understand. She delighted in listening to her words framed by his music. They saw a great deal of each other.[9]

The idea came up quite naturally, not only from Virgil but from Gertrude's friends, that she should write an opera libretto for him. Except for memories of being taken as a youngster to the "five-cent opera" in San Francisco, Gertrude knew nothing about opera. But the idea pleased her. Discussions with Virgil simply bypassed matters of staging and practicality, and moved directly to subject matter.

Virgil Thomson claimed that the theme for the proposed opera came from him and that Stein accepted it readily.

> [I]t was the working artist's working life, which is to say, the life we both were living. It was also my idea that good things come in pairs. In letters, for instance, there were Joyce and Stein, in painting Picasso and Braque, in religion Protestants and Catholics, or Christians and Jews, in colleges Harvard and Yale, and so on to the bargain basements of Gimbel's and Macy's. This dualistic view made it possible, without going in for sex unduly, to have both male and female leads with second leads and choruses surrounding them, for all the world like Joyce and Stein themselves holding court in the rue de l'Odéon and the rue de Fleurus.[10]

Since neither Stein not Thomson was interested in anything overly autobiographical or contemporary, and both wanted an opera that was stately in tone, they searched for a metaphorical setting that would express their theme. They considered Norse mythology, Greek antiquity. Just then on an American history kick, Stein wanted to do George Washington, but Thomson vetoed the idea on the ground that eighteenth-century colonial costuming makes everybody look alike.

They settled on Catholic saints as their operatic representatives. Like the saints of the church, the working artists of Paris lived simple lives consecrated to something larger than themselves. Medieval and Italian saints having been overdone, they chose Spanish saints, an idea that immediately energized Stein, who was fond of Spain ("nice place and nice people even if there aren't many").[11] Stein and Toklas had visited Spain in the humid spring of 1912. In Madrid they spent mornings studying the paintings of Goya and Velásquez, and evenings partaking of the nightlife in cafés and music clubs. Struck by the flamenco rhythms of Spanish songs, Stein experimented with a new direction in her writing, divorcing it more than ever from associative meanings and structuring her phrases with repetitious word rhythms.

So Spain suited Stein as a locale for her saints. However, a letter to Thomson suggests that she was working on the libretto before they had chosen specific saintly subjects and a historical era, although, almost by the way, Stein stumbles upon the eventual title of the opera.

> I have begun Beginning of Studies for an opera to be sung. I think it should be late eighteenth century and early nineteenth century saints. Four Saints in Three Acts. And others. Make it pastorale. In hills and gardens. All four and then additions. We must invent them. But next time you come over I will show you a bit and we will talk some scenes over.[12]

Next time was three days later for dinner. And many things must have been decided that night. The setting was shifted to the sixteenth century; the central characters were to be Saint Teresa of Avila and Saint Ignatius of Loyola. Stein had read and admired the autobiographical meditations of Teresa of Avila (1515–1582), a great mystic of the church and a leader of the Catholic Reformation, and someone Stein could identify with. Teresa combined radiant spirituality with managerial competence. A lovely, witty, strong-willed woman, Teresa had read chivalric novels and had youthful adventures with her older brother. She founded a reformed order of nuns in Avila, then a notorious hotbed of tolerance during the Spanish Inquisition. Moreover, her prose was prone, perhaps intentionally, to rather confusing ellipses, digressions, and alliterations. Gertrude and Alice, but particularly Alice, had loved Avila, a town enclosed by striking red stone walls built dramatically on the flat summit of a mountain that juts up from a treeless plain.

Saint Ignatius, the founder of the Jesuits, was a professional military man who converted, took vows of poverty and chastity, then devoted himself to education and missionary work, leaving to others the campaign to convert Protestants. Stein knew less about Ignatius, though she remembered fondly a San Francisco church that bore his name. But knowledge of her subjects would hardly seem to have mattered, judging from the libretto.

On first reading, the text seems typically hermetic. The Prologue begins, "To know to know to love her so. Four saints prepare for saints. It makes it well fish." But reading on, one gathers that the author is assessing out loud the task at hand, namely, to make an opera about saints: "In narrative, prepare for saints." At first, it would seem she has little to say about the matter: "Saint saint a saint. Forgotten saint." So she turns instead to a more familiar subject: "What happened today, a narrative," a chatty digression about herself and Alice. "We had intended if it were a pleasant day to go to the country it was a very beautiful day and we carried out our intention . . ." and so on, for three pages. Returning to the topic of writing the libretto and getting the saints on stage, the author by turns reassures herself ("Easily saints. Very well saints. Have saints") and gets quite worried ("Come panic come").

With Act 1, the opera proper commences, and Saint Therese (Stein chose to use the French spelling of her name) is introduced ("Saint Therese in a storm at Avila . . ."). Saint Therese is described as "half in and half out of doors," which conveys the historical Teresa, who enjoyed the mundane rituals of everyday life and thought them not incompatible with the mystical world of God. ("Among the kitchen pots moves the Lord," the good saint is thought to have said.)

The text is strewn with conversational pleasantries: "How do you do. Very well I thank you. And when do you go. I am staying on quite continuously." And Stein's poetry can seem incantatory: "How many saints can be and land be and sand be and on a high plateau there is no sand there is snow and there is made to be so and very much can be what there is to see when there is a wind to have it dry . . ."

Except for some fleeting stage directions in bold print ("REPEAT FIRST ACT"—"ENACT END OF AN ACT"), there is no discernible action. Well before he seems to appear, Saint Ignatius is anticipated and discussed: "Saint Ignatius needs not be feared. Saint Ignatius might be very well adapted to plans and a distance." The identity of the other two of the "Four Saints" is never entirely clear. Saint Chavez and Saint Settlement are the consensus choices. However, there are not four, but over twenty saints, almost all of Stein's invention: Saint Plan, Saint Matyr, Saint Evelyn, Saint Pilar, Saint Cardinal, Saint Selmer, Saint Answers, and others. And there are four, not three acts. In fact, a debate after the third act as to whether the opera should have a fourth act turns almost heated. ("How many acts are there in it.")

There are suggestions that one scene is a vision of a heavenly mansion, which the saints charmingly describe to each other ("How many windows and doors and floors are there in it"). And, though she refrained from telling even Thomson the meaning of her text, Stein did indicate that one long passage represented a procession: "in wed in dead in dead wed lead in led wed dead in dead in led in wed in said in said wed led . . ."), which the author James R. Mellow suggests may refer to the "Catholic custom of viewing the death of a woman saint as a wedding day, when she espouses the Heavenly Bridegroom."[13] Stein plays havoc with the conventions of structure, reducing whole scenes to one line and calling into question whether a completed scene has in fact happened.

Yet the text is not just self-referential jabber. Here, as in her earlier plays, Stein strove to present theater as "landscape," to depict life happening in the present with wonderment and mystery. The traditional devices of theater—suspense, storytelling, even character depiction—kept the audience separate, she felt, making it acutely aware of the passage of narrative time. Stein wanted the stage time to be the only reality, a theatrical landscape of reality that simply exists in the present. "A landscape does not move nothing really moves in a landscape but things are there, and I put into the play the things that were there." A model for her stage landscape was life in a convent. "I also wanted it to have the movement of nuns very busy and in continuous movement but placid as a landscape has to be because after all the life in a convent is the life of a landscape."[14] Given this aim, the Spanish saints were useful to Stein, as her friend and Stein scholar Donald Sutherland wrote, because they "afforded a stable metaphor on which to maintain and sustain her own generically poetic exaltation, her own vision of a world saturated with miracles."[15]

Thus, the challenge was to evoke an exalted, human landscape through the depiction of saints going about the business of their daily lives. "I think I have got St. Therese onto the stage," she wrote to

Thomson, "it has been an awful struggle and I think I can keep her on and gradually by the second act get St. Ignatius on and then they will both be on together but not at once in the third act. I want you to read it as far as it has gone before you go and come in about six Thursday."[16]

Stein's struggles might seem incomprehensible to the reader who glances at lines like "Believe two three. What could be sad beside beside very attentively intentionally and bright." But Thomson had an intuitive understanding of what Stein was up to. Clearly, he was a participant in Stein's creative process because she met with him regularly and sought his feedback. "Therese and Ignatius are in and out just like anything," she wrote in a note that spring, "which may be the first act and the third act and lots of scenes and I have a nice idea that Alice says you won't like at all, probably you won't, like it, at all."[17]

Yet, he did not ask Stein to elucidate her text. "The two things you never asked Gertrude, ever," Thomson recalled, "were about her being a lesbian and what her writing meant." However, in reading Stein, Thomson disengaged the part of his brain that demanded cogency. The way her words were liberated from associative baggage was the very quality he found so attractive for musical adaptation. When, late in the spring of 1927, Stein handed Thomson the completed libretto for *Four Saints in Three Acts,* he was thrilled with it. The text invited him to create a musical pageant, a latter-day, recitative-driven opera seria, something elegant and noble, not without whimsy and wit, but a thoroughly fresh, delightfully disorienting, and vibrant spectacle. However, unforeseen events were to put off his composing until November.

During the spring and summer of 1927, Virgil had no fixed address. He had temporarily taken a hotel room on the rue Jacob, which turned out to be his "definitive move to the Left Bank." The area was bohemian, filled with students from the nearby Université de Paris. Gertrude's feminist friend Natalie Barney lived down the street near a hidden private garden with a reproduction of a Doric temple where theatricals were put on and once, according to neighborhood rumor, the spy Mata Hari performed a belly dance in the nude.[18] Virgil's room was not large, and looked out upon a wall of buildings. But it was just large enough for a rented upright piano and incredibly cheap— about seventy-five cents a day.

With Gertrude's completed libretto in hand, he was anxious, in both senses, to begin composing—eager, but a bit worried. Then, an invitation to spend the last weeks of the summer in the French countryside came from some acquaintances, the Lasells, a moneyed Republican family from Massachusetts. This trip turned out to be pivotal: Virgil acquired a patron and righted his shaky finances.

In 1924, while a postgraduate instructor at Harvard, Virgil took a weekend church organ job in Whitinsville, a factory town southeast of Worcester surrounded by slooping hills and cranberry farms. There he met the Lasells, who lived in a baronial manor with winding hallways, a ballroom, and, outside, stables for trotters that Chester Whitin Lasell bred and trained. The matriarch, Mrs. Chester Whitin Lasell, "Jessie" to Virgil, had come originally from San Francisco. Virgil remembered her as "a naturally smiling woman midst tight-mouthed New Englanders,"[19] but in photographs she has a grimly aristocratic air. Jessie was kitchen-wise and well-read. Her daughter, Hildegard, thought herself a singer, though she seldom performed. Her husband, Sibley Watson, funded and oversaw a literary magazine, the *Dial*. Virgil was taken up by the family, lunching with them every Sunday after church. Hildegard and Virgil became quite close. He dedicated his *Five Phrases from the Song of Solomon* to her. She periodically gave Virgil money—for example, $100 in 1926 to offset expenses for his concert in Paris with Antheil.

However, the member of the family who attached himself to Virgil was Hildegard's cousin Philip Lasell, who was catty, homosexual, and professionally aimless. In the late fall of 1926, Philip moved to Paris and took a room next to Virgil in the 20 rue de Berne building. Virgil became Philip's tour guide to the intellectual life of Paris. It was Philip who introduced Virgil to Mary Butts. In his autobiography Virgil described Philip as "a playboy of wondrous charm." In a letter to Briggs, however, he was more blunt: "Philip has lived off my vitality now for three months. . . . I don't like to see him too much. He fatigues me. Like anybody with whom one ought to make love but doesn't."[20]

Philip's dependence upon Virgil provoked a "sort of ethereal Proustian quarrel" between them, as Virgil described it, a "marvellous quarrel conducted with the greatest dignity on both sides and the nearest to an open display of affection that we have ever allowed ourselves. A sort of tearful but indignant graduating exercise, Philip doing his best to be hard toward the institution he was so fond of."[21] Eventually, as a gesture of reconciliation, Philip offered Virgil ten framed gouache prints of Picasso. Realizing their value, even in 1926, Virgil kept them on his mantle for several months. But he gave them back, instead asking for Philip's painted wood wall sculpture by Arp, which he loved.

That summer of 1927 Hildegard wrote from America saying that her mother was planning a trip through Brittany and Normandy with a teenage granddaughter and wondering if Virgil would be willing to accompany them. He agreed. In late June, Virgil met Jessie Lasell and her companion in the north coastal town of Cherbourg. From there they motored through the Normandy countryside, stopping in cathedral towns, the eventual goal being Paris. They made it as far as Rouen when Jessie took ill with what seemed at first a headcold. A local doctor diagnosed mastoiditis, an inflammation of the space behind the ear which, if untreated, can cause loss of hearing, even death. Today, antibiotics can cure it. Back then surgery was necessary in bad cases.

Virgil drove back to Paris, taking the granddaughter with him to allow Jessie to recuperate. With the aid of his well-connected friend Madame Langlois, he secured an ear specialist, even though this was vacation month in France, and brought the specialist to Rouen. The doctor controlled Mrs. Lasell's infection, preventing the need for surgery. For several weeks Mrs. Lasell recuperated, but Virgil attended to her dutifully, as he explained in a letter to Briggs: "I loaf and take the granddaughter to see churches. I have a room with bath and the food is swell, but I'd rather be in Paris. I repose, and assume what masculine responsibilities arrive."[22] When she was able to travel, Virgil took Mrs. Lasell back to Paris, settled her in a comfortable apartment, arranged for her care, and visited her constantly.

It takes nothing from the account of Virgil's devotion to Jessie Lasell to note that he had every reason to anticipate that she would reward him for his troubles. She did. Mrs. Lasell sent him a monthly check of $125 for the next three years, as well as additional sums for special needs: putting on concerts, copying music. Her support came at a fortunate time, just as he was poised to make a career-defining leap. The creation of *Four Saints* would have been impossible without Jessie Lasell's patronage.

However, the experience took its toll. Virgil did not settle back in Paris until late October. He was exhausted, dispirited, creatively rusty, and still without a permanent place to live. Studio apartments being scarce at that time, he moved back to the Hôtel Jacob. Gertrude had heard of an available flat on the quai Voltaire. Virgil checked it out and decided on the spot to take it. He would live at that address, 17 quai Voltaire, eventually moving to a slightly larger apartment in the same building, until he returned to America permanently in 1940. By then he had purchased the apartment, which gave him a place to stay in Paris (and a place to let to friends) until he sold it in 1977.

"The quai Voltaire is a row of eighteenth-century houses standing between the rue des Saints-Pères and the rue du Bac and looking across the Seine to the Louvre," as Thomson later recalled with nostalgia.

> Just above it sits the seventeenth-century Institut de France, arms open like a miniature Saint Peter's for receiving daily its college of lay cardinals, the forty "immortals" of l'Académie Française. A farther short walk upstream brings the medieval world—the Conciergerie, Sainte-Chapelle, and Notre-Dame. Downstream one passes the 1900 Gare d'Orsay and the eighteenth-century Hôtel de Salm (Palais de la Légion d'Honneur) and looks across to the Tuileries Gardens before arriving at the Chamber of Deputies and Place de la Concorde, both dominating from on high excellent swimming-baths that sit in the Seine without using its water. The situation could not be more central or more historical.[23]

Next door, at the Hôtel du Quai Voltaire, Wagner had completed the libretto to *Die Meistersinger* and Oscar Wilde had lived briefly following his imprisonment in England. Thomson's address, no. 17, was actually two houses, each with its own courtyard and concierge. His studio, five flights up, was an octagonal room, with twenty-foot ceilings and high windows on the north and northeast covered with rose-patterned curtains from which he could see the Louvre, the Paris Opéra, and a tiny corner of the Seine. The studio was partly furnished—chairs, a table, a dish cabinet, all mahogany; a simple velvet-covered couch that doubled as his bed. Some long, horizontal stairs separated the bath (with its own gas for heating water) and a roomy dressing area built into a balcony. There was no kitchen, just an alcohol burner for making tea or coffee. Apart from a Persian chess table and some Chinese watercolors (both gifts from Mary Butts), Thomson didn't have much to bring with him, just books, manuscripts, and art—his Arp wall sculpture and, eventually, a gift from Christian Bérard, a larger-than-life portrait of a man Thomson didn't know, Walter Shaw, a dark, bleak, yet haunting, painting in almost black blues and browns, which covered an outlined figure on the canvas shaped in beeswax. It became one of Thomson's cherished works.

Shortly after moving in, Virgil acquired a rented upright piano from Pleyel and, with the first $125 from Mrs. Lasell, went on a shopping spree for clothes, all purchased in cash (earning him solid credit) at Lanvin—three suits, an overcoat, six poplin shirts, and matching underwear. He also laid in a supply of his favorite Lanvin cologne.

Madame Jeanne, the concierge of the building's other house, also tended to Virgil, washing his woolens, taking messages, ordering coal. But his meals were cooked mostly by her sister, Madame Elise, the concierge of his house, "tall, heavy, and beautiful, with blue eyes and white hair," a woman who smiled constantly, unless cooking. "Then she would hover, fluttering like a hen and barely breathing, as out of her left hand she would take with three fingers of her right a pinch of something and throw it in, then wait breathless, as if listening, till she divined the gesture a success."[24]

From his studio Virgil walked often to visit Gertrude and talk about the opera. At a purposeful pace this walk past the homes and outposts of many Left Bank literati took him twenty minutes. He would cut north one block out of his way so that he could walk along the bank of the Seine, looking across to the resplendent elegance and hedge-lined gardens of the Palais Royal, which once had been seized by revolutionaries as an outpost for the Rights of Man club. At the rue des Saints-Pères, Virgil turned right and headed south down this tree-lined boulevard, looking in the store windows at pictures and old furniture, past the lovely Restaurant Michaud, where Hemingway dined with Joyce when they felt like splurging. From here Virgil walked past the Romanesque church Saint-Germain-des-Prés with its dramatic flying buttresses, the oldest church in Paris, portions of it dating from 1163. From there, if in a hurry, Virgil would walk down the rue de Rennes, a bustling, noisy, main boulevard. When he felt more leisurely, he would cut over to the Place Saint-Sulpice, with its benches, its flowering chestnut trees, and the ornate fountain of four renowned preaching bishops, including the seventeenth-century Jacques Bossuet, whose polemical funeral oration for Queen Henriette-Marie de France Virgil later set to music. Gertrude enjoyed taking Basket there on walks, the sidewalks being wide and not crowded at midday. From here Virgil would usually go down the rue Férou, past the apartment building with the imposing stone sphinxes into which Ernest and Pauline Hemingway moved that year, past the office with the lead-trimmed display windows of L'Age d'Homme publishing company, which would one day bring out Thomas Wolfe's account of his experiences in Paris during 1925–26. Then he would enter the spacious Luxembourg Gardens. Walking west, he would leave the park, turn south onto the rue Guynemer, and walk the short distance to the rue de Fleurus, where, some four blocks down, he would stop at the glass-gated entrance to no. 27.

On November 1, 1927, Virgil moved into his quai Voltaire studio. On November 2, almost five months after receiving the text, he finally started composing *Four Saints in Three Acts.*

Thomson's approach to composing his first opera was almost as unorthodox as Stein's libretto. Seated at his piano, he would read the words aloud, over and over, until musical rhythms, contours, and shapes suggested themselves. He wanted music that was straightforward and water clear, music that would not just support but launch every nuance of Stein's words. Thomson tried out vocal lines, singing them in his reedy tenor, and fashioned contextual accompaniments. He wrote nothing down, reasoning that if he could not remember a setting solution from the previous day, then it was not good enough. When words and music meshed and a section of the piece kept coming out the same way, he knew he had it right. Only then did he jot down the music in sketchy form, just vocal parts and figured-bass lines, leaving inner harmonies to be filled in later.

Since Stein had assigned very little of her dialogue to anyone in particular, Thomson parceled out the text to the various saints. However, these choices were made only after each portion of the music had been composed. Because Stein had mixed into the text wordy personal digressions and constant asides about the progress of the opera, Thomson introduced two new characters, a Compère and a Commère, who act as host and hostess for the evening, talking to the audience and to each other about how the opera is going. As his composing progressed, the part of Saint Teresa (he restored the proper Spanish spelling of her name) grew large for one singer, he thought. So he boldly divided the part in two. But this wasn't simply a practical solution to a musical problem. The idea of Saint Teresa's having conversations and singing duets with herself seemed psychologically right. Various lines in the text would seem to endorse Thomson's decision. ("Two and two saints," "Saint Teresa and Saint Teresa too.") But the idea was his alone, and Stein found it charming.

The music that emerged during those first weeks of composition boosted Thomson's confidence in his procedures and inspiration. The opening lines ("To know to know to love her so. Four saints prepare for saints . . .") came out as a sort of hurdy-gurdy waltz for chorus. Yet something is askew here, the phrases of the chorus and the oompah-pah's of the accompaniment are out of sync. Before long, however, this endearingly clunky opening merges immediately into subdued music with sinewy vocal lines in shifting minor harmonies that announce the intention of the authors ("In narrative prepare for saints"). This builds to a declamatory choral outburst ("Saint saint a saint. Forgotten saint") that would be mock melodrama if it didn't segue with a start into the run-on narrative about the author's day ("What happened today . . ."), sung by the Commère with straight-faced seriousness on a monotone, like some urgent Anglican chant.

The varied musical materials and styles alternate constantly. Emphatic minor-key music sung by the chorus in full-throated block harmonies makes Stein's number games ("Four saints are never three / Three saints are never four") sound like delivered religious truths. A vocal quartet ("In some on some evening would it be asked") could be a slip of an English madrigal. There are foursquarish marches; sequential passages with plaintive melodies; unison chant for chorus that would echo Renaissance sacred music, were it not for the wondrously bizarre words ("There is no part parti-color in a house . . ."). Passages of neo-baroque recitative; bits of made-up hymns, chanteys, parlor dances, fanfares—Thomson's music is a beguiling jumble of materials. Yet the continuity and integrity of the musical line is never in doubt, and the tone, though humorous, is serene and sincere.

In Act 1 proper, Thomson displays his penchant for presenting basic musical elements in ways that make them seem sophisticated and unfamiliar. Saint Teresa is introduced in music that teeters between sweet innocence and disorienting repetitiveness. Thomson sets the text ("Saint Teresa in a storm at Avila there can be rain and warm snow and warm . . .") on a monotone chant with nothing but alternations of root-position tonic and dominant chords. As the phrase continues (". . . that is the water is warm the river is not warm the sun is not warm . . ."), at the words "not warm," the vocal line slips up a step and the chord changes to the simple subdominant. Any self-taught, three-chord rock guitarist knows these harmonies. But the way Thomson arranges them with the words, saving the sole subdominant chord for that "not warm" moment, creates an effect both tender and surprising.

But the wonder of the opera is its mix of music and words. Thomson's text setting is conversational, mimicking in its jerky, asymmetries the idiomatic flows of American speech. He later wrote that the special energy of the opera came from the contest in every vocal phrase between the two basic rhythmic patterns of music: lengths and stress.

> A pattern made up of lengths alone is static, and the stuttering of mere stresses is hypnotic. But together, and contrasted, they create tension and release; and that is the energy that makes music sail, take flight, get off the ground. By applying it to the text of Gertrude Stein, I had produced a pacing that is implied in that text, if you wish, but that could never be produced without measured extensions. Speech alone lacks music's forward thrust.[25]

By mid-December, Thomson had completed the Prologue and Act 1, about thirty-five minutes of music. The time had come to try it out for friends.

In late December, Virgil received a Christmas box of gourmet foodstuffs, a present from his patron Jessie Lasell, sent from Rosa Lewis, King Edward VII's former cook, "owner of the Cavendish Hotel, clubhouse for London's millionaire bohemia."[26] The box contained three large items: a Stilton cheese, a plum pudding, and a *fois gras en croûte* (decadently delicious, fat-saturated goose liver pâté baked in a pie crust). He was so excited by this manna from Cavendish that he decided to throw a Christmas Eve champagne party at his flat, a "stand-up-and-walk-around supper for twelve people." The menu was supplemented with items from a local hotel, including the "most marvelous chicken in the world," as he described it in a letter to his sister, Ruby.

> The chicken was really two chickens, big fat white ones with sliced truffles put between the skin and the meat and the chickens cut into nice pieces and then put together again to look like one large one with four wings and surrounded by little round jellies of a chopped vegetable salad in mayonnaise and the whole thing covered with transparent brown jelly. It was too beautiful for anything and heavenly to eat.[27]

The guest list, topped by Gertrude and Alice, included Russell Hitchcock, "Hitchy," as Virgil had taken to calling him, and an aspiring architect friend of Russell's named Peter Smith; Philip Lasell and his brother Josiah and wife who lived in Paris at the time; the Romanian-born godfather of Dada, Tristan Tzara, who for over ten years had been living in Paris writing poetry and criticism, and Tristan's Swedish wife; and Georges Hugnet, a sweet-tempered, young French poet whom Virgil had befriended and introduced to Gertrude, who adored him.

Virgil was pleased with the dinner, but ate very little. He was nervous and excited. For on this night he tried out the Prologue and Act 1 of *Four Saints* for his guests, playing the score on his piano and singing all the parts. (When he later finished composing the opera, Virgil was able to present the entire work in his one-man rendition, which Russell Hitchcock dubbed "the Paris production.")

This was the first time Gertrude and Alice heard a note of the music. Virgil recalled that both women were pleased as could be. Yet, in a letter written later to her close friend Carl Van Vechten, Gertrude seems optimistic, yet reserving of judgment: "I have written an opera and a rather amusing young American is making it put on the stageable. . . ."[28] But overall there is no reason to doubt Virgil's recollections:

> Tristan Tzara had told Hugnet he had been deeply impressed by a music at once so "physical" and so gay. I had wondered whether a piece so drenched in Anglican chant (running from Gilbert and Sullivan to Morning Prayer and back) could rise and sail. But no one else seemed bothered by its origins. On the contrary, they had all undergone a musical and poetic experience so unfamiliar that only their faith in me (for they were chosen friends) had allowed them to be carried along, as indeed they had been, as on a magic carpet.[29]

During early 1928 Virgil worked continually on the opera, usually all morning, sometimes in late afternoons as well, going out almost every day for lunch and dinner, but sometimes having meals sent up from the Hôtel de l'Université. "This was a good quarter of a mile from door to door; but a dainty waitress would trip it twice, bearing her platter up five flights with soup and roast, a second time with dessert."[30] Act 2 was composed by February. The entire work was finished and notated, though not orchestrated, by July.

The more Gertrude and Alice heard the music, the more enchanted they became. The subdued, harmonically soothing trio for the two Saint Teresas and Saint Ignatius ("They never knew about it green . . .") was transcendent. For Saint Teresa's speculations about the heavenly mansion ("To be asked how much of it is finished"), Virgil had provided gentle, oompah, patter music, with vocal lines clipped off at the ends just as one would speak them. "Pigeons on the grass alas" became a songful aria for Saint Ignatius, with snappy, long-short melodic notes so true to the verbal rhythms that they startle you. At the height of Saint Ignatius's spiritual query ("If they were not pigeons on the grass alas what were they"), the chorus breaks into a robust, meter-bashing, block-chordal answer ("They might be very well very well"), and then, as from on high, comes an offstage chorus, singing in short, steady, simple harmonies a celestial response ("Let Lucy Lily Lily Lucy Lucy let . . .").

Strewn through the score were bits of tangos and foursquare dances, a military march in which the men's chorus proclaims, "There is a difference between Barcelona and Avila"; a despondent, dirge-like dialogue between the Commère and the Compère to accompany the "in dead wed led" procession; and a consoling, full-voiced choral response, "With be there all their all their time . . . ," like some life-affirming Baptist hymn in the face of inevitable sorrow.

Gertrude had strong, provocative ideas about her plays, but had never been able to figure out how to get them on the stage. Virgil had lovingly set every word of Gertrude's obscure text, even the non-sensical stage directions (for example, "Repeat First Act"). But the opera had no plot and no indicated action. How could it be mounted in production? Before he could possibly entice a producer, he would have to solve this problem. Many things would happen—Virgil's return visit to America, dozens of one-man renditions of the opera for potential backers, and Maurice Grosser's pivotal help in devising a scenario—before the production process of *Four Saints in Three Acts,* like Gertrude's words and Virgil's music, took flight.

13 AMERICAN MUSIC AGITATORS

As Gertrude Stein was completing the text of *Four Saints in Three Acts,* long before Virgil Thomson had written a note of the music, she tried to secure financial support for him. Her hope, also her hunch, was that the opera could be a popular success ("perhaps we will get on the radio and the gramophone yet and have royalties and buy a prize Boddlington terrier and a telephone and pay for my new Ford car . . .").[1] Hoping that Virgil would make a good impression, she placed him in contact with patron friends who had helped to publish some of her books. Only one would help significantly, Emily Chadbourne Crane, a millionaire from Chicago. She told Virgil to write Crane immediately: "Nothing may come of it mostly does not of course but if she should write to you don't have it in your head that she's stupid because she isn't and if she interests herself and she has in many she is very generous."[2]

During the summer months of 1927, Gertrude courted Mrs. Crane's support for Virgil, acting as go-between. In July, when Mrs. Crane wrote to say that she was traveling to Paris and would be happy to meet the young composer, Gertrude wrote to Virgil with instructions: "I imagine you might write to her not too generously you and I have a bad habit of wanting to give it all to them but just so that she has your present Paris address. . . ."[3] Back in Paris on September 24, Gertrude sent news that the dinner meeting was finally arranged and that Emily Crane "seems possibly quite interested possibly." She advised Virgil to ease up on the cologne ("not too much Lanvin") and to behave ("just your own natural self and good luck").[4] He must have made a nice enough impression, for Crane gave him $1,000 toward the completion of the opera.

Ever the strategist, Virgil chose not to tell Jessie Lasell that he had acquired another American patron. In fact, when Jessie was visiting Paris that spring, Virgil requested a gift in addition to his regular monthly stipend. The time had come, he explained, to present a high-quality concert of his own music. Jessie endorsed the idea, arranged for $500 to be placed at his credit in a Paris bank, and left for home happy, Virgil having promised to spend Christmas with the Lasell family in Massachusetts.

Thomson arranged the entire concert, but did not perform in it. He hired musicians and rented the recently refurbished Salle d'Orgue, the concert hall of the old Paris conservatory built during the Napoleonic era, situated near the Folies-Bergère. The program opened with the *Variations and Fugues on American Hymns* for organ, this to commemorate the restoration of the hall's eighteenth-century instrument. The *Sonata da chiesa* was the only other instrumental piece, Thomson having wanted to showcase his vocal works, particularly those to Gertrude Stein's texts. Scouring the city for talent, he found four English-speaking male singers to perform *Capital Capitals* and a sympathetic French pianist. He wanted to present several Stein settings for soprano as well as his *Five Phrases from the Song of Solomon,* for soprano and percussion. However, Alice Mock, the American soprano who had given the premiere private performance of *Five Phrases* refused to have anything to do with Gertrude Stein. Miffed, Thomson replaced her with a French soprano, Madame Marthe-Marthine, "plumpish, blond, the classical soubrette."[5] He coached her to sing *Five Phrases* in English phonetically, and replaced the Stein works with three recent French-text songs, not wanting to expose his willing French soprano to "the comedy risks of pronouncing Stein with a foreign accent."[6]

The concert, held on May 30, was a mixed success. The audience was large and distinguished: Jean Cocteau, Nadia Boulanger, the composers Darius Milhaud, and the young American Roy Harris, later Thomson's good friend. Of course Gertrude and Alice came. The press, Thomson recalled, was "divided between those who found in my work 'exquisite sonorities' as well as 'a strong religious feeling boldly expressed' and those who heard in it only a 'maximum of cacophony' and judged my whole effort as 'no doubt sterile, certainly exaggerated.' " In general, he concluded, the "afterglow in musical circles was not warm." "Nobody said so in my presence; but I could feel it, smell it, know it for true that my music, my career, my position in the whole time-and-place setup was something the French power group did not choose to handle."[7]

Twenty years later, when Thomson was adjudicating the musical life of America from his powerful platform at the *New York Herald Tribune,* Milhaud would remark to a New York colleague that it was "curious you all find Virgil so powerful here; in Paris he was just that little man in a dark suit."[8]

Thomson did not let the cool reception rattle him. In the long run, he believed, it was probably beneficial.

> It kept me an American composer and removed temptation toward trying to be anything else. A French composer I could never be anyhow; I had always known that. It was all right to be a foreigner working in France, but not a pseudo-Gallic clinger-on. I had not gone to France to save French music, but merely to improve my own.[9]

Thomson had found two loyal French composer colleagues, both of whom attended the concert and were enthusiastic about the works performed. Henri Sauguet, silken haired, self-effacing, and five years Thomson's junior, had moved to Paris from his birthplace, Bordeaux, at the urging of Jean Cocteau, who became a champion. Sauguet befriended Satie, becoming a sort of protégé, though not a formal student. Sauguet and his music were similar: intelligent, soft-spoken, refined, and courteous. Like Thomson, Sauguet dared to buck intellectually fashionable modernism in favor of music that was accessible and elegant. He and Thomson became fast friends. "We showed each other our music, shared adventures and addresses, bound ourselves together by an unspoken credo (based on Satie) that forbade us to be bogus either in our music or in our lives."[10]

On the night of Thomson's concert, Sauguet erupted in a rare fit of anger. After the performance, as people drifted from the hall, he got into a screaming fight with his friend Christian Bérard, who had announced that he was going off, as usual, to smoke opium with friends. Sauguet shouted at Bérard to learn some self-restraint, creating a scene that Thomson, busy with postconcert schmoozing, tactfully ignored.

The other Thomson loyalist was Henri Cliquet-Pleyel, whose wife was the featured soprano at the concert, Marthe-Marthine. The Paris-born Cliquet-Pleyel, hollow cheeked and Hispanic looking, "save for the large, soft eyes, which could be only French,"[11] had been educated at the conservatory and participated in the notorious concerts of Les Six. Thomson was almost inexplicably loyal to Cliquet-Pleyel, on several occasions sharing patrons and concert programs with him, and writing articles about Cliquet-Pleyel's music that were extravagant with praise. By the time of his autobiography, however, Thomson had tempered his appraisal. "Cliquet was a pianist of unusual facility, a sight reader of renown, and a composer of willful banality. His music was a tender parody, his life a slavery to pot-boiling jobs."[12] Cliquet-Pleyel's marriage to Marthe-Marthine was steadfast but turbulent, he given to fits of rage in which he burned his manuscripts, she given to sulking and red wine, "quarts of it a day."

The support of both Sauguet and Cliquet-Pleyel in the aftermath of the Paris concert was heartening. Thomson was sure about the music he was writing, but it was good to have native composers who agreed with him. Yet, as if to shield himself from the pervasive negativity in Paris, he chose to leave for an extended working vacation. Just then his finances were flush, thanks to Hildegard Watson, Jessie Lasell's extravagant daughter, who thought herself a singer and had taken a fancy to Thomson. "Here's a little check for something to do for the concert, or after if you will a spree," she wrote in early May, with apologies that she would not be able to travel from America to attend. "Don't be insulted and I won't be if you will drink to me."[13]

So Thomson packed light clothes, his sketches for the last two acts of *Four Saints,* and stacks of manuscript paper and traveled to the Basque region of France, staying in Ascain, a small village six miles upcountry from the coastal town of Saint-Jean-de-Luz, to finish the opera and, only afterward, cross the border into Spain. During the next two months he would complete *Four Saints,* finish the last movement and orchestration of his long-neglected *Symphony on a Hymn Tune,* and soak up the sounds and scenic colors of northern Spain.

During this trip he would also compose the first two examples of a genre that would occupy him for the rest of his life: the musical portrait.

Composing musical portraits might seem to some a questionable exercise. How does a composer sketch in sound a likeness of a person?

The referential power of music can be vivid and visceral, but the only particulars music can evoke are other sounds or other music. Nevertheless, various composers have tried their hands at musical portraiture. In the early eighteenth century François Couperin composed pieces for harpsichord that he claimed were portraits of people. Schumann tucked into his large-scale piano suites representations of fiancées, friends, and colleagues. Anton Rubinstein did a suite of portraits for piano, composed while he was a guest at a house party in the resort island home of a wealthy friend—twenty-three portraits, one of each guest, and one more of the place itself. And one of the enigmas of Sir Edward Elgar's *Enigma Variations* was that each variation is a portrait of an unidentified person. (Musicological sleuths have since uncovered the identities of most of them.)

Thomson cited these composers as forerunners in the genre. But it was from Stein that he stole the idea for his own experiments. Stein had long practiced writing literary portraits, not descriptions of people, but verbal portraits, like abstract pictures fashioned from words. Yet they were not simply exercises in free association. Stein had studied psychology under William James at Radcliffe and spent three

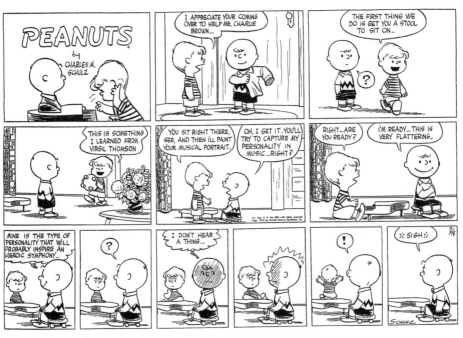

Peanuts Cartoon, 1954

years at Johns Hopkins Medical College, where her particular interest was brain anatomy. She was a keen observer of people and noted for the intensity with which she listened to those who interested her, which was just about everybody: grocers, soldiers, farmers, geniuses. She could do a portrait only after she had thought carefully about her subjects, trying to determine what she called their "bottom natures." Once the writing began, her method was an exercise in spontaneity: the portraits almost always came out in one sitting.

The immediacy of Stein's method intrigued Thomson, who was constantly trying to tap into his instinctive resources. When he finally completed the opera and symphony during his trip to Ascain, he was creatively spent. That's when the idea of trying musical portraiture, "practicing my spontaneities," as he called it, came to him. And just at that time, an ideal first subject presented itself.

A striking young Spanish woman who played the violin was staying at Thomson's residence. "She had a way of entering the hotel's dining-arbor with assurance," he later wrote, "her equally self-assured mother one step behind, that pleased me because this granting of priority to youth, in Europe uniquely Spanish, was also our American way."[14] When the young woman asked Thomson for a piece, he composed a musical portrait for solo violin, in one sitting, without recourse to any instrument, and called it "Portrait of Señorita Juanita de Medina Accompanied by Her Mother"—a short work, just two minutes, a fanciful piece with violinistic flourishes, subdued melodic bits, and fractured flamenco rhythms. Thomson was delighted not only with the music but the rejuvenating experience of composing it. He did another for solo violin on his way back to Paris in August, this time of his soprano friend Marthe-Marthine. At home that fall he did four more, again for solo violin, including one called "Miss Gertrude Stein as a Young Girl," and another of his patron "Mrs. Chester Whitin Lasell." Again, he was pleased. "Making portraits of people was just beginning to serve me, as it had long served Gertrude, as an exercise not only in objectivity but in avoiding the premeditated."[15]

That November he did a portrait of his composer colleague Sauguet. This time Thomson went one step further. He asked Sauguet to "sit" for him, just as a subject would sit for a painter's portrait. This piece he called "Sauguet: From Life." And thereafter, Thomson would never compose a portrait any other way but in the presence of the sitter.

The idea of having his subjects sit came, naturally enough, from

Thomson's many painter friends, who of course worked only "from life." As Thomson took up the practice more determinedly, he realized that having the subjects "pose" had nothing to do with trying to depict their physical selves in music. But it aided his concentration and fostered a state of almost psychic transference that he found essential to the creative process. While he "sketched" them, his subjects could read, or even sleep. It was not eye contact but "vibes" that he was after. Sometimes this worked almost too well, as in the case of Dora Maar, whose portrait Thomson composed on May 8, 1940. A photographer, artist, and, just then, the mistress of Pablo Picasso, Maar came to Thomson's Paris apartment to sit for her portrait. Out of curiosity Picasso came along as well and watched in silence this odd exercise. Naturally, being such a strong presence, Picasso got into the portrait. About two-thirds of the way through this whimsical piano piece, a rude motive in the bass register interrupts. Only after the fact did Thomson realize that this intrusion was the presence of Picasso.

During the course of his life, Thomson composed over 150 musical portraits. Most of his friends and colleagues wound up posing. Occasionally he worked on commission: Thomson did not have to know the subject at all, though his relationship to the subject could not but influence the outcome. Sometimes he found himself unable to compose a portrait, particularly when the subject was an "older women of a high social position that was largely fake." The façade was a wall to Thomson's powers of depiction.

The portraits tended to come in spurts, often right after Thomson had completed a major composition and was looking for a way to recoup his creativity. Most of them are short, one or two minutes, because he insisted on composing them in one sitting and could work for only ninety minutes or so before his concentration gave out. The majority are for solo piano, but there are portraits for violin and piano, cello and piano, brass quintet, four clarinets, wind trio, organ—even an entire concerto for flute and orchestra, a portrait of an intimate friend from the early 1950s, the painter Roger Baker. This portrait too was composed "from life," sketched in hour-long sessions over several days while Baker and Thomson were visiting with the composer Carlos Chávez in Mexico.

Though Thomson never made excessive claims for the success of these quirky works as depictions of people, he vouched for them as compositions. Yet the fact that they came out so differently from one another constituted his "circumstantial evidence" that they were indeed portraits. That said, he did not hesitate to toss out an unsuccessful effort, when, after letting it "refrigerate over night," he judged it lacking in musical interest.

This work confirmed for Thomson something he had been realizing: that his creative gift was one of observation and description, and that he was best suited to depicting people and places outside of himself. He was in his element composing operas, vocal works, landscapes, character pieces, and, eventually, theater music and film scores. He was less suited to the nonreferential forms of music: the symphony, the sonata. Similarly, as a writer he claimed no gift of invention. He was a describer, a critic. To him, as he once said, language was for telling the truth about things.

In October, pleased with the work he had completed during his trip, Thomson returned to Paris. He had promised to spend Christmas with Jessie Lasell and her family in Massachusetts, which would be his first visit home in three years. But other things were recalling him. In New York his colleague Aaron Copland was becoming an agitator for American music. Copland wanted Thomson to come join the fight. Thomson was skeptical, but decided that he had better get home and check out what had been going on in his absence.

Virgil Thomson and Aaron Copland liked and respected each other, but they were never especially close, being very different in temperament and background. They were both late starters in music, though Thomson's first efforts went toward performing (as pianist, organist, choir director) and Copland's toward composing. Like Thomson, Copland was homosexual, and though all his life he would be as publicly closeted as Thomson, Copland had more inner peace, less shame about his sexuality. He had nothing to prove. He was scrupulously private, but affable and unpretentious.

Copland was born in Brooklyn in 1900, the fifth child of Jewish immigrants. With his wide-set eyes and broad brow, he resembled his plain Russian-born mother, Sarah, rather than his handsome Lithuanian-born father, Harris. The Copland family lived on the third floor of a tenement above the family business, a dry goods store on a drab section of Washington Avenue in an ethnic neighborhood in Flatbush. They worked hard, but lived comfortably. The glory of the household was a Steinway upright piano. Copland's mother would play light classics, arrangements of arias, even ragtime now and then. But for the Coplands music was a gratifying diversion and no more.

Copland had no memory of ever being taken to a concert by a family member. His evolving passion for music seemed inexplicable to his parents. However, his determination to pursue a career as a composer finally won them over.

Copland studied piano privately and took harmony lessons from Rubin Goldmark, a New York–born, Vienna-trained composer who briefly taught George Gershwin in 1923 and soon afterward headed the composition department at the new Juilliard School. Goldmark was an excellent traditional teacher but an arch-conservative who warned Copland against the "moderns."

At that time in the states, to train for a career in music meant studying in Europe. Before the war it was Germany that Americans flocked to. After the war it was Paris. In late 1920 Copland read in a magazine of the establishment at Fontainebleau of a music school for Americans, to commence in the summer of 1921. He applied and, to his astonishment, was accepted. There he encountered Nadia Boulanger, whom he revered without reservation, unlike Thomson. Copland was impressed by Boulanger's "encyclopedic knowledge of every phrase of music past or present." She could sit at the piano and play excerpts from anything—a Mussorgsky opera, a Josquin motet—to illustrate her points. Mostly, he valued her ability to "inspire a pupil with confidence in his own creative processes."[16]

In Paris he also encountered the conductor who would become his principal patron in America, Serge Koussevitzky. Copland attended all of the Concerts Koussevitzky, as the Russian's programs devoted mostly to new music were called. He was energized by the modern works; even more, he was struck by the healthy climate for new music in Europe. New works were anticipated, celebrated, battled over, derided. But at least no one was neutral about them. Composers mattered. No such situation existed in his own country.

Copland did not have the inclinations of an expatriate. He returned home in June 1924, determined to develop a compositional voice that reflected the classical tradition but was as distinctively American as the music of Moussorgsky and Stravinsky was Russian. Back in New York, he found a small, hardy group of composers, administrators, and patrons who were challenging the status quo.

> As H. L. Mencken put it, "There are two kinds of music, German music and bad music." Right there was my reason for living in France.[17]

Virgil Thomson's autobiography is run through, as was his journalism and his conversation, with warnings about the smothering influence on American of the "German-Austrian musical complex," which he likened to an international cartel operating through the familiar techniques of "price-fixing, dumping, and pressures on the performing agencies."

> This situation, like the musicopedagogical machinery that had taught us all, had grown up after the nineteenth century had discovered what a gold mine in every sense were the classical masters. And the whole organization of it was central Europe's immortality machine. It was a conservative machine, its main merchandise Beethoven. Later composers like Brahms and Richard Strauss were tails to that kite. And Schoenberg the modernist, though a technical innovator, had kept his expressive content as close as possible to such standard Germanic models as the dreamy waltz, the counterpointed chorale, and the introverted moods of a *Liederabend*.[18]

Thomson's comments are characteristically sweeping. But by the end of the nineteenth century, the pervasive influence of the German music machine on America was indisputable. A young nation of immigrants, America had no concert music heritage of its own. Like English tea, French cognac, and Italian Parmesan, musical culture was imported from Europe. And Germany, having "led the world for two hundred years," as Thomson conceded, was the principal exporter.

The other culture to decisively influence American music was African-American, brought to the states by another vast population of transplanted people, in this case, transplanted by force. South America, by virtue of proximity, should also have been influential. However, its music arrived through the filter of the Caribbean. So even South American music was largely African-American in its character and impact. And the impact was enormous, though mostly on popular music, theater music, and jazz, all of which would soon galvanize the world.

However, the concert music culture in America was distinctively European. For three generations, immigrants from Germany and northern Europe had come to American cities, bringing with them musicians to play in America's growing roster of orchestras and opera companies, and audiences for the halls and houses. German musicians became teachers and cultural leaders. Arriving in New York in 1871, Leopold Damrosch, a conductor and composer from Posen, commandeered the city's musical life, establishing an oratorio society and, later, the New York Symphony Society, which presented the American premiere of Brahms's First Symphony. In 1884 he was given control of the Metropolitan Opera Company, which had run a $500,000 deficit after its inaugural season. Damrosch quickly sized up the mistake: the company had been founded as a venue for Italian opera. Under Damrosch, it became virtually a German repertory house dominated by the operas of Wagner, and flourished as such for two decades.

American composers and professors were not taken seriously unless they received certification in Germany from some *Hochschule* or *Akademie*. Some were enlightened and open-minded, like George Whitefield Chadwick. Having been trained in Leipzig and Munich, Chadwick espoused the great Germanic tradition. Yet he retained a rebellious streak from his days as a high school dropout and musical vagabond. During his long tenure as president of the New England Conservatory (1897–1931), he tried to loosen the stranglehold of German influence. In some cases it worked. Chadwick's student (later, Thomson's teacher) Edward Burlingame Hill established at Harvard a beachhead of toleration toward new developments in French and Russian music. In other cases it didn't. Chadwick's student Daniel Gregory Mason was a staunch conservative who believed in the absolute supremacy of Germanic composers and maintained that great music had died with Johannes Brahms—views he espoused for thirty-seven years as a professor at Columbia.

New works were being written by Americans, and the major orchestras dutifully performed them. But virtually all the chosen composers were from colleges and conservatories, a situation that still largely exists, and a support structure for the encouragement of new concert music was completely lacking. This became Aaron Copland's hope for his country: that after going to Europe to learn the tradition and hear the new developments, American composers would return home and develop a native voice. Irving Berlin and George Gershwin, the children of European Jewish immigrants, had reclaimed musical theater from its European trappings and invented something snazzy and fresh. Couldn't American composers do something similar in the concert hall?

However, what Copland found upon returning to New York in 1924 was that America was also importing the *contemporary* music of Europe and letting European composers take charge of the fledgling institutions established to support modern music. The new generation of American composers would have to change this situation if American music was to be rescued from foreign control. Within two years Copland had become the leader of an insurgent group of young composers. For over ten years Virgil Thomson largely absented himself from this assault. And the insurgents, except for Copland, responded by largely ignoring Thomson. Eventually, Thomson rallied to the cause, visiting America frequently during the 1930s and, from 1940 on, turning the chief critic's post at the *Herald Tribune* into a platform from which he delivered frontline commentaries.

In late November of 1924, just months after Copland returned to New York, he performed two of his solo piano works—the Passacaglia and the scampering character piece *The Cat and the Mouse*—at the inaugural concert of a series at a midtown art gallery presenting young composers. These were the first public performance of any of his music in America. The concert was sponsored by a fledgling organization called the League of Composers. The idea for the series had come from the league's director, Claire Reis, a small-framed, impeccably dressed, soft-spoken yet tenacious woman who, it could be argued, did more during this period to foster new music in America than any American composer.

Claire Raphael Reis grew up in Brownsville, Texas, an arid frontier town located at the southernmost tip of the state. But when her banker father died, Reis's mother, a petite woman of French ancestry, packed up her two girls (Claire was ten) and moved to New York, later traveling to France and Germany to round out her daughters' educations. Claire completed her schooling at the New York Institute for Musical Art, where she studied piano. Later, she met and married Arthur M. Reis, a successful New York clothing manufacturer and, for his day, an enlightened man, untroubled by his wife's feminist thinking and political activism. Claire Reis had been decisively influenced by two schoolmates: Walter Lippmann, already a committed socialist who would become an influential political columnist; and Paul Rosenfeld, a champion of contemporary music who would become a crusading music critic for the *Dial* and *Vanity Fair.*

Reis decried the elitism of classical music, believing that concerts should be accessible to working people. Her solution was to found the People's Music League of the People's Institute, which under her leadership from 1912 to 1922 presented free concerts, some six hundred a year at its height, in schools and settlement houses, and at Cooper Union, a progressive college in Greenwich Village. Yet in 1922 Reis was drawn into a field that some of her progressive friends considered thoroughly elitist: the promotion of contemporary music. Fortified by the populist ideals of Rosenfeld, Reis didn't see it that way. Earlier that year she had presented under the People's League a concert of works by six living composers, all of whom attended the event, introduced their works, and took questions from the audience. People had packed the hall at Cooper Union, sitting on windowsills and in the aisles. Reis was impressed by the audience's curiosity. She realized, as if in an epiphany, that in order to remain healthy, music needs to be continually reinvigorated with new works; that composers, especially young American composers, were being cut off from potential audiences.

The opportunity to do something about it presented itself to Reis in the person of Edgard Varèse, a visionary, autocratic, Paris-born composer. Varèse had won admiration and attention in the hotbeds of modernism in Paris and Berlin. But even these were too tame for his radicalism. He had begun to formulate new theories of music as "organized sound" and to explore the possibilities presented by the emerging electronic technology to create new instruments. In 1915 he moved to New York, a self-anointed messiah of modernism, looking for disciples. His initial successes were as a conductor: he led an ecstatically received performance of Berlioz's massive Requiem and started an orchestra for the performance of new music. In 1921, with his colleague Carlos Salzedo, a composer and harpist, Varèse, then thirty-eight, founded the International Composers' Guild, an insurgent outfit dedicated to presenting modern works. Together they issued a manifesto decrying the convention-bound performers and promoters who denounced as incoherent any piece they didn't understand and who, when they programmed new music at all, chose only the most "timid and anemic" works of "established names."[19]

Varèse's guild presented its first concerts in the drab Sheridan Square Theater. The programs were received with equal measures of bewilderment, outrage, and enthusiasm. Varèse was encouraged; but he couldn't run the guild alone. He needed a facilitator. At the suggestion of a colleague, he visited Reis and explained his mission. She was somewhat intimidated by this shaggy-haired, imposing European. But having grown up among gunslingers and *bandidos,* Reis figured she could handle Varèse. She accepted his proposal.

First she moved the performance venue for the concerts to the commodious, midtown Klaw Theater, which, thanks to her connections and savvy negotiating skills, she secured at a cut-rate price. The first concert was well attended and mostly well received, though one work set the audience jeering: *Angels,* a hauntingly dissonant piece for six muted trumpets by the flinty composer Carl Ruggles, the only American to enter Varèse's trusted inner circle, where he became a voice for undiluted radicalism, driving Reis to distraction.

> A report of good attendance at a concert was his cue to thunder that the reason for it was probably that we were not upholding our ideals. One evening he announced ominously, "I would prefer to see only six people at our concerts! If you had a full house last Sunday it only goes to show you've descended to catering to your public!"[20]

To Reis, Ruggles's attitude wasn't just impractical; it was elitist. The overbearing Varèse was elitist enough; Ruggles was making things worse. The strain between Reis and Varèse ripped open. She resigned, taking with her Mrs. Alma Wertheim, a patron she had induced to join Varèse's board, and several composers grown tired of Varèse's bullying.

That year, 1923, they founded the League of Composers, with Claire Reis as executive chairman. In announcing the organization, Reis tried to make it seem not like a rival group of disaffected Composers' Guild members, though to a large degree it was. The league's main goal, to "encourage and give support to the production of new and significant works," was indistinguishable from the guild's. However, from the start Reis wanted her group to be populist and educational. Winning the support of the public was the whole idea, not a sign of co-opted principles. To this end she persuaded musical laymen to join the board, not just patrons like Mrs. Wertheim but enlightened professionals: Stephen Bourgeois, an art dealer; Dr. Thaddeus H. Ames, a psychoanalyst; and Minna Lederman, a New York–based freelance music and dance critic. Varèse, who had declared war on the cultural establishment, never would have tolerated input from mere civilians. Reis welcomed it.

In her brownstone house on East Sixty-eighth Street, Reis converted a third-floor room, the former playroom of her now grown children, into the league's headquarters. The inaugural series of concerts, which began on November 11, 1923, were well attended; audiences, though sometimes perplexed, were curious and excited by the programs. The reactions of the critics were, with few exceptions, misinformed—patronizing at best, derisive at worst. Reis and her board recognized the need to educate the audience, including the critics, who, after all, were reporting on music they did not understand. From Europe came insightful monthly journals on music, art, architecture, contemporary literature. But virtually all the musical journalism in America was devoted to the music of Europe's past. The need for an American journal—an inside account, a forum for open debate—was clear. That journal, first named the *League of Composers Review,* was soon renamed *Modern Music.* The sole editor for its twenty-two-year run, who never drew a salary for her work, was Minna Lederman.

Nothing in Lederman's background—she had studied music, dance, and drama at Barnard and written some freelance criticism—had prepared her for launching a music magazine with no certain readership and woefully inadequate funding. But Lederman had a clear concept of what the purpose of *Modern Music* should be: "to rouse the public to a live appreciation of the new in music," as the opening page of the inaugural issue stated; and to give musicians, especially composers, a platform from which to describe, debate, defend, and debunk new music, including each other's. With the board's support, she set to work.

The magazine was born in a narrow spare room in the apartment of Lederman's parents, where she was then living; and there it remained. The office equipment, she later recalled, was a "hand-me-down brown desk, two typewriters, an old armoire to hold current material, a single shelf for reference books and dictionaries, and a telephone extension."[21] Lederman solicited articles from the leading European composers: Bartók, Schoenberg, Hindemith, Stravinsky, Milhaud. At first neither authors not translators were paid. Shortly thereafter, *Modern Music* established a fee scale of a penny per word, which would remain the fee scale until the last issue appeared over twenty years later.

Lederman would come to shudder at the thought of the inaugural issue (February 1924), with its "mawkish lack of design" and the "confusion of language and style." But it was an immediate success, particularly with those who mattered most, the critics.

> The mandarins of the New York and . . . Boston papers had an
> ambivalent attitude toward new music. The concerts of contem-
> porary works which they attended were legitimate prey for the
> ridicule they felt was acceptable to their daily readers. But litera-
> ture about this music appearing in the pages of an apparently
> exotic magazine was instantly recognized as a source for spec-
> tacular quotation. Advance copies were soon in great demand, and
> both the *New York Times* and the *New York Herald Tribune* began
> to compete for first go at our page proofs.[22]

Even in America the tradition of artists' reviewing each other existed in nonmusical fields. But only in Europe did this journalistic practice thrive in the domain of new music. Lederman wanted *Modern
Music* to fill that void. The magazine would champion no school or
dogma. All developments in new music were to receive scrutiny and
explication. In reporting on music, the American press had catered to
(and still does) performers and those who flak for them. *Modern Music*
would be first and foremost a forum for composers. Lederman invited
everyone to join the fray. No opinions fortified by clear analyses
would be softened or squashed. Lederman would simply referee to
keep the fight fair.

But in order to participate and be heard, emerging composers,
Reis felt, were going to need special support. Thus came her idea for
the Young Composers' Concerts, the aim of which was to advance
the cause of the "musical youngsters" from America, England, and the
Continent.[23] But before long it was dominated by American youngsters. And no one was more responsible for the growing American
tilt of this whole enterprise—the league, its concerts, *Modern Music*—
than the youngster who presented his first American performances
on that inaugural program in 1924: Aaron Copland.

Reis and her board, particularly Lederman, latched onto Copland,
recognizing in him a leader of the new American generation: the
young Brooklynite had European credentials and a persuasively clear
sense of the direction in which American music needed to move.
Moreover, they were mightily impressed by the fact that Copland had
a major premiere coming up.

Nadia Boulanger had been asked by the conductor Walter Damrosch (the son of Leopold) to appear as soloist with his New York
Symphony. She successfully petitioned Damrosch to commission a
new work for the occasion from her favorite American student, Aaron
Copland, who wrote his Symphony for Organ and Orchestra. The pre-

miere took place at Aeolian Hall on January 11, 1925. Copland's brash, sprawling work caused something of a sensation, partly as a result of an innocently intended comment by Damrosch prior to the performance. Turning to his audience, he said, "Ladies and Gentlemen. I am sure you will agree that if a gifted young man can write a symphony like this at twenty-three, within five years he will be ready to commit murder!"

Critics seized on Damrosch's words as evidence that he himself thought the work offensively radical. "Young Composer to Commit Murder!" ran one headline. The symphony pushed the boundaries of critics' tolerance. The music was daring and still sounds so: a ruminative first movement spiked with piercing dissonance; a skittish scherzo with squalling brass riffs; a "Wailing Wall" of a finale, as one review put it. Copland later deemed the work too European and derivative of Stravinsky ballet rhythms and modern French harmonies.

However, to Virgil Thomson, who was in the midst of his year as a teaching assistant at Harvard, the work was glorious. He had come to New York especially to hear the concert. Boulanger, spotting her former student backstage after the performance, asked Thomson how he had liked it.

> I replied that I had wept. "But the important thing," she said, "is why you wept." "Because I had not written it myself," I answered. And I meant that. The piece was exactly the Boulanger piece and exactly the American piece that several of us would have given anything to write and that I was overjoyed someone had written. For joy also had been there in my tears.[24]

Soon Claire Reis was coming to Copland for advice about concert programs, and Lederman turned to him for suggestions about authors and articles. Thomson later recalled this period with some resentment. "The league and Minna's magazine were controlled almost from the start by Aaron." This was not entirely true, although in her history of the journal Lederman acknowledged Copland's decisive early influence.

Having characterized the course *Modern Music* had set as "a vague, spread-out internationalism," Copland urged a decisive shift to something American—"contemporary music everywhere can be judged from the vantage point of the U.S.A." There were enough composers and critics in America, he assured her, to "effect a counterweight to the Europeans." Copland was confident and convincing.

From that early point he became, in her words, "an unofficial collaborator of the magazine."[25] She nurtured, encouraged, and edited a whole generation of American composer-critics, including Copland, Piston, Sessions, Antheil, Cowell, Carter, and, beginning in 1932, Virgil Thomson, who "more than anyone else brought a special resonance to the magazine."

But Copland did not join the League of Composers board until 1933, not wanting to bind himself to any one group. Thomson somewhat resented Copland's shaping influence on American music. But he had no right to complain. In the fall of 1925 Thomson moved to Paris, remaining essentially out of the loop during this formative period. Ultimately, it was impossible for Thomson to be jealous of someone who was so generous in sharing his growing access to performances and publication. In 1926 Copland published an article in *Modern Music* titled "America's Young Men of Promise." With little hope of being heard, his fellow composers "can at least be heard about," he wrote, proceeding to list and describe seventeen men between the ages of twenty-three and thirty-three: among them, Howard Hanson, Randall Thompson, George Antheil, Henry Cowell, the Oklahoma-born Roy Harris (whose full-bodied music reflects the "hills of his youth"), and Virgil Thomson. Copland wrote generously and accurately of Thomson's music, even though at the time of this writing, early 1926, not much of significance had been composed, not even the first Stein setting.

> At its best, his work displays a melodic invention of no mean order and a most subtle rhythmic sense growing out of a fine feeling for prosody. Certainly Thomson has not entirely found himself as yet. One waits with more than usual curiosity to see what he will do in the future.[26]

Obviously, it would have been bad form for Copland to include a self-appraisal of his own work in his article. He allowed himself to be represented in the roster only through a drawing—a playful caricature. However, implicit in his authorship of the article was the idea of Copland as the anointer of America's young men of promise.

In 1925 Copland had received the first-ever Guggenheim Fellowship in music, which was renewed the next year, stabilizing his finances—he had tried with mixed success to establish himself as a private teacher of composition—and allowing him to travel each summer to Paris, Berlin, London, Zurich. For all his fixation on the cause of American music, Copland did not want to lose touch with the latest happenings in Europe. In reporting on European new-music concerts for *Modern Music,* Copland was undaunted by international prestige. Schoenberg's Quintet for Wind Instruments "seemed to be nothing but principles and theories of composition leading to complete aridity," he wrote.[27]

During that same late summer trip, Copland visited Thomson in Paris, as well as Roger Sessions. Copland had included Sessions in his article on American's young men of promise, even though he himself knew of Sessions's work "only by reputation," as he wrote. During this visit and throughout the next year, Copland's respect for Sessions grew steadily. Curiously, he sensed in him a potential ally, even though their educations and approaches to music (and musical politics) were vastly different. By the end of this same year, Thomson had decided that Sessions was an enemy. And their mutual distrust would remain throughout their lives.

Unlike Copland and Thomson, Roger Sessions was a prodigy, not as performer but as composer, student, and intellectual. Born in Hadley, Massachusetts, in the same year as Thomson, he graduated from Harvard at eighteen, continued his studies with Horatio Parker at Yale, was teaching at Smith College by the time he was twenty-one, and then studied privately and profitably in New York with Ernest Bloch, the Swiss composer and pedagogue. Sessions also traveled to Europe to observe new developments and continue his studies, but not until he was twenty-seven and with nine years of college teaching behind him. He essentially remained in Europe from 1926 to 1933, supported by two Guggenheim Fellowships and other prizes, living mostly in Florence, Rome, and Berlin, with occasional semester breaks back in America to teach again at Smith College. The rise of fascism, which he witnessed, disturbed Sessions profoundly; in Thomson's letters of this period, there is scarcely a mention of current events.

It could not have been easy for Thomson to learn of this precocious peer who had completed his Harvard education five years before Thomson even began his. Moreover, Sessions was married at an age, twenty-four, when Thomson was pining hopelessly over Briggs Buchanan. But his dislike of Sessions can be traced not to envy but to a professional slight.

It concerned the concert in May of 1926 arranged by Nadia Boulanger to introduce works of her American students, the event that marked Thomson's public arrival as a composer. Sessions, recently arrived in Europe, covered it for *Modern Music*. Of the six composers performed—Copland, Piston, Antheil, Chanler, Elwell, and Thomson—Sessions proclaimed that three held "great promise" and two, "though somewhat less individual, obviously knew what they were about." Of the sixth he wrote,

> Virgil Thomson contributed a *Sonate d'Eglise* in three movements: chorale, tango, and fugue, for clarinet, trumpet, viola, horn and trombone. The music is in some ways sympathetic in feeling, especially in the chorale, with certain agreeable instrumental and harmonic sonorities, but on the whole seems decidedly *mal réussi*. There is intellectualism, lack of clarity, diffuseness, an uncomfortable sense of strain. Here again appeared the influence of Strawinsky, the Strawinsky of the *Octuor* and the *Symphonies for Wind Instruments*. The Russian's knowledge of this very difficult medium, however, is prodigious and not to be imitated lightheartedly. The viola in Thomson's handling seems superfluous, and succeeds only in muddying the clearer tones of the wind instruments, as does also the horn. One feels that he is by no means at home with his materials, and that the sonata has the air of an all too unsuccessful experiment.[28]

Part of the reason this review cut deep was that there was some truth in what Sessions wrote. This unorthodox sonata had been an experiment, Thomson's attempt to prove that he could produce something raucously modern. Yet, Thomson felt Sessions had completely missed the audacious humor in the music. Most upsetting was the charge that his piece was filled with "intellectualism," by which Sessions meant that the ideas were heavy-handed and self-consciously clever. Coming from a composer steeped in Germanic musical complexities, this was particularly galling to Thomson.

For the next two years the paths of Thomson and Sessions never crossed. But Copland brought them together, virtually by force, in 1928, for the project that became known as the Copland-Sessions Concerts.

For all the League of Composers' good work on behalf of new music, Copland still felt that young American creators were being short-changed. The only solution was to inaugurate his own concert series. Copland badly wanted Sessions, then ensconced in Europe, to codirect the project. Claire Reis knew what Copland was up to and, though somewhat nervous about it, did not object. But the machinations Copland went through in courting financial backers were more involved than she realized. Copland had approached Henry Allen Moe, the president of the Guggenheim Foundation, who had supported Reis's group. That Copland was keeping this solicitation secret is clear from a letter to Sessions in early 1928.

> I went . . . to see Moe. (If Mrs. R ever discovers this my "career" can be considered over!) To my astonishment he jumped at the idea of giving the concert without the L of C so that we need merely await developments. The final decision of the Trustees is tomorrow and he agreed to break the horrible news to Mrs. R.[29]

Later that year, to mollify Reis and protect his position of influence, Copland became an official member of the League of Composers. But plans for his own concert series proceeded. Sessions had to be won over to the idea. He considered Copland's espousal of American music to be misdirected. Indeed, he debunked the very notion that intrinsically "American" music even existed. Two years earlier in a letter, having expressed his great admiration for Copland's *Organ Symphony,* Sessions went on to give his new colleague "hell for two things." For one, he chastised Copland for taking "any interest whatever in other people's music and especially in the music of other young Americans" to the neglect of his own work. ("Can't you see that any two pages of your symphony are worth all the collected works of the 'jeune americains' (sic) that you so generously allow yourself to be interested in, and who have got to stand or fall on their own strength?") The second thing for which Copland deserved "hell, and even worse," was his "assumption of the title, and let us say, the obligations of a 'New York composer,' or even a 'young American composer.' " Sessions looked down upon all schools, groups, or collectives and thought Copland was wasting his own and others' precious time on "anything so vague and dubious as 'the future of American music.' "[30]

Yet, the more Sessions warned Copland about wasting his creative energy on others, the more Copland courted Sessions's support. Sessions was an intellectual of emerging influence, and Copland wanted his endorsement. Copland's pleas proved impossible to resist. Sessions signed on to the project, though he never felt quite comfortable with its title: the Copland-Sessions Concerts of Contemporary Music.

As it turned out, Sessions had little involvement with the performances, other than acting as a sounding board for Copland's ideas. During this period he was living in Italy, the result of having won the Rome Prize. In the spring of 1928, when the series was to be inaugurated, Sessions accepted a one-semester teaching post at Smith College, in Massachusetts, which at least brought him within a day's travel of New York.

For just $125 Copland had obtained the Edith Totten Theater, on West Forty-eighth Street near Times Square, for the first concert, scheduled for April 22, 1928. Copland thought it best to keep himself off the premiere program. Pieces by Theodore Chanler, Walter Piston, Carlos Chávez, and Sessions (his new piano sonata) were to be performed. Copland also had insisted that a work by Thomson be included, his *Five Phrases from the Song of Solomon,* for soprano and percussion. As a gesture of good will Copland had asked Sessions to play the rudimentary percussion part. Sessions agreed.

But, as the date approached, Sessions was struggling to complete his promised sonata. Frantic and full of regret, he wrote from Northampton to say that the work would not be finished in time. Chávez offered to perform a piano sonata of his own in its place. New programs were run off. As if this had not been enough, Sessions decided that in order to complete the piece in time for the second concert, scheduled for May 6, he would have to stay in Northampton and work. So Sessions did not attend the inaugural concert of the series that bore his name. Thomson, understandably, had sent his regrets from Paris. So Copland had to run the show himself, even playing the percussion part for Thomson's work in place of Sessions.

The modest hall was filled to capacity. Critics covered the event as real news. Though Thomson's *Song of Solomon* somewhat mystified the *New York Times* critic Olin Downes, it received the most attention as measured by column inches.

> Mr. Copland sat behind Miss Radiana Pazmor, beating the tam-tam, the cymbals, and using wooden drumsticks on a wooden drum or gourd, while Miss Pazmor ululated in the Indian manner over his rhythms. It seemed to us that this was realistic imitation of oriental chant rather than original and inspired music, and that the imitation had not quite its proper frame. If realism, why not a stage set in the Indian manner, and a singer with a turban or a hookah or whatever it is that Indian singers of the feminine sex employ during their performances?[31]

Sessions would never play a significant role in this now legendary series. After four seasons, a total of ten concerts (eight in New York, one in Paris, one in London), Copland was forced to abandon them. The concerts had been important not just for the music they brought to attention but also for the model Copland provided of composers promoting each other. In 1933 he joined the board of the League of Composers, his short-lived career as an independent producer over.

It was partly to attend one of the Copland-Sessions Concerts that Thomson returned to American in late 1928. Copland wanted to present *Capital Capitals* and had asked Thomson to coach the singers and perform the piano part. The unorthodox setting of Stein's crazy text just might stir up some interest in the press.

Moreover, Copland suggested again that Thomson show his *Symphony on a Hymn Tune* to Serge Koussevitzky. When the Russian-born Koussevitzky was appointed conductor of the Boston Symphony Orchestra, in 1924, he decided almost immediately that, among other obligations, he should use his important American post to promote new American music. No other conductor at that time shared Koussevitzky's sense of responsibility, and pitifully few have since. Naturally, American music was out of his ken. For this he relied on the advice of colleagues, in particular his friend from Paris, Nadia Boulanger. Of course she urged Copland on him. But Koussevitzky became genuinely enthusiastic about Copland's music. Soon he was turning to Copland for recommendations of other young American composers. Copland was strong in his beliefs, fair-minded, and not pushy. Koussevitzky trusted him.

Thomson trusted Copland too. When Copland visited Paris in 1928, he urged Thomson to come home at least for a while. Thomson had a symphony he wanted performed and an opera that needed backing. He was content in Paris and not anxious to leave his friends and colleagues. But his reception from the French musical machine had been chilly. Besides, the trip back would mean a chance to see Briggs. And even a visit with his family in Kansas City sounded pleasant. All this was worth a trip. In early December 1928 he began it.

14 THE FLOWERS OF FRIENDSHIP

Virgil was greeted like a member of the family when he showed up for the 1928 Christmas holiday at the Lasell manor in Whitinsville, Massachusetts. The days there were elegant and lazy. Everyone dressed for dinner, feasting on game that Chester Whitin Lasell had bagged himself, and drinking excellent wines stored since before Prohibition in the wine cellar. Christmas Eve dinner was a dress-up affair for sixteen with hot mousse of bay scallops, wild duck, and venison. For Christmas breakfast there were quails, strawberries, and champagne, and later in the day the traditional feast of turkey. Virgil had an indulgent holiday. But he was anxious to get to Boston, where he had arranged to meet with Serge Koussevitzky at the conductor's home in Jamaica Plain.

Virgil's review for the *Boston Evening Transcript* of Koussevitzky's 1922 Paris concerts had confirmed the favorable impressions the Boston Symphony Orchestra's board had acquired of the dynamic maestro. Koussevitzky was grateful to Virgil, but did not feel beholden, as his reaction to the *Symphony on a Hymn Tune* made clear.

> . . . I played it to him while he read the score. After one movement he said, "Good!" After two he said, "Very good!" After three he said, "Wonderful!" after the fourth, he threw up his hands and said, "I could never play my audience that." He was not articulate about his troubles with the fourth movement, but he seemed to find it not serious enough for a Boston public. He besought me

to salvage the work by writing another last movement. I thanked him for his graciousness and left.[1]

Somewhat bitter, Virgil wrote to Gertrude with the bad news: "Koussevitzky refused my symphony cold. I was a little surprised. I knew it was pretty good but hadn't really imagined it that good."[2] Gertrude replied with a consoling letter: "I am most awfully sorry about the symphony but then how could the Russian like it."[3] Gertrude was perplexed by Russians. Once, she wrote to Virgil complaining of a recent visit with a mutual acquaintance from Paris, the Russian-born painter Eugene Berman: ". . . as for the Russian well the Russian any Russian makes it difficult for one to like him, I suppose some day one must like some Russian."[4]

Gertrude's letter that January also contained a present, as she explained: ". . . we believe in you a lot as you can see from the profundity of the enclosed portrait, it has a new rhythm with sense. . . ."[5] The present was a literary portrait titled "Virgil Thomson." He appreciated the profundity of the piece and caught on to the rhythm. But the "sense" of it escaped him and continued to escape him for the rest of his life. It begins with verbal word rhythms that would seem to be celebrating Gertrude's artistic alliance with Virgil:

> Yes ally. As ally. Yes ally yes as ally. A very easy failure takes place. Yes ally. As ally. As ally yes a very easy failure takes place. Very good. Very easy failure takes place. Yes very easy failure takes place.
> When with a sentence of intended they were he was neighbored by a bean.
> Hour by hour counts.
> How makes a may day.
> Our comes back back comes our.
> It is a replica of seen. That he was neighbored by a bean.[6]

The portrait continues for another thirty-nine inscrutable lines. Virgil was flattered but frustrated. He knew that Gertrude sometimes buried in her abstract language negative descriptions of her portrait subjects. But he also knew not to question her about its meaning. For years thereafter he sought insights from friends and Stein scholars. At eighty-seven he was still perplexed, as he admitted in a note to this writer: "I have never been able to make much out of my portrait by GS. Have been looking at it lately with some intensity. So has Maurice. Neither of us can get very far. It is quite grand, but terribly dense. Do let me know what you make of it."[7]

From Boston, Virgil traveled to Kansas City for a visit home, where he was stunned by the winter weather, as he told Alice in a letter: "Oceans of slush froze last week and everything is now solid ice (motors waltzing). . . . [E]ven walking is impossible. Temperature at zero. Humidity at 100% (official reports). I write music at home and cure a cold and enjoy it all."[8] He was especially gratified seeing his ninety-seven-year-old grandfather, Benjamin Watts Gaines, who, he reported to Gertrude, was "full of wise political comment and people comment and questions about French life and agriculture."[9]

By February, Virgil was in New York, where he completed a male-chorus arrangement of the "Saints Procession" from *Four Saints,* which had been requested by the Harvard Glee Club for a March concert, and presented his one-man version of the opera for anyone who might possibly be interested or helpful. For two months Virgil lived the gracious life in New York, staying in the house of Hildegard Watson, the Lasell daughter who had become his friend and occasional patron. Hildegard lived most of the year in Rochester with her husband, Sibley, so her New York residence—a luxuriously appointed four-story town house on East Nineteenth Street—served as a hotel for her brother Philip whenever he was in town, and as a place for special guests. While there, a live-in caretaker attended to Virgil's needs, shopped for him, and prepared his breakfasts. The place was so spacious and splendid that Virgil often invited his own guests for gatherings in the drawing room, which boasted a beautiful concert grand piano.[10]

While in New York, Virgil tried out his opera one February night for a select audience, at the home of the arts critic and author Carl Van Vechten, one of Gertrude Stein's most devoted friends. Among some two dozen guests that night were the music patron and publisher Alma Morgenthau Wertheim, then involved with the League of Composers, and some "ladies of literary allegiance," as Virgil put it, including Blanche Knopf and Mabel Dodge Luhan, a wealthy salon hostess, sometime writer and arts patron. Dodge's conviction that Gertrude Stein was an utter genius ("it is almost frightening to come against reality in language in this way," she wrote of Stein) survived the cooling of their friendship in 1913. Also there were the two maiden sisters of Florine Stettheimer, which proved to be fortuitous to the future of *Four Saints.* A painter, and occasional poet, Florine Stettheimer, lived with her sisters and their invalid mother in a florid Gothic apartment building on Fifty-eighth Street and Seventh Avenue, just one block north of Carnegie Hall. Florine's pictures, delicate and brightly colored, were curious works filled with people and figurines all tumbled together. When Virgil later saw them—at her house, for Stettheimer rarely displayed her paintings in public—he found in her art a mock-naive quality that captured the witty innocence he had tried to achieve in *Four Saints*. He knew then that he had discovered a designer for his opera.

But it was the host of that private performance who would become pivotal to the opera's future. Carl Van Vechten, then forty-eight, had escaped a comfortable middle-class family life in Cedar Rapids, Iowa, to attend the University of Chicago, where he completed a Ph.D. in English and studied writing with William Vaughan Moody, who a few years earlier had taught Stein at Harvard. After an apprenticeship in Chicago as a cub reporter, Van Vechten was hired by the *New York Times,* first as assistant music critic, then as European correspondent, and then, in 1909, as the first dance critic working for a daily newspaper in America. He had met Stein in Paris, written articles about her work, pressured publishers to print her books, and become, in effect, her press agent. Though they were seldom together, Stein and Toklas and Van Vechten wrote each other constantly. So childlike was their familial devotion that they made up pet names for themselves: Papa Woojams was Carl; Mama Woojams was Alice; and Baby Woojams, whom Papa and Mama fussed over and worried about, was Gertrude. But the baby talk could not disguise the tenacious professional commitment they shared.

Gertrude trusted Carl's judgment completely. So she was delighted to receive this effusive letter in February 1929:

> Dear Gertrude,
>   Virgil Thomson came & played "Four Saints in Three Acts" to a select crowd that included Mabel Luhan, Muriel Draper, Les Stettheimers, Alma Wertheim, Witter Bynner etc. & everybody liked it so much that yesterday I cabled you. I liked it so much that I wanted to hear it over again right away. Mabel liked it so much that she said it should be done & it would finish off opera just as Picasso had finished off old painting—Well I cabled you but everybody loved it & I think your words are so right & inevitable in music. "Capital-Capitals" is being done next week.[11]

Capital Capitals was indeed done the next week, at a Copland-Sessions Concert on February 24, 1929, the second of the second season. Aaron had discovered four well-trained male singers, the Ionian

Quartet, whom Virgil coached and accompanied. The program included a pungent sonata for violin and piano by Alexander Lipsky, songs by Vladimir Dukelsky (who later became well known as the pop-song composer Vernon Duke), and a piano sonata by Roy Harris. *Capital Capitals* struck the audience as hilarious, so much so that at one point, seated at the piano, Virgil had to raise his hand like a traffic cop to stop the "obbligato of giggles, titters and roars of laughter," as one critic described it.[12] In terms of audience reaction and press space devoted to it, *Capital Capitals* stole the show. There were vivid accounts of the piece in *The New Yorker* and *Time* magazines. This is not to suggest that the critics knew what to make of the music. "It is a bit of a burlesque," wrote the *New York Sun* critic, "a travesty on inconsequential chatter such as one has to hear in many assemblies of entirely polite persons possessed of family pedigrees and college educations."[13] Comparing the experience of hearing the piece to that of observing patients at the Central Islip State Hospital for "the protection of the insane," the *New York Morning Telegraph* critic described the work as a "completely lunatic presentation."[14]

In depicting the performance as an absurdity, several critics wound up describing exactly the effect Thomson had intended. "Four men of solemn visage . . . projected the words in a manner not unlike the singsong of some primitive church chanting and ingeminations," wrote the reviewer from the *New York Evening Post*.[15] At least Virgil was pleased that in drubbing *Capital Capitals,* almost every critic conceded that it was the evening's liveliest work. "The only bright spot on an otherwise dreary program," wrote the *New York Herald Tribune* critic; his *New York World* colleague deemed the rest of the program "too nondescript for detailed mention."[16]

Roger Sessions, in Rome on a fellowship, did not attend. When word reached him of the riot-fest that had taken place, he was distressed. Sessions had become increasingly wary of having his name associated with programs with which he had so little to do, as he explained in a letter to Copland:

> The point is simply that I have no means of knowing the situation in any real sense when I am absolutely ignorant of some of the music that is being played. I have as much confidence in you as I would have in anyone; and yet—*in spite of the fact that I myself am wholly responsible for this situation*—I am beginning to realize the very great inconveniences as well as the risks involved in my being a completely irresponsible partner. I have to all intents

and purposes signed a blank page, and sponsored, as a musician and a composer, something for which I have no responsibility at all. . . .[17]

After this, no Thomson pieces were presented on Copland-Sessions Concerts in New York, though some were performed in the 1929 concert in Paris and the 1931 concert in London, in both cases with the composer presiding. At the London event, which turned out to be the final Copland-Sessions Concert, another go at *Capital Capitals* was tried. The London vocalists were resistant to the work and patronizing to Thomson. The performance was a dud.

From New York that spring of 1929, Virgil left for some "dates," as he always called his engagements, in Boston. "If New York had received me as a possibly acceptable invader, Boston and Cambridge took me as one of their own," Virgil wrote of the trip.[18] On March 17 the *Sonata da chiesa* was "performed in splendor of sound by first-chair men from the Boston Symphony," who had formed an ensemble called the Boston Flute Players Club. Two days later Virgil was the guest of the Harvard Musical Club, where he presented his music in an informal event. In the club's lounge, Virgil, wearing a rather garish shirt with large red-white-and-blue stripes, his thinning hair slicked back, performed several of his songs and Stein settings and presented his one-man rendition of *Four Saints*. "My merrier works were received with jollity, selections from *Four Saints* with awe (no reserves), my Symphony on a Hymn Tune, played in four-hand piano version, with frankly expressed bewilderment."[19]

The opera may have been received "with awe," but not by everyone. One dissenter was a Harvard music major named Elliott Carter. "Nobody liked *Four Saints*," he recalled. "People thought the music not very interesting musically, though the Stein text was interesting."[20] Even granting that some of Virgil's young listeners were as taken with the opera as he remembered, on balance he was disappointed with his visit to the States. Before leaving France, he had sent scores to the League of Composers hoping to get some performances, or a commission. No scores were accepted. No commission was forthcoming. Koussevitzky had turned down the symphony. New York critics had laughed at (rather than with) his *Capital Capitals*. Musicians in two cities had failed to grasp what was musically striking about the opera. Virgil attributed his exclusion to his bluntness: "I was forever blurting things out. Among my intellectual equals the habit was stimulating; but in a group of musicians banded together chiefly for capturing patronage, I was bound to be disruptive."[21]

That may have been a factor. More likely, the music was too eclectic to make much sense to musicians, especially composers trying so hard to be modern. With the opera in particular, the literary people tended to find the music enchanting and Stein's text to be nonsense. The musical people loved the absurdities and rhythms of Stein's words, but thought Thomson's music at best merely functional and at worst negligible. Thomson began to suspect that if his opera was going to be taken up, it would be nonmusicians—artists, theater people, choreographers, museum directors, writers—who would do the heavy lifting.

For now he was going back to Paris. The cause of American music would have to be left in Copland's charge. Virgil boarded a ship on March 29, 1929, taking with him memories of a warm New York reunion with Briggs, and also with Maurice Grosser, who would be returning that fall to Paris, and with baskets of fruit, boxes of candy, tins of caviar, champagne, books, bouquets—all farewell presents from friends—which crowded the corner space he had been assigned in his third-class cabin.

Resettled contentedly in his Paris apartment, Virgil Thomson composed music continually during the fall of 1929 and the winter of 1930. He revisited a technique that had served him well in his *Symphony on a Hymn Tune:* juxtaposing wildly contrasting materials in the same work, almost like constructing a musical collage. The trick was to take familiar, even banal ideas and, by scrambling and sequencing them in odd ways, to make them seem unfamiliar. He tried this technique in two piano sonatas, and in neither did it work as well as it had in the symphony. The Piano Sonata no. 1 is a curious work with its jumble of oompah-pah inanities, "wrong-note" counterpoint, fanfares, marches, and quixotic ruminations. It evolves in a discursive monologue, like a stand-up comic who segues from topic to topic with no setup. Should you laugh or be dumbstruck by the music's fractured oddities? Both, Thomson would seem to be saying. The piano textures are brazenly spare. When in 1931 he orchestrated the piece, calling it his Symphony no. 2, the textures obviously were thickened through his vivid instrumentation. Perhaps this was Thomson's concession that the bare piano writing was not successful or, even more,

his concession that there are only so many ways you can take familiar musical materials and jiggle them so that they come out sounding
fresh. Thomson had done that with brilliant originality in his *Symphony on a Hymn Tune.* Perhaps he couldn't do it again. After fash-
ioning this sonata turned symphony, he didn't compose another until
1972. And that work, Symphony no. 3, was also an arrangement of a
previously existing piece, his 1931 String Quartet no. 2.

The Piano Sonata no. 2, from early 1930, recycles from the first
sonata not only the same technique but some of the same materials.
Here the textures are even thinner, the music more naive, some of it
almost like a beginner's piano piece. But the effect is altogether different. There is a beguiling mix of resignation and whimsy in this self-
contained music. Thomson knew it would never mean much to
anybody, but it meant much to him. Thinking about the piece some
thirty years later, he decided that what he had composed was a self-
portrait: Virgil Thomson not acting himself, but just being himself, like
one of Gertrude's saints.

In 1930 he also wrote his only sonata for violin and piano. This
is decidedly a public piece. It opens with a musingly lyrical first
movement, followed by a Handelian andante that grows shockingly
intense, and a crash-bang waltz over in a flash. A contemplative soliloquy for the solo violin leads without pause to a flowing, impetu-
ous, gloriously diatonic finale with a mock-heroic ending.

The great Thomson work from this period remains unpublished
and little known: an elaborate, fourteen-minute cantata for high voice
and piano, a funeral oration with a commanding title, *Oraison funèbre
de Henriette-Marie de France reine de la Grande-Bretagne,* written
during April and May of 1930. Its impetus dates from 1923, when
Thomson's French painter friend Emmanuel Faÿ died ill and alone in
a New York City hotel room, possibly from an overdose of sleeping
pills. Thomson still felt remorse and guilt over the death of the moody
young man who had befriended him during his student year in Paris.

After Faÿ's death Thomson came across a long, polemical text by
the seventeenth-century pulpit orator Jacques Bossuet, a peroration
on the life and fate of Queen Henriette-Marie, the consort of King
Charles I of England. The marriage of Charles to the French Catholic
offended his Protestant subjects. It contributed to the hostilities that
incited the English Civil War. Bossuet's text is a confused, agitated defense of the maligned queen.

Only vaguely do Bossuet's sentiments reflect the situation of the brooding Faÿ, born to an aristocratic and ardently Catholic family. However, the text has proclamatory passion, and Thomson's musical setting with its long-spun phrases has poignant grandeur. Describing the work, Thomson wrote of its "declamatory melodies and high-arched Baroque curves, some of them pages long and all built to match Bossuet's long, florid, loose-hung, and as often as not quite il-logical Baroque sentences."[22] The piano part is restrained; the harmonic language, grounded. The vocal lines are not so much accompanied as coaxed and couched. The music is by turns inexorable, solemn, and tender. In some ways, this is Thomson's response to a work he revered, Satie's *Socrate,* which Thomson's *Oraison* matches in its quietude and dignity.

The *Oraison* was written with little thought of "career considerations," as Thomson later put it. It was not performed until the following year, when he received a windfall, a bonus for veterans of World War I, Virgil's share coming to $1,904, half of it paid right away. The money made possible a concert of his works on June 15, 1931, at the Salle Chopin in Paris.

However, the *Oraison funèbre* must have been circulated additionally among Thomson's musical colleagues, because Copland wrote of it with great respect in his 1941 book, *Our New Music.* Significantly, in later life Thomson did not put much effort into publishing the work, or even touting it to vocalists. Perhaps it was too intensely personal.

The friendship of Thomson and Stein had not been without tension. Having her words attached to the music and ambitions of a headstrong composer was a new experience for Gertrude Stein. She was excited about the prospects for success, but wary. Her inclination was to cede the responsibilities of production and promotion to Virgil. But she was uncomfortable in a dependent role and didn't trust his business know-how, though her own record in this regard was dismal.

One premonition of problems to come occurred in the fall of 1927. Virgil had dropped by for a visit with Gertrude and Alice. Later in the evening they were joined unexpectedly by a mutual friend, the Russian painter Pavel Tchelitcheff, who brought his sister Choura to meet them. Pavlik was boisterous and quick-tempered. Choura was gracious and demure. As they sat in the Stein salon, the conversation was strained. Pavlik seemed to be nursing some hostility toward Virgil. To break the tension, Virgil told everyone of a woman, an aspiring singer, who had arranged to come to him for coaching sessions on Satie's *Socrate,* but never showed up for her appointment. He had brought up the singer thinking that Pavlik surely knew her, since her regular accompanist was then sharing Pavlik's house. At the mention of the young woman, Pavlik froze, Virgil recalled. "I realized that his household suspected me of trying to win over a paying customer." This was untrue, but Pavlik denied knowledge of the incident and Virgil dropped the subject.

Gertrude would not. She pressed Virgil with irrelevant and repetitive questions: Where had he met her? How did he come to know her?

> Pestered, confused, embarrassed by the whole scene, and feeling set upon, I blurted out, "Through her having slept with one of my friends."
> In the silence that followed, Alice observed gently, "One doesn't say that." Whereupon I murmured regret and was allowed to remain quiet.[23]

After Pavlik and his sister left, Gertrude shared with Virgil the details of Pavlik's precarious household finances. This accounted for his testiness. But it did not excuse Virgil's impropriety before a female guest new to Gertrude's house. A week later he sent yellow roses as a token of remorse; the incident was forgotten. Tchelitcheff, who had become tiresome, was soon removed from Gertrude's circle.

Another quarrel, a short-lived one, concerned the potential publication of the *Four Saints* libretto. In May of 1929, two months after Virgil returned to Paris from his American visit, Gertrude wrote from the Bilignin country house to announce that, at her suggestion, the literary magazine *transition* would publish her opera text complete: "*transition* is printing the opera, and there is to be a note saying there is music your music and also a statement of what and when the Harvard Glee Club are doing."[24]

To Gertrude's surprise Virgil was not pleased with the proposal, fearing that this publication might interfere with a potential production and not wanting the libretto to have too active a life of its own. Moreover, having his contribution to the work relegated to a footnote was hard to swallow. When he told Gertrude of his objections, she replied like a mother calming the tantrum of an uppity child.

> There there you can never tell, I thought you would be pleased but you are not at all and yet I think you will be finally. You see they have as a footnote that the opera was written for you, then

> there will be a considerable notice in newspapers and that will
> reach the general public and make them curious and from past
> xperience I know that is a good thing particularly as it is the gen-
> eral public we are hoping to reach and they take a lot of prepa-
> ration, I am quite sure I am right and when I am quite sure I am
> right I very often am. . . .[25]

This crisis was averted for the time being, because the publication plans fell through.

By the early fall of 1929 Virgil and Gertrude were chummier than ever. Maurice Grosser had returned to Paris and was seeing Virgil constantly. At Virgil's request Maurice had undertaken the task of devising a way to get *Four Saints in Three Acts* on the stage. Gertrude shared Virgil's conviction that Maurice, whom she credited with uncommon sensitivity to her writing, was the man for the job. Inviting Virgil to dinner in November, she playfully reminded Virgil to bring Maurice along: ". . . I imagine Maurice an xtremely useful young gentleman and you not so useful but also a pleasure."[26]

What existed of the opera at that point was a complete text and musical score that seemed perfectly meshed; some scanty and terribly obscure stage directions; and Stein's vague suggestions that one short passage more or less depicted a vision of a heavenly mansion, and another more or less represented some kind of religious procession. Grosser took the words and music and literally imposed upon them a scenario of his own invention. This was not a plot, exactly, for very little happens in it. But the scenario provided some suggestions of activity, scenic imagery, and a means for mounting the thing on a stage.

Act 1 was to represent a pageant, a Sunday school entertainment taking place on the steps of the cathedral at Avila during which Saint Teresa, for the edification of other saints and visitors, would enact in a series of seven tableaux scenes from her own saintly life. At stage center, representing the portal of the cathedral, would be a gazebo-like structure closed off by a curtain, which could be pulled open for each tableaux. Stein and Thomson thought Grosser's tableaux were charming and just eccentric enough to seem right. In the first, Saint Teresa II is seen seated in the portal painting giant Easter eggs as she receives visitors and converses with Saint Teresa I. In the second, Saint Teresa I is holding a dove in her hand as Saint Settlement takes her photograph. In the third, Saint Teresa II is seated, while Saint Ignatius, kneeling, serenades her with a guitar. In the next, Saint Ignatius offers her flowers. Then Saint Teresa II and Saint Ignatius admire a model of a heavenly mansion. In the sixth, Saint Teresa II is shown in an state of ecstasy, an angel standing over her. In the last, she contentedly rocks an unseen child in her arms. The entertainment then ends with "comments, congratulations and general sociability."[27]

Act 2 would represent a garden party in the country near Barcelona during which the hosts for the opera, the Commère and Compère in evening dress, would observe the spectacle without entering into it. Saint Teresa and Saint Ignatius join the Commère and Compère in an opera box to witness a performance presented for their special pleasure: a dance of angels, and some party games organized by Saint Chavez. Left alone the Commère and Compère share a tender, transcendent scene of affection. The saints return and toast the happy couple. Saint Plan offers a telescope to the two Saint Teresas, who look through it and see a vision of the heavenly mansion. The saints kneel and rejoice in the wonderment of this vision. Saint Teresa I desires the telescope, but is denied it firmly but graciously by Saint Ignatius. Visibly disappointed, she is consoled by Saint Chavez, who is left alone to contemplate what has happened.

Act 3 takes place in a garden near a monastery on a seacoast surrounded by low trees and a garden wall. The male saints sit in a circle on the ground, repairing fish nets. Saints Teresa I and II walk slowly by discussing the monastic life with Saint Settlement. Saint Ignatius instructs the men to stop their work immediately, as he describes to them his vision of the Holy Ghost ("Pigeons on the grass alas"). The men are not convinced by Saint Ignatius's vision until they hear, like a confirmation from on high, a heavenly chorus ("Let Lucy Lily Lily Lucy Lucy Let . . ."). There is a military drill and a lecture from Saint Chavez. A chorus of sailors and young girls appear and dance in Spanish style for all the saints. Order is restored by Saint Ignatius. The female saints appear, doubting his vision, but he reproves them. The sky grows dark. Everyone is frightened. Together they form a processional line and sing an expiatory and devotional dirge ("in wed in dead in dead wed led . . ."), followed by a reaffirming hymn.

During an intermezzo, enacted before the curtain, the Commère and Compère discuss whether the opera is to have a fourth act. When they decide to proceed, the curtains part to reveal the saints reassembled in heaven looking radiant as they sing of their happy memories of life on earth.

Some of Maurice's ideas came from his taking quite literally images in Gertrude's text, as in the tableaux where Saint Teresa is seen being photographed: "Saint Teresa could be photographed having been dressed like a lady and then they taking out her head changed it to a nun and a nun a saint and a saint so." In fact, of the many mystifying sentences in Stein's text, this is one of the few she actually explained. Gertrude used to pass by the window of a shop on the boulevard Raspail in which the transformation of a young girl into a nun was depicted in a series of photographs. The girl's face was always the same, but her clothing changed picture by picture until at last she appeared in nun's habit. To Gertrude this suggested the spiritual process by which Teresa was transformed into a saint. Maurice, of course, knew nothing of this when he conceived his solution.

In other places Maurice simply used his imagination freely, or took his cues from Virgil's music, as in the tender scene between the Commère and Compère. In this passage Stein's words would seem to suggest yet another instance in which the opera debates with itself as to what scene had just commenced or been completed. In opposition to the implied bickering in the text, Virgil provided quiet lyricism, turning it into a gentle exchange between the Commère and Compère ("Scene eight. To wait. Scene one. And begun. Scene two. To and to. Scene three. Happily be."), supported by a sturdy, sustained, and unchanging harmony. This music—calming, content, somewhat sad—suggested to Maurice an avowal of affection between the opera's gracious hosts.

Gertrude might have been expected to object to Maurice's exercising his imagination so freely. On the contrary, she found his scenario to be emotionally and psychologically true to her own conception. She didn't want narrative, or a plot, nothing that would distract her audience from the actual "present experience" of her opera.

> A saint a real saint never does anything, a martyr does something but a really good saint does nothing, and so I wanted to have Four Saints who did nothing and I wrote the Four Saints in Three Acts and they did nothing and that was everything. Generally speaking anybody is more interesting doing nothing than doing something.[28]

This is what Maurice had given her—saints just being, going about their lives, doing simple tasks, exchanging cordialities, sometimes gently chastising each other, but never with agitation and always for the purpose of encouraging a fellow saint to return to the life of conse-cration and contemplation. Gertrude sent a cheerful note to Virgil.

> Alice and I are terribly pleased with the opera and I want to thank Maurice again for all he has done. As Alice says it not only sounds like an opera but it looks like an opera. May the saints have us all in their keeping and be good to us as we have been to them.[29]

Gertrude and Virgil freely shared their friends with each other. Gertrude had introduced Virgil to some amusing, brilliant people—Carl Van Vechten, Edith Sitwell and her two brothers, and the ever so helpful Mrs. Crane. Virgil had introduced Gertrude to Madame Lan-glois, whom she enjoyed immensely, to Maurice Grosser, whom she grew to respect, to the tumultuous Mary Butts, whom she grew to dis-like. But of all the people Gertrude met through Virgil, it was the young French poet Georges Hugnet whom she fancied with almost adolescent excitement.

When they met, Georges was in his early twenties, dark-haired, handsome, and feisty. Gertrude was enthralled by his looks, his lit-erary flair, and his appreciation of her work. His one shortcoming was a bad temper. Once, during a scuffle with friends in a Montparnasse bar, Georges heaved a chair at meek-mannered Christian Bérard, who had tried to prevent the outburst. The two artists had to be ousted by gendarmes.

Georges was given to bawdy humor. But even though she dis-approved of such behavior, Gertrude vicariously enjoyed it from Georges. Initially Alice liked Georges too. But as he became cozy with Gertrude, Alice felt threatened. She watched their emerging relation-ship warily, biding her time, waiting for an excuse to retaliate. But for now Gertrude was smitten. Once, after Georges visited at the coun-try house, Gertrude wrote to Virgil, ". . . we did love Georges he was so sweet and so gay and he is devoted to all he loves and on the whole he chooses his loves well I am awfully fond of him. . . ."[30]

With the financial backing of his father, Pierre, a successful fur-niture manufacturer, Georges had started a publishing venture, Edi-tions de la Montagne, which brought out limited, attractively designed and illustrated editions of poetry, his own and that of his friends. Georges also brought out two books by Gertrude, translated into French by himself and Virgil. The first was a selection of excerpts from Gertrude's novel *The Making of Americans*. Virgil's participation in the project ended when he left for his American visit in late 1928. But

Gertrude, writing at Christmastime, kept Virgil informed of the progress.

> Merry Christmas and Happy New Year and God bless our native land and how are you liking the templed hills, we are peacefully and completely translating it goes, I go alone and then Alice goes over me and then we all do it with Georges and then he goes alone and really it all goes faster than any one would think. . . ."[31]

By January the edition was ready for printing. Excited and encouraged, Gertrude sent the prospectus to Virgil: "We had a beautiful dinner at the Hugnet's in honor of the first outbreak of the edition, it looks as if it were going to be quite alright. . . ."[32]

The other publication was *Dix Portraits*, a translation into French, again by Georges and Virgil, of ten of Gertrude's word portraits: a lengthy one of Picasso and shorter portraits of various other artists and friends, including Satie, Apollinaire, and Virgil. The book, strikingly illustrated with sketched portraits and self-portraits by several subjects, was issued in 1930. Satisfied with the outcome, Gertrude pronounced the translations "darn good."[33]

That summer Virgil visited Gertrude and Alice at Bilignin, there setting to music a French-text work, the only scenario for a film that Gertrude ever wrote, *Deux soeurs qui ne sont pas soeurs* (Two Sisters Who Are Not Sisters). The film was to tell the story of Gertrude's acquisition of her poodle Basket. When the film project fell through, Virgil set the scenario as a vocal work, the accompaniment being, he claimed, a musical portrait of Basket sketched from life as the poodle was napping in the shade during a hazy, summer day in Bilignin.

While Virgil was visiting, Gertrude became very involved with a new project, a freely adapted translation of a series of reflective, atmospheric, and subliminally erotic poems by Georges called *Enfances*. Gertrude had never tried translating another writer's works. However, as she later explained in a letter to Virgil, her poems were no mere translations: "I have done Georges *Enfances*, I dunno I think its interesting its a mirroring of it rather than anything else a reflection of each little poem, well you'll see. . . ."[34]

By the time she sent off her adaptations to Georges, who was vacationing in Brittany, she was convinced she had opened a new dimension in her work. "The translation is more like a reflection," she wrote to Georges, "a true reflection from each moment to the next I am so pleased with you and with me, and sometimes I am a little afraid but all the same I am pleased with you and with myself."[35]

Georges was overcome by Gertrude's work and the honor it bestowed.

> Admirable Gertrude, what joy you give me in my solitude of sand and rock! I laugh at the sea which breaks out into white laughter all along the shore. This isn't a translation, it is something else, *it is better.* I more than like this reflection, I dream of it and I admire it. . . .
>
> I love you with all my heart for so brilliantly translating me and I send you the last thought of my 23rd and the first of my 24th year.[36]

Thinking Georges would be thrilled, Gertrude announced that the Boston-based literary quarterly *Pagany,* then being co-run by Virgil's friend Sherry Mangan, was planning to print the two sets of poems face to face in an upcoming edition; furthermore, Gertrude had interested a Parisian gallery director Jeanne Bucher, in publishing the entire work. To Gertrude's surprise Georges was disconcerted by the news. Though he was willing in private to acknowledge Gertrude's poems as far more than mere translations, and as independent works that were "even better" than the originals, he was not willing to do so in public. He feared that the greater renown of Gertrude's name, appearing in equal print size next to his, would confuse readers, making them question the authenticity of his poems.

Negotiations began. They were immediately strained. Georges proposed calling Gertrude's text a "translation." She preferred "adaptation" or "transposition." Georges suggested a compromise, "free translation." Gertrude rejected this, tabled the matter for the time being, and asked Virgil to negotiate. Virgil spoke with Georges, then reported back to Gertrude. He must have argued Georges' position too vehemently, for shortly afterward he sent an abject letter.

> Dear Gertrude,
>
> I've gone and done it again and I am sorry. Out of an overzealous and quite unnecessary loyalty to those absent I said an ugly thing to those present and that is worse because it hurt you whom I am ashamed to have hurt most of anybody and it was all so unnecessary on my part to hurt anybody especially my very dearest friend whom I love with all my heart.
>
> Yours very sorry, Virgil.[37]

As if this had not been enough, concurrently with the *Enfances* project, Gertrude had commenced another publication venture: to bring out a special edition of Virgil's music to be published by Georges' press, Editions de la Montagne. This was a generous offer, the expression of Gertrude's motherly interest in nurturing Virgil's career. Georges' father, Pierre, had agreed to put up $200 toward the costs of the project. Gertrude herself had pledged the remainder, which could have reached, it was estimated, $800, a significant amount of money for her. All that fall she had devoted time and energy to advancing Virgil's career, courting patrons for him, and exchanging letters with Carl Van Vechten in an attempt to entice Mary Garden into considering the lead in *Four Saints*. This proved fruitless. ("She aint going to sing any more, so now it will have to be another," Gertrude wrote to Virgil, after hearing the news from Van Vechten.)[38]

Nevertheless, Gertrude was naive about what she thought this publication project would accomplish. She wanted the book to do for Virgil "something like *Geography and Plays* did for me, make something definite and representative," she told him. But the meager returns and scanty sales of her self-subsidized *Geography and Plays* did not vouch for Gertrude's promotional savvy. She plunged with determination into the project. There were continual disagreements from the start.

As with Georges' other books, this one was to be printed by inexpensive methods on top-quality paper with illustrations by advanced artists. This was quickly agreed upon by all; also that it should contain only vocal works, this being the genre of Virgil's growing reputation (not to mention an easier sell for a publisher of literary works).

Four Saints was considered for inclusion but rejected, being far too long. Carl Van Vechten was asked by Virgil to write an introduction, which he agreed to do, "a preface extolling the virtues of you and Gertrude, marrying you in a kind of joint glory!"[39] However, Carl also had a lead on a potential publisher for the opera. So it was thought best to save him as a prefacer to that. He did suggest that, for the sake of marketing and programmatic sense, the book contain either Gertrude alone or French texts alone, but not a mixture. Virgil agreed. He proposed a trio of Parisian tableaux: *La Seine* (text by the duchesse de Rohan), *Le Berceau de Gertrude Stein* (a playful poem by Hugnet), and the setting of Gertrude's film scenario. Georges objected, not wanting to be sandwiched between two women. And Gertrude was unhappy with the inclusion of Georges' *Berceau,* which she thought unamusing and overly intimate. So Virgil proposed four vocal works: *Fable de La Fontaine, Phèdre* of Racine, Georges' *Valse grégorienne,* and Gertrude's film scenario.

Gertrude through *Valse grégorienne* would be fine. But she insisted that the book contain a substantial English text of hers. *Capital Capitals* was her first choice. Along with this she suggested the Bossuet *Oraison funèbre,* which she was fond of. These choices, she reasoned, "represented three distinct periods and would be saleable, and would show you at your heights," adding that she didn't mind at all being between two gentlemen.

When Virgil wrote to say that Georges was insisting upon all-French texts, Gertrude sent a testy reply.

> My dear my dear
>   Yes of course you have a weakness for french texts thats alright but we want to sell the damn thing and we got to have the reclame of English texts in other words mine to help sell it believe me it is not for anything xcept selling and also I definitely want some thing that has no words, this is a sample we are offering of one Virgil Thomson in whom we believe as well as a pretty book and we want it to reach as many people as possible and we want the samples as various as possible, no rather a few pages of the opera than any more french and cut down the artist illustration as much as possible, I don't think they will help sell this particular book a lot, and what I want is to have something that will reflect credit on the three of us as a book and will show you to best advantage, it really was a concession to Georges to have any painters at all I would much rather do more of you than that, think about it from that end, I personally think that the three periods and practically confined to that with the intention of your being shown in as much music as possible is my firm idea.[40]

Georges and Gertrude were at a standstill. By November, when Gertrude and Alice returned from the country, Virgil doubted that the book project would ever come together. To top it off, he had recently picked his own quarrel with Georges over not being sent a complimentary copy of a book that Georges had just published, a book of poems by Virgil's friend Pierre de Massot, a young opium-addicted writer who, it turned out, died before the year was out. Virgil confronted Georges, demanded a copy of the book, got one, and, feeling triumphant, went back to his flat, where he promptly took ill, his typical "frustration grippe," he called it, writing to Gertrude about the whole incident. She was not sympathetic.

Sorry about the grippe but look here I am not awfully anxious to mix in but you must not be too schoolgirlish about Georges and also after all he is putting down his 5000 francs of his fathers credit for your book and hell it is a gamble and he could do something with it that would be surer and after all nobody else is, its alright but nobody else is so remember the Maine. And even if there is a minority report you must not overlook this thing, and besides why the hell should not Pierre give you the book as well as Georges but anyway that is another matter, this is only to cure the grippe, anyway I love you all very much but I always do a little fail to see why anyone is such a lot nobler than any one else we are all reasonably noble and very sweet love to you and Maurice.[41]

By this point, relationships between the three of them were precarious. No doubt, behind the quibbling over these seemingly mundane matters lay unarticulated issues about loyalty, and Gertrude's need to be treated with deference by younger male admirers, and Virgil's exaggerated estimate of his skills as an arbitrator, and Georges' inability to acknowledge his ambition. Whatever was driving the ill will and paranoia, the three of them had hit an impasse. All the talk of the Virgil Thomson book ceased for now.

Yet there was still the matter of the publication of *Enfances*. Gertrude had left the arrangements with Georges. Just a few days after Gertrude mailed to Virgil her letter chastising him for being so "schoolgirlish" with Georges, she herself became thoroughly upset with Georges. The publisher Jeanne Bucher had sent her a sample subscription form for *Enfances*. It listed in bold type at the top the name "Georges Hugnet" and the name and the title of the work, "Enfances," under which, in smaller type it read, "Suivi par la traduction de Gertrude Stein."

Gertrude considered this an act of utter disloyalty; moreover, after all their discussions about it, she thought Georges' use of the word "translation" was intentionally hostile. Sides were taken in the entire Stein circle. But Gertrude's response was to simply withhold permission from the publisher to use her texts at all. When by chance at Madame Bucher's art gallery Gertrude and Alice encountered Georges, not wanting to quarrel in public, Gertrude refused his proffered hand. The break was now formal. "The last act of the drama was played this aft," she wrote to Virgil. "You have been very sweet about not saying I told you don't imagine I don't appreciate it."[42]

At this point, had Virgil dropped the entire matter, his relationship with Gertrude would likely have been salvageable. However,

Georges was in despair over the break and the collapse of the *En-fances* collaboration. He besought Virgil to intercede. When Gertrude heard of Georges' desire to reconcile the rift, she authorized Virgil to "act as agent," meaning *her* agent. This Virgil feared was an untenable position, since he was, in a sense, also acting as Georges' agent. However, quite reasonably, Gertrude agreed to consider any layout solution so long as both poets' names were of equal size and the word "translation" was not used. Virgil worked out exactly such a title page with the authors' names in type of equal size to be printed at top and bottom equidistant from the centered title. Hugnet, being author of the original texts, was to get top billing.

In the meantime Alice sent an urgent message asking that Virgil phone her immediately. When Virgil called from the lobby of his building, Alice specified that, to make clear it was not Gertrude who was instigating the negotiation, whatever proposal was offered be understood to come from Georges. Knowing that his stubborn friend Hugnet also had a face to save, Virgil was unsure he would be able to pull this off. But he promised to try. He brought the proposed title page to Georges, who examined it and wrote on the top corner, "I accept." Knowing that this did not conform to Alice's instruction, Virgil feared that Gertrude might reject it.

The climactic scene occurred on Christmas Eve in the Stein salon. Virgil had been asked for dinner; Maurice too. The night was dark, wet, and wintry; Virgil, feeling sickly, was depressed about the prospects for the evening and by this point quite fed up with everyone. Knowing there would be gifts, Virgil had brought one too, a white-framed picture for the summerhouse, a Victorian lithograph of two ladies in a swing. Walking with Maurice down the misty rue de Fleurus, Virgil dropped the picture on the street, breaking the glass in pieces. Virgil was distraught.

> But our hostesses were cheerful; a crèche with small statues from Provence had been set up beside the fireplace; in the tiny dining room, which with its octagonal Florentine table and equally massive Florentine chairs could seat just four, there was venison for dinner; and afterwards, back in the studio, there were neckties and silk scarves from Charvet. When all the ceremonies had been accomplished and well-being established (for nobody had a power like Gertrude's for radiating repose), I brought out the paper. Gertrude looked at it, did not bridle or seem to be suspicious. She merely said in a wholly relaxed manner, like a businessman sign-

ing a contract already negotiated, "This seems to be all right." Then she passed it to Alice, saying, "What do you think, Pussy?" And Alice, after seeing the two words written on it, said, "It's not what was asked for."[43]

The rest of the evening passed unexceptionally. Final Christmas greetings were exchanged toward midnight. Virgil and Maurice left. By the next morning Virgil was ill with his "frustration grippe."

Virgil was supposed to return on December 27 for another dinner party and bring three manuscripts lent him by Gertrude, one of them the fateful *Enfances* texts. Recalling this period in later life, he had no memory of attending that party, though he may have. He remembered returning the manuscripts via messenger. In the meantime, he nursed his cold, and also that of his bed-ridden elderly friend Madame Langlois, bringing a strong vegetable broth that her own hotel did not provide. As he got better, Virgil focused on an upcoming concert at which, among other works, some songs on Stein texts were to be performed. During the third week of January, not having seen or spoken with Gertrude since the New Year, Virgil dropped by unannounced one evening. Uncharacteristically, it was Gertrude who answered the door. She looked stiff and said only, "Did you want something?" "Merely to report on my absence," he replied. "We're very busy now," she said, nodding and closing the door. Not having told her of the upcoming concert, as he had intended, Virgil sent her an announcement along with his wish that she and Alice might be able to come. Her reply, dated January 21, 1931, was a formal off-white calling card, in size somewhat larger than three-by-two inches, with a matching envelope. At the bottom of the card in delicate print was her address. In larger print, centered, was her name, all in capitals: MISS GERTRUDE STEIN. Under this she had written in black ink, "declines further acquaintance with Mr. Virgil Thomson."

Virgil was stunned and upset, but also angry. He had done nothing more, he believed, than try to mediate a dispute between friends, both of whom were acting childish. The prospect of losing Gertrude's friendship was devastating. But he was not about to apologize. This time there would be no yellow roses and abject letters.

The break would last for nearly four years, until the fall of 1934, when Gertrude visited America with Alice to give her successful lecture tour and attend the Chicago production of *Four Saints*. Much later, in the early 1960s, long after Gertrude's death, finally talking about this incident with Alice, Virgil asked her why on that Christmas Eve she had intervened in this matter when Gertrude had seemed inclined to accept Georges' proposal. "I was only trying to protect Gertrude," Alice replied, adding, rather defensively, that Gertrude had indeed been "very disturbed by the separation" and relieved by the reconciliation.

For all of Alice's self-effacing support of Gertrude, it was clear to anybody who observed the relationship that Alice was in some basic way the stronger of the two. Gertrude was "Baby Woojams." Alice was "Mama Woojams," who knew what was best for Baby. Alice had her own agenda in shielding Gertrude from Virgil. She was always threatened by Gertrude's attachments to young men. Gertrude may well have regretted the split. She knew she had found in Virgil a sympathetic collaborator. Her stubbornness was as monumental as her physique. But even if her inclination was to patch things up, she would have found it impossible to oppose Alice. It had become too easy to defer to Mama's wishes.

Later that month Gertrude wrote to Carl Van Vechten and mentioned, as if in passing, her recent breakups.

> We have been having a hectic one might almost say lurid winter so far, there is this and many other things and then we have quarreled beginning with Bravig Imbs going on through [Kristians] Tonny and Georges Hugnet and ending with Virgil Thomson and now we don't see any of them any more, but we seem to be seeing almost everybody else such is life in a great capital, otherwise calm.[44]

Not wanting to lose the good will of valuable friends he had met through Gertrude, Virgil wrote to Van Vechten with his own account of the incident, to which Carl, by then an exponent of African-American culture, replied, "Your news is breaking me down—as we say 'en negre.' And your letter is both amusing and sad-making."[45] But Van Vechten did not try to dissuade Gertrude and Alice from their resolve. Papa Woojams knew better.

Soon thereafter, Gertrude published her adaptations of Hugnet's *Enfances* without his poems and called, pointedly, "Before the Flowers of Friendship Faded Friendship Faded."

Virgil was left with hurt feelings and an opera to produce; and this he would have to arrange by himself.

15 CONTACTS AND CONTRACTS

The two people who were most responsible for guiding *Four Saints in Three Acts* to production came not from the music but from the art world. They were convinced that the opera would proclaim a manifesto of the emerging American avant-garde. Yet their commitment was solidified before either of them had heard a note of Virgil Thomson's score.

R. Kirk Askew, Jr., seven years Thomson's junior, the son of a saddle manufacturer, was born and raised in the same middle-class Kansas City neighborhood as Thomson, though they never knew each other there. They met at Harvard, but their friendship didn't solidify until the late 1920s. Askew, slight of frame and solid, was a mercurial fellow, well-mannered and efficient, yet snappish and emotionally cool.

A. Everett "Chick" Austin, Jr., on the other hand, the pampered son of a doctor in Brookline, Massachusetts, was an adventurer. Since his early childhood, he had crisscrossed the Atlantic with his family almost every year. He entered Harvard in 1918 and immersed himself in art. He leapt at the chance to join an expedition to Egypt cosponsored by Harvard and the Museum of Fine Arts in Boston. Later he secured another leave to study in Siena with a skilled copyist of early Italian masters. Austin was a breezy, dashing dynamo, a "hunter," as Thomson later called him, both of paintings and of people.

218

Askew and Austin were protégés of the Harvard art historian Paul Sachs, who had escaped his obligations to the family firm, Goldman Sachs, and returned to Harvard, his alma mater, where he taught in the art department and codirected the Fogg Museum. His background in finance shaped his outlook on art. Sachs was convinced that the financial barons and wealthy patrons who had been collecting art-works, particularly modern art, would soon need new professional institutions to organize, care for, and validate their acquisitions. His mission at Harvard was to prepare young men to take over and establish those institutions; his means was a unprecedented course called "Museum Work and Museum Problems." From Sachs's class Alfred Barr, Jr., went off to Europe for a study trip then straight to the directorship of a new institution, New York's Museum of Modern Art, founded in 1929; Austin, just twenty-seven years old, assumed the directorship of the Wadsworth Atheneum in Hartford; and Askew was engaged by Durlacher Brothers, prominent London art dealers, to take over their New York gallery, on East Fifty-seventh Street.

Among the Harvard art historians Askew was the last to embrace modernism. But, open-minded and never intellectually pushy, he was engaged by people and fired by the exchange of new ideas. His home would become virtually the crossroads for the American avant-garde, or what some have called the upper-class bohemia, owing in part to the woman he married in 1929.

Constance Atwood came from a cultured, wealthy Stonington, Connecticut, family. She was eight years older than Kirk and had been through a divorce, which, though amicable, carried a social stigma in those days. Constance was a striking beauty, with her coils of sandy hair and ample bosom, " 'advanced' for the decade when breasts were just beginning to emerge," Thomson later wrote. "In a time when eyes still were tightly squinted and smiles were grins, Constance Askew's relaxed visage, as calm as that of Garbo, was deeply exciting to young men of her generation."[1]

Though he depended upon Constance for support, Kirk was a bisexual who maintained scrupulously discreet relationships with men. But if the marriage was unconventional, it was not uncommon among the smart set in which they moved. The Askews lived in a fine, four-story brownstone on Sixty-first Street and Third Avenue. That home, with its cork-lined library adjacent to a drawing room with imposing Victorian furniture and elongated windows overlooking a courtyard, became the site of celebrated gatherings eventually called the Askew salons. Every day at five business associates, friends, and friends of friends could drop by for tea or drinks to share artistic gossip and socialize. But the really elaborate affairs were the "at homes" every Sunday at six. Almost anyone could come, and almost everybody did. Artists, curators, writers, musicians, academics. The list of notables who frequented the Askew salon is a list of the prime movers in the cultural world from the 1930s: Aaron Copland, e. e. cummings, Agnes de Mille, Elizabeth Bowen, Carl Van Vechten, Alfred Barr. Lincoln Kirstein came to test out his idea of founding an American ballet company.

Not infrequently several dozen would show up. The drink during Prohibition was homemade gin diluted with ginger ale, or sometimes mixed with a nonalcoholic vermouth to make martinis, though olives and lemon peels and "other such nonsense," as Thomson put it, were never bothered about. Sometimes there was bootlegged scotch. John Houseman, who would become a frequenter, recalled the scene vividly:

> From time to time this human stream seemed to get caught against some physical object—the tail of the piano or the curve of a love seat—or it would become congested around some particularly eloquent or glamorous guest. Then Kirk Askew would appear, smiling and efficient, and start the traffic back into its normal flow. . . . Shoptalk was permitted up to a point; so were politics, if discussed in a lively and knowledgeable way. Flirtation (homo- and heterosexual) was tolerated but not encouraged. If it threatened to hold up traffic or disrupt the interchange of ideas it was soon ferreted out and broken up by the smiling, relentless and faintly malicious host.[2]

If Kirk was the catalyst of the salons, Constance was the anchor. A natural tendency to let people come to her kept her seated graciously on the drawing room couch. It was this quality that Thomson later captured in his musical portrait of Constance, "Sea Coast." This short piano piece gives the impression of swirling, cacophonous waves of events crashing and expiring upon a rocky coastline. "That was Constance," Thomson said. "A beautiful woman, but kind of rock-bound."

In 1932 two Askew salon regulars constantly talked up the opera that Gertrude Stein had written with Virgil Thomson. Henry-Russell Hitchcock, the historian of architecture, and another Paul Sachs protégé, had heard Thomson's one-man rendition of the work several times, and his enthusiasm was inexhaustible. Dressed in a tweed suit, though always somehow unkempt, and sometimes needing a bath, the bearded, bulky Hitchcock, who was hard of hearing, would bellow his praise of the opera at anyone who would listen. His judgment was confirmed by another Askew regular, Carl Van Vechten. Their talk fired the smart set at the Askew salon, especially Chick Austin, who always showed up whenever he was visiting from Hartford.

The Wadsworth Atheneum, America's oldest public museum, stood on Main Street in the heart of America's insurance capital—granitic, gray Hartford. But Austin was turning the museum into a hotbed of modernism. His board of trustees was a recalcitrant group. But Austin's enlightened acquisition of baroque Italian painting reassured them that their director was no loose cannon. His position was firmed up considerably when in 1929 he married the vivacious daughter of a prominent Connecticut family, Helen Austin, whose uncle was president and treasurer of the board. Even so, Austin's advocacy of the avant-garde was looked upon skeptically by the stuffy trustees. Yet, it was hard to resist Chick when he was carried away by a new enthusiasm. He used to say, audaciously, that the purpose of a museum was to entertain its director. And Thomson thought this a refreshingly enlightened view.

Austin believed a museum should be not just a repository, but a vital cultural center. To fulfill his vision he started a film series, threw costume balls, presented the first American exhibitions of Surrealism, showcased Buckminster Fuller's Dymaxion house. He organized a collective of patrons impishly called the Friends and Enemies of Modern Music and, through them, produced new-music concerts held mostly in private homes. By 1932, some stock holdings given to the museum in 1918 by Samuel Avery had tripled in value to over $700,000 dollars. The Depression had pushed construction costs to absurdly low levels. Austin proposed that a new wing for modern art be attached to the existing Beaux Arts museum complex. This wing would have a proscenium theater with a small orchestra pit. And the theater would be launched with the Thomson/Stein opera, this work that would demolish the boundaries that had defined modern music, writing, theater, and art. At the same time, the wing would house the first retrospective in America of paintings by Pablo Picasso.

It was a daunting plan, but Austin overwhelmed his board of trustees. Designs for the addition that reflected the best elements of International Style modernism and old-world elegance were approved

in June 1932. The opera project would have to be funded from separate sources, but Austin thought he could secure them from friends,
Thomson's patrons, and art dealer colleagues. This is where Askew
was essential.

   Four Saints in Three Acts became the closest thing to a unifying
crusade that the Askew salon ever launched. To prod the plans along,
Thomson would have to come from Paris for an extended visit, his
job being to engender excitement about the work and, more important, to impress the trustee-magnates attached to the Museum of Modern Art and the Wadsworth Atheneum, any of whom could discourage
contributors by turning a cold shoulder to the venture. "So Chick went
ahead with the opera plan," Thomson late wrote, "in the same way
he accomplished other things, not by seeing his way through from
the beginning but merely by finding out, through talking of his plan
in front of everyone, whether any person or group would try to stop
him. Then, once inside a project, he would rely entirely on instinct
and improvisation."[3]

Back in Paris, Virgil was eager to join his Harvard chums in their campaign for the opera. But just then he was broke. To his rescue came
Philip Johnson, a young friend for whom money was no problem.
Johnson, the middle child of a Cleveland real estate baron, had taken
seven years to complete his degree at Harvard, which he had entered
in 1923 at seventeen. He was passionate in his interests but un-
grounded, drifting from mathematical physics to poetry, piano, philosophy, classics. His education was interrupted by frequent summers
and semesters taken off for trips to Europe, or for time at home in
the posh Shaker Heights suburb of Cleveland, where he sometimes
recuperated from spells of nervous exhaustion and depression. His
distress was brought on in large part by his torment over his attraction to men.

   It would not be until the early 1930s that Johnson truly reconciled himself to his sexuality. But his professional drifting ceased
overnight when he chanced upon an article by Henry-Russell Hitchcock about the Dutch architect J. J. P. Oud, which fired his passion
for architecture. That spring, back in Cambridge to complete, reluctantly, his degree in classics, Johnson met Alfred Barr at his sister's
graduation from Wellesley College. It was clear to Barr that Johnson
was woefully uninformed about art and architecture. But his mind was
dynamic and his conversation, with its discontinuous leaps from sub-

ject to subject, was utterly engaging. Barr became Johnson's mentor. He introduced him to Hitchcock, sent him on a study tour of European architecture, and, upon his graduation, invited him to intern at the Museum of Modern Art. Johnson wound up writing with Hitchcock an influential book on the international style of modern architecture, which led to a pathbreaking exhibition.

While traveling through Europe in the summer of 1930, Barr and Hitchcock introduced Johnson to Virgil Thomson, who identified with Johnson's pugnacious intellectualism. Though just ten years older, Thomson became another authority figure. By this time Johnson was independently wealthy. In 1924 his father decided to parcel out the family holdings to his three surviving children. To his daughters he gave properties in downtown Cleveland, reasoning that women required ironclad income. To Philip he turned over issues of common stock in the Aluminum Corporation of America. The prognosis for the company was uncertain. In a few years, the ALCOA stocks so soared in value that by the time Philip graduated in 1930 he was wealthier than his father.

When, while visiting Paris in 1932, Johnson learned that Thomson lacked travel money to New York, he advanced him $200—the price of round-trip, third-class passage—and offered the use of his spacious, sparely furnished apartment in the genteel Turtle Bay section of East Side Manhattan. So Thomson found a temporary tenant for his Paris flat and boarded the *Ile de France* at Le Havre in wintry November.

It had been decided that Thomson would be passed back and forth between Philip Johnson and the Askews, who welcomed him to an upstairs guestroom. At the Askews that winter he became practically a member of the family. Constance, in particular, enjoyed Virgil's dry wit and clipped manner. Being around the house for days and weeks at a time, Thomson was able to proselytize for the *Four Saints* project at the Askew salons. Often, toward midnight, members of the party would head up to Harlem. "But the Askews seldom went along, though Constance might be itching to." And it was during such a foray in the early days of 1933 that Virgil made one of the pivotal decisions about the production of *Four Saints*.

The Harlem Renaissance of the 1920s was documented, written about, and celebrated in song and dance even as it was happening. But most Harlemites lived through it without noticing. It was a renaissance mainly for the downtown whites who frequented Harlem and for the black club owners, entertainers, and waiters who served them.

Traveling uptown in the 1920s, one entered just past 110th Street, the northern border of Central Park. From here Harlem was framed on the west by Columbia University, on the east by the streets that trailed off to the East River, and on the north by the old Polo Grounds, up near Washington Heights. Within those two square miles by 1930 lived over 200,000 Negroes, more to the square acre, it was determined, than in any other place on earth. Three main Harlem boulevards formed an H that rested on the northern edge of Central Park. Lenox Avenue to the east was home to immigrants from Africa, Latin America, Cuba, the West Indies. Here there was crime and violence, poverty and hardship. To the west was Seventh Avenue, the promenade of aspiring middle-class families, professionals—"strivers" and "dickties," they were called. Running the length of Lenox Avenue were streetcar tracks and attendant grit. But Seventh Avenue was divided down its length with a strip of trees and grass. These two parallel avenues were connected by 135th Street, where people regardless of class could meet, work, trade, and mingle. Cafeterias, general stores, and pawnshops dotted the neighborhood; also innumerable "skin-whitening" and "anti-kink" beauty parlors. Something approaching prosperity was possible in Harlem of the 1920s. It was not unheard of to find a domestic worker who had saved from her salary and purchased a brownstone for her family.

During the World War I years the night spots of Harlem had been for Harlemites. But in the 1920s whites from downtown discovered Harlem's gin mills and nightclubs, which were scattered on both sides of town. Clustered around Lenox Avenue were the Lenox Avenue Club, near 142nd; Cairo's, on Lenox and 125th; the Sugar Cane, on Fifth Avenue and 135th. Off of Seventh Avenue were Small's, near 135th; Connie's Inn, on 131st; the Bamboo, on 139th. Gradually these clubs started catering to whites. The Cotton Club, the most famous and posh of them all, on Lenox and 142nd, where Duke Ellington's band held court, was the first to all but officially close its doors to black patrons. It became the "Jim Crow Club," catering to moneyed whites and gangsters. This turned out to be bad for business. For whites, much of the fun of going to Harlem was in observing unthreatening black people dancing and laughing on their own turf. But Harlemites often resented the voyeurs. Much of what was observed was playacting for the white man. In clubs across Harlem white visitors played at black games, doing the Charleston, trying out the camel, the fish tail, the turkey, the black bottom, the scronch. And to many Harlemites this was a ridiculous sight.

Coming up on streetcars and taxis, white visitors sped by the jarring mix of poverty and modest prosperity. Boarded-up buildings stood right next to carefully maintained brownstones or well-appointed churches. This was an era when weekly rent was due on Saturday night and you were out on the street if you failed to pay. The rent party, often called the "social whist party," was an established institution of Harlem life. You would print up invitations to a whist at your flat, distribute them in the neighborhood, and hope enough people would turn up. Refreshments would be provided: Prohibition whisky, usually terrible, fried fish and pig's feet, usually delicious; and music—a piano augmented by a guitar or trumpet, maybe some drums. Guests paid a dollar or two, and with luck the rent was raised.

Harlem was also where whites with money could procure illicit pleasures: booze, tricks, drugs—though one needed a connection for these, a respectable supplier, not some hoodlum. When Ethel Merman in Cole Porter's *Anything Goes* sang that "some get a kick from cocaine," it was understood where "some" were likely to buy it.

For Van Vechten, Chick Austin, Russell Hitchcock, and, later, Virgil Thomson and the other habitués of Harlem from the Askew circle, the possibility of illicit pleasure was one of Harlem's attractions: it was where men could find men to have sex with. Like Askew, Van Vechten and Austin were maintaining what Thomson called "queer marriages." At the Askew salon, or anywhere in mixed company, one did not speak of this. But in Harlem, with its popular drag balls and a homosexual subculture that was more visible and less tormented, it was not difficult to procure men. Well-dressed, deferential Harlem gentlemen acted as discreet providers. This way of handling homosexual matters suited Thomson perfectly.

The Harlem Renaissance did not survive the Depression. With pervasive unemployment and despair, racial tensions were exacerbated. In 1935 there was a series of riots on 125th Street, the community's main commercial avenue. The alleged beating of a young Negro boy caught shoplifting in a white-owned store set off a night of looting and fires. The storefronts of white businesses were smashed, and merchandise was stolen. The police were admirably restrained, which helped to contain the furor. But a Negro Moslem agitator named Sufi Abdul Hamid, who headed the Negro Industrial and Clerical Alliance, turned the incident back on the white merchants. He organized picket lines on 125th Street to demand that store owners hire Negro workers and clerks, provoking countercharges of anti-Semitism from the merchants. Another emerging activist, the Reverend Adam Clayton Powell, Jr., joined Hamid's people on the picket line. The incident and its aftermath prefigured events and accusations that have continued to occur, most recently in 1994, and on the same street.

Virgil was usually eager to join the hangers-on at the Askew salons who headed for Harlem at midnight. One time in early January 1933, Virgil and Russell Hitchcock went to hear Jimmy Daniels, a light-skinned, impeccably dressed entertainer, not yet twenty-five and already popular in Harlem. Daniels sang beautifully—show songs by Gershwin and Arlen were his speciality—danced a bit, and served as host.

Virgil and Russell had heard him several times. On this particular night, Daniels was singing "I Got the World on a String" with his trademark style: a breezy rhythmic swing and free-and-easy vocalism. What struck Virgil was the naturalness of Daniels's diction: the words just came out clearly, as if he were speaking them, yet with no loss to the lyricism of the vocal line. This was not a matter of conscious enunciation. Words and voice were one.

Virgil turned to Russell and said, "You know, I think I'm going to cast my opera entirely with Negro singers."

Russell was about the biggest fan of Virgil's unorthodox opera. But this struck him as a bit gimmicky.

"You better think about that one overnight," he said. Virgil did. The next day it still seemed an excellent idea.

Later in life Virgil Thomson would list for anyone who asked the reasons for this unconventional decision. Like so many of his sweeping generalizations, the reasons could sound patronizing, even racist: blacks sing English beautifully, he would say emphatically; they are not afraid of religious subject matter; they do not overly intellectualize everything; they have dignity and bearing; and "you can dress them in anything and they look wonderful."

Thomson felt that all of these observations were fortified by his experience growing up in Kansas City. The churchgoing black Baptists of his youth cherished language. As children, they were brought up to recite and sing with reverence prayers and hymns they did not yet understand. To Thomson they seemed to accept religion unquestioningly. Virgil had worked with trained white singers who were embarrassed by, even contemptuous of Gertrude Stein's words. Surely black singers would offer no such resistance. And as far as "dressing them in anything," most fashion designers concur that African American skin tones complement even the brightest colors.

Yet this is a complicated issue. Throughout his life, Thomson never acknowledged that his sweeping comments about black people—and the proprietary tone that came through when he used phrases like "our blacks"—represented a plantation attitude. As the civil rights movement sensitized the country to its prejudices, any generalization—let alone Thomson's condescending notions of black people, say, accepting religious subject matter unquestioningly—was viewed as racist. Not only did Thomson deny this when it was suggested, he enjoyed provoking his white liberal friends by calling himself an "unreconstructed southerner." A similar controversy attached to Van Vechten. During the 1920s Van Vechten wrote with keen insight and deep respect of inner-city black culture and the Harlem Renaissance. Back then his writings were pathbreaking; reading them today, one finds it hard to disregard the slightly patronizing tone of his advocacy.

Thomson's decision to employ an all-black cast in his opera had another dimension relating to Mabel Dodge Luhan's prediction—her hope, really—that *Four Saints in Three Acts* "would destroy opera the way Picasso has destroyed old painting." Using an all-black cast in an opera not about a black subject was another way of flouting convention, of audaciously proclaiming that opera as it had been known was dated and that *Four Saints in Three Acts,* with its hermetic text and after-the-fact scenario, would be just the needed energizer. But even here the casting idea can be viewed many ways. To his credit, Thomson gave black artists an unprecedented opportunity to topple stereotypes and portray Spanish saints in what would be an elegant and historic production. However, the fact of their color was used to sully, in a sense, the rarefied white world of opera.

Two essential elements of the production were arranged during Thomson's stay in New York in early 1933. A conductor was chosen: Alexander Smallens, born in St. Petersburg, raised in New York City, formerly the music director of the Philadelphia Civic Opera, and currently the assistant to Leopold Stokowski at the Philadelphia Orchestra. A hearty character with bushy eyebrows, a thick mustache, and a voice that carried like a basso profundo, Smallens, then forty-five, was always a welcome guest at the Askew salons. He championed new music, having given the America premieres of Prokofiev's opera *The Love for Three Oranges* and Strauss's *Ariadne auf Naxos*. The sassy young American composers piqued his interest. Breaking down the elitism of the classical music world mattered to him. He would later in his career become a musical director at Radio City Music Hall. Smallens was intrigued by Thomson's curious opera and was willing to conduct it without fee—the arrangement that every member of the production team, including Thomson, would have to accept.

In addition, Florine Stettheimer finally agreed to design the sets and costumes. She had been considering the proposal since the winter of 1929, when her sisters told her of the one-man *Four Saints* that Thomson performed for a gathering at Van Vechten's place. A few weeks later he repeated it for Stettheimer at her Alwyn Court home, hoping to win her over. The interior of the Stettheimer residence, with "marble and gold and red velvet German-royalty style" furnishings, was ornate but "nowhere Gothic," Thomson recalled,

> There were crystal pendants everywhere and gold fringes and lace and silk curtains so much longer than the windows that they stood out in planned puffs and lay no less than two feet on the waxed floors. Throughout the house were pictures by Florine, a painter of such high wit and bright colorings as to make Matisse and Dufy seem by comparison somber.[4]

A married older brother, Walter Stettheimer, had made money as an underwear manufacturer in California and settled an income on his mother and three sisters in New York. Ettie, the youngest sister, was the most forceful and serious. She had a Ph.D. from Freiburg University and had published philosophical novels about the pursuit of intellectual beauty under a pseudonym, Henrie Waste. At home, Carrie, the eldest, was a gracious hostess for teas and parties. She was also the chief housekeeper, though unhappy about it. Reading, learning, and conversation were her pleasures. Carrie spent twenty years constructing an elaborate dollhouse, with a foyer, library, salon, kitchen, nursery, linen rooms, bedrooms, and baths; and with miniature paintings donated by artist friends, including a mini-version of Duchamp's *Nude Descending a Staircase* made by Duchamp himself. The dollhouse now reposes in the Museum of the City of New York.

Florine, the middle sister, was frail and petite. Prominent blue veins streaked her thin white arms. Yet, with her Prince Valiant hair and penetrating gaze, she was a formidable woman, unhappy with the heavy sense of Germanic responsibility that kept the Stettheimer sisters home with their mother, who never appeared at the socials. She refused to sell her paintings and only once displayed them publicly in a solo exhibit—at the Knoedler Gallery in 1916. The quizzical reactions to Stettheimer's fanciful work distressed her sisters, who, consequently, were against her venturing out again, especially in so public a venue as the theater.

But Florine's interest in Virgil's opera was apparent, because in the next year, 1930, she painted a whimsical yet mystical Virgil Thomson portrait with an evocation of Virgil playing his opera on the piano against a backdrop of heavenly tulle and fleece. In the lower right corner a lion chained to a rainbow sits on a podlike cushion, recalling the stone lions that are chained to the portal of the cathedral of Avila, which Florine had seen in a photograph and been much moved by. Sharp shafts of light flood upon apparitions of Saint Teresa and Saint Ignatius; "St. Virgil" and "St. Gertrude" and "Florine St." peer from a fleecy, tinseled heaven. And much of this imagery would wind up in Stettheimer's sets and costumes for *Four Saints*.

Thomson loved the painting, except for one embarrassing detail. Floating in the clouds of tulle are a toy theater, a dove of peace—and a black pansy, an obvious and playful reference to Thomson's homosexuality. Later in life he admitted to being worried at the time that people "would get it." But friends had assured him that the unknowing never would, and the knowing knew already.

Thomson was convinced that Stettheimer was the only choice for designer. The fact that she was distant from the subject matter, being a German-American Jew, and from the theater, having never designed for the stage, was to him an advantage. Her paintings were "very high camp," he believed, and "high camp is the only thing you can do with a religious subject"; anything else gets "sentimental and unbelievable"; whereas high camp taps into the innocence of true faith.

In many ways, Virgil was thriving. The New York modern-art distributors had taken him up as a cause. His champions, all shapers of the American avant-garde, were like-minded men who treated their varied homosexual inclinations not as shameful perversities but as curiosities to be explored discreetly. Being men of high social position, they felt entitled to indulge themselves and would not be judged by people with less intellectual accomplishment.

Although Virgil admired their way of handling themselves, even he didn't have that type of intellectual arrogance. Call it what you will, he still felt "queer." Resentments welled up in him. Yes, he was being taken up by the art museum world. But all this self-promotion was tiring. Whereas Copland was being championed by Koussevitzky and all but officially running the League of Composers, Virgil spent evening after evening courting museum trustees and patrons. With prospective backers he was appropriately charming. But he was surly and short-tempered with everyone else.

At Philip Johnson's apartment, the German-born manservant Rudolf threatened to resign if Virgil, "the man who came to dinner," came much longer.[5] Virgil won back favor in the household by helping Philip's younger sister, Theodate, with her singing career. After graduating from Wellesley in 1929, Theodate had studied voice in Boston. Now she wished to move to New York. Theodate "was getting set to be a singer," Thomson later wrote; "as a brunette with blazing eyes and a jacket of leopard skin, she was looking operatic absolutely."[6]

Philip offered to present Virgil and Theodate in a musical soiree at his apartment to which museum trustees would be invited. This might help Theodate and would certainly help the *Four Saints* campaign. Virgil engaged four string players from the New York Philharmonic, who performed the premiere of his String Quartet no. 2. Theodate sang his pensive, tender, and lyrically supple *Stabat Mater*, for soprano and string quartet, a work of just five minutes, but one of his most serenely beautiful. The *Stabat Mater* performance was so successful that it had to be repeated. Even though after the concert Virgil drank too much champagne punch and got embarrassingly sick, Mrs. John D. Rockefeller, among others, left smiling. When the evening ended, Philip told Virgil to consider his travel loan of $200 as a fee for services rendered.

Four days later in early April 1933, Virgil sailed for France. A dinner for twelve at the Askews had constituted his send-off party. He had done what he could for now to promote the opera. The next step was for Chick Austin to raise money and finalize the plans for his museum's new wing. Virgil's assignment was formidable enough: Gertrude Stein's approval of the production plans was going to have to be secured. Should she want to involve herself directly, well, Virgil was not sure whether that would be helpful or harmful. In any event, they had not spoken or communicated in over two years. Virgil was damned if he was going to make the first move. But, to his surprise, Gertrude spared him the trouble.

In January 1933, care of Philip Johnson's New York address, Virgil Thomson received a letter from William Aspenwall Bradley, Gertrude Stein's literary representative. The Hartford-born Bradley had served in France in World War I, met and married, at forty-two, a French-woman, and settled in Paris to become an editor and literary agent for some notable writers—Henry Miller, Ezra Pound, John Dos Passos, Thornton Wilder, among them. None were harder to handle than Stein.

Gertrude had heard of the plans for the premiere. So Mr. Bradley wrote a courtly letter to Virgil asking for details. In his reply Virgil told of his planned return to Paris and suggested a meeting, which happened in May. Following this, in a long letter to Gertrude, Mr. Bradley reported on the production plans to date, adding his observation that the "froid" between Gertrude and Virgil "seems to count for little or nothing" in Virgil's attitude and expressing the hope that he could serve as "peacemaker."[7] Gertrude's pointed reply, which Bradley copied word for word, was dated May 15:

> Dear Mr. Thomson,
>   Here is what Miss Stein says in comment on your letter which I sent her:
> Of course I can tell very little by description of what they are going to do, you can only tell when you see the maquettes, and I suppose they have good reasons for using negro singers instead of white, there are certain obvious ones, but I do not care for the idea of showing the negro bodies, it is too much what the English in what they call "modernistic" novels call futuristic and does not accord with the words and music to my mind. I liked Virgil's original Sunday school ideas on the whole better, but still it is up to them to make a success of the performance, I do not wish to be critical, the great thing is to get it done and successfully done for both his sake and mine.[8]

What she meant by the "certain obvious" reasons for using Negro singers is not at all clear (though it may have been a snide reference to Thomson's and Van Vechten's fondness for black men). Her distaste with the idea of exposing Negro bodies refers to Florine's suggestion that the cast be clothed in transparent costumes.

Virgil wanted to address Gertrude's concerns. It would have been possible to meet, for she and Alice had not yet left for their summer stay in the country. But Virgil and Gertrude had not even written to each other directly. What finally made him swallow his pride and write was that negotiations were threatening to break down, even with the tactful Mr. Bradley as buffer, over two contractual disputes. "I am taking the liberty of mentioning a business matter which I have already spoken of to Mr. Bradley," he wrote with caution and courtesy in a letter to Gertrude on May 30:

> At the beginning of my conversation with him I mentioned that although the usual practice was otherwise, I preferred, in view of the closeness of our collaboration and of the importance given to the text in my score, to offer you a 50–50 division of all profits. It has since been called to my attention by the Société des Droits d'Auteurs that such an arrangement defeats its own end and that the contract commonly made in France allowing two-thirds to the composer and one to the author is designed to establish that very equality;
>
> 1) because the manual labor involved in musical composition is so much greater than that of writing words that half the proceeds is an insufficient return for the composer, considering him as a joint worker,
>
> 2) because a literary work is perfectly saleable separate from the music and this brings further profit to its author, whereas the music is rarely saleable in any way separated from the text it was designed to accompany.
>
> The 2–1 division of profits is already, it would seem, to the advantage of the author in that an inferior text is assured of paying profits as long as the music lives, and a poem of merit is in no way injured in its independent literary career by the performance of an inferior musical setting. . . .
>
> In view of these considerations would you consider it just on my part to ask that our projected contracts (and any eventual publication of the score) be based on the 2–1 rather than the 1–1 division of profits, a proportion which, as I said above, is the one used in France to secure an equable division of benefits?[9]

Regarding Gertrude's fears of naked Negro bodies, Virgil added in a subsequent section,

> Naturally, if the transparent clothes turned out in rehearsal to be a stronger effect than we intended, petticoats would be ordered immediately for everybody. I think the idea is worth trying, however. If it can be realized inoffensively, the bodies would merely add to our spectacle the same magnificence they give to classic

religious painting and sculpture. One could not easily use this effect with white bodies, but I think one might with brown.

My negro singers, after all, are a purely musical desideratum, because of their rhythm, their style and especially their diction. Any further use of their racial qualities must be incidental and not of a nature to distract attention from the subject matter. . . . Hence, the idea of painting their faces white. Nobody wants to put on just a nigger show. The project remains doubtful, anyway, till I find proper soloists.

Gertrude's fears of exposing Negro bodies were largely calmed even before both this idea and that of using whiteface were dropped. Not so her displeasure with Virgil's suggestion for a two-to-one split of the profits. She was even more upset over another issue, the second reef upon which these negotiations nearly foundered.

It was standard practice in such ventures to stipulate that no production or publication of a joint work, in part or in whole, could be accepted by either author or composer without full acceptance by the other, "such acceptance not to be unreasonably withheld." Virgil wanted the protection of this "unreasonably withheld" clause because he anticipated that in this case most future productions would be secured by the composer, not the author. But Gertrude was not going to allow anything so intangible as her own or Virgil's reasonableness to become a contractual issue. In this matter Mr. Bradley was on Virgil's side. Furthermore, Gertrude had insisted that in all future productions Mr. Bradley be the agent for both herself and Virgil. This, Bradley carefully explained in a letter to Stein, was unfair.

It is quite conceivable that Thomson, who has been very nice in all this so far as I am concerned, might still for one reason or another wish to avail himself of the services of another agent at some future time for a second or third contract. I cannot, therefore, very well impose myself upon him in perpetuity, as would be the case were your instructions adhered to.[10]

Gertrude relented on this point. But she was immovable on the two major contractual disputes, though in a June 6 letter she tried to whisk away the unpleasantness with her practiced cordiality.

My dear Virgil,

Have just received your letter. I think, in fact, I wish to keep to the original terms of our agreement, half share of profits. It is quite true that upon you falls all the burden of seeing the production through but on the other hand, the commercial value of my name is very considerable and therefore we will keep it 50-50. The only point in the agreement between [us] is the one referring to the phrase, unreasonably withheld, Bradley will have told you that I think that we should take for granted one another's reasonableness. . . . As I xplained to Bradley long xperience had taught us that if we are to be together in this thing we are to be together all the way through.[11]

Virgil's response was immediate and withering:

Dear Gertrude,

Thank you for your kind and frank letter. If the only reason, however, of holding to a 50-50 division, aside from the natural enough desire to obtain as favorable an arrangement as possible, is the commercial value of your name, I should like to protest that although your name has a very great publicity value as representing the highest quality of artistic achievement, its purely commercial value, especially in connection with a work as hermetic in style as *Four Saints,* is somewhat less, as I have found in seeking a publisher for our various joint works, although I have found a publisher for other works of mine. Moreover, it is not the value of your name or the devotion of your admirers (I except Mrs. Chadbourne, who began very practically indeed but didn't continue very long) that is getting this opera produced, but my friends and admirers, Mr. Austin and Mr. Smallens and Florine and Maurice, who are all giving their services at considerable expense to themselves, and a dozen other friends, who are contributing $100 or more each to Mr. Austin's costly & absolutely disinterested enterprise. The value of your name has never produced any gesture from these people, whereas every one of them has on other occasions manifested his interest in my work by creating commercial engagements for me and by offering me further collaborations with himself. And dear Gertrude, if you knew the resistance I have encountered in connection with that text and overcome, the amount of reading it and singing it and praising it and commenting it I have done, the articles, the lectures, the private propaganda that has been necessary in Hartford and in New York to silence the opposition that thought it wasn't having any Gertrude Stein, you wouldn't talk to me about the commercial advantages of your name. Well, they *are* having it and they are going to *like* it and it isn't your name or your lieutenants that are giving it to them. If you hadn't put a finger on a sensitive spot by mentioning this to me, I should never have done so to you. However, I've got it off my chest now and the fact remains that even were the situation reversed a 50-50 contract would be, so far as I know, absolutely without precedent. . . .[12]

Gertrude was unflustered by Virgil's rebuke. By now she had a good rebuttal. Mr. Bradley's unceasing efforts on Gertrude's behalf had finally paid off. In January he placed Gertrude's most accessible book, *The Autobiography of Alice B. Toklas,* with two publishers, Bodley Head in England and Harcourt, Brace in America. Alfred Harcourt personally wrote to Bradley with an enthusiastic acceptance: "It is an extraordinary and extraordinarily interesting book and we are looking forward eagerly to the sensation its publication is apt to cause."[13] Moreover, in May and June, just as this dispute with Virgil was raging, the first two of four excerpts from the book were published in the *Atlantic Monthly.* So Gertrude finally could boast some commercial success, though she almost wrecked the deal with Harcourt by insisting that Bradley "force Harcourt's hand" to make them also publish her endless novel *The Making of Americans.* Fortunately, Bradley was able to talk her out of this ill-conceived maneuver.

Gertrude wrote to Virgil from the country to argue that everything had now changed.

> My dear Virgil,
>   Yes yes yes, but nous avons changé tout cela, but the important thing is this, the opera was a collaboration, and the proposition made to me in the agreement was in the spirit of that collaboration, 50-50, and the proposition that I accepted was in the spirit of that collaboration, 50-50 and the proposition that I continue to accept is the same. When in the future you write operas and have texts from various writers it will be as you and the precedents arrange, but our opera was a collaboration, we own it together and we divide the proceeds 50-50, and we hope that the proceeds will be abundant and we wish each other every possible good luck.
>
> Always,
Gtrde Stein[14]

Thomson caved in on this issue. Having "injudiciously proposed it" himself, as he later told Mr. Bradley, he could not correct the error when Stein objected. But he did get her to accept the "unreasonably withheld" phrase, which he considered a necessity. Before Thomson sailed back to New York in November, the contract was signed and witnessed. Mr. Bradley carried the papers from author to composer. They still declined to meet in person, even though Stein and Toklas had returned to Paris at summer's end.

The very month that Thomson set off to supervise the entire production, which had yet to secure a director, to choose a cast, and to transform Stettheimer's playbox miniature sets and costumes into a theatrical realization, the very month that Stein, who was not planning to attend, should have been most supportive of her composer colleague, she allowed a literary journal called *Story* to publish her only slightly fictionalized account of the breakup with Thomson and Georges Hugnet. In this version, titled "Left to Right," Hugnet is a man named Arthur William, who comes to the narrator with a joint-book proposal. The project causes a strain between them. Thomson is Generale Erving, a writer ("that is to say he had written not writing but something"), who offers to repair the damaged feelings and broker a compromise. It turns out terribly, with the narrator refusing to grant permission to the editor to issue anything.

> When I had waited a little longer I said to the editor that I was not giving her anything and so Arthur did not come to have anything and that was all over. I did however have something and I kept everything and I can use everything. I sent a card to Generale Erving and I said I did not want to have any further acquaintance with him.
>
> And now before I go out I always look up and down to see that none of them are coming. We were after that never friends or anything. This is all this true story and it was exciting.[15]

Everyone in the Stein and Thomson circle knew all about their argument. They would have recognized the lead players in this short story. Thomson knew that the piece had been written in the bitter aftermath of the events it chronicles. So he was prepared to overlook Stein's harsh depiction of his motives. But the timing of this publication was tactless and hurtful. Still, the contract was signed, and there was nothing left to do for now but plow on and try to be positive.

Chick Austin had come up with an unusual idea for sponsoring the *Four Saints* production. It had to do with the fledgling attempts by young Lincoln Kirstein, whom Austin had met at the Askew salon, to establish a school of ballet in America. Austin decided that this enterprising, visionary project must happen, and it must happen in Hartford.

Lincoln Kirstein was the grandson of a German Jewish radical who had exiled himself after the revolutions of 1848 to Rochester, New

York, where he became a lens grinder at the optical factory of Bausch and Lomb. Lincoln's father, uninterested in the family business, married the young daughter of a cultured Jewish family and eventually worked with great success for the Filene and Sons retail company in Boston, where the family lived in a splendid four-story Victorian home on Commonwealth Avenue in the Back Bay.

Tall, lanky, with angular features, close-cropped hair, a brooding nature, and restless intellect, Lincoln Kirstein entered Harvard in 1926 and came under the stern Presbyterian tutelage of Alfred Barr, Jr. For a time he thought he might became a painter. He studied dance seriously, but was too long-limbed and hulky for a professional career. His poetry was admired by Thomson's Harvard mentor, S. Foster Damon. But Kirstein grew to feel that his talents were organizational and conceptual. He founded his own journal, *Hound and Horn,* and for seven years turned it into a noted publication of arts and commentary, attracting support (and contributions) from T. S. Eliot and Ezra Pound. During repeated trips through Europe he saw the ballet company of Diaghilev and was seized with the idea of establishing an American counterpart. He had already been steered to the twenty-eight-year-old Russian choreographer George Balanchine as a potential artistic director. This is where Virgil Thomson played his pivotal role.

Kirstein had met Thomson through Foster Damon in 1929. Four years later, when Kirstein settled in Paris for a while, he made a point of situating himself in the Hôtel du Quai Voltaire, next to Thomson's building. Thomson introduced Kirstein to his Paris artist and author friends. More important, he became a sounding board for Kirstein's ill-formed and unrealistic ballet school plans. Night after night Kirstein climbed the five floors up to Thomson's studio and talked with him for hours.

"Virgil was a genius at social manipulation," Kirstein later recalled. "I don't know where or how he learned it. Perhaps from observing those aristocratic and socially agile French families—Bernard Faÿ, Madame Langlois."[16] Kirstein approached Thomson with a sketchy plan, big hopes, and small experience. Thomson disabused him of his wilder notions, Kirstein recalled, taking him through the means by which he must infiltrate societal structures to make his plan happen. The decisive influence of Thomson's tutoring is clear in Kirstein's published diaries.

July 19, 1933; Paris

> Virgil Thomson knows of my interest in an American ballet, but he made clear the importance of money: whose money? how much? how certain?
>
> . . . No one has understood the politics of lyric theater, painting or musical institutions as well as Virgil Thomson. His intelligence is analytical, surgical, cheerful, realistic; it is optimistic in spite of an unsentimental manner which is the passionate reverse of enthusiastic. Instruction from him let me see many factors in depth; his portraits of persons were objective and unromantic; his attitudes toward the company I hoped one day to form, helpful and cautious. He paid me the compliment of assuring that what I declared I wished to do could be done. In Paris I was dazzled by theatrical activity which for the first time I saw at first hand. He undazzled me. He revealed the skull beneath the skin of personages whom I tended to take on trust from their reputation. He showed me many ways to do what I wanted.[17]

Shortly after making this entry, Kirstein cornered Balanchine at the summer season of the Askew salon in London, courting him (a "headlong onslaught," he later called it) with promises of young blood, unjaded patrons, and free rein. Knowing that Chick Austin had expressed interest in the American ballet school, Kirstein sent a rambling, impassioned letter.

> My pen burns in my hand as I write: words will not flow into the ink fast enough. We have a real chance to have an American ballet within three years' time. When I say ballet—I mean a trained company of young dancers—not Russians—but Americans with Russian stars to start with—a company superior to the dregs of the old Diaghilev company.[18]

He spoke of his discovery, George Balanchine.

> He is personally enchanting—dark, very slight—a superb dancer and the most ingenious technician in ballet I have ever seen—I stake my life on his talent. . . . He could achieve a miracle, and right under our eyes. . . . Please rack your brains and try to make this all come true. . . . We have the future in our hands.

Chick Austin was smitten. Somehow, the triple premiere planned for early 1934—the opening of the new wing, the first Picasso retrospective in America, and *Four Saints*—had to become a quadruple premiere, including the inauguration of Kirstein's company at the Wadsworth Atheneum.

Meanwhile, Thomson must have suspected that Kirstein was holding out on him; for in their talks Virgil turned testy.

July 21, 1933

Lunch with Virgil Thomson. I had W. H. Auden's *Orators* with me; he picked it up; he asked me to tell him what it was "in one word." Made me furious; the greatest poem in English since *The Waste Land;* so I said nothing. And also nothing about Balanchine. He's so preoccupied with producing *Four Saints* he'd think I was trying to sabotage it with our ballet scheme for Hartford; he'd be right.[19]

When Thomson learned that Austin was considering letting Balanchine stage *Four Saints* as the inaugural event of his new company, he was not thrilled. Austin's promises to Thomson of money for part copying and subsistence had never materialized. *Four Saints* was an opera, not a ballet. Balanchine sounded like someone he could not control.

Thomson would not have to worry for long. In October, Balanchine, in poor health and impatient, visited Hartford and was stunned by its provincialism. Two Italian sisters who ran a ballet school whipped up opposition in the local press to this invading Bolshevik. Adequate funding had not been secured. Balanchine promptly left for New York.

Kirstein's persistence paid off. The School of American Ballet, with Balanchine as artistic and Kirstein as executive director, opened in New York in 1934. Afterward the two men started three successive companies: the American Ballet, the Ballet Caravan, and, in 1948, the New York City Ballet, which would change the face of international dance.

But for now, Austin's Hartford escapade with Balanchine and Kirstein was over. He could turn his attention again to supervising the construction of his new wing and to raising funds for *Four Saints*. For this he turned to his makeshift outfit, the Friends and Enemies of Modern Music, which had never produced anything beyond chamber music concerts in the roomier living rooms of Hartford's finer families.

16 A KNOCKOUT AND A WOW

Virgil Thomson arrived in New York on Halloween day, 1933, ready to commandeer the production of *Four Saints in Three Acts*. As previously arranged, he moved into the guest room at the Askews'. The opera was scheduled to open in Hartford at the end of January, but with construction of the new Avery Memorial Wing of the Atheneum behind schedule and so many details of the production yet to be determined, the January date was looking doubtful. Austin promised a budget of $10,000, but after receiving initial gifts from Jessie K. Lasell and Austin's art museum colleague Edward Warburg, the fund-raising campaign was petering out. Contributions from sympathetic individuals, like Paul Sachs of Harvard, were coming in dribs and drabs along with apologetic but well-wishing personal notes. A director and cast had yet to be selected, and Thomson had no clue how to proceed with either task.

In a sense, Thomson was reluctant to recruit a director with too much experience. He had very definite ideas about the desired style and look for his opera. This argued against using someone with too strong a creative personality. However, black singers with operatic experience simply did not exist. Assuming Thomson could even assemble an all-black cast, they were going to need skillful direction. A friend from Paris, Lewis Galantière, a multilingual French-American who was doing translations, knew someone he thought Thomson should consider—John Houseman, then thirty-one.

Houseman had little to recommend him. He was born in Bucharest, the son of a British mother of Welsh-Irish descent and a Jewish-Alsatian father, whose work in the international futures markets meant frequent household dislocations and volatile family finances. For stability, young John had been sent to Chilton, a proper English public school, where he acquired a high-class British accent that would serve him well in his early years as an international trader, and in his late years as a curmudgeonly character actor.

Houseman's success in school had pointed to an academic career. A scholarship from Trinity College was offered him, but a sense of duty to his widowed mother and a passivity born of his rootlessness propelled him into business. Somehow, this tall, pudgy, chronically insecure young man became a merchant prince of the international grain market, working as a dealer and speculator until 1929, when his New York export firm, his finances, and, eventually, his marriage (to a temperamental Hungarian-American actress, Zita Johann) collapsed along with the stock market.

For two years Houseman dabbled in the theater, coauthoring two plays fashioned from preexisting scenarios, working with Galantière as a play doctor to two more, and adapting a French farce for Broadway. This hardly amounted to a career.

> Through luck, shrewd associations and my knowledge of languages I had managed to gain a slippery toe hold in the theatre and to earn the few hundred dollars of option money and advances on which I was managing to subsist. But it was not a way of life and I knew it. Quite soon now I must find regular work in a profession in which I had a vague accretion of superficial knowledge but no training, no craft, no special skill or experience of any sort. In normal times there would have been little reason for anyone to employ me; in mid-depression with so many thousands of theatre people out of work, it was unthinkable—all the more since I myself seemed to have no clear notion of the capacity in which I was preparing to offer myself for hire.[1]

Since his days at Harvard, Thomson had had a way of overwhelming aimless younger men with his own certainty about the paths they should follow. Briggs Buchanan, Maurice Grosser, Christian Bérard, Emmanuel Faÿ, Philip Johnson, Lincoln Kirstein—all had experienced Thomson's onslaught of advice; all, at least for a while, had followed it. John Houseman was to be another in this line.

One day in mid-November 1933, Galantière brought Houseman

to the Askew salon, where he had arranged for him to meet Thomson. Houseman had admired some works by Gertrude Stein. Of Thomson and the opera he knew nothing. After greeting his hosts and accepting a drink, he was led to a "small, vivacious man" with a "pale face, a piercing voice, precise articulation and a will power that became evident within thirty seconds of meeting him."[2] Thomson steered Houseman through the crowd, taking him first to a nook of the piano, then moving to a sofa in the library, where he talked for close to an hour about his opera. Thomson was impressed by Houseman's international education and sophistication. "He asked me what I had done in the theatre," Houseman recalled, "and I told him the truth, which did not seem to disturb him."[3] The next day, they met at the Hotel Leonori, where a friend of Askew's had lent Thomson a studio with a piano. For two hours Thomson played and sang the entire opera in his reedy tenor voice. Houseman was perplexed but enthralled: ". . . I sat there trying to look intelligent and appreciative and hoping with all my soul that he would invite me to work with him."[4] He did so two days later. Houseman accepted, understanding that there was no money in it. So began "the busiest and most decisive weeks" of Houseman's life.

Given that *Four Saints* was a mystifying work and the Depression was sabotaging America's culture, Thomson was not exactly deluged with offers from experienced directors. Nevertheless, picking Houseman was a risky move. For the rest of his life, Houseman would admit that he was never really sure just why Thomson had wanted him. In an interview after Houseman's death, Thomson answered the question by extolling Houseman's intelligence, eagerness, and efficiency. But the bottom line, Thomson said, was this: "I could control him."

> Jack was never first-class as a director. He always had somebody around with quicker ideas, and he would use them as assistants. But what he could do with his smooth English manners was arrange compromises and rob one till and put it in another and make the money last when he didn't have enough, and find out who could get what for free and who were the very best people to bring together. He was a marvelous, creative producer. He didn't have original ideas as a director. And he knew it. But he didn't like it rubbed in.[5]

Thomson didn't rub it in. Though he would be listed as director on the *Four Saints* program book, Houseman understood his real role, to be "some sort of director-producer-impresario." Given his green-ness, this was daunting enough.

> We had ten thousand dollars and nine and a half weeks in which to find a cast, coach and rehearse them in two hours of unfamil-iar music and complicated stage action, execute scenery and cos-tumes, rehearse a new score, move to Hartford in an unfinished theatre with an orchestra of twenty and a cast of forty-three, set up, light, dress rehearse and open cold before one of the world's most sophisticated audiences. With the slightest theatrical experi-ence I would have realized the impossibility of our task. In my total ignorance I assumed the job in a mood of irresistible eu-phoria.[6]

Shortly afterwards, Houseman ventured with Thomson to the studio of Florine Stettheimer, downtown from her Alwyn Court apartment—a large single room overlooking Bryant Park, which ad-joins the New York Public Library. Stettheimer was fascinated with cel-lophane, then a new industrial material; her windows were curtained with it. The furnishings were exotic: white chairs, tables of glass and gold. In three boxes Stettheimer had constructed exactingly detailed models of the sets she wanted, with cellophane backdrops, crystal bead archways, emerald grass, and pink and white palm trees. Minia-ture dolls were draped in ecclesiastical robes, all in primary colors. Houseman thought the designs exquisite, but was worried about their execution. "Over tea and a homemade Viennese cake she listened while I expressed my admiration and tried to indicate (out of the depths of my inexperience) some of the problems we might en-counter in translating her delicate, diminutive models and special ma-terials to the theatre."[7] He suggested that a friend of his, Kate Drain Lawson, a technical director, formerly with the Theatre Guild, serve as executant. Lawson was a large-and-in-charge type who prided her-self on her ability to devise practical realizations of designers' and di-rectors' often impractical fantasies. As Houseman extolled Lawson's work, Stettheimer was torn. She did not understand why her ideas and the materials she wanted could not be exactly translated onto a stage. For now, she checked her concerns. But the working relation-ship between Stettheimer and Lawson was to be stormy from the start.

The time had come to recruit a cast and chorus. For this Thom-son would need one of those Harlem go-betweens. In later life Thom-son could not remember who put him in touch with Edward Perry. It may have been Carl Van Vechten, who seemed to know everybody in Harlem. More likely it was Edna Thomas, one of the most renowned black actresses in New York, who lived with her longtime lover, Olivia Windham, a British aristocrat with a modest inherited income. Like other prominent and professional Negroes, Edna Thomas was welcome at the Askew salon, though the unspoken but unbroken policy was that a black could come only as the guest of a white.

Edward Perry—impeccably dressed, chain-smoking, deferential—proved to be invaluable. Knowing that Thomson had been impressed by the all-Negro musical *Run, Little Chillun!*—a drama of conflict between Christian and African religious heritages, which had opened on Broadway in March of 1933 and starred Edna Thomas—Perry suggested that he contact the chorus for that show, the respected Hall Johnson Choir. But Johnson accepted singers who learned music by rote. Thomson wanted trained vocalists. Perry suggested calling Eva Jessye, whose singers, he had been told, could read music.

Eva Jessye, the daughter of slaves set free after the Civil War, was born the year before Thomson in Coffeyville, Kansas. Thanks to the sacrifices of her entire extended family, she was able to attend Western University, in Kansas City. She taught in segregated schools in Oklahoma, worked for a time on a newspaper in Baltimore, then headed to New York in 1922 to pursue a career as a choral director, an unprecedented leap for a black woman. She supported herself ironing shirts for thirteen dollars a week, and finally got a job as a warm-up singer in movie theaters. She formed a choir, trained its members hard, and secured them work on Broadway singing what white promoters thought of as Negro music: "Old Black Joe," "Massa's in da Cold Cold Ground," "That's Why Darkies Are Born." Her break came in 1926 when her ensemble started singing regularly on the *Major Bowes Family Radio Hour.* The next year she founded the choir that would bear her name for five decades. In 1929 she supplied music for a major Hollywood film, King Vidor's all-Negro epic *Hallelujah.* But she took whatever came along. The choir provided music for a religious program on radio station WOR called *Thoughts at Sunset.* In groups of eight they would perform at churches in all the boroughs of New York and be paid from the collection plate, maybe two dollars each, most times just one dollar. Sometimes Miss Jessye would hold out on them. "Who told you you were getting two dollars each?" she would yell. Her singers understood what was going on. Miss Jessye had to hold back. At least she was getting them work.

The Hall Johnson Choir, some sixty voices, was renowned for its robust sound and power. But the Eva Jessye Choir, usually just sixteen singers, never more than twenty, cultivated clarity and articulation. Tough and abrupt, Jessye was a taskmaster. "Evil Jessye," her singers sometimes called her. But how else could a black woman in the white male music world operate?

In late November, Edward Perry brought Virgil Thomson to meet Eva Jessye in her voice studio in a brownstone on 133rd Street near Seventh Avenue. She found Thomson conceited and condescending; he thought Jessye uppity. But they needed each other. Thomson doubted that her singers were as trained as she claimed. But he saw little alternative. Jessye did not know what to make of the opera that Thomson showed her. But she wanted this job. Prominent members of the white artistic world were promising a lavish production, and for once her singers would not portray demeaning racial stereotypes.

Thomson left Jessye with some sections of the score. It was arranged that he would return the next day at 10:00 A.M. to hear her singers sight-read the parts. Looking at the music, Jessye couldn't believe it: block-chord, church-harmony settings of incomprehensible lines ("Might have as would be as would be as within within nearly as out.") Her choir would be confounded. The truth was that not all of her singers could read music. So she told them to arrive at 8 A.M.; then she stayed up most the night deciphering the score.

The next morning Miss Jessye and her singers made much progress. She dismissed them at nine-thirty. Thomson showed up fifteen minutes later. When the choir members returned at ten and sang the parts right off, Thomson was reportedly staggered by their sight-reading skills. The subterfuge had been successful. The Eva Jessye Choir got the job.

Late in life Thomson dismissed this story, saying that all choirs, except for the top-rank professional ensembles, accept singers of varying skills, that it's traditional for less trained choristers to rely on others to learn their notes, and that he suspected the singers had practiced the parts beforehand. But a surviving member of the chorus confirmed Jessye's version of the story.

In any event, Miss Jessye had not finished negotiating. She insisted that her singers, who would have to give up daytime jobs and other musical work, be paid not only for performances but for rehearsals, an extraordinary request. Thomson balked, then gave in. The singers would be paid fifteen dollars a week, which, at the depth of the Depression, was very decent money. "We were thrilled with that," recalled one chorister, Tommy Anderson. "Why I could get five pounds of apples, three pork chops, five of those big rolls, a stick of butter and some jam for a dollar. You could live on $15 a week."[8]

Next, with Houseman's input, Thomson would have to cast the leads. Edward Perry was again the contact. Auditions were held either at the Askew's East Side house or at Eva Jessye's studio. One key role, that of Saint Ignatius, was quickly cast. Even Thomson had heard of Edward Matthews, a singer from Boston who already was enjoying as much of a concert career as a black American in the 1930s could hope to have. He was light-skinned and distinguished looking; though slight of build, he commanded the stage. His voice, though not enormous, was rich and incisive. A finely educated musician, Matthews later taught voice at Howard University and Virginia State College.

When Abner Dorsey showed up to audition, Thomson thought of him immediately as the Compère. Dashing and gracious, Dorsey had worked mostly in vaudeville. But he read music, his bass voice was lyrical, and he sang with conversational naturalness. He was perfect for the Compère, who is, essentially, the host for the opera. For his counterpart and cohost, the Commère, Edward Matthews suggested his wife, Altonell Hines, who was then singing with Eva Jessye. The Virginia-born Hines held a music degree from Livingstone College, in North Carolina, and a master's degree in education from Columbia. Other roles took longer to fill. Eventually, Bruce Howard was cast as Saint Teresa II. Though not so skilled a musician, she had a creamy contralto voice, worked hard, and never missed a rehearsal. She was strikingly beautiful. "The older boys would cluster around her and play gin rummy," Thomson recalled. "She was like a honey pot." Houseman remembered a darker side to Howard's life: "a voluptuous, lethargic girl whose lover, a liveried chauffeur, used to collect her at rehearsals and beat her from time to time."[9] Embry Bonner was cast as Saint Chavez, and this turned out to be a miscalculation. Bonner dressed in furs and silk scarves and put on airs. He was urged on Thomson by a friend, then a Chinese art authority at the Metropolitan Museum, who was Bonner's male lover. Bonner had a spectacular but out-of-control tenor voice and scant musical background. It soon became clear that he was in over his head.

Thirteen other named roles, most of them quite small, were eventually cast, some with members of Jessye's choir. But by the time rehearsals started at Jessye's studio, the lead, Saint Teresa I, had still not been selected, though Thomson had auditioned several contenders. Caterina Jarboro, the closest Harlem had to a Negro diva, was approached. She had just sung in a production of *Aida* at the Hippodrome. But she was not right—too much a diva and too expensive. Edward Perry talked up a young alto in Philadelphia, Marian Anderson. But Saint Teresa I was a high soprano; and, besides, Miss Anderson was perplexed by the prospect of being one of two characters named Saint Teresa.

Rehearsals proceeded without a Saint Teresa I. At first the members of the cast sat with their scores. Thomson insisted that they at least be able to get through their parts reading their scores before any blocking was tried out. It soon became clear that Jessye's studio was too cramped. She was given permission to rehearse in the basement of St. Philip's Church, down the street from her brownstone. The actual entrance to the church—a magnificent granite-and-brick building with an alabaster altar and panels of stained-glass windows built in 1911, the first church in Harlem designed by black architects—was on 134th Street. In the basement of the church was a large room, broken up by columns with radiators high up on the walls that clanked all winter and kept the space hot and arid. St. Philip's was the "hoity-toity Harlem church," Tommy Anderson recalled. "They liked the fact that all these fine Negroes and fancy white people were working there."[10]

Perry came up with another suggestion for Saint Teresa I, Olive Hopkins, a classically trained soprano who had begun singing jazz. But Hopkins was just then going off to Europe to sing on tour with Chick Webb's big band. She recommended a friend, Beatrice Robinson Wayne, who, it will be remembered, was disinvited by Thomson to his ninetieth birthday production of *Four Saints* more than fifty years later.

Beatrice Robinson Wayne was not given a private audition. Instead, she was told to come to a rehearsal at St. Philip's. At first sight, she was not striking. Stocky, pug-nosed, her hair pulled tight in a bun, she walked with a slight limp. She was in mourning for her mother and aunt—both had recently died—and wore a plain black dress, a black coat, and no jewelry. A devout Christian, she was still recovering from the breakup of her marriage to Ivanhoe Wayne eighteen months earlier. Thomson, who was directing the rehearsal from the piano, was dismayed. "Are you the soprano?" he asked abruptly. "Take a score and stand there."

Mrs. Wayne thought to herself, "What have I got here?" With his slicked-back hair and superior airs, puffing a cigarette through a long-stemmed amber holder ("A fool on one end and a fire on the other," was the way her grandmother, an ex-slave, used to describe people who smoked), Mr. Thomson made "the most ridiculous picture" she had ever seen.

The rest of the cast had gotten somewhat acclimated to this unorthodox opera. Mrs. Wayne looked at the nonsensical words and didn't know what to think. Thomson cued the cast to begin Act I proper, "St. Teresa in a storm at Avila." As Saint Teresa's first entrance approached, Thomson gestured to Mrs. Wayne. "Now," he shouted. She sang nothing. "Now! Now! Now!" he sputtered, in his snappish voice, jabbing his finger at the spot in the score where she was to have begun. The music stopped. Mrs. Wayne, who never swore, looked right at him and said, "What the hell's the matter with you?"

Bruce Howard turned and spoke to her softly. "You mustn't speak like that to him. He's the composer."

"I don't care who he is," Mrs. Wayne said.

Beatrice Robinson Wayne was eager to prove herself. Her musical career had been filled with obstacles. Born in New York, she was abandoned by her mother and raised by her "father's people" in Connecticut. Visiting family in New York when she was thirteen, she found her mother, had a tearful reunion, and lived with her for three years. She graduated from a Negro college in Virginia; she traveled with a touring evangelist, playing the piano and singing spirituals; she worked with choral ensembles at the Shubert and Ziegfeld theaters; most recently, as a member of the Donald Haywood Choir, she sang on the radio, where she was routinely lied to about the pay arrangements. Though she had no idea what this opera was about, she was determined to participate.

But Thomson's treatment of her was unfair. She was confident that, given time, she could learn anything. "When I hear the part, I'll be able to sing it," she told him, emphatically. Thomson must have realized that he was being rude. He wasn't used to people talking back to him. It proved effective. He calmed down and let her try again. Though she struggled, the sheer presence of her voice, shimmering with warmth and plaintive beauty, was undeniable. Her diction was impeccable. That night she stayed up studying the role diligently, and the next day things went better. Houseman was already enchanted. Her stolid appearance contrasted touchingly with her sublime singing.

She was positively saintly, a plain, strong woman who radiated inner beauty. She got the part, and no one, including Thomson, ever doubted the decision.

As Thomson questioned Houseman about his specific plans for staging the opera, he realized that his director had no strong ideas. Houseman needed help. What Thomson envisioned for this incantatory opera was closer to a baroque spectacle or religious pageant. He wanted his performers to be moved, not to be directed; he wanted them to have bearing, not to act. What they needed was a choreographer, and Thomson knew the man for the job—Frederick Ashton.

Thomson and Ashton had met the previous summer at the Askews' salon in London. At twenty-nine, Ashton was already doing choreography for the Sadler's Wells Ballet, but Thomson had not yet seen his work. Ashton's parents were English, but he was born in Ecuador and raised in Peru, where his father became an honorary consul. As a child, Frederick spoke more Spanish than English. Though not a Catholic, he attended a Dominican school and was immersed in the trappings and spectacle of the Catholic liturgy. "I still used to assist at all the masses in Lima Cathedral," he recalled. "I was the favorite acolyte of the Archbishop of Lima because I was a blond."[11] Religious pageantry had entranced him. Certainly he would comprehend what Thomson wanted in *Four Saints*.

Houseman agreed that Ashton should be sent for. When he received the cable, Ashton was completing rehearsals for his ballet *Les Rendezvous*. The *Four Saints* project was intriguing, and working with a Negro cast in New York City sounded stimulating. Ashton left for America on December 6, a day after his ballet opened to glowing reviews. ("One could ask for nothing lighter or more delicious than the new divertissement," wrote the *Daily Telegraph* critic.)[12]

Pleased with the musical progress, the Stettheimer sets, and the securing of Ashton, Thomson, forsaking all his animosity, wrote an excited letter to Gertrude Stein.

> . . . Miss Stettheimer's sets are of a beauty incredible, with trees made out of feathers and a sea-wall at Barcelona made out of shells and for the procession a baldachino of black chiffon and bunches of black ostrich plumes just like a Spanish funeral. . . . My singers, as I have wanted, are Negroes, and you can't imagine how beautifully they sing. Frederick Ashton is arriving from London this week to make choreography for us. Not only for the dance-numbers, but for the whole show, so that all the movements will

be regulated to the music, measure by measure, and all our complicated stage-action, made into a controllable spectacle.[13]

Ashton arrived on December 12, along with Maurice Grosser,
come over from Paris. Where Grosser stayed seems to have been forgotten. There was an extra bed in the Askews' guest room where
Thomson was living. That Thomson and his lover from Paris might
share a room in the Askew house was unthinkable, especially to
Thomson. Ashton got the extra bed.

The first task was to find dancers for the opera's garden party
entertainment scene, the dance of angels, and the Spanish routine for
sailors and young girls. With Edward Perry as guide, Ashton ventured
into Harlem to scout for some. At the Savoy Ballroom, three young
men doing the lindy hop impressed him. He and Perry approached
the dancers, who worked, respectively, as a pool lifeguard, a boxer,
and a cab driver. The dandified Ashton tried to explain his exotic project to these young black men. "At first they thought we were pulling
their legs," Ashton recalled. "None of them was trained, but naturally
like all Negro people they were very plastic and knew how to move."[14]
Eventually they found three young women who had had some elementary dance instruction.

The cast adored Ashton, with his funny mix of qualities: he was
campy and flamboyant, but athletic and agile; he had refined British
manners, but lost himself in outbursts of childlike enthusiasm. Just as
Thomson had wanted, Ashton choreographed the action, "standing, as
choreographers like to do, in center-stage and moving the singers
round him, at first with their music scripts in hand, so that movements
and music and words all came to be learned together."[15] He had a
habit, when caught up in work, of distractedly grabbing his buttocks,
which everyone thought hilarious. He devised movements and gestures for the cast, ways of holding their heads, positioning their feet,
walking and swaying. Ashton utilized the "natural plasticity" of his Negroes, taking cues from how they moved their bodies instinctively,
rather than imposing movements upon them. For the processional
scene ("in wed led dead"), Ashton, having been told how small the
Atheneum's stage was, devised something affecting: the cast members,
in two rows, swayed from side to side and shifted their feet in lock-
step, giving the impression of a heavy-footed funeral procession, but
in actuality hardly moving.

Musically, the rehearsals progressed steadily. Thomson shouted corrections at offending singers. But overall, he was pleased and said so. In a later account he characterized his working relationship with the black singers as "in every way rewarding," though the comments betray his plantation mentality and his proclivity for generalizations:

> Not only could they enunciate and sing; they seemed to understand because they sang. They resisted not at all Stein's obscure language, adopted it for theirs, conversed in quotations from it. They moved, sang, spoke with grace and with alacrity, took on roles without self-consciousness, as if they were the saints they said they were. I often marveled at the miracle whereby slavery (and some cross-breeding) had turned them into Christians of an earlier stamp than ours, not analytical and self-pitying or romantic in the nineteenth-century sense, but robust, outgoing, and even in disaster sustained by inner joy. . . .[16]

The Negro cast genuinely did take to the opera. Thomson's music and Stein's words fit so snugly that fifty years later surviving cast members could still sing whole lines from memory. These Harlem artists were liberated by the chance to premiere a work of such whimsical elegance and theatrical dignity. ("To think you were going to wear something besides overalls," Tommy Anderson recalled; "instead of falling down on your knees and waving your hands, 'Hallelujah!' It made a big difference in our attitudes.")[17]

But there was an undercurrent of resentment in the cast over the assumption among these educated white men that Negro people would simply accept language they didn't understand. There was something blithely patronizing, even racist, in Thomson's joy over his Negroes and the miraculous way that oppression and slavery had turned them into Christians unburdened with analytic scruples. If they accepted the opera as clever, beautiful nonsense, it wasn't for lack of intellectual curiosity, or because they possessed some ennobling simplicity. They had been given good work in terrible times. They had a responsibility to fulfill. And they didn't feel they had the right to question anything.

When Thomson, Houseman, and Ashton wanted to keep something to themselves, they spoke in French, which the cast members found intriguing but rude. Even good-hearted Maurice Grosser, who, as a southern gentleman, interacted comfortably with the black cast, was sometimes inadvertently condescending. Grosser decided he could be helpful in deciphering Stein. Though he meant well, he would rush up to the singers all anxious and fidgety, and start to de-construct the text for them ("this passage is about the spirit of America"). "That's what made me most sick," Anderson recalled. "Everybody trying to tell us what this *Four Saints* means." Eventually, Thomson felt that Grosser's constant explaining was making the cast nervous; so he ordered him to stay away from rehearsals.

One of a series of cast photographs taken by George Platt Lynes reveals the underside of the *Four Saints* story—a picture of Ashton and the lead male dancers (the lifeguard, the boxer, and the cab driver). Ashton, in a dark, three-piece suit, kneels, his upper body erect but relaxed, his head inclined down toward three young men, all of them naked, who encircle him. Two sit with their knees propped up; the other reclines, gazing up at the great white man, his legs entwined with those of his Negro brother. Ashton's left hand rests paternally on the arm of one; his right hand cradles the neck of another. From Ashton's bearing, he would seem to be saying, "How I love and care for these beautiful, simple black boys." The young men are compliant, but look not wholly comfortable, as if they had no choice. By the time *Four Saints* closed its Broadway run later that spring, Ashton had "slept with two or three of those dancers," Thomson later recounted. "They were pretty as hell, you know."[18]

That said, every surviving member of the first *Four Saints* cast talked about the experience with gratitude; and the excitement of it came alive again as they talked. "This show's no good unless everybody loves everybody," Thomson told Houseman during the heat of rehearsals.

With the stage and musical direction in good hands, Houseman was tending more to production matters. He refereed the fights between his besieged technical director, Kate Lawson, and her tormentor Florine Stettheimer, who simply could not understand why the tiny glass beads she had strung together to make archways in her models couldn't be translated into huge crystal balls on the stage, or why the proscenium couldn't be framed by genuine white lace, instead of Lawson's machine-made substitute, which Houseman explained was all they could afford. When creditors showed up, Houseman greeted them with unperturbable calm, a technique he had mastered when his grain export business was collapsing in 1929 and he went every day to the floor of the exchange, greeting people and blithely signing worthless checks.

In a savvy move, Houseman had signed up a "demon press agent," Nathan Zatkin, who drummed up curiosity about the goings

on in Harlem. Reporters started showing up at St. Philip's, like Geraldine Sartain of the *New York World-Telegram,* who wrote of this out-
landish opera with "its pink cellophane clouds, its all-Negro cast, and
its imported famous English choreographer," now scheduled to premiere in Hartford on February 8, 1934. Thomson was given several
column inches to expound on his notions of the Negro people and
their suitability for Stein. ("Negroes objectify themselves very easily,
and I think the explanation is all part of the 'threshold of consciousness' idea—they live on the surface of their consciousness.") He must
have entranced this reporter during the course of the interview by
playing and singing excerpts from the opera, for Sartain's description
of the "Heavenly chorus sounds" ("Let Lucy Lily Lucy let Lucy Lucy
Lily Lily") was ecstatic: "It was beautiful—soft, lovely, haunting music,
with the sound of words forming pictures in your mind. Further, you
heard each word, something unheard of in the usual opera, and
Thomson insists that each word shall be heard clearly to the last row
in the highest balcony."

Joseph Alsop, then a young reporter at the *New York Herald Tribune,* came several times, stoking the interest of readers with his articles.

> Arias and recitatives like no hymns that St. Philip's Protestant Epis-
> copal Sunday School children ever sang are echoing through the
> old church building. Beneath decorated texts in the dark basement,
> *Four Saints in Three Acts* is slowly taking shape and it begins to
> look as if the mysterious woman so long laughed at would at last
> be justified to the world—and by Harlem. . . .[19]

Notables started turning up at St. Philip's, merely to hear what
was going on: the playwright Maxwell Anderson, Mrs. Ira Gershwin,
and, at the invitation of Houseman, Harry Moses, who had made a
pile of money in Chicago as a manufacturer of ladies underwear, then
retired and moved to New York with his wife, who harbored artistic
aspirations. Moses had backed Broadway productions, most recently
The Warrior's Husband, which had made a star of Katharine Hepburn.
Just then he was looking for something to boost his intellectual prestige. *Four Saints,* Houseman thought, fit the bill.

Moses was impressed by the enterprise, with its egalitarian use
of Harlem singers, its fancy English choreographer. And, currently,
Gertrude Stein's name was in the news, because of the serialization
of *The Autobiography of Alice B. Toklas.* Moses agreed that for the

opera to have just five performances in a 299-seat theater in Hartford would be a waste. So, provided that the production was successful in Hartford, Moses agreed to bring the show to Broadway.

The cast worked with increasing confidence, especially after Alexander Smallens showed up to run vocal rehearsals. The singers couldn't believe the facility of the blustery conductor. In a flash, he would announce where he wanted to resume, sing out the notes for each part of the chorus, sputter instructions to soloists, rap his baton, and begin. He was a human pitch pipe. For his part, Smallens could not believe how tenderly and vividly the Negro cast sang.

On February 1, Thursday afternoon, Thomson and Houseman were driven up to Hartford for production week. The temperature had dropped below zero, where it stayed stuck for days. The Atheneum's new Avery Memorial Wing, a $600,000 project, was complete—and magnificent. The building enclosed a spacious central courtyard around which two levels of cantilevered, rectangular balconies rose. The plain white plaster surfaces of the balconies, with no structural vertical supports to break the clean lines or encroach upon the floor space, gave the interior a stunningly modern aspect. The Picassos were installed in the top-floor galleries, where the walls were painted white. However, the new wing boasted galleries for older works, elegant spaces with walls covered in fabrics: red brocades, cream silk damasks.

The theater was downstairs, off from a plush lobby and coatroom. It was a handsome facility, with curved rows of seats and no balcony. It was also terribly small, the stage no more than thirty by thirty feet with offstage space to the one side, but virtually no backstage area. Moreover, it was not yet equipped with the necessities of a functioning theater: rigging, ropes, cable. For two days trucks arrived from New York bringing lighting equipment, props, two hundred costumes, and, on Thursday, along with Kate Lawson, some 1,500 square feet of cellophane. On this stage with its low-lying ceiling, it was impossible to re-create the feeling of sky and space from Stettheimer's model. Lawson's solution was to drape the cellophane in curvaceous loops on a gridlike mesh, to which the cellophane had to be sewn.

Chick Austin greeted Thomson and Houseman, showed them the new wing and theater, brought them to his home, where they were to stay, served them an elegant dinner, and then, over brandy, broke the bad news: the Friends and Enemies of Modern Music had raised only $9,000 of the promised $10,000 budget, which meant that pay for the cast (which was to be $50 each) was going to have to wait until after proceeds from the house were collected.

Three days later on Sunday night the cast and crew, with Ashton as scoutmaster, arrived by train. Housing for the cast, arranged by the Negro Chamber of Commerce, had been found at the modest Hotel Avon and in black households all over town. Florine Stettheimer and her sister Ettie stayed at the old-world Hotel Heublein, where Carl Van Vechten and his wife had taken a room. Dress rehearsal was to occur on Tuesday, February 6; a preview for an invited audience on the seventh; and the official premiere on the eighth.

Each day, each hour, brought a new crisis. Abe Feder, the lighting technician, pronounced Florine Stettheimer's set with its diamond-bright cellophane background, "a creeping bitch" to light.[20] Soon it was Stettheimer herself he thought the creeping bitch. She was insisting that in certain scenes the stage be flooded in pure white light. Feder tried to explain, over and over, that no such thing existed, that all white light, as every theater technician knew, was a blend of primary colors in varying shades. Stettheimer's obstinacy was unrelenting. Eventually, Feder gave in, lighting the set with bare bulbs, producing a glaring light which finally satisfied her, and which Houseman, who had tried to deter her, had to concede looked indeed like white light. Maurice Grosser was overcome by the Stettheimer sets, a "sort of Schraft's candy-box version of the Baroque."[21]

Stettheimer had early on tried to prevent Thomson from using Negro singers, fearing that their skin colors would clash with her stage and costume colors. This was one fight she lost. She insisted, however, that everyone wear gloves, women and men, thinking that the exposed human hand was unattractive. This was agreed to. When Stettheimer finally saw the Negro singers on stage, she was delighted and surprised by how beautifully their dark skin took the bright colors of her costumes. This was a great relief to everyone. Right until production week, Stettheimer had been petitioning to have all exposed black skin covered with white makeup.

Late Monday morning, Smallens and his orchestra, two dozen players, most of them from the Philadelphia Orchestra, others from New York, arrived by bus. This was to be the first time the cast, who had rehearsed with a pianist, would sing with the orchestra. Monday's rehearsal turned out to be 16 hours of dissention and near calamity.

Because there was no budget to hire copyists, Thomson had had to prepare the orchestra score with Maurice Grosser's help. The previous summer on a Mediterranean island, Porquerolles, he copied out all the individual parts himself, marking the manuscript paper in pencil, averaging ten pages a day. Grosser kept pace, copying over Thomson's script in ink. There was no piano available to check for accuracy. But Thomson felt he didn't need one, having by this time adopted the practice of composing without recourse to any instument.

The parts contained countless mistakes, as was clear ro everyone when the instrumentalists struggled to read through the music for the first time. The hot-tempered Smallens was furious. Thomson, who had been such a bossy perfectionist, was devastated with embarrassment as he made correction after correction, wasting precious time and money.

The singers were stranded for long stretches on stage as the orchestra players, who barely fit into the pit, struggled with the unreliable parts. When the problems were finally straightened out, Smallens took complete control of the rehearsal, causing a major blowup, as Houseman remembered:

> the classic conflict of conductor and director over performers so placed on the stage that they had difficulty in following the beat. Smallens was a bully and a shouter. His yelling drove Freddy Ashton up the aisle in tears, stopping long enough to shout "I have worked with Sir Thomas Beecham! A genius! And he never spoke to me as you have!" before leaving the theatre. Since it was fifteen below zero outside, he returned almost immediately and the rehearsal continued.[22]

By Tuesday, though everyone was exhausted, things went much better. But another potential crisis was prevented thanks to Beatrice Robinson Wayne. Embry Bonner, who was singing a supporting role, Saint Chavez, had started out badly and gotten worse. Mrs. Wayne thought Bonner stuck-up and ridiculous. He would never make it through the production, she was convinced. She had taken a liking to Leonard Franklyn, a God-fearing, polite young tenor singing the minor role of Saint Ferdinand. "Leonard," she had told him a few weeks into rehearsal, "I want you to study the role of Saint Chavez. Don't tell anyone. Just do it." The pressure increased on Embry Bonner until, on the night of dress rehearsal, he finally cracked. What was left of his voice deserted him; Bonner walked off the stage during Act 1, abandoning the run-through. As the cue for Saint Chavez ap-

proached, Mrs. Wayne, standing in the wings, grabbed Leonard
Franklyn and coaxed him onto the stage. He started off shakily, but
sang the role quite ably. Thomson and Smallens were stunned and
grateful. Afterward, though he said nothing, Thomson gave Mrs.
Wayne a hug. Bonner was of course let go. Franklyn was now Saint
Chavez. And the few solo lines of Saint Ferdinand's part were distributed to various other saints, which made little difference.

Stoked by press reports and society gossip, the curiosity over *Four
Saints* had been building for weeks. That the advanced artists, writers, and theater people from New York and Boston were going to turn
up in Hartford for the invitation-only preview was certain. But the interest spilled into high society as well. The New Haven Railroad added
extra parlor cars so that the "New York fashionables" and the "international museum-and-dealer world" could travel to the Hartford premiere together.[23] Because a bartenders' convention and ball was
happening at the same time, hotel rooms were at a premium. Newspapers sent not only music critics but art critics, dance critics. The *New
York Herald Tribune* sent its society columnist, the foppish Lucius
Beebe, to cover the audience as well as the opera. His extravagant account of the Hartford invasion for the preview remains the most vivid.

> Since the Whisky Rebellion and the Harvard butter riots there has
> never been anything like it, and until the heavens fall or Miss Stein
> makes sense there will never be anything like it. By Rolls Royce,
> by airplane, by Pullman compartment, and, for all we know, by
> especially designed Cartier pogo sticks, the smart set enthusiasts
> of the countryside converged on Hartford Wednesday evening for
> the dress rehearsal [sic].[24]

Clare Boothe and Dorothy Hale in "shimmering evening dresses," escorted by Buckminster Fuller, made the most spectacular entrance,
arriving fifteen minutes before curtain time in the first specimen of
Fuller's Dymaxion car, "black and shiny and shaped like a gigantic
raindrop," Beebe reported.

The cast was remarkably calm. John Houseman, though terrified,
was too busy rushing about backstage preparing to supervise en-
trances and props to notice. Thomson, Stettheimer, and Grosser sat
in the audience. Smallens walked out, bowed curtly, and cued the
snare drum roll that commences the opera. When the bright red curtain was pulled apart, revealing Edward Matthews as Saint Ignatius,

"there was a gasp of astonishment and delight," so reported the *New York Sun* art critic, Henry McBride, who had been sending dispatches to his paper virtually by the hour.

> This audience all knew something about pictures and could see at once that the Saint kneeling in front and clad in voluminous purple silk was quite as ecstatic as anything El Greco had ever devised in that line, and that the costumes of the two St. Teresas as well as the effect produced by the cellophane background and the remarkable lighting were all addressed to the painter's eye.[25]

At the first intermission, Lucius Beebe reported, the conversation was guarded.

> Nobody wanted to admit he didn't know what it was all about and take a chance that he was talking to Miss Stein's publisher, but as soon as the Messrs. Kirk Askew and Julien Levy burst into unabashed tears because "they didn't know something so beautiful could be done in America" the hysteria was on and a blizzard of superlatives was in progress. Little groups let down their back hair and cried quietly in corners for beauty.
> . . . After the amazingly abrupt last curtain there was an uproar that would have brought the police from Central station in a jiffy if Mr. Austin hadn't warned them in advance.[26]

The curtain calls went on and on. Henry-Russell Hitchcock rushed down the aisle, crushing his opera hat, ripping open his shirt collar, and shouting "Hoorah! Hoorah!" Thomson, summoned to the stage, was cheered deliriously. Then Chick Austin was called up, who "made a bow to Bedlam and a sea of fluttering handkerchiefs."[27]

Afterward there was a champagne reception at the home of Chick and Helen Austin. The composer Nicolas Nabokov pounded out Russian folk songs on the piano in the parlor, sung by a boozy Archibald MacLeish. At Austin's bash, everyone was talking about the glorious Negro singers. Of course, none of the cast members had been invited to this elite affair. But on the last night of the run, the cast was honored with its own party, hosted by the Negro Chamber of Commerce. The only drink was "pale rum punch in paper cups"; but there was "Southern-style jazz in a big bare hall,"[28] and the dancing lasted until the band packed up at five. Thomson, Houseman, Grosser, Ashton, and others from the production team, who were naturally invited, turned up; everyone, even Thomson, who was no dancer, took to the floor.

Fifty years later, Thomson would learn that one of those who attended *Four Saints* was the Hartford resident, full-time insurance company executive, and part-time poet Wallace Stevens. Although Stevens had a love-hate relationship to Gertrude Stein's writing, this curious opera moved him strangely. However, he detested the whole smart-set crowd, as he explained in a letter to a friend:

> . . . I reached Hartford in time for the opening performance of Gertrude Stein's opera. While this is an elaborate bit of perversity in every respect: text, settings, choreography; it is most agreeable musically, so that, if one excludes aesthetic self-consciousness from one's attitude, the opera immediately becomes a delicate and joyous work all around.
> There were, however, numerous asses of the first water in the audience. New York sent a train load of people of this sort to Hartford; people who walked around with cigarette holders a foot long, and so on.[29]

Notably absent from the Hartford festivities were Gertrude and Alice. But Carl Van Vechten, completely overcome, wrote to Baby Woojums immediately.

> Dear Gertrude,
> *Four Saints,* in our vivid theatrical parlance, is a knockout and a wow. . . . It was a most smart performance in this beautiful little theatre. People not only wore evening clothes, they wore sables and tiaras. Henry McBride sat just in front of me (and was really wild with delight). I haven't seen a crowd more excited since *Sacre du Printemps*. The difference was that they were pleasurably excited. The Negroes are divine, like El Grecos. More Spanish, more Saints, more opera singers in their dignity and *simplicity* and extraordinary plastic line than *any* white singers could ever be. And they enunciated the text so clearly you could understand every word. Frederick Ashton's rhythmic staging was inspired and so were Florine's sets and costumes. . . . The manager who is taking it to New York expects it to be a big success and I am sure it will be something. . . . I really think you should see, hear, and feel *Four Saints*. Maybe you and Alice can be persuaded to try it out. . . .[30]

The Broadway run of the opera, now assured, was to open on February 20 at the Forty-fourth Street Theater for at least four weeks. An extension, Harry Moses made clear, could be added if the box office was strong. There was even talk of taking *Four Saints* on the road. When the cast and crew packed up and returned to New York, they had about one week to transfer a production created for a 299-seat minitheater to a musical-comedy house of 1,400 seats. The cast members adapted well to the Broadway theater, easily filling the reverberant space with their voices. Ashton was delighted to be able to expand the movements of his choreographic staging. However, to prevent the Stettheimer sets from seeming "pitiably flimsy and small," in Houseman's words, a black velour portal was used to frame them and the cellophane sunburst was doubled. Otherwise, the transition went smoothly.

Until exactly fifty hours before the curtain was scheduled to rise.

An officious New York City fire marshal, alerted by press accounts of the cellophane sets, walked into the theater, took out a penknife, cut a strip of the cellophane, set a match to it, and dropped it to the floor before flames burned his hand. The entire set, every bit of it, was condemned. Harry Moses had already invested $10,000 in the show. Opening night was sold out. Lawson went white. Feder bit his mustache with his lower lip. No one spoke. Until a young man from the theater staff suggested coating everything with a new fire-resistant chemical called water glass.

The set and props were coated with a thick, smelly glop. The lovely tarlatan trees sagged; the cellophane colors grayed. New netting had to be added to the mesh to hold up the extra weight. But, when the fire marshal was summoned again, it did not burn. Grudging permission was given for the show to proceed. All during the course of the run, Houseman remembered, as the coating baked under Feder's lights, "there was the constant faint sound of falling rain as thousands of little globs of crusted water-glass flaked and dripped off the cyclorama onto the stage floor below."[31] But there was nothing to do. Furtively, before each performance, Lawson substituted some uncoated tarlatan trees for the drooping coated ones, then locked them up as soon as the show was over. This would be the first and last time that cellophane was sanctioned for use on a Broadway stage.

The New York run created incredible hoopla. Everyone came: Gershwin, Toscanini, Cecil Beaton, Mrs. William Rockefeller, Dorothy Parker, who had her own play at the Bijou, *After Such Pleasures.* Twenty-nine shows competed for audiences on Broadway, including O'Neill's *Ah, Wilderness!* with George M. Cohan at the Guild; Walter Huston in Sinclair Lewis's *Dodsworth* at the Shubert; Maxwell Anderson's *Mary of Scotland* with Helen Hayes at the Alvin; a new Jerome

Kern musical, *Roberta,* at the New Amsterdam. But *Four Saints* commanded the highest ticket price, $3.30 for the best seats.

Some reviewers were perplexed; some were ecstatic. None was indifferent. Henry McBride in the *Sun* called *Four Saints* "an overwhelming, an inescapable success."[32] John Martin, the dance critic of the *New York Times,* proclaimed it the "most interesting theatrical experiment that has been made here in many a season and the most enlightening." However, the *Times*'s music critic, Olin Downes, countered with a long (thirty-two column inches), severe, dismissive piece. "The trail of foppishness and pose and pseudo-intellectuality is all over it," he wrote. Because for the most part those who attended *Four Saints* came not from the concert music crowd, whose defender he considered himself to be, Downes violated a long-standing principle of criticism—Never review the audience.

> Every snob and poseur in town swelled the gathering at the first night, strutted his or her hour in the intermissions and followed the immemorial custom of certain Americans who think themselves artistically smart in being present on an occasion that apes from a distance and across a decade or two the poses of certain Parisians. This is one aspect of the "opera," if such it is to be called, that was performed with such eclat for the precious last Tuesday night in the Forty-Fourth Street Theatre. But it is not the sum of the matter and it would be intolerant to behave as if it were.[33]

Downes ridiculed Stein's text as "far from an innocent or naive creation"; rather, it is "a specimen of an affected and decadent phase of the literature of the whites." The prospect of a new opera, Downes wrote, had whetted his appetite for "something reasonably contemporaneous, practical and observant of basic principles of opera writing." Thomson "wore lightly what is obviously a real knowledge of prosody and a great skill in combining music with texts." But the defects of Thomson's equipment, "resultant upon a lack of technical underpinning and flimsy orchestration and the slapdash way of it all," proved too pronounced to overlook. He concluded that *Four Saints* was "nine-tenths farce and exhibitionism, but there is a little truth in it, and there are some lessons that American opera composers could well take to heart."

What rankled Thomson most was not Downes's negativity but his blindness to the exciting idea that creative people from outside the music sphere—artists, museum directors, choreographers, Harlem entertainers—might have something to teach the opera composer.

There, in light-bulb letters on a Broadway marquee were the names of Gertrude Stein and Virgil Thomson, down the street from those of Jerome Kern and George M. Cohan. This tainted the opera for Downes. But Thomson thought, "Why shouldn't composers and poets have their names in lights on Broadway?" Downes could not dismiss the piece with complete legitimacy. Even he knew that Thomson was not pandering. For all its musical straightforwardness, *Four Saints* was too radical to be condemned as a crowd pleaser.

However, at least a segment of the crowd flocked to *Four Saints*. And the fashion industry caught *Saints* chic. In one magazine advertisement, Bergdorf Goodman announced a tea gown with dramatic sleeves called "Saint" in five colors, because "it looks like one of the thrilling costumes in the much-talked-of Four Saints opera." Another store advertised a new series of mandarin coats made of cellophane combined with rayon and called "4 Wraps in Cellophane." With apologies to Gertrude Stein, the ad copy extolled the creation:

> Might it be silver if it were not cellophane.
> Wrap number one red lacquer red red silver lacquer
> Wrap number two in white.
> And bright.
> And right.
> And quite.

Four Saints was selling well, the gross receipts averaging between $12,000 and $14,000 a week, this during the worst winter of the Depression. Though Harry Moses still complained that the opera was ruining him, he offered to extend the run for two additional weeks. But the Forty-fourth Street Theater was previously booked, so the production would have to be moved to the posh and popular Empire Theater, three blocks away. There, one Sunday evening, Houseman recalled fondly, he had the honor of escorting Saint Teresa, Mrs. Robinson Wayne, to the leading lady's dressing room, once occupied by Helen Hayes, Katharine Cornell, and Ethel Barrymore. Alexander Smallens, with prior commitments, had to withdraw before the final week at the Empire, so those performances were conducted by Thomson. Six weeks on Broadway represented the longest run ever for an opera; only *Porgy and Bess* and *The Medium* would eventually exceed it.

For John Houseman, *Four Saints* had been a life-altering experience. The waves of applause after opening night on Broadway unhinged a floodgate in his psyche. Houseman had discovered what he must do with his life. He experienced overpowering relief, but also deep gloom. How would he be able to continue such work? That night, when the cast and crew left and he was alone on stage, where "only a single, bare worklight remained burning," he found himself with his "face down against the splintered wooden floor, sobbing like a child."[34]

While *Four Saints* was enjoying its Broadway run, disputes were erupting over finances and future performance plans. The Hartford production had run up a $2,000 debt, which was covered personally by Houseman, Austin, and Askew. But this was a loan and would have to be repaid. Moses was covering all the costs of the New York production. He wanted to take the show on the road. But Stein, through her agent, Bradley, was quibbling over the royalties. Thomson warned Stein that pushing Moses too hard would scuttle the plans entirely. Moreover, he was insisting that Maurice Grosser, who had worked without pay, now receive at least one-half of one percent of the royalties for any future production or publication of the score. Moses could cover this expense out of his own share; or, better yet, Thomson suggested, it could be deducted from Stein's share, which was only fair, he argued, since she had left the responsibility of producing the opera to him.

Once again Bradley became a go-between. By the time the show closed, in April, the Moses-sponsored tour idea had been dropped. Stein was disappointed but unrepentant about refusing to budge. "Moses and Houseman may be alright," she wrote to Bradley, "but you have to remember that they were chosen by Virgil and they may be very easily playing his game."[35]

In May, Thomson made a victorious return trip to Kansas City. He gave a morning interview to the *Kansas City Star* from his family home on Wabash Avenue dressed in black pajamas, black robe, and lounging slippers. Invited by the Vassar Club to lecture at the Kansas Citian Hotel, he obliged with a ninety-minute peroration titled "Music for the Modern World." Borrowing a phrase of President Roosevelt, he proclaimed a "new deal in music," and "a revolt against the complicated hyperbole of the exaggerated romantic period which is a tumor on the body of music."[36]

Having returned to New York, Thomson left for Paris on May 19. Once there, neither he nor Stein made any attempt to see each other.

That November, Grace Denton, a statuesque, six-foot-three impresario in Chicago, produced four performances of *Four Saints* in the monumental Sullivan Auditorium.

The cast was rehired. Though the sets had been stored, they had grown stiff with their fireproof coating. So new cellophane sets (with no fireproofing) were run up at the Sullivan, though how Denton managed to clear this with the Chicago fire marshal Thomson never learned. Smallens being not available, Thomson conducted, keeping the orchestra to twenty-six players, as in New York, but situating them against the back wall of the spacious orchestra pit for maximum resonance.

The day of the Chicago opening, Thomson attended a luncheon in his honor given by the ladies of the American Opera Society. Miss Emily Larned, the "toastmistress," as the *Chicago Daily News* called her, introduced the musical entertainment (arias from *Madame Butterfly* and *Carmen* sung in English) and then presented Thomson with the David Bispham Medal, whereupon, the *News* reported, he made a speech. " 'I am highly honored and touched,' he said, 'particularly that you have given me a medal without having heard my music.' Then, without apologies, he pushed for the door, detouring slightly for his coat."[37] Some days later, Thomson gave the David Bispham Medal to his adolescent niece.

In Louis Sullivan's downtown auditorium, a "shabby golden shell with its huge stage opening,"[38] some of the impact of the opera was lost, Houseman felt. However, the performances sold out and the reviews were enthusiastic, though, viewed with hindsight, painfully prejudiced. "No race is so gifted in simplicity as the Negro. The Negro is childlike. Miss Stein's verse is reminiscent of the processes of every child's mind in a contented, a soliloquizing, a creative but inert state."[39]

Thomson's parents, Quincy and May, now the owners of an automobile, drove from Kansas City to attend a performance. Of course they were proud of their son, conducting his opera from the pit of the famed Sullivan Auditorium, and impressed by the lavish production; some of the music reminded them of beloved Baptist hymns. But, all told, they were utterly mystified by *Four Saints in Three Acts*.

The Chicago production boasted one new element, the presence of Gertrude Stein. When Stein learned that an American lecture tour

she had accepted coincided with the Chicago plans, she and Alice decided to attend. Neither had been in her native country for twenty-
seven years.

They arrived in New York on October 17, 1934. By now they were
celebrities, so reporters came aboard the ship for photos and interviews. At Carl Van Vechten's suggestion they checked into the Algonquin Hotel, favored by writers and literary people. He had arranged
nightly dinner parties and receptions. At one they met George Gershwin, who played excerpts for them from the new opera he had written. They were driven to New Haven to attend the Yale-Dartmouth
football game. And, on October 30, for the first time in three years
and eight months, Gertrude, Alice, and Virgil visited together. The
greeting was stiff, but Virgil said several times how glad he was to
see them both.

Since they were staying in New York for a month, they decided
to fly to Chicago for the opera, their first trip ever in an airplane. Curtis Air offered them free tickets. Naturally the women were thrilled
with the opera and its reception. Some of the cast went to Stein's hotel
to make a courtesy call. Mrs. Robinson Wayne did not go, not wanting to be forward (and a bit bothered that Stein had not come backstage to visit with her). But she did telephone Stein, who greeted her
warmly: "Oh, my lovely Saint Teresa!"

Stein and Thomson were now speaking again. But their relationship would never completely recover. In the aftermath of the *Four
Saints* premiere, several strands of the story took ironic and interesting turns.

George Gershwin was so taken with Alexander Smallens's conducting, and with Eva Jessye's Negro choir, that he employed them
all the next year when his opera, *Porgy and Bess,* opened in Boston.

Thomson felt a lingering, and seemingly unreasonable, animosity toward Eva Jessye. For years he complained about "Eva Jessye's
trying to insinuate herself into the history of *Four Saints."* In his 1966
autobiography he does not refer to her by name, writing only, "for
hiring choristers I moved uptown, engaging there, for access to these,
a Negro woman who had the best of them under contract."[40]

H. T. Parker, the long-reigning music and drama critic for the
Boston Evening Transcript, the man who had given Thomson his start
in journalism, came from Boston in mid-March to catch a performance
of *Four Saints.* He was enthralled with the work, and told Thomson
so. Parker returned to Boston, promptly came down with pneumo-

nia, and died ten days later, March 30, 1934. He had started, but never finished, writing his review of *Four Saints*.

On July 19, 1934, finally fed up with Gertrude Stein's "abusive letters" and her charges that he had done her publishing program "incalculable harm," the long-suffering William Aspenwall Bradley resigned as Gertrude Stein's literary agent.

17 THE COMMANDO SQUAD

For the most part, celebrity did Virgil Thomson little good. No professional lecture agent signed him up. Librettos were offered, but they were "invariably low-grade comic scripts."[1] No publisher made a bid for *Four Saints,* nor did any existing opera company. *Four Saints* had been a rallying cry for a contingent of the American avant-garde and a popular success on Broadway. Yet Thomson's reputation in the select sphere of modern music had, if anything, taken a hit. It's telling that the composer Arthur Berger, then a young man studying in New York, despite having some sixty chances to hear *Four Saints,* did not bother to attend. "It was on Broadway," Berger would later explain. "The serious composers—many of us simply didn't pay attention to things on Broadway." Thomson must not have held this against him. Twelve years later Berger was hired as one of Thomson's assistant music critics at the *Herald Tribune.*

Some composer friends had been genuinely enthusiastic, especially Aaron Copland. "I didn't know one could write an opera," he told Thomson afterward, meaning, that he didn't know one could rescue opera from its European trappings and make it something fresh and American. Some of the most perceptive reactions came from musicians outside the concert music world. Oscar Levant, the stylish pianist and raconteur, a close friend of Gershwin and a celebrity in Hollywood, wrote lovingly of *Four Saints* in his 1939 memoirs, calling it a "historic event in American music."

It brought the American composer for the first time into the commercial theater; and, moreover, with a work of considerable commercial appeal. To be sure, it had the advantage of a collaborator named Gertrude Stein; but curiosity trade alone would not have sustained the work as long as it ran. Some part of that success was definitely the contribution of Thomson, in his creation of a truly delightful theatrical atmosphere, in the lilt and flow of the music, and above all, with the demonstration once again of his superlative ability in setting English.[2]

No review upset him more than Theodore Chanler's in *Modern Music*. Chanler had been Thomson's admiring colleague during the early Paris days. After the New York premiere, Chanler had congratulated his old friend Virgil with seeming sincerity. But his review was dismissive. Minna Lederman, *Modern Music*'s judicious editor, had sent two reviewers: one, Gilbert Seldes, to cover the production, and Chanler to focus on the music. Seldes, though not without reservations, found the opera delightful, likening the Act 3 procession to a "magnificent funeral cortege—positively Shakespearean in the poetic trappings of woe."[3]

Chanler's piece, a long article discussing several other recently premiered works, devotes only one paragraph to *Four Saints*. His comments are offered with some reluctance; but his description of the music is devastating:

> Since *Four Saints* is reviewed as a "show" elsewhere in this issue by a more competent critic of the theatre than I can claim to be, I have confined myself to estimating the value of the music alone. This is perhaps unfair. In his assembling of the various elements that lend the music plausibility, as part of a homogeneous theatrical ensemble, Virgil Thomson has shown a resourcefulness, a consistency of purpose, an imagination, even, which, if these qualities are all wanting in his music, he should at least be given credit for in the field in which he has exerted them. He has accomplished the proverbially impossible task of making a silk purse out of a sow's ear.

After this Thomson wanted nothing to do with Chanler, though for years he was perplexed and hurt. Eventually, the truth came out: Chanler had been pressured to change his opinion by Roger Sessions. "He was five years my senior, and I was very much under the spell of his remarkable mind." This was how Chanler later justified himself to Thomson's biographer Kathleen Hoover, who had written to him in 1948 requesting his recollections. As if to assuage his lingering guilt, Chanler confessed the whole story.

> I was very much moved by his *Four Saints*. I heard the first per-formances in New York, and reviewed it in *Modern Music*. Sessions was there too and we met afterwards at a reception. He simply pulverized me with scorn and indignation at having dared to like it. I was intimidated and wrote most unfavorably about the work in my review. This of course made a rift between Virgil and myself. It was not until some years later that I regretted my weakness and meeting Virgil one evening explained the matter to him. His playful answer was "Come home! All is forgiven!"—but he evidently meant it, for he has shown me great kindness since. We are by no means at opposite poles. In his music I admire his daring, as in the ending of the first movement of his First Symphony, the fleeting tenderness, the sense of not knowing what will come next. My reservations about it are those of a man who whole-heartedly prefers his own music to that of any one else writing today.[4]

While Thomson was swept up in the production of *Four Saints,* the campaign to establish a support structure for new music in America was going on all around him. Copland had become the movement's benevolent leader. But Sessions was a powerful, outspoken lieutenant. Fostering good will among the troops was one of Copland's top priorities. He knew of the animosity between Thomson and Sessions. But now that Virgil was back in America, Copland wanted him to quit the bickering and stay. Virgil had removed himself too long from the fight; Copland wanted him in the front lines. This was one reason Thomson remained in America far longer than he had planned.

In later life, by way of enhancing his image as an expatriate, Thomson used to state that he had lived in Paris for fifteen years, from 1925 until 1940. Sometimes, tossing in the time he spent there as a student—two months on tour with the Harvard Glee Club and a year on fellowship—he'd inflate his total time abroad to twenty years, more or less. In fact, during the 1930s, though his permanent address remained 17 quai Voltaire, Thomson lived on and off in New York at various addresses for sixty-one months, over half the decade.

Realistically, in 1934 there was little to sustain Thomson in Paris, other than friends, a pleasant flat, and a familiar way of life; and there was much to be wary of, not the least of which was Hitler's incendiary rhetoric. In New York there were colleagues like Houseman, with his grand plans, and Copland, with his proven connections, who were urging Thomson to stay. So, after the Chicago run of *Four Saints,* Thomson decided, for the time being, to do just that.

When Thomson spoke of the "commando squad" that invaded the established musical order in America (primarily during the period between the two world wars), he had in mind five composer colleagues all born within a few years of each other: Aaron Copland, Roger Sessions, Walter Piston, Roy Harris, and himself. In principle (and in public) the commando composers were collectively committed to fostering a healthy climate in America for modern American music. But behind the scenes they formed a very contentious group.

Walter Piston was no radical. Since 1926 he had been ensconced as a teacher at Harvard, and he thrived in academia. He had cultivated a working relationship with the Boston Symphony Orchestra and its conductor Serge Koussevitzky. By 1934 three major Piston works, including his Concerto for Orchestra, had been premiered at Symphony Hall. The Harvard–BSO connection would remain beneficial to both institutions. Even today, when the orchestra wants to lure subscribers, it touts its celebrity soloists and devotion to essential mainstream repertory. But when the orchestra needs its intellectual prestige validated, it turns to the Harvard faculty—or their students—and commissions a piece.

Piston thought Thomson's compositions were at best iconoclastic and at worst negligible. Thomson thought Piston a pompous pedant, embarrassed by his Italian heritage (the original family name was Pistone), who took on Boston Brahmin airs. Yet, in his 1970 book *American Music since 1910,* Thomson summed up Piston's achievement fairly: "A neoclassical composer of Parisian cast, skilled technician of the orchestra, a valued pedagogue, and author of today's best book on harmony."

Roy Harris, the laconic Oklahoman, had settled in Los Angeles, where he supported himself through part-time teaching and writing music criticism. Thanks to Copland's intervention, Koussevitzky had premiered Harris's Symphony no. 1 in 1933 to public acclaim (making Thomson the only Koussevitzky reject among these five emerging Americans). Like the man, Harris's music had a homespun authenticity that was hard to dislike. Though eager to support Copland's efforts any way he could, he moved constantly after 1935, taking guest professorships in numerous cities. Only some summer-term teaching stints at the Juilliard School brought him to New York for extended periods during the 1930s.

Roger Sessions had already established himself as the group's uncompromising intellectual. He supported all of Copland's efforts to organize composers for the purpose of promoting performances, recordings, publications, and the collection of royalties. But he debunked the whole idea of an "American school" and thought all music should be held to the most rigorous international standards. While Copland was prodding the League of Composers to favor the cause of American music, Sessions in 1934 took over the presidency of the United States branch of the International Society for Contemporary Music, an organization dominated by Germanic Europeans and their intellectual American disciples, those Thomson derided as "the Schoenbergians and the Bang-Bangs." In 1935 Sessions accepted a post at Princeton, where, except for a nine-year stint at Berkeley following World War II, he remained until he retired in 1965.

If Copland was the leader of the fractious commando unit, it's because he was the one person everyone else trusted. Copland valued Sessions's intellectual rigor and high standards. He considered himself a modernist, but didn't want the old orthodoxy replaced with a new one. Thomson sent all his works to Copland and appreciated Copland's appraisals, which were models of positive criticism and usually on target, as in this discussion (only part of a long letter) of Thomson's 1930 Violin Sonata:

> I don't know whether you want a "criticism" or not. Anyway, I think it has lovely things in it—particularly the second movement, but I also think that you are often much too easy with yourself as for instance the too-Handel-like beginning of that 2nd movement, or the theme with arpeggio accompaniment of the 4th movement that sounds like Grieg perhaps. What I like about the piece are those moments of a seemingly effortless musicality which are utterly simple and deeply charming. I see them mostly in the 1st and 2nd movements. (The measures before the end of the second movement please me most of all—except for the final four measures which again suddenly seem too easy.)[5]

What Copland now needed from Thomson that nobody else could provide was Thomson's savvy regarding musical politics, his knowledge of how the musical world worked, of who was pulling the strings and who was being pulled. Both Copland and Thomson thought that composers should be in charge of their own affairs—

should run the publishing houses, put on the concerts, disperse the commissions, collect the royalties. For that matter, they should run the orchestras and opera houses! Why not? Who would be better suited to this work? Business executives?

To this end, Copland had been organizing. When the Copland-Sessions Concerts collapsed in 1931, he persuaded the trustees of the Yaddo artist colony in Saratoga Springs to sponsor a similar series, featuring Americans, which started in 1932. As an insider at the Cos Cob Press, and as an adviser to the Boosey & Hawkes publishing firm, Copland ushered into print the works of his colleagues, including Thomson's first two published works: "Susie Asado," and the *Stabat Mater,* for soprano and string quartet. He organized around himself a group of junior colleagues, called, simply, the Young Composers Group, which he introduced to the public as a group in a performance at the New School in New York in January 1933. Among the composers on the program were Paul Bowles, Israel Citkowitz, Henry Brant, Lehman Engel, Elie Siegmeister, Vivian Fine (the first woman to break into this male bastion), and Bernard Herrmann (who would become famous as a composer of film scores, especially that for Hitchcock's *Psycho*).

This was an era where collective activity, organized resistance to exploitation, and radical left-wing politics were rampant in America. Copland saw no reason why American composers should not also put their faith in collective action. But if all this organizing was to sustain these young composers, then people would have to be paid properly. That's where Thomson, always comfortable talking money, came in.

In 1936 the performers—singers, dancers, instrumentalists—organized themselves into an effective union, the American Guild of Musical Artists. Even the managers had pooled forces in organizations like Columbia Concerts Corporation. But the performing-rights association that since 1914 had collected and distributed royalty fees for composers—the American Society of Composers, Authors and Publishers (ASCAP)—was largely uninterested in the problems of composers working in the classical tradition: there was not enough money involved. So in 1935 a band of composers, spearheaded by Copland, started meeting to form their own organization. Through Copland's insistence, Thomson became a major player in this effort. A large dinner for some one hundred composers was arranged by Milton Diamond, a sympathetic and savvy lawyer. Many thought this the "dawn of a new day." Not Thomson, who "figured that Diamond and his associates were probably moved less by our interests than by theirs." Along with a few others, Thomson was elected by his colleagues to meet with Diamond for the drawing up of bylaws.

> . . . I went to every meeting, asked embarrassing questions, and confused the lawyer, who knew lots about mergers but very little about authors' rights, into revealing that he was not completely on our side. When these negotiations failed, as I had been determined that they should, the desirability of a composers' society remained. Over the next three years the plans for this were worked out, partly by me, who had in my European years learned something about authors' rights, and partly by Copland, who could mold them into forms acceptable to others.[6]

The result was the American Composers Alliance, incorporated in 1938. That same year the publishing efforts and the existing catalog of Cos Cob Press, which had been languishing, were taken over by a new venture, Arrow Music Press, founded by Copland, Thomson, Marc Blitzstein, and Lehman Engel, for the specific purpose of publishing and distributing contemporary American music. (Arrow Press did essential work until 1952, when, unable to sustain itself or attract further backing, the catalog was acquired by Boosey & Hawkes.)

The rights of composers were fortified by these organization efforts during the 1930s. But if the concertgoing public was to be reached, it was the composers who would have to extend the hand. Copland and Thomson believed that American composers belonged out there in American society, not walled up in the concert hall, or sheltered in the university. This was not a question of pandering. Anywhere fine music was needed—for a school chorus, for music students, for a play or a film, for a civic occasion—professional composers should be hired to provide it. One could always compose complex chamber pieces for select audiences. But writing a fanfare for the dedication of a new town hall was a perfectly proper and thoroughly professional activity, and the attendant visibility would help to demystify the composer, would make the concert music world not so elitist. This utilitarian conception of the composer's place in society found a powerful ally, President Franklin D. Roosevelt.

When Roosevelt took office in 1933, the number of Americans on public relief (amid cries of communism and bolshevism) had grown to twenty million. Midway through 1935 a plan emerged from the administration that involved a radical shift of thinking. Relief programs, thought to engender defeatism, dependency, and despondency, would be changed over to work relief programs. The federal government would put people with essential skills and trades back to work (amid further cries of communism and bolshevism). By September the Works Progress Administration, administered by Harry Hopkins, was launched with a budget of $5 billion, to be spent in blocks of $420 million a month.

Significantly, the arts were embraced under the definition of "essential" work. Never more than one percent of the WPA budget went to the arts, but their very inclusion was unprecedented. Naturally, the artistic work had to have some utilitarian cast. So a painter might be put to work designing posters or painting murals. Of all the arts, the one that most easily justified itself as a cooperative enterprise providing public enjoyment and enrichment was the theater. Within one year of its formation the Federal Theater Project of the WPA had over fifteen thousand men and women on the payroll—actors, writers, scenic painters, technicians, costumers, composers—most of them earning exactly $23.86 a week. During the program's four years of operation, over two hundred resident Federal Theater Project companies and traveling troupes would present productions in auditoriums, public schools, city squares, and parks to over thirty million Americans.

The Federal Theater Project was directed by Hallie Flanagan, a tough, visionary midwesterner whose mission was twofold: to put thousands of creative people to work and to foster theatrical ventures so "excellent in quality and low in cost, and so vital to the communities involved that they will be able to continue after Federal support is withdrawn."[7] Early on, Flanagan decided to direct some funding to inner-city ghettos. The New York WPA Negro Theater Project was the result, which began operations in mid-September 1935.

The idea of a federal theater project based in Harlem galvanized the community into three factions: there were the professional black stage people who had produced shows and kept small companies running through the early Depression years without any outside help and were understandably suspicious; there were the well-intentioned and somewhat condescending government and civic leaders who wanted to bring theater to Harlem as the benevolent gift of concerned whites; and there were the left-wing agitators—the communists who published a Harlem edition of the *Daily World* called the *Liberator,* radicals long hostile to patronizing white do-gooders. To steer the Negro Theater Project through this hotbed of agitation, Hallie Flanagan turned to Rose McLendon, the respected black actress. However, feeling she lacked administrative experience, McLendon accepted the post on one condition, that John Houseman, her trusted friend, be appointed codirector. Since the production of *Four Saints,* Houseman had continued to straddle the roles of director and producer for a few marginally successful productions. But the good will he earned from *Four Saints* had lingered in the Harlem community. His application—as emergency, nonrelief, executive personnel—was approved. "With only a confused awareness of its hazards and implications," Houseman started work at a salary of fifty dollars a week.

The Negro Theater, Houseman decided, would have two branches: one to produce indigenous black works in familiar settings; the other, following the example of *Four Saints,* to produce classical and modern plays with Negro actors chosen for their artistic merit, presented in interpretations that made no concessions or references to color.

For help, Houseman turned to a new colleague, a nineteen-year-old, moon-faced actor named Orson Welles. In December of 1934 Houseman attended a Broadway production of *Romeo and Juliet;* and it was not Katharine Cornell's fervent Juliet or Basil Rathbone's polite, middle-aged Romeo, but Welles's furious Tybalt, "death, in scarlet and black, in the form of a monstrous boy—flat-footed and graceless, yet swift and agile; soft as jelly one moment and uncoiled, the next," that left Houseman overwhelmed.[8]

Houseman sought out Welles and established an oddly interdependent relationship: the brilliant, reckless Welles, presuming his place in the theater world; the efficient, deferential Houseman, a gifted facilitator. Their first collaboration was the premiere of *Panic,* Archibald MacLeish's verse play, a leftist indictment of Wall Street greed. Welles, with his "pale-pudding face," donned a wig and putty nose to play the lead, McGafferty, a sexagenarian tycoon whose world collapses amid the banking crisis of 1933. Reviews were mixed, but Houseman was convinced of Welles's talents. Now he wanted Welles to direct a production for his pathbreaking Negro Theater Project.

The other person Houseman turned to—for guidance, for stability, as a roommate to share temporary apartments (five during the next three years), and for music—was Thomson. Among composers, Thomson was uniquely positioned for inclusion in WPA projects. The very fact that he had been ostracized, to some degree, from the established orchestras and chamber ensembles freed him of elitist taint. In conceiving *Four Saints*, hiring black singers, and bringing the production to Broadway, he had already accomplished what the Federal Theater Project was created to foster. Thomson was a theater man, the first composer of his generation to welcome WPA work; and, at least in this case, Aaron would follow Virgil's example.

The project that proved irresistible to Thomson and Welles was an all-black version of Shakespeare's *Macbeth,* to be set on an island that could have been Haiti at the time of the black emperor, Jean Christophe, with the witches as voodoo priestesses and the soldiers bedecked with epaulets and military caps adorned with feathers. This was to be not some Negro adaptation of an Elizabethan classic but a forthright reading of the text, transplanted to a modern locale with daring contemporary imagery, a production that would strive to capture the play's occultism and mystery.

But first, the dilapidated Lafayette Theater, on Seventh Avenue just north of 132nd Street, had to be restored. The Negro Theater Project had taken on 750 men and women: actors, carpenters, electricians, seamstresses, office workers, and various others who claimed such skills. All descended upon the Lafayette, turning this abandoned theater, with its rotting carpets, flaking plaster, and rat-infested seats, into a functioning performance space and headquarters. The members of the technical crew, continually refused admission to the Stagehands Union because of their color, were exuberant over the chance to equip and run a professional facility, complete with miles of new ropes and cables, and six portable dimmer boards, all requisitioned by Abe Feder of *Four Saints* fame, whom Houseman had appointed the project's technical director.

For the four leading roles, Welles recruited experienced professional actors. Jack Carter, who had created the role of Crown in the original play version of *Porgy and Bess,* was Macbeth; his ruthless lady was Edna Thomas, a frequenter of the Askew salon, whom Thomson had admired in *Run Little Chillun!* Canada Lee, a New York–born son of West Indian parents, formerly a boxer, was Banquo. (In 1941 Lee would win acclaim on Broadway as the hero of *Native Son,* adapted from Richard Wright's novel.) Eric Burroughs, who had trained at the Royal Academy of Dramatic Arts in London, played Hecate, a composite role pieced together by Welles from bits of witches' dialogue. The cast was complemented with sundry soldiers and apparitions.

Houseman recruited a troupe of authentic African drummers, commandeered by an Oxford-educated African named Asadata Dafora Horton (who later became the minister of culture in the Republic of Sierra Leone). The lead drummer was a genuine witch doctor, a dwarf with gold and diamond teeth named Abdul, who demanded twelve live black goats, which were slaughtered and their hides stretched into skin for devil drums. Sometimes during rehearsals Abdul would fall into a restless trance from which not even his fellow witch doctors could arouse him.

Thomson's task was to provide not just incidental music but sound effects. Besides the sizable pit orchestra there was a backstage percussion group with a bass drum, a thunder sheet, a wind machine, gongs. Using these, Thomson amplified the actors' voices during stormy scenes, underlining words with thunder claps, rattling drums, and swooshing wind effects. He also provided ready-made pieces: arrangements of Viennese waltzes by Joseph Lanner for the banquet scene, trumpet fanfares, military marches. But, denying Welles's request, Thomson wrote no original music for the production, as he explained to Houseman in a subsequent letter:

> He was never hateful or brutal with me, though I was a little terrified of his firmness. He was extremely professional and he knew exactly what he wanted. He knew it so well and so thoroughly that I, as an older musician with a certain amount of pride, would not write him original music. I would not humiliate myself to write so precisely on his demand.[9]

The African drummers provided authentic music for the voodoo scenes; or so they said. When they first demonstrated their music, Thomson and Houseman thought it rather tame.

"Is this stuff really voodoo?" Thomson asked Asadata.

"Oh, yes. Indeed. This is absolutely authentic voodoo."

"It don't sound wicked enough," Thomson insisted.

All that afternoon Thomson argued with the Africans. Finally Asadata admitted that the chant and drum music his troupe had been playing was not real voodoo, just some spells to ward off the beriberi; for had he dared to use the real thing, Asadata explained, it would have worked.

The *Macbeth* troupe—actors, understudies, technicians, costumers, children—grew to 137. Welles took complete control, ordering Houseman, clearly in a producer's role, to stay away from the initial rehearsals, lest the cast be confused as to who was in charge. Welles was alternately tyrannical and patronizing. At that time Welles was also committed to a radio job in the evenings, reading poetry on the *Fleishman Yeast Hour.* So he got Houseman to agree that daily rehearsals would not begin until close to midnight. Frequently they lasted until dawn. Welles was easily exasperated with the cast, calling his soldiers "dumbbells" when they were slow to execute his formations. At other times he was like some baby-faced father figure. Tommy Anderson, a veteran of the *Four Saints* chorus who was acting as an unofficial assistant to Welles, had an infant girl whom he sometimes brought to rehearsals. Welles used to walk around the theater with the child in his arm, issuing commands to the tech crew and calling the cast to attention.

For all his brilliance and bluster, Welles needed help, and he knew it. In staging the Act 4 storm scene with the three witches ("Round about the cauldron go; in the poison'd entrails throw"), Welles had the not terribly original idea to move his witches, in this case witch doctors, in a circle. It wasn't working. "Tommy," he told Anderson one day, "take some time and straighten this out." Anderson choreographed the actors to emphasize certain phrases ("Eye of NEWT, and toe of FROG") with thrusting gestures and accentuated steps, creating a movement within a movement. Naturally, Anderson's contributions were uncredited in the program.

Expectation built up in the Harlem community and spilled into advance reports by Bosley Crowther in the *New York Times.* On opening night, April 10, 1936, the theater was sold out; all press seats were taken. (One critic wrote to request that he and his wife, if possible, not be seated "next to Negroes.") Before dusk two detachments of band musicians from the Benevolent and Protective Order of Elks started marching through the streets of Harlem, heralding the play. An estimated ten thousand people crowded around the theater. Northbound street traffic "was stopped for more than an hour," the *Times* reported. Finally, well past schedule, Thomson took the podium to begin. Five minutes into the play, Houseman, surveying the house, knew "that victory was ours."

However, the reviews were equivocal, condescending, and, some of them, racist. In an article titled "Macbeth in Chocolate,'" Robert Littell wrote, "In watching them, we capture briefly what we once were, long centuries ago before our ancestors suffered the blights of thought, worry, and the printed word." Edward R. Murrow, writing in *Stage* magazine, faulted the production for its "blackface attitude," exactly the quality the creative team believed it had avoided. Murrow expressed the desire to see instead Negro theater that "would show the passion, beauty, cruelty, suffering, aspiration, frustration, humor, and yes, the victories of a deeply emotional race." However, the most important critic, Brooks Atkinson in the *Times,* was the most positive. Making the witches scenes work with the usual make-believe magic effects of the "polite, tragic stage" is a perpetual challenge in Shakespeare's *Macbeth,* he wrote. "But ship the witches into the rank and fever-stricken jungle echoes, stuff a gleaming naked witch doctor into the cauldron, hold up Negro masks in the baleful light—and there you have a witches scene that is logical and stunning and a triumph of the theatre arts."[10]

The production ran for ten weeks in Harlem and two weeks on Broadway, then went on the road to Hartford, Bridgeport, Dallas, Indianapolis, Chicago, Detroit, and Cleveland, a total of 144 performances. But the negative reviews rankled the cast, particularly the witch doctor Abdul. Percy Hammond, the caustic critic of the *Herald Tribune* had been dismissive ("one of your benevolent Uncle Sam's experimental philanthropies"; "an exhibition of deluxe boondoggling"). Particularly angering was his unctuous expression of surprise over "the inability of so melodious a race to sing the music of Shakespeare."[11]

After the article appeared, Abdul asked Welles, "This critic, is he a bad man?" "Yes, he is," Welles said. "You want we make beri-beri on this man?" Abdul asked. "Go right ahead," Welles said; "make all the beri-beri you want to."

That night the performance went beautifully. Wells was elated. But afterward the sounds of ranting drums and baleful chanting emanated from the Lafayette Theater, seemingly all night. For a few days Hammond continued about his business unaffected. But on Sunday, April 19, he was taken ill suddenly at his apartment in the Hotel Algonquin. Two days later he was hospitalized. On April 25, ten days after Abdul's horrific all-night ritual, Percy Hammond died at sixty-three of what the papers reported as lobar pneumonia.

Virgil Thomson was now a professional theater man. His success with *Four Saints* and the WPA led to work in the commercial theater. Among other projects that summer was Leslie Howard's *Hamlet,* directed by John Houseman, not well received by critics in New York, but a box office success on national tour. For this Thomson made a ballet-opera out of the Gonzaga's murder episode, arranging the actors like players in a roving medieval troupe, using onstage, costumed musicians with tiny drums and cymbals and bamboo recorders.

Throughout 1936, as Thomson accumulated theater credits, he started working in another nonconcert medium, one that would eventually take him to a Pulitzer Prize in music—film. And the man who inaugurated Thomson into this work was comparably inexperienced as a filmmaker.

Pare Lorentz, then thirty, was a noted film critic, writing for *Vanity Fair* and *McCall's*. Born in Clarksburg, West Virginia, to a cultured family, he moved as a young man to New York, where he soaked up film, theater, opera, and concerts and married a professional actress. Early on, he developed a strong social conscience and examined the social impact of film in a book he wrote with the civil libertarian Morris Ernst, *Censored: The Private Life of the Movies*. An ardent supporter of Roosevelt, Lorentz had gathered materials for a film he hoped to produce. The film was never made; but the materials—photos of dust storms, protests, and breadlines, accompanied by Lorentz's insightful text—were published as *The Roosevelt Year: 1933*. This book won him an appointment as a political columnist for King Features, a Hearst syndicate. But in an early column Lorentz dared to praise a New Deal farm program, resulting in his immediate dismissal via telegram from William Randolph Hearst himself.

However, Lorentz had already decided to turn this material into a film. He had never directed a film, but had a comprehensive knowledge of film history. Articulate, handsome, and physically imposing, Lorentz tried to sell his idea to producers. Hollywood, condescending toward the documentary genre and suspicious of the subject's socialist taint, was not interested. But the U.S. Resettlement Administration, a division of the Department of Agriculture, looking to justify its program of aiding refugee families from areas devastated by floods, droughts, and dust storms, was very interested. Rexford Guy Tugwell, the director of the Resettlement Administration, hired Lorentz and provided a budget of $6,000, a measly sum, for a film eventually titled *The Plow That Broke the Plains*.

It would be a half-hour history of the Great Plains, from the days of the first cattle drives to the punishing drought, which was then entering its sixth year, a story told with "an emotion that springs out of the soil itself," Lorentz later wrote.[12]

Lorentz hired first-class professional cameramen: Ralph Steiner,

Paul Strand, and Leo Hurwitz. Starting in Montana and moving south-east through to Texas, they filmed dust storms, which were then destroying millions of acres of farmland. Lorentz and his cameramen quarreled over the shooting script. The members of the crew, avowed New Dealers, thought the grassland's rape should be ascribed not just to human nature, economic catastrophe, and natural causes but also to rapacious capitalist greed. Lorentz was sympathetic to their view. But being a government-funded project the film had to have a positive message: that something could and would be done.

The film was in the cutting stage when Lorentz began searching for someone to compose a musical score. He approached Aaron Copland and Roy Harris, neither of whom struck him as right. John Houseman, whom Lorentz had met, recommended Thomson. What sold him on Thomson, despite his having heard not a note of his music, was the composer's refreshing pragmatism. It's a story Thomson loved to tell.

> He first explained his film, asked could I imagine writing music for it. My answer was, "How much money have you got?" Said he, "Beyond the costs of orchestra, conductor, and recording, the most I could possibly have left for the composer is five hundred." "Well," said I, "I can't take from any man more than he's got, though if you did have more I would ask for it." My answer delighted him. "All those high-flyers," he said, "talk about nothing but aesthetics. You talk about money; you're a professional."[13]

As it turned out, they didn't have to debate aesthetics, because they agreed on everything. Lorentz had set his mind on "rendering the landscape through the music of its people," which was Thomson's idea as well. Through viewing the uncut footage and poring over collections of cowboy songs and settler folklore, Thomson gathered tunes and ideas. When the film was completed, twenty-five minutes of music were needed; and they were needed in a week. Thomson, already committed to a short-lived arts festival that Chick Austin was launching in Hartford, said he would need two weeks. He fashioned a score that used cowboy songs ("Laredo," "Git Along Little Dogies," "Houlihan"), sometimes simply, sometimes as themes for fugal episodes; there are dances and tangos, hymnal passages, spacious harmonies, and bumptious rhythms; the drought is evoked in bare, restrained, neo-medieval, two-part counterpoint. The familiar tunes are sometimes deployed for their associative value. For example, during a 1918 war sequence, as the narration explains that farmers were being pressed to turn grazing land into wheat fields, we see tractors coming over a hill, almost like a military maneuver. Thomson accompanied this montage with the marching song of American troops, "Mademoiselle from Armentières," making the point that the farmers were being inducted into the war effort. The score is an eclectic but cogent patchwork.

To the standard orchestra he added saxophones, guitar, a banjo, and, for evoking a down-home church music, a harmonium. With the help of Henry Brant, a young Canadian composer whom he had hired on the recommendation of George Antheil to assist in copying out the parts, Thomson delivered the score on time. For the recording sessions in New York, he hired the conductor hero of *Four Saints*, Alexander Smallens, and an orchestra of thirty, recruited from the New York Philharmonic and the Metropolitan Opera Orchestra. When mistakes turned up in the newly copied parts, causing delays and costing, by Lorentz's stopwatch, an additional $500, Smallens was not surprised. This time, however, he checked his temper. Thomas Chalmers, a Metropolitan Opera baritone, was hired to read in resonant tones Lorentz's quasi-poetic text:

DROUGHT

A country without rivers . . . without streams . . .
with little rain . . .
once again the rains held off and the
sun baked the earth.
This time nongrass held moisture against the
winds and sun . . . this time millions of acres
of plowed land lay open to the sun.

The film ended with a peroration about the desperate farmers and field-workers, tens of thousands every month, who only ask "for a chance to start over."

And a chance for their children to eat,
to have medical care, to have homes again.
50,000 a month!
The sun and winds wrote the most tragic chapter in
American agriculture.

Lorentz was so impressed by the score's structural impact, that he re-cut sections of the film to accommodate Thomson's music. For thirty years the government had been producing instructional and informational films. But a film that illuminated a national problem in powerfully vivid terms, with film footage, photographs, narration, and music working in tandem, was unprecedented.

As word got out from selected previews, congressional opponents of Roosevelt's farm policy protested. *The Plow That Broke the Plains* was branded New Deal propaganda, which of course it was. The distribution was also threatened by the deficit Lorentz had amassed: the $6,000 venture had cost $19,260. Moreover, sensing competition, the Hollywood industry was refusing to allow the film into its distribution system. But one former Paramount executive, Arthur Mayer, now the manager of New York's Rialto Theater, decided to show the film to capitalize on Hollywood's antagonism. Billed "The Picture They Dared Us to Show!" the film opened on May 28, 1936. Audiences cheered it nightly. Soon the opposition caved in to public demand. Bookings, arranged theater by theater without Hollywood's help, followed in Philadelphia, Washington, Boston. Eventually over three thousand theaters screened it. While some critics chided the film's hamstrung production ("a wheezy, badly handicapped little effort," said the *Herald Tribune* critic), the reviews were superb overall.

> What the government has been saying about dust storms in the newspapers was said here in 30 minutes of unforgettable pictures.
> —*Nation*

> Pare Lorentz turned in a classic. Demand it at your local theater.
> —*Esquire*

> Brilliantly photographed and with a superb musical score.
> —*Cleveland Press*

> There is more serious drama in this truthful record of the soil than in all the "Covered Wagons" and "Big Trails" produced by the commercial cinema.
> —*Baltimore Sun*

Though the politics of the film were to Thomson a "matter of supreme indifference," he was delighted to have been associated with a work considered so provocative. He had had a solid success in the film business, and by the end of 1936 his prospects for other projects looked good. Yet, as the winter approached, he felt called back to France, at least for a visit. He would turn forty on November 25 and wanted to be with his friends in Paris.

There he engaged a projection theater and showed a print he had brought of *The Plow That Broke the Plains*. Hugnet, Cocteau, Gertrude, and Alice and other friends came and admired. He gave a joint concert with Cliquet-Pleyel in his studio apartment. But Europe was engulfed in tumult.

> Paris itself had turned political; the leftist Popular Front was a success. The Spanish were embraced by civil war. The King of England had resigned for love. Hitler has caused henchmen to be shot down. Russia was disciplining Shostakovich. In Italy liberals had joined the Fascist party.[14]

Opportunities for Thomson lay in America, not Paris. His self-identity as an expatriate would have to be adjusted. But shortly before he went back a pink slip arrived terminating his employment with the Federal Theater Project. Thomson had left the country without notification. There would be no more WPA projects with Houseman, but other work was calling. He arrived in New York on New Year's Eve.

Pare Lorentz, exhilarated by the success of his first film, thought he should quit while ahead. In mid-1936 he walked into the office of his boss at the Resettlement Administration, Rexford Guy Tugwell, intending to resign. He wanted to return to New York and resume writing. As he turned to leave, he saw on the office wall a framed profile map of the Mississippi River valley. If you ever wanted to do another film, he told Tugwell, there's your subject: a film about the Mississippi River. It would be the story of the devastation brought by unchecked cotton cultivation, reckless timber cutting, the abuse of land, the building of cities on river banks. It could depict the misery of sharecroppers, the wreckage of punishing floods. It could also show what the Roosevelt administration was doing about it: reforesting barren fields, rehabilitating stricken citizens, conserving forests, developing power in the valleys. In other words, Tugwell realized, the film could be terrific propaganda for New Deal programs that required constant promotion to a recalcitrant Congress. Such a film, Lorentz said, could even have, literally speaking, a narrative flow: "We would start at Lake Itasca and follow a drop of water, in effect, to the Gulf of Mexico." Tugwell was hooked. As he spoke, Lorentz had had a kind of cinematic epiphany. Asked what the film might cost, Lorentz suggested $50,000. Within thirty minutes, Tugwell had secured the budget from President Roosevelt. Lorentz would make another film; this time, however, he would receive a salary: $30 per day.

By January 1937 the shooting of *The River,* as Lorentz called the film, had been completed and his six-man crew disbanded. Then, winter floods along tributaries of the Mississippi augured that a catastrophe was about to happen. Two of the top cameramen, Willard Van Dyke and Floyd Crosby, were called back, the Department of Agriculture provided additional funding, and off they went to shoot 80,000 more feet of film. The floods, though devastating to the region, were fortunate for the filmmaker and the cause of the New Deal. When they returned to New York on February 24, Lorentz and his men had covered 22,000 miles in the Mississippi valley.

Of course, Lorentz wanted Thomson to rejoin his production team. Thomson was wary. Lorentz was "talkative, ambitious, truculent, ever a battler." So was Thomson, of course. This time their work together was fractious.

> For seven months he battled with me over music, money, aesthetics, every single point of contact that we had. Nor do I think he was not mainly right. I merely note that battling was for Pare a way of life and that even in creating he warred with his teammates. He did not bicker; his tone was gentlemanly; our weekly all-night conferences were warm. But Pare's film was his brainchild not yet born, and he could not be stopped from going on about it.[15]

For Thomson, this film would be an altogether more difficult project. "Its landscape of streams and forests was pastoral, static. Its historical narrative covered a century, its geographical perspective half the continent." If Thomson was to incorporate indigenous musical source materials, as he had in *The Plow,* he would have to do some research. Thomson had examined with fascination a book by George Pullen Jackson, a professor of German at Vanderbilt University, who had identified and brought to attention the wealth of music called "white spirituals"—the ancient Scottish and Irish tunes that America's southern and western forefathers learned in the rural districts of the British Isles and brought with them to this continent as their musical heritage. Negro spirituals are the Africanized offshoots of this heritage, derived from Scottish sea chanties and hymnal melodies in ancient modes, and familiar to southerners as folk hymns, camp-meeting tunes, and revival choruses. In 1933 Jackson published his first book on the subject, *White Spirituals in the Southern Uplands;* Thomson kept and utilized a copy of this book all his life. While researching the score for *The River,* he wrote to Jackson, asking for access to the hymnbooks that were his sources. Jackson sent the main ones and, on his way to Europe, stopped in New York to play for Thomson recordings of the music as authentically performed.

But Thomson wanted more. Maurice Grosser was just then in the midst of an extended visit with family in Chattanooga. So Thomson wrote him, asking if Grosser could somehow obtain a rare copy of *The Southern Harmony,* as the principal hymnal was called. The white spiritual heritage was largely an oral tradition. The notation system used was that of "shape notes," where pitch was identified not only by a note's place on the staff but by its shape: a round, a square, a triangle, a diamond. Grosser and a family friend from Huntsville, who knew something about the subject, drove all over Alabama and central Tennessee, stopping at farmhouses to ask if anyone knew where a copy was to be found. Eventually they located one, in bad condition, which the owners were reluctant to lend until they were told of the intended purpose. When Grosser returned to New York with his find, Thomson had him put on the federal payroll, and hired him to transcribe by hand the entire book.

Thomson was to have been put on Lorentz's payroll, too, for twenty-five dollars a day, starting on February 1, 1937. But no checks arrived. Via wire, Thomson threatened to resign. Lorentz replied with a pointed telegram, complaining that Thomson was being unreasonable, that the floods could not have been foreseen, that Thomson could not be paid to write music for a film that, at the time, did not exist.

Soon thereafter, however, Lorentz returned with new footage, the film was cut, Thomson's checks started coming, and he composed his score, working to meet Lorentz's sudden deadline in July, churning out fifty pages of manuscript a day for a week. Some of the tunes employed plaintive melodies he had found in the white spiritual source books. Yet, for all Thomson's hard research, most of the tunes that wound up in the score were familiar from his youth, including, "How Firm a Foundation," "My Shepherd Will Supply My Need," "Yes, Jesus Loves Me," and "Hot Time in the Old Town Tonight." The finale of his *Symphony on a Hymn Tune* was recycled as a five-minute sequence that concluded the film. But the arrangement of materials as they were assembled and orchestrated made an integrated whole. Once again the score was recorded by Alexander Smallens and pickup players from the Philharmonic.

Lorentz's script, again narrated by Thomas Chalmers, strives for an incantatory poetic power. Names of places, rivers, and trees are invoked; the phrase "we built a hundred cities and a thousand towns" recurs like a musical refrain. In one passage describing the destruction of primeval forests, Chalmers's chesty voice intones, "Black spruce and Norway pine; Douglas fir and red cedar; scarlet oak and shagbark hickory—we built a hundred cities and a thousand towns, but at what cost!" In another passage a litany of tributaries is read like some Homeric epic: "Down the Yellowstone, the Milk, the White and the Cheyenne; the Cannonball, the Muscleshell, the James and the Sioux . . ." Given the poetic text, the undulant imagery, and Thomson's vivid music, it's no wonder that Lorentz often called the film an "opera."

This time, in a major breakthrough, Paramount Studios agreed to distribute the film, which opened in late 1937. Along with studio films like *Scandal Street Murder,* with Lew Ayres, or *The Awful Truth,* with Cary Grant and Irene Dunne, moviegoers saw *The River* as an extra added attraction. The documentary demonstrated unexpected box office pull and garnered several awards, including that of best documentary at the Venice Film Festival. The reviews were excellent. *Time* magazine wrote, "Like the mighty Mississippi that is both hero and villain of the picture, *The River* has a powerful locomotive quality that is pointed up by a Virgil Thomson score based on bright scraps of locality music, matched in tempo by a cadenced narrative written by Lorentz."

Garrett D. Byrnes, writing in the *Providence Journal,* praised the film ("a superb achievement"), but warned that it was propaganda for the New Deal. And though few Americans object, he wrote, to what the government is doing to rehabilitate the eroded Mississippi valley, Byrnes feared that this set a dangerous precedent.

> [O]bserving what other governments have done in the way of propaganda on the screen, one is inclined to wonder whether American governmental productions if continued will deal always with such non-controversial matters as are treated in *The River,* or whether, bit by bit, the government will introduce more and more propaganda into its publicly-financed releases.[16]

Roosevelt's political and corporate opponents were outraged: the German Führer had his Leni Riefenstahl; now FDR had his Pare Lorentz. Shown the film at a private screening in Hyde Park, President Roosevelt turned to Lorentz and asked what he could do to help. The result was the formation of the U.S. Film Service. Lorentz took charge, but the next year the House of Representatives scuttled its budget, ruling that movies were not an appropriate use of relief funds. With the emerging European war commanding his attention, Roosevelt was in no position to take on this fight.

After this project Thomson again found work in the theater, this time in a well-financed commercial venture, a sumptuous production of Shakespeare's *Antony and Cleopatra* starring Tallulah Bankhead. It was a notorious flop. The play opened in Rochester and closed four days later. Tallulah "was fine in comedy scenes such as that with the messenger from Rome," Thomson wrote, "but a tragic stance she could not quite assume."[17] Bankhead went through rehearsals bellowing, "What this show needs is cunt! And that's what I've got." But Thomson thought her take on the play was utterly wrong. "It is a political tragedy and can only succeed as that. Played for love, it is all build-up and no showdown."[18]

Thomson's other major project from this period started with a suggestion from Lincoln Kirstein. Their relationship had chilled since the days when Kirstein tested his ideas for forming an American ballet company during late-night talks with Thomson in Paris. But Kirstein still respected Thomson and was grateful for his guidance. With George Balanchine as artistic director, Kirstein had founded the American Ballet. An offshoot of this was the Ballet Caravan, founded in 1936 to encourage American creators and dancers to collaborate on works with American themes.

Though Kirstein had been moved more by the spectacle than by the music of *Four Saints,* he had devised a ballet scenario, called *Filling Station,* for which he thought Thomson would be an ideal composer. Thomson was enticed. This would be the first thoroughly American modern ballet; the subject, scenario, music, choreography, costumes, and scenery were all by Americans; the dancers were American-born.

The traditional hero of the classical European ballets was a mythic figure of some sort. Kirstein wanted a modern American equivalent, a youthful, self-reliant everyman. Who better embodied these qualities than a resourceful gas station attendant who services our cars, offers respite to weary travelers, and keeps his washrooms spic and span?

When the curtain opens, Mac, our *Filling Station* hero, dressed in a white translucent coverall and cap (created by Paul Cadmus), is whiling away the lonely hours of the night reading a newspaper. He puts down the paper and starts to dance, vigorously, restlessly. He is then visited by a series of customers. First comes a motorist in a garish golfing outfit, looking for directions, later joined by his wife, a huge blonde in tacky slacks, and their constantly whining daughter. Two truck drivers show up; and with Mac they do an athletic pas de trois. A state trooper arrives, with a stern warning for the truck drivers, whom he has clocked speeding. An intoxicated young couple on their way home from a party drop in and dance a limp adagio. As the young woman gets a second wind, she wants to dance with everybody. At the height of the partying, a gangster shows up, pulls out a gun, lines up all the people, and orders them to hand over their cash and jewelry. Mac sneaks away and turns out the lights. The stage is plunged into darkness. But Mac has found some flashlights, which he distributes to his customers. As the gangster is searched for, a frenzied dance begins, lit only by crisscrossing flashlight beams. Panicked, the gangster shoots blindly into the dark. When the lights go up, the partying woman has been shot dead. The state trooper enters, arrests the gangster, and the slain woman is carried off in a funeral cortege. As she is hoisted high, however, she wakes from the dead and waves at Mac, left alone again to contemplate his evening and return to his newspaper.

Thomson loved the mock-heroics of the story. Once again, a score of indigenous American music seemed called for, and he fashioned one, deliberately derivative but skillfully assembled: a patchwork of waltzes, tangos, a fugue, a Big Apple dance, a holdup episode right out of the gangster movie genre, a funeral dirge—all aimed, in his words, "to evoke roadside America as pop art." The choreography was by Lew Christensen, who also danced the role of Mac, who "filled the stage with his in-the-air cartwheels and held us breathless with his twelve-turn pirouettes."[19] Erick Hawkins, who later became Martha Graham's partner in work and life, danced the gangster. Eugene Loring was one of the truck drivers.

Filling Station opened in Hartford at Chick Austin's increasingly booked Avery Memorial Auditorium on January 6, 1938, sharing the program with two other American ballets: *Show Piece* (music by Robert McBride, choreography by Erick Hawkins) and *Yankee Clipper* (music by Paul Bowles, choreography by Eugene Loring). All were performed with only a solo pianist playing orchestral reductions. Thomson, a hero in Hartford, won the best notices and the loudest ovations.

When Ballet Caravan took the show to New York, the sponsor was the WPA Federal Music Project of New York City. By now Thomson had been restored to the good graces of the WPA. The production was handsome and well attended; the scores were performed by the WPA-sponsored Greenwich Orchestra. Thomson's music was only a qualified success with the New York critics, and there was the typical grumbling among Thomson's more cerebral colleagues that his music was mere pastiche. However, Edwin Denby, writing in *Modern Music,* who was on his way to becoming America's most respected dance critic, was delighted by the whole venture.

> The ballets . . . taken together . . . show that an American kind of ballet is growing up, different from the nervous Franco-Russian style. . . . None of these ballets is imitative or artificial, and there is nothing pretentious about them. Hawkins shows us good-humored inventiveness, Loring a warmth of characterization, and Christensen a clear logic of movement that are each a personal and also specifically American version of ballet. I think this is the highest kind of praise, because it shows the ballet has taken root and is from now on a part of our life. And the dancers themselves have an unspoiled, American, rather athletic quality of movement that is pleasant.[20]

But Thomson had decidedly influenced one colleague—Aaron Copland. In later life, Copland openly acknowledged having been affected by Thomson's example of writing more simply. In some ways what Copland was influenced by was the example of writing functional music. Simplicity came naturally as a result of the serviceability. Copland had had one unhappy experience with ballet—*Hear Ye, Hear Ye!*—which he wrote in 1934 for the choreographer Ruth Page in Chicago. But *Filling Station, The Plow That Broke the Plains,* and *The River* had convinced Copland that composers could, after all, be central to the cultural life of mainstream America. When Lincoln Kirstein approached him in 1938 to write a ballet about Billy the Kid, Copland at first declined. What did a Brooklyn Jew know about cowboys? But Kirstein answered that the real-life Billy the Kid was a New

York–born hustler named William Bonney. If Copland could employ Latin American sources with confidence, as he had in *El Salón México,* why not try writing a cowboy ballet with real western tunes?

Billy the Kid, presented by the Ballet Caravan, with choreography by Eugene Loring, premiered in Chicago on October 6, 1938. Although the score was played only in a two-piano arrangement, the ballet was a wild success. A young dancer named Jerome Robbins, who had a small part in the ballet, made a point of complimenting Copland on his music. The next month in Los Angeles, Ballet Caravan presented *Billy the Kid* on a triple bill with *Yankee Clipper* and *Filling Station.* The success of these works sank in even among the young American composers who took themselves very seriously. The next year in a New York production, *Billy the Kid* shared a program with *Pocahontas,* a new ballet in a lighter style by the brainy young Elliott Carter. The subsequent refusal of Serge Koussevitzky to perform a suite from *Pocahontas* steered Carter away from experimenting again in a popular format. But Copland had begun his career as an enormously successful composer of ballets, theater music, and film scores.

By 1938 Thomson was feeling that the "good time" for him was over and that he had better get back to France. The theatrical thirties had been engaging. But his most original and important works, he believed, were his songs, his *Symphony on a Hymn Tune,* and his opera; yet his songs were seldom sung, his symphony remained unperformed, and *Four Saints* was by now more known about than known. From time to time talk flared up about reviving it; but, as he wrote to Stein, he doubted a revival would happen anytime soon: "The epoch isn't right. The original production isn't forgotten enough. All of a sudden one day it will be forgotten and then *Four Saints* will start its natural life as a classic repertory piece which I know will be a long life."[21] Perhaps back in Paris he could at least create another *Four Saints.*

During this period in New York, Thomson had gathered around him a group he called his "little friends," two of whom enchanted him for years. Harry Dunham and Paul Bowles had first appeared in Thomson's life at his Paris flat in the summer of 1931. They were intensely close, but an odd pair: Bowles, the sickly, winsome, nervous son of an abusive New York dentist; and Dunham, the dashing, confident, Princeton-educated son of a wealthy doctor. Thomson was dazzled. "Was it the radiance that they both brought with them, both nineteen, both in camel's hair overcoats, both with yellow hair and yellow cashmere scarfs?"[22]

Actually, Bowles was then twenty-one, and though he had already published poetry, he was an aspiring, though unformed, composer. In New York, Copland had taken Bowles under his care and given him lessons. Copland was worried that Bowles was undisciplined. "If you don't work, by the time you're thirty no one will love you," Copland used to tell him. As much as Copland let himself fall for anyone, he fell for Bowles, although Bowles was a reticent sexual being. Dunham, on the other hand, was an exuberantly promiscuous homosexual whose exploits left Bowles in awe. Dunham basically subsidized their adventures in Paris and Berlin in the spring of 1931 and, come summer, in Morocco, the ancient desert country that Bowles later extolled in his bleak, exhilarating fiction and eventually adopted as home.

Paul was entranced by Marrakech, with its white-hot sun and endless sky, and its streets and squares shaded by eucalyptus and date palm trees, lined with buildings in browns and maroons, and teaming with dark-skinned turbaned people. Beautiful Arab chamber boys, whom Harry adored, brought pomegranates to their hotel room for breakfast. In Tangier they took a house near the top of the cliffs that overlooked the Straits of Gibraltar. On all these expeditions, Harry was the leader, Paul the acolyte.

That fall of 1931 they settled in Paris—Harry for adventure, Paul to study, at Aaron's suggestion, with Nadia Boulanger, though Virgil tried to dissuade him from this. In the winter Harry took a flat in Virgil's 17 quai Voltaire building and invited Paul to live with him for free. Harry was a passionate but superficial and reckless young man. During this period he spent time in Berlin, where he was swept away by the euphoria over Hitler and attracted to the Nazi youth movement. Paul and his friends were horrified by Harry's Nazi talk. Soon Harry did a complete turnaround, joining the Communist Party, even financing leftist agitprop. Virgil was amused by Harry's flip-flopping politics, but he too was relieved when Harry renounced the Germans.

During this period in Paris, while Virgil was banned from the Stein household, Paul became a virtual member of it. Gertrude was fascinated by Paul, with his golden locks, refined manners, eclectic interests, and curiously detached attitude. Paul enjoyed Alice's mothering and Gertrude's advice: Gertrude told him to forget all about poetry and become a composer. Gertrude and Alice adored Paul, their precious "Freddy," as they called him.

Though miffed by Paul's sudden thickness with Gertrude, Virgil grew terribly fond of him that year. In the summer of 1933, when he and Maurice went to the island of Porquerolles to copy out the score and parts of *Four Saints,* Paul went along, to work on his music under Virgil's guidance.

Back in New York in 1933, Bowles and Thomson became colleagues as well. Bowles was a big booster of *Four Saints,* writing constantly to update Stein, sending her packets of clippings, and skewering those who resisted it. In 1936, when Bowles was hired to compose music for a French farce that Houseman was directing for the Federal Theater Project, a work roughly translated as *Horse Eats Hat,* he wrote a score full of vitality and color. Thomson had to orchestrate it, Bowles being too unskilled. By the time they shared the billing for Ballet Caravan productions, Bowles was his own orchestrator, and a good one, for which Thomson took credit.

By 1937 Thomson's "little friends" group had picked up new members. John Latouche, just nineteen, a fleshy-faced, handsome writer of light verse and show songs from Richmond, Virginia, was attending Columbia University. Eventually Bowles and Dunham both entered into "queer marriages." In February 1938 Bowles married Jane Auer, a high-strung, mop-haired daughter of a moneyed Jewish family from New York City who was almost defiantly lesbian. Jane walked with a limp, the vestige of surgery for tuberculosis in her knee. "A strange and elaborate marriage," Thomson called it. "They probably never slept together. Oh, they may have tried it once or twice. But they were terribly devoted." Harry became engaged to an unambiguously heterosexual woman who was attracted to homosexual men, Marian Chase, the daughter of a former army colonel and scientist and his Louisiana belle wife.

In late 1937 Harry, who had taken up photojournalism, went off to capture the Spanish civil war, taking Marian along. Paul and Jane, right after their marriage in February, left for Panama and France. Latouche would also marry a lesbian woman, Theodora Griffis, the daughter of Stanton Griffis, the U.S. ambassador to Spain. The one thing this eccentric group of "little friends" had in common was devotion to Virgil, whom they often called Papa. But the absurdities of the relationships among them and the undercurrents of Harry's attachment to Virgil can be gleaned from a morose letter he wrote to Virgil in 1937 while on another adventure, this time in Nanking, China.

> It boils down to hating to be in bed alone.
> And the least objectionable partner I've ever found is Latouche.
> If you were here we'd have problems, to bed or not to bed.
> If Paul were here we'd have hungry genius to be fed.
> If Marian were here I should be profoundly bored.
> But if Touche were capering around that bathroom and running naked about the place, I should be pleased as Punch and twice as grouchy. . . .
> I've decided I know why we resent each other. You're mad because you don't really like that big brother role at all—even tho you got yourself into it.
> You don't see where the "big" comes in and you're quite right. You were crazy and even a little trite when you said you got vitality from me. You're twice as alive and a good deal younger than I am. I'm so often bored. I'll be an old maid before you will.[23]

Not surprisingly the Latouche-Griffs marriage ended in divorce. Latouche went on to achieve success as a Broadway playwright and lyricist; but he grew pudgy and shiftless and and died at thirty-eight of a massive heart attack. Harry married Marian in 1940. In 1943 Lieutenant Harry Dunham was shot down while flying a voluntary scouting mission over New Guinea. During the 1940s in New York, Marian decided for a while that Virgil was the homosexual she was destined for. Virgil used to boast of this involvement, but little in fact ever came of it.

In any event, by 1937 Thomson's intense group of "little friends" was disbanding.

Meanwhile, Thomson's old friend Sherry Mangan, working in Norwood, Massachusetts, as a printer and engraver, was growing restless with his staid, suburban life. Having been divorced by his first wife, the highborn Kate Foster, he was now living in a pine-surrounded cottage with Marguerite Landin, a nurse who had treated him during one of his hospitalizations for depression. His "Margretta," he wrote to Virgil, "if not the paragon of beauty, is at least the perfection of devotion—very soothing to the Kate-abandoned vanity."[24] As he became more committed to Trotskyist politics, Sherry wanted to be close to the action, which meant returning to Europe. So Margretta cashed in her life insurance, and they moved that spring to Paris.

Maurice Grosser had gone there in January, having earned some money from a series of portrait commissions in Chattanooga, and from many government-paid-for hours of copying the score and parts to *The Plow That Broke the Plains*. Theodate Johnson announced that she would move to Paris in the fall with the intention of studying singing.

Virgil Thomson "had been busy (and in America) long enough."[25] His little friends were scattering about. His old friends were regrouping in Paris. So in June 1938 he returned there.

WHO DOES WHAT TO WHOM AND WHO GETS PAID

W hen Virgil Thomson arrived in Paris in late June of 1938, he found Maurice ensconced in a studio on the rue Bonaparte, just a few blocks south from Virgil's flat. Maurice's place was a single square room, five flights up, sparsely furnished, and newly equipped with a basin and taps and a hard-coal Franklin stove. Maurice, now thirty-five, trim and productive, was selling paintings for small sums. Virgil thought Maurice's work elegant and exotic: paintings of "over-life-size fruits and bread and vegetables in high bright colors"; and sensual portraits, for which commissions kept coming.

They were happy to be together again. Virgil still lost patience with Maurice's fidgetiness; Maurice found Virgil's bullying hard to take. But they were each other's primary person, though they never said so. Officially, each was free to engage in other affairs. Jealousy was not to be tolerated.

Just as Virgil was starting to find his flat at 17 quai Voltaire too cramped, a large apartment in the building—the whole third floor— was vacated. The landlord planned to divide it into small units to be rented furnished. Virgil asked that two rooms be set aside unfurnished for him, for which he would pay a yearly rate of $200. The landlord's work lasted through September; Virgil's renovations took another month: a washbowl with running hot water (electrically heated) was installed; walls were painted (sunlight yellow, bottle green, Bordeaux red); carpets were laid atop the oak floors; silver draperies were hung the full length of the thirteen-foot walls—all accomplished for just $200.

But from July through September, Virgil had time to fill. Since railway fares that summer were reduced for foreigners by two-fifths, he and Maurice headed for the country with no particular itinerary. The highlights of their wanderings was Lamoura, a grassy village with thick-stone houses atop a flowery plain in the Jura Mountains. There on three successive days in August, Virgil and Maurice made portraits (musical and painted) of three French boys. Claude Bias and Louis Lange, both about ten, were cute, sweet kids who agreed to pose for a small fee. The third was Maurice Bavoux, a young man of nineteen, handsome, delicate, with penetrating eyes and wavy blond hair. Virgil made an extra copy of the portrait as a gift for Bavoux. Over half a century later, Bavoux, long retired from his job as a customs officer, was astonished to learn that Thomson's portrait, suggestively titled "Maurice Bavoux: Young and Alone," had been published, cataloged in a book, and recorded on a compact disc.

This summer trip was supposed to be a working vacation. Maurice got a lot of painting done, but Virgil accomplished little. Before leaving New York, he had agreed to provide incidental music for a production of *The Duchess of Malfi* that Orson Welles was scheduled to direct. The production fell through, but Virgil thought this swashbuckling play might make a good opera libretto. He tried to fit it with music that summer, but soon deemed the play's blank verse hopeless for vocal setting.

During this trip Thomson was supposed to be working on another sizable project. He had sold the idea of a book of breezy essays—accounts of culture from both sides of the Atlantic, reports of the European war that in mid-1938 seemed about to erupt—to Thayer Hobson of the William Morrow publishing firm. But the book was not coming out the way he had planned it.

Thomson's success as a writer on music predated by years his success as a composer. He had partly subsidized his student year in Paris by writing reviews for the *Boston Evening Transcript*. When he moved there in 1925, he lived off the fees from his articles for *Vanity Fair*. By then H. L. Mencken, delighted with Thomson's explications of jazz for the *American Mercury*, invited him to submit anything he wanted on any subject. This open-ended invitation resulted in Thomson's one early failure: a straight-faced discussion of the erotic imagery in a standard 1917 collection of Baptist hymns. Thomson breaks down the 205 hymns into ten groups:

> 36 of these hymns are evangelical exhortations,
> 28 explain the benefits of conversion,
> 25 anticipate or describe Heaven,
> 13 are for children,
> 6 are prayerful,
> 4 are military,
> 3 predict the Judgment Day,
> 1 is about Mother,
> 1 recalls with pleasure a little brown church in the wildwood,
> 91 confess erotic feelings for the person of Jesus.[1]

He then proceeds to dissect the texts for their erotic content, specifically, an "eroticism turned inward by social taboos and converted thus to auto-eroticism." God moves in "no mysterious way for these illumined writers," he writes. "In fact, God the Father scarcely interests them. Jesus, the perfect, though very human 'lover of my soul' is the deity." By assembling bits of text, Thomson illustrates his point.

> Love is the theme, "love for you, love for me." It is the "old, old story." "Tenderly pleading," He waited, "all the night long," "knocking, knocking at the gate." Those who had "tasted his delights" called to me "in His name." "Heed," they cried. . . . "Resist Him no more!"

In this case, the problem was more than Thomson's penchant for sweeping generalizations. The subtext of his argument would seem to be that closeted erotic feelings are to be found everywhere, but that only he has the daring to point them out in church hymns. Mencken was not buying it.

> I can't rid myself of the feeling that you actually say nothing here. Your investigations of the hymns are a bit shaky to begin with and you discover nothing new about their contents. I believe that a discussion of the music would be far more interesting than any possible treatise on the words.[2]

The article was rejected.

In 1932 Thomson wrote his first article for *Modern Music;* during the 1930s he would become one of the journal's most essential and important commentators.

That first piece was an essay on Aaron Copland. The idea of inviting composers to write on each other came from Minna Lederman,

Modern Music's editor. Thomson writing on Copland seemed an obvious choice. However, when the article arrived via airmail from Paris, its "blunt, almost brutal tone" gave Lederman "a shock":

> This was a complete departure from the reverent tone of earlier profiles. How can I publish it, was my reaction. On second reading, the question was, How can I not? It had what I immediately recognized as Instant Style, with a clarity and concentrated brevity of judgment that made most other writing about music seem, by comparison, garrulous.[3]

The article begins audaciously.

> Aaron Copland's music is American in rhythm, Jewish in melody, eclectic in all the rest.
>
> The subject matter is limited but deeply felt. Its emotional origin is seldom gay, rarely amorous, almost invariably religious. Occasionally excitation of a purely nervous and cerebral kind is the origin of a *scherzo*. This tendency gave him a year or two of jazz-experiment. That has been his one wild oat. It was not a very fertile one.
>
> He liked the stridency of high saxophones and his nerves were pleasantly violated by displaced accents. But he never understood that sensuality of sentiment which is the force of American popular music nor accepted the simple heart-beat that is the pulse of its rhythm, as it is the pulse of his own rhythm whenever his music is at ease.
>
> His religious feeling is serious and sustained. He is a prophet calling out her sins to Israel. He is filled with the fear of God. His music is an evocation of the fury of God. His God is the god of battle, the Lord of Hosts, the jealous, the angry, the avenging god, who rides upon the storm.[4]

After further comments about the music's gentleness ("like an oriental contemplation of infinity") and tension ("the screaming of piccolos and pianos evokes the glitter of armaments and swords"), Thomson backpedals:

> All this I write is bunk, naturally. But I put it down because it seems to me to provide as good an evocative scheme as any for fitting together the various observations one can make about the way his music is made.

The article then describes in an incontrovertible tone the exact way Copland's music is made. By the end the reader is swept away by Thomson's tough critical analysis of the music, not just because the author is so sure of his insights, but because he seems so solidly in Copland's corner.

> If Copland's simplifications are perhaps not radical enough for my taste, they are important simplifications all the same.
>
> Because he is good, terribly good. A European composer of his intrinsic quality would have today a world-wide celebrity and influence. It is a source of continual annoyance to me that his usefulness and his beauty are not fully achieved because he has not yet done the merciless weeding out of his garden that any European composer would have done after his first orchestral hearing.
>
> The music is all right but the man is not clearly enough visible through it. An American certainly, a Hebrew certainly. But his more precise and personal outline is still blurred by the shadows of those who formed his youth.

Thomson manages to say that Copland is terribly good, but would be even better if he were more daringly radical (meaning simple, as Thomson is) and tenaciously true to himself (as Thomson is, by writing simply). The piece is both an encomium to what Copland has done and a clarion call for the man to do better. Copland responded graciously and, it seems, gratefully: "Thanks for the article. All my friends thought it very swell. It made me understand *your* music much better. And it will help me make mine better I hope."[5] Other reactions were not so gracious. One faction leapt on the piece as evidence of Thomson's anti-Semitism. Even Minna Lederman conceded that some of Thomson's comments could be so construed. The anti-Semitism charge would dog Thomson all his life. Viewed in context, his comments about Jews were no more sweeping than his comments about almost anything: the French, Baptists, organists, the rich, or, when he was courting controversy, our blacks, queer boys, and so on. He knew (and in his Copland article, even admitted) that his generalizations were sometimes "bunk." But making generalizations was an effective technique in the art of debate (when taking on opponents) or conversation (when talking with friends). Thomson's statements could be enraging, discombobulating, puzzling, amusing, exhilarating. Whatever the effect, he was usually able to keep his listener (or reader) off balance and seize the upper hand. There was something in his "Maxims of a Modernist" bluster that invited outrage. When confronted with the charge of being anti-Semitic, he would respond with another generalization: "They always accuse you of that!" If pressed, he would answer by listing the Jews (or those of partial Jewish background) who were his intimate associates: Maurice Grosser, Gertrude Stein, John Houseman, Florine Stettheimer, Morris Golde.

In later life, harboring some residual bitterness that the League of Composers ("that League from top to bottom was Aaron's baby") had considered him more a powerful critic than an important composer, he would unabashedly refer to it as "The League of Jewish Composers." Lederman remembers Thomson proposing for *Modern Music* an article on the thirteen Jews who ran music in New York, an idea she quickly quashed.

Thomson's Jewish friends defended him against the charge of anti-Semitism. But to generalize about Jews in the 1930s (or blacks in the 1960s, or queers in the 1970s) was to be politically incorrect. Thomson reveled in it. Besides, his comments about the Hebraic character of Copland's music were echoed by Jewish musicians who revered Copland, notably Leonard Bernstein, who called him "the stern prophet," a "Moses," who led music in his time to "a land full of promise."

Thomson thought the best critical writing on music came from composers, who are by nature "authoritative and passionately prejudiced." That was his own approach; and he unabashedly used his platform at *Modern Music* to support his allies and settle scores. In later years he credited Lederman with being his most influential editor. Though impressed by Thomson's brilliance and style, she worked hard to tame his tone, to weed it of blatant hostility or agendas. It worked. His articles, though still provocative and irreverent, grew more tactful and, consequently, more effective. Thomson's was becoming an essential voice.

He filed articles from Paris on new music and new trends; he wrote about film music in Europe and in America. There were two more explications of "Swing-music." Perhaps the most talked-about article from this period was Thomson's 1935 profile of George Gershwin, the substance of which is a precanonization analysis of Gershwin's then new opera, *Porgy and Bess*. Thomson demands that *Porgy and Bess* be taken seriously by the concert music establishment.

> When a man of Gershwin's gift, experience, and earning capacity devotes in the middle or late thirties three years of his expensive time to the composition of a continuous theatrical work on a serious subject, there is no reason for supposing that it represents anything but his mature musical thought and his musical powers at near their peak.[6]

In the middle of this long article is the nub of Thomson's argument in one pithy paragraph.

> *Porgy* is none the less an interesting example of what can be done by talent in spite of a bad set-up. With a libretto that should never have been accepted on a subject that should never have been chosen, a man who should never have attempted it has written a work that has some power and importance.

Operas by the "more conventionally educated composers" have been getting produced for years, Thomson says. Yet "nothing ever happens in them." Gershwin "does not even know what an opera is; and yet *Porgy and Bess* is an opera and it has power and vigor." There are regrettable shortcomings, of course. The play and the libretto derived from it are "full of hokum." The folklore is artificial: "Folk-lore subjects recounted by an outsider are only valid as long as the folk in question is unable to speak for itself, which is certainly not true of the American Negro in 1935." Moreover,

> his prose declamation is all exaggerated leaps and unimportant accents. It is vocally uneasy and dramatically cumbersome. Whenever he has to get on with the play he uses spoken dialogue. It would have been better if he had stuck to that all the time. . . .
>
> There are many things about it that are not to my personal taste. I don't like fake folk-lore, nor fidgety accompaniments, nor bittersweet harmony, nor six-part choruses, nor plum-pudding orchestration. I do, however, like being able to listen to a work for three hours and to be fascinated at every moment. I also like its lack of respectability, the way it can be popular and vulgar and go its own way as a real professional piece does without bothering much about the taste-boys.

The expected charges were leveled against Thomson. The article was patronizing, offensive both to Gershwin's Broadway fans and to Thomson's concert music colleagues; it was anti-Semitic. But *Porgy and Bess* was initially a failure; it ran for only 126 performances and did not recoup its investment. So, on balance, Thomson's article was an impassioned defense of the opera. He insightfully exposed the opera's authentic achievements and shortcomings three decades before they were generally accepted by most other critics.

Thomson's *Modern Music* work (from 1932 to 1939 he wrote eighteen articles), was winning him notoriety and respect. The idea of writing a book had been urged on him by friends and musicians who admired his writing. Thomson wasn't sure he had a book's worth of things to say. But he was attracted to the idea of making some money. Before returning to France, he offered his vague proposal to three publishers, got three bids, and took the highest: $1,000 from William Morrow. But as he traveled in France that summer with Grosser, the book floundered atop the mountain plains of the Jura region. It was not until he returned to Paris and moved into his newly refurbished flat that a compelling new twist to his original slapdash idea came to him—in large part, from talking late into the nights that fall with his old friend Sherry Mangan.

Life was cozy at 17 quai Voltaire in the fall of 1938. Maurice, living nearby, was loyal and loving and not underfoot. And Theodate Johnson, Philip's sister, had come to Paris, ostensibly to study singing. Four years earlier Virgil had participated in her official New York debut, a Town Hall recital that received mixed but encouraging notices. Samuel Chotzinoff in the *New York Post* found her Brahms and Handel wooden, but approved of her French group. With Virgil playing percussion, Theodate had also performed his *Five Phrases from the Song of Solomon.* Walking onstage all solemn and pudgy, carrying his drum sticks, Virgil looked like "a field mouse from *Alice in Wonderland,*" Theodate recalled. The audience tittered. Chotzinoff reported of the performance that "Miss Johnson applied herself with the required ecstasy and a good deal of virtuosity."[7]

Wanting to be near the friend who had supported her vocal ambitions, Theodate leased a flat one flight up from Virgil's, a sunny place with two balcony windows. She made some progress with her singing, winning small roles with the Royal Flemish Opera Company. The prospects for a successful career were not high. However, she was vivacious, attractive, and generous with the modest family stipend that supported her. Friends could count on her when they needed a good dinner. Virgil enjoyed having her around.

Sherry Mangan was also around that fall, employed as a correspondent for *Time,* which "had discovered that his trainings as research scholar and as revolutionist were valuable for news analysis."[8] Eventually he ran the Paris bureau and, feeling prosperous for a change, moved with Marguerite, whom everyone had taken to calling just "M," into 17 quai Voltaire, taking a spacious top-floor suite with three balconies. As in Harvard days, Virgil was delighted with Sherry's company. Marguerite was mousy and plain, but devoted to her boisterous, attractive, hard-drinking husband.

Sherry's journalistic career was taking off. He wrote influential cover stories for *Time* on the Socialist French premier Edouard Daladier, on Picasso, and on James Joyce. But he was leading a stressful double life: he was an ambitious and frustrated poet and linchpin of the Paris artists set; he was also an underground activist in the Trotskyist Fourth International. Fearful that his radical politics would jeopardize his journalistic career, he wrote for leftist periodicals under pseudonyms, Terence Phelen being one.

But all that season Sherry and Virgil talked politics. For Sherry, devotion to Trotsky and his followers had taken the place of devotion to the Jesuits. Virgil, though apolitical, was struck by Sherry's clear-headed explications on the economic determinism of practically everything, his faith in collective action, and his analysis of capitalist exploitation. Virgil had a sophisticated understanding of social and artistic politics. Some of it he had gained by befriending wealthy families (the Lasells, the Faÿs, the Askews and their salon group) and by following the money trail. How did they invest? Which art and institutions were deemed worthy of patronage? He had fought in the trenches of the new-music movements; he had been involved with every aspect of the theater: patron supported, government supported, and commercial. He had associated not only with writers, poets, and painters but with publishers, bookshop owners, literary agents, union lawyers, picture dealers, and everyone engaged in the "pseudo-philanthropic museum racket."

In no way did Virgil accept Sherry's leftist take on these matters. But it did encourage him to lace his analysis with a more provocative and deterministic view of the musical state. By October, in a letter to Thayer Hobson, Thomson finally was able to announce the subject of his book:

> It is to be a complete account of the musical world (no less) and include esthetics, economics, politics, and even some technical matters, the whole show in fact from pedagogy to opera and movies, including the business politics of symphony orchestras and an exposé of the pseudo-educational rackets.
>
> Not an encyclopedia of course. Just my opinions about all these things. But still I have to do lots of explaining in order to have my opinions make sense. I've written 15 or 20 thousand words and

ABOVE: Virgil Thomson at thirty-one, in 1927. Photo by Man Ray. RIGHT: Sherry Mangan, poet, journalist, and Trotskyite revolutionary, at twenty-three in Paris, 1927.

ABOVE: Virgil Thomson and Gertrude Stein going over the score for their opera *Four Saints in Three Acts,* at her home in Paris, probably in 1929. OPPOSITE, TOP: Virgil Thomson and Maurice Grosser in Paris, 1930. OPPOSITE, BOTTOM: A. Everett "Chick" Austin, Jr., director of the Wadsworth Atheneum in Hartford, Connecticut, whose vision it was to present the premiere of *Four Saints in Three Acts* in a specially built new wing of his museum.

ABOVE: Florine Stettheimer in 1925, New York, a reclusive painter whom Thomson asked to design the sets for the premiere of *Four Saints in Three Acts*. RIGHT: John Houseman, Thomson's choice to direct *Four Saints in Three Acts,* at thirty-two, in 1934.

ABOVE: Frederick Ashton, the British choreographer, whom Thomson recruited to create movements for the all-black cast of *Four Saints in Three Acts*. Pictured here with three members of the cast, a controversial photograph by George Platt Lynes. LEFT: Beatrice Wayne Godfrey, the original Saint Teresa I, cast photograph for *Four Saints in Three Acts*, 1934.

ABOVE: *Four Saints in Three Acts,* 1934: Act 1 tableau. OPPOSITE, TOP: Saint Teresa I and II serenaded at a garden party. RIGHT: Procession in Act 3.

Four Saints in Three Acts, 1934: Saint Teresa I and II observe the Compère and the Commère in a tender moment.

that is practically all introduction. I haven't touched the main meat of the book which is my economic-esthetic theory. No doubt I shall do later a good deal of pruning and transposing in what I've written but at the moment there is no use. Nor am I doing any travelling around until I am nearer the end and need some flashy bits of news and scholarship for embellishments.[9]

With the topic now sighted, Virgil worked obsessively all winter, from nine to one and from one-thirty to five or sometimes seven, turning out whole chunks of text every day. Once in a while for diversion, he practiced the piano. But he wrote no music. And by the springtime he had finished *The State of Music.*

The main thesis in *The State of Music,* if a relatively short book so sprawling in its subject matter can be said to have one, is that the musical world is an "island home" not quite like anyplace else; and that if everybody understood this, including musicians themselves, the inhabitants of that island home and their customers (and noncustomers) from the outside would get along a lot better. Thomson describes the entire gamut of the musical world in relation to the other arts and the rest of society—the "whole works." The actions, daily routines, artistic interests, and economic motivations of everyone involved, Thomson argues, can be explained in terms of their position in a cultural matrix.

Thomson begins with a description of "Our Island Home," or "What it feels like to be a musician."

> Every profession is a secret society. The musical profession is more secret than most, on account of the nature of music itself. No other field of human activity is quite so hermetic, so isolated. Literature is made out of words, which are ethnic values and which everybody in a given ethnic group understands. Painting and sculpture deal with recognizable images that all who have eyes can see. Architecture makes perfectly good sense to anybody who had ever built a chicken coop or lived in a house. Scholarship, science, and philosophy, which are verbalizations of general ideas, are practiced humbly by all, the highest achievements of these being for the most part verifiable objectively by anyone with access to facts. As for politics, religion, government, and sexuality, every loafer in a pub or club has his opinions, his passions, his inalienable orientation about them. Even the classical ballet is not very different from any other stylized muscular spectacle, be that diving or tennis or bull-fighting or horse-racing or simply a military parade.

> Among the great techniques, music is all by itself, an auditory thing, the only purely auditory thing there is. It is comprehensible only to persons who can remember sounds. Trained or untrained in the practice of the art, these persons are correctly called "musical." And their common faculty gives them access to a secret civilization completely impenetrable by outsiders.[10]

From this introduction Thomson moves to a description of the surrounding neighborhoods—painting, poetry; but the bulk of the book is devoted to "Life among the Natives" in the island home: musical habits and customs; the civic status of musicians; a chapter titled "How Composers Eat, or, Who Does What to Whom and Who Gets Paid"; and, in the book's most provocative section, a straight-faced explication of how musical style is affected by the financial setup of a composer's life, called "Why Composers Write How, or, The Economic Determinism of Musical Style."

The book abounds with prescriptions, particularly in the final sections, when Thomson wrestles with the question of group action through guilds, leagues, and associations. While it is essential for musicians to pool their power, to act collectively in order to protect themselves, the labor union models are not ideal for musicians, he argues, since the functions and interests of the executant (the performer) are so essentially different from those of the composer.

However, for all its calls to action, *The State of Music* reads like a descriptive, not a polemical, book. The polemics are neatly nestled into the audacious, brilliant, and wickedly funny descriptions. Thomson's technique is to seduce the reader through his writerly charm into going along with his generalizations, and into agreeing with his polemics.

Here, for example, is Thomson on why painters, unlike musicians, who are orderly by nature, value disorder in their lives:

> because disorder, both material and moral, is of the essence in a painter's life. Their incomes and their love-lives are as jumpy as a fever chart. Their houses are as messy as their palettes. They view life as a multiplicity of visible objects, all completely different. A dirty towel in the middle of the floor, wine-spots on the piano keys, a hairbrush in the butter plate are for them just so many light-reflecting surfaces. Their function is to look at life, not to rearrange it. All of which, if it makes for messiness in the home, also makes for ease in social intercourse. This plus the fact that they all have perfectly clear consciences after four o'clock, or at whatever hour the daylight starts giving out. . . . The painter's whole

morality consists of keeping his brushes clean and getting up in the morning.[11]

Here is Thomson on why composers make good husbands for wealthy women:

> After all, if a lady of means really wants an artistic husband, a composer is about the best bet, I imagine. Painters are notoriously unfaithful, and they don't age gracefully. They dry up and sour. Sculptors are of an incredible stupidity. Poets are either too violent or too tame, and terrifyingly expensive. Also, due to the exhausting nature of their early lives, they are likely to be impotent after forty. Pianists and singers are megalomaniacs; conductors worse. Besides, executants don't stay home enough. The composer, of all the art-workers in the vineyard, has the prettiest manners and ripens the most satisfactorily. His intellectual and his amorous powers seldom give completely out before death. His musical powers not uncommonly increase. Anyway, lots of composers marry money, and a few have it already from papa.[12]

Even today, few composers who make their living from teaching in a university can read without wincing Thomson's picture of how working in the pedagogy business determines their compositional styles.

> As everybody knows, school-teachers tend to be bossy, pompous, vain, opinionated, and hard-boiled. This is merely their front, their advertising. Inside they are timid and over-scrupulous. Their music, in consequence, comes out looking obscure and complex. Its subject-matter, its musical material are likely to be over-subtle and dilute. When we say nowadays that a work is "academic" we mean all that and more. We mean that the means employed are elaborate out of all proportion to the end achieved.
>
> . . . Teachers tend to form opinions about music, and these are always getting in the way of creation. The teacher, like the parent, must always have an answer for everything. If he doesn't he loses prestige. He must make up a story about music and stick to it. Nothing is more sterilizing. Because no one can make any statement three times without starting to believe it himself. One ends up being full of definite ideas about music; and one's mind, which for creative purposes should remain as vague and unprejudiced as possible, is corseted with opinions and *partis pris*.[13]

The most prescient passage in the book may be Thomson's skewering of the complex "international style" of contemporary composition and the resulting alienation it has caused among musical creators,

promoters, and consumers. Written in 1939, this insightful analysis
could be applied to the troubled situation as it exists today.

> The international-style music world used to be a well-organized
> going concern, with its own magazines, its "contemporary music"
> societies, its subventions, its conspiracies, and its festivals. Of late
> years business has not been so good. Private commissions are
> scarce, institutional funds diminished, the societies defunct or
> moribund, the public fed-up. The high-pressure salesmanship that
> forced into the big orchestral concerts (by pretending that an in-
> ternational movement should be supported on nationalistic
> grounds) music that was never intended for anything but prize-
> winning and the impressing of other musicians, has given a black
> eye to all music written since 1918. The general music public and
> the trustee class have both revolted. The conductors have seized
> the occasion to pull all the cover over to their side of the bed, thus
> leaving quite out in the cold the problem of contemporary com-
> position in large form (which presupposes as an essential factor
> in the equation the presence of a large general public). . . . Every-
> where the preceding decade's chief offender (the international
> style) is taboo. . . . The new pieces most orchestras play nowa-
> days are in the vein of pre-war post-Romanticism. They are chiefly
> by school-teachers and children just out of the conservatories. They
> are often tuneful and pleasing. They seldom get a second perfor-
> mance, however, even when the first goes over big, as it does not
> infrequently. I don't think the conductors quite want any composer
> to have a very steady success. They consider success their domain.
> And their success depends on keeping orchestral performance a
> luxury product, a miraculously smooth, fabulously expensive, and
> quite unnecessary frame for sure-fire classics.[14]

Thomson has little sympathy for the proposed remedies to this
dilemma. If anything, he views the cultivation of a healthy musical
life as undermined by patrons who claim to love music.

> These women are not stupid; they are just not very musical. . . .
> What they like about orchestral concerts mostly, I think, is (a) the
> conductor and (b) the resemblance of the musical execution's
> super-finish to that of the other streamlined luxury-products with
> which their lives are surrounded. They feel at home, as if they were
> among "nice things," and as if the Revolution (or whatever it is
> that troubles rich people's minds) were far, far away.[15]

He debunks the whole effort to court audiences. Nor does he
have much good to say about the "appreciation racket" and its ac-

companying literature, which "transmits no firm knowledge and describes no real practice."

> The basic sales technique in all these manifestations is the use of the religious technique. Music is neither taught nor defined. It is preached. A certain limited repertory of pieces, ninety per cent of them a hundred years old, is assumed to contain most that the world has to offer of musical beauty and authority. . . . It is further assumed (on Platonic authority) that continued auditive subjection to this repertory harmonizes the mind and sweetens the character, and that the conscious paying of attention during the auditive process intensifies the favorable reaction. Every one of these assumptions is false, or at least highly disputable, including the Platonic one. The religious technique consists in a refusal to allow any questioning of any of them.[16]

And so on.

At the very moment Thomson was writing these words, a music appreciation book written by Aaron Copland was published by McGraw-Hill. *What to Listen for in Music* was taken from a series of fifteen lectures that Copland delivered during the winters of 1936 and 1937 at the New School for Social Research, in New York. Copland had an avuncular lecture style, and he made concert music seem unintimidating to his audiences of lay listeners. The book was equally successful. Thinking his old friend Virgil would want to see it, Copland sent a copy off to Paris. But to Thomson, the book was exactly the kind of mealy-mouthed nonsense that he decried, as he said in a stinging letter.

> Your book I read through twice and I still find it a bore. Marian writes me it sells swell and that is a good thing of course. Not that the book doesn't contain a hundred wise remarks about music. But it also contains a lot of stuff that I don't believe and that I am not at all convinced you believe. Supposing you do believe that analytic listening is advantageous for the musical layman, it is still quite possible and not at all rare to believe the contrary. It even remains to be proved that analytic listening is possible even. God knows professional musicians find it difficult enough. I suspect that persons of weak auditive memory do just as well to let themselves follow the emotional line of a piece, which they can do easily, and which they certainly can't do very well while trying to analyze a piece tonally. In any case, I find it a bit high-handed to assume the whole psychology.

I find similarly unproved assumptions in the musical form chapter. I do not believe, for instance, that the loose and varied sonata form practiced by the great Viennese has very much relationship to the modern French reconstructed form that d'Indy made up for pedagogical purposes. . . . You know privately that it is the most controversial matter in all music, has been so since Beethoven. I find it a little dull of you and a little unctuous to smooth all that over with what I consider falsehoods. . . .

I'm not trying to write your book for you. I'm just complaining that you didn't write it for yourself. Almost any music teacher could have written it. Maybe not so smooth and high-toned. Certainly not nearly so clear and authoritative as when you give your own answers to things. But that is far from always.[17]

After some professional gossip and congratulations for the success of Aaron's new ballet *Billy the Kid,* Virgil ends by saying, "My book gets toward being finished. I like it better than yours. I only hope it sells as well."

Poor Copland had never anticipated such a reaction. But it clearly rattled him.

Dear Virgil,

It was lots of fun to get that long letter from you. . . . I enjoyed reading your strictures on the book more than much of the praise that it has had. All the wrong people like it very much, which makes me suspect you must be right. I won't argue the merits of your sonata-form analysis—this is hardly the moment. My tendency always is to stress the similarities of things rather than their differences. The whole book is a kind of outline of musical facts. It never occurred to me that anyone would look for original contribution to musical theory in it. I quite agree that any music teacher could have written it. The damn thing was never meant for you to read in the first place—so it doesn't surprise me to know that you found it a bore. Still, I'm glad you read it and sent me the low-down on it. I was about to think that so much praise must be deserved when your letter arrived. Thought I: we can always depend on Virgil.[18]

In the spring of 1939 Thomson sent his manuscript, typed by Sherry Mangan, to William Morrow and Company. *The State of Music* was published in the fall, with a fanciful jacket cover depicting a balding, tuxedo-clad composer strumming a golden harp on his island home, surrounded by three neighbors—a poet, a writer, and a sculptor—standing waist-deep in the lapping ocean waters. By March of 1940 only 2,045 copies at $2.75 had been sold; thereafter sales dwindled to almost none. But the arts world buzzed with talk of Thomson's book, and the reviews were sensational.

> . . . as pithy and entertaining a monologue on music and life in general as one can possibly hope to read in a lifetime. . . . Mr. Thomson writes breathtakingly about music. Any one who had tried to write about music knows that there is no subject more elusive, more potentially resistant, more baffling and more boring. Mr. Thomson writes about music as if it were a rational subject like literature or the condition of overseas commerce. . . . Take it from one who has written a lot of baloney about music, Mr. Thomson's "The State of Music" is as refreshing as a thunder shower and as cleansing.
> —Samuel Chotzinoff, *New York Post*

> . . . Virgil Thomson can not only compose music but can write about it, so that the drums and cornets, as well as occasional violins and flutes, sing in his sentences.
> —Lewis Gannett, *New York Herald Tribune*

> . . . Mr. Thomson's wit, independence of thought and his gift for the fresh and telling phrase pervade this book, and even if you are not at all interested in the state of music he manages to entertain you. If you are interested in the state of music, Mr. Thomson will delight you or make you furious. He is a man with opinions, not only about music but about other arts. He expresses them pointedly and pungently, delicately and piercingly. Whatever else this book does to the reader, it is not a soporific.
> —Howard Taubman, *New York Times Book Review*

Perhaps the most insightful and valuable assessment was Copland's for *Modern Music*. Copland writes as one living on that island home. He points out the subtext to the book that the noncomposer reviewers missed.

> For once the composer is treated as a human being, with not merely a craftsman's interest, but also economic, political and social interests. . . .
>   Thomson has an almost medieval sense of the composer's professional community of interests—both financial and artistic.[19]

Copland manages to work in a gentle barb at Thomson's taking on of the dissonant "international modern music style," pointing out that it "has served as the perfect foil for the simplicities of Thomson, Sauguet and Co." However, despite Thomson's trashing of *What to*

Listen for in Music, Copland was mightily impressed by the book and said so.

> Virgil Thomson has written the most original book on music that America has produced. *The State of Music* is the wittiest, the most provocative, the best written, the least conventional book on matters musical that I have ever seen (always excepting Berlioz). If you want to have fun, watch how people react to this book. It will undoubtedly be taken too solemnly by some, not solemnly enough by others. It will make many readers hopping mad. It will simply delight others. It will be quoted and discussed everywhere.

Reacting to all the reactions, Thomson wrote to Briggs Buchanan.

> The music world seems to be swallowing The State of Music with considerable smacking of lips. I expected a wry face from Harvard, it's only natural. But I guess they all read it, from what I hear. The poets and painters like it too. The only anger has come from the exploiting worlds. The symphony trustees are shocked and silently thankful, for both my sake and theirs, that I didn't mention Toscanini. The ladies who run the Metropolitan Opera Guild are openly furious, as if they had been made to look a little ridiculous. The Museum of Modern Art opines the book is brilliant but fallacious. You see all that is just side issues. The book was aimed at the profession and seems to be hitting its mark surprisingly. And in spite of the continual wisecracking in it, it isn't supposed to be controversial. It's supposed to be just God's truth every word of it and time somebody said same out loud.[20]

With his book done, Virgil intended to return full-time to composing. But life in Paris was unsettling. Throughout 1939 the French press and government had treated the threats of the Germans as just more Nazi bluster. Maurice Grosser, for one, bought the press propaganda. "The newspapers were very reassuring: The Germans had no generals, they had no gasoline, the Maginot line was impenetrable. It was beautifully engineered and very comfortable. All one had to do was to wait and eventually the Germans would get tired and go back home. We believed it all."[21] Virgil was equally blasé.

In early September 1939 the Germans invaded Poland, as Sherry Mangan had warned his apolitical friends they would. France and England immediately declared war on Germany. That was it for Maurice. "He stayed in France just long enough to show he was not afraid," Virgil wrote, "and to be assured that his French friends, at home or mobilized, had no need of him."[22] Maurice had no money for staying on and no prospects for making any. Just then, fortuitously, he was offered a show by Julien Levy, who ran the most advanced of New York's galleries. The only safe way to transport his pictures overseas was to travel with them. Of course he should go.

Moreover, Maurice had contracted a case of syphilis from sexual adventures with promiscuous young men. Fortunately, Virgil was not infected. And Maurice was responding well to treatments in Paris. But he was worried about continuing them in wartime conditions. All this compelled him to return. In late October, Virgil, Sherry, and his wife, Marguerite, took Maurice to a farewell dinner at a Left Bank café known for its veal kidneys cooked in port. Virgil walked him to the train station, and Maurice left for Bordeaux, there to board a New York–bound steamer.

After war was declared, Virgil wrote to Gertrude Stein, who had gone that summer with Alice to her country place in Bilignin and thought it wisest to stay on. Virgil and Gertrude had seen each other infrequently since his return from America. They were cordial, but some tension from their quarrel lingered. Virgil wrote to ask if Gertrude and Alice were safe and in need of anything. Gertrude answered that they were fine and spoke of a disturbing new acquisition.

> For the first time in my life I have had a radio in the house and it does discourage one about music, why should there be so much of it, it going on all the time in the air certainly has something to do with the world's troubles, well, anyway, it will be nice seeing you again and I hope the book is going well.[23]

Ironically, as the war effort mobilized, Virgil's spirits lifted. He was enjoying immensely his neighbors: Sherry and Marguerite, and Theodate, who was nursing a barely disguised crush on Sherry. Almost every night they ate together. Afterward there were drinks and talk. Sherry always had an open bottle of Grand Marnier on his mantle. Marguerite joined the group but seldom spoke. Sherry was tortured by the war news and exhausted by his double life: journalist by day, clandestine agitator for the French Trotskyists by night, who now had to reconfigure themselves into an underground organization. But he still loved drinking and debating with Virgil, whom he lectured fruitlessly about the oppression of Jews, the scourge of fascism, the plight of the smaller countries Hitler was vanquishing, and the hopes of the radical left. He found Virgil shockingly detached. Virgil thought the forces that controlled history were immutable and there was little to be done about them.

To Virgil the excitement and danger of a country at war was stimulating. He, Sherry, and Theodate all found radio work translating French programs and dispatches into English. Wartime Paris, Virgil wrote to Briggs, had "never been sweeter and quieter and pleasanter and kinder and more sensibly reasonable about everything."

> The war itself, of course, is rarely mentioned. Neither are those tiresome old peacetime subjects that we worried around for 20 years, such as the surrealist quarrels and the perfidy of Salvador Dali and the bad manners of G. Stein and the death of J. Cocteau and the extreme elegance of Christian Bérard's never washing and the superhuman excellence of P. Picasso, our local and equally tiresome Toscanini.

Every Friday evening Virgil hosted a poetry salon:

> I admit painters because they are fun, but we never mention painting (I've heard enough about that in the last 19 years of Paris residence); I discourage musicians from coming too. And I won't have any of those unhappy women whose husbands are at the war or anybody who knits.[24]

Yet, as the sounds of sirens summoning everyone to air raid drills grew routine and the newspapers reported the defeatism of the French generals, it became harder to ignore the approaching chaos. Sherry was working days at a time in isolation, growing despondent and constantly complaining about his health, which exasperated Virgil, who never could tolerate other people's health complaints. By February he was annoyed with his old friend, as he wrote to Maurice: "The Sherrys lead a secluded life devoted entirely to journalism and marriage with a touch of hypochondria thrown in."[25]

Some of the growing distance between Virgil and the Mangans was no doubt related to Sherry's impatience with Virgil's political aloofness. By now Virgil's best French male friends, Christian Bérard and Henri Sauguet, had been conscripted into the military. Yet Virgil's letters to Maurice are filled with chitchat about his physical culture regimen and resultingly trimmer body, reports of how fine foodstuffs (chestnuts, oysters) were still surprisingly available, news of his piano practicing routine, and gossip.

There seems to be lots of marrying here too. . . . But the sex life is about as uninteresting as I've ever seen it. I haven't much interest that way myself and nobody else seems to have either. The war seems to act in the opposite way to what one might have expected. I seem to be perfectly happy practicing the piano and making new friends and trying on suits.[26]

However, all the marrying going on around him must have had an effect on Virgil, who was still unhappy in his singlehood, especially in terms of public perception. Despite his cavalier talk, it seemed inevitable that the war would compel his return to America. He was forty-three; the time had come to stop playing boy games and settle down with a suitable mate, which meant acquiring a wife.

One night, after dinner with his neighbors, Virgil lingered alone to talk with Theodate. With no lead-up, he announced that they should marry. Theodate's career was going nowhere, he bluntly pointed out; she would make an excellent wife and be happy in her role; they both had intelligence and charm. Theodate was completely taken aback.

"Virgil," she said; "I can't marry you. I'm too fond of you to marry you. I know you too well."

He was insistent. Theodate started getting annoyed. Virgil was a brilliant man and good friend. But she found him rather homely. Of course she knew about his relationship with Maurice. Moreover, from the stairwell she often heard the sounds of Virgil coming home in the middle of the night with various men he picked up. Like all of Virgil's good friends, Theodate understood and accepted his private life but never mentioned it. Even as he was being obnoxious and pressing her to marry him, she was reluctant to mention it out loud.

"Virgil," she said firmly. "I can't marry you and you know why I can't." She told him to forget the whole idea and go down to his place immediately. It was late. She was tired. She was going to take a bath and go to bed.

Virgil left through the back door, which led to a rear stairwell that connected their apartments. Theodate's flat had two floors; the bath was on the lower floor. She bathed, toweled herself, put on her robe, and climbed the stairs to her bedroom. In her bed she found Virgil, naked.

"We're going to get married!" he shouted. "And we better get used to it."

Virgil, still naked, started chasing Theodate around the room.

Theodate was never really frightened; but she was furious. She pushed him away, pointed to the door, commanded him to take his clothes, leave, and not come back. He left. For almost six weeks Theodate would not speak to him. Sherry and Marguerite found out what happened. Marguerite was shocked, but Sherry thought the whole escapade hilarious.

Unlike Virgil, Theodate was impressed by Sherry's sermonizing. At his suggestion, she volunteered for the Belgian Red Cross in France, receiving refugees at the Gare du Nord, eventually directing a medical and surgical relief unit in Bordeaux. Virgil later wrote dismissively of Theodate's decision to remain at her post that spring before the Germans invaded, shouting instructions in makeshift facilities to huddled refugees: "By waiting for that outcome, she added nothing to her usefulness, merely lost her voice and a large part of her luggage."[27] Perhaps his remark was motivated by guilt; Theodate remained in France longer than Virgil, doing important and dangerous work and paying a price. Her voice was permanently damaged. Years of vocal therapy in American helped, but failed to restore it.

In April and May, as the German troops approached, Virgil spent hours in his flat practicing Mozart piano sonatas, seized by a theory he devised of how the pieces work compositionally. He wrote to Maurice about it.

> They are not camp, as I had thought, or just sort of routine writing, as most musicians think; they imitate things. Sometimes they imitate symphonies, which makes them easy to understand; but then sometimes they imitate music-boxes and wind-instrument pieces and are not personally expressive at all except unconsciously, so those have to be played like music-boxes or wind-instrument pieces and then they come out not dull at all but sharp and lovely and terrible fun and quite loud and rich.[28]

As Parisians scurried past Virgil's building—stocking supplies, arranging to leave, closing down shops—they were amazed and incensed by the sounds of Virgil pounding away at Mozart's piano sonatas. Virgil's notion that these works were imitative pieces may have been influenced by his musical state of mind. During the months of April and May, he went about the city visiting friends and composing their musical portraits, twenty-one in all during eight weeks. It was becoming clear that he would have to leave France. Just as a painter or photographer might do farewell sketches or take parting shots, Virgil composed pieces to remember his French friends by. Among them were a somber, contrapuntal portrait of Sherry with Scottish snaps in the rhythmic figures; a "Poltergeist" of the Dada artist Jean Arp; an industrious piano invention of Theodate; a sultry tango for the lovely seventeen-year-old daughter of the violinist Yvonne de Casa Fuerte; a brilliant depiction of Picasso called "Bugles and Birds"; and a short but proper three-movement piano sonata, a portrait of his eccentric art collector friend Peggy Guggenheim.

On May 29 the Germans bombed the Renault factory on the Seine. The war had gotten so close that from his top-floor windows Sherry could see the air raids. Virgil was reluctant to leave, but he had little money. On May 6 he had written to Briggs asking for a $500 loan, and Briggs had deposited that amount in a French-American bank. However, to be caught behind German lines without escape money, even for a citizen from a neutral country, was too big a risk.

He packed his luggage, twelve suitcases full of his winter clothes, household silver, and musical manuscripts. He arranged for two boxes of artworks to be shipped ahead. But they missed the connection and were never sent, remaining behind in storage at a Paris train station until 1944, when it became possible for Virgil, sending a baggage check from New York, to reclaim them. He arranged to keep his flat for a rate of $200 per year. There he left his printed music and books, which would have been impossible to take.

By June 14, when the Germans marched into Paris and draped a Nazi flag from the Eiffel Tower, Virgil was at the home of Miss Gertrude Newell in Moumour, a bucolic village in the Pyrenees. A New Yorker with literary connections, Newell had invited Virgil and other artistic friends to be refugees from the city at her country home. By July, Virgil had overstayed his welcome. The trains were running again with German officers manning the stations. It was still risky, but now possible to make the trip. Virgil, twelve suitcases in tow, traveled to Biarritz, where he ran into an old friend from Paris, the photographer Man Ray. Together they made their way through Spain, to Lisbon, where they boarded a New York–bound American ship. The crew was rude; the food was frozen. They slept, more than sixty men, on the "floor of the library, Man Ray with cameras under his pillow."

Soon after arriving in New York in late August, Virgil heard from his conductor friend Alexander Smallens, who had a place in Stamford, Connecticut. Virgil must come right away, Alexander said. There was someone he wanted Virgil to meet. Geoffrey Parsons was the editorial-page editor and overseer of all things cultural at the *New York Herald Tribune*. The paper was still searching for a chief music critic to replace Lawrence Gilman, who had died the preceding September. Parsons followed Virgil's articles in *Modern Music* and had been impressed by *The State of Music*. He wanted to meet its author.

19 THE TRIB

In 1910 there were fourteen daily newspapers in New York City competing for readers and advertisers. By 1940 the number had dropped to eight; but most of these claimed a stable share of the market. The tabloid *Daily News,* with its snappy writing and penchant for covering seamy local stories, led in circulation, over two million per day. There were two Hearst papers: the *Mirror,* a *Daily News* wannabe (with about half the circulation) kept afloat by the intense popularity of the celebrity columnist Walter Winchell; and the flashy *Journal-American,* the best-selling evening tabloid. By 1940 the arch-conservative, but warm and fuzzy evening *Sun* was starting to flounder. By 1950 the *Sun* had been bought and folded into the *World—Telegram.* The *Post* trailed the tabloid field.

The *New York Times* strived to be the journal of record. Its hallmarks were comprehensive coverage of international affairs, equitable accounts of American politics, disdain for "trend" stories and celebrity profiles, substantive coverage of the arts, and unsensational design (the *Times* did not employ front-page photos until 1965). Then as now, the *Times* had unshakably loyal readers.

During the 1920s through the early 1950s, its chief rival was the *Herald Tribune,* generally considered to be the best-written, best-edited, most lively and literate newspaper in the business. The *Tribune* never caught up with the *Times* in circulation and advertising. During the 1940s the weekday circulation of the *Times* grew from about 450,000 to 550,000. During the same period the *Tribune*'s dropped from over 70 percent of the *Times*'s figures to under 60 percent. There was room for both papers. The *Herald Tribune* targeted a slightly different market: socially liberal, non-isolationist, civic-minded, fiscally conservative Republicans. The *Tribune* strongly endorsed all four of Franklin Roosevelt's Republican opponents. The Republican-Liberal mayor Fiorello La Guardia was considered a sell-out to the paternalistic social welfare policies of the New Deal.

The Liberal Republican politics of the paper reflected the outlook and affluent lifestyle of Ogden Reid, its owner and editor. Reid inherited the *Tribune* from his father, Whitelaw Reid, who had fortified the family fortune by marrying a millionaire, Elizabeth Mills. Ogden was his parents' pride and despair. At Yale he was the star of the swimming and water polo teams, but an indifferent student—a party boy, forgetful and reckless. He had scant powers of concentration and none of his father's business savvy. The Reids were relieved when in 1911 Ogden married Helen Rogers, a diminutive, plainspoken woman who had been the essential personal secretary to Mrs. Reid. But at the *Tribune* Ogden became an absentee editor, not infrequently found collapsed on his desk after a night of boozing with his writers. Helen tried to compensate for Ogden's neglect, but mostly turned her fuss-budgety attention to the advertising department. Both were devoid of the business instincts, the literary acumen, and the tenacity that might have navigated the newspaper through the changing postwar times, when the *Tribune*'s core readers started moving to the suburbs and got their news from television. The *Herald Tribune,* having been passed on to the Reid's feckless sons and from them to the earnest but unsuccessful John Hay Whitney, finally died in 1966.

But during its heyday the inattentiveness of Ogden and Helen Reid ironically allowed the *Tribune* to thrive. Ogden Reid had no choice but to surrounded himself with brilliant editors; and they took full advantage of the leadership vacuum to recruit and support first-class talent. Reid was a tightwad; staff salaries and support services never approached those of the *Times*. Its physical plant was actually two buildings. In 1923 the *Tribune* moved to its new, state-of-the-art, seven-story building on West Fortieth Street, between Seventh and Eight Avenues, just three blocks from the *Times* and around the corner from the old Metropolitan Opera House. This facility immediately proved inadequate. A twenty-story addition was constructed fronting Forty-first Street, which became the main entrance. The unneeded top floors would provide rental income. The building opened in 1929, just before the crash. By 1930 it was difficult to find takers for the extra office space. By the time Thomson showed up, in 1940, the office areas were chronically grungy. William Zinsser, who in 1946, at just twenty-four, was thrilled to be hired as a reporter by his favorite boyhood newspaper, has given a vivid account of the place:

> For one thing it was grimy. Our desks were all in one enormous room, the city room, which was as wide as a city block. It was painted in eye-rest green, which was repainted periodically, but not periodically enough, in a less restful shade of eye-rest green. The air was foul with the smell of cigarettes and cigars. During the summer it was stirred sluggishly by ancient fans with dangling electric cords that looked like the exposed wires you see lying on the road after an ice storm. Of course there was no air conditioning, but we were conditioned to bad air because we were newspaper men.
>
> The typewriters we wrote on were as antique as the fans, and the desks were mottled with stains from coffee that had been swilled, or spilled, from cardboard containers since the early 1920s. In the middle of the room the city editor, a terrifying giant from Texas named L.L. Engelking, who was obsessed by his quest for the grail of perfection, roared in a tremendous voice his constant displeasure with the day's work. I thought it was the most beautiful place in the world.[1]

In those days, when *Tribune* staffers left the complex, they mostly used the back entrance, on the ground floor of the seven-story tower, which led, conveniently, to the paper's quasi-official watering hole at 213 West Fortieth Street: the Artist and Writers Restaurant, whose name, in Olde English letters, appeared on a swinging door out front. The decor was imitation British pub, with overhead timbering, stuccoed walls, high-backed booths, oak-top tables, and a forty-two-foot-long bar in the front room. Most of the regulars, which from noon until closing time at 3:00 A.M. included a steady sampling of the *Tribune* staff, called it Bleeck's, after its owner, a stolid bloke from St. Louis, John Bleeck (pronounced "Blake"), who opened his pub to women, reluctantly, only after Prohibition was repealed in 1933, and still did his best to discourage the patronage of blacks. One story of his racial sensibility, a classic among the *Tribune* staffers, was recounted by Richard Kluger in his definitive history of the paper.

> The king of Siam, who was not exactly black, but looked that way to Bleeck, was a house guest of the Reids in 1931, when he came to America for an eye operation; Ogden Reid and his new executive assistant, Wilbur Forrest, brought the king downstairs to

enjoy a little local color and a libation. "Mr. Bleeck," said Forrest, "I'd like you to meet the king of Siam." Bleeck, often the butt of practical jokes, replied, "Mr. Forrest, get that nigger out of here."[2]

The *Herald Tribune* was a hard-drinking paper. A bottle of scotch and a stack of paper cups on a writer's desk during deadline crunch was not even commented upon. After that day's edition had been laid to rest around 12:30 A.M., writers gathered at Bleeck's to drink, perhaps to eat (the food, writes Kluger, "was vaguely German and generally digestible"), and to await fresh-off-the-press copies of the paper. The walls of Bleeck's vibrated slightly as the presses rolled.

The staff in those days was an eclectic collection of virtuoso writers, hard-bitten reporters, and eccentrics, the last mostly holdovers from the time when Reid involved himself in hiring. Virtually no one got fired. The operation was a "gentleman's paper," as Thomson recalled, run more "like a chancellery than a business." The highest concentration of eccentrics was in the drama and music division, which, for some reason, was cordoned off from the rest of the expansive fifth-floor city room by waist-high partitions. The most striking eccentric was Lucius Beebe, the café society columnist who had covered the premiere of *Four Saints in Three Acts,* though he reported on the audience and the ambiance, not the opera. Beebe was an Oscar Wildean character, a tall, foppish figure who sported a derby, smoked long, thin cigars, and strutted with a silver-tipped walking stick. Beebe's prose was a thicket of rococo excesses; but one had to admit it had an identifiable style. He was an unalterable opponent of labor unions and the fledgling American Newspaper Guild, which resembled one to Beebe. His beat almost necessitated that he get drunk twice a day: interviewing a gossip source at lunchtime, and attending some social function at night. Next to Beebe's desk was that of Walter Terry, the dance critic, who, "when he stood up to stretch," Zinsser recalls, "often stood in Fourth Position."[3]

Nearby was the domain of Francis D. Perkins, from an old Bostonian family and an unlikely newspaper man. Maintaining files was an obsession with him. He kept indexed scrapbooks of all the reviews and stories relating to music that appeared in all the papers. He was often observed sitting at his desk reading railroad timetables from across the country—just reading them. He spoke rapidly, sometimes bursting into a boardroom of editors with some distressing update that no one could understand, then exiting just as suddenly. He smoked a pipe that was constantly turning over, setting his clothes or his papers on fire. Keeping records straight, laying out the music pages, and writing his own reviews kept him frequently at the paper until the early morning.

Presiding over this department was only a sideline for Geoffrey Parsons. In 1924 Parsons, a Queens-born graduate of Columbia Law School, was appointed chief editorial writer. In 1928 he wrote a well-received one-volume history of the world, *The Stream of History*. His editorials earned him a 1942 Pulitzer Prize. Parsons took a particular interest in the arts department at the paper and was granted by Reid the authority to hire critics and shape the coverage. When he approached Virgil Thomson in 1940, Parsons was sixty-one, a venerated newspaper man who knew what he was looking for.

Their initial meeting at Alexander Smallens's Connecticut house was convivial and conclusive. Parsons was delighted with Thomson's informal performance that day of a Mozart piano sonata and was engaged by his talk about music and wartime Europe. He offered Thomson the job on the spot. At first Thomson demurred. His friend Theodore Chanler's experience during a brief tenure in 1934 as music critic for the *Boston Herald* had warned him off newspaper criticism as a profession. As Thomson recalled it, Chanler had dared to write of the Boston Symphony Orchestra "as if it were a human organization possibly capable of error," and had written "daily-press criticism as composers would like to see it written." Through representatives, Koussevitzky complained bitterly; Chanler was fired. Mrs. Olga Koussevitzky was affronted that Chanler's dismissal was slowed down at all by professional protocol. "In Europe," she confided to Thomson some time afterward, "we handled these situations more efficiently." Parsons listened to the story but discounted it, telling Thomson, simply, "I think you are not familiar with the ways of a metropolitan newspaper."

Most editors at that time would have rejected Thomson as a candidate for the chief critic's post because of his active professional involvement in music. How could a composer, conductor, and contemporary music activist who had maintained a prominent creative presence in America despite living on and off in Paris, and who fully intended to revive his New York career, issue disinterested assessments of musical compositions, performances, and institutions?

In the late nineteenth century, when the modern metropolitan daily was born, newspapers were fiercely partisan. Today they strive to assure readers that their reporting is absolutely objective, unbeholden to any interest group or ideology. In 1940 this pendulum shift was in midswing. The responsible papers maintained a partisan cast, but avoided obvious conflicts of interest. So, hiring as the chief critic a composer with such well-documented and brilliantly stated prejudices was audacious.

Parsons had a different take on the issue. He wanted an insightful and captivating voice. The *Tribune*'s previous critic, Lawrence Gilman, had been a judicious commentator. But Thomson was far more immersed in the contemporary currents of the time, not just in music but in art, literature, theater, and film. So Thomson had provocative opinions? Then let him state them forthrightly in his columns and support them with description and analysis. "Always attack head-on," Parsons later advised. "Never make sideswipes and never use innuendo. As long as you observe the amenities of controversy, the very first of which is straightforward language, the paper will stand behind you."[4] As far as Parsons was concerned, Thomson's professional activity, far from compromising his authority, enhanced it. All he was worried about was whether Thomson could learn to write under deadline pressure without his partisan opinions coming out surly and mean-spirited. Thomson would not be asked to tame his opinions, but he would have to tame his style, learn the art of persuasion and gentlemanly discourse.

Parsons's concerns, it turned out, were not unfounded. All this was broached that afternoon at Alexander Smallens's house. Thomson, won over, agreed to an informal luncheon interview with Mrs. Reid and to a get-together meeting with the music staff.

In addition to Francis Perkins, the *Tribune* employed two full-time classical music critics. Jerome D. Bohm was a fastidious young man, a bit of a sad sack, who had conducted opera in Berlin during his student days there. A singer, he still did occasional vocal coaching on the side. Bohm was German trained and German oriented. But Thomson thought this might provide some balance to his own Francophilia. The New York–born Robert Lawrence, then twenty-eight, was already itching to become a conductor. In 1943 he left the *Tribune* to serve with the army in Italy. Afterward he remained in Europe, commencing what would become a successful conducting career. In 1940 Lawrence was already a fervent Francophile, who was entranced by Thomson's tales of Paris. Francis Perkins was deeply disappointed not to have been appointed chief critic himself. But he acknowledged Thomson's brilliance and became an immediate ally. After the meeting Thomson's sociability was tested over drinks at Bleeck's and found suitable.

At the luncheon with Mrs. Reid, Thomson was asked, "How does it seem to you, the idea of becoming our music critic?" "I replied that the general standard of music reviewing in New York had sunk so far that almost any change might bring improvement. Also I thought that perhaps my presence in a post so prominent might stimulate performance of my works."[5] Mrs. Reid was not used to such bluntness. The friction that would underlie their future relationship started at that luncheon meeting. "I almost invariably rubbed her the wrong way. My impishness and my arrogance were equally distasteful, and something in my own resistance to her dislike of being rubbed the wrong way led me over and over again to the verge of offense."[6]

However, Mrs. Reid had to agree with Parsons that Thomson was an impressive character. She gave her approval to the appointment, effective October 10, 1940, about six weeks before Thomson's forty-fourth birthday. His starting salary was to be $5,800 per year, a substantial sum, though not as high as he had bargained for. Parsons assured Thomson that once his value was established, his salary would grow steadily. By 1944 his yearly salary was $7,800; and by 1953, the last full year of his tenure, $11,700, this at a time when a $10,000-per-year job was enough to support a family in suburban comfort with money left over for investments and savings.

When Thomson sent word of his new job to his parents, they were greatly relieved. Quincy Thomson had always been bewildered by his only son's vagabond musical life. Seeing *Four Saints* in Chicago in 1934 had, if anything, left him more bewildered than before. But a steady job at a major newspaper was solid, respectable work, something he could understand and explain to his friends. Maurice was proud and delighted. "You'll have to take me to things," he said. The most poignant response came from Leland Poole, Thomson's old army buddy, the man he had pined for at a time when revealing such feelings, even to himself, was impossible.

Leland and Virgil had drifted apart during the 1920s. The intensity of their friendship did not survive the geographical distance (Leland was living in San Francisco) and the entry of Briggs Buchanan into Virgil's life. But they stayed in touch. Leland lurched from one job to another, mostly midlevel, dead-end positions at banks and investment firms. His youthful charm had given way to chronic sadness. Occasionally during the 1930s he wrote to Virgil, long letters filled with nostalgia for the old days, complaints about his health, and requests for small loans, this during a period when Virgil's income was irregular at best. News of the *Tribune* job prompted Leland to write with recollections of the time when, awaiting orders from their respective army units, they shared a room at a New York hotel.

> Dear Virgil,
>   Do you remember the dough you advanced me when I was in New York before I went with the Moseley firm? You probably have written it off. You were so damn swell to me and I never could pay it back before. Thank you again.
>   To say I am happy about your swell new job is to be guilty of understatement. I am proud as well as pleased. What I would like to do would be to buy you a pretty pink comforter like they had at Newburgh way back in 1918. Wasn't that long ago and far away? I often think of you and other days. Will write again but I am pretty sunk today so why depress anyone else.
>
>   As ever, Prim[7]

Over the next decade Leland's letters grew increasingly self-pitying.

> When you come and then when you leave I always feel a little sad because you are of course so tied up with my life when it was young and gay. And each time you are just a lot more successful and each time I am in such contrast. I do not want you to think I begrudge your success. I enjoy every bit of it. (August 5, 1945)

> Is Maurice coming this summer? My friends like him so much. It must be wonderful to have talent. Youse guys is lucky. (April 14, 1946)[8]

To Virgil, Leland became more a bothersome obligation than a valued old friend. In 1946, about to lose another job in an accounting firm, Leland wrote to ask if Virgil would help him land a position in New York. Virgil sent an all-purpose letter of recommendation on *Herald Tribune* stationery, said that there were no positions available at the *Tribune* (which was not what Leland had asked for), and told him to shape up (one "must learn to be modest at fifty"). Virgil continued to send loans and, in 1949, a cash gift that covered Leland's doctor bills and allowed him to "enter 1950 with NO accounts payable! Whoopee!"

Virgil would continue to help Leland financially. And whenever

Virgil was in Los Angeles, where Leland eventually settled, they would visit. Leland died, a humbled man, in 1966.

For nine months during 1936–37, when Thomson was doing theater and film work, he lived in a rented room at New York's colorful Chelsea Hotel, on West Twenty-third Street between Seventh and Eight Avenues. And it was to the Chelsea that he returned in 1940, renting at first a small flat on a lower floor, but moving in early 1943 to the ninth-floor suite where he lived for the rest of his life.

When the Chelsea Hotel was built, in 1883, it was, at twelve stories, the tallest building in Manhattan, and an architectural mongrel: part Victorian, part Edwardian. It also marked the city's first experiment in cooperative apartment buildings; but it went bankrupt in 1903, then reopened in 1905 as a hotel with long-term leases available. The conversion had involved subdividing the apartments in sundry ways. No two units in the Chelsea share the same floor plan.

From the start the Chelsea attracted eccentrics and offbeat artists. At various times Eugene O'Neill and Dylan Thomas lived there. Arthur Miller, a resident during the 1940s, recalled, "The Chelsea was not part of America, had no vacuum cleaners, no rules, no taste, no shame. It was a ceaseless party."[9] In 1940 the look and daily routine of the place was much as it is today. The lobby was shabby, but its tall walls were filled with artworks and its ceiling hung with constructions. Residents were constantly carting canvases and sculptures and musical instruments in and out. Thomson's eventual apartment, 9-C, had basically three rooms: a spacious salon with rosewood paneling, a closetless bedroom, and a rectangular connecting room that functioned both as office and as dining area. This room contained the apartment's only closet. There was, however, a four-by-five-foot pantry with shelves and a built-in floor cabinet with three drawers. Eventually Thomson would cram a small refrigerator, all of his dishware, glasses, vases, his sister Ruby's hand-painted china, and household tools into that space. With no room for a stepladder, he reached the items on the top shelves by pulling out the three drawers and climbing up them like stairs, which he did into his late eighties. The kitchen was really a converted three-by-seven-foot closet with a small sink and a small squarish stove. As Thomson's tubby midriff grew in later years, he could just barely squeeze between the sink and wall. The kitchen opened into the bedroom. Eventually he acquired as a gift from his friend Henry-Russell Hitchcock a three-piece bedroom set that had been left him by his grandparents: an American rococo revival walnut bedstead, washstand, and marble-topped bureau, all circa 1865. The bureau, located just outside the kitchen door, wound up serving as a food preparation area. All of Thomson's fabled dinner parties were prepared on that slab of marble. The bathroom had a porcelain tub. (Thomson would never install a shower.) Eventually he found places for everything. His shoes were kept in neat pairs lined up on the floor before the nonfunctioning bedroom fireplace. His cousin Lewis Blackburn built wall shelves in the salon, in the bedroom, in the dining room, in every conceivable corner of the place where they would not impede mobile living. Books and manuscripts were stacked to the ceiling, eventually organized in green file boxes. Also stuck up high were five amazingly sturdy Louis Vuitton leather suitcases, part of the luggage with which Thomson moved from France. They would last him for the rest of his life. Even in 1940, with many possessions and all his books still in Europe, the Chelsea apartment was crowded. But Thomson loved the ambiance, the wacky vitality, the stimulation of the place. It reminded him of the Left Bank. He never considered moving anyplace else.

On Friday, October 11, 1940, the headlines of the *Herald Tribune* proclaimed, "U.S. Sends Reinforcements to Hawaii, Asks Industry to Speed 21,000 Planes, Consults Britain on Far East Situation." Other front-page stories reported on the presidential campaign ("Willkie Insists He Can Make Jobs for All, Says New Deal Defeatism Is All That Stands in the Way") and on France's shameless Nazi collaborator Marshal Petain ("Petain Reveals Totalitarian Aims of Vichy, Says New France Rejects Traditional Friendships, Offers Amity to Hitler"). There was a photograph of the altar at London's cherished St. Paul's Cathedral buried under rubble from a Nazi aerial bomb attack. The day's lead editorial, written under the supervision of Geoffrey Parsons, was yet another morale booster for the Wendell Willkie campaign: "If ever indomitable courage, tireless energy and the confidence of right showed in a human being, they belong to Wendell Willkie today."

And on page 19 in the upper left-hand corner was the debut column by the *Herald Tribune*'s new chief music critic. The subject was the season-opening concert by the New York Philharmonic-Symphony Orchestra, conducted by John Barbirolli at Carnegie Hall the preceding night. The program consisted of Beethoven's *Egmont* Overture,

Elgar's *Enigma Variations,* and Sibelius's Symphony no. 2. Since Arturo Toscanini had retired in 1936, the opinion among many critics was that the Philharmonic had slipped in quality, although by and large the *Times* critic Olin Downes was supportive. Barbirolli was a steady and solid musician, but not a dynamic conductor.

Thomson brought Maurice Grosser to the concert with him, sat through it, took no notes, parted from Maurice, and went to the desk that had been assigned him in a specially cordoned-off section of the drama and music division. Geoffrey Parsons was at his desk trying to look busy. In fact, he was there to monitor the launch of his new critic. He knew that Thomson had never written for a nighttime deadline. On most nights copy was due no later than 11:45 P.M., though it could, if necessary, be extended until past midnight.

That night, Thomson established the writing pattern that he would stick with for fourteen years. *Tribune* writers were expected to type their articles on special, padlike paper, five small sheets interspersed with carbons and bound together, one to go to the copy desk, one to the editor, one to the pressroom, and so on. The paper could hold no more than two large paragraphs. Once filled, the writer called for a copyboy to send each installment of the piece down the chute to the fourth-floor copy editors and typesetters. Thomson, who could not type, ignored this practice. He wrote his articles with pencil in longhand on yellow legal pads. When he got to the bottom of a sheet, even if in midsentence, he called for the copyboy to take it away.

Thomson did not object when Parsons asked to look over the article when the galleys showed up. There on the page was that vivid voice that Parsons admired. The writing suffered in places from haste, and from lapses in tone, which Parsons, for now, let pass. His only suggestion, accepted without objection, was that Thomson delete his reference to the Philharmonic's "undistinguished audience." The review read, in part:

> The Philharmonic-Symphony Society of New York opened its ninety-ninth season last evening in Carnegie Hall. There was little that could be called festive about the occasion. The menu was routine, the playing ditto.
>
> Beethoven's overture to "Egmont" is a classic hors d'oeuvre. Nobody's digestion was ever spoiled by it and no latecomer has ever lost much by missing it. It was preceded, as is the custom nowadays, by our National Anthem, gulped down standing, like a cock-

tail. I seem to remember that in 1917 and 1918 a sonorous arrangement of "The Star-Spangled Banner," by Walter Damrosch, was current at these concerts. After so long a time I couldn't be sure
whether that was the orchestration used last night. I rather think
not. Last night's version seemed to have more weight than brilliance. It had the somber and spiritless sonority of the German military bands one hears in France these days. That somberness is
due, I think, to an attempt to express authority through mere
weighty blowing and sawing in the middle and lower ranges of
the various orchestral instruments, rather than by the more classic method of placing every instrument in its most brilliant and
grateful register in order to achieve the maximum of carrying
power and of richness. I may be wrong about the reasons for it,
but I think I am right about the general effect, unless my seat was
in an acoustical dead spot of the hall, which I do not think it was.
The anthem, to me, sounded logy and coarse; it lacked the buoy-
ancy and the sweep that are its finest musical qualities.

. . . Twenty years residence on the European continent has
largely spared me Sibelius. Last night's Second Symphony was my
first in quite some years. I found it vulgar, self-indulgent and
provincial beyond all description. I realize that there are sincere
Sibelius lovers in the world, though I must say I've never met one
among educated professional musicians. I realize also that this
work has a kind of popular power unusual in symphonic literature. Even Wagner scarcely goes over so big on the radio. That
populace-pleasing power is not unlike the power of a Hollywood
Class A picture. Sibelius is in no sense a naif; he is merely provincial. Let me leave it at that for the present. Perhaps, if I have to
hear much more of him, I'll sit down one day with the scores and
really find out what is in them. Last night's experience of one was
not much of a temptation, however, to read or sit through many
more.

The concert, as a whole, in fact, both as to program and as to
playing was anything but a memorable experience. The music itself was soggy, the playing dull and brutal. As a friend remarked
who had never been to one of these concerts before, "I understand now why the Philharmonic is not part of New York's intellectual life."[10]

The next day, Thomson traveled to Boston for the season-
opening concert of the Boston Symphony Orchestra, conducted by
Serge Koussevitzky, a program including *A London Symphony* of
Vaughan Williams and the Fifth Symphony of Beethoven. The review
began grandly.

BOSTON, Oct. 11—And so, in cerulean sunshine and through indescribable splendors of autumnal leafage, to Boston—the Hub
of the Universe, the home of the Bean and the Cod. The home,
as well, of the Boston Symphony Orchestra, the finest by all-
around criteria of our resident instrumental foundations.[11]

Of the *London Symphony* Thomson wrote,

The first two movements are long, episodic, disjointed. The third
is short, delicate, neatly sequential, compact, efficacious, charming. The finale is rich and varied. Its musical material is of high
quality, its instrumental organization ample and solid. Also, it is
not without expressive power....

Making a program out of only that and the Beethoven, out of
one live Englishman and one dead German, classic and great
though he be, is an obvious reference to current events and sympathies. The reference might have turned out in its effect to be
not nearly so gracious as in its intention, had those last two movements of the "London Symphony" not been in themselves so impressive, the finale so moving and deeply somber. It was written
in 1913, I believe. It might have been written last month, so actual is its expressive content.

The Vaughan Williams symphony served also as a vehicle for a
display of orchestral virtuosity on the part of Dr. Koussevitzky and
his men such as few orchestras are capable of offering their subscribers. Not that the piece itself is of any great difficulty; it is only
reasonably hard to play, I imagine, but the Boston organization is
in such a fine fettle after its Berkshire season that every passage,
any passage, no matter what, serves as a pretext for those constant miracles of precision and of exact equilibrium that a first-class
modern orchestra is capable of.

The Beethoven symphony performance, Thomson remarked,
was distinguished by Koussevitzky's putting his effort into "a rhythmic exactitude that adds to Beethoven's dynamism a kind of monumental weight that is appropriate and good." But he questioned the
conductor's attempt to achieve more weight by forcing the strings beyond their optimum sonority.

[A]t the back of every conductor's mind is a desire to make his orchestra produce a louder noise than any one else's orchestra can
produce, a really majestic noise, a Niagara Falls of sound. Sometimes in the course of nearly every concert this desire overpow-
ers him. You can tell when it is coming on by the way he goes
into a brief convulsion at that point. The convulsion is useful to

the conductor because it prevents his hearing what the orchestra really sounds like while his fit is on. But if you watch carefully from the house you will usually find that the sound provoked out of a group of exacerbated musicians by any gesture of the convulsive type is less accurate in pitch and less sonorous in decibels than a more objectively conducted fortissimo.

Thomson's debut itself received an incisive review from the man responsible for hiring him: Parsons. When Thomson arrived at the office some days later, a memo from Parsons dated October 14 was waiting on his desk. The memo is virtually a compendium of guidelines on how to practice the art of daily newspaper criticism on the highest level.

> Dear Virgil:
> Your Boston review was such peaches and cream from every point of view that I hesitate to revert to the Philharmonic piece at all. You struck the exactly right note in Boston—of wise, modest, generous, urbane, constructive comment—and I'm not worrying about the future. But having jotted down these notes, chiefly for my own clarification, I hand them on to you as written on Friday.
> Yours faithfully,
> Geoffrey

> Notes on the Almost Perfect Critic
> 1. The first principle of newspaper criticism has long been, "Never criticize an audience." I don't know just where the ancient saw came from. But I feel sure it is sound as sound—in 999 cases out of 1,000. Perhaps the reason is about the same as that expressed in (2). The audience that a critic knocks is, after all, largely composed of the very people he wants to have listen to him and insulting them merely makes them walk out on him.
> Reporting an audience's reaction is, of course, quite another matter. Whether a hall is filled or empty, whether an audience applauded or hissed or walked out is quite often significant news.
> 2. Checking up on the Philharmonic piece, I reached the conclusion that the Sibelius paragraph was the one considerable blunder in it. Added to the general abruptness of the style and the too many first personal pronouns—due to the harassment of making a deadline, I know, since your natural writing is quite other—you unintentionally committed the one cardinal sin of criticism, that of appearing to condescend.
> When you cited the opinion of "musically educated" people, you made every illiterate and amateur who disagreed with you simply snort and quit. "What the hell, the experts have always been

wrong in estimating the importance of creative work. Here's another cocksure wiseguy. Provincial is Sibelius? Well, then, that's what I like." And so on.

Looking backward it seems clear to me that, holding the views that you do of Sibelius, you should have reserved comment upon him until later, registering only your general attitude. For what you had time and room to say that evening was not an effective way to cope with the Sibelius cult. (In your haste you also left the reader wondering what right you had to criticize Sibelius at all since you boasted of knowing very little about him. I know that compression gave this misleading twist—but there it was.) I think you will discover very soon that the huge audience available to you in the Herald Tribune can be reasoned with endlessly but that it will resent being "told." I do not mean that you should alter in the slightest degree your convictions or tone down their expression. But a cult is a cult and must be approached patiently and calmly—the way you would a nervous horse, let's say. You're up against a real cult in the Sibelius people and I don't know a better job that needs to be done than its gradual persuasion to the light. But you've first got to understand the cult, its sources, etc., and make clear to its members that you understand the power of its appeal, before you can get any distance in coping with it.

Ditto about almost everything else. I guess. When you come back to the Philharmonic, for instance, now that you have thrown down your gauntlet, the real problem remains of convincing the Philharmonic supporters. It is no trick to persuade the real music lovers—they were already persuaded and had deserted the Philharmonic for the Boston and Philadelphia, from orchestra seats to gallery. Your job now is to make clear to every subscriber who can read words of more than one syllable, that so far from being a Young Pedant in a Hurry, with a Paris condescension, you are a fair, patient judge, anxious to help. It is a great tragedy for the city that the Philharmonic should have relapsed into such stodginess. It hurts you more than it does Barbirolli. You search and search for what is good—Barbirolli did a good job with the Purcell last season, for instance,—and your anger is a nothing to your sorrow. Well, I write as an old specialist in pleading, rather than a critic. But there is the direction in which you can best build up a large reading public and do musical service, I am sure.

You'll have to get the feel of it yourself. The opportunity is utterly different from that of "Modern Music," let us say. You have before you in the pews not only the educated and the partly-educated, but also the illiterate, musically speaking. When you write such swell prose as the Boston piece, believe me you can talk also to a huge audience composed not only of music-lovers

but of countless folk who are glad to know what is going on anywhere in the intellectual world, provided the tale of it is told simply and entertainingly—as you tell it.[12]

Parsons concluded with two sensible suggestions: to treat gin-
gerly the subject of nationalism, "loaded today with so much preju-
dice and passion"; also, to take some time to check up on his
predecessor Lawrence Gilman's predilections and, "when disregard-
ing them as you must, of course, unhesitatingly do whenever you disagree with them, slay them as politely as you can."

Thomson later wrote that Parsons's memos during this period
were "not, of course, unjustified, merely out of proportion to the visible fault." Parsons was "committed to making a success of me, since
my appointment had been wholly his doing."[13] However, he acknowledged that Parsons's instruction was invaluable. In 1940 Thomson was cocksure of himself, but he was no newspaper man; Parsons
turned him into one.

Parsons recognized that music criticism was perhaps the most difficult writing discipline because music resists being written about.
Moreover, even the technical terminology that has been devised to
describe music is largely unavailable to critics because so few readers, even passionate concertgoers, really understand it. The typical
crowd at a baseball stadium is far more informed about baseball than
the typical audience at a concert hall is informed about music. Baseball writers can assume a tremendous amount of knowledge on the
part of their readers. Music critics cannot. Thomson understood this.
So did Parsons, who acknowledged from the start that Thomson
could describe the way music actually sounds in the most homespun,
nontechnical language—a rare skill.

Thomson's literary method, as he later wrote, was to seek out
the precise adjective.

> Nouns are names and can be libelous; the verbs, though some-
> times picturesque, are few in number and tend toward alleging
> motivations. It is the specific adjectives that really describe and that
> do so neither in sorrow nor in anger. And to describe what one
> has heard is the whole art of reviewing. To analyze and compare
> are stimulating; to admit preferences and prejudices can be help-
> ful; to lead one's reader step by step from the familiar to the sur-
> prising is the height of polemical skill. Now certainly musical
> polemics were my intent, not aiding careers or teaching Appreci-
> ation. And why did a daily paper tolerate my polemics for four-

teen years? Simply because they were accompanied by musical descriptions more precise than those being used just then by other reviewers.[14]

To understand the impact such pointed, perky reviewing had at the time, one need only compare Thomson's debut piece on the New York Philharmonic-Symphony with that of the *Times* chief critic, Olin Downes. Ten years Thomson's senior, Downes had held the *Times* post since 1924, wielding considerable influence. Downes's tastes were well informed and traditional. From the start, Thomson relished being in the minority and debunking conventional wisdom. Downes, as the insightful critic Joseph Horowitz has stated, "cherished the majority, whose viewpoint boosted the resonance and security of his own. Downes' ideal critic was one who so identified with an audience as to disappear into it. His reviews are packed, as Thomson's are not, with information about a huge constituency of shared feeling and experience."[15] Downes's writing style was plodding and officious; he used the third person exclusively. Thomson's reviews were spiked with his first-person pronouncements and ignited by the friction between his own reactions and accepted opinion.

Whereas Thomson had dismissed the Philharmonic's season-opening program—Beethoven's *Egmont* Overture, Elgar's *Enigma Variations,* Sibelius's Symphony no. 2—and the performances in one sentence ("The menu was routine, the playing ditto"), Downes intoned that "mere accident could not have shaped the heroic character of the program which John Barbirolli arranged for his opening Philharmonic-Symphony concert last night." To Thomson, Beethoven's *Egmont* Overture was "a classic hors d'oeuvre. Nobody's digestion was ever spoiled by it and no latecomer has ever lost much by missing it." The same work inspired Downes to a lofty call to arms for all defenders of liberty:

> Beethoven never produced more compact, dramatic and powerful pages. And when the audience listened to that proud and passionate music, and that exultant cry of liberty in its final pages, they must have thought of the tyranny and terror that stalk today in Beethoven's own land, and taken heart from the sure prophecy of his pages.

(Almost certainly, Thomson's quip in his review the following day of the Boston Symphony Orchestra concert—to the effect that making a program out of only two works by two composers "one live Englishman and one dead German . . . is an obvious reference to current events and sympathies"—was his not-so-veiled attempt to deflate Downes's grandiosity.)

Whereas Thomson had described Sibelius's Second Symphony as "vulgar, self-indulgent and provincial beyond all description," and Barbirolli's performance as "dull and brutal," Downes called Sibelius the "only living composer whose spirit is equal to the need of the time," praised the work as a "paean to the unconquerable spirit that is in man," and hailed the performance for its "sensitive treatment of details . . . fine proportions . . . haunting instrumental effects."

Subsequent generations of critics have tended to side with Downes's appraisal of Sibelius as an original voice. But Downes's praise is vague, emotive, and unconvincing, whereas Thomson's re-proof is incisive, immoderate, and engaging. Perhaps, as Parsons had argued, Thomson's approach in taking on the "Sibelius cult" was in-effective. But his writing was irresistible. He had arrived not like a playground bully taking control of the game, but like the brightest boy in class who has claimed the largest swath of the playground for himself to make up his own game with his own rules. Thomson was writing as a professional musician unimpressed by the trappings of celebrity performers and unemotional about the composer icons of music's past. But his reviews were vividly accessible to lay readers.

Just six days on the job, in a review headlined "Velvet Paws" (Thomson titled his own reviews), he vividly deflated the charge that the famed string sound of the Philadelphia Orchestra had "gone off" since their former conductor Leopold Stokowski had been succeeded by Eugene Ormandy.

> Nowhere else is there such a string choir; one would like to stroke its tone, as if the suavity of it were a visual and a tactile thing, like pale pinky-brown velvet. If memory does not trick, that luxurious and justly celebrated string-tone is less forced, less hoarse and throaty than it was in the days of the all too Slavic ex-King Leopold, now of Hollywood.[16]

In subsequent weeks, he praised the pianist Josef Lhevinne for his "complete authority":

> Any authoritative execution derives as much of its excellence from what the artist does not do as from what he does. If he doesn't do anything off color at all he is said to have taste. Mr. Lhevinne's taste is as authoritative as his technical method. Not one sectarian

interpretation, not one personal fancy, not one stroke below the belt, not a sliver of ham, mars the universal acceptability of his readings. Everything he does is right and clear and complete. Everything he doesn't do is the whole list of all the things that mar the musical executions of lesser men. (November 18, 1940)

Thomson's description of Mozart's *Don Giovanni,* from a Sunday column in December titled "Mozart's Leftism," illuminates in just three peppery paragraphs the inherent paradoxes of this astonishing work more insightfully than most scholarly tomes on the subject.

Don Giovanni is a tragicomedy about sacred and profane love. Its dramatic tone is of the most daring. It begins with a dirty comic song, goes on to a murder, a series of seductions, a sort of detective-story pursuit of the murderer in which one of the previously seduced ladies plays always a high comedy role; a party, a ballet, a supper scene with music on the stage, a supernatural punishment of the villain, and a good-humored finale in which everybody reappears but the villain and the corpse, by now long since become a statue.

The villain is charming; the ladies are charming; everybody in the play is charming. Everybody has his passion and character; everybody acts according to his passion and character. Nobody is seriously blamed (except by the other characters) for being what he is or for acting the way he acts. The play implies a complete fatalism about love and about revenge. Don Giovanni gets away with everything, Donna Elvira with nothing. Donna Anna never succeeds in avenging her father's murder. Punishment of this is left to supernatural agencies. Love is not punished at all. Its sacred (or at least its honorable) manifestations and its profane (or libertine) practice are shown as equally successful and satisfactory. The only unsatisfied person in the play is Donna Elvira, who is not at all displeased with herself for having sinned. She is merely chagrined at having been abandoned.

Mozart is kind to these people and pokes fun at every one of them. The balance between sympathy and observation is so neat as to be almost miraculous. *Don Giovanni* is one of the funniest shows in the world and one of the most terrifying. It is all about love, and it kids love to a fare-ye-well. It is the world's greatest opera and the world's greatest parody of opera. It is a moral entertainment so movingly human that the morality gets lost before the play is scarcely started. (December 14, 1940)

The real mettle of music critics, Thomson used to say, was tested by their dealings with contemporary music. This is the music critic's most important function: to introduce new compositional voices to the ongoing discourse of music. In reviewing a new piece by Roy Harris, *American Creed,* performed by the Chicago Symphony at Carnegie Hall, Thomson was grappling with the work of a colleague who had achieved popularity with audiences despite his lack of academic certification. Thomson knew that his nemesis Roger Sessions had been disparaging Harris in private. Thomson shared many of Sessions's reservations, but aired them in public. In some ways, of course, this was more damaging. But by dealing with Harris openly and substantively, Thomson was deeming the work worthy of discussion, thereby lending it stature. Let us fight our battles out in the open, Thomson was saying.

> Mr. Harris's "American Creed" invites kidding, as all of his programmistically prefaced works do. If we take his music as he offers it, however, we risk refusing a quite good thing. No composer in the world, not even in Italy or Germany, makes such shameless use of patriotic feelings to advertise his personal product. One would think, to read his prefaces, that he had been awarded by God, or at least by popular vote, a monopolistic privilege of expressing our nation's deepest ideals and highest aspirations. And when the piece so advertised turns out to be mostly not very clearly orchestrated schoolish counterpoint and a quite skimpy double-fugue (neither of which has any American connotation whatsoever) one is tempted to put the whole thing down as insincere and a bad joke.
>
> The truth, however, is other. Mr. Harris, though the bearer of no exceptional melodic gifts and the possessor of no really thorough musical schooling, has an unquenchable passion to know and to use all the procedures of musical composition. He has pondered over the medieval French melodic line and over the problem of continuous (nonrepeating) melodic development, and he has come by this road to understand where the crucial problem lies in America's musical coming-of-age. . . .
>
> He knows that musical material, even folklore material, is as international as musical form and syntax, that localism is no more than one man's colorful accent. He knows this so well that he avoids, as though it were the devil, any colorful accent whatsoever. He puts his musical effort on serious problems of material and of form. He does not always get anywhere in his music; but it is serious music, much more serious than his blurbs would lead one to believe.[17]

Geoffrey Parsons was delighted with the piece.

November 29, 1040

Dear Virgil,

I hear such warm and friendly words talked about you—"the new Virgil," as one of my friends put it. I explained that there was only one of you, etc. etc. Then I got to thinking what it was that your last months' writing has that your early weeks with a hatchet, hacking your way through the musical jungles of Manhattan, didn't have. . . . The point is not at all one of the amount of praise or criticism that you dole out. It is a question of human understanding of the enormous difficulties involved in any musical composition or performance, of explaining those difficulties to the reader and of stating your criticism, however severe, in relation to this human effort. Take your piece on Harris, as an illustration. You certainly didn't leave his composition very much when you got through but you did give me my first clear notion of what the man was trying to do and what specifically was wrong with his work. . . . Looking back to your earlier reviews, I think they were dry and crackly and lacked juice and life in comparison with these later ones. Neither sparkle of wit, nor the one word of apt slang, nor the justest of definitions, can hold the reader, make him believe in you, and educate him, as can sympathy, good nature, generosity, and all the other traits that go to demonstrate understanding of the human animal.[18]

Two months to the day after Thomson's first review appeared, Carl Van Vechten, a former *New York Times* critic, wrote to his old friend Gertrude Stein to tell her the news: "Dear Baby Woojums, Did you know that Virgil is the music critic of the N.Y. Herald-Tribune and has made a sensation?"[19]

In his choice of what to cover, Thomson was announcing that musical events would be reviewed according to their intrinsic merit, not the power of the publicity machine that promoted them. His third review was of a gifted woman conductor, Frédérique Petrides, leading a thirty-piece chamber orchestra in a new work by David Diamond. He covered a Brazilian music festival at the Museum of Modern Art, and used the striking authenticity of the pieces performed to poke fun at the pompous public image of the museum. Yet the celebrated violin virtuoso Jascha Heifetz was amusingly debunked for his glamorous executions of trifling showpieces, his "justly remunerated mastery of the musical marshmallow." And the electrifying pianist Vladimir Horowitz was dubbed a "master of distortion and exaggeration," a charge that would stick for the rest of

the pianist's career. Thomson praised the integrity of a makeshift ensemble called the Nine O'Clock Opera Company, comprising young
singers just out of Juilliard who had performed Mozart's *The Marriage
of Figaro* in English with piano accompaniment; and he skewered
the pretensions of the Metropolitan Opera. The New York Philharmonic, the visiting orchestras, the Met, the touring recitalists—all
these were covered responsibly, but not reverently. He challenged
the cult that sustained Arturo Toscanini not by dismissing his work,
which had undeniable greatness, but by subjecting it to coolheaded
analysis. The maestro's performances, Thomson wrote, had admirable
qualities: "detailed clarity, sequential coherence and avoidance of
adolescent sentiment." But Toscanini was "essentially a reactionary."
And his conducting style

> is very little dependent on literary culture and historical knowl-
> edge. It is disembodied music and disembodied theater. It opens
> few vistas to the understanding of men and epochs; it produces a
> temporary, but intense, condition of purely auditory excitement.
> . . . No piece has to mean anything specific; every piece has to
> provoke from its hearers a spontaneous vote of acceptance. This
> is what I call the "wow technique."[20]

The breadth of Thomson's reach was unprecedented. He wrote
about Paul Bowles's music for *Twelfth Night* on Broadway, student
orchestras, Maxine Sullivan singing at a nightclub, a black preacher
in New Jersey who played swing music on an electric guitar (as an
Easter Sunday piece), an economic and sociological report from Columbia University on the "hit" trade in popular songs. He treated the
piano concerto of the Hollywood pianist and raconteur Oscar Levant
as a work to be taken seriously. He poked fun at the cerebral compositions of the composer and pedagogue Paul Hindemith ("dogmatic
and forceful and honest and completely without charm; . . . a style
rather like that of some ponderously monumental and not wholly in-
commodious railway station").

He chastised New York's major performing institutions for their
neglect of new works, which he considered an abrogation of responsibility. He unabashedly advanced his Francophile sympathies.
When taking on New York's powerful managers, concert promoters,
and boards of directors, Thomson was backed up fully by the *Tribune*. However, taking on an amateur orchestra in the suburbs was

another matter entirely. Thomson's slip this time resulted in a severe rebuke.

> My questioning the civic value to Stamford, Connecticut, of a quite poor symphony orchestra brought two strong letters from Parsons. Conflict with Manhattan millionaires, I could read between the lines, was permitted, but not with country clubs. Suburbia had long supplied the nut of our liberal Republican readership, and the paper's eventual drama of survival came to be played out against the sociological transformation of those neighborhoods. Discouraging suburbia about anything, I understood, was imprudent. For suburbs, like churches, accept only praise.[21]

However, Parsons's rebuke was directed more at a journalistic error than at Thomson's choice of target.

> Memo of May 2, 1941
> Sometimes I almost despair of your ever becoming a newspaper writer. . . . The essential fact was that in your review your pen and foot slipped and you wrote as follows: "It has never seemed to me that amateur symphony orchestras accomplished much for anybody." If this was the truth, then your whole expedition into the hinterland was nonsense and you should have stayed at home. The sentence stuck out like a sore thumb in an otherwise beautiful and accurate piece. . . . Anybody with a modicum of newspaper training would have seen this and said to himself, "How can I best turn this from a minus into a plus?" By seizing upon the sentence, redefining your point of view, discoursing about the amateur idea generously, humorously, etc., you could have re-captured all the irritated people and turned a defeat into a victory.[22]

Parsons's reviewing of Thomson's reviews continued regularly for two years and less frequently after that. One slip Parsons would not countenance was any use of slang. Thomson's review from November 25, 1942, of the Boston Symphony Orchestra contained the sentence "The Martinu Symphony is a beaut." Parsons responded immediately.

> I regret to disturb your Thanksgiving Day peace of mind but in justice to the paper as well as yourself, I feel I must tell you how badly I think you slipped in the last week or so.
> I suspect that if I had been Managing Editor I would have fired you out of hand for putting that word "beaut" in that otherwise excellent review of the Boston concert. At the least I would have notified you that if ever again a word of slang appeared in any of

your reviews, you need not report for work the next day. I assure you that all your strongest admirers feel about such a sour note exactly as I do. . . . Incidentally, if I see the word "amateurish" in your column again I shall scream. I haven't the faintest idea of what you mean by the word, and I don't believe you have. If a performance lacks style or distinction, or is stilted or stiff, or what not, say so. To my ear the use of "amateurish" is a lazy generalization for the lack of the more accurate word.[23]

With Parsons always around to make him behave, Thomson was enthralling readers, and not just in New York. Allen Hughes, who later became a Thomson protégé and music critic at the *Times,* was an organ student at the University of Michigan when Virgil became the *Tribune* critic. In Ann Arbor they didn't get the daily *Tribune.* But every Monday Hughes's music history professor would come into class with the Sunday *Tribune* to discuss Thomson's column. "We weren't even hearing the concerts being discussed," Hughes recalled; "but here was this refreshing tone and point of view. To say that it was stimulating is not enough. It opened up the world for us. We young musicians felt that here was someone who understood what it was really like to be a musician."[24]

Thomson's writing was winning public praise even from his competitors. In a *New York Times* review of Thomson's Symphony no. 2 in 1941, a diplomatic Olin Downes prefaced his negative treatment of the work by calling Thomson "the music reviewer whom all his colleagues must envy for the wit, the force and concision of his style, and the originality of his thinking."[25]

Within less than a year, Thomson had assumed a position of leadership among his colleagues, a position made official in June of 1941 when the Music Critics Circle of New York, an organization initiated by Thomson, elected him as its first president. Thomson's idea, agreed to by his colleagues, was to "promote a better understanding between writers on music and those concerned with the presentation of music," as the press release announced. The aims of the organization, the statement continued, would be as follows:

First, to award a testimonial to the American composer of a work composed during the last twenty-five years, and publicly performed for the first time in New York City during each current season in each of three fields of composition.
Second, to encourage the establishment of an American repertory by giving suitable recognition to a previously performed work

in each of the three fields, composed since 1900 and re-heard during the season.[26]

The awards went not to performers, or orchestras, or opera companies, but to American composers. No one before had even thought of organizing critics for such a purpose. By supporting Thomson's idea, the board of officers (Olin Downes of the *Times,* Donald Fuller of *Modern Music,* Oscar Thompson of the *New York Sun,* and Miles Kastendieck of the *Brooklyn Eagle*) acknowledged Thomson's leadership.

From the start of his tenure at the *Herald Tribune,* Thomson's rattling of the status quo enraged the powerful New York promoters and managers. Just how much it enraged one of them, Thomson was not to find out until some two years after the incident, or so he always claimed.

Arthur Judson was the Louis B. Mayer of the concert music business. He reached the zenith of his power in the years from 1930 to 1936, when he simultaneously managed the Philadelphia Orchestra, the New York Philharmonic, and the summer concerts series at Lewisohn Stadium in New York and at Robin Dell in Philadelphia; was the president of Columbia Concerts Corporation, the largest artists representatives agency in America, which included in its holdings his personal artists agency Arthur Judson, Inc.; and was the second-largest stockholder in the Columbia Broadcasting System.

A Dayton, Ohio, native, born in 1881, Judson had tried to be a concert violinist. But, married young and with a child to support, he moved into management. Early on, he predicted the marketing potential of radio and with three partners bought a moribund low-power station. That venture initially lost Judson $300,000; it grew into the Columbia Broadcasting System. Eventually, in 1941, to avoid a government investigation into monopolies, Judson sold his share of CBS to William Paley, the son of his original partner.

A hefty, six-foot, broad-shouldered man, Judson relaxed by chopping wood at his summer camp in Canada. When friends complimented him on the healthy color in his cheeks, he answered gruffly that it was due to the permanent rage induced by dealing with so-called artists. Virtually every major conductor from the 1920s through the 1950s, except for Arturo Toscanini, was handled by Judson. As a manager of orchestras, he was responsible for booking soloists. Naturally, they came from the roster of his own agency. By 1938 he was the sole owner of Columbia Records. Judson ran his empire as a business. Marketing celebrity performers in familiar repertory was the most profitable approach.

By 1940, when Thomson began his tenure, Judson had relinquished only one of his positions: manager of the Philadelphia Orchestra. Thomson's very first review deplored the sad state the Philharmonic had fallen to. Judson was incensed. There seemed to be no predicting what this upstart would do next, what with his carping about the neglect of contemporary music, his sympathetic coverage of exotic Brazilian music, women conductors and such, and his giddy deflating of the carefully (and expensively) inflated reputations of star soloists, all within days of his arrival.

The breaking point came two weeks to the day after Thomson's debut. Thomson reviewed a recital by a Judson artist, the soprano Dorothy Maynor. The review was negative, one of those early pieces that Parsons thought too "dry and crackly." Maynor, just thirty, was already a respected singer, one of the few black artists with a chance for a successful recital career. The review reads as if Thomson was making sure readers understood that he wasn't going to cut an artist slack just because she was an admirable young black woman from Norfolk, Virginia, who had made it to New York's Town Hall. Thomson's appraisal seems fair, but his tone is condescending. There is no direct mention of her race, but his observation that Maynor is not "at home" in French and German repertory has an unfortunate implication. He seems to be up to mischief here, almost trying to provoke a charge of racism, a charge he must have assumed could not stick, given that he had cast his only opera with black singers from Harlem. The article read, in part,

> She is the possessor of what is commonly called a "lovely voice." She sings softly with ease. She seems to have had good lessons, too, though probably not enough. . . . Her French and her German diction, though schooled, are quite incomprehensible. She is not at home in either of these languages or in their repertories. Her English diction is excellent. It is with English vowels and English meanings that she is inspired to exploit the surprising gamut of color, from very light to very dark, that she is mistress of.
>
> . . . Miss Maynor is not a refined musician. Her best numbers are broadly effective rather than sharply pointed or delicate. She has more musicianly schooling than she has musicianly style. I

imagine that some of that concert-style schooling will wear off before long.

She is immature vocally and immature emotionally. She has the makings of a singing actress, however, and a very good one. I doubt if lieder and oratorio, her present stock in trade, offer a congenial medium for the expansion of her broad humor and her warm folksy intimacy.[27]

Of course, exactly how Thomson expected Maynor to fulfill her potential as a singing actress is unclear, since it would be 1955 before a black artist, the contralto Marian Anderson, finally broke the color barrier at the Metropolitan Opera. That said, Thomson's evaluation of Maynor's work, however exacting, was shared by at least one member of the audience. A friend from Paris days, the poet e. e. cummings, sent a note: "Congrats on the Maynor review. Eye 2 was there."[28]

Judson had carefully cultivated Dorothy Maynor as a recitalist. When the review appeared, he held a meeting at which he compelled his staff into supporting his call for an ultimatum: either the *Herald Tribune* removes Thomson from the critic's post, or Columbia Concerts Corporation will withdraw all its advertising from the paper. Evidently Judson was careful. Nothing seems to have been put in writing. It was all done through phone calls and underlings.

Word got around to Ira Hirschmann, who ran a weekly chamber music series called New Friends of Music, but worked full-time as the advertising manager at Bloomingdale's. On principle Hirschmann was offended by Judson's chest-pounding and threats. He offered to match, line for line, any lost advertising, should Judson carry out his threat. The boycott would have been self-destructive, since *Tribune* readers formed an important market. The editors at the paper did not budge. Judson's scheme fizzled.

It's hard to believe that Thomson, as he claimed, was not told about this for two years. However, records that contradict his account have not been found. Parsons must have felt that at least some of Judson's complaint about the Maynor piece was justified. But the *Tribune* was not going to bend to a bully. As a result of the incident, Judson became Thomson's sworn enemy. There would be other incidents.

While Parsons kept calling Thomson to task for his occasional slips, and even so minor an infraction as using slang brought forth indignant memos, he never once seems to have challenged Thomson in regard to his most glaring offense: conflict of interest. Thomson's new prominence and influence was winning him new champions. All of a sudden, important artists whom Thomson praised in his reviews, musicians who had not previously demonstrated interest in his music, started performing Thomson's works in prominent venues, particularly conductors like Eugene Ormandy, Eugene Goossens, Vladimir Golschmann, even Arthur Rodzinski with the New York Philharmonic (Arthur Judson's orchestra!). Thomson's ten-year-old Symphony no. 2 finally had its world premiere on November 17, 1941, with the Seattle Symphony under no less an international musical celebrity than the conductor Sir Thomson Beecham. When during the next week Sir Thomas conducted the Philadelphia Orchestra in its hometown and in New York, he again presented Thomson's symphony. Thomson and Beecham, who genuinely enjoyed each other's company, would cultivate a chummy relationship throughout Thomson's tenure at the *Tribune.*

Overall, the performers and orchestras performing Thomson's works could count on having him in their corner. This assessment from a 1944 article was typical of the coverage Ormandy consistently received from Thomson, who was his most ardent champion.

> The Philadelphia Orchestra, which last night at Carnegie Hall opened our indoor orchestral season, has a sound that is pungent and mellow like the smell of fall fruit. No other instrumental assembly has quite the quality of impersonal, almost botanical beauty that this one possesses; and none of the other conductors who appear regularly before us has quite Eugene Ormandy's way of offering really excellent workmanship without personal insistence.[29]

Whenever a New York concert included a work by Virgil Thomson, even when he conducted himself, an assistant critic from the *Herald Tribune* was sent to review it. Without exception the reviews were well considered and positive. Writing of Thomson's performance with the Philadelphians of *The Plow,* Jerome D. Bohm called the music "carefully wrought and effectively orchestrated . . . American in feeling without self-conscious efforts in that direction"; of Thomson's performance, he added, "Thomson conducted as though conducting was his daily job. His beat was firm and clearly outlined, his movements graceful and restrained." Reviewing the soprano Doris Doe's singing of Thomson's *Air from Racine's "Phèdre,"* Francis D. Perkins praised the music's "flexible, vital musico-dramatic speech, its projection and enhancement of the ebb and flow of emotion in the protagonist's poignant utterance."

Thomson's protocol was to assign the reviewer to cover the concert, telling him to say whatever he wanted. No overt pressure was applied, but no writer working with Thomson ever tested him by criticizing his pieces in print. At most, a critic would attempt to demonstrate his impartiality by withholding praise and simply describing the music in detail. Of course, this implied that the piece warranted thorough consideration. Sometimes reservations were expressed indirectly, as when Bohm said of Thomson's *The Plow That Broke the Plains* that "the finest movement is indubitably the final 'Devastation,' " which obliquely suggested that other movements may have been less fine. Perhaps Thomson's staffers genuinely admired his music. But the writing in these articles is always strained. And the impropriety, at least the appearance of it, was dumbfounding.

The impropriety was explicit on those several occasions early in his tenure when the reviewer Thomson assigned to cover his music was himself. Sometimes he tried to turn the exercise into a bit of a joke, but it was no less outrageous. Of a New Jersey Symphony Orchestra concert on which a piece of his was played, Thomson wrote,

> It is scarcely appropriate that I should comment on the Scherzo of my own Symphony no. 2 as a musical work. It is only just to state, however, that its execution was satisfactory to the composer. The orchestra played clearly and correctly, and Mr. Pensis had already taken pains to consult both the written notes and the author's intentions. The result sounded very much, indeed, as I had intended that it should.[30]

Thomson did not *always* find it "inappropriate" to comment on his own music.

> The Philharmonic menu of yesterday was definitely on the easy-to-digest side. The Sibelius Violin Concerto and my own "Filling Station" were the meat and salad of it, Weber's "Euryanthe" overture and Strauss' "Till Eulenspiegel" the entrée and dessert. . . . My piece came off well in balance and in sound. Rhythmically I found it a bit unstable, especially the Tango.[31]

One can only imagine how Arthur Judson must have reacted to reading Thomson's review of his own composition on a program performed by Judson's orchestra conducted by Judson's client, this just six weeks after Judson backed down from his ultimatum to the *Tribune*. There is no evidence that Parsons was troubled by the conflict-of-interest issue. However, his attitude should be understood in the context of those times.

In journals and magazines, the tradition of artists' reviewing fellow artists has a long heritage. Berlioz, Schumann, and Debussy were influential critics. While recognizing that the function and protocol of a daily newspaper is essentially different from than of an arts journal, Parsons valued that critical heritage. To Parsons, having a composer writing about other composers harked back to that tradition. Who knows more about music than composers? Besides, with so many newspapers covering music in New York, other voices were there to balance out Thomson's. Olin Downes, for one, seldom shared the opinions of the *Tribune* staffers when it came to Virgil Thomson's music.

Nevertheless, Parsons was allowing Thomson to push the boundaries of propriety. Parsons was apparently sold on the idea of using composers as critics. For when Thomson needed an additional freelancer, Thomson, with Parsons's approval, hired his friend Paul Bowles, another composer pursuing a career in New York, and someone with great admiration for Thomson's music, an admiration he was given many chances to express in the pages of the *Herald Tribune*. Of the harpsichordist Ralph Kirkpatrick's performance of a group of Thomson's musical portraits, Bowles wrote, "The little pieces gave the impression of having come from nowhere, and moved airily in and out of the focus of consonance like breezes through a pagoda. They were perverse, sinister, mincing, imperative and lyrical one after the other, and always carefully expressive."[32]

Curiously, far from carping about the burgeoning musical activities of the *Tribune*'s staffers, some critics from rival papers extolled them; for one, Louis Biancolli of the *New York World Telegram*, who wrote a jocular piece about Thomson's performance of his suite from *The Plow That Broke the Plains* with the Philadelphia Orchestra.

These days anything can be expected of music critics. The Tribune staff fairly blooms with conductors and composers, and there must be others secretly nursing an urge to beat symphonic time. Mr. Thomson's sudden emergence as batonist is no novelty. In the old days critics usually stayed put. Today they show conductors and composers a thing or two at their own game. . . . In a way, Mr. Thomson is the kind of conductor critics cry for. No fuss, no calisthenics, no Boris Karloff scowls. Strictly business-like. The film music reflected drought-stricken areas and lugubrious wanderings, and Mr. Thomson's podium style no doubt suited it perfectly. But stretches of the homespun score about the Okie migrants perk up smartly.[33]

Among Thomson's composer colleagues, opinion was divided over how effectively he used his powerful position. It all depended on whose ox was being gored just then. Aaron Copland, on balance, was delighted to see such influence accrue to his old friend and co-conspirator in the cause of American music. Copland was still spear-heading the collective-action organizations started in the 1930s: the American Composers Alliance, Arrow Music Press, the League of Composers. Thomson offered advice, sometimes attended meetings, and helped plot strategy. Then he would mount his post and spread the word. Copland was taken aback that Thomson used his columns for such shameless self-promotion. And to his intimate friends Copland would confide that he never really felt personally comfortable with Virgil, what with his airs, his cigarette holder, and his effeminate mannerisms. Thomson was too flamboyant for the self-contained, scrupulously closeted Copland. But having Thomson around to promulgate the gospel was an incredible break.

In 1942 the two composers were thrown together in an unusual commission project. The conductor André Kostelanetz, who had gained celebrity performing programs of light classical works on radio and in film, was engaged to present a series of summer concerts with major orchestras. Since becoming an American citizen in 1928, the dashing Russian-born conductor had turned into a devout patriot. With America now at war, Kostelanetz wanted a series of patriotic works. Having heard of Thomson's musical-portrait idea, Kostelanetz proposed to personally commission Thomson, Copland, and the Broadway legend Jerome Kern to compose "a musical portrait gallery of great Americans." The subjects Kostelanetz suggested were mythic in size: George Washington, Paul Revere, Walt Whitman, Henry Ford, Babe Ruth. Though not particularly engaged by the proposal, Copland thought he could render Whitman. But when Jerome Kern chose Mark Twain as his subject, Kostelanetz suggested that Copland do a statesman, not another literary man. When Copland confided that he was thinking of Lincoln, Thomson warned him that Lincoln would be impossible—far too eminent and imposing a figure. Thomson, of

course, would render only subjects who would sit for him. So Kostelanetz suggested Eleanor Roosevelt. But the first lady, busy with the
war effort, declined. So Kostelanetz suggested Mayor La Guardia and
Dorothy Thompson, the *Tribune*'s dynamic political columnist: he
thought the two of them might equal Mrs. Roosevelt. Both agreed,
but the mayor was too busy to actually pose. So Thomson sketched
his portrait at city hall, while His Honor was at his desk, running the
affairs of New York.

Copland stuck with his Lincoln idea because he devised a way,
he thought, to avoid the pitfalls of nationalistic pieces, which he
found bombastic and maudlin: by using Lincoln's own words spoken
by a narrator. The *Lincoln Portrait* stole the show at the premiere in
Cincinnati, May 16, 1942. The piece went on to become Copland's
most famous and profitable composition. Dozens of politicians and
actors have leapt at opportunities to narrate the work and profess their
culture and patriotism. Recent speakers, from left to right, have included Senator Edward M. Kennedy and General Norman Schwarz-
kopf.

Thomson was dissatisfied by his contributions to the venture: the
Mayor La Guardia Waltzes and *Canons for Dorothy Thompson*. Neither was ever published; they are seldom performed. Moreover, the
Tribune arranged for a roving freelance reviewer, Goddard Lieberson,
to cover the premiere in Cincinnati. The result was one of the few
negative reviews of Thomson's music ever to appear in the pages of
the *Tribune*. "Baffling," Lieberson called the mayor's piece, "simple
in the extreme," although the "obvious humor of the piece is highly
infectious." On the other hand, he called Copland's *Lincoln Portrait*
"one of the most masterful works yet produced by an American composer."[34]

Needless to say, Lieberson's association with the *Tribune* as
music critic was short-lived. However, he had already started working for Columbia Records. By 1956 he would become the company's
president and transform the entire classical recording industry.

Back at the *Tribune* the music department was getting shaped up.
With the expansion of staff and coverage that Thomson instigated,
Francis Perkins, the music editor, was no longer able to manage the
secretarial responsibilities by himself. The department was awarded
a coveted prize at the *Trib*: its own secretary, Miss Julia Haines.

Julia was a jolly and sharp-tongued Irishwoman who from having been around some twenty years was on girl-to-girl terms with the secretaries of Ogden Reid, Helen Reid, and Geoffrey Parsons. Her discretion was complete, and so was her devotion to me. She told her colleagues all the favorable news, showing them admiring letters from prominent persons and unusually skillful replies of mine to the opposition.[35]

Miss Haines typed all Thomson's private correspondence, answered all letters of inquiry, and sifted through the reams of promotional materials that arrived every day from concert managers. She also kept for Thomson a scrapbook of his clips. Every review and article he wrote was pasted into thick black books, which, by the time of his retirement, totaled seven volumes. With her help, Thomson was able to respond to almost every letter from his readers, be it an encomium or an attack. Some of his replies are lengthy discourses on assorted topics: the state of Jussi Bjoerling's singing; the misuse of the word "passionate"; the "cut-throat antics" of the harpsichord-playing world. The short letters to readers are textbook demonstrations of how to deflect criticism tactfully, but unflinchingly.

I thank you for your letter. The intensity of your feeling on all these matters is proof of their sincerity and I hope that you will not take my occasional violence of expression as anything essentially different. (October 23, 1940)

I thank you for your extremely indignant letter. I am afraid I do consider Schumann to be a greater and more original composer than Brahms. (February 20, 1941)

I don't follow any special etiquette about applause. I applaud if I feel like it, just as anybody else does, and just as I would if I had paid for my ticket. (March 13, 1942)

I thank you for your charming letter. German music has been smelling bad for a long time. It is largely from this fact that I concluded it must be dead. It will take a little time, however, to get it buried. (January 19, 1944)

I am sorry to have forgotten about Brooklyn in my seasonal review. Music critics nearly always forget about Brooklyn. A thousand apologies. (January 24, 1947)

I did not notice the misprint "Angus Dei." Theologically the cow might as well have been adopted by the Deity as the lamb. Both are peaceful beasts. (February 14, 1947)

You really should not use such language in front of my secretary, who is a lady, and who opens my mail. (April 12, 1951)

Ultimately, the most striking aspect of Thomson's tenure at the *Herald Tribune* was the element of surprise he brought to the job. You never knew what Thomson was going to do next as a critic. The Metropolitan Opera would mount a major new production, and Thomson would send a stringer to cover it. A little-known, unglamorous soprano would sing songs of Liszt and Ravel in a college auditorium, and Thomson would devote a Sunday column to it. People began to feel that anybody could be reviewed by Virgil Thomson. He was not interested in building or busting careers. He liked to spread praise around equitably. No one, he felt, should get too much. Not Stravinsky. Not even Beethoven. Certainly not Toscanini, a mere executant. Composers should be treated as human beings capable of writing pieces that work and pieces that don't. No composer should be turned into a going concern with a group of vested supporters. Perhaps there was a self-serving aspect to his approach. If the praise got spread around, then he would get his share. But it was also an enlightened attitude. And an empowering one, both to musicians and to audiences.

20 329 PACIFIC STREET

When the staffers at the *Herald Tribune* spoke of the "eccentrics" in the music and drama department, this was code for homosexuals. Tolerance prevailed at the paper because no one, especially the eccentrics themselves, ever talked about homosexuality openly. Both sides engaged in a conspiracy of silence.

The foppish Lucius Beebe was understood to be homosexual. He even had a male companion, another dandy type, whom he often brought to events he was covering. Not only was Beebe closeted; his political and social views were adamantly conservative, even intolerant. He would have been aghast, had any homosexual openly discussed his private life in public.

Jerome D. Bohm was closeted in terms of talking about himself. But, more than any other staffer, Bohm thrust his sexuality into the faces of his colleagues. He maintained a weekend house in Bethel, Connecticut, with his longtime companion, Paul Engel, a successful dress designer who specialized in formal concert dresses. And circumstantial evidence suggested that artists who purchased their gowns from Engel were guaranteed good reviews from Bohm.

Paul Bowles, whom Thomson had hired as a stringer, just added to the cast of characters. Bowles was maintaining a "queer marriage," as Thomson called it, with his manic-depressive wife, the writer Jane Bowles. Paul was essentially homosexual; Jane was thoroughly lesbian. They were living in a brownstone on Tenth Street with Jane's older, moneyed friend Helvetia Perkins, who was very possessive of Jane—a true domestic drama, from which Paul found needed relief at the *Herald Tribune.*

Francis Perkins, a workaholic prone to mumbling and nervous fits, was a lifelong bachelor married to his job. And keeping everyone in order was the efficient Miss Haines. When Thomson wrote of his secretary that "her discretion was complete," he meant that Julia Haines was no fool, and no prude. She understood what was going on about her. But she would not have articulated this understanding even, in a sense, to herself. One did not think about such things.

Virgil Thomson fit comfortably into this closeted milieu. He had his foppish side. But this was offset by his pugnaciousness. His cutting wit cracked up many a gathering of hard-drinking, tough-guy *Tribune* staffers after hours at Bleeck's. Thomson maintained his personal life with punctilious propriety. Maurice Grosser was living on West Fourteenth Street, and they saw each other often. Virgil brought Maurice to concerts and operas with him. They took vacations together, including one country tour on Maurice's motorcycle.

Maurice had taken up motorcycling shortly after returning to America in 1939. His first bike was a small Indian Junior Scout, a "June Bug" unequipped with headlights that Maurice totaled one night on a dark road in Chattanooga. After this he graduated to a Harley-Davidson, a compact yet perky vehicle on which he had another accident, this time breaking his arm, thereby affirming his official initiation into the bonded circle of cyclists. ("A rider who had not yet had an accident is not yet afraid of his machine, does not respect its limitations," Maurice later wrote.)[1] During the summer of 1941, Virgil's first summer vacation from the *Herald Tribune,* Maurice took Virgil on a motorcycle tour of New England. The only mishap occurred one day when Virgil, not wearing his helmet, got badly sunburned on the balding patches of his head and complained about it for days.

Maurice was never secretive about his relationship with Virgil, but he insisted on having the freedom to pursue other affairs and keeping them to himself. Virgil, on the other hand, was nervous about being perceived as Maurice's lover. Now that he was before the public, he developed a circle of New York women friends, some of them married, whom he could call on as "dates" when he covered events. He loved being seen with attractive women. Theodate Johnson, back in New York, her voice mostly gone but her striking looks intact, became one of his regular companions at concerts. He also called on

Minna Lederman, whose husband, Mell Daniel, though over forty, had enlisted in the army after the attack on Pearl Harbor.

Virgil projected an air of assurance about his work and his life. He had power within the musical community, admiring colleagues, plenty of enemies to keep him sharp, good friends, and a reliable private relationship. But suppressed drives still unsettled him. Now a prominent person, he was reluctant to engage in promiscuous sexual relationships, as he had in Paris. He knew the illicit places where one could find exciting men. But he was too cautious and conflicted for that. However, there was one place he had discovered that he did patronize, a discreet place in Brooklyn.

At 329 Pacific Street, within walking distance of the Brooklyn Navy Yard, was an unremarkable, three-story, brick house owned by a Swedish-born naturalized American citizen named Gustave Beekman. Then fifty-five, Beekman identified himself as a professional gardener and florist. In fact, he ran a gay bordello at his home. The house was frequented by a cross section of New York professional men; investors, warehouse managers, switchboard operators, city employees, and a butler were among the regulars. They came to mingle socially and to meet young military men who flocked to the place, mostly sailors, but also marines, soldiers, and merchant seamen. The house was not exactly a den of prostitution. There is no evidence that anyone ever paid Beekman for arranging sexual encounters. There was an entry fee; and upstairs bedrooms could be rented by the hour. If money was involved, people made their own arrangements with each other. On the lower floor were sofas and stuffed chairs, tables with coffee and snacks, sometimes buffet suppers and drinks. Beekman was a paternal figure to the sailors and soldiers. He greeted them with affection and bade them farewell with a kiss or a pat on the backside. Sometimes he had sex with one of them, never by force and seldom for money. The young men were apparently willing participants.

The comings and goings of so many strangers, all men, aroused the suspicion of neighbors. They alerted the police, who in turn alerted the Bureau of Naval Intelligence. Government sleuths set up a surveillance operation in a room on the fifth floor of Holy Family Hospital, diagonally across the intersection from Beekman's place. After five weeks of spying, a raid was ordered. There were two imperatives for action: Beekman was clearly supplying his clients with young servicemen who were being tempted into acts of unlawful and abominable sodomy; in addition, there was evidence that some of the clients were foreigners, including Germans and German-born nationals who were suspected Nazi sympathizers, possibly Nazi agents. The foreigners were plying sailors with liquor and asking lots of questions about maneuvers and battleships.

On the evening of March 14, 1942, plainclothesmen from the New York Police Department's Eleventh Division accompanied by naval intelligence officers raided Beekman's house. They arrested Beekman, two sailors, several regular clients, some younger nonmilitary men, and other habitués of the place. One of those arrested was Virgil Thomson.

Thomson was taken to the local Brooklyn precinct. For several hours he was intimidated by investigators and thoroughly frightened. Allowed to make a call, he phoned Geoffrey Parsons, who came immediately. A bail bondsman in Brooklyn was contacted. Thomson was released. His record of arrest would stand, but no charges were filed.

The day following his arrest Virgil stayed at home and tried to relax. He called friends to chat nonchalantly. To Maurice and some other intimate friends, he told the truth. The next day, March 16, he was scheduled to cover the concert at Carnegie Hall by the National Symphony, conducted by Leon Barzin. He phoned Minna Lederman and asked her, practically ordered her, to accompany him that night. He told her that she must get "dressed up all fancy," that he was dressing up and the evening was going to be stylish. Minna didn't understand what made this evening so exceptional. But she did as asked, wearing an elegant red chiffon dress, something completely inappropriate, she felt, for a routine symphony concert. Virgil, dressed in a dark gray, three-piece French suit with an evening hat and white gloves, picked Minna up uncharacteristically early. At Carnegie Hall they mingled in the lobby, greeting acquaintances who passed by, which was also uncharacteristic behavior for Virgil. After the concert, instead of rushing off to write the review as he normally did, Virgil insisted that they linger in the lobby. Eventually, Virgil hailed a taxi, got out on Forty-first Street near the *Herald Tribune* building, and told the cabby to take Minna home. He went to his desk and wrote his piece.

The next day, Minna was visited by her friend Herbert Weinstock, a writer on music, editor, and translator. She told Herbert about Virgil's peculiar behavior the previous night. Herbert, who was also a friend of Virgil's, said that he could explain. Virgil had been arrested,

Herbert said. Word had gotten around. Virgil was, rather pathetically, trying to boost his public image as a man who went about town with well-dressed women.

Throughout the ordeal Geoffrey Parsons was tactful and supportive. He did not lecture or issue warnings. Virgil was shattered enough. This was the fulfillment of his worst fears, an almost inevitable result of "being queer" in God-fearing America. It could have been worse. He could have gone to prison like Henry Cowell, his colleague from California.

Henry Cowell was a visionary composer whose eclectic pieces using unconventional instruments and ethnic musical sources had made him something of a celebrity during the early 1930s. But in 1936 Cowell, then thirty-nine, was arrested and charged with performing oral sodomy on a seventeen-year-old male. A sweet-tempered, cheerful, and almost naively honest man, Cowell had a swimming pond in the back of his Menlo Park home. Young men in the neighborhood used to come by to swim. In his defense, Cowell stated that the boys, the youngest of whom was sixteen, had actually been the instigators, and that in no instance did he force anyone to do anything. But a jury trial would mean calling the young men to testify, which he would not do. So Cowell signed a confession and was sentenced to San Quentin prison, where he remained until June of 1940. The case became fodder for the Hearst tabloids.

In prison Cowell taught music to over fifteen hundred inmates, organized a prison orchestra, composed fifty pieces, and wrote a book on melody and several journal articles. Upon release in 1940, he was able to establish himself in New York as a composer, teacher, and new-music organizer. Eventually, he made himself indispensable to the war effort by fostering working relationships and good will with South American composers. In 1942 he was granted a full pardon.

Yet he never shook off the stigma. Many of his closest colleagues broke off ties with him, including Charles Ives, whom Cowell had come to regard as practically a father. Only after Cowell married in 1941 did Ives agree to see him again. But everyone in the cultural community knew of Cowell's shame; creatively, he never fully recovered.

Thomson feared that his arduously established reputation would collapse. But Geoffrey Parsons brought all the prestige of the *Herald Tribune* to bear. At first, no report of Thomson's arrest appeared in print.

However, the story spread at the paper, among Thomson's circle, and even beyond. Just when Thomson was beginning to put the affair behind him, everything threatened to explode. Government investigators had initially kept the incident from the press. But some four weeks later, two tabloids, the *Brooklyn Eagle* and the *New York Post,* started dropping hints of a government higher-up who was implicated in a raid at a "house of degradation" for men in Brooklyn. The mystery man was identified as "Senator X." For over a week the papers teased readers about the identity of this person.

After his arrest, Beekman had been pressured by the FBI, the Naval Intelligence Service, and Judge Samuel S. Leibowitz, a liberal jurist who was trying the case, to cooperate. Judge Leibowitz announced that evidence collected during the investigation suggested that enemy agents had used Beekman's establishment to entice information from servicemen. Only Beekman's complete cooperation, including the naming of names, would prevent his receiving the maximum sentence.

Beekman decided to talk. He listed all the men he could remember who frequented his house. At the top of the list was a regular whom everybody called "Doc" but who was, Beekman knew, David Ignatius Walsh, the sixty-nine-year-old senior senator from Massachusetts, a New Deal Democrat, a friend of organized labor, and the chairman of the Naval Affairs Committee. Until Pearl Harbor he had been a recalcitrant isolationist. Now he was fully on board with the war effort and essential to it.

Walsh was an influential leader with a inspiring story. The ninth of ten children of an Irish immigrant, he lost his father at twelve, worked his way through high school selling newspapers, graduated from Holy Cross College and Boston University Law School; he served two terms as governor before winning a senate seat in 1918, the first Democratic senator to be elected in Massachusetts in seventy-five years. He was outspoken on behalf of women's suffrage and mine safety.

However, his personal life left him vulnerable to the charge of homosexuality. A bachelor, he lived with four maiden sisters and enjoyed the company of women, he once told an interviewer, as "nonromantic companions." His closest relationship seemed to be with a Filipino houseboy who had served him for thirty years. To investigators Beekman gave details of the senator's frequent visits to Pacific Street: government work or train trips back to Boston took him often through New York; the senator preferred the company of young navy men, Beekman said; he usually came about seven in the evening and stayed an hour or two, bringing sailors upstairs.

Walsh denied the accusations, saying he had been in Brooklyn only three times in his life, in each instance to make a speech. This "Doc" person was obviously someone else. Beekman's story was weakened by the fact that during the weeks of surveillance, Walsh was not seen entering the house. What probably happened, according to recently uncovered FBI reports, is that Walsh, as chairman of the Naval Affairs Committee, was tipped off to the investigation. The last time Beekman claimed to have seen Walsh just happened to be two days before the surveillance operation began.

However, other Pacific Street regulars, also under threats to co-operate, backed Beekman's story and identified Walsh as "Doc." Their descriptions matched Walsh exactly: a stout man in his sixties, just over six feet, over 200 pounds with a "good-sized belly on him," a "good-sized jaw," a ruddy complexion, and a slight limp.[2] One merchant seaman knew exactly where Walsh had ripples of fat and where he didn't.[3]

Finally, on May 7, the *New York Post* named Walsh as "Senator X." According to some sources, word was sent down from Roosevelt himself to save Senator Walsh. An official FBI investigation of the charges was requested by Attorney General Francis Biddle. The Senate majority leader, Alben W. Barkley (who would be elected vice-president in 1948), approved but did not officially endorse the investigation. Everyone wanted these malicious charges against the esteemed senator from Massachusetts repudiated. In the final report, J. Edgar Hoover—a man who, we now know, understood what it meant to be homosexual, closeted, self-loathing, and hypocritical—issued a summary dismissal of Beekman's testimony and asserted that Walsh was not the notorious "Doc." The inflammatory *New York Post* headlines about Beekman's revelations ("Links Senator to Spy Nest") made the job of clearing him easier. Senator Walsh was indisputably not a stooge for Nazi spies.

On May 20 Senator Barkley took the Senate floor to report on the FBI findings. At the climax of a long speech, his voice ringing with righteous indignation over the "undignified, malicious, degrading" accusations leveled against his honorable colleague from Massachusetts, Senator Barkley declared that the Federal Bureau of Investigation had concluded that there was not the "slightest foundation" for the charge that Senator Walsh "visited a 'house of degradation' in Brooklyn" in an effort "to connive or to consort with, or to converse with, or conspire with anybody who is the enemy of the United States."[4] To that specific charge Walsh was clearly innocent.

The reactions of the press were predictable. The *Boston Globe*'s headline read, "Senator Walsh Story Denounced as Absolute Fabrication." The *New York Times* was more equivocal: "FBI Clears Walsh, Barkley Asserts." The *New York Post* proclaimed, "Whitewash for Walsh." And, in this instance, the tabloid was probably closest to the truth.

The case was dropped. Walsh's reputation was salvaged. In 1948 he ran for a fifth term, but was defeated by the Republican Henry Cabot Lodge, Jr., who had resigned the junior Massachusetts Senate seat in 1946 to enlist in the army, and returned, a decorated hero, to challenge his former colleague. Walsh died the next year at seventy-four.

Gustave Beekman had cooperated in good faith with the investigators. But they reneged on their promises of leniency. Accused of just one charge, sodomy, Beekman was convicted and sent to Sing Sing, where he served a full sentence, twenty years. He was released on April 1, 1963. He was seventy-eight.

Virgil Thomson could only watch and worry as this sordid story claimed the tabloid headlines for weeks. The papers kept mentioning "others" who had been arrested or implicated in Beekman's activities. Finally, on May 14, 1942, Walter Winchell, a gleeful queer baiter, slipped a sly reference about Thomson into his *Daily Mirror* column:

> The ad-libbers are having fun with the yarn about Brooklyn's spy nest, also known as the swastika swishery. What are the suspects going to claim they were doing there if not spying? Like the gal in the police court who accused the guy of snatching her purse from her stocking. When Hizzoner scolded her for not resisting, she pouted: "I didn't know he was after my money."
> . . . That musician mentioned in the Brooklyn house will embarrass his employers. He's got many gunning for him, and this will give them a very loud haw-haw. . . .[5]

The next week Thomson read with dismay of the speech by Senator Barkley, who described the activities at Beekman's house as "too loathsome to mention in the Senate or in any group of ladies and gentlemen."[6] But Thomson's name never surfaced. His friends never mentioned it. With Walsh cleared and Beekman in prison, the story faded away.

Relieved, he settled into his work. Before long, Geoffrey Parsons was back on the job as Thomson's editorial watchdog, sending caustic memos. One, dated November 25, 1942 (Thomson's forty-sixth birthday), refers curiously to a slump Thomson had fallen into during the spring.

> Last spring you were at the bottom of the valley—the bottom of the brook, if you prefer. You had gradually crawled out until you were, say, one-third of the way up the slope. In these last weeks I feel you have slipped clear to the bottom again. The thing that readers most want from a critic is a reliance on his judgment. When you use slang, or become petty and personal in your criticism, you compromise yourself with all your readers. What the hell's the matter with you?[7]

Was Parsons elliptically referring to Thomson's personal slump as well? Despite his humane handling of Thomson's indiscretion, it cannot have been easy for this proper professional man to use the clout of the *Herald Tribune* to rescue Virgil from this affair. His memo could be read to have a subtext: "Virgil, as we both know, last spring you learned what it means to be utterly humiliated; so just remember how it feels before you go humiliating others."

One year later, Virgil's father, Quincy Alfred Thomson, child of a Civil War widow, died at eighty-one. He came down with pneumonia, declined steadily, but stayed at home. Feeling he was becoming a burden to his family, he asked to be brought to a hospital. Once there, he said, "I'm all right now," then died in peace. Virgil did not rush to Kansas City when the news of his father's illness came from his sister. He traveled home for the funeral in April. He later wrote tenderly of his father's death.

> My personal regret (for my father and I were warmly attached, though without the possibility of much ease) was that now I could never let him know my shame for harsh things said in adolescent years. But he must have known and long since forgiven me, for he was a Christian and a loving one; and though the former I was surely not, he had always understood me and spared reproach.[8]

This reflection is lovely, but idealized. Quincy Thomson, no doubt, supported his son; but he never understood him. Virgil had long ago moved into an intensely private and, literally, foreign world. Quincy must have had his suspicions of what that world was about. But he never asked. Virgil was not just private; he was intimidating.

Yet, if there was not "much ease" between them, there was certainly warmth and respect. In recounting his son's accomplishments to his friends and family, Quincy spoke with special pride of Virgil's having been a soldier. All the men in Quincy's family had served in the military, but when Quincy came of age he had a widowed mother to care for. Military service was the one manly obligation he never fulfilled. That his son carried the Thomson name into World War I, even if he never saw combat, had been a comfort.

Virgil Thomson's letters from the World War II years seldom mention the overseas conflict, or the domestic support effort. Friends remember him as being almost detached about it. Even before D-Day, on June 6, 1944, Thomson was trying to finagle his way back to Paris for a visit. War references did make it into his columns; mostly these were jocular attempts to boost readers' morale. "Private Samuel Barber's *Essay For Orchestra, No. 1* is a pretty piece but not a very strong one," he wrote in April 1943 of his younger colleague, who just days earlier had been drafted into the army.[9] In a Sunday piece on March 18, 1945, when the surrender of the German army seemed imminent, Thomson wrote of the usefulness of Beethoven's Fifth Symphony as a call to arms. The occasion was a performance by the conductor George Szell with the New York Philharmonic.

> If thinking of the work as embodying faith and hope has helped conquered nations to resist tyranny, that is all to the good. An energizing moral result is more valuable than any misreading of the composer's specific thought is dangerous. Besides, the piece will recover from its present military service just as easily as it has from its past metaphysical and political associations. But as a musician I was interested to observe the amount of distortion that Mr. Szell was obliged to impose on the work in order to make it seem to be representing military struggle and final victory.[10]

During the early war years Thomson's personal and professional circle in New York was joined by three young Americans, all of whom for various reasons had managed to escape the draft. Two of them, John Cage and Lou Harrison, arrived from the West Coast seeking fame and fortune in New York. The other, Ned Rorem, was trying to extricate himself from a confining academic regime at the Curtis Institute of Music, in Philadelphia. All three would play significant roles from then on in Thomson's life.

In March of 1939 Virgil Thomson, still living in Paris, got a letter from a young man associated with the Cornish School, a progressive institution for the arts in Seattle, Washington. The writer, who misspelled Thomson's name ("Dear Mr. Thomsen"), had heard some years earlier in New York a performance of Thomson's *Five Phrases from the Song of Solomon,* for soprano and percussion. He had recently presented a percussion concert in Seattle and was organizing another.

> For this next concert Johanna Beyer has written 3 movements for percussion, Henry Cowell has written a new work, Lou Harrison has completed his 5th Simfony. We would like very much to present some work of yours. Rehearsals begin April 10th. We have five good players, and three not so good (they could play easy parts). We have 7 gongs, 3 cymbals, 4 tom-toms, two timpani without pedals, many wood blocks, and can improvise instruments from junk yards or construct things, given specifications of sorts, etc.
> Please let me know about this as soon as convenient for you.
>
> Very sincerely,
> John Cage[11]

Thomson did not respond. Two years later when he heard from Cage again, he was intrigued by this unorthodox composer, soon to be thirty. Cage wanted to play for Thomson studio records—enormous discs that had to be played on professional studio turntables—of some radio plays he had composed and produced for a CBS workshop in Chicago. The plays, which mixed sound effects, speech, ambient noise, and excerpts of other music, had created a stir when broadcast. Thomson agreed to meet Cage.

Born in Los Angeles in 1912, Cage was the son of an inventor. Among others devices, the senior Cage had invented a gas-propelled submarine, a hydrophone for submarine detection, an inhaler for treating colds, and the first radio powered by alternating current so that it could be plugged into an electric light system. As a boy at Los Angeles High School, young John Cage excelled in Latin and oratory and was fascinated by audio technology and radio broadcasting. At twelve, a Tenderfoot in the Boy Scouts, Cage persuaded a radio station to let him produce a Boy Scout show. He brought in friends to sing, play trumpet or piano, and talk of scouting adventures. Every week there was a guest from a local church or synagogue who delivered an inspirational message.

Cage's musical studies had taken him to Paris, Berlin, and Madrid; in 1933 he took classes with Henry Cowell in New York, where he lived in a succession of cheap furnished rooms and earned money washing walls in a YWCA. The next year, at Cowell's suggestion, he returned to Los Angeles for lessons with the Teutonic Arnold Schoenberg, who pronounced Cage more an inventor than a composer, a label Cage did not object to. ("I am essentially not very talented as a musician," he always said of himself in later years.) Cage's interests went well beyond music: he wrote poetry, took dance classes, studied painting, and considered becoming an architect.

When war was declared in the aftermath of Pearl Harbor, John Cage, Sr., was working on a device for submarine detection and on radar systems for airplanes in fog conditions. Both projects were deemed essential to the war effort. Because John, Jr., with no musical work at the time, was assisting his father, he was deferred from the draft.

The next year he moved to New York, where he pursued his friendship with Thomson, who enjoyed him immensely. ("Cage has a wit and breadth of thought that make him a priceless companion.")[12] Thomson was entranced by Cage's radio plays and percussion pieces—almost random-sounding assemblages of sounds; but it was Cage's frontal attack on the musical status quo that excited him. Like the senior Cage, who had come from Tennessee mountaineer folk, the "lanky and freckled red-haired big-boned son was distilling a clear-as-water musical moonshine without the stamp of any Establishment."[13]

In 1942, having heard that the League of Composers was sponsoring a series of new-music concerts at the Museum of Modern Art, Cage sought support for an all-percussion program featuring many of his own works and performed by his own ensemble. Copland, by now the all-but-official head of the league, not knowing what to make of Cage, was against it. But when Thomson took up Cage's cause, Copland gave in.

The concert, which took place on February 7, presented three works by Cage, two by Lou Harrison, and one each by Henry Cowell, José Ardévol, and Amadeo Roldán. The twelve-person percussion ensemble, conducted by Cage, included Xenia Cage, his wife of seven years (one of six daughters of a Russian Orthodox priest from Juneau, Alaska), and Merce Cunningham, a young dancer Cage had met at the Cornish School. Xenia and Merce were crossing paths in Cage's life, for he was then in the process of separating from Xenia and beginning what turned out to be a lifelong relationship with Merce.

The concert was a scandalous success. Even *Life* magazine, titillated by this unorthodox "concert" at a modern art museum, sent a reporter and photographer to cover it.

> At the Museum of Modern Art in New York City a few Sundays ago, an orchestra of earnest, dressed-up musicians sat on the stage and began to hit things with sticks and hands. They whacked gongs, cymbals, gourds, bells, sheets of metal, or bells, Chinese dishes, tin cans, auto brake drums, the jawbone of an ass and other objects. Sometimes instead of hitting they rattled or rubbed. The audience, which was very high brow, listened intently without seeming to be disturbed at the noisy results.[14]

The reporter described percussion music as "going back to man's primitive days when untutored savages took aesthetic delight in hitting crude drums or hollow logs." Cage believes, the article continued, that when people begin to appreciate his music "they will find new beauty in everyday modern life, which is full of noises made by objects banging against each other."

That *Life* magazine covered Cage's concert only confirmed the suspicions of the musical establishment that this had not been a purely musical event. Not surprisingly, a critic from the *New York Times,* Noel Straus, dismissed it entirely: "[P]ractically all the 'music' . . . had an inescapable resemblance to the meaningless sounds made by children amusing themselves by banging on tin pans and other resonant kitchen utensils . . . could not be taken seriously enough to require detailed comment."[15]

Thomson attended but did not review the concert. Instead he sent Paul Bowles, an ideal choice, given Thomson's desire to support Cage effectively. In Tangier, Bowles had slept in rooms at the top of the cliffs at Gibraltar listening all night to the distant sounds of African drums; he had sat in cafés in Algiers smoking hashish and drinking goat's milk while Arab women danced to music of reed flutes, drums, and guitars. Among New York critics, he had a unique understanding of non-Western music; his article was insightful and sympathetic.

> The concert was good for the hearing; it was an ear massage. Fourteen persons, 125 instruments and about fifty sticks to hit them with. When things were not beaten or tapped they were shaken, rubbed, pulled or immersed in water. There was an ominous audio frequency oscillator, recorded sounds went on and off, and both thunder sheet and marimba were equipped with electric pick-ups.
>
> [In John Cage's *Imaginary Landscape* no. 3] Oriental and African elements dominated. . . . [T]he effects strove to approximate those of the ritual music of the far parts of the world. Even the figures used by Mr. Cage in his delicate "Amores" for piano transformed with screws and clips were reminiscent of Bali, and often the passages of ensemble work were suggestive of the gamelan music of that same island.
>
> . . . Sometimes the level of excitement reached was below the obviously prodigious amount of energy expended to obtain it. The complicated rhythmical juxtapositions sounded neither complex nor simple, but desultory and accidental. But there were few of these dry spots. The music's principal aim was to achieve a maximum of sonorous effect, and the composers involved were adept at it.[16]

Bowles's final point was that Cage's greatest contribution lay in pointing new directions for "Occidental art music." Thomson agreed. Moreover, he was heartily for anything that managed to rattle the support structure of the musical establishment, and Cage's percussion pieces for auto brake drums did the trick. Thomson took up the cause. A review from January 22, 1945, the first penetrating analysis of Cage's procedures, lent enormous credibility to Cage's work.

On this particular program, presented at the New School for Social Research, Cage had introduced his pieces for "prepared piano," an ordinary pianoforte, Thomson wrote, "prepared by inserting bits of metal, wood, rubber or leather at carefully studied points and distances between the strings," resulting in an "even greater variety of sounds" than in his previous pieces for tin drums, electric buzzers, and such. The effects produced Thomson likened to gamelan orchestras and to the futuristic experiments of such gleeful noisemakers as Varèse, Cowell, and Antheil. His most provocative observation was to compare Cage's procedures to those of the pioneer of atonal modernism, Arnold Schoenberg:

Mr. Cage has carried Schoenberg's harmonic maneuvers to their logical conclusion. He has produced atonal music not by causing the twelve tones of the chromatic scale to contradict one another consistently, but by eliminating, to start with, all sounds of precise pitch. He substitutes for the chromatic scale a gamut of pings, plunks, and delicate thuds that is both varied and expressive and that is different in each piece. By thus getting rid, at the beginning, of the constricting element in atonal writing—which is the necessity of taking care to avoid making classical harmony with a standardized palette of instrumental sounds and pitches that exists primarily for the purpose of producing such harmony—Mr. Cage has been free to develop the rhythmic element of composition, which is the weakest element in the Schoenbergian style, to a point of sophistication unmatched in the technique of any other living composer.

. . . That these procedures do not take over a piece and become its subject, or game, is due to Cage's genius as a musician. . . . His work represents, in consequence, not only the most advanced methods now in use anywhere, but original expression of the very highest poetic quality.[17]

Here was Thomson using the iconoclast John Cage, the master of the thunder machine and flowerpot, to skewer Schoenberg and his disciples. Roger Sessions at Princeton was outraged. Even Copland thought Thomson had gone too far. Cage was exultant: "genius as a musician . . . sophistication unmatched . . . most advanced methods now in use anywhere." This was heady praise. However, the review of that concert that he treasured came from Thomson's mother.

Now that May Thomson was a widow, she visited New York almost once a year. Virgil usually arranged for her to stay in a vacant room at the Chelsea. Sometimes she accompanied Virgil to events. One was this all-Cage concert at the New School. During the pieces for prepared piano, May Thomson listened attentively, then applauded politely, but said nothing. Virgil asked her, "So, Mother, what did you think?"

"It was very interesting," she answered. "I wouldn't have thought of it myself."

Forty-five years later, long after his relationship with Thomson had soured for good, Cage told that story with delight, laughing so hard at the punch line that his eyes teared.

The Portland-born Lou Harrison, four years younger than Cage, had studied with the same teachers: Cowell and Schoenberg. Their friendship grew when they worked with Bonny Bird at the Cornish School. A plump, affable young man, Harrison was also a musical iconoclast, drawn to the music, instruments, and philosophy of the Far East. From the start his music was willfully unconventional, mixing styles, techniques, and instruments from Western and non-Western sources. Like the man, the music was vibrant but not pushy.

In 1943 Harrison was studying with Schoenberg in Los Angeles. But when a boyfriend at the time, the dancer Lester Horton, joined a troupe in New York, Harrison decided to drop everything and relocate. There he maintained himself with sundry jobs: florist, store clerk, poet, dancer, music copyist. Through Cage he met Thomson, which he had long wanted to do. Harrison knew few of Virgil's compositions; but he had been impressed by *The State of Music*.

Thomson was pleased with his young West Coast friends, who were ardent fans and charming conversationalists ("the three of us provided for one another, with Europe and the Orient cut off by war, a musical academy of theory and practice . . .").[18] He introduced them to Satie's *Socrate,* singing and playing the work at the piano, an experience which moved Harrison, but profoundly changed Cage. Like Thomson, Cage grew to revere Satie.

That year Thomson tried out Cage as a stringer at the *Tribune,* but his style was too idiosyncratic. Cage had little interest in whole epochs of music's past and could not write on deadline. But he hung on Thomson's reviews. ("Virgil made it necessary to buy the paper. I would leave my apartment early every morning just to read his writing.") Harrison, however, became a sharp and valuable critic. His first New York articles were done for *Modern Music,* where Minna Lederman turned him into a clear-thinking writer. Having proven himself, Harrison was invited by Thomson to review for the *Tribune*. He had to learn everything: how to type (a black minister boyfriend from Harlem taught him in one weekend); how to operate at concerts (Francis Perkins gave him a stopwatch so that he could time new pieces). Like Cage, Harrison had great holes in his knowledge of the standard repertory. ("I was terribly happy when I could review, say, the *Waldstein* Sonata as though I'd heard it more than once.")[19] But in Eastern music—from India, Japan, Java, Bali—Harrison became the *Tribune*'s resident expert.

Virgil was struck by Lou Harrison's blasé attitude about being homosexual. He thought it masked some inner sadness or turmoil. Lou battled inner demons. However, they were stirred up not by discomfort over his sexuality but by the shock of Hiroshima and Nagasaki, which knocked him flat. In Los Angeles he had read a novel about a meltdown in an atomic factory. He seemed to be the only one in his New York circle who really understood what had happened at Hiroshima, the actual physics of atomic exposure. By early 1947 he was having periodic symptoms of mental breakdown.

One morning he went to the *Tribune* office in a distracted state. He stood by Virgil's desk and told him that he was hearing voices. Virgil said, "Lou, you're having a tizzy." He sat Lou down and, with calming certainty, gave him a talking to about guardian angels.

"You see, Lou, we are all born with three guardian angels. But people keep getting born and there are not enough angels to go around. If you're having troubles, it's because one or more are off taking care of other people. That's the reason everything is going to hell. You mustn't squirm. You must sit quietly and wait for the guardian angel to return."

Completely absorbed by Virgil's explanation, Lou asked if there were some people without any guardian angels. Yes, there are, Virgil answered. "But you are not one of them."

Virgil gave Lou some spending money and told him to take the day off. Lou went to the Bronx Zoo, feeling as if he were floating on the cushiony wings of protective angels.

But Lou's angels must have been needed elsewhere, for shortly thereafter he had a serious breakdown. He showed up at Virgil's door at the behest of inner voices and spent a night on Virgil's couch. John Cage and Virgil arranged for a psychiatrist to visit. Lou was checked into an upstate sanatorium. Eventually he was moved to the Psychiatric Institute and Hospital at the Presbyterian Medical Center in New York, where he remained for nine months. Virgil and Maurice helped defray Lou's expenses. So did Charles Ives, who heard of Lou's problems from Cage. Shortly before this incident, Lou had met Ives and agreed to work for him as a copyist. Then seventy-three, Ives had been in failing health since 1930. ("I want you to be my eyes," Ives had said at the interview.)

The diagnosis given Lou Harrison was a type of schizophrenia. It would take ten years before he felt fully comfortable in company. But shortly after his return from the hospital, Lou was back at the *Tribune,* at Virgil's insistence, working productively and supporting himself.

Ned Rorem's parents were staunch pacifist Quakers. As a decorated army lieutenant, C. Rufus Rorem had observed World War I close up; his wife, Gladys, had lost a younger brother to it. That was enough for them. So when Ned was called up for his draft physical, his father urged him to avoid service any way he could: "Father . . . felt pragmatically that since war was unrelated to morality, why be moral about methods for avoiding it."[20] After his exam in 1942 Ned, then a composition major at the Curtis Institute, was given a temporary student deferment. Called back twice, in 1943 and 1947, he told the truth about his sexuality and was branded 4-F.

This left him free to continue his adventures, personal and musical, in New York City, to where he moved in early 1944, abandoning his scholarship, much to the dismay of his father, who was a professor of economics at the University of Chicago during Ned's youth. C. Rufus Rorem was an early proponent of prepaid health care whose pioneering work led to the creation of Blue Cross and Blue Shield; and he believed without reservation in higher education.

Rorem had been unhappy at Curtis. The courses were calcified; his composition teacher, Rosario Scalero, was a conservative taskmaster. He found himself making frequent forays by train up to New York, for concerts, stimulation, and sex: ". . . I went there mainly to cruise, bedding about, catch as catch can. I've no remembrance of how the days were spent beyond using the private washrooms of the Winslow bar on Lexington for my personal toilet (I didn't yet shave much, still don't), and subsisting on milkshakes and apples."[21] In New York he was befriended by Leonard Bernstein, who introduced him to Aaron Copland, both of whom were fabulously more exciting than any of his Curtis colleagues. So when he learned that Virgil Thomson was looking for a copyist, he made an appointment to meet him. Rorem had heard Thomson on a panel in Chicago, on the topic "Music in Our Changing Society."

> Opening volley: the obligatory struggle to define music. The others were falling back on Shakespeare's "concord of sweet sounds" when Thomson shrieked: *"Boy, was he wrong!* You might as well call painting a juxtaposition of pretty colors, or poems a succession of lovely words. What is music? Why, it's what we musicians do." That settled that. His unsentimental summation was the first professional remark I'd ever heard—music is what musicians do— and could well have marked my semiconscious acceptance of myself as French and not German.[22]

On the appointed day Virgil escorted Ned, just twenty and uncommonly handsome, onto the sofa in his salon and asked, "So what's your sad story?" Rorem's first impressions, recorded with his trademark bluntness in his beguiling autobiography, offer a vivid portrait of Thomson in 1944, at the crest of his success.

> I was prepared for the swishy voice because of the lively round table in Chicago a year or two back, but not for the patronizing friendliness and icy impatience, a mixture I later found to be native to uppercrust French females. His eyes were quick, his head balding, his cravat a hand-tied butterfly bow, his cigarette holder a nonfilter, his stomach already paunchy (his was forty-seven, a year younger than Father), his housecoat maroon, his slippers plush, and his manner sardonic and adult. I was intimidated. Not because he was a famous composer (I didn't know a note of his music), nor because he was a redoubtable critic of the *Herald-Tribune* (I never read newspapers, but *The New York Times*'s Olin Downes was more nationally known). I was intimidated because I'd never met anyone like him, so brusquely precise, so businesslike about music—and hence didn't know how to behave. The intimidation would never entirely go away and proved to be a good thing.[23]

Virgil gave Ned an assignment to test his copying skills. Ned managed to translate Virgil's penciled, squiggly manuscripts into legible, even somewhat ornate, fair copy. A deal was struck. Ned was to become a New Yorker.

When he heard the news, Ned's father was not pleased. If Ned quit Curtis for good, his father promised, he would be cut off financially. Still, Ned went ahead with his plans and moved into the apartment of a young man and sometime lover he had known since 1941, Morris Golde. Husky and energetic, Morris was a New Yorker through and through. Born there in 1920, educated at New York University, he was then working for the family business—a direct-mail and printing press business run by his older brother—and living in Greenwich Village on the top floor of a four-story brick building on West Eleventh Street. Every morning Morris rose early and caught the IRT local to his office on West Forty-fifth Street, and Ned walked twelve blocks north on Seventh Avenue to the Chelsea Hotel. Ned worked five days a week, four hours a day—from ten till noon, and one to three—copying parts, and also accompanying Virgil to rehearsals when the parts had to be distributed and corrections made. For this work he received twenty dollars a week, of which five went to Morris for rent and five to a savings account, leaving ten for "concert tickets, music, books, groceries, subways, and beer." Virgil was impressed with Ned's financial efficiency.

From his vantage point Ned observed Virgil running the musical affairs of New York from his bed, sleeping until noon, calling up Paul Bowles to admonish him for a slip of tone in that day's review, or arranging get-togethers with Thomas Beecham, Oscar Levant, Peggy Guggenheim, and innumerable other luminaries. Almost every day, sitting at the other end of the chrome-legged table where he worked was the cook, a "humorless old-world Negro woman named Leana," who never made conversation, but grunted sarcastically about the improper goings-on at Virgil's: sleeping to all hours, wasting money on French cologne for men, talking gossip.

Morris made a lasting impression on Virgil the first time they met. Ned had just finished adding a missing accidental to the thousand extant copies of Virgil's just published Second String Quartet and packed them into a footlocker, which he was to transfer to the American Music Center, on West Fifty-seventh Street. "I said that my friend Morris Golde would help with the cab. When Morris showed up, all tough and eager, he hoisted the footlocker like a feather onto his shoulders, and off we went. Virgil was thrilled."[24]

Morris was exactly that type of unpretentious, open-minded intellectual Virgil found refreshing company, someone who loved music but was not a musician, someone who enjoyed Virgil's wit and wisdom but wanted nothing from him, no recommendations, no introductions. In fact, in later years, when Morris started earning good money, it was he who helped out Virgil, underwriting performances, never failing to contribute to a Thomson project. From their first meeting, Ned would later write, Morris and Virgil "hit it off like long-lost Jewish cousins, and remained close—closer than I ever was with Virgil, or at least in a different, noncompetitive way—until the end."[25]

Soon Ned was comfortably established as worker and honorary son of the Thomson circle. Virgil showed off Ned one weekend at Briggs Buchanan's New Jersey home, where they arrived with taffy apples for the Buchanan boys, and where Ned, somewhat uncomfortably, shared a room with Mr. Thomson, as he still called him. That weekend, Virgil played his favorite piece, Satie's *Socrate,* singing the French text and accompanying himself at the piano. Immediately, Ned joined the roster of people—Gertrude, Alice, Paul Bowles, Lou Harrison, John Cage—who had been moved profoundly by the music and Virgil's devotion to it: "During that half hour I felt my notion of the world's musical repertory change shape, swell, shrink, and ensconce itself in my ken where it would permanently lodge, along with *The Rite of Spring*, as one of those three or four artistic experiences against which I would judge all others in the coming years."[26]

Virgil was charmed by his handsome copyist and young charge. "Ned doesn't have to work," Virgil one time piped at Maurice, who at a Thanksgiving dinner had shouted at Ned, reclining on the sofa, to make himself useful. "Ned doesn't have to work; Ned's a beauty." Although Virgil gossiped and even flirted with Ned, only once did he make a pass at him.

> One winter afternoon, when I had to stay late to make corrections in something I'd botched, Virgil said:
>
> "I'm going to take a nap. Will you wake me at exactly four fifteen."
>
> At four fifteen I opened the door into his darkened room.
>
> "It's four fifteen."
>
> "That's no way to wake Papa. Come over and wake Papa with a kiss."
>
> Am I supposed to say no? So I leaned down, as upon a great lady—a great, *doughy* lady like, say, Nero—and kissed him on the lips.
>
> "That's how to wake Papa," he said, quickly realizing he'd maybe done the wrong thing. I still hear the wistful voice now as he turned toward the south window through which the light was fading fast over our grimy city.
>
> "It looks like Barcelona out."[27]

If Virgil feared he had "done the wrong thing," it was because he felt responsible for Ned, having tempted him to give up a Curtis scholarship and his parents' approval. It would take some cooling-off time, some diligent familial negotiations, and a meeting with Virgil, but eventually Mr. Rorem accepted Ned's career choices. By the summertime, Ned wrote to Virgil with news of the arrangement he and his father had struck.

> Father was in town last night and I had another long and slightly harrowing talk with him, the final result being: that I can study here (with individual private teachers as you and I had planned) with the provision that I continue working four hours a day for you (which would give me the $20 a week which I told him was the amount necessary for my education), and he will give me $20

a week to live on. . . . If I manage to get lessons for less, I can keep the difference.[28]

Mr. Rorem was impressed with Virgil when they met in New York. Ned's parents had admired the Chicago production of *Four Saints in Three Acts,* and Mr. Rorem, wanting to learn more of his son's employer, had read *The State of Music.* This sense of obligation to Mr. Rorem was perhaps what motivated Virgil to give Ned lessons in orchestration for free. Virgil's pragmatic know-how made the lessons invaluable. "[D]uring the eighteen months I worked with Virgil," his pupil later wrote, "I was to learn more than during the long years, before and after, spent in the world's major conservatories. . . . I can recall today as on a disc each word he spoke during our lessons fifty years ago."[29]

Virgil sat Ned down and in clipped instructions that allowed no argument explained the mechanics of orchestration: the flute can do this, but not this; it does this in the high register, this in the low; three flutes together can hold their own against a trumpet *mezzo forte* but not a trumpet *forte.* And so on. For six months he had Ned orchestrate anything except his own music: Schumann piano works for just brass; Beethoven piano sonatas for just strings; later Debussy piano preludes for combinations of his choosing. The purview of the lessons eventually included critiques of Ned's compositions—pragmatic feedback, not instruction. Thomson never claimed to have been anyone's composition teacher.

Rorem has written that from the beginning he was perplexed by much of the music he was copying ("Virgil's sappy stuff . . . Virgil's dumb solo flute sonata"). But a fan letter from 1946 suggests that he was genuinely affected by certain Thomson works.

> Meant to tell you in my other letter that I recently bought a copy of your Stabat Mater which I had never heard (or even seen) before and while playing it through on the piano I found it so natural and perfect in prosody, so beautifully simple, and so unornately religious, that when I reached the last page where the strings have their two little finishing measures, I was moved to the point of weeping.[30]

Eventually, pressure from his father to acquire certifiable credentials (namely, a degree), pressure spiced with financial inducements (an offer to pay tuition, rent, and allowance), proved too great for Ned to resist. In 1946 he enrolled in the Juilliard School. His association with Virgil as employee and student ended. So did his domestic association with Morris. One night, when Morris was away, Ned brought home a sailor and made love while the phonograph (playing his beloved Billie Holiday) blasted into the courtyard. Morris was "kind but firm." He wanted Ned out. Immediately. Ned resettled into a tiny flat on Twelfth Street. He juggled friends (including Morris, with whom he remained close), course work, piano practice, and composition. He continued to cultivate his relationship with Virgil. The Ned Rorem file in the Virgil Thomson Collection at the Yale School of Music Library is filled with greetings, congratulatory notes, and frequent requests for letters of recommendation.

One of the first works Rorem copied for Thomson—full score and orchestra parts—was the *Symphony on a Hymn Tune,* completed in 1928 and as yet unperformed. His inability to arrange for its performance had been Thomson's biggest career disappointment to date. Finally, an offer came from, of all quarters, the New York Philharmonic-Symphony, still under the management of Arthur Judson, Thomson's announced enemy. The concert on February 22, 1945, presented the Polish-born keyboard artist Wanda Landowska playing a Mozart concerto on piano and a Haydn concerto on harpsichord, and short works by Rossini and Ibert, conducted by Arthur Rodzinski. Thomson took the podium to lead the premiere of his own symphony.

Olin Downes, his tact tested from over four years of competition with Thomson, dismissed the piece as "too trivial and inconsequential, too unoriginal in its material and flimsy in its structure to merit discussion."[31] Oscar Thompson in the *Sun,* seemingly perplexed, called the symphony "capricious," wanly described some of its events, then concluded that it "lacks continuity."[32] On duty that night from the *Herald Tribune* was Paul Bowles. It's hard to imagine that the musical community considered Bowles's review to be impartial; but it's equally hard to imagine a more insightful description.

> The piece is as American and ungainly as the woodstove and pump in the kitchen on the farm; it eschews the slick and insists on the homely. There is none of the streamlined mindlessness and spurious culture of present-day urban life. Its sounds are dry, with no suggestion of the lush or exotic. Sometimes one is reminded of the fact that the composer has written extensively for percussion; the music becomes wholehearted noise-making. The hymn tune passages suggest the untrained voices of the backwoods.

Often there is very little for the orchestra to do, but always there is something unexpected happening somewhere among the instruments. It is music which is awkward, droll and rough, but it is not static.[33]

If the reviews of his symphony were by and large poor, the reviews of his first collection of *Herald Tribune* articles, *The Musical Scene,* published in March by Alfred A. Knopf, were raves: "astonishing range of interests and vision . . . exceptionally well-organized mind . . . epigrammatic quality of his style . . . musicianly and unhackneyed analyses . . . uncompromising exposition of all the ills that harass our musical life . . ."

In addition, that April saw the release, at long last, of Thomson's first recording: a suite of his musical portraits orchestrated and conducted by the composer. Eugene Ormandy, alert as ever to cultivating his ties with Thomson, had spearheaded the project, putting his own Philadelphia Orchestra at Thomson's disposal.

Also that spring, on April 12, President Roosevelt died just eleven weeks into his fourth term. But the war in Europe, it was now clear, would soon end. On August 6 President Truman introduced the world to atomic warfare at Hiroshima, giving horrific reality to the prophetic question Gertrude Stein had posed in *Four Saints in Three Acts:* "If it were possible to kill five thousand Chinamen by pressing a button would it be done. St. Teresa not interested."

With the end of the war, Thomson managed to return to Paris, though this was not easy. It took the intercession of the French consulate, which offered Thomson a "mission," an arrangement whereby foreigners who could provide some service to France were granted visas and free transportation. Since Thomson had been virtually an emissary for French music and aesthetics, the mission was approved. He agreed to send back weekly Sunday articles on the state of French culture and music, anything except war and politics. His editors thought that *Tribune* readers would find such articles refreshing.

In mid-August, Thomson wrote to Grosser from Paris with impressions of battered but victorious London, and of his beloved but humbled Paris. Oddly absent from the letter is any mention of the bombed-out blocks of London or the humiliation of Paris, now liberated from Nazi occupation.

Left New York last Sunday. Got to London on Monday. Stayed till Friday with two days in the country chez Beecham. Flew to Paris in Army plane. London rich still act & think rich, though their food is bad and their shirts are darned. I think all classes are a little tired.

Tribune is lending me a car & chauffeur. . . . Getting around is not too hard, because Metro works, though nothing else does. Life is difficult but not impossible, prices astronomic, people full of muscular energy, walking all the time, limited food admirably cooked, the city incredibly beautiful all dirty white stone in clean white light. Weather perfect, tempers very sweet. I am moving to the Ritz, I believe, in a few days. I like the neighborhood better than the Champs-Elysées. There are only a few hotels where transient Americans can go. Gov't keeps this reserved for missions and business—visiting civilians. Everything else full permanently.[34]

Thomson would remain in Paris through November, staying at hotels while he waited for his own flat, which had been sublet to tenants after the landlord died in 1943, to be made available again. This was a long time to be away from his job. But the state of arts in France was "better than one had any right to expect," and his articles were lively.

In the meantime, there was business to talk over with Gertrude, always a dicey proposition. Virgil had been offered a production of a new opera. And he had an idea he was sure she would jump at.

21 WHAT IS THE QUESTION?

Columbia University's Brander Matthews Theater, on the main campus just east of Broadway at 117th Street, was an efficient facility of 280 seats, although the orchestra pit's placement under the proscenium brought the conductor uncomfortably close to the front rim of the stage. It was run with unchallenged authority by Milton Smith, who prided himself more on his working theater experience than on his doctorate in theater history. Smith turned Brander Matthews into a training school for drama and musical theater, rather like a provincial German repertory opera house. Sitting at his rolltop desk cluttered with scripts, clippings, props, and cigarette butts, the crusty Dr. Smith directed a program that taught all the essentials: acting, directing, building scenery, costume making, stage design, even how to paint posters, run a box office, and tend to publicity.

He battled constantly to protect the program from Columbia academics with pretensions to the theater. But in the music department there was one person he could talk shop with, Douglas Moore, the chairman since 1940, an urbane theater professional whose American folk opera, *The Devil and Daniel Webster,* had been produced successfully in 1938. Smith pretended to find musicians nothing but trouble, what with their half-baked notions of musical theater and their noisy instruments that drowned out the actors. Actually, he collaborated effectively with the music department, helping to run an opera workshop program and putting on full productions of lesser-known, small-scale operas.

The year Moore became chairman, Alice M. Ditson, the widow of the prominent music publisher Oliver Ditson, left a gift to the music department. The bequest stipulated, rather vaguely, that the money be used "for the encouragement and aid of musicians." Naturally, Professor Paul Henry Lang, who was trying to build the department into a musicology empire, wanted to underwrite additional scholarships and faculty posts. Moore wanted to support composers, both younger Americans and older composers who had been overlooked or were in need, and his view prevailed. In its first year the Ditson Fund provided a sinecure at Columbia for Béla Bartók. The next year, 1941, it funded the premiere production of a new opera, *Paul Bunyan,* with a text by the poet W. H. Auden and music by an emerging English composer, Benjamin Britten. Dr. Smith, who had been skeptical of the whole idea, was wildly enthusiastic about the Britten opera. Critics were not. In his *Herald Tribune* review Virgil Thomson described the libretto as "flaccid and spineless" and the music "sort of witty" but mostly "undistinguished." Britten withdrew the work, his first opera. His second, *Peter Grimes,* which opened in London in 1945, would bring him international renown.

Given the critical reaction, Smith and Moore were surprisingly upbeat about their opera project. When in 1944 the composer Otto Luening joined the faculty of Barnard College, Columbia's sister school, he also became music director of the Brander Matthews Theater. And for the next fourteen years the Ditson Fund was used to commission yearly a new opera to be produced in the spring semester. Given the dimensions of the auditorium, the opera had to be modestly conceived. Professional singers would be recruited for major roles. But Columbia and Barnard students, as much as possible, would be used in supporting roles; the student orchestra would be supplemented with first-chair players from conservatories.

This venture contrasted mightily with the American opera companies' abandonment of American opera. Commissions and productions of new works had become largely token gestures to sustain a veneer of intellectual prestige for the opera house as museum. If new works were going to be developed, they would have to come from alternative venues: smaller companies and, in particular, universities.

Among the first composers commissioned under this arrangement was the Italian-born Gian Carlo Menotti, an innate opera composer (he had already written two operas before he entered the Milan Conservatory at thirteen) who was demoralized by the situation in the major opera companies. Menotti had been acclaimed in Philadelphia for his comic opera *Amelia Goes to the Ball*. But he was so disturbed by the wrongheaded way the Metropolitan Opera had produced his tragic opera *The Island God* in 1942 that he would accept the Ditson Fund commission only if he could direct the work himself. In this case Dr. Smith, who usually claimed directing rights, was willing to defer. He didn't have much faith in the piece, a melodrama called *The Medium,* about a spiritualistic phony who one night is made to think that her fraudulent seances might be real. It called for only five singers, a dance mime, and a chamber orchestra of fourteen players. Otto Luening, who conducted, thought the opera was theatrically superb. The premiere on May 8, 1946, was triumphant. Thomson called it "the most gripping operatic narrative this reviewer has witnessed in many a year."

Even while *The Medium* was in the planning stages, Professor Moore, Dr. Smith, Otto Luening, and his new assistant, Jack Beeson, a young composer from Muncie, Indiana, sat down to select the next Ditson Fund opera composer. The committee wanted Copland. But, busy with other projects and unsure of his footing on the opera stage, Copland turned them down. Luening suggested that Virgil Thomson and Gertrude Stein be commissioned. Douglas Moore, who had loved *Four Saints* on Broadway in 1934, leapt at the idea. That Luening was the one to suggest it is curious.

Born in Milwaukee of German parents in 1900, Luening moved to Munich at twelve and enrolled at fifteen in the city's music academy. Luening was German trained, but not doctrinaire about it. Moreover, he was a skillful theater man who had spent the war years in Zurich working as an actor and stage manager with the James Joyce English Players. Upon returning to the States, he joined the American Grand Opera Company in Chicago, conducting operas in English translation, a sensible practice that he defended against attacks from purist critics. Luening had composed music for silent films, arranged gospel for export to Japan, and directed musical comedy productions in New York.

However, he had never heard *Four Saints*. Yet from his experience with Thomson's songs, some of which he had performed with his wife, Ethel, a soprano, he knew that Thomson was a master of prosody. And earning the gratitude of the powerful *Herald Tribune* critic, already well disposed to the Columbia opera program, seemed a fine idea. So the commission was offered, $1,500 ($1,000 for Thomson, $500 for Stein), which would have been a substantial sum had it come from a professional company, let alone a university. Knowing that Stein was anxious to do another opera, Thomson accepted.

In 1938 Gertrude and Alice had been forced to leave 27 rue de Fleurus so that the landlord could make their pavilion into an apartment for his newly married son. They moved to a handsome flat with elegant wainscoting in a seventeenth-century building at 5 rue Christine, a short, narrow, dull street in a low, damp district near the Seine. Picasso owned a seventeenth-century house nearby. Along with their other belongings, Gertrude and Alice had brought 131 paintings, including five Picasso canvases that had not yet been put onto stretchers. The walls provided space for 91 paintings; the rest were stored in a closet.

During the summer of 1945 Gertrude was enthralled with American GIs. Every day when she walked Basket in the park, she picked up soldiers, sometimes by the dozen, brought them home to Alice's cake and homemade chocolate ice cream, and closely observed their slangy, plainspoken talk, which delighted her. In August she incorporated the rhythms and sounds of their speech into a wistful book, *Brewsie and Willie.* The GIs were facing a world without answers, Gertrude felt. Soon they would go home, take off their uniforms, and never be so happy again, because at least they had been "carefree among other men" and because "men loved fighting."[1] The soldiers had a quality, like the nuns and saints who fascinated her, of just being, of "standing and doing nothing standing for a long time not even talking but just standing and being watched by the whole French population."

One of her favorites, Captain Joseph Barry, born in Scranton, Pennsylvania, had studied journalism at the University of Michigan and done graduate work at the Sorbonne. Well-spoken and gregarious, he became virtually Gertrude and Alice's "adopted nephew." After the war, when Katherine Anne Porter suggested in *Harper's Magazine* that Gertrude Stein had been surly and condescending toward her American GIs, Barry wrote an indignant letter to the editor.

In the four years of my army life, I have never seen anyone—officer, enlisted man, or civilian—listen so attentively, so patiently, to the American soldier. Far from "smacking down" any GI who appeared "to be thinking in her presence," Miss Stein encouraged it constantly.[2]

The GIs reciprocated by taking Gertrude and Alice on adventures, as Gertrude recounted in a letter to Carl Van Vechten.

We just had a most xciting time with the Glenn Miller Band, they took us over to hear it with the troops, then I talked to the band afterwards, gave them a little address and they were delighted and then they came over one afternoon ten of them with their instruments including drum and bass viol and played for us in the house here, it was fine and Alice made them chocolate ice-cream supplied by the American army in the shape of chocolate and tinned milk, it was lovely.[3]

The next day, Gertrude added, the GI friends were going to "an evening of jitter bugs given for the army and they are taking us, so we will know."

To Gertrude Stein, World War II signified the true end of the nineteenth century with its social protocols, lofty language, and civilized wars. It was partly nostalgia for this past era and sadness over her departing GIs that attracted Gertrude to Virgil's idea for an opera "about nineteenth-century America, with perhaps the language of the senatorial orators quoted." At first, Gertrude suggested George Washington. But Virgil vetoed the entire eighteenth century. ("Everybody dresses alike; you can't tell one from another.") Virgil wanted the nineteenth century, preferably something set between the Missouri Compromise and the impeachment of Andrew Johnson. And, he told Gertrude, "let's not have any foolishness about putting Abraham Lincoln onstage. That can't be done."[4]

Virgil and Gertrude were enamored of nineteenth-century American political rhetoric. During this era the lifeblood of the nation was captured in grandiloquent political orations, stem-winders rich with metaphor, classical allusions, and quotations from Shakespeare. This was a time when citizens routinely traveled long distances to town squares and fairgrounds to hear politicians and statesmen debate for hours, proclaim policy, memorialize the dead, or inaugurate a new building, a new administration, a new era.

Thomson later wrote that when he proposed his idea as a subject for the opera, Gertrude "hardly thought at all, just started writing."[5] In fact, she thought, read, and researched quite extensively and took several weeks to settle on a protagonist. At first she studied the accounts of President Andrew Johnson's impeachment in 1868, thinking that she might view the event through the perspective of the Frenchman Georges Clemenceau, a young journalist at the time of the impeachment who would become the French premier during World War I. Gertrude emptied the Paris libraries of books in English on nineteenth-century America. "I have achieved quantities of literature about the period," she wrote to Virgil, who was staying temporarily at the Ritz in Paris, "and am now reading Clemenceau about the impeachment, he might be the hero, you know he was there, might make a nice hero."[6] Two weeks later, Gertrude was still accumulating books requested from abroad: "[T]hey seem to be sending me from the New York Public Library all the literature of the period, if it comes off it will be a most erudite opera."[7]

By October she had definitely settled on her subject: Susan B. Anthony, like Saint Teresa and Stein herself, a pioneering woman misunderstood in her own time. Born in 1820 in the small Berkshire town of Adams, Massachusetts, to a principled Quaker father and a devoted but withdrawn mother, Susan B. Anthony was raised to be a homemaker. She rebelled against this life, becoming a schoolteacher, then a tenacious leader of women's causes. She founded the first women's temperance association, and helped to secure the first laws in New York guaranteeing women's rights over their children and property. From 1892 until 1900 she was the president of the Woman Suffrage Association. For years she was the most reviled woman in America. In 1871, during a speaking engagement in San Francisco, Anthony was shouted down at the podium and condemned in the regional press for daring to say that a young prostitute convicted of murdering a local official had acted in self-defense. Anthony maintained a nearly fifty-year loving relationship with her co-suffragette Elizabeth Cady Stanton, who was married but devoted to Anthony, a relationship that brought scorn and whispered scandal to both women. Anthony had an ardent following; but for the most part her work was contentious, even among the majority of women.

Anthony died in 1906, fourteen years before her dream of suffrage for women became a constitutional reality. Her life and struggle resonated deeply within Stein. In choosing her subject, Stein was reaching not to the dim past but to someone of her grandmother's generation. Perhaps she anticipated that Anthony would increasingly be viewed as a hero by later generations of strong women. Susan B. Anthony truly was "the mother of us all," as Stein would title her libretto. In any event, the opera has remained topical.

Gertrude was so enraptured by her work on the opera in the fall of 1945 that her notes to Virgil, still in Paris, are uncommonly affectionate. "I made out a list of the characters for the Mother of us all, they came out kind of funny and there is a kind of prelude, well one meeting more Virgil is almost necessary, bless us all, Always Gertrude and again so many thanks."[8] In December, after Virgil had returned to New York, Gertrude was immersed in the project: "[N]ow I will quiet down and think about the opera," she wrote to him; "I know a lot now about Susan B. and I am beginning to Webster, lots of love Always Gtrde."

Gertrude was keenly interested in Anthony's dilemma over the rights of Negroes. Anthony was an ardent Abolitionist; but after the Civil War, as a tactic in the struggle, she opposed granting suffrage to freedmen unless it was granted to women as well. When former male slaves won the vote but women were still denied, the irony embittered her.

The opera was certainly turning out "kind of funny," as Gertrude remarked. She peopled her text with a menagerie of characters. Some were historical figures, a few of whom had associated with each other in life, but most of whom came from completely different periods. The text borrowed lines (taken out of context and modified) from speeches of the period, including Anthony's. Susan B., as she is called, is presented in a domestic relationship with a devoted woman called Anne, probably meant to be Anna Howard Shaw, the younger suffrage leader who lived with Susan B. Anthony toward the end of her life. Just as in *Four Saints,* where Gertrude's strong female protagonist, Saint Teresa, has a sometimes contentious relationship with her male counterpart, Saint Ignatius, in this opera Susan B. battles with Daniel Webster, senator from Massachusetts, loquacious orator, defender of the Union, and a politician whose ideology shifted with the changing times. Gertrude begins the opera with a political rally at which Webster (who died when Anthony was thirty-one) and Anthony debate the issue of women's suffrage. However, their rhetoric, though grand, is nonsensical. "Youth is young, I am not old," Susan B. begins. To which Daniel Webster replies, "When the mariner has been tossed for many days in thick weather, and on an unknown sea, he naturally avails himself of the first pause in the storm."

The politicking is spiked by the appearances of other statesmen and activists: President Andrew Johnson and Thaddeus Stevens, an Abolitionist active in Johnson's impeachment; Anthony Comstock, born in 1844, a self-righteous crusader for Christian morals who was responsible for the destruction of 160 tons of "indecent" literature and pictures. A gruff, intolerant General Ulysses S. Grant shows up, who proclaims, "He knew that his name was not Eisenhower," and demands that "everything and every body be quiet" when the general colloquy gets out of hand. The actress Lillian Russell interrupts the action from time to time to waltz about the stage accepting compliments for her beauty. And Gertrude presents John Adams (John Quincy Adams, most likely) as a romantic gentleman whose courtship of the gracious Constance Fletcher is constrained by his high station.

Adams's operatic love interest was a real-life acquaintance of Gertrude and Alice's. A writer of novels and an intimate of Oscar Wilde's, Fletcher met them only one time, in 1911. Once a beautiful woman with golden curls, she was by then massively overweight and terribly nearsighted. But she made a lasting impression on Gertrude, who found her forceful and intelligent. In the opera Constance is, as John Adams bluntly says, "blind as a bat and beautiful as a bird."

In October, Gertrude and Alice discussed the progress of the opera with Virgil, the GI Joseph Barry and Donald Gallup, then thirty-two and also an officer in the American army who was planning, if all went well, to resume his position as a librarian and professor at Yale. All three of Gertrude's male friends—Barry, Gallup, and Virgil—wound up in the opera.

Joseph Barry appears as a rootless, good-hearted character named Jo the Loiterer, referring to an incident from Barry's student days in Michigan when he was charged by the police with loitering. Jo the Loiterer is paired in the opera with a fictional character, Indiana Elliot, and much banter is devoted to the issue of whether Indiana Elliot will take Jo's last name when they marry, something she is loath to do. Jo's sidekick, also fictional, is Chris the Citizen.

Gertrude was fond of Donald Gallup, who admired her work and came to visit almost every Thursday evening. When he returned to America after the war, she inscribed a book to him, "in memory of such pleasant Thursdays, there was Donald all through that cold winter after the liberation here was Donald himself and packages, full of comfort and packages, Dear Donald, he was a Thursday child, and we were the happier welcomers of the Thursday days. . . ."⁹ Gallup's role in the opera is tiny, but he has one classic Steinian line: "Last but not least, first and not best, I am tall as a man, I am firm as a clam, and I never change, from day to day."

Acting as a kind of host and commentator, much as the Compère did in *Four Saints,* is a character called Virgil T. The cast is a dotty and charming bunch. Yet despite the whimsy, we see Susan B. in action: crusading for women's rights, debating patronizing statesmen, leading meetings, and officiating at marriages. In a touching epilogue at a ceremony to unveil a statue of Anthony next to those of other leaders in the women's suffrage movement, our heroine speaks from the grave in words that could be Gertrude's eulogy to herself: "In my long life of effort and strife. . . . Life is strife, I was a martyr all my life not to what I won but to what was done. Do you know because I tell you so, or do you know, do you know. My long life, my long life."

Gertrude worked on the opera text through the winter and spring of 1946. By March she was finished. Virgil had already written of his intention to return to Paris in the summer, and had promised to bring Alice a much wanted kitchen gadget. Gertrude had entrusted the contract negotiations to the wife and partner of her former agent William Bradley, the man she had so alienated that he resigned after the production of *Four Saints.* Bradley had died in 1939. Over time Gertrude reconciled with his pleasant French widow, Jennie. This time Gertrude was in no mood to be obstructionist. A letter to Virgil, dated March 20, 1946, spills over with enthusiasm.

> It will be nice seeing you again, the opera finished, registered, is on the way to Carl, put at the post four days ago, I hope it gets there before you leave, I think I did make her quite magnificent, well we'll see, and when you get here I have a very good agent, Mrs. Bradley is doing all my theatricals in American, Alice is most xcitedly looking forward to her can opener, pleasant days Always Gtrde.¹⁰

On April 15 Virgil wrote back,

> The opera is sensationally handsome and Susan B. is a fine role. . . . She is practically Saint Paul when she says "let them marry." And the whole thing will be easier to dramatize than *4 Saints* was,

much easier, though the number of characters who talk to the audience about themselves, instead of addressing the other characters, is a little terrifying. Mostly it is very dramatic and very beautiful and very clear and constantly quotable and I think we shall have very little scenery but very fine clothes and they do all the time strike 19th century attitudes.[11]

Two days after receiving Virgil's letter, Gertrude heard from Carl Van Vechten, who vouched for Virgil's enthusiasm.

> . . . I talked with Virgil AT LENGTH about The Mother of Us All, over the telephone, and "sensational" was the word he used. . . . He is enchanted with it and I've no doubt it will inspire him to terrific efforts of creation. . . . Virgil thinks Mary [Garden] hasn't voice enough any more for this and at the same time he finds her too sexy. But he'll dig up something tremendous, I predict. This all adds up to a newer and BETTER Four Saints.[12]

Virgil arrived at the Paris railway station on May 10. By chance, Gertrude was there, waiting to greet the young black author Richard Wright, whose writing she admired. Gertrude seemed out of sorts. Virgil noticed her weight loss, but was not particularly alarmed. He promised to be in touch as soon as he settled into his flat.

But just a few weeks later Gertrude wrote to Van Vechten, "Virgil as yet answers nothing new about the opera, we have cut him out as a character and I think that is right."[13] Carl wrote back that he was sorry to see Virgil gone from the opera. Eventually Stein agreed. For in the version she authorized for publication, Virgil T. is restored. Perhaps talking contract details with him upset her. And she had yet to hear a note of music. Still, Gertrude's irritability was due, no doubt, to the increasing fragility of her health.

In November 1934, when Gertrude and Alice attended the Chicago production of *Four Saints,* John Houseman was seated next to them at a postperformance supper. He was troubled by dark spots on Gertrude's lips much like those that his father had when ill with Addison's disease. Perhaps, Virgil later speculated, "Gertrude was cancerous already."

However, in the fall of 1945 Gertrude "was happy with her GIs and her opera subject," Virgil recalled. She had agreed to entrust her papers to the Yale University library, Donald Gallup having won her confidence. "No thought of death was with her, I am sure," Virgil later wrote, "for she planned, come spring, to buy a car again."[14] Come spring, she did just that—a second-hand Simca.

But during that fall constant visits with her GIs, including an arduous trip to Brussels, had tired her. She complained of intestinal troubles and abdominal pain. A doctor told her to adjust her girdle, which seemed to help. Advised to see a specialist, she refused. On February 3, 1946, she turned seventy-two. Her appetite was chronically poor. To Alice she seemed terribly thin.

Some two weeks after their chance meeting at the railway station, Gertrude and Virgil saw each other again. Virgil hosted a dinner party at his flat. Besides Gertrude and Alice, the guests included a Russian-born man whom Virgil always referred to as "my French gangster friend," who sold armaments and traded currency on the black market, but comported himself with impeccable breeding. The gangster courted Virgil's friendship because his wife was a singer with career ambitions. His brother, who ran one of Paris's fanciest restaurants, had sent over a heavy game dish for Virgil's dinner party—jugged hare, or rabbit cooked in its own blood, a delicacy Alice adored. Gertrude was quite taken with the French wife, whom she invited to the house to view the paintings. With everybody in high spirits, Virgil got into a teasing mood. But when he joked with Gertrude, Alice leapt to her protection: "Don't scold her. She may cry."

Virgil then became busy with professional "dates." He conducted a concert of his music at a radio station in Luxembourg, where he encountered, for the first time, a magnetic tape recorder; he rehearsed a program of his chamber works for broadcast in Brussels; he heard Flemish opera in bombed-out Antwerp, visited musician friends in Milan and Venice, and consulted with the director of an opera company in the troop-filled seaport of Trieste. It was on July 28 in the Trieste railway station, while awaiting a train to Paris, that he picked up a Paris edition of the *Herald Tribune* and read about Gertrude.

To build herself up that summer, Gertrude had accepted the long-standing offer of Bernard Faÿ to use his country house, a priory at St. Martin in the Sarthe, 125 miles southwest of Paris. Bernard, of the pedigreed Faÿ family that had befriended Virgil during the 1920s, was one of Gertrude's three or four closest friends. He had been decorated for valor at Verdun in World War I, studied at the Sorbonne, and become a professor of history. During the occupation he served as an adviser to Marshal Pétain. When the Germans were routed in

1944, Bernard was arrested, charged with collaboration, and sentenced to life imprisonment. Throughout his ordeal, Gertrude's constancy never faltered.

So she went to his country house, promising to walk in the hills and recoup her strength. Joseph Barry drove Gertrude and Alice there in the new car. After settling in St. Martin, they took an excursion to Azay-le-Rideau, a lovely town where the women had once considered buying a house. There Gertrude became seriously ill. Rather than return to St. Martin, they took a room at the town hotel. A local doctor ordered her to see a specialist immediately. Alice called Gertrude's nephew Allan Stein, the only child of Gertrude's brother Michael, and asked him to meet them at the Paris railway station. The next day they boarded an early-morning Paris-bound train. Gertrude paced the aisles and stared through the windows at the passing countryside. In Paris, Gertrude was taken to the American hospital at Neuilly, "both of us full of hope, planning to return to the Sarthe in September," Alice later wrote to Carl Van Vechten. The doctors recommended surgery for what, by now, they surely suspected was uterine cancer. But when told she would first have to build herself up, Gertrude waved the doctors away, as Alice recalled: "She was furious and frightening and impressive like she was thirty years and more ago when her work was attacked."[15] The operation was delayed for several more days. Gertrude's spirits lifted when the first two copies of *Brewsie and Willie,* just published in New York, arrived at her hospital room. The doctors pronounced the surgery too risky, given Gertrude's precarious condition. Clearly, the cancer had spread and was inoperable. Gertrude protested angrily, "I was not meant to suffer."

At Gertrude's insistence the operation was scheduled. As a precaution she made her will. Alice and Allan Stein were to be executors. She left Picasso's portrait of her to the Metropolitan Museum in New York. As arranged, she left her papers to the library at Yale, and instructed her estate to pay Carl Van Vechten whatever sums he deemed necessary to oversee the publication of her unpublished works. The remainder of her estate she left:

> to my friend Alice B. Toklas, of 5 rue Christine, Paris, to use for her life and, in so far as it may become necessary for her proper maintenance and support, I authorize my Executors to make payments to her from the principal of my Estate, and, for that purpose, to reduce to cash any paintings or other personal property belonging to my estate.[16]

The operation took place on Saturday, July 27. In her memoir Alice later recalled their last moment together.

> By this time Gertrude Stein was in a sad state of indecision and worry. I sat next to her and she said to me early in the afternoon, What is the answer? I was silent. In that case, she said, what is the question? Then the whole afternoon was troubled, confused and very uncertain, and later in the afternoon they took her away on a wheeled stretcher to the operating room and I never saw her again.[17]

At five-thirty that afternoon Gertrude slipped into a coma. At six-thirty she was pronounced dead. "And now she is in the vault of the American cathedral on the Quai d'Orsay—and I'm here alone," Alice wrote to Carl four days after Gertrude's death. "And nothing more—only what was. You will know that nothing is very clear with me—everything is empty and blurred."[18]

"Those who knew her only through the greatest of her work will never know how great she could also be in friendship," Carl wrote to Alice. From his prison cell, Bernard Faÿ, sent a loving letter: "She has been one of the few authentic experiences of my life—there are so few real human men and women—so few people really alive amongst the living ones, and so few of them are continuously alive as Gertrude was. Everything was alive in her, her soul, her mind, her heart, her senses."[19]

Upon arriving in Paris, Virgil went straight to Alice. He found her "lonely in the large high rooms, but self-contained."[20] In later life, he spoke of Gertrude's death with perceptible defensiveness, as if he should have recognized the severity of her condition and been more attentive. After their acrimonious breakup and tortured reconciliation, Virgil avoided delving into Gertrude's personal affairs, thinking it safer. But, clearly, he felt guilty for having missed the signs of her illness.

In comforting Alice, he promised to make *The Mother of Us All*, Gertrude's last completed work, an opera she would have been proud of. Twelve years earlier, when Virgil was struggling to get *Four Saints in Three Acts* produced, Gertrude had been at best unhelpful and at worst obstructive. Now Virgil would have the free hand he had wanted then. Yet he missed his grand, impossible, and unforgettable old friend.

In September, Virgil Thomson returned to New York and to work at the *Herald Tribune*. He immediately set his attorney, Arnold Weissberger, to the task of finalizing the rights to *The Mother of Us All* with the estate of Gertrude Stein. This time all the provisions that Gertrude had refused during the *Four Saints* negotiations, including the standard division of royalties (two-thirds to the composer, one-third to the author), were accepted without protest by Mrs. Bradley, who had never agreed with Gertrude's objections in the first instance, and by Alice, who was too numb to get involved.

Douglas Moore and his colleagues at Columbia were delighted with the libretto. A production for May 1947 was planned, even though, as of September 1946, Thomson had yet to compose a single note. But he had been reading the text aloud, trying out its verbal rhythms, and sifting through songbooks of nineteenth-century Americana. When he began to compose on October 10, he was confident. On November 25, 1946, the day he turned fifty, Thomson put in a full afternoon's worth of work on the opera and then went to a small dinner with Maurice Grosser and some other friends. By December 10, exactly two months after he began, he had completed the entire piano-vocal score with the exception of the epilogue in the Congressional Hall, where the statue of Susan B. reflects on her long life. Before composing that scene, he needed time with what he had written so far, to "find out how it moved and learn its ways."[21] It was completed in January. Scoring and orchestrating the work would be arduous, tedious, but straightforward.

As he had for *Four Saints,* Maurice Grosser devised a scenario for *The Mother of Us All;* in this case there was much less to do. Although many of Stein's lines were comparably hermetic, she had provided a fairly cogent narrative structure. Only two scenes needed fleshing out. Grosser made Stein's prologue and opening scene of Act 1, which seemed to present a political meeting of some sort, more explicit. Crowds gather to hear Virgil T. address them with a rabble-rousing and utterly confusing preliminary speech. ("Pity the poor persecutor.") We meet all the secondary characters. Jo the Loiterer tells Chris the Citizen about the wife he doesn't have and about their domestic spats. We meet Angel Moore, the apparition Daniel Webster loves. There is much milling about and chatter as everyone awaits the main event, a debate between Susan B. and Daniel Webster. The other scene Grosser tinkered with was the epilogue. The sculptured group of Susan B. Anthony and her allies in the fight for women's suffrage, a monument that actually exists in Washington, is simplified: we see only a statue of Susan B. Anthony.

More significant, Grosser and Thomson cut scenes from Stein's libretto, trimmed others, and reversed the order of the first two. The political-meeting scene comes second. Thomson begins the opera with an "Interlude," as Stein called it, showing Susan B. and Anne at home on a quiet evening. In Grosser's scenario Anne is knitting and Susan B. is pasting press clippings into a scrapbook. The scene as written so lovingly captured the atmosphere of Gertrude and Alice's domestic life that Thomson could not resist beginning with it. Moreover, not only is Virgil T. retained as a character; Thomson shifted some of his lines to another character of his own invention: Gertrude S. Like the Commère and the Compère in *Four Saints*, Virgil T. and Gertrude S. host, comment upon, and occasionally participate in the opera as it progresses.

Thomson's music evoked sounds familiar to all Americans in 1947: a concert band playing waltzes in the park, military marching bands on the Fourth of July, a church organ, parlor songs sung around the piano, schoolyard ditties, gospel choirs sounding forth from Negro churches. Yet, with the exception of one quotation ("London Bridge Is Falling Down"), all the tunes are original. Bugle calls and foursquare fanfares are built into the contours of the vocal lines. Yet there is a continuous and supple lyrical thread that runs through and holds together this entire score. Susan B. sings ruminative melodies as she ponders her life and work. Pungent passages of bitonality depict moments of tension both comic and somber: cold weather, premonitions of defeat for the cause, Ulysses S. Grant's bluster.

In setting the text to music, Thomson took the musings and prattles of the characters seriously. Moment after whimsical moment turns tender, taking listeners by surprise. When Susan B. complains, "Men are so conservative, so selfish, so boresome, and they are so ugly, and they are so gullible, anybody can convince them," she does this to pointed music in a minor mode. Suddenly, her outburst seems all too justified and terribly sad. After Jo the Loiterer explains to Chris the Citizen, in music that suggests a bumptious bugle call, just what it means to be funny—"To be funny you have to take everything in the kitchen and put it on the floor, you have to take all your money and all your jewels and put them near the door. You have to go to bed then, and leave the door open"—Chris asks, "Was she funny?" referring to Jo's wife, a wife he does not have. "Yes, she was funny," sings Jo, in sighing music that turns mournful in the space of one measure, making him seem lovable and pitiable, and setting up effectively the introduction with strummed harp and strings of the angelic Angel Moore.

In the romantic scenes for John Adams and Constance Fletcher, Thomson reclaims the dated genre of the love duet for high lyric tenor and ingenue soprano. Adams switches nervously from outpourings of lyrical bliss ("Dear Miss Constance Fletcher, it is a great pleasure that I kneel at your feet") to peppery protestations of his inability to do so ("But I am an Adams, I kneel at the feet of none, not any one"). The chorus, observing the courtship, is distressed. In an utterly serious, block chordal proclamation, they sing, "If he had not been an Adams, he would have kneeled at her feet, and he would have kissed one of her hands and then still kneeling, he would have kissed both of her hands still kneeling if he had not been an Adams." It's a disarming moment, one of many in the score.

In late January, Thomson went uptown to the Riverside Drive apartment of Douglas Moore to show the completed opera to the Brander Matthews Theater production team: Moore, Milton Smith, Otto Luening, who was slated to conduct, and Willard Rhodes, the director of Columbia's opera workshop, who was hoping to cast some of his student singers in minor roles. Thomson played through the entire score with clumsy "composer's pianism," as Luening called it, singing all the parts with his impeccable diction and makeshift voice. Luening and Moore were charmed and excited. Brandy was brought out, toasts were made, and planning sessions scheduled. But when Thomson left, Smith, who had been rather silent, spoke up. The opera made no sense; he had no idea what to do with it as a director; he didn't want to oppose it; he just wanted out of the venture. When informed, Thomson was not displeased. This allowed him to pick his own director. With Luening's help he found someone ideal, John Taras, a choreographer who had worked under Lincoln Kirstein. As in *Four Saints,* his singers would be moved and placed, not directed, which was Thomson's preference.

Auditions were held at Thomson's apartment. He, Luening, and Taras heard close to two hundred singers. Even though this was a workshop production and nobody involved was being paid, every singer in town, it seemed, wanted a part in the new opera by the powerful music critic of the *Herald Tribune*. Thomson wouldn't listen to anything not sung in English. He asked for airs from Handel's English oratorios, and he got them. Jack Beeson, who was Luening's assistant and rehearsal pianist, sat at Virgil's piano sight-reading Handel for days.

Some of the singers who were chosen for this nonpaying production had considerable professional experience. William Horne, a dashing, diminutive leading tenor with the City Center Opera Company, who had sung the title role in Britten's *Peter Grimes* the previous summer at the Berkshire Festival, in Massachusetts, won the role of Jo the Loiterer. Alice Howland, a German-born, Juilliard-trained mezzo-soprano, who had just toured Canada in Gounod's *Roméo et Juliette* with Jeanette MacDonald, was cast in the soprano role of Constance Fletcher, but sang it beautifully. Daniel Webster was given to a strapping young bass from Maine, Bertram Rowe. With twenty-eight singing roles, there were opportunities for several Columbia Opera Workshop students.

In order to cast two small but significant roles, Thomson had to reactivate his Harlem connections. In one scene Susan B. muses bitterly that her work has helped bring the vote to Negro men, but still not to women. She sees a young couple, called Negro Man and Negro Woman, and asks, "Negro man, would you vote, if only you could vote and not she?" The man replies, "You bet!" Since Thomson would have to recruit black singers for these roles, he decided, partly as a homage to his wonderful *Four Saints* cast, to fill out the ensemble with a few black dancers in nonsinging roles. So he, Taras, and Maurice Grosser visited the Harlem studio of the choreographer Katherine Dunham, watched several classes, and selected four statuesque young men: Dale Burr, Vernon Van Dutton, James Hunt, and Isaiah Clarke, all war veterans, now studying dance and hoping for careers in the theater.

Miss Dunham explained to her dancers that this short, snappish composer with a cigarette holder was a powerful man and that being in his opera in any capacity could be very beneficial. They needed little convincing. Most of them knew *Four Saints* by reputation and had heard the stories of John Houseman and the glory days of the WPA Negro Theater Project. Every day after classes at Dunham's, they went down to Columbia for rehearsals. Two of the dancers, Hunt and Van Dutton, were trained singers who could participate during the choral ensembles. Burr, muscular and agile, and Clarke, who worked on the side as an artist's model, just danced, looked good, and mouthed the words. Backstage they would joke with each other about the wacky Stein text.

As in the case of *Four Saints,* by the time rehearsals for *The Mother of Us All* started, they had still not found a singer for the title role. Several possibilities were urged on Thomson by his colleagues; none satisfied him. He called people at the Metropolitan Opera for a suggestion, and they recommended someone they had just auditioned: Dorothy Dow, a twenty-six-year-old soprano from Houston, a Juilliard graduate who had recently made her operatic debut in Buffalo as Santuzza in *Cavalleria rusticana.* She had an opulent voice with a rich, distinctive color, but a tremulous quality that troubled Luening; and Taras found her somewhat stiff. But Thomson thought Dow had a dignified carriage that would be perfect for Susan B. She wasn't mannish or asexual, just solid and self-contained. Luening and Taras gave in.

Once rehearsals were under way, Thomson wrote to Alice B. Toklas with all the news.

> Dear Alice,
>
> The opera is finished and its orchestral score is finished, 500 beautiful pages. We are in rehearsal. I have wonderful singers, all of them young people around 30. . . . Even the small roles are handsomely sung. . . .
>
> Everything is under control, and I am very happy about it all. Everybody loves the work and believes in it. There will almost certainly be a downtown production next winter. I have a publisher too, for both the Mother of Us All and Four Saints. Also for Capital Capitals.
>
> . . . I do wish you were going to be here for the performance. Perhaps next year, if all goes well, you might be induced to come over. Constantly I regret that Gertrude cannot hear it. It would make her very happy.
>
> . . . I am sorry not to have written you more often in the last few months. I have worked literally day and night finishing the opera score and casting the work, all the while keeping up my regular duties; and so I have rather counted on Carl to keep you informed of my progress. . . . Do let me hear from you. I have worried about you and the Paris heating problem. . . .
>
> Love and always devotedly,
> Virgil[22]

Keeping up his "regular duties" at the *Herald Tribune* was not easy for Thomson during these months. He grew to depend on the help of Theodate Johnson, who became virtually the godmother to *The Mother of Us All*. Theodate was living at the time in her brother's two-story apartment on Forty-seventh Street and Third Avenue. Her brother, Philip, had gone back to school at Harvard to study architecture. Since returning from Europe and her refugee work, Theodate had grown to accept that her ambitions for a singing career were impossible. She was still searching for a fulfilling career path and living off her modest family income. Helping Virgil get through this bruising spring schedule was something she could do. Theodate recruited sponsors to underwrite the cost of publishing the score. Virtually every day she came to the afternoon rehearsals, then left early for home, prepared supper, fed Virgil when he arrived, and more often than not returned with him to the theater in the evening. At rehearsals she was good at keeping Virgil calm, which became increasingly urgent.

Jack Beeson and Otto Luening had kept Thomson from the cast until they knew their parts perfectly. Once there, he was an unrelenting taskmaster on the matter of textual clarity. "Diction! Diction!" he would shout from the back of the hall. Once, when Dorothy Dow muffled the words of a tender, pianissimo phrase, Thomson screamed the words at her: " 'Hush, I hush, you hush, they hush, we hush. Hush!' Let me hear those hushes!" Finally, after one outburst, Bertram Rowe, the towering young baritone singing Daniel Webster, could take no more: "Mr. Thomson, if you keep carrying on like this we won't be able to sing at all." Luening took Thomson out into the corridor and sternly but calmly told him to knock it off: the singers were young and were doing their best. Chastened, Thomson spoke to the cast. "Have I been naughty? I'm sorry. I'll behave myself."[23]

The orchestra of sixteen players comprised mostly Columbia students with three principal players from Juilliard. Overall, they were not a strong group, and rehearsals went badly. Luening was confident that he could get them to play the score properly, but Thomson was being a nuisance. So as not to cover the singers, Luening had had the stage crew mount a piece of canvas curtain in front of the pit. During one choral scene Thomson came running down the aisle shouting, "Louder, Louder!" Grabbing the canvas with both hands, he ripped it right off. The orchestra players sat motionless with fright. Luening told his players to calm down, then whispered, "Play everything *fortissimo*." "Virgil came back to the podium again," Luening recalled, "and said to me through the din of the orchestra, 'I think it's a bit too heavy, Puss.' From then on everything went beautifully."[24]

The week of the opening, Luening had to deal with one last crisis. His lead, Dorothy Dow, was a chronic complainer. Before every run-through she told Luening that she might not be able to get through the last act. Luening decided to call her bluff. Dow's understudy was Teresa Stich, a lovely, nineteen-year-old soprano from Connecticut with a clear-toned voice, good diction, and stage charm. Being only a student in the workshop, she had a tiny part, Henrietta M., whose only solo line was one of the opera's most peculiar: "Daniel Webster needs an artichoke." But Luening had coached Stich in the role of Susan B., and she knew the part cold.

There were to be four run-throughs of the opera for invited audiences and five performances from Wednesday through Saturday nights, May 7 through 10, including a Saturday matinee. When Dow announced that she could not sing both performances on Saturday, Luening said, "Fine. I've got a very good girl all ready to go." Later, Dow announced that her voice was better and that she would, after all, sing twice on Saturday. Luening refused to let her, until she returned with a letter from a doctor attesting to her good health.

On opening night the small Brander Matthews Theater was thick with critics and musicians. Edward Johnson, the managing director of the Metropolitan Opera, was there; so were seven of the most important conductors working in America: Dimitri Mitropoulos, Eugene Ormandy, Sir Eugene Goossens, Alfred Wallenstein, Serge Koussevitzky, Alexander Smallens, and Leon Barzin.

The physical production, though modest, was handsome. Paul DuPont created evocative costumes from simple materials. Jo the Loiterer and Chris the Citizen were dressed as discharged Union soldiers with ragtag outfits; John Adams wore ornate men's finery with a stove-top hat; Susan B. wore a prim, red velvet dress with lace collar trim and a bonnet and carried a reticule. The sets, constructed by Columbia students, were minimal, with painted murals and simple furniture salvaged from other productions.

The performance was broadcast live and recorded by WNYC radio. The recording reveals the technical limitations of the orchestra, but the music lilts by with suppleness and shape, and the cast sings confidently. Thomson's bullying about diction paid off, for the text comes through vividly. The audience laughs and is struck silent in the appropriate places.

Naturally, it was reviewed everywhere. Robert A. Simon in the *New Yorker* called Stein's libretto "original, entertaining and provocative" and pronounced Thomson's musical setting "right on every count."[25] Richard Watts, Jr., the drama critic for the *New York Post,* wrote,

> Mr. Thomson, who long ago destroyed the old sneer about the critic being a frustrated creative artist by writing music as brilliant as his criticism, seems to be just the man Gertrude Stein needed to bring out the bite, humor and odd charm of her eccentric English. . . . "The Mother of Us All" is just what I think an amalgamation of modern opera and the drama should be.[26]

Irving Kolodin in the *New York Sun* called Thomson's score

> a sophisticated affair, always listenable, often entertaining, occasionally even expressive. His idiom, in the main, parallels hymn tunes and popular songs of the nineteenth century he was portraying, but with a cultivated wit and a conscious musicianship that mark the difference between a platitude and an epigram.[27]

The critic from *Variety* predicted, correctly, it turned out, that the prospect for a commercial production of the opera was poor:

> Despite the gay spirit, its humor and wit, the work isn't Broadway. For all its appeal in story line and situation, and its original approach, this is still an esoteric parlor-piece. It's strictly longhair chamber music.[28]

To Francis D. Perkins of the *Herald Tribune* staff fell the task of reviewing his colleague's opera. Perkins made no pronouncements, choosing, wisely, to describe the music ("gives an impression of simplicity and tunefulness"), praise Thomson's masterful prosody ("a successful solution of the often vexatious problem of recitative and lyric declamation in English"), and congratulate the youthful cast. As if determined to demonstrate his independence, Perkins registers a few reservations about the last act:

> Here the progress of the opera comes to occasional halts; there is a sense of dwelling overlong at a given point, although the final tableau, leaving Susan in her meditation, is effective. The last two scenes, however, are somewhat weaker than the earlier ones.[29]

In his long review for the *New York Times,* Olin Downes, straining to appear fair and intellectually rigorous, describes the opera as a "piece of admirable metier and integrated style," an "arresting period piece." Stein's words, with their "indirect associative purposes, unlinked from their customary coordinates and employed not only for mental images, but for their sounds and rhythms," are a "natural match" for "a composer of such literary propensities as Mr. Thomson." Of that music Downes finally concludes,

> In the sum of it the textual setting is very adroit, entertaining, expressive. The question that remains is whether the very literary style of opera, for all its skillfulness and sensitivity, affords enough musical substance, contrast and climax to sustain interest through a full three acts; whether a text which is always discursive and chopped up, and in the late scenes over-polemical, gives the composer enough opportunity for his score to stand as a unit in itself, and keep its place in the repertory.[30]

In other words, the Thomson/Stein collaborations, however ingenious, were primarily of literary importance and not musical masterpieces to lay, like slabs of stone, atop the expanding edifice of music history. This view was shared by the academic composers who did not dismiss Thomson's music outright. To some degree, it still is. This is why Thomson was "touched so deeply" when Jack Beeson, who knew every note of the opera from having accompanied all the rehearsals, showed keen interest in the key system Thomson had employed.

Ironically, it is within the universities where many such academics teach that *The Mother of Us All* found its most commodious homes. Too "esoteric" for Broadway, as the man from *Variety* pointed out, and too literate and intimate for most grand opera houses, the opera is an ideal student work. There are lots of little parts that want singers with theatrical flair but do not require operatic-sized voices; the opera provides a field day for a director. Before he died, Thomson estimated that he had received royalties from over one thousand productions of *The Mother of Us All,* most of them in colleges or small opera companies.

Wishing to honor Thomson for his achievement, but not wanting to appear parochial, the Music Critics Circle voted *The Mother of Us All* a special award. Thomson was pleased, but he would have preferred to see the proposed Broadway production materialize, or to see one of New York's major companies produce either of his Stein operas.

The aftermath of the premiere of *The Mother of Us All* brought turns in many personal stories, some of them surprising, some of them predictable.

Dorothy Dow never sang at the Metropolitan Opera. She did sing major dramatic roles—Elizabeth in *Tannhäuser*, Marie in *Wozzeck*, Lady Macbeth, Ariadne—at the Zurich Opera, La Scala, Glyndebourne, and Venice. But her performing career did not last beyond the 1950s. Her understudy as Susan B., Teresa Stich, later Teresa Stich-Randall, came to the attention of Toscanini, who used her for his broadcasts and recordings of *Aida* (as a High Priestess) and *Falstaff* (as Nanetta). She went on to a major career with the world's leading opera companies, including the Metropolitan. Alice Howland became a distinguished concert artist, a favorite of American composers. In 1950, with Aaron Copland at the piano, she gave the premiere performance of Copland's *Emily Dickinson* songs.

At Yale University, Donald Gallup spent thirty-five years as the curator of the Collection of American Literature, now housed in the Beinecke Rare Book and Manuscript Library. He published books on Stein, organized her papers, and tended to her affairs at Yale like the devoted "Thursday's child" he always was to Gertrude and Alice.

Joseph Barry became a prominent Paris-based journalist, manager of the Paris edition of *Newsweek*, Paris bureau chief for the *New York Times* from 1949 to 1952, and the author of five books on Paris and its people.

Virgil Thomson lived to regret that he never wrote another opera with Gertrude Stein. "It never occurred to either of us that we would die," he used to say. "Otherwise, we would have written an opera every year!"

22 POLITICS AND PRIZES

During Virgil Thomson's first weeks on the job at the *Herald Tribune,* in 1940, he asked his seasoned colleague Francis Perkins how long it would take to get over being unduly elated or unduly depressed by a musical event. Perkins answered, "About six years." Perkins turned out to be right. By the end of 1946 Thomson was established in his authority and secure in his routine. ("I could write a review, go off to bed, and wake up in the morning with no memory of where I had been or what I had written.")[1] The battles had been fought, the big issues engaged, and the status quo rattled all during the first six years of his tenure. After that he fashioned his schedule in a way that allowed maximum time for composition and travel. He worked full-time only seven months each year, producing, on the average, one Sunday article and two reviews a week, not a demanding schedule, certainly not in comparison with that of Olin Downes, his prolific counterpart at the *New York Times.* During the five warm-weather months Thomson traveled and sent back Sunday pieces, including essays on culture in general and accounts of his nonmusical adventures. Even then he took six weeks of complete vacation. From 1948 until 1952 he did not return to Europe. Instead, he crisscrossed the United States and traveled through Mexico and South America.

Back at the paper, the Reids and the senior editors, to the consternation of Thomson's rivals, continued to support their chief critic's other career as a composer and conductor. Not only did they encourage his months of wandering; they provided extra help to cover the New York beat. So, when Paul Bowles quit his freelance post in early 1946 ("I wanted to write music instead of having to write about it," he told his friend George Antheil),[2] he was replaced, at Thomson's urging, with a full-time critic, another young composer.

Arthur Berger, then thirty-four, born and raised in New York, was was bright, excitable, and, like his boss, a Francophile. After college he joined the Young Composers Group formed by Aaron Copland, took a master's degree at Harvard, studied with Boulanger in Paris, and taught at Mills College, in California, as a colleague of Darius Milhaud. His music was American neoclassical, influenced by Stravinsky and Copland, but with a distinctive, spiky rhythmic character.

Berger's articles were sometimes too erudite for Thomson's taste. But he relied on Berger's professionalism, gained from three previous newspaper jobs. Berger became a valued and knowledgeable critic. Thomson encouraged him to relax at concerts. Once, while having dinner with Thomson before they attended different events, Berger declined a drink. "I drink only after I've written my review," Berger said. "No, no," Thomson replied. "You should drink *before* the concert. That way you get a good nap *during* the concert."

Thomson was not kidding. His habit of dozing unabashedly during concerts he was reviewing was notorious. Sitting in a critic's aisle seat, he would drift off, upright, eyes closed, immovable, as if he were meditating. Yet, inevitably, his critique was filled with detailed description and lucid commentary. Theodate Johnson, who often accompanied him to events, had "elbow privileges," which meant that if Virgil dozed he was not to be disturbed, but if Virgil snored she was allowed to elbow him awake.

Early in 1947, while Thomson was under pressure to complete the composition and scoring of *The Mother of Us All,* two stories that demanded coverage arose within weeks of each other. On January 11 Minna Lederman, the editor of *Modern Music,* announced that this esteemed journal was discontinuing publication. For all its intellectual prestige, *Modern Music* had been run since its inception from the home of Lederman's parents. But they were aging, and this arrangement could not continue. Moreover, production costs were rising. Some grants and gifts, including $500 from Charles Ives, who requested anonymity, kept the journal afloat through 1946. Ironically, this assistance just exacerbated the magazine's internal politics. *Mod-*

ern Music was sponsored by the League of Composers, whose finances were also dire. So why, the league chairman wanted to know, should gifts be directed solely to this one venture and not to its overseeing organization?

The obituaries in the musical press were heartening and personally flattering to Lederman, none more so than Thomson's titled "A War's End." This revealing article addressed more than the legacy of a valued journal. Thomson used the occasion to pronounce the battle for acceptance of contemporary music essentially won. The fight would now be over the "division of the spoils."

> Modern Music, distinguished quarterly review edited by Minna Lederman and published by the League of Composers, has ceased publication after twenty-three years. Musicians and laymen who are part of the contemporary musical movement will of necessity be deeply moved by this announcement, because Modern Music has been for them all a Bible, and a news organ, a forum, a source of world information and the defender of their faith. . . . In the atmosphere of sharp esthetic controversy that pervaded the magazine and with its constant confrontations of authoritative statement and analysis (for there is practically no living composer of any prestige at all whose works have not been discussed in it and who has not written for it himself) wits became more keen and critical powers came to maturity. . . . My own debt to her is enormous. . . . Her magazine was a forum of all the most distinguished world figures of creation and of criticism; and the unknown bright young were given their right to speak up among these, trained to do so without stammering and without fear.
>
> The magazine's "cessation of hostilities," as one of its European admirers refers to the demise, is explained by its editor as due to "rising costs of production." Considering previous difficulties surmounted, I should be inclined to derive the fact from a deeper cause. After all, the war about modern music is over. Now comes the division of spoils. . . . No student in a library, no radio program maker, dallying with [Miss Lederman's] priceless back issues, can avoid recognizing the vast fertility, the originality, ingenuity, and invention that music has manifested in our time.
>
> This is all admitted now, and modern music is played everywhere. There is no war about it any more. Our century's second half, like any other century's second half, will certainly witness the fusion of all the major modern devices into a new classical style. That fusion, in fact, has already begun; invention is on the wane, comprehensibility within the modern techniques on the in-

crease. And the public has ceased resisting them as such. The stabilization of modernism's gains is the order of the next few decades. . . .

No other musical magazine of our century . . . and no book has told the musical story of its time so completely, so authoritatively, so straight from the field of battle and from the creative laboratory. Its twenty-three volumes are history written by the men who made it. For the history of music in any epoch is the story of its composers and of their compositions. Nobody ever tells that story right but the composers themselves. What Haydn thought of Mozart and Beethoven, however wrong as opinion, is true as musical history. What Heine thought of Beethoven, however right, is literature and belongs to the history of another art. The subsequent recounting of musical history from documents of the period belongs, of course, to still another. Thanks to Modern Music the last quarter century has probably a better chance of being written up convincingly than any other, save possibly those years between 1820 and 1845, when Schumann, Berlioz, Wagner, Liszt, Weber and Jean-Paul Richter (himself a composer) all wrote voluminously about their contemporaries.[3]

Lederman, very touched, wrote Thomson a note of thanks:

Dear V,

You made me weep at my own wake—especially the sweet flattery about being indebted to me when it was always the other way around. The most fun I ever had out of MM was breaking open those envelopes from 17 Quai Voltaire.

Love,
Minna[4]

History has proven Thomson partially right that by 1947 the battle for contemporary music was essentially over. The European innovators had radically altered musical language and substance. The Americans, indebted to the European heritage but free to rebel from it, had put their own sassy spin on things. The next decades would indeed be more about consolidation than about continued innovation. But the "fusion" that Thomson predicted did not take place. The disparity of styles that existed in 1947, if anything, increased. The only "fusion" that occurred produced a dissonance-saturated international style of modernism that was highly complex and often faceless. And though the public may have ceased resisting modern music in terms of questioning its validity, the public wasn't exactly buying it either.

Thomson's assessment of the state of music in 1947 reads like wishful thinking. Earlier, in his more polemical days, he had decried the production of cerebral modern music that "was never intended for anything but prize-winning and the impressing of other musicians." "The general music public and the trustee class have both revolted," he warned. He debunked the "international style" as "God's gift to pedagogy"[5] and cautioned composers about the dead end of excessive complexity. But by 1946, in a respectful article about atonality in France, Thomson is conciliatory, calling the ingenious young composer Pierre Boulez the "most brilliant of all the Paris under-twenty-fives." Privately, however, he warned Boulez of the trap he was slipping into.

> I said to him, "By using carefully thought out and complex ways, you produce by thirty a handful of unforgettable works. But by then you are the prisoner of your method, which is stiff. You cannot handle it with freedom; so you write less and less; at forty you are sterile. This is the trap of all style-bound artists. For without freedom no one is a master."[6]

In 1947 Thomson was even more disturbed by other trends in the contemporary music sphere. The organizations that composers had founded during the 1920s and 1930s to promote and protect themselves were struggling. Composers were taking refuge in universities, which, to Thomson, was both good and bad. Having security was good; being sheltered from the need to win the public's ear was bad. But in his eulogy for *Modern Music,* he appears to be calling for a truce. There are many ways to be modern, the subtext of his piece suggests; Roger Sessions practices the modernism of complexity; I practice the modernism of simplicity. There is room in the marketplace for everybody to set up a stand.

Thomson believed, no doubt, that in his own writings he treated the music of colleagues who wrote in complex styles, even the music of Sessions, a personal enemy, with respect simply by describing it, placing it in context, and affirming its technical excellence. But it's hard to imagine that Sessions was content with Thomson's 1947 review of his Piano Sonata no. 2. Sessions's compositions, Thomson wrote,

> are learned, laborious, complex, and withal not strikingly original. They pass for professor's music, and the term is not wholly unjustified. Because the complexity and elaboration of their manner is out of all proportion to the matter expressed. Nevertheless, they

are impressive both for the seriousness of their thought and for the ingenuity of their workmanship They are hard to take and even harder to reject. They represent the most embarrassing problem in American music, because though they unquestionably have quality, they just as certainly have almost no charm at all. And we have no place in our vast system of musical distribution for music without charm.[7]

In part, Thomson's declaration that the war had ended was prompted by his wish to have his place acknowledged and move on. He was tired of arguing that the simplicity of his music was radical, not negligible. That he was sensitive about this is clear from a letter he wrote in response to a query from an author preparing an article on Thomson's operas for *Harper's Bazaar*.

> I am not too happy at seeing my score called whimsical. Also, I think the idea that Miss Stein and I are primarily wits is, if you will permit me, both antiquated and inaccurate. . . . I am sorry to be so critical, because I know you have spent a great deal of thought on the paragraph which you sent me. But since you have asked for my cooperation, I should be most grateful, and so would Miss Stein if she were living, for some word that would not place us quite so definitely with the amusers.[8]

The one man in the musical world who made Thomson's conflict-of-interest issue look tame by comparison was Arthur Judson. By 1947 Judson's management agency Columbia Concerts was grossing over $5 million per year. So the salary he earned as the manager of the New York Philharmonic ($15,000) meant little to him. Running the orchestra was a convenience and a shameless power move. By controlling the Philharmonic, he could provide his conductors and soloists bookings with the most important orchestra in America. (Some thirteen million people listened to its Sunday broadcasts on CBS radio.) All but a stubborn handful of the international conductors who wished to work in America were under contract with Judson, who extracted commissions of up to 20 percent, two notable exceptions being Toscanini and Koussevitzky.

Another important holdout was Arthur Rodzinski, a conductor of Polish descent. In 1947 Rodzinski was being proclaimed the savior of the New York Philharmonic. After Toscanini left in 1936, the orchestra floundered under Sir John Barbirolli, a fussy interpreter with scant interest in new music. Once Thomson arrived on the scene in 1940, his tough critiques helped drive Barbirolli away. Rodzinski took over in 1942. Facing an ensemble of frustrated and bitter musicians, he began a complete overhaul: he fired fourteen players, including the concertmaster, reorganized the rehearsal schedule, and revitalized the programming. Though exacting, he was a psychologically savvy father figure who invited the musicians to his home for one-on-one talks about musical and domestic concerns. Orchestra work, he used to say, was maybe 75 percent psychology. Though he lacked the incandescence of Toscanini or Stokowski, and though the orchestra often played with more inspiration for dynamic guest conductors, Rodzinski was an insightful musician devoted to his orchestra. The Philharmonic had not sounded so good in years.

But Arthur Judson was not pleased. Rodzinski, formerly a Judson artist, had signed with another agent. As the Philharmonic's manager, Judson was making what Rodzinski thought were inappropriate demands about programming, guest conductors, and the choice of soloists. Faced with the option of signing a three-year contract that undermined his authority, Rodzinski announced that he was quitting America's most prestigious and best-paid musical position (over $85,000 yearly, including revenues from radio and recordings).

The resignation made front-page headlines. *Time* magazine described it with novelistic drama.

> Last week a pent-up man eased his big frame into a desk chair in a plainly furnished 16th-floor office in Manhattan's Steinway Building. The man was Dr. Arthur Rodzinski, conductor of New York's renowned Philharmonic-Symphony. His small eyes, almost concealed behind thick glasses, took in his audience: seven tense members of the Philharmonic's executive committee. . . . Grey-maned Arthur Rodzinski had a lot to say. . . . His speech rose to a bitter, excited tirade that accused Arthur Judson, the handsome, leonine manager of the Philharmonic, of trying to run the orchestra and hamstringing the conductor. Mr. Judson, who was present, listened with interest.[9]

More jaded commentators suggested that Rodzinski's resignation was less principled than it appeared, for while he was negotiating with the Philharmonic he was being courted by the Chicago Symphony Orchestra. Virgil Thomson did not see it that way. The Chicago post paid less than $50,000 and was considerably less distinguished. Thomson was outraged by Judson's strong-arming and exhilarated by Rodzinski's response. The conductor's bold announcement made explicit what had been going on covertly for years: rapacious managers were trying to run artistic institutions like international corporations, test-marketing and standardizing the product for maximum profit and efficient delivery. Thomson had been a solid Rodzinski supporter, not least because the conductor had allowed him to conduct the Philharmonic in the premiere of his *Symphony on a Hymn Tune.* In his Sunday column called "The Philharmonic Crisis," Thomson took on Judson in a coolheaded, incisive, and withering attack.

> Arthur Rodzinski has gone and done it. For years the knowledge has been a secret scandal in music circles. Now he has said it out loud. That the trouble with the Philharmonic is nothing more than an unbalance of power. . . . He points to Arthur Judson, a powerful business executive who manages the orchestra as a side line, as the person chiefly interested in weakening the musical director's authority. He is right; he is perfectly right; he could not be more right. An orchestra can use one star performer and one only. And such a star's place is the podium, not the executive offices. . . .
>
> The Philharmonic case is simple. Arthur Judson is unsuited by the nature and magnitude of his business interests to manage with the necessary self-effacement a major intellectual institution doing business with his other interests. . . . Arthur Rodzinski has done more for the orchestra . . . than any other conductor in our century has done. . . . Today the Philharmonic, for the first time in this writer's memory, is the equal of the Boston and Philadelphia orchestras and possibly their superior. . . .
>
> What awaits [Rodzinski's] successor is anybody's guess. Dramas and heartbreaks probably. . . . In any case, the Philharmonic will decline as an orchestra as inevitably as winter will return. There is only one way to have a first-class orchestra and that is to let the conductor run it. If he fails, he can be replaced. But while he lasts he has to be given full musical authority as that is understood in the major symphonic establishments. . . .[10]

Judson was enraged. He had always considered Thomson an enemy. But recently, mollified by Thomson's consistently good reviews of Rodzinski, he had actually considered a suggestion by his client (and Thomson champion) Eugene Ormandy to take charge of the critic's burgeoning sideline career as a guest conductor. Thomson had not encouraged Ormandy's idea, but had not closed the door on it either. In any event, "The Philharmonic Crisis" quashed such talk.

Meanwhile, congratulatory letters arrived by the dozens at Thomson's office. The reaction of the composer Ernst Bacon was typical:

"Your statement about the Judson-Rodzinski case Sunday was magnificent. You can't imagine how good it makes us feel that there is one writer who has not only the courage but the literary artistry to bring such issues as these to the fore."[11]

Thomson was particularly gratified to hear from other artist representatives, small-timers who had long ago resigned themselves to Judson's power. Ermine Kahn, an artist manager working in the same Steinway Hall office building as Judson, sent a jubilant letter:

> We truly have occasion again, today, to thank you with our warmest hearts for your courageous, clear, and I think decisive voice, against a cynical commercialism which has no conscience and no mercy.
>
> I well remember that it was you, single-handed, who—among many other rescues—delivered us from Barbirolli: and I have a feeling that we will continue to thank you—silently or otherwise—for many more deliverances in the world of a living music.[12]

Rodzinski, feeling vindicated, wrote Thomson in triumph:

> Dear Virgil,
> Congratulations on your wonderful Sunday story. You are the real hero of the day. I am receiving countless telegrams, telephone calls and letters of congratulations, and the public support is tremendous. All of them refer to your great Sunday story.
> Of course, the job is not yet finished and we will have to go to the very bottom of it. . . .[13]

Rodzinski accepted the Chicago post, but remained for several months in New York to finish "the job." He issued more press releases and wrote letters to the editors of newspapers and music magazines. Thomson took up the larger issues of management in five Sunday pieces over the next two months. Nevertheless, in May, Rodzinski asked Thomson "to ventilate the story once more." ("It is not too late. . . . As a matter of fact, it may be a good idea to open it up because I feel it died out a little too quickly.")[14] Thomson agreed with his editors that overkill would only hurt the cause.

Rodzinski's first season in Chicago, 1947–48, was a critical triumph. But with his penchant for last-minute program changes and by breaking the budget with semistaged operatic productions in place of symphony concerts, he alienated the orchestra's trustees and was not rehired.

At the New York Philharmonic, Rodzinski was succeeded by the revered German-born Bruno Walter, who agreed only to be musical adviser, meaning that he planned the season with Judson but turned over a majority of programs to guest conductors. This ill-defined arrangement lasted two years. Dimitri Mitropoulos, the next full-fledged music director, outlasted Judson, who gave up managing the orchestra in 1956. In 1958 the Philharmonic appointed the first American ever to lead a major American symphony orchestra, a just-turned-forty dynamo named Leonard Bernstein.

Having ushered into production his second opera and marshaled the musical troops in a battle against managerial tyranny, Thomson was looking for another high-visibility project when he returned from his European vacation in the fall of 1947. That project turned out to be another film.

Robert Flaherty's pioneering work in documentary film was fore-shadowed by his pioneering exploits as a youth. He grew up among the mining camps of northern Michigan and Canada, where his father, an engineer and prospector, was hired by corporations to search the wilderness for minerals. Working with his father, young Flaherty explored the northern reaches of Canada, mapping subarctic Eskimo country and learning the techniques of frontier survival.

In 1910, at twenty-six, Flaherty was hired as an explorer by a Canadian railroad company, a transporter of minerals and pulpwood. Three years later his boss suggested that, since he was going to un-mapped regions of the Northern Territories, he might want to bring a film crew with him. Excited by the idea, Flaherty took a crash course in cinematography. Within two years making movies became the lifework of this physically imposing frontiersman.

The film that would make him famous and set the mold for feature-length narrative documentaries was *Nanook of the North,* which examined an Itivimiut Eskimo tribe living on the northern border of the great Hudson Bay. Flaherty's innovation was to focus his film on the story of one hunter, Nanook, as he stalked walrus, tracked wildlife, built sleds, and raised a family. Nanook and his tribe cooperated fully with the crew, taking them along on walrus hunts, even building an oversized igloo with one side missing to enable the cameras to film interior shoots with natural light, scenes which, though staged, at least replicated authenticity. During months of shooting the crew survived blizzards and isolation. One day Flaherty's camera dropped into icy water. It had to be taken apart, piece by piece, dried, and reassembled; film footage had to be laid atop driftwood to dry in the sun. The life the film documented was somewhat idealized. Even in this remote region of Canada, the influence of industrial civilization was seeping in. However, nothing like this dramatic documentary had even been done before. When, after rejections by four major film distributors, *Nanook of the North* was accepted by the French-based Pathé organization and screened at New York's Capital Theater on June 11, 1922, the reaction was unprecedented. "Beside this film," wrote the *New York Times* critic, "the usual photoplay, the so-called 'dramatic' work of the screen, becomes as thin and blank as the celluloid on which it is printed."[15]

In 1947, then sixty-three, Flaherty approached Virgil Thomson about writing a score for a film that was already completed and edited, his first in six years. He had admired Thomson's scores for Pare Lorentz's films, and he loved music. On location, whether in arctic territories or on tropical islands, he took along his violin and portable phonograph. Thomson viewed Flaherty's film, called *Louisiana Story,* which still had no soundtrack, and was captivated by its vivid imagery, the work of Flaherty and a young cinematographer, Richard Leacock, and by the ingenious way Flaherty's scenario made a compelling narrative out of "found" materials.

Set in the lush, exotic, sparsely populated bayou country of Louisiana, the film jogged Thomson's memories of traveling to this primordial region when stationed for three months at Fort Gerstner in 1918. It told the story of a young Cajun boy who rafts through the overgrown, alligator-infested marshes, leafy bogs, and blackened rivers, and watches with wariness the infiltration of industry in the form of oil rigs and massive derricks. The boy lives in the bayou with his parents, speaking French at home, hunting and fishing for food. This was another instance of Flaherty's staged authenticity. The boy who "played" the lead was a photogenic twelve-year-old, Joseph Boudreaux, a sharecropper's son who was found in a schoolroom by the producer's wife. His parents were portrayed by other bayou natives whom Flaherty hired.

Flaherty was not comfortable having his film about the invasion of industry into the pristine Cajun region funded by one of the invaders: the Standard Oil Company of New Jersey. Company executives were forthright about their intentions: they wanted a film that depicted their interest in the region as beneficial to progress and benign to the environment. So the company kept its sponsorship off the credits, while Flaherty concentrated cinematically on the bayou's natural splendors and idealized the industrialization.

In one scene, as a well is being drilled, there is a terrifying blowout, with fearsome jets of oil spewing into the air. But in a balletic sequence of images—shining metallic drill pipes, gushing oil, brawny men covered with black slicks—the laconic and commanding crew members cap the leak and protect the land, winning the admiration of the lonely boy who had feared them. Their work done, they leave the land as they found it. With the money the boy's father has earned from licensing part of his property, he gives his son a present—a shiny new hunting rifle.

Flaherty was ambivalent about blurring the conflict between industry and the environment, but the pragmatic Thomson, who knew how to finesse conflict-of-interest issues, was a pillar of support. Musically, Thomson employed a comparable technique for ennobling the isolated Cajun people: he incorporated their own music into a beguiling orchestral score, searching through Louisiana French folksong collections by Alan Lomax and Irene Therese Whitfield to find plaintive melodies, lilting tunes, and bumptious dances. These materials are alternated with Thomson's landscape music that evokes the dark, murky beauty of the marshy land with its dangling overgrowth. In the opening sequence the Cajun boy, standing on his raftlike "marsh buggy," sinking his long-handled oar deep into bog, winds his way through inky waters and moss-covered trees. Thomson's music shimmers with an eerie, almost ominous tranquillity: against a progression of tremulous string chords, all sturdy modal harmonies, an inexorable pattern of ascending harp arpeggios evokes the lapping waters and the steady strokes of the oar. Eventually, a mournful tune gets passed from oboe to flute to violins.

However, Thomson used similarly resonant music to characterize the industrial intruders. In one pivotal scene, as the boy frolics to a jocular Acadian scherzo, he is struck still by the sight of invading oil derricks, creeping down the Mississippi River on massive barges. The boy's frolicking music is cut short, replaced by a serene chorale of root-position chords that make unorthodox harmonic shifts and build to a swelling climax. The music, like the sight of the oil derricks, is fearsome yet reassuring, unfamiliar yet uplifting. This is progress in action, the film sequence reassures us, disruptive, disconcerting, but nothing to fear.

In depicting action sequences, Thomson made some daring musical choices. In a harrowing scene when the boy fights with an alligator and is saved just in time by his father, Thomson captures the snapping and wriggling in a vigorous fugue with a jagged and diabolical theme. He depicted the racket of oil-well drilling with the recorded noises of actual machinery, which he used like compositional materials to fashion a long (nine minutes) and deafening sequence.

When finished, Thomson's score provided music for nearly sixty of the film's seventy-seven minutes. Except for his operas, it was Thomson's longest composition. To record it he hired Eugene Ormandy and the Philadelphia Orchestra. Since the film had little spoken narrative and Flaherty thought the music so illustrative, he saw no reason not to emphasize it up to the point where its volume became a distraction to the visual imagery. The film had been budgeted at $175,000; cost overruns brought the final tally to $258,000. It opened at the Sutton Theater in New York on September 18, 1948, and soon played across the country. Reviews were uniformly excellent: "should be seen by all those who savor original and arresting screen craftsmanship," wrote Howard Barnes in the *Herald Tribune*. Bosley Crowther of the *Times,* like several other critics, noted the irony of Flaherty's turnaround regarding the role of industry in modern life.

> Heretofore, Flaherty's pictures have been more or less romantic studies of individuals in primitive walks of life. . . . But now, in "Louisiana Story," Flaherty accepts the intrusion of machinery in the individual's life. And he even finds beauty in the rhythms and in the energy of the machine.[16]

That the film would provide "invaluable public relations material" for Standard Oil of New Jersey was not lost on several critics.

> The firm has no rights and no identification in the film, but stands to get across the idea that oil companies are beneficently public-spirited, their employees honest, industrious and amiable, and their operations productive and innocuous.[17]

Thomson's score was hailed ("a triumph of movie music"—*Vogue*). John Houseman talked up the film and his old friend's score to his associates in Hollywood. Both were mentioned around town as possibilities for Academy Award nominations. But the only nomination that came through was in the writing category, a curious choice in that the script by Flaherty and his wife, Frances, was so minimal.

Thomson was not about to let nearly sixty minutes of music remain forever attached to a movie. He fashioned two suites from the score. *Acadian Songs and Dances,* the second of these, used seven segments of the score that borrowed themes from bayou songbooks. In 1952 George Balanchine adopted this suite for his ballet *Bayou* at the New York City Ballet. Though the decor by Dorothea Tanning was stunning, the ballet was not. The dance critic Edwin Denby praised the gentle gracefulness of Balanchine's choreography; but, Denby added, Balanchine

> missed the originality of the score, its subtlety in candor, the sense it gives of clear repose in a secret spot. The liquid continuity of the music, the easy breathing of the melody, the transparency of the harmony, the unelliptic, unabridged, so-to-speak circular or stanzalike forward motion it has—these are peculiarities of structure that might have looked beautiful reflected in dancing.[18]

The other composition Thomson extracted from his film, called, simply, Suite from *Louisiana Story,* used four substantive and original episodes: a prelude ("The bayou and the marsh buggy"), a chorale ("The derrick arrives"), a passacaglia ("Robbing the alligator's nest"), and a fugue ("Boy fights alligator"), making a twenty-minute, four-movement, minisymphonic composition. The work received its premiere in late November 1949 by Ormandy and the Philadelphia Orchestra at their hometown Academy of Music, and was repeated on November 30 at Carnegie Hall, in New York. The suite had a flurry of subsequent performances that winter. Walter Hendl conducted it with the New York Philharmonic; William Steinberg, in Buffalo; Efrem Kurtz, in Houston. The reviews were among the most satisfying of Thomson's career. The *Philadelphia Inquirer* critic called it one of Thomson's "finest, most spontaneous and refreshing scores." The critic John Briggs of the *New York Post Home News,* no admirer of Thomson's music, wrote a glowing review.

> It is always a pleasure to revise one's estimate of a composer upward. This reviewer, having long since pegged Mr. Thomson as an amusing but rather superficial dabbler in musical composition, was bowled over by "Louisiana Story." It is a first-rate piece of work. Its solid craftsmanship was no surprise; Mr. Thomson has shown himself to be a competent technician even in such ephemera as his "Hymn Tune Symphony," "Four Saints in Three Acts" and "The Mother of Us All." But in "Louisiana Story" there is something more—a new depth and power of musical expres-

sion. The score is no musical pot-boiler; it has weight, dignity and something that frequently approaches grandeur.[19]

The score also brought Thomson the most prestigious accolade of his career to date: the Pulitzer Prize in music.

From the time of its inauguration in 1917 as an award for outstanding achievements in journalism, the Pulitzer Prize had also been given in certain areas of arts and letters. There were yearly awards for fiction, drama, history, and biography. In 1922 an award for poetry was added. An award for an outstanding musical composition was not begun until 1943.

The Pulitzers were guided by the principle that no one knows a given discipline better than those who practice it. A jury of three experts in each field selected three finalists for each award, designating one as the winner and passing their choice to the overall Pulitzer board for approval. The board reserved the right to select another winner from the finalists, but rarely exercised it. Within the fields of arts and letters there had always been the typical grumbling about the selection system, namely, that it was inbred, that rotating rosters of artists and authors were making awards to their favorites and friends. The small circle of American composers was especially chummy.

Consequently, it was a wise decision when a conductor, Chalmers Clifton, was made chairman of the jury that awarded the first Pulitzer Prize in music. Clifton, then fifty-four, was a mainstay of the New York musical community. Neither a star nor a powerhouse, he worked behind the scenes—teaching, organizing orchestras, and making performances of new music happen. Many composers were indebted to him. It was Clifton who had invited Thomson in 1923 to participate in his conducting class in New York. Clifton was a good arbitrator who brought fairness and nondogmatic intelligence to the Pulitzer selection process. That first year he was joined by another conductor and American music champion, Alfred Wallenstein, and by the Yale-trained composer Quincy Porter, then the director of the New England Conservatory, a composer of Thomson's generation, but someone who had not been part of the Copland-led "commando unit." The first award went to a younger member of the American composers group, William Schuman, then thirty-three, for his Symphony no. 3.

Clifton remained the chairman of the music jury though the first years of its existence, and there was surprisingly little dissent about the results. The next year, he was joined by Otto Luening, who had just started teaching at Columbia, and Philip James, a composer, organist, and chairman of the music department at New York University. The award went to the Symphony no. 4 by Howard Hanson, another composer based in academia: the Eastman School of Music, in Rochester.

In 1945 Clifton and Luening welcomed Henry Cowell to the panel. Just two years earlier Cowell had received an unconditional pardon for the sodomy charge that had sent him to San Quentin prison during the 1930s. Cowell, basking in the good regard of his colleagues, was honored to have been asked to join the jury. The prize went to a work that had just slipped in under the deadline for the 1945 prize: Aaron Copland's ballet *Appalachian Spring* was premiered in Washington. D.C., on December 30, 1944. An article announcing the Pulitzers, including, in the third paragraph, Copland's, made the front page of the *New York Times* on a day when the world news might have been expected to push it off. On May 8, 1945, the bold headlines read,

THE WAR IN EUROPE IS ENDED!
SURRENDER IS UNCONDITIONAL;
V-E WILL BE PROCLAIMED TODAY;
OUR TROOPS IN OKINAWA GAIN

In 1946 a committee consisting of Clifton, Copland, and Hanson gave the prize to Leo Sowerby, in the year he turned sixty, for his sacred cantata *The Canticle of the Sun*. Thomson had secretly hoped that his *Symphony on a Hymn Tune* might win. Though completed in 1928, the work had received its premiere in February 1945. However, there was no precedent for making an award to a long-existing composition.

The next year such a precedent was established. Clifton, acting as a committee of one, persuaded the Pulitzer board that the music prize must go to the Symphony no. 3 ("The Camp Meeting") by Charles Ives, a work written in 1904 but premiered on April 5, 1945, by the New York Little Orchestra Society conducted by Lou Harrison. Then seventy-three and quite ill, the pioneering composer was recognized only by a select group of American composers, no one more so than Clifton. Much later, Thomson called Ives "the father of us all."

The 1948 Pulitzer went to Walter Piston for his Symphony no. 3, a piece Thomson grudgingly respected, but a choice that rankled him. But the next year was to be Thomson's. The Suite from *Louisiana Story* had received strong reviews even from academics who tended to treat

Thomson like some gadfly. The groundswell for Thomson was strong. Still, the vote was not unanimous. Chalmers Clifton and Henry Cowell voted for *Louisiana Story*. The third member of the jury, Beveridge Webster, a distinguished pianist teaching at Juilliard, voted for another film score, Copland's music for *The Red Pony,* based on the John Steinbeck story. The Pulitzer board accepted the majority vote. Thomson's award was announced on May 2, 1949. Most newspaper accounts the next day gave it second billing after the award for drama, which went to a play that had created a sensation, *Death of a Salesman,* by the thirty-three-year-old Arthur Miller.

As of this writing, Thomson's award remains the only Pulitzer Prize ever given to music from a film, something he was always proud of. It vindicated his conviction that composers had to get involved with the everyday world, that music for a popular medium could be as challenging to compose as music for a chamber music society. Among American concert music composers, Thomson had led the way to the film studio with his ambitious scores for Pare Lorentz's documentaries.

The next year, however, his ego was bruised a bit when on March 23, 1950, Aaron Copland won an Academy Award for his musical score for the 1949 Paramount Pictures film *The Heiress,* which also took a best-actress Oscar for its star, Olivia de Havilland. But publicly he was full of good will for his old colleague and competitor: "This is to tell you how pleased I am that the Oscar people have recognized your music," he wrote to Copland three weeks after the ceremony.[20]

In the late 1940s Thomson was at the peak of his powers. With the imprimatur of the Pulitzer, *Louisiana Story* started to be programmed by major conductors everywhere—George Szell in Cleveland, Pierre Monteux in San Francisco, Charles Munch in Boston. Within six months of its premiere, *The Mother of Us All* was published as a piano-vocal score. Thomson had never had so little trouble getting an expensive score into print. That same year, 1947, RCA Victor brought out a recording of *Four Saints in Three Acts,* conducted by Thomson, a frustrating but important project.

RCA was unwilling to record the entire opera. Forty-five out of ninety minutes of music, ten 78-rpm disc sides, was their limit. With Maurice Grosser, Thomson made cuts that pained him, but maintained a linear continuity in the remaining score. A chorus was assembled and prepared by Leonard De Paur, the dynamic choral director who had worked with Thomson and Houseman on the WPA Negro Theater production of *Macbeth*. He was currently the director of the De Paur Infantry Chorus, which was under contract to Columbia Records and toured extensively. De Paur was a skilled musician who was so enamored of *Four Saints* that he used bits of it as warm-up exercises for his infantry men ("Let Lucy Lily Lily Lucy Let . . ."). He also recruited the soloists, including four of the leading singers from the 1934 cast. Abner Dorsey and Altonell Hines, the original Commère and Compère, returned, as stylish as ever. Edward Matthews, who was having success in musicals and on the concert stage, returned as Saint Ignatius. And Beatrice Robinson, the original Saint Teresa, who since the *Four Saints* premiere had been teaching privately in Corona, Queens, came that spring day to New York's elegant Town Hall to record the role she had created.

When Thomson arrived, he was upset to learn that only ten hours had been set aside for recording, and the orchestra and chorus had already been positioned onstage near to twelve individual microphones. The balance would have to be achieved by the recording engineer. Thomson objected strongly to this setup. When they broke for lunch and listened to the playbacks, the balances were off and the recording sounded unnatural. Annoyed at having lost three hours, Thomson took charge, arranged the orchestra and singers onstage as they would be in a performance, and ordered one large microphone to be placed back near the balcony and one smaller microphone near the downstage chorus to pick up diction. This way he was able to control the balances himself. Everyone felt the pressure to complete the recording in the remaining time, but the results were glorious: the sound was natural and present; the diction of the soloists and chorus was a marvel; Thomson's tempos were supple and undulant. The performance, sadly only half of the opera, has never been equaled. "I have the test pressings of our *Four Saints* records and they are quite wonderful," Thomson wrote to Alice B. Toklas late in December. "I have not heard such good choral diction before on discs."[21]

In his first years at the *Tribune*, while adjusting to his new career, Thomson had written little music. But after the war, in addition to the opera and the film score, he produced a sizable list of works. There was a film score for *Tuesday in November,* a documentary commissioned in 1945 by the Office of War Information for use as propaganda in countries where free elections were little understood. For separate commissions Thomson composed three orchestral portrait pieces, or musical landscapes: *The Seine at Night, Wheat Field at Noon,* and *Sea Piece with Birds,* atmospheric and quizzical evocations that he conducted on a recording as a suite of three. *The Seine at Night,* in which one hears the softly steady flow of the river, the shimmering of mist, and the flare of skyrockets in distant Montmartre, was written for a commission from Thomson's hometown orchestra, the Kansas City Symphony. In his program note for the 1948 premiere, Thomson wrote that, having spent his "second twenty years in Paris" writing music that was, in one way or another, about Kansas City, he now wished to offer to "the other city that I love, and the only other one where I have ever felt at home, a sketch, a souvenir, a post-card of the Seine, as seen in front of my own house, a view as deeply a part of my life and thought as Wabash Avenue, where I spent my first twenty years."[22] There were the elegant *Four Songs to Poems of Thomas Campion,* and the poly-stylistic *Five Songs from William Blake,* the latter for baritone and orchestra. The Blake songs were written expressly for the robust, articulate voice of Mack Harrell, the American baritone, who later recorded them with Eugene Ormandy and the Philadelphia Orchestra, a record that became one of Thomson's most popular.

However, no piece from this period was more important to Thomson than his Cello Concerto, begun in 1946, completed in 1949 after extensive input from a friend, the virtuoso cellist Luigi Silva, and premiered in 1950 by the Philadelphia Orchestra with its brilliant twenty-three-year-old principal cellist, Paul Olefsky, as soloist. On the surface the music is genial and bumptious. The first movement depicts, Thomson wrote, "a horse and rider on the open plain." The second is a set of muted yet fetchingly colored variations on a tender hymn tune, "Death, 'tis a Melancholy Day." The finale, a vivacious depiction of children's games, plays musical games, at one point stealing a theme from the finale of Beethoven's Piano Sonata no. 6, in F major, and showing us how suspiciously close is Beethoven's theme to the tune of "Yankee Doodle." Thomson's academic colleagues and the more cerebral music critics, while acknowledging the work's striking orchestration, dismissed the piece as, at best, a diversion, and at worst, drivel. But the admirers of this concerto found in it what Thomson did: music that is structurally ingenious, with its fractured phrase lengths and peppery rhythms; music that uses everyday elements but dislodges them from their everydayness; music that explores the resources of the cello in fantastical ways. At first, the work received some fancy performances, including one with the cellist Anthony Pini, the conductor Sir Thomas Beecham, and the Royal Philharmonic Orchestra in Edinburgh in the summer of 1950; another with the cellist Pierre Fournier and the conductor Fritz Reiner during his Chicago Symphony years. Yet the piece has been largely neglected. That his Cello Concerto did not join the standard repertory was one of Thomson's great disappointments in later life. "It may be just too hard for the cello," he used to say, searching for an explanation.

In the midst of this activity, Thomson was cheered to learn that a proposed Broadway revival of *Four Saints in Three Acts,* to be co-produced by the American National Theater and Academy and a private patron, Ethel Linder Reiner, had come through. The opera would be presented for two weeks as part of a five-play season by ANTA, the country's only nationally charted theater, at the Broadway Theater, on Fifty-third Street. Thomson was given complete artistic control. He decided, unwisely, it turned out, to try to reproduce as closely as possible the production from 1934.

Since cellophane, even if it had been affordable, was prohibited by the fire department for use in a theater, it was decided to copy from sketches and pictures Stettheimer's cellophane sets by using a woven plastic material that Thomson found "droopy, greasy, its blue-green color dismal." Stettheimer's costume designs were also copied by the designer Paul Morrison, but the colors were flatter, the textures less rich. Relying on the original prompt books and Maurice Grosser's memory, the new choreographer, William Dollar, tried to replicate Frederick Ashton's movements, with some success. Basically, the production was directed by Thomson and Grosser, who was listed as "Book Director."

Mrs. Godfrey auditioned once again for the role of Saint Teresa I. But in the eighteen years since the premiere, her radiant voice had faded. Only two members of the original cast were chosen: the ageless Edward Matthews was once again Saint Ignatius; and Altonell Hines, his wife, sang the Commère. His sister, Inez Matthews, who had sung on the RCA recording, was cast as Saint Teresa I. Most of the other singers were fresh out of music school and happy to be singing opera for pay. One promising soprano, Leontyne Price, just turned twenty-five, who had recently distinguished herself as Alice Ford in a Juilliard School production of Verdi's *Falstaff,* was cast in the tiny role of Saint Cecilia. Miss Price had come from Laurel, Mississippi, where there was no network radio station capable of receiving the national broadcasts of orchestras and opera from New York and Chicago. From Laurel she had gone directly to Wilberforce College, in Ohio, and from there, on scholarship, to Juilliard. Her role in *Four Saints* was her first paid, professional job. Recognizing the excellence of her voice, Thomson asked her to understudy the role of Saint Teresa I. But given the brevity of her solo part, no reviewer singled her out for mention.

The other impressive young singer, a twenty-two-year-old Ohio-born mezzo-soprano who had just graduated from the Hartford School of Music, was Betty Lou Allen, who was cast as Saint Teresa II. The previous year she had been chosen by Leonard Bernstein to sing in a performance of his *Jeremiah* Symphony. Despite her youth, Allen was already a mature artist with clear diction, an open and resonant voice, and striking stage presence. Later, as Betty Allen, she became a noted singer and pedagogue, the innovative director of the Harlem School for the Arts, and one of Thomson's closest colleagues.

The production, which opened on April 16, was not as ecstatically received as the fabled 1934 premiere. Several critics faulted the sets and costumes for their gaudy colors and gilt. The reviews of the opera itself, however, were, if anything, more consistently admiring:

> a refreshing experience of real and distinguished theater art
> —B. H. Haggin, *Nation* (May 3, 1952)

> as fresh as it was in 1934, as simple and naive in its nice confusion as it will always be . . . an opera in the extraordinary sense. . . . Thomson achieves a marriage of word and note that is exceptional. . . .
> —Miles Kastendieck,
> *New York Journal American* (April 17, 1952)

There were dissenting voices. The music critic Irving Kolodin wrote that *Four Saints* was "significant for what it was rather than for what it is" and that "purposeless double-talk no longer registers in a time when the purposeful kind, on an international level, possesses ominous overtones." The *Times* drama critic Brooks Atkinson, just as puzzled as he was in 1934, wrote that people in search of an explanation for the opera "had better not look to this column."[23]

In June the cast and crew traveled to Paris, where the production was presented at the Champs-Elysées theater as part of its Twentieth Century Exposition of the Arts. Thomson again conducted; a good orchestra, that of the Concerts Colonne, and sufficient rehearsal time had been made available. But the players themselves were restless and rude.

> Enthralled for certain by the Negro girls, my men half the time would turn their backs to me. For every entry of a soloist or section, I had to snap my fingers a good two measures in advance. That they could cooperate, however, was revealed at the last performance, when Inez Matthews had a cold. "Don't try to go on," I had said to her. "Leontyne knows the role." But she did go on. So I said to the orchestra, "Please take care with my soprano; don't make her sing loud all the time." Their anti-American resistance to me (three-fourths of them were commies) disappeared at once; and they followed lamb-like, hushing volume at my slightest indication, their eyes on me instead of on the stage.[24]

The Parisian audience and critics were wildly divided about the piece. Many had expected an American opera to sound like Gershwin. Those who prided themselves on some knowledge of English were exasperated by Stein's text. Sarcastic reviewers savaged the work. How could a critic of Thomson's stature, so the line went, write such puerile music? What were all these sequences of major and minor triads, hard, clean, and symmetrical? Was the opera satirical? Serious? Naive? Knowing? A vocal minority was captivated, but the singers were downcast. However, for many the trip to Paris was a dream come true. And everyone enjoyed mingling with Miss Alice B. Toklas, the tiny, dark, chain-smoking lady who had lived with Miss Gertrude Stein. Miss Toklas gave a party for the entire cast at 5 rue Christine. She served tea and punch and *petits pains au paté* and made four luscious cakes.

The *Four Saints* revival decisively set in motion the early career of Leontyne Price, thanks to Alexander Smallens, who had conducted the 1934 premiere. The year after the first production, Smallens conducted the premiere of another all-black opera, *Porgy and Bess*. In 1953 there was to be a revival of Gershwin's opera at the Ziegfeld Theater, which would kick off a two-year international tour. Smallens was to conduct again. When it came time to cast the role of Bess, he remembered the striking young Saint Cecilia with her lustrous voice with whom he had just worked. Price would be his new Bess. She sang the role in New York and toured the world, and one of the greatest careers in opera was launched.

During this time of intensive music making, Thomson sometimes complained to his friends that he was losing his touch as a critic. Yet his reviews from the early 1950s were as sharp as ever; for example, this hilarious description of a concert by the New York Philharmonic under the conductor Dimitri Mitropoulos, a musician sympathetic to Thomson's music who in 1950 had conducted the orchestra's first performances of his Symphony no. 2. Here, Thomson complains that Mitropoulos's agitated gestures on the podium during Schumann's *Rhenish* Symphony revealed a "personal excitement, bordering on hysteria."

> Actually, when the conductor, in moments of calm, conducted straightforwardly and with a minimum of motion, his orchestra followed with a maximum of beauty and with the authority of style that is our Philharmonic's way. But for the most part he did everything to the orchestra but conduct it. He whipped it up as if it were a cake, kneaded it like bread, shuffled and riffled an imaginary deck of cards, wound up a clock, shook a recalcitrant umbrella, rubbed something on a washboard and wrung it out. Really, there were very few moments when a film taken of the conductor alone, without sound, would have given any clue to the fact that he was directing a musical composition.[25]

For Thomson, reviewing performances may have become routine, but, clearly, he had not tired of battling managers. In a December 30, 1951, column, he dissected the comments, recently aired in a Metropolitan Opera radio broadcast, of the company's imperious Austrian-born general manager, Rudolf Bing, who had come to the Metropolitan in 1950 by way of the Glyndebourne Opera, in England. In his discursive and tactless remarks, Bing tried to account for the dearth of contemporary opera in the company's repertory. He stated that it was "a regrettable fact that so few new operas of real musical consequence are being offered" today; and that "no one in the world of the theater puts on any show unless he is convinced that it will either be a 'hit success' or at least attract sufficient public acclaim to justify the effort. I cannot see why this sound principle, which is commonly accepted in the theater, should become a criminal offense when applied to opera."

In his blistering point-by-point refutation, Thomson suggested that somebody on the Metropolitan board should "explain to the general manager that the Metropolitan Opera Association is not engaged in show business, that it is a nonprofit society vowed to the advancement of musical art and of public taste," and, as such, is exempted from real estate taxation and the federal amusement tax, and that gifts to the Metropolitan are tax deductible.

> I have long found [Mr. Bing's] program regrettable; and I found his radio speech of two weeks back acceptable only for the frankness of his admissions, shocking as they were. He admitted his lack of faith both in the music of his own time and in the public's aspirations regarding this. . . .
>
> All the same, he plans to take a flyer next season with the new Stravinsky opera. "We shall then see what the public reaction will be," he added. Does this mean that he is giving contemporary music just one chance to compete with *Carmen?* Really, one has heard double-talk before from Metropolitan spokesmen but nothing quite so cynical as this.[26]

The new Stravinsky opera the following season was *The Rake's Progress;* Thomson gave it a glowing review.

In the midst of all his professional hustling, something happened that shook Thomson badly and made him take stock.

Jerome D. Bohm, Thomson's junior colleague at the paper, was arrested and sent to prison. Bohm lived in Manhattan with his homosexual partner, Paul Engel. They also had a country house in Bethel, Connecticut, where they spent free weekends and vacations. At their Connecticut place they frequently entertained teenage boys, who had the run of the house. Keys were left under the doormat; there was always beer in the refrigerator. That spring, however, one of the boys, the son of a town official, was questioned by his doctor during a routine exam about some abrasions around his anus. Under pressure to talk, the boy told of the goings-on at Bohm's house.

Bohm and Engel were arrested, charged, and convicted. None of the story appeared in any New York newspaper. No explanation was given in the *Herald Tribune* for the sudden disappearance of Bohm's columns. The editors knew what had happened; Thomson also knew, but said nothing. Arthur Berger remembers a staffer coming in one day with copies of a paper from Danbury with reports of the scandal. Evidently Bohm had contacted Thomson and asked him to be a character witness at his trial. This Thomson could not do. To refuse pained him, but to testify would have been impossible. Thomson had barely escaped a similar fate. This was the price one paid.

Exactly just what went on in that house was never discovered. Bohm spent two years in Wethersfield prison, in Connecticut. When he returned to New York, he complained bitterly to friends that society had handed him an injustice. He considered going to the writers' guild to fight for reinstatement at the *Herald Tribune,* but realized it would be impossible and agreed to resign. Demoralized, he took a job in the fall of 1954 for $1.25 an hour at Joseph Patelson's, a family-run music store across the street from Carnegie Hall. There he sold scores to performers he had once reviewed.

Bohm's case was a personal tragedy, and Thomson felt powerless to do anything about it. He was a fighter, willing to use his reputation and column for a worthy cause, but only in his chosen field. Opera house impresarios, orchestra managers, and celebrity performers with inflated reputations he was always ready to skewer. But politics he would not touch. In the early 1950s American artists were being called upon to stand up for political freedom. This Thomson refused to do even when it involved his colleague Aaron Copland.

For the inauguration of President Eisenhower on January 20, 1953, the Inaugural Concert Committee had requested that Copland's *A Lincoln Portrait* be performed by the National Symphony with the actor Walter Pidgeon narrating. However, after Congressman Fred E. Busbey, Republican of Illinois, alleged that the composer had associated with Communist front groups, the committee dropped the work from the program two days before the concert. Commenting afterward, Busbey said, "There are many patriotic composers available without the long record of questionable affiliations of Copland. The Republican party would have been ridiculed from one end of the United States to the other if Copland's music had been played at the inaugural of a President elected to fight communism, among other things."[27]

The League of Composers issued an indignant public letter on behalf of the man who had composed *Rodeo, Billy the Kid, Appalachian Spring,* and other works of "pure Americana," urging that the decision be reversed:

> No American composer, living or dead, has done more for American music and the growth of the reputation of American culture throughout the civilized world than Aaron Copland. To bar from the Inaugural Concert his music, and especially a piece about Abraham Lincoln, will be the worst kind of blunder and will hold us up as a nation to universal ridicule.[28]

Copland, who sympathized with liberal causes and had many left-wing friends (Marc Blitzstein, Lillian Hellman), admitted openly, with some humor, to having cast his vote for Adlai Stevenson. But he had never been an official member of any political party. For all his public composure, the charges stunned him. "I can not for the life of me see why the cause of the free countries of the world will be advanced by the banning of my works," he said in a statement to the press. Music critics rushed to print in his defense: Howard Taubman in the *New York Times;* Paul Hume in the *Washington Post*. The historian Bruce Catton in a long piece for the the *Nation* sarcastically commented that at least the assembled Republican politicians at the concert will be saved from hearing Lincoln's brooding words: "Fellow Citizens, we cannot escape history. We of this Congress and this Administration will be remembered in spite of ourselves."

Everyone in the cultural community was waiting for Virgil Thomson's strong voice. But publicly he was silent. His social attitudes were essentially conservative. Just the year before he had castigated the Parisian orchestral musicians who were disrespectful during rehearsals of *Four Saints* as a bunch of "commies." Asked about the Copland incident by his editors at the *Herald Tribune,* he advised them to leave the story alone, which, as a Republican paper, they were disposed to do anyway. In private, Thomson's advice to Copland's friends and supporters was to let the incident pass. To the composer Ernst Bacon, who was still advocating some organized protest four weeks after the concert occurred, Thomson wrote,

> . . . I thought that publicizing the incident might be more disad-
> vantageous to him than protesting about it. It all happened so
> quickly that no practical advantage could be derived from offer-
> ing more support to the conductor who had chosen to program
> the piece. Roy Harris has been having similar troubles in Pittsburgh
> all winter, and I have not publicized them either. If this sort of thing
> diminishes, my policy will have been proved to be the right one.
> If it increases, then we must all get together and do something ef-
> fective. We might even, if necessary, boycott the organizations
> guilty of discrimination. I do not think individual action is ever very
> effective and I know that agitational or editorial protest can be a
> two-edged weapon.[29]

This "sort of thing" did not diminish. In May, Copland was called to testify in a closed hearing before Senator Joseph McCarthy's intimidating subcommittee. Ten years after this event, with President

Kennedy in the White House, Copland conducted the National Symphony on the West Lawn in a Fourth of July concert that included his own works. What the events of 1953 had made clear, however, was that Virgil Thomson, the scrappy critic, picked his battles judiciously.

Perhaps the events of early 1953 rattled Thomson more than he admitted, for by the summer he decided the time had come to leave the *Herald Tribune*. More performances of his work than ever before were taking place. That May his ballet *Filling Station* was successfully revived by the New York City Ballet with its new male star, Jacques d'Amboise, as Mac, the station attendant. Invitations to conduct kept coming in. If he were free of the critic's job, surely he would be able to accept and generate more. To the owners of the *Herald Tribune,* and to his mentor Geoffrey Parsons, the idea that Thomson "would relinquish a post so little demanding, so honorific, and so powerful was unbelievable."[30] But he told them he planned to resign that fall. Only the announcement by Arthur Berger that he had been offered a professorship at Brandeis University, a position Thomson advised him to accept, delayed Thomson's plans. He did not wish to saddle the paper with two simultaneous vacancies. Thomson agreed to put off his departure until the following fall.

Given the events of April 1954, Thomson would have been wise to question his plans to earn a living from conducting. That spring he went to Europe for an international music festival organized by the Russian-born composer Nicolas Nabokov. Prior to the formal festival events in Rome, Thomson conducted an all-American program with an orchestra in Barcelona at the Gran Teatro del Liceo. The program, which he introduced to the audience with comments in Spanish, was a demanding one: Barber's *School for Scandal* Overture, his own Cello Concerto, *Three Pictures for Orchestra,* and *Louisiana Story,* and Copland's *Appalachian Spring.* It proved to be beyond his abilities, given the constraints of the rehearsal schedule. The reviews were enthusiastic, but the experience was unsettling. That summer, Thomson kept conducting the Copland work, along with his own Cello Concerto, on programs in Paris and Vienna. When the Copland performance continued to go awry, he blamed the piece. "The orch. boys all crazy about the concerto," he wrote to Maurice Grosser. "Everybody hates Appalachian Spring—some very pretty material in it but a choppy piece and quite unnecessarily difficult."[31] Nevertheless, Copland, who wanted to do more podium work himself, was impressed by Thomson's burgeoning new career: "Pleased as punch at your various conducting activities. Make a nice wide swath thru which we can all travel after you!"[32]

Only once during Thomson's fourteen-year tenure as the *Herald Tribune*'s chief music critic was one of his articles held back from publication: a Sunday piece discussing the treatment of the paying public by the performing institutions in New York. Town Hall, Carnegie Hall, and the Metropolitan Opera were praised for the efficiency and courtesy of their house staff. The City Center of Music and Drama was faulted for its treatment of visiting artists. ("Backstage it is full, like City Hall, of political appointees who hate their work and never smile.") As a concert venue the Museum of Modern Art was slapped hard. ("[T]he museum has lots of valuable property around, but that does not . . . justify treating every patron as a thief.") In "planned rudeness," he concluded, Radio City "yields to no institution." Mrs. Reid, whose wealthy lady friends served on the boards of several of these institutions, protested. The article was pulled.

Otherwise, he took on concert managers, star performers, even, in one piece about a papal encyclical on the use of music in religious services, the Vatican. But the time had come for a "cessation of hostilities." Thomson reaffirmed his decision to leave and told his editors that he should have no say in picking his successor. He soon changed his mind and recommended Paul Bowles, then living in Morocco. But the decision had already been made. Having supported an upstart practitioner with an insider's point of view, Parsons thought it would be healthy to have someone completely different in temperament and outlook. Thomson's replacement would be the sober, erudite, Budapest-born music historian from Columbia University, Paul Henry Lang, the author of the scholarly 1,043-page *Music in Western Civilization*. In a *Time* magazine article about the the changing of the guard at the *Trib*, a friend of Professor Lang's was quoted as saying, "He thinks music ceased to exist at the death of Schubert."[33]

During the search for his replacement, Thomson was approached by one of the younger composer-critics he had hired as a stringer in 1948, Peggy Glanville-Hicks, an Australian, recently become a U.S. citizen, and the only woman music critic then working for a major paper in New York. Glanville-Hicks believed that "all the world was out to crush women composers," Thomson later wrote. That her belief was justified can be deduced from Thomson's affectionate yet rather patronizing account of her tireless musical activism.

She wrote for the *Herald Tribune* and for magazines; she copied music; she managed concerts; she ran everybody's errands; she went on lecture tours by bus in the Dakotas; she composed documentary films for UNICEF; she made musicological trips to India for the Rockefeller Foundation; she saw other people's music . . . through the perils of recording. She made her own clothes and dressed charmingly. . . . She wrote a great deal of music, got it published and recorded, grew as a composer from modest beginnings . . . into an opera writer of marked originality. . . .[34]

Seeing male conspiracies in every corner, "she complained, she stormed, she telephoned." Yet for Thomson she was an indispensable colleague.

One day in that spring of 1954, when the search for a new chief critic was under way, Glanville-Hicks approached Thomson at the office to put herself forth as a candidate. If she was to have any chance of replacing him, given the conservative male editorial board, she would need his strong support. She spoke of her musical philosophy, of her work, which was strong, and of the fresh perspective she might bring to the post. Rather as a joke, she added that being the chief critic of so influential a paper would no doubt be a boon to her own career as a composer. Thomson grinned, looked her in the eye, and said, "Baby! I've sucked that lemon dry."

23 ROGER

Leaving the *New York Herald Tribune* was a risky decision for Virgil Thomson. Influence, money, the allegiance of renowned performers, invitations to lecture and conduct—all this had come as he accumulated power in this visible post. But his self-confidence was due in part to a new person in his life, Roger Baker, a painter twenty-nine years his junior.

Roger Baker was born in Troy, West Virginia, a rural town of fewer than two hundred people on a tributary of the Ohio River. Roger came from settler stock. His father, Harry Claybourne Baker, was a schoolteacher, later an engineer. Harry was mystified by his dreamy oldest child's passion for drawing. He considered it a stage that Roger would grow out of. When Roger entered the Army Air Force Cadets in 1943, his father assumed that wartime military life would put an end to his interest in art. Before being sent to England, Roger was injured in a plane accident and reassigned first to India and then China, where he managed a billeting quarters for overseas officers. This experience far from the front lines only enhanced his feeling for the exotic and the artistic.

After the war, thanks to the GI Bill, Roger attended Ohio State in Columbus, where his parents had moved. There he felt out of place. His war experience in Asia was unlike that of the other ex-GI students, and he felt little in common with the adolescents who had come directly from high school. Impatient to get through with his education, he took a double load of courses and graduated in two years, majoring in art history, since there were no qualified teachers of applied art at the school. Roger was largely a self-trained painter.

At twenty-three Roger had his first one-man show, at the Butler Institute of Art in Youngstown. After college he traveled through North Africa, England, and France, taking art classes in Paris. In 1950, at the Galerie Jean Robert, he had his first Paris show, reviewed favorably in *Le Monde* and *Le Figaro*. His paintings were representational, a throwback in style; yet they were vibrant, richly textured, and somewhat ominous. Jean Genet came and complimented him profusely.

Eventually he returned to the States, intent on becoming a New York artist. Notwithstanding his success abroad, in New York Roger felt like some awe-struck youth, and his looks—he was short, trim, boyishly handsome with sandy hair and sad blue eyes—just enhanced the sense of innocence he projected. People instinctively wanted to father him, to listen to his troubles. And Roger had a gift for befriending people, especially older well-established men, who could help him.

Through a dancer he had met in Europe, Roger fell in with the New York City Ballet crowd, eventually becoming friendly with Brooks Jackson, a dancer with Balanchine, and Pavel Tchelitcheff, Virgil's old Paris friend, who was doing successful stage designs. Roger took odd jobs, worked as an usher at the City Center, did silk screen press work for Lincoln Kirstein. He found a loft on West Forty-seventh Street just off Fifth Avenue, in the midtown diamond district. On opening night of the ballet in the fall of 1951, Roger attended a postperformance party. Among the guests was W. H. Auden. Roger introduced himself to the great man, who was enchanted by this attentive young painter. The next day, while Roger was working in his studio, there was a knock at the door. It was Auden. "I was in the neighborhood," Auden said. "I thought you might give me some coffee. I'd like to see your paintings." Roger had that kind of effect on people.

In January of 1953 Roger gave a party at his studio for his friends the gregarious duo-pianists Arthur Gold and Robert Fizdale, who were in the midst of a concert tour. Another friend, the singer Alice Esty, who could not come, sent a case of Dom Pérignon, which Roger put in the bathtub with ice. Roger had been circulating very effectively among the established New York artists, of whom the most active networkers were gay men. The attendees at the party that night, either invited by Roger or brought along by his guests, included Barber, Menotti, Copland, the young conductor Thomas Schippers, Tennessee Williams, and Virgil Thomson, whom Roger had never met. However, assured by mutual friends that Virgil would enjoy coming, Roger had called him.

Roger was then twenty-eight; Virgil, fifty-seven. As in the old days with Briggs, Virgil sensed immediately that this attractive young man needed a mentor. Other artistic luminaries had counseled and courted Roger. But that night Virgil took over. Roger was astonished by Virgil's knowledge of art, not just of styles and techniques, but of patronage, marketing, and distribution. Virgil seemed to have a repository of names from the art world: artists for Roger to contact, and gallery dealers Virgil promised to speak to on Roger's behalf. Virgil was overwhelming in both senses of the word: a font of brilliance and an engulfing presence. But Roger was willing to be engulfed. And if Virgil dominated the relationship intellectually and psychologically, Roger had qualities that Virgil yearned for: youth, beauty, and promise.

Not long after meeting him, Virgil flattered Roger by asking him for important advice. One night he told Roger, "You know, I'm bored to death with writing criticism. I'm tempted to leave. What do you think?" Most of Virgil's other friends had told him he'd be crazy to quit. Not Roger. "Virgil, you set out to be a composer. You have enough money. You're entirely capable of making a living. For God's sake, yes! Leave!" Roger's encouragement proved decisive.

That spring of 1953 Roger was awarded a Guggenheim Fellowship. According to Baker, Auden had urged him to apply and offered to write a letter of support. But the only letters in the Baker file at the Guggenheim Foundation are from Basil Petrov of the Knoedler Gallery, the painter Leonid Berman, and the composer Alexei Haieff. However, this list and Roger's work were clearly distinguished enough to win him a fellowship, then seldom given to artists so young.

To Roger the award of $3,500 seemed a windfall. It meant that he could accompany Virgil on trips, since travel had been part of his proposal. So they went to Paris, where, for discretion's sake, Virgil stayed in his flat, while Roger stayed with an eminent friend he had met through Copland, the baron Henri-Louis de la Grange, who later wrote a massive biography of Mahler. During the spring and summer of 1954, while Virgil conducted in Barcelona and participated in Nicolas Nabokov's Rome festival, Roger came along. Virgil sent back chatty reports to Maurice, who was vacationing in Greece. "I'm enjoying the outside of Rome, haven't looked inside the churches or museums, though Roger has been chasing Caravaggios. Food & wine fair, fresh peas wonderful."[1]

Long months together and daily exposure to Roger's slack work habits eventually took a toll on Virgil's patience. In July, writing to Maurice with news of Paris, Virgil sounded relieved to have settled Roger into his own place for a while. "Six months is a lot of Europe these days. R. moves today to his old rooming house. He seems to have started painting finally. In August we will be in Austria, at Kitzbühel, then Venice for my flute piece. . . ."[2]

Still, overall Virgil was proud to be traveling with an impressionable and handsome young man. And Maurice, far from being jealous, was delighted for his friend of over thirty years. Maurice had a highly charged libido and had always found young men of his own, especially young black men, including a couple of dancers from the cast of *The Mother of Us All*. Maurice talked blithely of his sexual escapades. In a letter from Morocco he reported to Virgil about the ready availability of "tail" (young men for hire) in Tangier.

> There are two beaches, one on the Mediterranean just below the town, fine sand and no surf, and the other about ten kilometers away, on the Atlantic with surf which extends I believe to the Cape of Good Hope. It is fairly deserted and one can do nude bathing, if you wish. The other is full of people and bathing establishments and is where the boys go. The tail is easy, good-natured and very pleasant and costs 50 to 160 pesatas, though one is supposed to be able to get away with 35. I confess that I have not done much of it.[3]

Once Roger entered the picture, Maurice inevitably ended his letters to Virgil with "Much love to you both."

The "flute piece" Virgil referred to was the Concerto for Flute, Strings, Harp, and Percussion, a seventeen-minute work that is the longest by far of the Thomson musical portraits. For some years after its composition, Virgil kept its subject secret. He later admitted that the subject was Roger.

The piece was composed over several days in June of 1954 in Acapulco. Virgil and Roger were the guests of the composer Carlos Chávez, whose house in the shadows of the Sierra Madre del Sur overlooked the Pacific Ocean. They stayed in a room with bunk beds. When they weren't sharing one, Roger slept up top, while Virgil, from below, "sketched" his lover's portrait. Roger was not consciously posing, but Virgil knew that this extensive piece was a musical portrait. The orchestration was worked out later that summer in time for a September premiere in Venice with the flutist Elaine Shaffer and the Orchestra del Teatro La Fenice.

Thomson kept other winds and brass out of the orchestration so as to "make the solo part sound prominent and beautiful." The first movement is for solo flute, a two-minute cadenza by turns ruminative and fitful, marked *rapsodico*. The slow second movement is among Thomson's most harmonically complex works, with parallel layers of chromatic harmonies in muted strings over which a flighty solo flute line hovers and twitters like an exotic bird. The propulsive third movement, with its fractured dance rhythms, is intense and unsettled, yet strangely engaging—all qualities that could be ascribed to its twenty-nine-year-old subject.

Back in the States that fall, Roger had his first one-man show in New York. Stuart Preston from the *Times* wrote an encouraging review:

> Roger Baker, a young painter of pronounced romantic tendencies, is making a debut at the Karnig Gallery with some figures and landscapes whose picturesque mood is deeply dyed with attractive desperation.
>
> It is easy enough, and only natural, to detect influences here: Berman, Bérard, and even Stuempfig. But the artist's personality is not submerged by his artistic godparents and he has a seductive way with oil paint that should do him good service once he comes into his own.[4]

During this same period Virgil's career faltered. To no one's surprise but his own, performances of his works by top-name artists and orchestras dropped off after he left the *Herald Tribune,* and invitations to conduct declined. He grew increasingly dependent on speaking engagements, and even then had to accept some modest forums: the Asolo Theater in Sarasota, the Midwest Music Conference in Ann Arbor. The main professional event of 1955 was a trip through South America as part of the State Department's International Educational Exchange program. Virgil's baggage, loaded down with scores and recordings of his works that he hoped to distribute to interested musicians, was one hundred pounds beyond the weight stipulated by the State Department. On the tour he conducted his flute concerto, attended concerts of South American composers, and lectured in Spanish and English on various topics: "The Music Reviewer and His

Assignment," "Memoirs of a Music Critic," "The State of Music Today," and "Words and Music." Before departing, Virgil had written to the Brazilian pianist Guiomar Novaës, an artist not known for her interest in American music, hoping to arrange a meeting. It had been a long time since Virgil Thomson had had to lobby a performer so solicitously.

The nadir of 1956, the year Thomson turned sixty, was the New York premiere on April 19 of his Concerto for Flute, Strings, Harp, and Percussion, as the work was formally called. The orchestra was the New York Philharmonic; the conductor, Dimitri Mitropoulos, still well disposed to Thomson despite his having been the occasional recipient of some cutting Virgilian criticism. The reviews of the flutist John Wummer were splendid. But Thomson's music fared poorly. In the very space that Thomson's *Herald Tribune* column once occupied, his successor, Paul Henry Lang, dismissed the work.

> Mr. Thomson's flute concerto completely baffled me. It surely is an unusual specimen of this venerable genre, for it begins with the cadenza—the flute playing all by itself. Upon reading the program notes I discovered that the cadenza was actually the first movement; well, I stick to my own impressions.
>
> The second movement I found quite monotonous with its contrived harmonic scheme, while the third, full of rather aimless runs and whatnots, struck me as mortally fatigued music. In a word, this is not one of Mr. Thomson's good pieces.
>
> Mr. Wummer, a distinguished artist, played with his wonted skill and beautiful flute tone. He had my sincere admiration for remembering his part.[5]

Lang's style was pedestrian, and he evinced little sympathy with or understanding of the work. But the review stung.

The most steady and well-paid work of these years came from the theater. John Houseman had become artistic director of the American Shakespeare Festival, a summer festival in Stratford, Connecticut. Houseman hired the friend who had given him his start in the theater to write incidental music for *King John* and *Measure for Measure* in 1956 and, in 1957, *Othello, The Merchant of Venice* with Katharine Hepburn as Portia, and *Much Ado About Nothing* with Hepburn and the dashing Alfred Drake. Brooks Atkinson in the *Times* called Thomson's *Much Ado* music a "beguiling score that begins with some Lone Ranger music and includes dainty madrigals, sweet dance music and an enchanting overture to a wedding."[6]

But if the test of professional success is income, a criterion the author of "Who Does What to Whom and Who Gets Paid" would certainly endorse, Thomson's immediate post-*Tribune* career was a failure. In 1954, his last year at the paper, Thomson's pretax income was close to $30,000, a princely sum for the time. In 1955 he earned half that amount; after deducting meticulously recorded expenses, he declared a net loss of $583.83; 1956 was comparable, with a net loss of $489.48; in 1957, with $2,450.00 from the American Shakespeare Festival and over $8,000 of royalties from ASCAP, Thomson earned over $27,000 but reported a net income of only $9,616.04, a considerable drop from the *Tribune* days, but a living wage, all of it earned from professional activities as a musician. It was not until 1959, when some investment decisions made with the advice of a friend from the Bank of New York (including stock in AT&T, American Tobacco Company, Du Pont, Standard Oil, US Steel) started earning him dividends, that Thomson's financial situation turned around. For the rest of his life, those stocks continued to provide dependable income.

During that winter of 1957, Virgil kept his financial setbacks and career frustrations from his mother, who was ninety-two and not well. Clara May Thomson had never really understood her only son and his artist friends. She had wanted a grandson to carry on the Thomson name, but knew that some men were just not the marrying kind. She was saddened that Virgil never took to religion, but proud of his success and renown. Virgil let nothing shake her confidence in his achievements.

Every winter May Thomson went to Pittsburgh, where her daughter, Ruby, lived with her husband, Roy Gleason. Come spring, she always went home to Kansas City. But this winter, when she took ill in Pittsburgh, Virgil went to see her.

> "I hadn't planned it this way," was her apology. "I shan't get over this one. But that's all right. I've had a good life." Since I was to conduct shortly in Berlin, at the opening of the Kongresshalle, my sister wondered whether I should go. "Of course I must; Mother would think it foolish of me not to. And surely I can count on her for the tact not to die while I'm away." So I went to Berlin and came back. And then she did die, murmuring, "Open the door." And we took her to Missouri. And I went back to Europe for another engagement.[7]

This account from Thomson's autobiography skirts the facts. For May Thomson, ill as she was, did return that early spring to Kansas

City, where she died on April 6. Virgil was back in the country, but not at his mother's side. She was comfortable and cared for at home, and there was no telling how long she might linger. Virgil returned to Missouri to see his mother laid to rest beside her industrious, God-fearing husband in the hilltop Baptist cemetery in Slater, the rural town her grandfather Reuben McDaniel had prospered in.

In recent years, May's regular visits to New York had been difficult for her son. But this birdlike woman, "barely five feet, though plump," had been a formidable influence. "She never raised her voice. But in her gentle way she was a driver. She saw no reason for accepting in oneself, unless God forced it, any remediable imperfection such as ignorance, poor health, or a lack of manners."[8] Virgil had at least one imperfection that for all he knew was "forced by God" and was certainly unremediable. But he had managed to keep it from his mother.

By the summer the combined effects of financial stress, career uncertainty, and personal loss undermined Virgil's tolerance for Roger's chronic confusions and relationships with other men. Still, Virgil's friends were surprised to hear him starting to complain about Roger's superficiality and dependency. "All would be fine except that I miss you terribly and don't understand why I've not had a word from you," Roger wrote to Virgil while on a study trip to Italy in the summer of 1956. "This upsets me and leaves me at a loss."[9] Virgil was a pudgy, pugnacious sexagenarian. Roger was a dashing, star-struck still-young man. Perhaps Virgil was secretly embarrassed by the relationship, or too distressed by his shaky career to keep it going, or afraid that sooner or later Roger was sure to reject him. To his friends, Virgil was never very clear about the source of his dissatisfaction. But by 1957 he was dissatisfied.

The breakup was precipitated by a curious event from Roger's past.

When Roger was in China during the war, in Hangchou, an exquisite village two hundred kilometers southwest of Shanghai, one misty afternoon he climbed through a bamboo grove to the Temple of the Sacred Fish. Suddenly, a presence spoke to him, a voice not his own, but within him. He was overcome by a sense of profound peace. The voice explained that everything is part of everything, a rock, a tree, a river, and that he too must complete his cycle. Roger asked the voice some questions: May I stay in this place? No, the voice answered. You must go back. Will I live to see 2000? Yes. What will

I die of? Heart disease, the voice answered, unfazed by the question's specificity. Roger felt as if all the pain he was going to feel in his whole life welled up within him. It was unbearable and unforgettable. But he told no one about it.

Some thirteen years later, while staying in Venice in July 1957, Roger was introduced to a handsome young painter from a wealthy Pennsylvania family named Alba Haywood III. They made an appointment to see some Carpaccio paintings in Venice the next day. When the time came, Roger, who arrived thirty minutes late, made up some excuse for his tardiness. Alba said, "No, that's not what you did." Alba seemed to know exactly how Roger had spent every minute of the morning. Alba insisted that Roger ride with him to Rome, where he was going to meet the painter Pavel Tchelitcheff, who had been friendly with them both.

On the train, just below Florence, at dusk, alone together in a compartment, Alba's face went white. "Roger," he said, "listen carefully. Once you were climbing a mountain in China." Stunned, Roger immediately knew what Alba was going to say. In exact detail he described what had happened to Roger that day at the Temple of the Sacred Fish. As they traveled on, Alba recited prayers Roger had been taught as a child, told stories of Roger's family. It was terrifying and exhilarating. That night they joined Tchelitcheff for dinner in the town of Frascati. Going back on the bus to Rome, Alba broke down and sobbed. "Pavlik will be dead within a month," he said. Two weeks later, on July 31, Pavlik had a heart attack, his first, and died.

Roger was entranced by Alba, but was afraid to tell anyone about what had happened. Later that summer Virgil visited him in Venice. Unable to keep his feelings to himself, Roger spilled out everything to Virgil. Hearing this "utter nonsense," Virgil was derisive and hostile. That fall, when Roger returned to New York, Virgil went to Roger's apartment for dinner. Virgil was calm, friendly, but not at all affectionate. After dinner with no explanation, Virgil said, "I don't want to see you any more." Roger was upset by the rejection, but far more crushed by the brutality of Virgil's manner. He left, and Roger cried all night.

In Venice that summer, Roger had been told by his friend Tanaquil LeClercq, the prima ballerina and, at the time, the fourth wife of George Balanchine, of a new vaccination for polio. Everyone in the company had had the vaccination but LeClercq. Three weeks later this magnificently beautiful dancer was in an iron lung, struck down by polio. That fall in New York, Roger decided he should be vaccinated. Auden suggested that he go to the office of a young doctor friend who had just completed his residency and started a private practice. Soon after receiving the vaccinations, Roger was taken ill: he was bedridden and paralyzed. It turned out that the doctor had used a contaminated vaccine from the Cutter Laboratories. Tens of thousands of people were mistakenly given this compromised virus. Many of them came down with some form of polio. The doctor later destroyed his records and died in a fire while drunk. Eventually Roger recovered, but nerves in Roger's legs had been permanently damaged. By 1970 he would need a cane to walk.

When Virgil heard of Roger's illness, he deliberated, then phoned him to express concern. He did not apologize; but he did ask, sheepishly, "Would you like to come back?" It was too late. Roger said no, and never doubted his decision. He did not even want Virgil's friendship. "Virgil was terrible around sick people" Roger later explained; "he was useless."

For years they did not see each other. Roger's career prospered, relative to that of other struggling New York painters. In 1958 he was given a Louis Comfort Tiffany Award; the following year, at the request of Auden, he designed decors for a production in Spoleto of Auden's play *Dark Valley*. His paintings and drawings were presented in one-man shows at the Hazlitt Gallery in London (1960) and the Seiferheld Gallery in New York (1962). For years he and Virgil did not speak to each other. But the hostility cooled, for in 1970 Virgil wrote on Roger's behalf to the Ingram Merrill Foundation.

> I have known Mr. Baker and his paintings for some fifteen years. He is an authentic artist, a slow producer, but a steady one. His draftsmanship is remarkable and his color both delicate and stable.
>
>   At this time a health emergency which does not interfere with his working but which involves some expense, makes it appropriate, I think, for a foundation to come to his aid.[10]

Roger drifted from relationship to relationship. In 1972 he met "the great love" of his life, Phyllis Olivieri, born Phyllis Goodhew Konta in Boston, a painter, sculptor, and a poet who had studied with Auden. Phyllis, who looked like the young Vivian Leigh, even in her fifties, married into an immigrant family that had prospered in politics. Her son, Anthony Olivieri, was a Manhattan assemblyman and a firebrand liberal who was being talked of for statewide office, but he died of a brain tumor at thirty-nine. When Phyllis died in December 1979, after two years of illness, Roger was devastated. He started drinking heavily. Confronted by an actor friend on June 22, 1982 ("my re-birthday"), Roger entered Greymore, a clinic run by the Franciscans, for a three-week recuperation. After that he spent a month in a veterans hospital. Released from the hospital, he was jobless and homeless. Step by step, through all twelve steps of Alcoholics Anonymous ("a very good way to live"), he rebuilt his life. During the 1980s he and Virgil visited each other, not often, but amicably.

In the early 1950s Virgil Thomson felt that his position within the matrix of American music needed a boost. His biggest detractors were the academics. Getting a book written about himself, a comprehensive life-and-works biography, would confer substance and scholarly prestige on his career. To get his book, Thomson turned to John Cage.

In 1949 Thomson's collegial relationship with Cage was at its peak. Though in later years he talked dismissively of Thomson's music, in the late 1940s Cage wrote to Thomson with seemingly genuine enthusiasm about his work. And he always found Thomson an engaging conversationalist. "Anyone who enjoys ideas, language, as I did, enjoyed being with Virgil," he later recalled. "So many cooks have only a few recipes. Virgil had countless. With Virgil you never thought of saying, 'Oh, you *would* say that!' He always surprised you."[11]

Cage loved the way Thomson talked with command even when he did not know what he was talking about. One day while Cage was visiting, Thomson got a call from an Englishman in New York who had been urged to call Thomson by a mutual friend, so he claimed. The caller, whom Thomson had never heard of, wanted a letter of introduction to a composer Thomson knew on the West Coast. "I can't write a letter of introduction for someone I've never met," Thomson said, testily. The Englishman explained that he could not come in person that day, he was sorry to say, because he was at that moment on his way to Berkeley, California, which he pronounced, "Bark-ley." Thomson corrected him pointedly: "You mean, Berkeley!" (Pronounced "Berk-lee.") The caller said, "Well, in England we say 'Barkley.'" Thomson shot back, "Not in the eighteenth century you didn't!" Completely flustered, the caller apologized and ended the call. Upon hearing the whole story, Cage asked, "How did you know how

Berkeley was pronounced in eighteenth century England?" "I didn't," answered Thomson. "But I knew he didn't either."

As a critic Thomson had given Cage consistent support. In 1949, thanks largely to Thomson's strong recommendations, Cage received an award from the National Institute of Arts and Letters and a Guggenheim Fellowship. No sooner had the awards been announced than Thomson told Cage that he wanted a book written about himself and he wanted Cage to write it.

> He put the two together. I was made to know that I was indebted, and I was asked to do this for him. I could only say yes. And so I said yes. I don't mean to say that I was unhappy to say yes or that he forced me. He simply made a circumstance in which I could not have acted differently.[12]

Cage plunged into the project with "willingness and heart." He interviewed Thomson at length, asking precise and rather peculiar questions about his life. Not about his private affairs, but about, for example, the way his mother kept house in Kansas City. Was she as meticulous as Thomson? Did she back then, like her son today, surround herself with fine objects? When he finished the first three chapters, he read them aloud to Thomson and Maurice Grosser. Cage was attempting to relate the style and character of Thomson's music to the specific events or household customs of his childhood and youth. Thomson was amused. He was flattered by having a theory proposed, even a far-out one, about the sources of his creativity. But Grosser felt the writing and approach trivialized Thomson. Cage must stop at once. Thomson was persuaded. Cage's analyses were provocative, but the attitude that came through was "definitely unfriendly," Thomson said. And so the whole project was dropped.

What Cage later learned was that, prior to his discussion with Thomson about the biography, Thomson had been approached, quite independently, by a matronly woman author, Mrs. Kathleen O'Donnell Hoover, who also proposed to write a biography of him. Hoover was from a prominent family of journalists and authors. She had attended piano classes given by Leschetizky in Vienna, and studied at the Sorbonne. But shortly after that she gave up performing and turned to music history, which she studied with Paul Henry Lang at Columbia. In 1948 H. Bittner and Company brought out Hoover's book *Makers of Opera,* a collection of essays about eighteen major opera composers, from Jacopo Peri to Richard Strauss. Although her essays uncovered no new territory, they were reputable and written with her well-bred prose; the book was handsomely designed and illustrated. Hoover had underwritten the entire venture with her own money. She now proposed to underwrite her biography of Thomson.

Thomson was delighted with Hoover's interest and ready funding. Figuring that controlling her would be relatively easy, he sanctioned the proposal with the proviso that she hire at her own expense a musician approved by Thomson to "assist" with the discussion of his works. Though wary of the suggestion and unhappy about the added expense, Hoover agreed. In the spring of 1949 she sent out letters of inquiry to Thomson's friends and colleagues asking for memorabilia and letters, which she promised to have copied and returned.

Collecting the documents and researching the story of Thomson's life consumed Mrs. Hoover's time. The search for a musician to analyze Thomson's works was left to Thomson, who first approached Otto Luening. Though fearful of alienating his powerful colleague, then still at the *Herald Tribune,* with a refusal, Luening demurred. He did not see how he could write an objective evaluation of the music with Thomson standing over his shoulder. In 1955 Thomson approached Cage again, asking him to resume the project, this time defined as primarily a study of the works, not a full-fledged biography. Cage agreed on condition that Thomson not read the manuscript until it was completed. Thomson went along, believing that, if need be, he could bully Cage into making any changes he wanted.

Once again, Cage interviewed Thomson. Once again, Cage completed a manuscript and sought Thomson's approval of it. That text, comprising 167 carefully typed, double-spaced, footnoted pages, dated March 1956, was mailed to Thomson from Stony Point in Rockland County, New York, a sleepy town on the west bank of the Hudson, where Cage was living. When they later met at the Chelsea to discuss the manuscript, Cage was suffering from a severe case of poison ivy. He was weak and irritable, his skin was swollen, itchy, and covered with a pasty medicinal ointment. Overall, Thomson was pleased with the manuscript. Cage had analyzed every scrap of Thomson's music, from his shortest musical portrait to the two full-length Stein operas. Of course, Thomson added matter-of-factly, the manuscript would have to be completely changed.

For one thing, the analysis of musical politics in New York City during the late twenties and thirties would have to be removed. Taking his account directly from conversations with Thomson, Cage depicted the scene as "virtually musically determined" by Aaron Copland, who used his position as de facto head of the League of Composers to "kill-off" the competing American Composers Guild, "the Jewish question having been raised against the Copland organization in a city where it is suicide so to further one's interests." Cage's account contained other incendiary charges, which no doubt came from Thomson, but could not judiciously be publicized.

> Realizing that the musical world was generally "sewed-up," Virgil Thomson looked about for places where it wasn't, finding first Opera, then Film, then Ballet. After each one of his successes in these freer fields than that of the concert halls, Aaron Copland made similar departures, writing *The Hurricane, The City,* and *Billy the Kid.* He was not willing, however, day after day to follow Thomson into a newspaper office. . . . For nearly one quarter of a century, composers promising serious competition to Copland's position of power in New York City either left town of their own accord or indirectly received honorable positions in distant places.[13]

Cage had compounded the problem by adding in a footnote that Thomson's take on musical politics was not shared by the author and should be taken with a "grain of salt."

Moreover, in his text, which was supposed to be an examination of the works, Cage had dealt with aspects of Thomson's life. These would have to be removed, Thomson said, because another writer was covering the biographical side of the story. Cage later claimed that he knew nothing of Hoover's participation in this project until that day in the spring of 1956 when he arrived at the Chelsea to discuss his completed manuscript. Apparently, Thomson was keeping both prongs of this project hot, hoping that at least one of them would ignite. That this was always his strategy is clear from a letter he wrote to Alice Smith, his Mormon friend from junior college days in Kansas City. In 1949, seeking information on Thomson's youth, Mrs. Hoover had written to Alice asking for recollections. Not knowing whether to cooperate, Alice wrote to Virgil for guidance. Virgil wrote back, basically endorsing Mrs. Hoover's project.

> My only reserves about Mrs. Hoover come from the fact that she is older than I and I don't really know her well. Also that she is a very slow worker, not in good health, and may take years to get through the chore. If she shows signs of getting on with the book,

I shall give her everything. If not I shall withhold material and give
it to someone else, since there are several similar projects in the
air. . . .[14]

Actually, Hoover was only one year older than Thomson and
would remain active until her death in 1977. But for the time being,
Thomson was caught between the two authors he had played against
each other. Cage was outraged, but at this point there was nothing to
do except agree to work with Hoover. However, when they met they
immediately disliked each other. Cage thought Hoover an "old biddy."
She thought Cage acted more like some backwoods character than a
composer and author. Cage thought Hoover was snippy and rarefied;
Hoover thought Cage was weird and arrogant. Moreover, she was convinced that Cage didn't really like Thomson's music, that he despised
it. She pleaded with Thomson to approach Luening again. She contacted the Columbia University musicologist William J. Mitchell, who
expressed interest but said he was too busy. No, the book would be
coauthored, Thomson insisted; but it would be divided into two sections: Hoover's account of Thomson's life, and Cage's discussion of
the music.

The project, with attendant bad will and turmoil, lurched through
the next three years. That Thomson had his controlling hands over
every aspect of this work is clear from an urgent letter Hoover sent
him on May 27, 1955.

> Dear Virgil,
>   It is very important to me that you see and correct the three en-
> closures before you take off for South America.
> *No. 1* is my estimate of you as a critic, minus my quotes from your
> reviews. You said you wanted to develop my point that you
> viewed NY of the forties as a prolongation of Paris of the twen-
> ties. There is nothing about this in the Hudson Review article about
> you, so let me know how you want it developed, or rather please
> develop it!
> *No. 2* is my paragraph about your theatre music, which you haven't
> yet seen.
> *No. 3* discusses your landscape pieces, your Blake Songs, your con-
> ducting, and your withdrawal from criticism. . . .
>   All your corrections in the earlier part of this chapter, dealing
> with *Four Saints, Mother,* etc., have been wonderfully helpful.[15]

Thomson coerced Cage into making countless and constant
changes in his text. Cage was humiliated, but still afraid to alienate

his powerful protector. Writing from Stony Point, Cage talks of having spoken with Hoover about making major cuts in his portion of the book, which, he adds, "will be beneficial." He concludes the letter with a plea for work: "My financial situation is again approaching zero. If you hear of any jobs (my attitude towards writing is somewhat different than it used to be) on magazines or newspapers, would you think of me. I could also write music now and then! Very devotedly, John."[16] By that summertime Virgil, in Paris, is reporting to Maurice, "The Cage book still hanging fire. I expect it will be abandoned, which is a pity, because it is very good. But he is neurotic about editorial changes, even small linguistic ones. And Mrs. Hoover hates him. . . ."[17]

Thomson's changes were seldom just "editorial" or "linguistic." Cage's equivocal statements were emboldened by Thomson. Peculiarly recounted anecdotes from Thomson's life that Cage thought relevant to Thomson's music were cut out entirely—for example, this incident from 1928, which reflects on Thomson's studies with Nadia Boulanger:

> It was also at Thonon-les-bains that Virgil Thomson, in a hotel room, lying on a down quilt he had placed on the floor for sun bath purposes, received the revelation that "Music makes no sense." He had, of course, been preparing himself for such a revelation in all his previous work. For, if one can break the rules given by a strict teacher and receive, nevertheless, the teacher's congratulations, obviously music makes no sense.[18]

By the summer of 1957 an edited version of Cage's manuscript was finished. Cage's discussion of the works still dwarfed Hoover's account of the life, but Cage refused to alter his text further. Hiring an editor was suggested. Minna Lederman was asked, but she, sensing trouble, turned down the job. Thomson beseeched his friend Herbert Weinstock, who accepted. Cage later stated that the page proofs he received had been drastically edited not just by Weinstock but by Thomson. "My writing style is too recognizable," he told Thomson. "People will see that there's something funny going on here." But finally, Cage didn't care. He simply wanted his involvement with the project to end. Hoover, told that Weinstock's changes meant that the entire book would have to be retyped, complained that there was no money for this. She had to type it herself, a task that "sprained her back and ruined her eyesight," she later told Thomson.

By now the book was threatened not only by squabbling between the co-authors and subject but by the increasing recalcitrance of the publisher Hoover had secured, Thomas Yoseloff of New York. Thomson had made unprecedented demands for a book of which he was only the subject, including a requirement that he be paid "25% of all royalties received by the joint authors in excess of $1,000 dollars," and "50% of all sums paid the authors for sales of the book (or any part of it) to magazines, to book clubs, to reprint firms or to foreign dealers or publishers."[19] Negotiations had dragged on for three years. In early 1958 Thomson's own lawyer, Arnold Weissberger, warned that Yoseloff was threatening to abandon the project even though Hoover was largely subsidizing it:

> Mrs. Hoover states that Mr. Yoseloff is only mildly interested in getting your biography, and he told her that he had checked on the sale of your other books and found that they were not remarkable. Mrs. Hoover was of the opinion that a letter making many demands upon Mr. Yoseloff would sour him on the deal, and I would be inclined to agree with her. . . .[20]

Moreover, Yoseloff, who thought Cage an utter eccentric, had protested his involvement in the book from the start. Cage's arrangement with Hoover, Weissberger had promised Yoseloff, would not require him "to have any dealings with Mr. Cage."

Even Thomson's own preface to the biography was a source of contention. Mrs. Hoover "doesn't want to use it now on various pretexts," Thomson wrote to Grosser that summer, "but really it talks too much about Cage for her liking."[21] The preface was dropped. *Virgil Thomson: His Life and Music,* by Kathleen Hoover and John Cage, was finally published in the spring of 1959 at a list price of six dollars.

Upon first holding it in his hands and reading it through, Thomson was pleased. It was a handsome book, with a dramatic black-and-white cover photo of Thomson intently conducting the Philadelphia Orchestra, and sixteen pages of illustrations. An appendix contained a comprehensive catalog, prepared by Cage, of Thomson's works—a "bibliographical triumph," Thomson later called it. Hoover's biographical chapters are reverential, as her account of Thomson's hapless military career makes clear:

> When Thomson entered the army in February, 1917, his friends and foes alike speculated on the effect of an environment so fatal to eccentricity and conceit. Speculation gave way to astonishment

as he rose to the highest rank attained by a Junior Collegian in the first World War: second lieutenant in the United States Military Aviation Corps.[22]

Reading through her biographical portrait, one gets not a glimpse of Thomson's intimate life. In fact, the truth is camouflaged with suggestive accounts of Thomson's attachments to women, particularly the troubled Mary Butts. "She penetrated the Chinese Wall of his creative ego, took him out of himself, opened his eyes to new values, gave him fresh perspective. She even dispelled his inveterate skepticism about romantic attachment."[23]

By the time Cage's text reached the printed page, it was substantially changed. Nevertheless, his analyses as presented are frequently insightful, invariably detailed (especially regarding rhythmic content), and often engaging. To be sure, there are eccentricities that reveal more about Cage's preoccupations than about Thomson's music. We are told exactly how many times in a piano miniature a particular pitch is struck. In some passages, even when Cage seems to be extolling a work, there is a suggestion of condescension in the writing, as when he states that *Four Saints* "leaves few traces" in the memory. Sometimes whole groups of works are wearily dispatched: "All these songs are pleasing, but they add nothing new to Thomson's musical language."[24] Yet, overall, the music is discussed with respect and, as often as not, affection. Which makes all the more striking Cage's sudden disassociation from it in the concluding paragraph:

> We know now the great variety and all but intangible nature of Thomson's work. What position has it in the field of contemporary music? Obviously, one of popularity. In my personal panorama it has today little place.[25]

However, this dismissal is genteel in comparison with the text as Cage originally wrote it:

> "What position has it in the field of contemporary music?" That of popularity, obviously. Whether this has been brought about by extra-musical (political) pressure or not is beside the point. It is a fact. But, quietly, in the country, "What position has it?" It interests me little. . . . Beyond his heterodoxical use of the twelve tones, what about his music could interest me? His tunes? No. His hymns? No. His canons? No. His abrupt shifts of tonality? No. His stacked-up thirds? No. And so on. It is not where I am. Nor, I must say, is much of the rest of contemporary music. . . .[26]

Given the overt hostility in this passage, it is interesting to speculate why Thomson insisted upon Cage's participation in this project at all. If Cage was not interested in Thomson's music, he would have been no more interested in, say, Copland's, maybe even less. Thomson could easily have found a compliant writer to produce a book about his works. The tradition of authorized analyses and vanity biographies controlled by the subject still flourishes.

But that was not the type of book Thomson wanted. Cage interested him because Thomson was irresistibly attracted to original minds. When he selected stringers at the *Herald Tribune,* he turned to composers like Paul Bowles and Lou Harrison, who were original thinkers but unconventional critics. Thomson wanted his works discussed by a provocative analyst, which he thought Cage would be. But he also wanted loyalty. His mistake was in not understanding that loyalty and originality are usually incompatible.

By commandeering the project, Thomson had managed to remove the animosity from Cage's text before it was published. Or so he thought. Over time he discerned in the subtext of Cage's discussion his barely disguised contempt. Hoover had been right, after all. The rift between them was painful. But it healed. They missed each other's company. During a dinner party at the home of Thomson's music-loving friends Judge Julius and Betty Isaacs, about two years after the release of the biography, Cage dared to mention it. "I know that book caused no end of troubles," he told Thomson. "I know you're not so happy with it, but I think it came off well and will do you good." Thomson agreed and thanked him for his work, which had stretched over ten years.

The book received mixed reviews. Oliver Daniel in *Saturday Review* wrote,

> Miss Hoover approaches her task with zest—but with little style or real penetration. The reader will hardly recognize the Thomson personality from this account. Cage . . . approaches the music knowingly, and writes of it with perception and skill.[27]

The respected London *Times Literary Supplement* gave the book rather backhanded compliments:

> On the face of it, Virgil Thomson seems a small figure to have a book devoted to him. Yet this book was worth writing and is worth reading: for Thomson is not merely a minor composer, he is also

a part of social history. . . . Miss Hoover's biographical contribution is consistently interesting, nicely written, but on occasion a bit fulsome. . . . Mr. Cage, writing specifically of the music, in musical terms, claims less but convinces more.[28]

And so Cage and Thomson put the venture behind them.

However, as Cage's career prospered and his frontal challenge to the musical establishment made him increasingly pivotal, Thomson grew resentful. In 1970 he wrote an influential article for the *New York Review of Books* called "Cage and the Collage of Noises," a piece he later admitted was his "revenge for the malice in that book."[29] Thomson's piece was an exposé and overview of Cage's aesthetics and the essentially destructive agenda, as he saw it, of Cage's work. Provoked by a performance at the University of Illinois, at Urbana, of *HPSCHD,* a gargantuan multimedia installation for fifty-two tape machines, fifty-nine power amplifiers, fifty-nine loudspeakers, and 208 computer-generated tapes, with comparable numbers of accompanying slides, projections, and silent films, Thomson wrote that Cage's idea of making musical compositions out of noise was not new, but that no previous creator had believed in it "as a destiny." "The ultimate aim," Thomson charged, "was to produce a homogenized chaos that would carry no program, no plot, no reminders of the history of beauty, and no personal statement." Thomson demystified Cage's music with its games-of-chance procedures and philosophical trappings. In fact, he argued, Cage, much like Gertrude Stein, "selects his materials casually and then with great care arranges them into patterns of hidden symmetry." The article, though an incisive indictment, was so audacious and engaging that even Minna Lederman, as perceptive an editor as ever was (and Cage's good friend), missed the malice in it upon first reading. She merely thought Virgil was up to his old tricks, being wicked and amusingly clever. But Cage was not amused.

> . . . Cage's aim with music, like Samson's in the pagan temple, has long been clearly destructive. Can he really pull the whole thing down around him? You never know. He might just! And in that way himself reach immortality. . . .
> It could happen, though. For Cage, like Samson, is a strong one; and he has helpers. They admire what he does and, what is far more dangerous, believe what he says. The young, moreover, seem to be yearning nowadays after a messiah. And a musical one might be the likeliest for them to follow. Indeed, Cage's rigid

schedule of beliefs and prophecies, his monorail mind and his turbine-engined, irreversible locomotive of a career all make it easy for the young to view him as a motorized and amplified pied piper calling out, "Get on board-a little children; there's room for a million more."[30]

When this article reached him, Cage was in Venice, staying in the palazzo of his friend Peggy Guggenheim. After he read it, he went out into the courtyard and vomited. Cage loved to laugh, but was admittedly sensitive to criticism and took himself very seriously. Their friendship never recovered from this attack. Thomson compounded the offense by twice reprinting the article in later collections of his writings. Cage and Thomson made passing attempts to patch things up that came to nothing. Twenty-one years after Thomson's article appeared, Cage, quite seriously, said of his onetime mentor and champion, "Virgil is the devil."

Dale Burr was one of the four young black dancers whom Virgil and Maurice selected in 1947 from the roster of students at Katherine Dunham's school in Harlem to appear in *The Mother of Us All*. Dressed, as Dale recalled, like "colored boy jockeys" in green silk pants and caps and boots, they didn't do much dancing in the production. They moved scenery, served champagne at Lillian Russell's garden party, "digged a ditch" and "digged it deep" for Daniel Webster during the political rally scene, and stood in motionless wonderment as Susan B. mused on her life of strife during the dream sequence. But to be in this high-visibility production was thrilling. *The Mother of Us All* changed Dale Burr's life.

Born in Columbus, Mississippi, in 1924, Dale was educated at Negro colleges in Texas and Virginia and served as a typist in the Supreme Headquarters Allied Expeditionary Forces in Paris, then in Rheims, where he saw General Eisenhower almost every day but never once spoke to him. Appearing in *The Mother of Us All* was a sufficient credential to get Dale into other auditions. He did the revival of *Carmen Jones* and won a bit part in *Finian's Rainbow* on Broadway. But there was a limit to what a black man could accomplish in show business. Dale was the first black dancer to appear on the *Voice of Firestone,* a popular television entertainment show. He portrayed a guard before an Indian temple while Roberta Peters, as the priestess Lakmé, sang the "Bell Song." When Dale turned thirty, in 1954, the only work he could get was dancing in Harlem night-clubs.

While working in *The Mother of Us All,* Dale made friends of Virgil and Maurice. Virgil sometimes hired Dale to serve cocktails at his dinner parties. Usually, after everyone was attended to, he told Dale to mix with the guests, keep things moving, make sure everyone had a drink in hand. Maurice also hired him for household jobs. And now and then each of them had sex with Dale. Maurice found Dale exciting, this limber black man with his sculptured back—the "most beautiful back I've ever seen," Maurice said. Dale was flattered and amused by the attentions of these smitten older men: Virgil, a "plump little man with them fire blue eyes," and Maurice, "compact, in surprisingly good shape, and very sexual."[31]

In 1950 Dale moved into a third-floor apartment on West Seventeenth Street, not far from Maurice's place on Nineteenth Street, and just six blocks south of Virgil's flat. He was getting by with nightclub work and odd jobs and was mostly content. Then in 1957 he woke up one morning and couldn't see. Friends took him to the veterans hospital, but no one could determine the cause of the problem. Twenty-five doctors (Dale counted them carefully) examined him; some thought it might be psychosomatic. Dale was not totally blind; he could make out shadows and figures. But he was severely handicapped and, for the only time in his life, terrified.

Needing money, he asked Virgil for $200. Virgil gave him $1,000 and told him to pay it back whenever he could. This was 1957, when Virgil was reporting a net income loss to the Internal Revenue Service. Maurice also helped out with small gifts: $25 or sometimes $50. But Dale was not willing to weave baskets and make brooms. He wanted a new trade. Thinking the perfect work would be massage, he applied to a program at the Swedish Institute, but was turned down. They had never had a blind student. It took him two years to convince them that the one thing you didn't need in order to practice Swedish massage was sight. Once admitted, he graduated with the highest scores in his class. He worked first for Jack La Lanne's fitness center and then the YMCA and the YMHA. Eventually he set up a private practice in his ramshackle one-room apartment, a homey little place with a rooftop garden off the back-door window.

In 1958 Maurice painted Dale's portrait. Though he had taken a series of striking nude photos, he painted Dale clothed, straddling an armchair, facing the viewer, with his handsome back hidden. Maurice wanted to capture the unfocused but calmly intent look of Dale's face. Hearing about the finished painting he could not see, Dale was very honored.

By the fall of 1959 Dale was adjusted to his new life. He had his own apartment, friends, a mostly reliable young black lover, and a satisfying trade. On Thanksgiving night, as Dale was preparing to go out, there was a knock at his door. It was Virgil, who had arrived unannounced. He asked to come in, saying something he rarely confessed: "I'm lonely."

There was no sex that night. All Virgil wanted was a massage. Dale worked for an hour on his famous friend, just turned sixty-three. Afterward Dale said he was going out to join friends at a gay bar, Club 19 on Nineteenth Street. Would Virgil like to come? Virgil walked Dale to the door of the dimly lit club, then said, "I think I'll go home. Maybe another time."

There was too much on his mind. Virgil had to jump-start his career. The only major work he had written since leaving the *Herald Tribune* in 1954 was a score for a 1957 Paddy Chayefsky film, *The Goddess,* an absorbing drama about an aspiring Hollywood actress loosely based on Marilyn Monroe, starring Kim Stanley in her film debut. Virgil needed to sink himself into a major composition. He was searching for the right project. He was lonely that night, but had been burned by such a place before. Suppose there was a bust? Suppose he met another young man, like Roger, someone he would lose control over? That was almost the more frightening scenario.

Virgil thanked Dale for the massage and the company, then turned away and walked home.

24 IT'S A SOFT EGG, BABY!

Virgil Thomson's colleagues often wondered why, after his success with *Four Saints in Three Acts* and *The Mother of Us All,* he did not write more operas. He wanted to, but knew that the Stein operas had been exceptional collaborations. Stein's nonsensical verse found an ideal mate in Thomson's deceptively simple music. Now that Stein was gone, the widower was hard-pressed to find a suitable new spouse.

Thomson thought that few writers had the combination of gifts to make a good librettist. Only the poets, he believed, write the type of lyrical verse that can sing from the stage. But poets are seldom theater people; they don't know how to make a text stageworthy. On the other hand, the theater people, who know what works on stage, tend to write in the banalities of everyday speech. Thomson wanted a poet who was also theater-wise, and such a person was hard to find.

For ten years after composing *The Mother of Us All,* he sought and was sent numerous librettos and seriously considered several of them. Stein's "opera," as she called it, *Doctor Faustus Lights the Lights,* intrigued but baffled him. His former Harvard tutor S. Foster Damon urged him to consider several librettos. One of them, Damon's adaptation of *The Bacchae,* engaged him for several months in early 1952. "It appeals to me enormously," he wrote to Damon, "in spite of the transvestism, which is hard to do on a stage without going into low comedy."[1] A possible commission from Juilliard was discussed; but Thomson lost interest.

He considered librettos and plays by Robert Lowell (*The Old Glory*), Langston Hughes (*Love from a Tall Building*), and Truman Capote (*A Christmas Memory*). All were ultimately rejected. Francis Ferguson, a professor of literature at Princeton, sent an adaptation of *Huckleberry Finn,* which Thomson read and enjoyed, but rejected as unsuitable for the "purely lyric stage," as he wrote to Ferguson. "I do not imagine the full operatic treatment of so many accents and dialects as propitious. I cannot imagine what one would do with Huck. Is he a boy soprano or a lady mezzo with hips?"[2]

Eventually, Thomson found the fellow he thought he could write an opera with, Kenneth Koch. A Harvard-educated poet, Koch had come through stints in the military and in psychoanalysis to take a prominent place in the circle of young New York poets and artists of the 1950s. Neither he nor Thomson could recall the exact occasion they first met. They simply remembered seeing each other at parties given by mutual friends—Larry Rivers, Frank O'Hara, Ned Rorem—during the mid-1950s, when Koch was about thirty. Thomson had admired Koch's published poems and was elated when Koch showed him some of his unpublished things. One night at the Chelsea, Thomson showed off to friends the young poet he had "just found." He said, "This is Ken Koch. He writes just like Gertrude, except it makes sense." This quip was actually a perceptive description of Koch's art.

Koch's poetry "wanted music," Thomson felt. And Koch was a theater man, who had written some plays in verse that had excited his circle, admittedly small, of New York poets and artists. By late 1958 Koch and Thomson had decided to collaborate on an opera. For its setting they chose two things they both loved: Paris and the nineteenth century. Koch's assignment was to go off and think about Paris and come back with fictional characters, historical characters, or, as in the Stein operas, a mix of both.

Koch ensconced himself in the New York Public Library to investigate nineteenth-century France. He wasn't used to doing research for his work. During his twenties he got an idea to write a poem about Einstein and planned to do background research. But the poem got written before Koch ever made it to the library. This time he immersed himself in books on the period, and soon got excited by the life of Baron Georges Eugène Haussmann (1809–1891), the French prefect and city planner who persuaded Napoleon III to allow him to remake the city of Paris. Haussmann was largely responsible for the city's present layout and appearance, with its expansive vistas, luxurious parks, and broad boulevards radiating like the rays of a star from the Arc de Triomphe; he even designed the elaborate sewer system. Koch loved the "crazy heroism" and "wild egomania" of Haussmann, who once proposed moving all the buried bodies out of Paris into one enormous cemetery on the Oise, to which a special train would transport mourners. He loved the idea of Haussmann dramatically issuing orders to slice through city blocks and reshape or remove entire buildings. Mock-heroic lines kept coming to him.

> *Here, put that building back! It's sticking out*
> *A good three inches farther than the rest!*
> *What do I care if it's the Hotel Vair?*
> *Chop off the front so that it evens up!*

With his hero selected, Koch needed a heroine. He was then enthralled by the Italian Renaissance epic poet Ludovico Ariosto, whose language was so grand, beautiful, and extreme. Koch's first commercially published work, which came out in 1959, was a contemporary homage to Ariosto, "Ko," an epic poem about baseball written in strict *ottava rima*. So, in looking for an opera heroine, Koch turned again to *Orlando Furioso*. In that work, Angelica, the most beautiful woman in the world, is sent by the Saracens to undo their enemies, the French Christian soldiers, who indeed fall in love with her, to their eventual demise. Koch would have his nineteenth-century Parisian epic presided over by the spirit of beauty, called Angelica. He went further, inventing two other spirit guides who compete for Angelica's love: Edouard, the spirit of visionary progress and civic improvement, and Jean, the spirit of poetry and art. Beneath the gaze of these three spirits, a panorama of nineteenth-century French artists, poets, scientists, and generals pass by: Napoleon and his British nemesis Wellington, Lamartine, Baudelaire, Pasteur, Offenbach, Delacroix, Napoleon III, Monet, Pissarro. Edouard and Jean intervene in the human life they witness, trying to make their respective domains of civic progress and the arts prosper and dazzle their beloved Angelica; with Edouard carving out boulevards and causing cathedrals to be built; with Jean inspiring the outburst of impressionism, and so on. In Koch's fanciful conceit, the entire history of nineteenth-century France was reduced to a struggle between forces embodied in these dueling spirits. The text was full of mock-humor. A disconcerted Delacroix says, "Victor

Hugo! Ah, must you go?" But, much like *The Mother of Us All,* which also playfully mixed historical figures, the concept inspired Koch to flights of whimsical yet never hackneyed lyricism. Describing his vision as Angelica watches, Haussmann says,

> *Paris should be filled with air,*
> *Interstellar spaces where*
> *Everything is clear as air.*
>
> *But now beneath the street I hear*
> *A sweet music gently clear,*
> *As I walk, my soul's seduction—*
> *The gay sound of sewer construction!*[3]

Koch shared his ideas and drafts with Thomson, who was encouraged. He loved the language, the parade of historical figures, the mix of fancy and elegance. But he was troubled that the three spirits were emerging as the leading roles. What were the substantive qualities of such insubstantial characters? He grilled Koch with questions about Angelica: How old is she? What kind of clothes does she wear? How does she feel about the boys? What does she eat? Koch wasn't sure. "I got the feeling that the spirits weren't enough like the people he knew," Koch later recalled. "Of course, I thought, neither were Gertrude Stein's saints. I guess he just wanted to understand the psychology of the characters. I had little talent at the time for depicting characters' psychology."[4]

Thomson must have decided that the character details could be filled in later by his music and by an imaginative director. Basically, he was delighted with Koch's work and told him to finish it up. Meanwhile, as a good-faith gesture, he set some existing Koch poems to music—first, in the spring of 1959, a text called *Collected Poems,* which reminded him of Stein's *Tender Buttons.* Koch's work was a series of bold-text titles and fanciful one-line poems:

> *BUFFALO DAYS*
> *I was asleep when you waked the buffalo.*
>
> *THE ORANGE WIVES*
> *A mountain of funny foam went past.*
>
> *GREAT HUMAN VOICES*
> *The starlit voices drip.*
>
> *COLORFUL HOUR*
> *A few green pencils in a born pocket.*[5]

And so on, for another thirty-seven "poems." Thomson cast the work as a duet with piano—a baritone sings the titles, and a soprano sings the poems—set to music of oompah-pah rigor and arpeggiated elegance with shifting keys and fractured meters. (He later arranged *Collected Poems* for vocal duet and chamber orchestra.)

The other work was a setting of four poems, chosen by Thomson from then unpublished works of Koch, and grouped together under Thomson's title, *Mostly about Love*. Thomson cut bits out of three of them. Like any poet, Koch was perturbed about having his work tampered with. But Thomson was an imposing elder statesman of the arts; Koch was the chosen younger colleague with a scant reputation outside of poetry circles; so he could not protest. Besides, to get his way, Thomson turned on the old charm. ("It's more beautiful this way, sweetie. Don't say the same thing three times.")

Yet, not since his collaborations with Stein had Thomson's music so embraced a poet's words, like the effusive and wonderfully wacky language of "Love Song" ("I love you as a sheriff searches for a walnut / That will solve a murder case unsolved for years / Because the murderer left it in the snow beside a window / Through which he saw her head, connected with / Her shoulders by a neck, and laid a red / Roof in her heart . . .").[6] Thomson set the poem with music of ardency and earnestness. Each of the four songs in the group addresses a different aspect of love. "Love Song" is a declaration of love, "Down at the Docks" is a discourse on love, "Let's Take a Walk" is an invitation to love, and "A Prayer to St. Catherine" is a supplication for love or, preliminarily, for saintly intervention to cure the supplicant of heartache and shyness. The music gives lift and point to every word and phrase. There's whimsy, but also disarming tenderness that comes from Thomson's use of proper church hymn harmonies.

By now Thomson and Koch were great colleagues. Thomson was very fond of Koch's wife, Janice Elwood, and their precocious daughter, Katherine. Thrilled by Thomson's settings of his works, Koch worked that spring and summer to complete his libretto. In July of 1959, from a rented beach house in Southampton, Long Island, where he was staying, Koch wrote to Thomson, who was in Paris that summer, to apologize for the delay with the libretto, which was "being very difficult to finish." But Koch assured Thomson that he would have a text to mail within two weeks. ("If there's anything you want to say about Angelica before she is produced in carbon copies, hurry!")[7] He also wrote with the news that he had accepted a post at Columbia University, which Thomson had urged him to take.

Just over two weeks later Koch wrote again:

> It was lovely to hear from you and, as usual, most inspiring—it produced a grand new scene. I think I could go on working on this libretto forever, I've gotten to love it so. But since everything seems to me pretty much in order, I think what I had better do is type it up and send it off and let you look it over.[8]

Koch finally mailed the libretto on August 11. In a separate letter he acknowledged that it was no doubt too long, and most certainly could be shortened. Groping for a title, he had proposed "Angelica in the Air," "The Air of Paris," "The World May Fall Apart, Angelica," "Angelica Disappears," which is what happens at the end. Or "Paris after 1815," like a mock-title of a college course. He settled, simply, on "Angelica." Even before receiving the final carbon copies, Thomson was elated. On August 1 he wrote, "What by the way is the subject of our opera number 2?" Immediately after reading Koch's draft, Thomson, who had just moved back into his renovated Paris apartment, sent a rapturous reply:

> Dear Kenneth,
>   The Angelica is beautiful, ever so beautiful and sings all the way. I love it all. But I do imagine it will need cutting. We can face that next winter. Now it is too handsome to castrate. I am taking it to Provence where I shall visit Greek friends for two weeks. This means the flat is finally finished and I am in it. All summer so far no work done but that. . . . I leave the next day with Angelica my love.[9]

Ten days later Thomson wrote to say that Angelica "improves on acquaintance if that is possible, in any case, she doesn't disappoint."[10]

Koch was filled with fantasies of becoming famous in an entirely new dimension. It was a heady sensation. "When you're a poet people don't get all dressed up to read your work. It doesn't get in the newspaper. Glory! That was my fantasy."[11] It was a not unreasonable fantasy. Thomson was clearly inspired. Koch would take the place of Gertrude Stein. He and Virgil would start writing operas together.

Several weeks passed. By September, Thomson was in New York. But Koch had still not heard from him. Finally he telephoned Thomson: "Virgil, How's the opera coming?" Thomson, without preparation or sympathy, simply said, "You don't really want me to set that, do you, baby? It's a soft egg." Koch was flabbergasted. And rather furious. "Virgil, I don't understand at all. What do you mean?" In his most clipped and pointed voice, Thomson said, "It won't work. It's not an opera, not a libretto. Can't set it." Koch insisted that they meet for lunch and talk, which they did, at El Quijote, a Spanish restaurant adjacent to the Chelsea Hotel lobby. It was an exasperating meeting. Thomson was insistent that the libretto was unusable, but unspecific about his objections. Koch was furious, but too stunned to fight.

Some time prior to this meeting, Thomson detailed his objections to the libretto in a scene-by-scene critique, handwritten and undated, which he never showed to Koch. The criticisms are severe. Yet the comments concerning Act 1, for example, read like notes for a work in progress:

Sc.   1)   Why does Napoleon speak to Edouard?
               Why does Edouard speak to Napoleon?
               Napoleon's language is frivolous.
               Crowd is not needed.
Sc.   2)   Alleges that Ed. can control events.
Sc.   3)   Napoleon still frivolous, also full of self-pity.
Sc.   4)   Crowd not needed.
               Angelica shows she is a silly woman.
Sc.   5)   A. still a silly woman.
Sc.   6)   Might become a soliloquy.
               If E. can talk to Nap., why not to H?

Clearly, the mix of history and fantasy as presented bothered him. The spirits talk to the real characters at some times but not at others; they are sometimes visible, sometimes not. And alleging that Edouard could control events depletes the plot of dramatic tension. If Edouard has such powers, why doesn't he simply twist events to his own ends?

But the problem that caused him to reject the libretto outright was the character of Angelica. Thomson liked strong women. He liked to have them around him in public; he liked them sitting by his side at the dinner table; he liked them in his operas. In some ways Thomson's psychological alter ego was a strong heterosexual woman. Angelica is a "silly woman," the classic pursued, passive, pretty object of male desire. Strong male characters take the stage in Koch's libretto, Baron Haussmann, Napoleon III, Pasteur. But the main story concerns the contest between two love-struck male spirits for the love of a beautiful, frivolous woman. Angelica is no Saint Teresa, no Susan B. Anthony. She is not like the women Kenneth Koch met at Thomson's

Chelsea apartment: Lotte Lenya, Lillian Hellman. By Scene 1 of Act 2 on Koch's libretto, Thomson scrawled in his notes to himself, "Angelica's silliness complete."

Yet why did Thomson not notice this flaw sooner? And why, since he obviously loved so much of the language and the characters, did he not talk with Koch about rewriting the work? Clearly, that summer of 1959, someone got to him in France, someone who made him see Angelica's true nature. A strong possibility is that Thomson showed the libretto to Alice B. Toklas. Having no tolerance for silly women, Alice would have seen right through Angelica's feminine façade. Thomson may have been annoyed with himself for not recognizing the problem immediately. This would explain his sudden, hostile rejection of a libretto he had adored.

Thirty-two years later, when Koch reread Thomson's love letters of praise for "my beautiful Angelica," it all came back to him. "What a heartbreaker," he said. "It almost makes me cry. It's really at-the-altar stuff."[12] Shown Thomson's notes for the first time, he acknowledged the problem. ("I wish he had told me. At that time I didn't know how to make a female character who was as subtle as a male character, I tended to see women as inspirations, objects of desire.") Yet he was confident that if Thomson had continued to work with him, he could have recast the libretto to deal with Thomson's objections. Haussmann could have been the main character. Much of the language that, as Thomson put it, "sings all the way," could have been salvaged. But it was not to be. The rejection was complete. All that remained of this two-year collaboration was *Collected Poems* and *Mostly about Love,* two of Thomson's finest vocal works, and the momentarily dashed hopes of a young poet. After some time the bad feelings were patched up. "How could you stay mad at him?" Koch later said. "I had a good ride even though I wound up back in the garage." But Thomson never set another poem by Kenneth Koch (though Koch would write librettos for Ned Rorem and other opera composers). Three years passed before Thomson met the man who would become the librettist for his third and final opera, a ten-year project from inception to production.

In the five years after leaving the *Herald Tribune* in 1954, Thomson had written incidental music for the theater, some remarkable songs, shorter chamber works, and a film score, but no substantial concert work. He had hoped to make a major statement with "Angelica," but over twelve months of plotting with his librettist had produced nothing. However, 1959 was not a total wash. The State College of Education at Potsdam, New York, commissioned a major work for chorus and orchestra. In the spring of 1960 Thomson delivered his *Missa pro defunctis,* a forty-five-minute requiem mass for double chorus (women's and men's choruses, divided and singing on opposite sides of the stage) and full orchestra. The mass is a thick, imposing piece; layers of counterpoint get piled up so deep that the textures turn murky; passages of block chordal, root position, parallel harmonies heave and surge inexorably. Thomson conducted the May 14 premiere in Potsdam with a chorus of three hundred and an orchestra of ninety. The work clobbered the audience. That it never caught on was yet another hurtful disappointment. But it served its purpose: after completing the requiem, Thomson later wrote, "I knew that my reconstruction time was over."[13]

He still ached to write another opera. Time was running out. In 1961 he turned sixty-five. In the meantime he was gratified when in late 1962 Betty Allen, the mezzo-soprano who had given such an impressive performance in the 1952 revival of *Four Saints,* asked him to compose a song cycle for her. Allen had received a grant from the Ford Foundation to commission a work for a recital at the Metropolitan Museum of Art. Since the *Four Saints* revival, Allen had been a devoted interpreter of Thomson's music. He had a definite idea of the kind of cycle to compose. "You always sing my religious songs," Thomson told her; "so I'm going to give you some love songs." Some weeks later, Allen, now living in Stamford, Connecticut, with her husband, Edward Lee, received a packet of poems by D. H. Lawrence, the texts Thomson intended to set. Now, Miss Betty Allen was a lady. She once auditioned for a production of *Porgy and Bess* and was turned down before she sang a note. "You're not Catfish Row," the director told her. Allen had to agree. "My mother would have called the people of Catfish Row godless. I mean, here is Bess sniffing cocaine." So, when she read the Lawrence poems, Allen was shocked.

> They were poems about carnal love, one about a woman standing in the doorway gazing longingly at her husband, stripped to the waist, handsome in the fields; she is practically panting for him to come to her. Most of the poems were about mammals copulating. I remember one about elephants.[14]

Instead of responding, Allen brooded. After some time another packet arrived from the Chelsea, with a note, saying, "I see you don't think much of the Lawrence poetry. I'm sending you some religious poems. You can't find fault with the Bible!" These would become *Praises and Prayers.*

Strictly speaking, the five texts, though they borrow biblical lines, are not from the Bible. There is a "Canticle of the Sun" by Saint Francis of Assisi; an anonymous prayer, "My Master Hath a Garden"; an excerpt from a hymn by Richard Crashaw; a beloved children's bedtime verse; and some anonymous stanzas quoted in the "Meditations of Saint Augustine." The songs range from the grandeur and directness of the Saint Francis "Canticle" with its arching lines of declamatory power for the singer and churchly part writing for the pianist, to the tender innocence of "Before Sleeping," though even here the gentle melody is given body and emphasis through the word setting, with its striking syncopations so evocative of plainspoken English.

Allen's recital took place at the Grace Rainey Rogers Auditorium on October 24, 1963. The pianist Paul Ulanowski accompanied her in songs by Ravel, Schubert, and Grieg (sung in Norwegian); the Kohon String Quartet participated in a performance of Respighi's *Il tramonto.* Thomson insisted upon accompanying the world premiere of *Praises and Prayers,* and it turned out to be a mistake. As a recording of the performance, later released on the CRI label, reveals, his playing, though full of character, was clinker-prone and rhythmically unreliable. In the final song he jumped an entire measure ahead of Betty Allen, in glorious voice, who sounds astonishingly unrattled. The critic John Gruen from the *New York Herald Tribune* praised the work and Miss Allen:

> Mr. Thomson has given us all a lesson on how the English language can be put to music. The new cycle is no exception. Appended to a rare and deceptively simple harmonic structure, he has fashioned a unique prosody that is a study in clarity and economy. . . . In Miss Allen the composer has found an ideal and dedicated interpreter. Her diction is faultless, her musicianship never less than gratifying, and her voice an instrument of great resourcefulness and strength.[15]

The *New York Times* did not send a critic that night, a slight it must have felt needed righting, because eleven days later when Allen, with the composer at the piano, performed an all-Thomson program for the Overseas Press Club, the *Times* critic Raymond Ericson covered it glowingly, even though this event was virtually a private affair and Thomson had only a spinet at his disposal.

Eighteen days after this review appeared, President John F. Kennedy was assassinated in Dallas. Thomson, who never owned a television in his life, spent hours watching the coverage in the lobby of the Chelsea, where a television had been set up. Though famously apolitical, Thomson had met the president and liked him immensely. The occasion was the White House concert given by Pablo Casals with the pianist Mieczyslaw Horszowski and the violinist Alexander Schneider. At seventy-seven, Casals had played magnificently, Thomson thought. After congratulating Casals in the greenroom, Thomson found himself nose to nose with the president.

> "Hello," he said. "What did you think of the music?" When I told him I had never heard the old man play more beautifully, nor Horszowski either, nor Schneider, and that their special excellence had been all for him (it could only be that way), he listened intently as if wondering, "Can I use this?" Then with a charming grin and a slight leer of complicity, as if asking for the low-down, he leaned toward me. "Is he really as good as he ever was?" he wanted to know. For answer I described his bow-arm control. "Say, that will interest my wife. Let's tell her. Jackie, listen to this."[16]

During the early 1960s Virgil Thomson's domestic life was tranquil and satisfying. Maurice was thriving. In an era when abstract expressionism was pushing the boundaries of modernism, Maurice's vibrant realism was hardly fashionable. But his paintings sold steadily, if for modest prices, and he was content in his work habits. Following Virgil's lead, Maurice had written books. *Painting in Public* (1948), a comprehensive and witty examination of the mechanics and procedures of the artist and his professional life, was indebted to Virgil's *The State of Music,* something Maurice acknowledged outright. More successful were two books of criticism, *The Painter's Eye* (1951) and *The Critic's Eye* (1962), both filled with Maurice's demystifying discussions of the leading painters of the time. His writing was refreshingly pragmatic. Few of Maurice's critic colleagues thought to explain why Mondrian's recent paintings were deteriorating more quickly than the earlier ones.

> The earlier ones, painted with more spontaneous brushwork on a rougher canvas, are still handsome, clean and well preserved.

The later ones, executed in smooth paint on a smooth canvas prepared with heavy priming, already show the irreparable cracks
which such a ground will suffer from even the slightest blow.[17]

Maurice considered himself lucky. He traveled the world, visited
his countless friends, did whatever he wanted. Virgil's constant fretting about his reputation seemed to Maurice a waste of time and spiritually damaging. By now their sexual relationship, most likely, had
ended. Virgil used to brag of his "twenty-six years of sex" with Maurice, which would put the cutoff year around 1952, just before Virgil
met Roger. Occasionally there may have been quick trysts for old
time's sake. But in the 1960s their friendship was more solid than ever.

Theodate Johnson was happy in love and in work. Back in 1953,
when Virgil was still entertaining the absurd fantasy of marrying her,
Theodate married, rather impulsively, Tony Kloman, dashing and
shiftless, putatively a painter, but in reality a mooch. The breakup of
this marriage was a relief to everyone. "Theodate is divorcing and
madly happy," Thomson wrote in 1954 to one of their mutual friends
from Paris, the conductor Manuel Rosenthal. "I must say it is a great
pleasure having her back in New York again."[18] By 1960 Theodate
had become the publisher of *Musical America*. The next year, she married her lover, Scott Severns. As a wedding present, her brother, Philip
Johnson, thriving as an architect, presented them with the deed to a
spacious apartment in the coveted Dakota apartment building, on Central Park West. While Virgil was possessive about Theodate, he welcomed her good news. "Theodate got married to her young man, the
dentist twenty years younger who loves her," Virgil wrote to Maurice.[19]
Without her dentist, she was still available now and then for accompanying Virgil to concerts or dinner parties. But during this period his
favorite "date" was Carol Truax.

Carol, three years Virgil's junior, was born in Manhattan, the
older daughter of Charles Henry Truax, a New York State Supreme
Court justice for twenty-eight years, and Caroline Sanders, the judge's
second wife. This prosperous and flamboyant family lived in an elegant East Side town house just off Fifth Avenue. Judge Truax was a
gourmet, a wine connoisseur, and a gargantuan man, "nearly seven
feet tall, if you include his high silk hat," Carol later wrote, "and you
should because he almost always wore it. It went with his striped
trousers, his voluminous frock coat, and the gold hawser across his
double-breasted waistcoat."[20]

ABOVE: Scene from *Macbeth,* presented by the WPA's Federal Negro Theater Project, 1936. RIGHT: Orson Welles and Virgil Thomson, 1936, during a rehearsal break for *Macbeth*.

ABOVE: Virgil Thomson, at the piano, rehearsing the members of the all-black cast for the 1952 revival of *Four Saints in Three Acts. Left to right:* Calvin Dash, Elwood Smith, Altonell Hines, Betty Allen, Rawn Spearman, Inez Matthews. Photo by Vic Shifreen, ANTA Playhouse.

OPPOSITE, TOP: Geoffrey Parsons, Pulitzer Prize–winning chief editorial writer at the *New York Herald Tribune* and Virgil Thomson's mentor there. At his desk in 1944. OPPOSITE, BOTTOM: Listening to the playback during the recording session for Virgil Thomson's film score to *Louisiana Story,* 1948, New York. *Left to right:* Helen Van Dongen, editor; Eugene Ormandy, conductor; Robert Flaherty, director; Bob Fine, recording engineer; and Virgil Thomson.

ABOVE: *The Mother of Us All*, Act 1; Columbia University, Brander Matthews Hall. With Belva Kibler as Anne *(left)* and Dorothy Dow as Susan B. Anthony. LEFT: Roger Baker, the young painter with whom Thomson had one of his deepest relationships during the early 1950s. At his studio in Paris in 1951.

RIGHT: George Reeves and Jack Larson on the set of *The Adventures of Superman* television series in the 1950s. Jack Larson, who played Jimmy Olsen, was a poet and playwright who later provided Thomson with the libretto for his last opera, *Lord Byron*. BELOW: Jack Larson and Virgil Thomson at the Chelsea Hotel when their collaboration was announced to the press in 1965.

ABOVE: Scene from *Lord Byron,*
Juilliard Theater, 1972. *Left to right:*
Grayson Hirst, Jean Fuerstenau,
Barbara Hendricks, and Ann Farr.
LEFT: Virgil Thomson and his close
friend Norma Flender, attending a
fund-raising reception for the
MacDowell Colony at the Plaza Hotel
in New York in 1972.

ABOVE: Virgil Thomson in his
parlor at the Chelsea, 1978. LEFT:
Virgil Thomson, composing in bed
at the Chelsea Hotel in the 1960s.
Photo by Mottke Weissman.

Virgil Thomson at eighty, outside the Chelsea Hotel in 1976.

One day, when Carol was a senior at the Horace Mann School, she started bleeding from her throat. The cause was a hemorrhage from tuberculosis, then considered a dirty disease among the wealthy. Carol's condition was hushed up, and she was sent to a series of sanatoriums in Arizona and Colorado Springs. It took her ten years to recover, but she grew into a big-boned and boisterous woman. In Colorado Springs she started a bookshop, later ran the bookstore at Colorado College, and eventually became the executive director of the fine arts department. A tough-talking, take-charge woman, Carol was just what the effete arts faculty needed to shape things up. Soon she was running the summer program and arts festival, and became an ally of Walter Paepcke, who helped to establish the Aspen Music Festival in 1949. It was during these years that Carol met Virgil, who came to Colorado Springs and then to Aspen to conduct and lecture. Carol was a lot like Virgil: bossy, opinionated, impossible, and outrageously delightful company. Their temperaments differed: Virgil was dry and pointed; Carol was loud and dramatic. They could drive each other crazy. But they cooked together, threw parties together, and enjoyed each other immensely.

In 1951 Carol moved to New York, where she was hired to establish and manage the music programs of the entire State University of New York system, thirty-three campuses. During the fifties she continued to spend summers in Colorado Springs, where she produced the Broadmore International Theater festival season, booking classical and popular musicians and singers (Van Cliburn, Helen Traubel, Liberace, Nat "King" Cole). But cooking increasingly took over her life. In 1947, with her friend Lillian McCue, Carol wrote and published *The 60 Minute Chef,* which was a big success. Carol would produce another twenty-three cookbooks, which mixed recipes with embellished anecdotes about her colorful life and famous friends. Her accounts of cooking with her father in *Father Was a Gourmet* annoyed her family, since most of it was made up. The judge died in 1910, when Carol was eleven.

Virgil loved taking Carol to concerts and parties. On one outing in 1962 they met a young couple, Norma and Richard Flender, who quickly became and remained among the closest of Thomson's friends for the rest of his life.

Norma came from bucolic Uniontown, Pennsylvania. Her father was a dentist, but also a poet who encouraged his three children to study the arts. Norma, a pianist, won student competitions and studied at Juilliard. But it was always expected by her parents and, consequently, by Norma, that she would marry well and raise a family. Richard Flender, born to a New York family that had prospered in the investment field, was a lawyer when Norma met him. Later he began a successful banking career at Morgan Guaranty. Married in 1960, they were a striking couple. Poised and capable, Norma was lovely with long dark hair; Richard, though slight of frame, was athletic and radiated a quiet confidence.

In 1962 they bought a town house on East Sixty-ninth Street and renovated it completely. The next year they were visited by Norma's friend from India, Vanraj Bhatia, a composer she had met in Paris when they both were studying with Boulanger. Vanraj was courteous, sweet but rather nervous, no doubt as a result of his tightly closeted homosexuality. He had met Virgil Thomson in 1962 when Virgil was traveling through Bombay. Virgil liked Vanraj, who was then struggling; so he lent Vanraj $500, money he never expected to see again.

However, in New York the next year Vanraj was prepared to pay back this loan. After a concert they all attended at the Metropolitan Museum, Vanraj, with Norma's permission, invited Virgil and Carol, his companion that night, back to the Flender house for a postconcert party. There they sat around the kitchen table eating escargots, dipping bread in the shells, and drinking wine. Virgil enjoyed this young, handsome, cultured couple. Between the two of them he could discuss three of his favorites things: food, France, and money. Virgil loved talking with Richard about the stock market, the American economy, the banking business. To Richard's mind, Virgil's sympathies had a distressingly leftward tilt, what with his concern for the unemployed and his suspicion, dating from the Depression years, that capitalism was no friend to the workingman. Richard would jocularly try to persuade Virgil differently. Virgil, pleasant but firm, resisted. This banter over economics continued for close to twenty-six years.

Theirs became a friendship of complementary interests. Richard and Norma loved to take people on trips; Virgil loved to be taken. The Flenders brought youth, breeding, and generosity to the friendship; Virgil brought glamour and brilliance. Norma soon moved to the top of the list of Virgil's "dates." He loved having Norma on his arm in public.

Driving to Pittsburgh to visit Norma's sister, Doris Hackney, an actress who lived with her husband in a roomy house, became a regular ritual for Virgil and the Flenders. By then Ruby was living there with her husband, Roy Gleason. Before this, spending time with Ruby and Roy had always been strained. Now Virgil could go to Pittsburgh with his New York friends and stay with Doris and Bill Hackney. Doris was lively; Bill was a fancy cook. Visits there were one big party. But Norma and Doris would always take Virgil to see Ruby for a few hours, which was just enough time. The siblings would sit together on the couch like two stones—Ruby small and compact, Virgil small and rotund. Ruby was as blunt and direct as Virgil. Her subject matter included family life, needlepoint, china painting, the travels of friends, weddings past and to come, and rising prices.

If Virgil's relationship with the Flenders, like all his friendships during this period, had a utilitarian aspect, it did not mean he was insincere. Virgil knew people were drawn to him at least in part, sometimes in large part, because of his fame. He expected something in return. Affection, as opposed to marriage, "is the feeling we entertain toward persons who are useful to us in a more limited way." This was one of Virgil's modernist maxims from his private 1925 manifesto. Forty years later he might have blushed at his brashness, but not at his candor. As long as the balance between giving and taking was tilted slightly in his favor, Virgil could be the most generous and charming friend. He was even capable of being sentimental. But tilt that balance toward yourself, or overstep the accepted parameters, and Virgil could yank you back into line. Every good friend of Virgil's experienced this. The Flenders were no exception.

Close as they were, one subject that simply did not come up, not with Richard, certainly not with Norma, was homosexuality. They both understood perfectly well what Virgil's life was, and neither felt the slightest discomfort about it. Yet once, early on in the friendship, Norma made the mistake of alluding to homosexuality, not in regard to Virgil, just to the subject in general. They were having dinner with Virgil, Maurice, and Carol Truax at the home of Carol's niece and her husband, Carolyn and Hunter Frost. Vanraj had just left New York, and Norma was talking about him. Vanraj used to flirt innocently with Richard, whom he found adorable, which Norma thought amusing. In a playful mood that night and, no doubt, trying to demonstrate that such subjects did not trouble her, Norma said at the dinner table: "You know, Vanraj never could understand why we—Richard, Vanraj, and I—could not have a ménage à trois."

Virgil turned grim and barked at her angrily, "You should be busy having a child!"

In telling her playful story, Norma was indicating that for her homosexuality held no stigma. In a way she was prying open the topic. Not that she was inviting Virgil to talk about himself; she was simply trying to lighten the tension. Virgil crushed her. Norma had crossed a line; he did not want her to do it again.

But his tactic was purposely cruel. At that time—and Virgil knew this—Norma and Richard were trying to conceive and were beginning to face the possibility that they could not. Norma was stunned by Virgil's put-down. But the tactic worked. She never even hinted at the topic again in Virgil's presence.

Virgil was still nursing shame about being homosexual. To be with cultured, prosperous heterosexual friends like Norma and Richard was a great relief. When he walked into a public event with Norma on his arm, Virgil could entertain for a moment the fantasy that he was a proper member of straight society. For Norma to destroy his illusion with a risqué remark was intolerable. Norma now understood this. It did not excuse his behavior; but it explained it.

Eventually Norma and Richard did adopt two baby children: Charles, who was born in late 1965 and came to them in February of 1966, was an extraordinarily handsome child with blond ringlets and dimples. Sylvia was born in July of 1967 and arrived at the home of her parents at six weeks old.

During this period the day-to-day routine of Virgil's apartment was under the efficient control of Wendell Dorne, a black domestic employee from the South who served Virgil as cook extraordinaire, bartender at cocktail parties, shopper, errand runner, and masseur. Wendell was tall, striking, cheerful, courteous, and discreet. The circumstances of his private life were never clear to Virgil's friends. There seemed to have been a couple of children in his recent past. He and Virgil were cagey about their own relationship. Most people assumed that something was going on. But, without explicitly forbidding it, Virgil made clear that this subject was not to be raised. Twice when Virgil went to Paris, he brought Wendell along as a valet. Once they rented a car for travel in the country, and Virgil bought Wendell a chauffeur's uniform. In the mid-1960s Wendell disappeared from Virgil's life as suddenly as he had entered it. When asked what had happened to Wendell, Virgil professed not to know.

Although Virgil never mentioned homosexuality among his respectable straight friends, within a coterie of younger gay artists, he could be catty and campy. During these years he enjoyed the company of Edward Albee, Gore Vidal, and, when they were in New York, Christopher Isherwood and his young lover, the painter Don Bachardy, who lived in California. Through Ned Rorem and Kenneth Koch, Virgil had met the sexually ambidextrous painter Larry Rivers, the gay poet Frank O'Hara, Joe LeSueur, a Mormon from California who lived with Frank for ten years in an East Village cold-water flat, and the blond, stunningly handsome, and rather aimless J. J. Mitchell, who, since coming to Manhattan after a Harvard education and a stint in the navy, had been befriended by Frank and Joe. Then working as a fact checker for Grolier's encyclopedia, J. J. had aspirations to be a writer.

Frank O'Hara, guru to a large circle of New York poets and painters during the fifties and sixties, practiced friendship, courtship, and conversation as an art form. He was famously curious about people. Virgil, with his constant pontificating, got on Frank's nerves. But Frank was fascinated by this brilliant curmudgeon and impressed by his work. O'Hara later wrote that Thomson's two Stein operas were "the most important thing that has happened in American prosody," that Thomson brought about an "Americanization of diction" that liberated poets from Anglicized models.[21]

One night, out on the town in New York, Frank got a glimpse into how Virgil operated. At dinner that night, Frank joined Joe, J. J., their friend the poet Kenward Elmslie, and Ned. Virgil was the featured guest. But the main attraction was a black hustler named Joe, who called himself Miss Dietrich from Hollywood. The evening, as O'Hara recalled in a letter to Larry Rivers, was memorable, as was the hustler.

He was of course 6'2, gorgeous and ended up screwing—you guessed it—Virgil. He liked my chest but money more. Virgil at first tried to talk him out of any fee by saying, "Well, baby, it's a noble thing to be a negro, but it's an ignoble thing to be a whore, right?" To which this Harry Belafonte substitute smiled gently and replied, "Ah don't know as ah understand quite what yuh mean." Ned was quite huffy to him since he thinks *he's* Miss Dietrich. After we were kissing in the kitchen the hustler opined that it was a pity I was a "poor poet," a piece of information he picked up from that sand-bagging bastard Joe L. Anyhow, I thought you'd be interested to know how we cultural leaders who remain in New York amuse ourselves and each other.[22]

Though he never became his close friend, Virgil was a party to the tragedy that befell Frank O'Hara in the summer of 1966.

Smarting from one of his periodic fights with Joe LeSueur, Frank was looking for a place to have some weekend fun with J. J. He called his friend Morris Golde, who was heading that weekend to his summer bungalow on Fire Island, a gay mecca, technically not an island, but a thirty-two-mile-long beach barrier strip off the south coast of Long Island. Frank had been to Morris's place many times, which was cozy but nothing fancy, a cedar cabin on stilts in a sparsely settled area of Fire Island unserved by electricity. Morris kept house there with kerosene lamps, a propane gas stove, and lots of candles. Morris had already invited his old friend Virgil to stay the weekend. "You know, I've never really gotten to know Virgil well," Frank said. He asked if he and J. J. could join them, and Morris was happy to oblige.

On Friday, July 22, they drove out late in the afternoon in Morris's Mustang, then boarded his small boat for the trip across Great South Bay to Water Island. Arriving late Friday night, they ate a simple dinner and went early to bed. The next day was balmy and beautiful. With his bathing trunks pulled up above his beachball belly, Virgil looked a little ridiculous. But for a man four months from his seventieth birthday, he was surprisingly limber. Nothing could keep him out of the surf that day, until one wall-high wave knocked him over and towed him under. Frank had to run into the water to help Virgil get on his feet. After that, a bit shaken, Virgil conceded that he had better quit for the day.

That night an elaborate dinner was prepared mostly by J. J., but under the supervision of Virgil: a gigot, prepared à la Alice B. Toklas, corn sheared from the cob, and Moulin à Vent ("the Belgian rule," Virgil insisted, "seven bottles for six people"). Frank and Virgil liked to engage in verbal repartee. But that night Frank was deferential and quiet; Virgil was expansive and rhapsodic. "It was a night of quintessential Virgil," J. J. later wrote in a memoir; "prompted by the bonhomie of the occasion, he delivered a long monologue on life, love, and friendship which left Frank, Morris, and me stunned in silent awe."[23]

"He was positively Homeric," Morris recalled. Virgil's theory was that being gay was not a diminution or perversion of manliness, but just the opposite, a call for heightened, bonded manliness. When Virgil concluded his sermon, there was a long silence. "Thank you for letting me be brilliant," he said, breaking the spell. "Now let's go look at the animals."

What he meant was that the four of them should hail a beach buggy, the covered jeeps that were licensed to transport Fire Islanders on the ocean shoreline, and head to Fire Island Pines, where there was a hotel on the harbor with a gay disco that was always hopping. There they took a table on a terrace overlooking the ocean, drank stingers, greeted friends, and watched the action on the dance floor. All except Virgil, who, as easily as if he had been sitting at a string quartet concert, took a nice nap. His ability to shut out sound that bothered him was the one advantage of the gradual hearing loss that, like many older people, he had begun to experience in his sixties.

Around one in the morning Morris and Virgil decided to return to the bungalow. Frank and J. J. said they would stay a while longer. So Morris and Virgil left. When later Frank and J. J. decided to return, the only available beach buggy was overcrowded with tourists. En route the taxi threw a rear tire. No one was hurt. But everyone had to disembark and wait in the darkness as the driver radioed for another taxi. Frank wandered off from the group closer to the ocean. There is some disagreement about what happened next. Apparently, a twenty-one-year-old college football star, not a licensed driver, and his girlfriend came speeding by in a beach buggy. The driver, who later claimed to have been blinded by the headlights of the idled jeep, veered toward the shore and plowed into Frank, who was knocked cold, as J. J. later recounted.

> We all run to his aid. The taxi radios for the police and the Pines doctor. We examine him. He is unconscious, but beginning to stir, moan. It doesn't look disastrous. (Frantic inner denial of the worst, hope for the best.) The young summer resident doctor arrives, miraculously fast. He takes his pulse, probes with his fingers. Frank's leg is definitely broken; contusions, abrasions, but no immediate evidence of internal damage.[24]

But it was disastrous. With J. J. at his side, Frank was taken by police launch across the bay to a small private hospital at Mastic Beach, on Long Island. Back at the bungalow, Morris stirred awake close to dawn and woke Virgil to say that the boys were still out. Virgil told him not to worry. As the sun rose, the phone rang. It was J. J.

Morris and Virgil arrived at the hospital at midmorning. J. J. had called Frank's friends, who rushed from New York: Joe, Kenneth Koch, Larry Rivers, Willem de Kooning "with a big checkbook, wanting to pay for everything." But there had been internal damage, which had necessitated emergency surgery. They could only wait. Virgil, notoriously useless around illness, yet fascinated by the particulars, took the train back to New York and wrote a letter, a "disaster letter," he called it, filled with bad news, to Maurice, who was on summer vacation.

> I spent the weekend with Golde at Water Island; and Frank O'Hara, also a house guest, was run over on the beach by a jeep. A broken leg and facial plus other lacerations are not important, but liver injury which caused the loss of a quarter of it (most of the left lobe) give him, it seems, less than a 50-50 chance to live.[25]

The letter is dated July 25, 1966. At 8:50 P.M., Frank O'Hara died at the age of forty. As O'Hara's reputation as poet and art critic grew in subsequent years to legendary status, Virgil increasingly inserted himself into the history. They had never been close friends. But Virgil presided over O'Hara's final dinner, almost as if bestowing a final benediction. "It's as if Frank's death was foreshadowed during that dinner," Morris recalled. "Frank was calm and contemplative. And that was really thanks to Virgil."

The week of the tragedy of Fire Island, Virgil Thomson received advance copies of his new book, an autobiography, five years in the making and about to be released. The idea had come from Blanche Knopf, wife of the publisher Alfred A. Knopf, and one of Virgil's biggest fans. Knopf had published Thomson's first two collections of articles from the *Herald Tribune*. Knopf had balked at a third, which went to Henry Holt. This book, *Music Right and Left,* sold the poorest but garnered the best reviews. Blanche Knopf lured Thomson back to Knopf with the idea of an autobiography, something Thomson had shied away from, not wanting to discuss publicly his private life. But when Knopf suggested that he could cast the book as a memoir of life on two continents during the 1920s and 1930s, Thomson was intrigued by the proposal. He signed a contract in August of 1961, accepting a healthy advance of $15,000, and promising to complete it within three years. But he had trouble finding an appropriate tone; his writing was by turns guarded, combative, and saccharine. By the summer of 1964 he had over 200 typed pages of sometimes compelling, but more often discursive, recollections heavily weighted on the early years. Herbert Weinstock, the editor who had been the savior of the Hoover/Cage biography and was Thomson's editor at Knopf, tried to be encouraging. But he was not pleased, and said so in a September 1964 letter: "We feel that to publish it about as it stands now would be self-defeating, could result only in puzzled and perhaps niggling reviews, indifferent sales and sorrow all around." Weinstock recommended two major alterations: a condensation by as much as 50 percent of the first 110 pages, dealing with the early years, material that in Thomson's telling moved "molto adagio," Weinstock said; and additional chapters on Thomson's tenure at the *Herald Tribune*. The manuscript seemed to be "cut off in mid-stream," Weinstock added, as if "to provide you with an excuse for writing a second, later volume." "Unless you write this added section we will be unable to take any but a rather dim view of the book's possibilities in today's extremely competitive market. With the added section, we'll be ready to be as enthusiastic now as when the contract was signed."[26]

For once, Thomson was worn down by another's strong argument. Reviewing the manuscript, he had to agree with Weinstock. The long analyses of his compositions from the late 1920s were cluttered with technical jargon and, worse, defensive in tone. ("All these works confuse reviewers who have usually taken their suave harmonic syntax for an innocence of modernistic ways. Actually they have borne scrutiny under that charge.") And his recollections of Kansas City were filled with sentimental and implausible tales of heartsick crushes on pretty girls: "I took other girls to the games and dances, the hayrides, and the weenie roasts, made my companionship with them as if I were a perhaps just-slightly-flirtatious brother; but I could not play the mating game so long as Martha's image was in my thoughts."[27]

All this had to come out. With Weinstock's guidance, Thomson cut and rewrote. He extended the story to the present. Though he devoted only one chapter to the *Herald Tribune* years, it was brilliant, wry, and revealing. By the following summer Weinstock wrote Thomson to congratulate him on his progress. By the spring of 1966 Virgil wrote to Maurice from Los Angeles to say that he had showed his draft to Christopher Isherwood, who proclaimed it "a masterpiece."

The book, called, simply, *Virgil Thomson,* was released in the fall of 1966, 432 pages with index and pictures, priced at $7.95 and handsomely designed. Thomson, in a not unprecedented practice, had written his own jacket blurb:

Salty, witty, warm, and beautifully written, as they tell of a Kansas City childhood, a Harvard education, a Missourian's adventures in Boston, New York, and Paris, Virgil Thomson's memoirs are authentic Americana. But they are also authentic history, a participant's account of the artistic life of Europe and America between the two world wars. These amazing decades, as lived through by a composer who was also a performer, a theater man, and a music critic, are brilliantly evoked through Thomson's running commentary on his own life and further lit up by sharp word-portraits of such leading characters as Christian Bérard, Nadia Boulanger, Aaron Copland, Marcel Duchamp, John Houseman, Pare Lorentz, Picasso, Poulenc, Schoenberg, Gertrude Stein, Alice Toklas, and Orson Welles. The full text, the very numerous illustrations, and their carefully integrated captions present a unified picture of a richly enjoyed, unusual, and extremely productive life. Penetrating, powerful, and quirky, the book shows Virgil Thomson not only as an international gadfly stinging where he pleases but also as one who was certain to leave an indelible mark on the times that he so vividly recounts.

"The book is a beauty to look at and to feel," Thomson wrote to Weinstock. To Alfred A. Knopf he sent a lovely note, for Blanche had died earlier that year, and the work, he wrote, was really "Blanche's book. . . . She was responsible for my undertaking it, and my last word from her in the spring was a fan letter."[28]

Virgil Thomson sold well and was reviewed everywhere. The reception spanned the spectrum. Those looking for a travelogue through the life and times of a "provocateur of the musical scene" were rewarded. Those looking for a revealing personal story—a traditional autobiography—were frustrated. The consensus was that the memoir, though fascinating and written with a distinctive voice, lapsed into name-dropping and glib recollections.

Some of those closest to Thomson, like Alice Smith from Missouri, were thrilled to find themselves "immortalized." Others were hurt to be largely left out, like Leland Poole, languishing in Los Angeles, a professional failure who considered his intimate, long-ago friendship with Virgil a highlight of his life. Thomson was not simply exercising "tactful respect" in protecting the public images of his closest friends, he was manufacturing a public image of himself. To have left out all explicit mention of his homosexual life was completely understandable, given the times, Thomson's history, and the lingering scars of the Brooklyn catastrophe. But he includes stories of affairs with women that are at best exaggerated and at worse dishonest.

The person with the greatest cause for grievance was Ned Rorem, who was completely cut from the memoir. Rorem believed that this was purposeful, and he knew why. Earlier that year Rorem's first book, *The Paris Diary,* had been released. His beguiling and trenchant commentaries on the arts and artists were admired; but his unabashed accounts of his homosexual life made the book a succès de scandale. Rorem became an instant hero in the underground gay world. Naturally, Thomson, a recurring figure in Rorem's life, was a recurring presence in Rorem's book. Thomson was unhappy about his presence in such an explicitly "queer" book. Clearly, he did not want to be publicly associated too closely with Rorem; so he excised Ned from his own memoir.

If the autobiography was not a triumph upon its release, it did thrust Thomson back into the public arena of American arts and letters. Within that world everyone was talking about the book. But Thomson was counting on another project to reposition himself in the cultural community. During the period he was writing the book and jousting with the editors at Knopf, he was planning an opera. He had met, through Ned Rorem, ironically, a young poet and playwright, Jack Larson, who, after years of collaboration, had given him the "gift of a perfect libretto." By 1966 putting that libretto to music, as Thomson stated in his book's last paragraph, seemed "vastly urgent."[29]

25 A LORD, A GENIUS, A MILLIONAIRE, AND A BEAUTY

Growing up in the early 1940s in Montebello, a working-class Los Angeles suburb, Jack Larson was a bad boy. His parents—his father was a milk truck driver; his mother, a Western Union clerk—tried to be patient with their rambunctious son. But he was always getting into trouble and skipping school to go bowling, which was his passion. Only one thing kept him quiet: reading. He loved tales of King Arthur, anything with knights and suits of armor; and comic books, which he bought, read over and over, and never threw out. Piles of them cluttered his room.

Eventually Jack was admitted to a special public school for underprivileged youngsters from East Los Angeles who were difficult but had creative potential. Seizing on his interest in reading, his teachers turned Jack on to literature, especially Shakespeare. Two books changed his life. He came across Gertrude Stein's *Lectures in America* and started reading everything by her he could find. He even named his dog "Susie" after a favorite Stein poem, "Preciosilla," which ended with the line "Toasted Susie is my ice cream." He would speak these words sweetly to Susie, and she would wag her tail. Larson later found out from Virgil Thomson that the poem is considered one of Stein's most pornographic.

The other book was *The Canterbury Tales,* which started Larson's mania for verse. He discovered he had a knack for poetry and began writing plays in rhymed verse. By this time he had switched over to a school in Pasadena that merged the last two years of high school with the first two years of community college; there he put on his plays in verse, acting in and directing them himself. During one production, a play called *Balguna del Mar* (about college students on spring break in Laguna and Balboa beaches), an agent from Warner Brothers spotted the impish teenage actor and offered him a contract, which of course he signed. He was fifteen. At the studio he met Debbie Reynolds, also fifteen, who had been signed up the same week. They hung out together and sneaked onto the lot where John Huston was directing Humphrey Bogart in *Key Largo*.

At Warner Brothers, Larson made "mostly forgettable" films, including *Fighter Squadron,* directed by Raoul Walsh, which introduced Rock Hudson, and *Battle Zone,* starring John Hodiak and Stephen McNally in a love triangle in which the vying men take time out to fight Commies in Korea. Larson began to realize that one of the reasons for his tumultuous childhood was that he was gay. Hollywood was then a tightly closeted place, but there was an underground gay life that he began to explore.

By 1951 Larson was restless and unhappy in Hollywood. He wanted to move to New York, where he could write plays and act on stage, and his manager was sympathetic. So when Larson was offered decent money for what looked like a one-shot job in television, he grabbed it. The job involved filming twenty-six episodes of a new show. "It's just for kids, nobody will see it," his manager assured him. "They don't even have sponsor for it yet. It may never even air." Larson figured he would take his money, $250 per episode, move to New York, become a playwright, maybe do some theater acting. The show was *The Adventures of Superman.* Jack Larson played Superman's pal, the cub reporter Jimmy Olsen.

When the filming of *Superman* was finished, Larson returned to New York and took, sight unseen, a tiny, dark basement apartment on East Eighty-third Street. To his delight, he was befriended by the poet Frank O'Hara, "the Apollinaire of the New York art world," as Larson called him. O'Hara took Larson to galleries and introduced him to artist colleagues—a "private education" that taught him more than any college could. And Larson was having some success with his verse plays, which were presented in loft readings where the arbiters of New York's beat culture hung out.

Then, in 1953, the producers of *Superman* found a sponsor and the show was aired. It was a huge overnight success. And more even than the man of steel, it was Jimmy, the adolescent everyman who seemed always to be getting himself and Lois Lane ensnared in perilous mix-ups with nefarious no-goods, Jimmy, with his "Golly gee, Miss Lane" manner and sad-sack eyes, that America took to heart.

Larson was mortified. "I thought I was ruined as a serious playwright. As an actor, I feared I would be typecast forever." However, a successful television series provided a good livelihood. Life in New York was dynamic but penurious. So he returned to Hollywood and made six more seasons of *Superman,* until the filming was halted in 1959 because of the apparent suicide—Larson never completely accepted that it was suicide—of Superman, George Reeves. During this period he was excited by a relationship with Montgomery Clift, the brooding, darkly handsome film star thirteen years his senior. But Larson was tormented about his career. He fulfilled his responsibilities to the show. But, the bad boy once again, he refused to do publicity tours or interviews. He kept up his New York contacts, traveling back and forth and continuing to write. He also took occasional movie roles. In 1957 he had a small part in *Johnny Trouble,* a story of an elderly woman living alone, played by Ethel Barrymore (her last role, it turned out), who befriends the boys at a nearby college and talks continually of her long-missing son. In the cast was James Bridges, an aspiring actor and writer from Arkansas, gentle, perceptive, and just turned twenty. Larson and Bridges became fast friends. Within a year they were lovers. Their lifelong relationship would become one of the most admired domestic partnerships in Hollywood.

Larson needed Bridges's stabilizing influence, for after *Superman* ended he was bitter. The most he had ever earned was $350 per episode, and in those days residuals were not paid to actors when shows were rebroadcast. Larson devoted himself to his writing and, though living in Los Angeles, traveled regularly to New York. But he could not shake off his Jimmy Olsen past. "I was enormously famous. I couldn't go places. I hid out and acted like a nut."

Then, in 1962, he met Virgil Thomson.

Ned Rorem, on his first trip to California, was spending two months in Los Angeles at the Huntington Hartford Foundation, which provided space and support for artists to work. Frank O'Hara had told Ned to contact his friends Jack Larson and Jim Bridges. They got together and liked each other immediately. Rorem decided to use some Larson verse in a song cycle, *Poems of Love and the Rain.* A few weeks later Thomson arrived, having been invited to the foundation to work on his autobiography. Bridges, who was then a directing assistant to John Houseman in a professional theater company affiliated with UCLA, had met Thomson when the composer attended a production of *Measure for Measure* for which Houseman used Thomson's music. Larson, who had worn out his recording of *Four Saints in Three Acts*, longed to meet Thomson. So Rorem arranged a dinner. Thus started a series of memorable evenings that continued through Thomson's stay. In September, Larson wrote to Thomson, who was back in New York, to thank him for the "happy privilege" of meeting him. "Those were marvelous dinners and talks, *and,* of course, you know I fully appreciate you being interested in what I've written. That you liked it and want to see more of it is wonderful for me."[1]

He sent Thomson some recent plays, including *The Candied House*, a retelling of the Hansel and Gretel story. Larson did more than simply put the story in verse; he transformed it. The characters are introspective and complex. As Larson presents them, the parents who desert their children in the forest are victims of poverty, delirious with hunger, fear, and failure. Obsessed with the myth of Romulus and Remus, who were raised in the wilderness by a wolf that rescued and suckled them, the parents convince themselves that their children will be cared for by the creatures of the forest. When they realize the scope of their delusions, they are sick with remorse. Even the witch is a complex character, who reflects on the nature of evil and the roles some are given to suffer. Larson's verse is resonant, beguiling, and humorous. Here is the witch in an exchange with the caged Hansel, whom she intends to fatten up for dinner:

> HANSEL
> *Please don't! Please! I'm sure I'd be bad to taste.*
>
> WITCH
> *You would be now, you're all sinewy waste.*
> *But with care you'll be a digestible joy;*
> *A meaty, well-nourished muscular boy.*
>
> *When your skin swells sweet with muscles and meat,*
> *When your veins seem to flood with rich red blood,*
> *When you're fed till you're an Adonis of food,*
> *Then dear, you'll be most delicious to eat.*

In mid-November, Thomson wrote to Larson, "I have read your plays with great pleasure. There isn't anything that I can do about them except to admire."[2] By then the idea that Larson should write a libretto for Thomson was no longer provisional. Resolved not to do "another opera with a hermetic text," Thomson asked Larson to begin work on a subject he had been toying with for years: the Sixth Baron George Gordon Noel Byron, renowned as Lord Byron, the early nineteenth-century Romantic poet. To Larson, getting onstage the man whose very name was a synonym for grandeur ("Byronic") was an intimidating prospect. But, not yet thirty, he was in no position to object.

The idea of writing an opera on Byron, Thomson always used to say, came to him through a boast by his acquaintance Gore Vidal that, for a play on the great poet, he already had a second-act curtain line: our hero would declare himself father of a child by his sister. However, already in 1935, flush from success with *Four Saints,* Thomson considered making on opera of *Byron a Play,* a 1933 work by Gertrude Stein. Virgil "directly and indirectly wants to do it," Stein wrote to Carl Van Vechten, "it would take a lot of stage imagination to put it on, but it does move and it is a romantic tragedy."[3] Thomson eventually rejected the idea.

Twenty-five years later, Vidal's teaser rekindled Thomson's interest. He could not imagine a stage play on Byron, but he thought the subject ideal for a "poetic drama with music." Byron was of mythic size, a "lord, a genius, a millionaire, a hero, a lover, and a beauty!"

> That's an awful lot for one man to carry, even with his club foot to hold him down. But with all that, I think he rather had to misbehave every day a little . . . to cut himself down to size. . . . He had a Scotchman's violence, and the poet's independence. He simply would not be told how to behave or how not to behave.[4]

He asked Vidal if he would be interested in writing a libretto, but the writer had "no bent toward musical collaborations."[5] Looking for other poets with theater sense, Thomson approached Robert Penn Warren and Robert Lowell. Both declined. Putting aside his misgivings, Jack Larson accepted. "I've read everything by and about Byron I can find," he wrote to Thomson in late November. "I'm very excited about it and believe I can do it."[6]

At first Larson feared that any stage representation of Byron would be a pale reflection of the legendary poet. Moreover, would a verse libretto set itself up for comparison with Byron's own poetry? And if one decided to include Byron's verse, as Larson thought he must, how would one get it on the stage? Larson quickly found a solution and wrote to Virgil with his idea. In 1817, to escape the scandal his brazen private life (the rumors of an affair and child by his half sister and notorious accounts of romances with young men) and to distance himself from his wife, who had renounced him, Byron traveled to Venice, where he had an affair with Contessa Guiccioli, and then to Greece, where he joined the battle for Greek independence from Turkey. There he died in 1824 at the age of thirty-six from an illness (probably influenza) that was mistreated by local doctors (who bled him). When his body was brought back to England, the public proclaimed him a hero, and his friends began a campaign to get Byron interred in Poet's Corner of Westminster Abbey. The Church of England would not hear of it. Larson's idea was to begin the opera after Byron's death.

> The line I imagine it taking is the pursuit, intrigues and battles between his wife, his publisher, his sister, his friends and his Italian mistress, to get in possession of, and burn, those memoirs Byron had written, telling all, which in fact, as you know, they did burn. . . . In every scene there'd be a bust surrounded by house palms and ferns, or a statue of Byron, and as the other characters argue, read, rhapsodize and plot, Byron's bust can sing out his wonderful, witty poetry. I wouldn't be writing them, my lines for a genius, but could let his own genius sing about his world.[7]

The indirection of Larson's approach appealed to Thomson, who was not interested in writing a swashbuckling romantic opera. But he was bothered by the notion of a singing statue. Still, he believed Larson's concept was promising. For the next eighteen months they consulted by letter, occasionally met, and refined their ideas. There would be a statue of Byron and statues of his fellow poets honored in Poet's Corner. But visible singers, full-fledged characters, would sing the roles of Byron and his poet colleagues, not as singing monuments but as "the still living spirits of themselves separate from their statues." As the memoirs are read by Byron's friends, events from his life would be retold in memory scenes. Almost all the lines spoken by Byron would be quotation from his verse, diaries, and letters. Thomson thought Larson's original verse so elegant that "you can not tell what is Byron and what is Larson."

By summer 1964 Larson had obtained Thomson's permission to show his text to John Houseman, who was enthusiastic and had several constructive suggestions. Larson then sent Thomson a complete two-act text. On September 10 Thomson wrote back, "Dear Jack, Have been re-reading Byron and singing it to music in my mind. It does sing and it also speaks if I want it to. You never told me what Houseman's reaction was. I'm beginning to be quite attached to your rhymed couplets. All the characters are different, wonderful for acting." And two weeks later: "The second act is lovely and especially the love scenes. I get happier and happier about it all."[8]

In May of 1965, as Virgil was passing through Los Angeles, Larson arranged a reading of the libretto with a cast drawn from his Hollywood actor and writer friends. There was no audience. Everyone just sat about the living room table at the Brentwood house where Larson and Bridges lived; a technician from UCLA tape-recorded the event for the archives. The cast was dazzling: Christopher Isherwood read Byron incomparably; the writer and critic Gavin Lambert read John Hobhouse, Byron's close friend, and James Bridges read John Murray, Byron's devoted publisher. The actresses Betty Harford and Antoinette Bower split the three major female roles: Augusta Leigh, Byron's married half sister, now lady-in-waiting to the Queen; Lady Byron, Byron's wife, the former Annabella Milbank; and Contessa Guiccioli, Byron's last mistress and the wife of Count Gamba, Byron's companion in the Greek War of Independence. The painters Jim Gill and Don Bachardy helped out with smaller roles. Larson read the stage directions, and Thomson scored a triumph in a short but climactic role, the dean of Westminster Abbey.

In the final scene Byron's friends, having read the racy memoir, decide they must destroy it if they are to have any hope of placing the statue in Poet's Corner. The dean, come to inspect the statue and pronounce his ruling on the suit, enters the abbey and sees the pages burning in the brazier. Sizing up the situation, he says, "The statue is very fine. As for its being here, in your burning his memoir, you'll find your answer. The man whose life is not fit to be read / Is not fit to be publicly honored, dead."

The way Thomson read these lines the dean is neither upset not indignant, just calmly dismissive. Thomson's performance suggests something of the reasons for his attraction to this subject. No doubt, he got a vicarious kick out of his hero's wickedness, and relished the way Byron skewered the "smatter and chatter" of British drawing room society and the "blue-stocking" ladies, one of whom the poet had married so unhappily. Byron could have coauthored Thomson's youthful manifesto "Maxims of a Modernist." But Byron flaunted his wickedness in proper society. For this he had to pay a price. Of course he could not be honored in Westminster Abbey. Thomson would have agreed with the dean.

After the reading everyone went for a festive Chinese dinner at a downtown restaurant, Man Fook Low. A few days later Thomson wrote Larson from San Francisco, "Successful visit. But nothing like L.A. The gift of a perfect libretto. Write me for fun."[9]

Thomson's gratifying note seemed to indicate that Larson's work on *Lord Byron* was over. But Thomson gave no indication of when he might begin composing. While in New York for a visit that winter, Larson was out one night with Thomson when an acquaintance came up to them and asked after the opera. "What opera?" Thomson said. Larson did not speak, but started to panic. He had heard from Frank O'Hara the story of Kenneth Koch's "Angelica." During that visit Larson was hyperactive and drinking too much. Thomson disapproved. Back home in January, Larson wrote to apologize.

> As you might have guessed, I've been sick as hell ever since I got back from New York and as I know you know, I was certainly sick there. Certainly, I was behaving, what you called, "over-stimulated." The main reasons are different from what you think, though. I get total anxiety through the disparity of wanting to be "taken" only for the work I do now, and being hounded on the NYC streets for my "past" as "Superman's pal." I won't go on about it. We'll talk of it sometime if you like.[10]

As it happened, there was no cause for alarm. Thomson was working intensely on his autobiography and not composing. Meanwhile Larson was getting high compliments from heady sources. "Don Bachardy gave my play *Angel Flight* to Lincoln Kirstein," Larson wrote to Thomson, "who's since overwhelmed me with letters about it. He says it's 'absolutely marvelous and could be a whopping commercial success.' "[11] Through Thomson he learned of Alice B. Toklas's enthusiasm for the libretto. While visiting in Paris during July, Virgil had read the first draft to Alice, who, Virgil reported via postcard, "kept saying 'wonderful' but added that it would be hard to add music to a text so complete in every way."[12]

Alice was in a bad state. After Gertrude's death she had become a Catholic, thinking it the only way to be together again with Gertrude. Being an atheist and a Jew, Gertrude had never entertained the idea of an afterlife. But Alice knew that, despite herself, Gertrude was immortal. So "Alice had no choice but to take on immortality," as Virgil explained it. "Since in her case that could not be done through genius, her only chance was through the Christian faith."[13] In 1960 she spent ten months at a monastery in Rome with a Canadian order of nuns. Her eyes were poor, her frail and bony body ached with arthritis. But she was happy in her cloistered life with the sisters.

When she returned, she discovered that the children of Allan Stein, the coexecutor of Gertrude's estate who had died in 1951, had removed all the paintings from her rue Christine apartment, those that belonged to the estate and those that belonged to Alice. They had gone to court to declare the works "endangered" by her absence. In addition, Allan Stein's widow alerted the authorities that Alice was in violation of a law stating that no rented apartment could stay empty for more than four months a year. So, in 1963, nearly blind and eighty-six, Alice found herself evicted. If she had contacted her influential friends earlier, the eviction might have been stopped. Though informed late of her troubles, a group of friends—Thornton Wilder, Janet Flanner, Jo Barry, the scholar Donald Sutherland, and Thomson—provided some financial support. Alice was moved to a new apartment in an elevator building near the Eiffel Tower with efficient heating, but with no character and thin walls.

Jim Bridges had gone to Paris in the summer of 1965 to write a script for a Louis Malle project, a film called *Choice Cuts,* which never got made. Offered Thomson's Paris flat, Larson joined Bridges that fall. After several days he called Alice, who invited him to come the next day at four. Larson resisted the temptation to bring her a rose, opting instead for a potted cyclamen. He was sad to see the fabled furniture from the photos of the 27 rue de Fleurus salon crammed into Alice's drab modern rooms. Now bedridden, Alice was sitting up in a brass bed by a window on a courtyard.

> She looked small yet vital, and though her cropped hair and bangs were very gray, her trace of moustache was still dark enough to be very there. She looked at me through thick eyeglasses, and as she explained she was recovering from cataracts, she introduced a young Englishman she employed to read to her. They had been reading *Figaro* and feeling concern about a possible workmen's strike. She was pleased with the cyclamen but feared for its life as it seems her maid was very bad about watering plants. A chair was brought for me next to her bed, and soon a tray was set up with rosé wine and buttered honeybread. She told us she'd developed a taste for the bread when she'd been with "the Sisters."[14]

Larson spent three afternoons in October with Alice B. Toklas, the ful-fillment of a fantasy. He told her that his friend poet John Ashbery was in Paris then and would love to meet her. Alice declined. But she agreed happily to meet Jim, who came by one afternoon for an ex-hilarating visit. By then, Alice, recovered from her cataract procedure and fitted with new glasses, was reading by herself, *The Spoils of Poyn-ton,* by her beloved Henry James. "I'm not just reading it," she said, "I'm rereading it. I always read it again as soon as I can forget it. . . . He's wonderful. All his young ladies are so sad." Alice was very cu-rious to hear news of Virgil's progress on his autobiography. "She told me that she and Virgil had never been such friends while Gertrude Stein was alive, 'But since Gertrude died, he's been one of the best friends to me. I know why too. He's repaying me for what Gertrude did for him.' "[15] That fall, in the last note Larson received from Tok-las, she asked about Virgil's autobiography. "How is the book on Gertrude coming along? Let me have news of you."[16]

Five months later Alice B. Toklas died at eighty-nine. As she had requested, Alice was buried at Père Lachaise in the same tomb as Gertrude, with her name and dates inscribed on the back of Gertrude's headstone so as not to distract visitors who had come to pay homage to Gertrude.

By mid-November, summoned to the Chelsea Hotel, Larson was finally reassured that Thomson intended to begin work on the opera. On Sunday, November 28, 1965, the headlines of the *New York Times* reported on a march in Washington ("Thousands Walk in Capital to Protest War in Vietnam") and the ominous national debt ("7 Billion Federal Deficit Seen as Spending Nears 105 Billion"). That day in the music section was an intriguing article titled "Lord Byron in Three Acts." Under a striking picture of Thomson and Larson, seated together in Thomson's mahogany confidante with the velvet upholstery, ran an article by the music critic Allen Hughes announcing plans for the Lord Byron opera. Tactfully, the specifics of Larson's acting career were left unspecific. Hughes merely mentions "a period in the 1950s when he worked in motion pictures and television. He insists that all that is behind him now." Thomson is quoted as saying that he had yet to begin composing, but was at the "terminal point" of writing his memoirs and would soon "be free to get to the opera."

The article attracted great attention. Inquiries started arriving from various opera companies. Then, in early 1966, a solid offer to commission the work came from a surprising source: the Metropolitan Opera. That the Met wanted to commission its former tormentor seemed inexplicable. Thomson's last years on the *Herald Tribune* had overlapped with the first years of Rudolf Bing's tenure as general director, which began in 1950. Thomson had used his column to attack Bing's antipathy to contemporary opera. Bing was still on the job, his control more pervasive than ever.

However, much had changed in the twelve years since Thomson had left the paper. Bing had acquired an assistant, the German-born John Gutman, who had genuine sympathy for contemporary music. Gutman made Bing understand that the company would lose intellectual prestige if it did not at least occasionally put its estimable reputation behind new works. In addition, Thomson had recommended the Metropolitan Opera Studio, a roster of young Met singers who presented concerts in smaller venues, to the director of a series at the Library of Congress, which resulted in regular, well-received concerts in Washington and elsewhere. Bing must have concluded that it would be advantageous to the Met to make peace with this elder statesman of American music.

Finally, however, the decision came down to money. Gutman knew where to get it: the Ford Foundation had a program to enable performing arts institutions to commission new works. To date, only two new operas had been commissioned during Bing's tenure: Samuel Barber's *Vanessa* was premiered in 1958; and Marc Blitzstein, backed with a Ford Foundation grant, had been commissioned in 1960 to write an opera on Sacco and Vanzetti. But while in Martinique in January of 1964 Blitzstein was bar-hopping one night with three queer-bashing sailors, two Portuguese and one Martinique native, who stripped him, robbed him, beat him, and left him to die.

In 1966 the Metropolitan was moving from its old home on Fortieth and Broadway to its new complex in Lincoln Center. Gutman convinced Bing that this occasion demanded the production of new works. Three composers were approached: Samuel Barber, whose *Antony and Cleopatra,* starring Leontyne Price, opened the house on September 16, 1966; Martin David Levy, whose *Mourning Becomes Electra,* featuring a young baritone named Sherrill Milnes, was performed in March of 1967; and Virgil Thomson, whose *Lord Byron* had been announced so notably in the *Times.* With the Ford grant boosted by some money from the Koussevitzky Foundation, the Metropolitan Opera was able to offer Thomson a commission of $18,000, two-thirds of it for the composer, one-third for the librettist.

Thomson accepted eagerly and asked his well-connected lawyer, Arnold Weissberger, to draw up a contract for Larson to sign. Stein had been a stubborn negotiator, but Larson was in no position to question Thomson's stipulations, even clause 5, which placed the "composer in charge of both artists' rights in musical, visual and all other production matters," although the composer, it continued, "will consult and satisfy where possible the author." A Metropolitan Opera production meant that Thomson's last opera, and he sensed that this was to be his last, would have to be his most ambitious work. Thomson expected Larson to be thrilled by the news, but he wasn't. Larson had always assumed that *Lord Byron,* like the two Stein operas, was to be a literate, conversational piece ideally suited to productions in smaller companies and colleges where Thomson's ability to bring words to life through music would have its greatest impact. But now, it seemed, *Lord Byron* was to be a grand opera. The Metropolitan's move to Lincoln Center demanded certain changes in conception and scope. The management did not present them as requirements. But failure to fulfill them would diminish the work's attractiveness and endanger its future at the Met, as Larson recalled:

> Their audience needed two intermissions so Virgil needed a three-act libretto. The huge stage would require larger scenes with a bigger cast. It would be advantageous to include a large chorus. And, it seemed, a ballet. Since there would be grand set changes it would be impossible to have a fluctuating change of time and place between the Abbey and the character's memories; the opera would have to open and end in the Abbey with the memories combined into scenically manageable flashbacks.[17]

As a matter of professional pride, Thomson was determined to meet the Met's requests. Larson didn't know where to begin rewriting. Thomson urged him to consult John Houseman, whose advice was to bend to Virgil's wishes. Then, just when his confidence needed a boost, Larson had a wonderful success. In the last week of February, his play *The Candied House* opened the new 602-seat theater at the Los Angeles County Museum of Art. The production, directed by James Bridges, was lavishly praised. This experience decisively turned Bridges from acting to directing, though writing would remain his first love. Margaret Harford of the *Los Angeles Times* wrote,

> Larson is a young writer with a poet's gift and an actor's theatrical eye. In a day when the ugliest words in the English language

are perpetrated on stage in the guise of realistic drama, it's a joy
to hear from a man who loves and respects words and does not
see language as the enemy of images.[18]

Clyde Leech of the *Los Angeles Herald-Examiner* called Larson's verse
the "most sensitive, lyrical and beautiful language I have encountered
recently from the pen of a contemporary playwright."[19]

By way of a congratulatory note, Thomson turned on the charm
to win his librettist's compliance:

> Dear Jackiewakie,
>   The news of success and more productions is beautiful. House-
> man and you seem inclined to humour me in Byron matters and
> that is beautiful. A big opera needs a solid structure. And this will
> be a big one.[20]

For the next two years Larson wrote and rewrote, sometimes "just a
jump ahead of Virgil's needs for the music."

> I bogged down completely sometimes, lost grasp of any concept
> of the work, and could barely keep it from unraveling. Once, John
> Houseman had to mediate the placement of the new act breaks.
> Another time, Virgil sent me a four-page outline of the new dra-
> matic arrangement of the libretto with everything by page num-
> bers that was in or out or needed.[21]

Meanwhile, Thomson composed steadily and happily. During the
summer of 1966 he went to the MacDowell Colony, the rustic arts
colony in New Hampshire where twice before he had been granted
residencies. "I began the very first day and write rapidly every day,"
Thomson wrote to his young collaborator in August; "I could not be
more pleased with you and me."[22]

But the commission from the Metropolitan decisively changed the
nature of the opera and the spirit of the collaboration, as Thomson
ruefully recalled ten years after these events. In the beginning the "enterprise had gone forward in good will and mutual confidence; and
I was enchanted by Larson's longer script when I received it." But as
the Met became more involved, the work "was beset by disputes, mis-
understandings, deceptions, concealments, delays, wrong decisions,
and plain stupidities."[23]

Larson worked on the libretto continually to accommodate Thomson's ever-changing demands, extraordinary in their specificity. His
letter to Larson of June 16, 1967, asking for changes in a crucial

speech where Byron's publisher announces the existence of the tell-all memoir, is typical:

Dear Jack,

I phoned you last night and shall again soon, but I need to explain about Tom Moore's speech introducing the flashbacks.

I've made 1 1/2 versions and don't like either of them. I think the trouble is the stilted nature of the poetry (surely Moore's own) With rhymed ten-syllable iambics, elegant but uninspired, I can't make the melody take off as it should do in a place where nothing else (but sceneshifting) is taking place. I need to hold attention with a soaring Irish air of some sort.

Could you possibly take the meaning of Moore's lines (or whatever other meaning you might like him to express) and write me a lyric poem (5 stanzas maximum, maybe 4) that I can set to music in the Irish lyric vein?

Moore himself was at his most memorable when he wrote new words for old songs, for the Irish ones, as Burns had done for the Scottish.

Use a simple rhyme-scheme like ABAB or AABB and 4-line stanzas of either 4-4-4-4 feet or 4-3-4-3. I don't say this is the only set-up. But surely something just as plain. And with plain rhymes.

Moore's own verse is not good enough to hold an aria. You will do something with quality. Compact and meaningful.

Byron's pentameters are possible to set because of their constant surprises and rigorous thought. Moore is hopeless and garrulous and in the end only genteel.

What is the possibility?

Virgil[24]

Ever obliging and resourceful, Larson wrote four stanzas that the grateful composer set to the tune of "Those Endearing Young Charms," a popular Irish air.

MOORE (Unwrapping the Byron Memoir)

Remember, the poet we knew with our heart
Is known only to others in books.
There are thousands who cherish each word of his art
As we cherished his voice and his looks.

What those thousands would give to read of his life
That we who lived with him ignore!
They might find in his genius the seeds of his strife
Penned there by the hand they adore.

Remember, that genius that gleamed in his verse,
Gleamed as bright in the life of the man.
He has left us the prose of his life, not a curse,
A witness we've no right to ban.

How often he spoke of his muse as the truth,
While he followed its Lorelei song.
What he sought in his art from his laurel-wreathed youth,
He sought in himself his life long.

Larson grew to realize that "writing a libretto is like working in-side someone else; the words have to make the bird sing or they're of no use." A librettist can do his best work imaginable, but if it doesn't inspire the composer, it's useless and that's that. But Larson's verse did inspire Thomson, from the opening chorus of Londoners who be-moan Byron's death, which Thomson set with music of unusually deep emotional resonance (the chorus wails in heaving parallel chords of stacked-up tritones), to the final scene at Westminster Abbey when spirits of the entombed poets emerge to welcome their deceased friend Byron in a merry madrigal.

On May 7, 1968, Anthony Lewis reported in the *New York Times* that finally, a century and a half after his death, Lord Byron was to have a plaque in the Poet's Corner of Westminster Abbey. Three pre-vious efforts to secure this recognition had been rebuffed. The last, on the centenary of Byron's death in 1924, was firmly rejected by the then dean of Westminster Abbey, Bishop Herbert E. Ryle, who cited the poet's "openly dissolute life" and "licentious verse," and his "world-wide reputation for immorality." The successful effort in 1968 was spearheaded by the poet laureate of England, Cecil Day-Lewis (whose son Daniel would become the Academy Award–winning actor). Thom-son and Larson considered the news a good omen. It certainly made the opera topical.

More good news came that fall when Larson received a grant from the Rockefeller Foundation. Thomson had submitted an eloquent let-ter in support: "He is a master of a seemingly relaxed style of writing in meter and rhyme that is ever so becoming to theatrical use, since it rides high above the banalities of merely naturalistic speech with-out ever becoming mannered or obscure."[25]

A crucial tryout of *Lord Byron* took place on the afternoon of April 9, 1969, in a large rehearsal room at the Metropolitan Opera. Nine young singers from the Opera Studio program and two guest artists performed four extended scenes, almost sixty minutes of music, accompanied on piano by John Ryan of the music staff. The invited audience of over one hundred was composed mostly of Met patrons and board members. Thomson had invited just a few of his friends. Larson's guests included Lanford Wilson, Terrence McNally, John Ashbery, Andy Warhol, and the film legend Myrna Loy. The Lord Byron was Grayson Hirst, a wholesomely handsome tenor from California, not yet thirty, who had studied at Juilliard with the renowned Jennie Tourel. His voice was not enormous, but he had clarion sound, effortless technique, and a wide, flexible range.

From all accounts, including a tape recording, the tryout went splendidly. Thomson made introductions and set up the scenes. His dry descriptions of Byron's indiscretions inspired much laughter. Speaking of the early scene where Byron's friends debate what to do with the memoir, Thomson said that he associated this situation with Wagner's *Das Rheingold,* "which is one long discussion about contracts." The singers performed with skill and palpable involvement.

The music was not what might have been expected of an opera about this quintessential Romantic. The long scene in which Byron's friends debate the fate of the memoir evolved in long spans of conversational, lyrical yet not particularly melodic vocal lines. There was wit and playfulness in the rendering of the text, with its clever wordplay and mock-poetic flourishes. The music was straightforward, clearheaded, more bracing than emotional. Yet there were episodes of real fervor. Byron's pugnacious entrance music ("A mighty mass of brick and smoke and shipping, dirty and dusky, but wide as eye can reach," he sings of London town) was dispatched by Hirst with ringing tone and a triumphant high C. There was prolonged applause after the dreamy Act 2 trio for Byron, Lady Byron and his half sister Augusta Leigh; and complicitous laughter during the scene when the same trio sang the wickedly witty ensemble "Kisses, kisses, give your baby kisses, kisses from his Mrs., kisses of his sis's."

Yet during the entire presentation Rudolf Bing stood poker-faced, sometimes talking to a Met patron, someone he was hoping, Thomson always suspected, might back the *Lord Byron* production. To this conservative Austrian manager, Thomson's music was perplexing: This is our grand opera about Lord Byron? With all those words so meticulously set to music? And what are all these musical quotes doing here? A contrapuntal rendering of "Auld Lang Syne? A fugal, polytonal treatment of "Ach, Du Lieber Augustine"?

Moreover, to Bing the story was shocking. It would be one thing if Thomson had characterized the lechery through tortured chromaticism and dissonance. But the blithely cavalier musical treatment seemed nonjudgmental.

Afterward compliments and congratulations were bestowed on the creators during a champagne reception. Bing approached Thomson, shook his hand firmly, and said, "We shall be seeing each other soon. Meanwhile, you will make arrangements with Mr. Gutman." But Thomson felt uneasy. He asked Gutman, who was extremely enthusiastic about the opera, whether everything was as favorable as it appeared to be. Gutman said, "It might not be so sure. We'll talk."[26]

Five days later, on April 14, 1969, Thomson received from Bing the following letter:

Dear Mr. Thomson;

I hear that you will be out of town next week and as thereafter I will be on tour with the Company for six weeks and in New York only for occasional short days before my departure for Europe, I thought I better let you have a line about my views.

Needless to say I was extremely interested in hearing your new opera, but if you want me to be frank, I have grave doubts whether this is a piece suitable for a 4000-seat house. An overwhelming portion of the work consists of dialogue between two or three people—dialogue which it is essential to understand and this of course is always difficult in a house of our size.

I think John [Gutman] has already told you that the next two seasons had to be planned because nowadays if we want prominent conductors, directors and singers, one has to plan two years ahead. This leaves, as the earliest possibility, the season 1971/72 which, as things stand at the moment, may be my last season in the House. It would be premature for me at the moment to make commitments already for that season.

John tells me that you asked whether we would object if the work was first done somewhere else—I think he mentioned Dallas—not at all. On the contrary I would welcome it to see what effect the work has in a large Opera House and, indeed, we are more and more inclined to lend and borrow scenery amongst Opera Houses to reduce the ever increasing cost of productions.

I very much hope that we will find a chance to meet and discuss the matter within the next month, but in any case I felt I should not keep you waiting and let you have these observations.

Thank you very much for having made it possible for us to listen to this interesting reading and I hope you will feel, as I do, that Mr. Ryan and all the singers did a splendid job.

With kind regards,

Yours sincerely,
Rudolf Bing[27]

Thomson was somehow not surprised. "Until I'm in my seat watching the curtain go up I never believe that productions of my operas are actually going to happen," he used to say. A Metropolitan Opera premiere was almost too good to be true. He considered rebutting Bing's letter point by point. One could argue that *Die Walküre* is an opera that consists overwhelmingly of "dialogue between two or three people," dialogue which is "essential to understand." But it seemed pointless. Instead he stewed at home, complained to friends, and wrote to Maurice who was in Europe.

> D.M.:
> The Met's (in effect) refusal of my opera has been a shock. Bing himself seems to have been pleased with it till a rich trustee said no. It seems that *both* incest & pregnancy (and among the highborn) are considered bad taste. Anyway, I now know from the unanimous (but one) enthusiasm that the piece is sort of dynamite. Nicolas N[abokov] is taking a tape of the reading-audition to East Berlin, where they do handsome productions and where corruption among the high life is believed to be true. We may have to wait a bit for a production. San Francisco and others are approached. The tape is excellent.
> Meanwhile I am back at my book.*
>
> Love,
> V[28]

For years thereafter Thomson consoled himself with the fact that the Metropolitan Opera never formally refused the work: the company commissioned it, showcased it in tryouts, but never brought it to production. He assumed that Bing's primary reason for rejecting it was financial. However, in his 1972 memoir Bing was blunt, in a way he had not been with Thomson, about his reason for not producing *Lord Byron:*

> Twice, with money from the Ford Foundation, we commissioned American composers to write operas for us but did not stage the results—once because there were no results (Marc Blitzstein was bizarrely murdered in the Caribbean before completing any but a

---

*American Music since 1910, published in 1971.

fraction of *Sacco and Vanzetti*), once because, frankly, we did not like the results (Virgil Thomson's *Lord Byron*).[29]

Thomson had tailored *Lord Byron,* some would say inflated it, to Metropolitan Opera–sized proportions. Now there would be no production. This was and remained the most demoralizing setback of Thomson's career.

Meanwhile, Jack Larson's dejection was assuaged by another theatrical success. Jim Bridges, now working as a director at the University of Southern California's Festival Theater, had organized a summer residency at the Edinburgh Festival in Scotland, and one of the plays presented was Larson's *Cherry, Larry, Sandy, Doris, Jean, Paul.* The play is a romp in verse, a modern-day answer to Restoration comedy. Set in 1960, it concerns a triangle of friends, two gay guys, Larry and Sandy, and the domineering matriarchal Cherry, who is legally (though not carnally) married to Sandy. They are traveling in England, staying at the boardinghouse of Mrs. Pacellis, and they are all constipated. Everything gets loosened up when they meet Doris and Jean, two young American women, and Paul, a handsome bisexual GI on leave from his base in Germany. The characters, though eccentric, are earnest and delightful. During the summer of the Stonewall uprising, when "gay play" meant the self-loathing characters of *The Boys in the Band,* Larson produced a play in which gay situations are presented with matter-of-factness. The reviews were excellent ("natural, charming, completely without self-pity and hysteria . . . written in bubbling but unobtrusive rhymed couplets"). The success was duplicated in September when the troupe returned to the USC theater.

But a venue to introduce *Lord Byron* was not forthcoming, and Thomson was getting worried.

Since *Lord Byron* had been conceived for the Metropolitan Opera, a college production no longer seemed suitable. But when in early 1971 composer Peter Mennin, the president of the Juilliard School, offered the auspices of Juilliard's American Opera Center for the premiere, there were good reasons for Thomson to change his mind. Though officially students, the gifted Juilliard singers were burgeoning professionals. Moreover, with no one being paid, the rehearsal schedule could be extensive. The orchestra was first-rate. Best of all, since 1966 Thomson's friend John Houseman had been running Juilliard's theater department and would be available to direct. Finally, Mennin promised Thomson artistic control, which no professional opera house would have. So Thomson accepted. The production would be presented in April of 1972 in the new 933-seat Juilliard Theater, less than one-fourth the size of the Met, but a handsome, efficient facility.

Such was the state of music in America that the roles of the professional companies and the conservatories had gotten reversed. During the nineteenth century, the glory days of opera, it was the professional opera houses that introduced new works. The highlight of every season at La Scala or Teatro La Fenice was the new Verdi opera. The conservatory, as its name suggests, was where the great tradition was maintained and passed on. But a century later, it was the major American opera houses that, to their discredit, had become merely curators of the repertory. The colleges and conservatories, freed from commercial obligations, took on the responsibility of extending that repertory. So *Lord Byron* would be produced across the plaza at Lincoln Center from the Met at Juilliard, where at least Thomson would find a supportive musical climate. Or so he hoped.

That spring in London, Thomson sounded out Frederick Ashton about coming to New York to direct *Lord Byron* choreographically, as he had done in 1934 for *Four Saints*. Ashton agreed. Thomson also asked the painter David Hockney, Larson's good friend, to design the production; Hockney also accepted. The team was shaping up impressively.

Finding a conductor proved more frustrating. Thomson asked Alfred Wallenstein, who had conducted a supple live radio broadcast of *Four Saints* in 1942. When Thomson completed the orchestration of the opera in the fall of 1971, Wallenstein examined the score and agreed to conduct. Then his wife had a heart attack, necessitating their move to California for her recuperation and the cancellation of all his obligations. Thomson approached other eminent conductors and was turned down. Finally, he settled on Gerhard Samuel, German-born, American-trained, then the associate conductor of the Los Angeles Philharmonic, a man highly recommended by Mennin but unknown to Thomson. Though uneasy about the decision, Thomson at this point had no other choice.

Then the "cavalcade of catastrophes," as Thomson called it, began. For "reasons still unknown to me" Peter Mennin "simply delayed writing to Ashton and Hockney," who were awaiting official confirmation of their hiring. In fact, Mennin was sidelined in Iowa that summer undergoing serious foot surgery, something Thomson did know. In any event, three months passed with no word to Ashton. By that time, having waited long enough, Ashton accepted an engagement for early 1972 in Australia. Since Ashton was not to be on the team, Hockney also declined. Thomson had wanted Ashton not just for his grace in moving singing actors around a stage but also for a ballet sequence, an idea that arose during *Lord Byron*'s courtship with the Metropolitan Opera. Stuck with fantasies of operatic grandeur, Thomson would not relinquish the idea. The ballet would take place between the last two scenes, "between Byron's leaving England for Italy and his return from Greece dead." It would depict the events of the seven years that transpired: his affair with the contessa, his friendship with Shelley, Shelley's death, Byron's exploits in Greece, the Greek War of Independence, and Byron's death. Both Larson and Houseman argued that an inserted ballet would seem exactly that, inserted. Moreover, though the opera was completed, Thomson had not written a note of the promised ballet. But he would not hear of abandoning it. *Lord Byron* was a grand opera, grand operas wanted ballet, so *Lord Byron* would have a proper ballet, and that was final. Approaching his seventy-fifth birthday, Thomson had not the energy or inspiration to compose something new. Rather than give up the idea, he orchestrated his String Quartet no. 2, a jocular and lyrical work, but unrelated stylistically to the opera. Even the orchestration of this music was too much to handle. So he farmed out the job to Hershy Kay, virtually the house orchestrator at the New York City Ballet. The resulting ballet, hastily choreographed by Alvin Ailey, who was busy with his own company, and danced only adequately by students from the dance division, turned out to be an embarrassment.

In the fall of 1971 Thomson auditioned the Juilliard singers and selected his cast. Mennin and Houseman were very concerned about Thomson's taking over this critical task, for the hearing problems that had troubled him since the early 1960s had become serious.

Like other elderly people, Thomson had experienced a growing deterioration of volume in his hearing. But he also had a less common problem: pitch distortion. He heard all low pitches (basically, all the notes below middle C) as flat by a full halftone; and in the treble range, in place of each sounded fundamental pitch, he heard an overtone. Music became a jumble of false pitches.

For decades Thomson had composed away from the keyboard by choice, hearing music in his head, much as Beethoven did. So his worsening hearing did not prevent his composing. Of course, he could no longer conduct or play the piano, "still less the unspeakable pipe organ which put me through college."[30] Even listening to recorded music was virtually impossible. However, auditioning singers was something he stubbornly maintained he could do. After all, he could at least tell whether a singer had a lustrous sound, accurate rhythm, long-spun legato, and, most important, clear diction. His production team colleagues were not so sure.

Yet the results of Thomson's auditions were excellent. Thomson selected twenty-eight Juilliard singers, several of whom would have international careers. For John Hobhouse he picked a baritone from North Dakota, Lenus Carlson, who in two years would debut at the Metropolitan. For the small role of the poet Thomson he cast a dark, handsome, twenty-two-year-old New Yorker, tenor Neil Shicoff, who would one day triumph as Offenbach's Hoffmann at Covent Garden and the Metropolitan. For the minor part of Lady Charlotte, he cast a young black soprano from Stephens, Arizona, with an agile, lyrical voice, Barbara Hendricks, who became a radiant Sophie and Nannetta at the Met. Thomson insisted that Grayson Hirst be his Byron, and everyone concurred. The tenor had made a successful New York debut singing in a 1970 concert performance at Carnegie Hall of Donizetti's *La Fille du régiment* with Beverly Sills as Marie. In order to sing the premiere of *Lord Byron,* Hirst had to break a contract with the Geneva Opera.

With his cast selected, Thomson, who was fretting like a worried parent, managed to relax enough to enjoy a fancy seventy-fifth birthday bash thrown for him in early November by his lawyer Arnold Weissberger, a black-tie affair at his East Side town house. Weissberger serviced many celebrity clients from the world of entertainment and the arts, and he invited several to come that night. Carol Channing and Alexis Smith showed up; Leonard and Felicia Bernstein talked Broadway gossip with Ethel Merman; Ned Rorem wound up escorting home Maureen Stapleton, who had drunk too much. There had been other commemorative affairs, concerts, and broadcasts. But Thomson was preoccupied that fall with making *Lord Byron* a success, and he was already sensing trouble.

With his plans for securing Ashton derailed, he, rather reluctantly, turned the stage direction over to Houseman, who always blamed himself for the unanticipated problems that ensued. "Around Juilliard I had acquired a reputation for decisive and, sometimes, overbearing behavior. Throughout the preparations for *Lord Byron* I astonished everyone by being accommodating to the point of weakness." But Thomson, who, Houseman recalled, "was in a state of nervous anxiety that I had never encountered before and that made it impossible for anyone to reason with him,"[31] was more at fault.

During the nearly forty years of their working together—from *Four Saints,* through the WPA Negro Theater, the Office of War Information films, and the productions at the American Shakespeare Festival—Houseman and Thomson had a curious working relationship. Though usually Houseman was the employer and officially "the superior," as he described it, Thomson "played the role of elder statesman and guru," while Houseman acted as "his energetic and worldly disciple."[32] During the production of *Four Saints* "Virgil had a crystal clear and compelling idea of exactly what he wanted it to be," Houseman recalled.[33] In the case of *Lord Byron* Thomson's ideas were muddled; the rejection from the Metropolitan had rattled him. Instead of working with his colleagues to find the ideal tone and style for *Lord Byron* and using the Juilliard situation to its best advantage, Thomson seemed intent on settling scores with the Met, as if he were trying to prove that *Lord Byron* was indeed a grand opera. In reverting to old form and giving Thomson autonomy, Houseman surrendered his own authority and betrayed his expertise.

Complicating the situation, Houseman was distracted with other work. He had been sidelined for weeks in Washington, where two projects that he had directed were playing simultaneously at the Kennedy Center: a revival of Clifford Odets's *The Country Girl* with Jason Robards and Maureen Stapleton; and the Washington Opera Society's new production of Verdi's *Falstaff.* In addition, that spring Houseman's first book of memoirs, *Run-Through,* was released to dream-come-true reviews. But he was compelled by Simon and Schuster to travel the book-tour circuit, taking him away from *Lord Byron* when he was most needed. "I should have been in New York, pounding some sense in Virgil about the sets."[34]

The opera's scenario opened and concluded in Poet's Corner of Westminster Abbey. Those scenes involved a large cast of soloists, a chorus and boys choir, plus a statue of Byron that needed to be wheeled on and off the stage in a cart. An impressive and realistic set seemed essential and Juilliard's house designer David Mitchell produced something deemed both "stunning" and "buildable." But the Poet's Corner scenes framed a series of flashbacks: a morning party at Lady Melbourne's; a victory ball at Burlington House to celebrate the defeat of Napoleon at Waterloo; a double-party scene on the night before Byron's wedding where the ladies chatter with the bride-to-be and, simultaneously, the men throw Byron a bachelor's party at his club. To satisfy Larson's original concept of a "continual interplay between the present and the past," Houseman had visualized a production of which "the permanent setting was an atmospheric, all-encompassing Abbey background—a frame within which it would be possible to suggest, with light changes and a minimum of realistic scenic movement and delay, the various locales and remembered scenes. . . ." However, "Virgil stuck stubbornly to his Metropolitan dream and refused to consider any suggestion for what he contemptuously called a 'unit set.' "[35] What they ended up with was a series of unwieldly, hastily executed sets that had to be laboriously moved on and off the stage. These would be described by Harold C. Schonberg in his *New York Times* review as "some of the tackiest, scrappiest, ugliest sets seen hereabouts in a long time."[36]

On top of everything else, the conductor Gerhard Samuel arrived late from California (having just been to Russia) and was virtually unprepared. Yet Samuel was unapologetic and unperturbed. A solid professional, he learned the score while rehearsing it and soon seemed to know its shapes and moves. But his initial tentativeness contributed, Thomson felt, to the rambunctiousness of the orchestra players. The musicians were young Juilliard hotshots with dreams of glory. Several would go on to major careers: the flutist Carol Wincenc and the violinist Eugene Drucker, the concertmaster, who became a founding member of the Emerson Quartet. Sitting in the third row of the cello section was a sixteen-year-old, Paris-born, Chinese cellist named Yo-Yo Ma, who was amused by the mischief but was not an instigator. Overlong rehearsals were keeping him out past the 11 P.M. curfew his strict parents had mandated. All he could think of were the "terrible things that would happen" whenever he got home too late.

The orchestra musicians had been conscripted into playing this curiously unmodern (to them) opera by a famous former critic. They thought this roly-poly old man with his sputtering temper was a little ridiculous. They'd play a passage, and Thomson would come trundling down the aisle shouting, "No! No! No!" Switching to his sweetest far-off voice, he'd lift his gaze, raise his arms, twitter his fingers and say, "It should sound like leaves falling from trees." The Juilliard kids would smirk and laugh. That Thomson treated Gerhard Samuel contemptuously in the presence of the orchestra did not help matters.

Intruding into Houseman's domain, Thomson insisted that all the singers face front when they sang. ("This is for you, Jack," he'd say; "I want your words to be heard.") Houseman thought this was mannered, but he caved in. Unlike the orchestra players, the singers were serious and hardworking. But Thomson's instructions were often unclear and sometimes bizarre. At one rehearsal, when Byron and three of his fellow poets were trying out the tight-fitting nineteenth-century breeches that had been designed for them, Thomson, seemingly in complete seriousness, bounded toward the stage, pointed at their crotches, and shouted: "Everybody hang to the left, hang to the left!" Too stunned to laugh, the men looked to Houseman, who simply shrugged. Embarrassed, they attempted to arrange their bulges in some semblance of conformity.

In the calm center of it all was Jack Larson—courteous, diplomatic, and encouraging. To the Juilliard students he was a celebrity. All of them had grown up watching *The Adventures of Superman,* and Larson's presence created a sensation at the school. "Those Juilliard kids," Thomson would recall, "they were hard to impress. They had had masterclasses with Callas, Heifetz, Casals. But, oh boy, were they excited when Jimmy Olsen showed up!" Everyone wanted Jack's autograph, or to have a photo taken with him. The same thing happened when, at Houseman's request, Larson met with the students from the acting program. Not even Helen Hayes, a recent visitor to the school, had gotten such a turnout. Being at Juilliard was pivotal to Larson's evolving attitude about his past. He grew to realize that people everywhere loved Jimmy Olsen. The peculiar nature of pop culture celebrity in America meant that Larson would always be known as Jimmy Olsen. But maybe that wasn't such a bad thing, maybe it was a privilege. "I've shared my life with Jimmy," Larson would say. "And he's been a good companion."

During the last two weeks of rehearsals, the tension grew so great that Houseman, for the only time in his working relationship with Thomson, fought with him in front of a cast. The next day, Thomson called Larson to the Chelsea Hotel and told him, "I'm not coming any more. I'm staying away, for the good of the piece. Now it's up to you." He added, "I've done all that I can do." That was all too true. Houseman, greatly relieved to be on his own, smoothed out the staging and threw out whole chunks of scenery. But it was too little, too late. The performance was basically set. Thomson was back, and basically behaved, for the dress rehearsal. The world premiere was the next night, Thursday, April 20, 1972.

The mythology that has grown up around *Lord Byron* holds that the reviews were universally poor. Actually, they were divided; some were extremely positive. Herbert Kupferberg in the *National Observer* called it "nothing less than the most thoroughly enjoyable new American opera of recent years. *Lord Byron* confirms Thomson as America's most original operatic composer."[37] Alan Rich in *New York* magazine thought the opera "an honorable and often eloquent piece of craftsmanship which proves, if nothing else, that the old fox can still jump over the lazy dog."[38] However, he wrote, Larson's rhymed couplets were "fluent," but also "pompous and fatuous, and there are far too many of them." Yet the critic from the *Neue Zürcher Zeitung* called Larson's libretto "utterly distinguished." Robert Commanday, whose *San Francisco Chronicle* assessment appeared a few days after those of colleagues across the country, wrote that the opera "had more to recommend it than its critics have thus far recognized. Thomson has written an opera for singing, not a strong dramatic piece, but a lyric and sensitive study."[39] But the influential Harold Schonberg in the *New York Times* slammed it. He objected to the depiction of Byron as "the original swinger—a heterosexual, a homosexual, a man who enjoyed a heavy spot of incest to vary his pleasures." Of the music, he wrote, "To all this Mr. Thomson has provided a very bland score . . . distressingly banal (those waltzes!) and frequently gaggingly cutesy."[40]

Three months later a penetrating appraisal by Patrick J. Smith appeared in *High Fidelity/Musical America*. Smith notes the seemingly curious decision to depict so Romantic a figure through such literate, lyrical music. "It is precisely this intellectual stepping-back and looking at the subject through a quizzing-glass which disturbs audiences in search of 'honest emotion.' " Rather than stemming from the heritage of Italian *melodramma* or any psychological twentieth-century approach, *Lord Byron,* Smith suggested, beckons to a "discredited genre," the French nineteenth-century *opéra*.

> It is verbose, as French operas tend to be, on mundane subjects; it has a large and varied cast, few of whom are sketched in more than minimally, and it has the "obligatory" ballet in the third act.

. . . Yes, one can pick numerous faults. . . . And yet it is a masterpiece. It handles the problem of word and music in the grand line from Monteverdi to Mozart, Bellini, and Richard Strauss, and is, for all its coyness and masks, a genuine musical entity of great beauty. . . . I know of no finer opera to have been written by an American composer since *The Mother of Us All* (unless Stravinsky is considered as American). Whatever its final standing in relation to the Stein operas, *Lord Byron* is a credit to our premier opera composer.[41]

The negative reactions, Thomson felt, were to be expected. He wrote music straightforwardly at a time when extreme complexity was intellectually fashionable. Having himself dished out a lot of criticism over the years, he knew there were enemies waiting to settle scores. Even Harold Schonberg's piece, though the blow hurt, was part of a fair fight. But Ned Rorem's lengthy review in the *New Republic* was another matter. Ned was a former pupil and friend. Some oedipal angst seemed to generate Rorem's derision.

Reviewing *Lord Byron* was a difficult exercise in diplomacy for Rorem because he had personal associations with both creators, although such attachments had never inhibited Thomson. Part of what rankled Thomson was that Rorem's writing was so Virgilian: his sweeping appraisals were presented with such certainty that it was difficult to object. The main theme of his critique is that Thomson's work is indirect and guarded, one could say, closeted. As Rorem once put it in a diary entry, "Virgil keeps himself one step removed from the fatal crime."[42] Rorem's article concluded,

. . . Virgil Thomson's composing gift has never relied on interesting ideas, but on the uses to which dull ideas can be put. Displacing the ordinary, he renders it extraordinary—that is his stock in trade. His music has little to do with romance or the grand statement, for it is as removed from the scene of action as cherubim are removed from the scenes they decorate. . . . Thomson's lifelong effort would seem to have been to cleanse his art of meaning in the Beethoven sense, of sensuality or suffering or what we call self-expression, seeking instead, like pre-romantics such as Mozart, to delight.
. . . One cannot know whether Thomson intends his music as satiric, yet most of it for 50 years does sound that way. And for 50 years it has not changed much. Whatever the secret of Thomson's message, the message remains the same and the composer believes continually in it.[43]

There are hints in Rorem's diaries that he regretted coming down so hard on his former mentor. "Have I become merely contemptible?" he wrote four months later; "someone who settles crabby scores in *The New Republic?*"[44] However, the score settling worked. In October 1972, six months after *Lord Byron,* Thomson attended a recital of his sacred organ works at the Chapel of the Intercession performed by the organist and choir director James Holmes. Since 1967 the companionable, Kansas-born Holmes had been Rorem's devoted younger companion. Thomson, who thought him a fine musician, attended the recital and was touched by Holmes's genuine involvement with the music, as Rorem recounted:

> Afterward in the choir sacristy, Virgil, very manic, bestowed enthusiasm on all but me. . . . Six months is a long time to hold a grudge, especially for one who retained his cool during fifteen years of dishing out put-downs for all the world to read. Meanwhile, in *The New York Review of Books* his review of an old friend Paul Bowles' autobiography. . . . is so nonconstructively mean that mine seems indulgent by comparison.[45]

If Rorem's intention was to eventually patch up the squabble, this entry, which continues with an extended put-down of Thomson as composer (and which was published in 1974), did not help. He concludes with a virtual sign-off to "camaraderie of three decades' standing," stating, "I owe you a lot, Virgil. But I owe you for what I took, not for what you gave. You deserve your glory, but your music does not."[46]

The rift was healed, after a fashion. Rorem had become too important for Thomson to disavow. But he pushed Rorem out of the inner circle. After this, when Thomson birthday affairs and such took place, Rorem was conspicuously absent.

Back in Los Angeles, Jack Larson, hugely let down by the response to *Lord Byron,* which had occupied ten years of his life, sat home trying to sort it out. "I have been feeling quiet and being quiet and don't have any news at all," he wrote to Thomson in July, "but I wanted to send you my love."

Thomson used to say that his works were like children. The ones that were successful and popular he was proud of, but a bit bored by. It was the troubled ones, the ones no one else seemed to appreciate, that he loved the most. For the rest of his life, *Lord Byron* was his most troubled child, the one he worried about and deeply loved.

26 MAKING YOUNG FRIENDS

Of all the criticisms *Lord Byron* sustained, the one most upsetting to Virgil Thomson was the charge that, here and there, he had simply piled dissonances atop an essentially conservative "white-key" score in an attempt to make the music seem modern. But in Thomson's view the self-consciously modern music was being written by composers enslaved to complex methods, especially twelve-tone techniques. By this time "academic serialism" (or some variant of twelve-tone technique) was the orthodoxy. No composer wishing to be respected by his academic peers dared to write tonal music.

After the Second World War the efforts of Copland and his colleagues to establish a viable role for American composers in contemporary society dissipated. Most composers exacerbated the problem by barricading themselves in college music departments. Surrounded by academic colleagues doing cutting-edge research, the composers followed suit. By the mid-1960s attending a contemporary music concert at a university was like attending a scholarly convention: you practically had to be another composer to make sense of a new piece. Overwhelmingly, students who yearned to be taken seriously felt compelled to write in a musical language derived from the twelve-tone system. Young Americans who grew up listening to doo-wop and Beatles songs composed music nostalgic for the artists' garrets of Vienna in the 1920s.

When Stravinsky began composing twelve-tone works, Thomson

was not the only observer to wonder whether the composer's adoption of his rival Schoenberg's procedures reflected intellectual curiosity or a strategic maneuver to remain in the front rank. Even Copland felt compelled to try serialism. But the effort sapped him. By the early 1970s Copland all but officially ceased composing.

In 1973 Leonard Bernstein outraged the academic musical community when he attacked the twelve-tone system in his Norton Lectures at Harvard. He had come to grips with the procedures in the mid-1960s, composing and then discarding several twelve-tone works. With his *Chichester Psalms* in 1965 he in effect announced his recommitment to tonal music. When Harvard invited him to deliver America's most prestigious lecture series in the arts, Bernstein used the platform to codify and validate his thinking about tonality.

Drawing on the ideas of the linguistic theorist Noam Chomsky, who had speculated about the common roots of all languages, Bernstein proposed that there was a common root of all musical languages: tonality. Even the music of Asian and African cultures, however disconcerting to Western ears, was essentially tonal. The entire experiment with twelve-tone procedures and atonality, however ingenious, was doomed to oblivion; the nature of sound and the physiology of hearing demanded it. Bernstein did not deny that enduring works had been written by means of twelve-tone techniques. But he rejected the idea that such writing represented the natural next step in the evolution of musical language. History would record the twentieth century's exploration of twelve-tone technique as an interesting, influential offshoot.

University composers belittled Bernstein's televised lectures with their multimedia trappings. This was no serious composer speaking, they argued, but a glamour-boy conductor, Broadway's darling. But Thomson was delighted.

> Now that I have been through the Norton lectures (three by video, all six by reading) it is clear that your skill in explaining music is also tops, as indeed it was when you used to do it at Carnegie Hall.
>
> I find nothing reprehensible about your bringing in linguistics. You needed an authority to support an "innate musical grammar" and Chomsky's heavy artillery is surely that. Especially since postwar researches in the physiology of hearing, though they do support a syntax based on the harmonic series as unquestionably built into the human ear, are being treated by the Germanic twelve-tone world and the French-based solfeggio world as "controversial."[1]

Thomson had been ominously warning of the pitfalls of complexity since Bernstein was in grade school. Yet he regretted the battling among his peers and maintained respect for composers who used complex procedures. In 1971 he served for the first time on a jury for the Pulitzer Prize in music. His copanelists were Copland and the conductor Robert Craft; the prize, supported by Thomson, went to Mario Davidovsky's daunting Synchronisms no. 6 for Piano and Electronic Sound.

In return for his public support, Thomson coveted intellectual respect for his own choice, which was to stick with straightforward tonal techniques. Writing *Lord Byron* had been Thomson's attempt to demonstrate the continuing vitality of these procedures. Now seventy-seven, he would have to step aside and let the Bernsteins take up the cause.

Yet there was a backlash building against the "complexity boys," as Thomson called them. Philip Glass, who had proper university credentials, renounced the timidly modern works of his student days and started writing luxuriously diatonic music with mesmerizingly repetitive materials, music that was being dubbed, not by Glass, minimalism. And Glass pointed to Thomson as a creative godfather. Like Thomson in his early days, Glass was being championed not by other composers but by visual artists, theater people, and dancers.

Mission control for this movement was downtown New York, in clubs and performance spaces far removed in spirit from the cultural palaces of Lincoln Center and the music theory classrooms of Columbia University. The "downtown composers," as they were called, were winning young, enthusiastic audiences. They had a champion at the *New York Times* in the renegade critic John Rockwell, who was a Thomson admirer. All this activity emboldened those composers at the universities who by instinct and preference had resisted serialism.

What this meant for Thomson was that, although the academics were his harshest critics, less doctrinaire composers embraced him. Invitations to attend events in his honor came regularly from the colleges. To commemorate his seventy-fifth birthday, in 1971, concerts of Thomson's works were presented at New York University, Carnegie-Mellon, and even, thanks to Otto Luening, Columbia University, whose music department was controlled by serialists. The University of Bridgeport presented a week-long festival, including a fully staged production of *Four Saints* and an open reading of *The Mother of Us All*. And Thomson began accepting short-term, lucrative teaching residencies, which usually involved giving lectures and work-shops, sometimes a seminar in criticism or prosody. During this pe-riod he had short-term associations with Carnegie-Mellon, Trinity College, California State College at Fullerton, UCLA, and Yale. Trav-eling to distant college campuses, attending tributes he couldn't hear, and mixing at dinners with the local elite was hard work. But while in residence Thomson's music got performed—his top priority. So hus-tling to campuses became the primary activity of his last years. There were side benefits, as he commented: "Almost anything I choose to do at my age is deductible."

Meanwhile, partly as a compensation for the debacle of *Lord Byron,* the Metropolitan Opera offered to present *Four Saints* as part of a new venture called the Mini-Met. The proposal came from Rudolf Bing's successor as general manager, the Swedish director and ad-ministrator Goeran Gentele. He wanted the Metropolitan to present a series of smaller-scale works—chamber operas, baroque operas, ex-perimental works—in a modest-sized theater. The plan was nearly scuttled when the enterprising Gentele died in a car crash just weeks before his first season was to begin in the fall of 1972. But Schuyler Chapin, his successor, found funding for the project and invited Thom-son to participate.

The first season, three-weeks long, alternated two programs: *Four Saints* and a double bill of Purcell's *Dido and Aeneas* paired with *Syllabaire pour Phèdre,* a recent work by the Paris-based composer Maurice Ohana. Thomson was pleased with the Met's offer of Alvin Ailey as director and choreographer. Ailey had choreographed the ill-fated ballet in *Lord Byron;* but Thomson had still been impressed with Ailey's work. And having one of the hottest choreographers in the business, who happened to be a leading artist from the black com-munity, made strategic sense in terms of cultural politics. But Thom-son soon had reason to regret the decision.

Ailey was stymied by Stein's hermetic text. Sensing their direc-tor's skittishness, the singers, most of them young and only some of them black, lost confidence. At first Ailey suggested a tongue-in-cheek approach to the opera, but Thomson shot down that idea: he wanted it straightforward and "saintly." Eventually Ailey coped with the piece through a mixture of "free associations and literal interpre-tations of ideas," he told the *New York Times* prior to press night.[2]

Ailey found the cramped performing space an obstacle. The Forum Theater of the Vivian Beaumont complex in Lincoln Center was a 272-seat facility with no proscenium stage or orchestra pit. The instrumentalists had to play from a balcony above and behind the singers, who could see their conductor, Roland Gagnon, only through a video monitor. The small space necessitated using the simplest of sets. Costumes were equally minimal, just brightly colored satin simulations of monks robes. But the cast was excellent. Betty Allen was the Commère. Saints Teresa I and II were the young sopranos Clamma Dale and Hilda Harris. Barbara Hendricks, who had sung in *Lord Byron,* sang the small role of Saint Settlement.

On opening night, February 22, 1972, the Mini-Met performance went surprisingly well. All the critics came; Thomson received a standing ovation; *Four Saints* was again in the news. But Ailey's discomfort with the piece came through in the put-on earnestness of some singers and the heavy-handed comic bits. His direction diminished the piece, playing right into the hands of the *Times* critic, Harold C. Schonberg, who extolled the work in a classic example of backhanded praise. He wrote that the opera was at its premiere and still is "wonderful camp," the "campiest thing" about it being its harmonic language, which he described as "avant-guard in reverse . . . a white-key opera made out of Satie . . . an American hymn tune, folk song opera with more plagal cadences than can be found in a year of Sundays."[3]

Thomson was gratified by the enthusiasm of the audiences, but ultimately humbled. Four decades after the premiere of *Four Saints* he had to contend with critics who still misconstrued the opera's radicalism. On top of everything else, Ailey failed to return an item from the 1934 production that Thomson had lent him: Frederick Ashton's original prompt book. Despairing of an answer from Ailey, Thomson wrote to their mutual attorney, Arnold Weissberger.

Dear Arnold,
  I am leaving tomorrow for a bit of Western touring, to be back on April 27.
  Meanwhile, I should be most grateful if you would speak to your client Alvin Ailey about the *Four Saints* prompt book which you got me from England with some trouble. I lent it to him at his request for use in connection with the Forum Theatre production. I also lent him a book and some tapes.
  These latter he has returned. The prompt book he has endeavored not to return and when questioned has admitted that it is in

poor shape and needs repair. This repair he gives me no assurance will be done. Neither that anything is to be done about the volume itself other than being kept "in security" at his apartment.

Having done two shows with this gifted choreographer, I know him to be undependable about promises. I am not trying to reform his character, merely to get back an irreplaceable item.

If you have any influence, I do hope you will help me to recover the prompt book.

Ever warmly and best,
Virgil Thomson[4]

Though it took a month of lawyerly letters, the prompt book, tattered but intact, was returned to Thomson.

Maurice had never been as consumed with his career as Virgil was with his. He cared too much for traveling and fun. For years Maurice rented an apartment in Tangier (at fifty dollars a month) in the same building as his friend Paul Bowles, and every summer he took extended working vacations there. Virgil came twice, staying at the Intercontinental Hotel, but did not enjoy it. It was too hot, too dull, too exotic. Virgil was frightened by the young boys Maurice found so alluring. And the Moroccans who seemed always to be hanging around Paul were rather creepy, with their talk of witchcraft and their constant smoking of mood-altering grasses.

In 1970 Maurice traveled through Central Africa. Virgil tried to stay in touch, but tracking him down was difficult.

> d.M:
>
> Every day of its life the NY Times prints a map of Nigeria but not on any of these do I find the places you live in or travel to. The rain forest you describe fits with descriptions of where there was a civil war but I can't figure out where you are. Anyway you are somewhere in the South and on your third tropical disease not counting conjunctivitis. . . .[5]

By now even Paris was no longer tempting Virgil. In 1977 he sold his apartment for "a very good price" ($50,000) and invited Maurice to come along for one last fling to see old friends, which he did. Though just seven years younger, Maurice was open to adventure and change in a way Virgil was not. Change had come in September of 1973, when Maurice, then seventy, met a lecturer at the Museum of Natural History, Paul Sanfaçon, just thirty-three, and fell in love.

Paul Sanfaçon was the fifth of ten children from a devout Catholic family in Grand Isle, a small town on the northern border of Maine just across the St. John River from the shores of New Brunswick, Canada. It was a farming region where school closed every fall for three weeks so that the children could help harvest potatoes. In Grand Isle the boys played hockey without any rules. You could tell who were the best players from their missing teeth. Paul, slight of frame and gentle by nature, was not one of them.

French was the language of Paul's home; English, the language of his school. Hoping he might become a priest, Paul's mother sent him to a convent school in St. Agathe, twenty miles away. Paul loved singing chant and religious rituals. But his sexual attraction to several of the brothers made him realize that the priesthood was not for him.

Paul attended Saint Francis Xavier University, where he became the school rebel and was thrown out after three years. He went into the army, serving in Texas, and, for eleven months and two days (he kept track), in Vietnam, working in a military office where his knowledge of French was valuable. In the army he became a voracious reader. After the service he applied himself to his studies at the University of Maine and graduated Phi Beta Kappa. Though English was his major, Paul was hooked by an elective course in anthropology. Hoping to shake up his life, he moved to New York, found work as a proofreader at McGraw-Hill, and received a scholarship to the master's program in anthropology at New York University. After graduation he won a job as a lecturer at the Museum of Natural History over candidates with doctoral degrees and published articles. With his leather coats and flippant manner, Paul was a rambunctious character around the museum. But he was articulate, well traveled, and bilingual. His engaging lectures on the Middle East and Morocco and his courses on comparative religion were well subscribed. With a starting salary of $6,000, Paul felt like a big success.

But personally he was still inhibited. He nervously cruised gay hangouts, but fled from involvements. Shortly after beginning his new job, he was approached in an adult-male movie house by Carl Preston Green, who was sixty but looked much younger. Paul was powerfully attracted to older men. Soon Paul moved from the Excelsior Hotel into Carl's apartment and into Carl's life. A radio announcer for a children's program, Carl was kind, calm, and, at times, amusingly campy, an ideal person to lead Paul out of the closet. They were together until Carl died in July of 1973.

Two months later, though still grieving, Paul was back in an East Village movie house, Variety Photo Place, a grungy gay pickup site. Looking down from the balcony, he noticed an attractive older man. It was Maurice Grosser.

Maurice came upstairs and sat in a nearby row. Paul moved to the adjacent seat and introduced himself. He was immediately attracted to Maurice, but Maurice, wary of this intense young man, suggested that they meet in two days on the corner of West Fourteenth Street, not far from his place. On the appointed day, a bitter cold November afternoon, they met and went to Maurice's apartment. Paul was excited by Maurice's work. (The paintings of trees with their intertwining branches, Paul would say, captured what it was like to have sex with Maurice, who enveloped you in his limbs.) Paul was entranced by Maurice's stories of Morocco. And Maurice was thrilled that this dynamic young man was smitten with him.

Maurice and Paul became inseparable. Paul all but officially moved into Maurice's rent-controlled apartment, which, thanks to Maurice's long occupancy, cost $92.50 per month. Eventually Paul took a small apartment on the Upper West Side so that he could sometimes have privacy and be closer to the museum. But he seldom stayed there. Paul had heard of Virgil Thomson, but didn't know his music or even that he had been a famous critic. Virgil thought Maurice looked a little foolish, love-sick over someone thirty-seven years his junior. But he got a vicarious kick out of Maurice's romance. And Virgil thought it perfectly natural for a young man to be attracted to an old one.

Paul had more difficulty with Maurice's other friends. Norma Flender thought Paul was cheap, with his tight pants and leather, his youthful irreverence. As she saw it, Paul was purposely playing the "enfant terrible." He thought himself clever for ridiculing people's cultured airs and well-bred ways. To Norma he was simply bad-mannered. Over time her feelings, along with Paul's behavior, changed. "Maurice taught Paul manners, and taught him to be less arrogant," Norma later said; "Maurice was Paul's salvation."

The two men became frequent guests at both the Manhattan and the Long Island homes of the Flenders. And the children adored Paul, who was boisterous, uninhibited, and full of stories about Africa and witchcraft. One winter he taught them how to ice-skate on a neighbor's pool in Easthampton.

Carol Truax took an immediate disliking to Paul, and that proved to be the undoing of her friendship with Virgil and Maurice. The friends who loved Carol for her gregarious personality had to put up with her bossy behavior. But Paul hated her. Once, Carol had dared to accuse Maurice of being unfair toward a young black man he had hired for household work. Paul used this as an excuse to turn Maurice against her. With Paul constantly complaining about her, Virgil, who always found Carol difficult (he liked to be the bossy one in any relationship), also turned against her. What finally provoked a split between Virgil and Carol was her marriage to the respected musicologist Gustave Reese, whom Carol had known since they were in the fourth grade together. After Reese's wife died, he and Carol kept company, as she put it. In October of 1974 they married; they were both seventy-five. This was Carol's first marriage. Virgil, who was possessive of his female friends, was indignant. "If I had known Carol was interested in getting married, I would have married her!" he told almost anyone who asked. The marriage lasted for three years; Reese died in 1977. Carol was terribly upset by the break with Virgil and Maurice. But it was never patched up. She died in 1986, six months after suffering a stroke.

Paul was deeply content with Maurice. Over time he mellowed and won over all of Maurice's friends, who were impressed, even moved, by Paul's devotion. Their relationship was never strictly monogamous. Now and then Paul visited the Greenwich Village bathhouses. During summers in Morocco, it was impossible to keep Maurice from the beaches. But their relationship was accepted in the Thomson circle.

During this period when Maurice was thriving, Thomson faced hurtful losses of others from his life. On May 4, 1973, Jane Bowles died in Málaga. For sixteen years she suffered mental instability, neurological disease, and strokes. For all her enormous talent, Jane was "frighteningly self-destructive," Virgil wrote to Paul Bowles upon learning the sad news. "My love to you, dear Paul, and do tell what I can do to be of help to you or to Jane's posthumous glory."[6]

On December 10, 1976, Briggs Buchanan, the golden boy of Harvard days, the first person Virgil lost himself over, died in a Connecticut nursing home at the age of seventy-two. He was survived by his wife, two sons, five grandchildren, and two sisters, whom he supported all their lives.

On June 5, 1979, Virgil's sister, Ruby, nearly ninety-four, died in Pittsburgh. She had always been proud of her brother's achievements, though she understood little of his work and even less of his life.

Thomson's health was basically good, except for chronic problems with his hearing. "My own pitches are so completely falsified by now," he wrote to an old friend, "that I cannot listen to music under any circumstance and get a believable report of it from my ears."[7] Yet he continued to compose shorter works and musical portraits. In 1975 one large-scale project came along. Thomson selected a suite of American songs, marches, and parlor pieces from the Federal period (not folklore but "published polite music") and scored it for seven instruments for use in a comic ballet commissioned by Erick Hawkins: *Parson Weems and the Cherry Tree,* a spoofing of George Washington, Martha, the Delaware—the whole works. Though it was not an original composition, completing this bumptious score was laborious for a man of seventy-nine.

During this decade Thomson became a sought-after lecturer. There were two time-tested talks that he purposely did not publish, because they made him more money on the circuit. One was an explication of music criticism and the other an introduction to prosody. There was also a graduation ceremony speech that was a surefire success: an erudite and humorous talk about history, the constant factors versus the changing ones, and their applications to an individual's life. By now he had many opportunities to give this speech, for honorary degrees kept coming his way. There were two in 1978, one from Columbia University, one from from Johns Hopkins. Along with these came two elaborate academic outfits, one powder blue with pink velvet bands, the other gold with black bands. ("My academic gowns can be worn in academic parades or as bathrobes," Thomson wrote to Maurice.)[8] That spring he also gave the commencement speech at the Peabody Conservatory, in Baltimore, the same speech, it turned out, that he had given there in 1952. ("I didn't tell them and nobody recognized it. It was a huge success.")

Thomson also entered a new field: radio. In 1970, at the invitation of David Dubal of WNCN, Thomson presented a series of peppery broadcasts from his apartment that lasted for a year. There were interviews with composers, concert tapes, and recordings of works, old and new, that interested him.

But Thomson's apartment was becoming so cluttered with materials—manuscripts, published and unpublished music, letters, programs, books—that it was increasingly unsuited for living in, let alone for radio broadcasts. Piles of papers and materials were stacked under the piano, behind the furniture, atop the bookcases, underneath the living room couch. These would have to be deposited in a research library where they would be accessible but safe. However, first they would have to be cataloged. For this Thomson needed a secretary. He had always hired part-time assistants and copyists for short-term projects. Now he needed a full-time assistant. In 1973 he found one.

Victor Cardell was a bookworm. Growing up in Wethersfield, Connecticut, he used to spend hours at the public library browsing through books and leafing through the record bins. At Trinity College he was a music major, even though the only instrument he played was the phonograph. But the idea of becoming a music librarian had already occurred to him. After college Cardell was living at home with his family, working as a security guard and feeling glum, when a professor, aware that Thomson was looking for a secretary, suggested that Cardell apply for the job. Thomson wanted somebody who could type, who knew music, and was interested in cataloging and who could read and write French. Vic Cardell fit the bill. When they met, Thomson liked this husky, shy, young gay man; and Cardell thought that living in Manhattan and working for Thomson would be liberating.

When he started on January 2, 1974, his duties involved merely typing correspondence and answering the phone. But as Thomson became more trusting, Cardell started organizing files, keeping books, and doing household chores: making the bed and going to the market to see if there were any vegetables that looked "amusing," as Thomson put it.

Needing a copyist, Thomson paid for Cardell to take a course at Juilliard with a professional copyist. In addition, knowing that Cardell was interested in library school and wanting his collection to be properly catalogued under his own supervision, Thomson offered to pay Cardell's tuition. Thomson had proposed his plan to an old friend and longtime patron, Louise Crane, who provided funding through the family foundation. Cardell completed a master's program at Columbia, then began doctoral studies at New York University, also with Thomson's financial support. And here began what Thomson called his "adventures with libraries."

Prior to Cardell's coming to work, Thomson had contacted his friends on the NYU faculty to ask about the possibility of donating his papers to the library. Excited by the prospect, the university offered to renovate an entire room for the Thomson Collection on the upper floor of Bobst Library on Washington Square. In turn, Thomson, again with support from the Crane Foundation, offered to provide funds for Cardell to catalog the papers as part of his academic work. In effect, Thomson transferred the funds to the university, which would pay Cardell, keep accounts, and supervise the work. A contract was signed, and, for a while, things progressed smoothly. At the Chelsea the correspondence was cataloged; proper filing boxes (over one hundred of them) were purchased and labeled; cartons of materials were stacked in order about the apartment. At Bobst Library the Virgil Thomson Room was shaping up. Display cases were installed; attractive paneled doors and moldings were constructed. But Thomson still was unhappy with the pace of the work. Then he discovered what he thought was "funny business" going on, as he would later describe it:

> At my first checking of these accounts, I found charges I had not authorized and certain purchases not related to the project. After inquiring these were removed, and the music librarian, Ruth Hilton, thereafter helped me to keep expense-items correct without betraying any effort of her superiors toward cheating a bit.
>
> I did not know then that all colleges cheat. Handling lots of money transactions, it is easy for them to charge off minor items against some neighboring account. Indeed accounting in government, as in corporations and in philanthropy, flourishes as an art on just such legerdemain. The universities, moreover, in handling capital gifts for a specific purpose, always hold back a part of what it is earning, often up to fifty percent, for unspecified handling charges. Ignorant of these practices and shocked by them, I no doubt made a nuisance of myself by complaining to the librarians. Moreover, I did not trust the word of certain library officials or believe in the intelligence of others. Further, I had learned that were I still free to do so I could no doubt sell my relics for a sizeable sum. So I asked Aaron Frosch, who had been my lawyer in making the N.Y.U. gift agreement, whether I could get out of it. His reply was, "Only if you can show that the university has failed to observe its promises."
>
> Then, after examining the five-year history he spoke to the university's lawyer, who agreed that negligences had occurred. As a result I was released from my gift contract. I remained on the best of terms with Ruth Hilton, to whose music collection I later gave all the books I owned of which the music library had no copies. The university itself seemed not unhappy to be rid of me.[9]

Having learned that there was money, potentially a lot of money, to be made from his relics, Thomson hired a dealer to peddle them. There were no immediate takers.

Then Yale University entered the picture. Thomson had approached a friend from Paris days, Donald Gallup, who had been one of Gertrude and Alice's favorite American GIs. Now over sixty, Gallup was the curator of the Stein Collection, which was housed at the Beinecke Rare Book and Manuscript Library, a massive, marble-walled, climate-controlled facility. Thomson was impressed with the way Yale handled materials. The idea of having his relics alongside Gertrude's was appealing. He respected the jovial head of the School of Music Library, Harold Samuel ("Sammy Wammy," Thomson called him). Moreover, the idea of his collection's winding up at Yale, where he was being courted, rather than his alma mater Harvard, by which he felt ignored, was very satisfying.

But what decided him was money. Samuel thought it would be possible to secure a sizable gift to purchase the collection. When Thomson met Anne-Marie Soullière of the Yale School of Music, who had just become the school's executive secretary, the deal was clinched. Soullière, French-Canadian by heritage, was "pretty and utterly charming," as Thomson said; "we became very thick." Soullière was responsible for writing the successful application to the Booth Ferris Foundation, which awarded the Yale School of Music a grant to purchase and process the Virgil Thomson Collection. Thomson was to be paid $100,000 dollars for his music manuscripts, 10,000 pages of the composer's pencil holographs. Thrilled with this news, Thomson decided to "throw in his correspondence for free." When a crew from Yale arrived at Thomson's flat to pick up the materials, the manuscripts filled five large moving cases, and the correspondence some twenty-five more. At Thomson's insistence, library workers spent an entire summer photocopying the complete letters and papers so that he could keep copies of everything in his apartment.

Thomson's association with Yale grew steadily. In the spring term of 1976 he gave a criticism class at the School of Music. Money was raised to establish a scholarship in Thomson's name. In the spring of 1979, with the collection cataloged and officially opened, the school presented a two-day festival, ending with a concert at Sprague Memorial Hall at which Ned Rorem delivered a tribute to "Thomson as Teacher."

During this period, while Virgil was preoccupied with housing his materials, his routine at the Chelsea continued with remarkable equanimity, considering the sometimes crazed happenings at the hotel. During the sixties and seventies the place became a mecca for rockers, including Jimi Hendrix and Janis Joplin. There the Jane Fonda movie *Klute* was filmed, and the British punker Sid Vicious of the Sex Pistols murdered his American groupie girlfriend Nancy Spungen.

Virgil was completely unperturbed by it all. He had good friends in the building, especially "the boys downstairs," as he called them, Gerald Busby, a composer, and his partner Sam Byers, who was successful in the advertising business. Gerald was a gregarious Texan who composed film scores (Robert Altman's *Three Women*), ballets (Paul Taylor's *Runes*), and songs that Virgil admired for their clarity of expression. And Sam and Virgil shared a Missouri heritage and a love of cooking. Sam and Gerald were Virgil's helpful neighbors who kept keys to his apartment and would watch things when he was away.

During his late seventies Virgil attracted a coterie of young gay male friends. Christopher Cox was a charmer from Gasden, Alabama, who wrote novels and took jobs at publishing houses. A remarkable typist, Christopher sometimes worked as Virgil's secretary when Victor was in school or extra help was needed. Craig Rutenberg, born in New Haven, was a pianist and vocal coach of international experience: the Opéra Comique in Paris, the Glyndebourne Festival in England. When he became the head of the music staff at the Metropolitan Opera, Virgil was not surprised. That such an impressively accomplished opera man loved his Stein operas greatly gratified Virgil. Craig was also a fine cook, a masseur, a trained therapist, and fluent in several languages, just the sort of professional gay man Thomson could mix with his proper society friends. Christopher Beach, a genial fellow from Pittsburgh, was mad about theater. He became a theater administrator, but, reluctantly, had to return home to rescue the family finance business. With Christopher, Virgil liked to go to foreign movies (the only kind he could watch, because of his deafness). They would nestle together, act a little silly, and sometimes hold hands in the dark. Mark Beard was a painter from a Mormon family in Utah. "Mark is incredibly handsome," Virgil said; "he has muscles in all the places where you wouldn't think anybody could have them." When Thomson did Mark's musical portrait, he called it "Never Alone." Mark didn't like to be alone, Virgil believed; and of course he didn't have to be. On the West Coast there was Ron Henggeler, a boyish yet intense Nebraskan who had escaped a confining Republican family and moved to San Francisco. There he worked as a waiter, poster artist, and photographer. Ron doted on Virgil and took hundreds of striking photographs, some of the best from Virgil's old age.

Virgil enjoyed being sought out by such vital young men. Their openness about "being queer" seemed to him an enormous mistake. He chided them about queer politics and refused to use the word "gay." Sometimes someone would try to argue with him that things were changing. Mostly the topic was avoided.

The year of Thomson's eightieth birthday, 1976, also the American bicentennial, saw a flurry of productions of that most American of operas, *The Mother of Us All:* in Boston, at the Iverness Festival, in San Anselmo, California, at the Peabody Conservatory, in Baltimore, at Queens College, in New York. The most prominent production occurred that summer at the Santa Fe Opera in its spectacular opera house partially opened to the mountainous New Mexico sky. Elaborate sets bedecked in bunting and vividly colorful costumes with body streamers to identify all the characters were designed by Robert Indiana, to whom Thomson had been introduced by his Greenwich Village artist friend Bill Katz. This would be Indiana's second production of *The Mother,* and he was enchanted, "almost obsessed," Thomson once said, with the opera. The orchestra was led by the eminent British conductor Raymond Leppard; a studio recording of the performance was funded by the Rockefeller Foundation, which had inaugurated a company, New World Records, specifically to make recordings of seminal American music available free to libraries and colleges.

Thomson never made it to Santa Fe. In June he suffered from a spinal disc pinching a nerve that controlled muscles in his right leg, which made walking painful. He spent much of the summer in Roosevelt Hospital diagnosed with sciatica. George Balanchine was in the next room; same disease, same doctor. Surgery eventually corrected the problem.

He heard mixed reports of the Sante Fe *Mother.* The sets were so grand that some critics found them smothering. The casting of Mignon Dunn as Susan B. was controversial. Though a renowned operatic artist, Dunn was a dramatic mezzo-soprano, not a soprano, as the role requires. Thomson had expressed his objections to no avail.

When the recording was released, he was mollified somewhat. He thought Dunn "musically convincing," and her "sheer vocal presence" was impressive. But, from what he could tell with his impaired hearing, she was overmiked. "The recording ends up by suggesting a cast with little dramatic purpose beyond giving cues to Susan B.," he wrote to the record company president.[10] Leppard's conducting was labored. Finally, a Thomson opera had been elaborately produced and recorded complete with international-caliber artists and adequate funding, and to Thomson the results were still intensely frustrating.

One of the individuals who made this recording possible was a wealthy woman friend of Thomson's from Los Angeles, Betty Freeman, who contributed $10,000 to the project. Thomson had met Freeman shortly after the premiere of *Lord Byron* when the conductor Gerhard Samuel, then with the Los Angeles Philharmonic, played a tape of the performance for a gathering at Freeman's Beverly Hills home. Thomson was always eager to court potential patrons, especially one as unaffected and open-minded as Betty Freeman. She thought Thomson, with his "salt and pepper personality," was a fabulous character, and enjoyed his opinionated conversation and cantankerous charm.

Born in Chicago in 1921, Betty Freeman had studied music seriously during her youth; but she was equally drawn to the visual arts and later took up photography, which led to successful shows at galleries and museums. In the 1960s, she produced a series of contemporary music concerts at the Pasadena Art Museum. When the museum closed, she moved these events to the sunny and spacious salon of her home, where the walls are lined with huge paintings by friends like Roy Lichtenstein, David Hockney, and Frank Stella. Her musicales became renowned within the contemporary arts world. In 1980, with the help of her music critic friend, Alan Rich, she formalized the musicales. Composers would introduce live performances or recordings of their works and take questions. Before the presentation only bubbly water was served. Afterward there would be wine, fruit, cheese, and panettone. The leaders of Los Angeles culture and distinguished visitors would attend, listen, talk, and plot. A soft-spoken, bright-eyed woman, Freeman was not a pusher. She was a facilitator. She brought people together and let things happen naturally.

Like a "modern-day Medici," as the composer John Adams has called her, Freeman supports her chosen composers and artists directly, not through institutions or foundations. Over the years John

Cage, Harry Partch, Luciano Berio, Elliott Carter, Pierre Boulez, and Ned Rorem, to cite just some, were presented at Freeman's musicales and benefited from her patronage. After they met, Thomson joined the roster. Whenever a Thomson project was in the works, Betty Freeman was approached for help. She seldom refused.

Betty and Virgil grew quite chummy. For several years she spent time in Paris working on her photography and making musical contacts. Virgil let her use his apartment for free. During summers he joined her in Italy for trips through the Tuscany hills, to Verdi's home at Busseto and to the villages of Umbria. Every year he met Betty and her companions in the resort town of Montecatini, where he would stay at a health spa. He did not exercise like the other guests, but ate the spa's low-fat, low-calorie meals and took steam baths and massages. Every summer he would lose some fifteen pounds, then resume his routine eating habits at home and put it back. But he claimed the treatment made him feel fit.

The trips together ended abruptly after one disastrous experience in the summer of 1981. By this time Betty had married Franco Assetto, a courtly Italian sculptor, painter, fountain builder, and architect. At seventy, Franco, compact and limber, was a vigorous and striking man, with his clean-shaven head and penetrating eyes. Franco enjoyed Virgil's company; or at least he thought he did, until the events at Corfu.

Franco and Betty had rented an apartment on the Greek Island of Corfu, in the Ionian Sea. Their place at the Villa Moro, situated on a bluff surrounded by olive and cypress trees, overlooked the turquoise bay at Paleokastrizia, twenty miles from the city. There were four double bedrooms with baths, a large kitchen and living room, and a glass-enclosed terrace facing the sea. Since Betty was not going to be at Montecatini, she asked Virgil if he would like to visit with them at Corfu. At first he politely declined. Hanging up the phone, he muttered to his secretary, "The problem with patrons is they give you a bit of money, then expect you to earn it at the dinner table."

In early July, Virgil telephoned Betty from New York to say that his plans to spend August in central Italy had fallen through, that he had no place to go and would like to visit Corfu after all. Betty said yes, he could come. Then Virgil informed her that, since his return flight at the excursion fare was set for September 2, he would be staying for five weeks. Betty was nonplussed. She had already invited another couple to stay, but felt she could not refuse Virgil.

Virgil's letters to Maurice that summer seem to indicate he was having a relaxing and productive time:

> Corfu is very satisfactory. . . . I am writing a piece for string orchestra, commissioned by a Missouri student organization. It goes good. Betty and Franco go to beaches and I stay home. We cook or go out. The sea-and-mountain air reminds me of Villefranche. I don't sun or climb, though thinning has made walking a pleasure.[11]

This is a decidedly slanted account of the visit. Virgil had arrived from Montecatini slimmer by fifteen pounds and ready to start putting it back. But Corfu had a limited supply of fresh produce, and the market was twenty miles away. Betty had hired a housekeeper but no cook. She and Franco prepared all the meals; Virgil did little but complain about the menu. "You are not feeding me well," he would state. "I'm getting tired of tomatoes and eggplant." One day Betty was lucky to find some chicory at the market. She knew Virgil liked its leafy bitter taste. After soaking the chicory, which was typically muddy, and removing the firm portions of the stems, Betty served the dish as a steamed vegetable at lunch one day, which met with approval from Franco and her other guests, the Wrights from California. Afterward Virgil poked his head in the kitchen and said, "The chicory was quite nice, but next time remove all the stems." Betty responded, "Next time, how about if you remove all the stems?" Virgil, a bit miffed, agreed. When Betty returned from the next shopping trip with two kilos of chicory, Virgil spent a morning cleaning and stemming the greens. Served steaming and buttered at lunch, everyone enjoyed it, but without any special comment. After lunch Virgil erupted. He had spent all morning in the kitchen; no one had thanked him for this special dish; from now on he was quitting kitchen duty, and it would be best if Betty bought no more chicory.

Exasperated with Virgil's constant complaining, Betty decided that they should eat out more often, everyone paying his share. Virgil, annoyed about having to pay for his meals, agreed this would be best. By this time, however, Franco was furious with his houseguest's boorish behavior. He could not believe that a man would speak so rudely to a lady; he was appalled by Virgil's table manners. Virgil ate with his fingers, even slices of tomato and melon; he belched shamelessly, even pridefully; he picked at his teeth, not bothering to "cover this intrusion," as Betty tactfully put it. One day Betty placed a box of toothpicks near Virgil's plate. "I see you are giving me a hint," he said, mockingly. Once or twice he used them. Then he reverted to his fingers.

Betty thought this was classic passive-aggressive behavior. Virgil was provoking them, testing the limits of what he could get away with. By this point in his life, Virgil Thomson acted in all situations as if advanced age excused him from the protocols of proper conduct. He bellowed at waiters, sometimes clapping his hands and shouting for attention, "Hey! Hey!" He ridiculed merchants who did not understand his questions. Walking at night in New York with friends, he would suddenly announce, "I've got to pee!" Then he would nestle near the wall of a building and pee on the sidewalk. His prostate problems were admittedly frustrating; but he acted as if entitled to pee on the pavement.

Needless to say, when early September arrived in Corfu, Betty and Franco were hugely relieved to see Virgil depart. To catch an early-morning flight, he had to leave at five-thirty. The caretaker of the villa appeared at dawn to load Virgil's baggage into the car for the trip to the ferry and then to the airport. Virgil neither thanked nor tipped him. When Betty remarked that it was kind of the man to arise so early to help, Virgil shrugged. The departure at the airport was equally unemotional, Betty later recounted:

> I was hoping that Virgil would say he had enjoyed being at Corfu or at least had had a good rest or even would say he felt well. No, no such word much less a word of thanks in any form. Only, "Well, goodbye, I'll see you in New York." And off he went, lugging his own heavy-as-rocks ancient Louis Vuitton wood luggage, a little round figure, strong-willed and tough as a cock.[12]

Betty Freeman would continue to support and befriend Virgil Thomson. But there were no more trips together.

In Corfu that summer Thomson composed every morning the way he always had, without recourse to any instrument. He completed that choral piece for the Missouri students, titled *A Prayer to Venus,* and composed musical portraits of Betty, Franco, and their California friend John Wright. Back in New York he continued to compose, mostly short portraits. But at least he was composing; Copland, four years his junior, had stopped long ago, as Thomson liked to point out.

But for the most part during this period, Thomson's workday was devoted to projects that buttressed his reputation or furthered the availability of his music. He cooperated with a filmmaker, John Huszar, who had done a documentary he admired about Robert Indiana. Huszar produced a sixty-minute film about Thomson. Hoping to enable Huszar to include excerpts of *Louisiana Story,* which he felt was being forgotten about, Thomson wrote to the Robert Flaherty Foundation, "I should be wretchedly unhappy if this highly important work of both Flaherty and myself should have to be omitted from John Huszar's film."[13] Permission was denied. But Huszar's film won good reviews when shown on public television. There is one poignant sequence of Thomson seated at his piano and looking straight ahead into the camera as he sings in a creaky voice excerpts from *Four Saints,* accompanying himself just as he did fifty years earlier for friends and possible producers.

And there were always interviews to give, though too often the focal point was someone else. He complained about this in a letter to Paul Bowles:

> D.P.
>   Very happy with good reviews of your story book. I am well. Ditto Maurice. People visit constantly for writing books about us all. This month it's mostly Nadia Boulanger. But there is lots of George Antheil too coming up. So far I am more a source than a subject.
>
> Everything ever everbest
V.T.[14]

27 THE ABSENCE OF THE PRESENCE

I met Virgil Thomson in the spring of 1979, became over time a colleague and friend, and remained close until his death. I had just completed my first year as an assistant professor of music at Emerson College, in Boston. A small private college with majors in communication fields, Emerson seemed concerned more with how to communicate than with what to communicate. But it was a lively, if unscholastic, place.

I met Virgil through my faculty colleague Scott Wheeler, a Connecticut-reared composer. Balding, baby-faced, perky, and brilliant, Scott was a latecomer to classical music, having grown up playing show music in piano bars and electric keyboards in a rock band. Later he studied composition at Amherst College and earned a Ph.D. from Brandeis University, which had a strenuously academic music program. But Scott remained a pragmatic musician with wide-ranging interests. He could play virtually any Broadway show song in any key, transposing at sight, something that few of his colleagues who had sat through classes on set theory analysis could do.

With his background in musical theater, Scott was fascinated by the art of mixing words and music. No one practiced prosody better than Virgil Thomson, with whom Scott had struck up an association. So, in his first year as director of the college chorus, Scott presented an all-Thomson program, including choral excerpts from *Four Saints*. Virgil came up for the concert and approved of it all. "Invite me back

524

anytime," he told us during dinner at the Park Plaza Hotel on his last night. Two years later we did.

Very ambitiously, perhaps recklessly, we decided to put on *The Mother of Us All.* Emerson had a thriving musical theater department, but no classical music program to speak of. Though many of the theater students had robust voices, few were musically trained. But they could project words vividly and they could act, two things most opera singers are notoriously bad at. So we put on *The Mother* and invited Virgil to attend. Scheduled for February 1981, our production would be among the first acknowledgments of Virgil Thomson's eighty-fifth-birthday year.

Teaching the piece to the cast was a daunting task. The Susan B., Beth Bornstein, had iron lungs and compelling presence, but she virtually had to be taught the part by rote. Some cast members had extensive acting experience; some were recruited from the college chorus and had never been on a stage. Our director, John Horvath, a graduate student, had imagination and skill but no experience in opera.

What this meant was that Scott and I could take charge, assuring that musical matters were the chief focus. So we drilled that cast until every bit of that score was mastered, and every word was, as the *Boston Globe* critic Richard Dyer later wrote, a "living presence." Moreover, after being initially nonplussed by the Steinian nonsense, the students got hooked on it. Like the original cast members of *Four Saints,* they went around talking to each other in bits of Steinese.

Five days of events were planned for Virgil Thomson's visit to Emerson. He was the guest in a course fortuitously scheduled for that semester called "Paris in the Twenties." At a special ceremony in the music room, Virgil Thomson was awarded an honorary doctorate degree. Off campus, escorted by his energetic Boston friend Christine Gratto, Virgil did media interviews. On a local television show, *Good Day,* he was asked by its vacuous hostess, "So, what is your music like, Mr. Thomson? Is it like Brahms?" Virgil handled this ridiculous question with wit and tact. "No, no. After a war everything gets up-to-date! I went through *two* world wars!"

But Virgil's main mission was to attend the final two rehearsals in the small theater of a local church where his beloved opera would be presented. The night he was scheduled to hear his first rehearsal, Virgil arrived after Act 1 had started. We were using the existing reduction of the orchestra part for trumpet, percussion, piano, and harmonium. Scott was conducting; I was playing the piano. With the run-through in progress, Virgil took a seat in the first row and started barking at the singer cast as Virgil T. ("Don't wave your arms!" "Don't smile!") Gradually, as Virgil settled down, he started silently mouthing every word of the text.

During the break Virgil was formally introduced, to nervous applause from the intimidated students. It had taken him some time to adjust to John Horvath's kinetic directing style, but he was won over by the energy and earnestness of the actors. Most of all, he was impressed by the singing, which (with two exceptions) was not remotely operatic. But it recalled the sounds of well-drilled Missouri church choirs, which was not inappropriate. And Virgil had seldom heard Gertrude's words come through so clearly. "I feel I know you all very well already; you've got a beautiful show," he told the cast members, who laughed with relief and pride.

The next day Richard Dyer, who had come with Virgil to the rehearsal, reported in the *Boston Globe* that Virgil Thomson called the upcoming Emerson College production of *The Mother of Us All* the "most imaginative I have seen." This ignited a rush for tickets. The run sold out. Yet Virgil was not eager to attend the public performances. Sitting in the first row during rehearsals he could involve himself. But as a member of the audience he would be unable to hear anything properly and would have no input. His creative work was done. In attending the show, he was putting in an appearance and demonstrating support. But he did come, and promptly fell asleep. At intermission he walked over to Scott and me to offer congratulations: "Everything's going just perfectly. If anything had gone wrong I would have woken right up."

After the final performance Virgil climbed five flights to the Back Bay apartment of our Jo the Loiterer, Jimmy Boutin, to attend the cast party, where star-struck students, including quite a few handsome gay men, sat at his feet and relished his every word. As he left, I told him that I would miss having this music in my life every day. I meant it.

Virgil's anniversary year was marked by the release of a book he had instigated, *A Virgil Thomson Reader,* a collection of his writings (early and recent articles, a generous selection of reviews from the *Herald Tribune,* and excerpts from three books), which was published by Houghton Mifflin in Boston. To edit it Virgil chose the *New York Times* critic John Rockwell, a formidable voice on behalf of post-modern American music. Rockwell viewed Thomson as a pioneer who, in his music and prose, "has given us as profound a vision of American culture as anyone has yet achieved."[1] Having in one handsome volume such a compendium of Thomson's writings made the impact of his work more apparent than ever. The reader won the National Book Critics Circle Award for criticism.

That September, to honor Virgil, Roger Sessions, who was also observing his eighty-fifth birthday, and Aaron Copland, who was one year past eighty, a Composer's Showcase Concert at the Whitney Museum presented a performance of Stravinsky's *Histoire du soldat* with these three eminences of American music enacting the dialogue. Virgil took the part of the devil, Sessions was the soldier, and Copland was the narrator. The grudge match between Thomson and Sessions had not subsided. But for this historic occasion they behaved with civility. Andrew Porter wrote it up in *The New Yorker:*

> It was a nostalgic, affectionate runthrough of the piece; it was not without wit, and offered the unusual spectacle of one of America's greatest composers [Sessions] calling another [Thomson] a "dirty, rotten cheat." Mr. Copland was the most coherent speaker and Mr. Thomson the most perky, but Mr. Sessions' soft, bewildered protestations won the heart.[2]

On November 13, twelve days before his birthday, the Thomson festivities culminated at Carnegie Hall, where a concert version of *Four Saints in Three Acts* was presented by the Orchestra of Our Time with Joel Thome conducting. The decision had been made to use only black singers in the cast and chorus, which proved to be a troublesome restriction. Virgil was touched that Betty Allen, a colleague for nearly thirty years, sang the Commère. But he was not happy with Thome's conducting. "Everything's backwards," he complained; "the choruses and ensembles are draggy, and the recitatives and chants are rushed!" Though displeased with the Carnegie Hall performance, Virgil pronounced himself satisfied with the Nonesuch recording that was made afterward, a success, he said, thanks to Maurice, who "went over and yelled at everyone until things were straightened out."

But the deeper cause of his lingering resentment over this commemorative performance was that no one else had managed to present *Four Saints* in an opera house, which is what he felt the occasion demanded. There had been inklings of possible productions, including talk that the avant-garde director Robert Wilson was interested, which Virgil wanted badly to happen. (It finally did, seven years after Virgil's death, to commemorate the Thomson centenary.)

The day after the Carnegie Hall concert, Virgil, though tired, had a pleasant and productive visit with Anne-Marie Soullière, now working for the Yale development office. Anne-Marie had come to have her musical portrait composed and then to stay for a late lunch. The portrait took about ninety minutes—a whimsical, waltzing, miniature piano piece, which Virgil called "Something of a Beauty."

After that, Virgil moved to the kitchen, where lunch was keeping on the stove: his fabled Irish stew, watercress salad dressed with only olive oil and salt, a whole bottle of Côte Rôtie, and a pear. Later, as they washed the dishes together, the talk turned intimate. Though cheerful by nature, Anne-Marie was somewhat self-contained and had never mentioned any special male friend. So Virgil, uncharacteristically, asked her if perhaps she liked women better. Anne-Marie was amused and not at all offended. She said that she understood how Virgil might have been confused since she was rather private, that she had been married before, that she was now dating a Chinese-American lawyer named Lindsay Kiang, the chief attorney for Yale University, and that, no, she was not a lesbian. Virgil, pleased to hear all of this, smiled and said, "Well, you know, I'm 98 percent queer."

This is the only occasion I know of where Virgil Thomson volunteered information about his homosexuality to a female friend. Anne-Marie eventually married that distinguished-looking lawyer. Virgil heartily approved. He liked for people to do somewhat unconventional things. And to Virgil's mind Anne-Marie's marrying an Asian was unconventional.

Earlier that year, in June, for the first time in nine years, Virgil composed a musical portrait. Bill Katz, his artist friend, was the subject, and Virgil was pleased with the result: a sort of bumptious, jerky, contrapuntal piano piece called "Wide-Awake." This unleashed a spree of musical portraits, fifteen more that year alone, all for solo piano, including portraits of Norma and Richard Flender, Gerald and Sam, his old friend Morris Golde, Christopher Cox, and Craig Rutenberg. That June he also did a portrait of Scott Wheeler, an industrious, quirky two-part-invention-like piece called "Free Wheeling," which uncannily captured Scott's sprightly yet well-organized character. Scott had been spending time in New York that summer taking lessons from Virgil in text setting and orchestration. When Scott gave me a copy of his portrait, it got me interested in the larger questions

Virgil Thomson's manuscript for his musical portrait "Tony Tommasini: A Study in Chords," composed in 1984.

regarding Virgil's unique approach to composing musical portraits, of which there were already well over one hundred. At the time I was completing my doctorate at Boston University and was searching for a dissertation topic. I asked Virgil about examining his musical portraits, and he, pleased for a change to be a subject rather than a source, promised to cooperate.

By that time, as I began visiting the Chelsea regularly to interview Virgil and search through manuscripts, there was a new secretary: Louis Rispoli, then twenty-nine, a native New Yorker raised in East Harlem and educated at Stony Brook and Chapel Hill. Lou was a gifted writer, an efficient organizer; he was easygoing and, best of all to Virgil's mind, direct. Soon after starting work, Lou's home life stabilized when he started living with his lover Danyal Lawson, a Juilliard-trained pianist born in Arizona of an American father and a Turkish mother. Though he did not read music, Lou had been working for a concert artist manager. So he understood the machinations of the music business.

Lou was especially good at defusing Virgil's tantrums. He did not shout back. But when Virgil was being impossible, Lou spoke firmly and called him on it, and Virgil almost always stopped. Lou found the right balance between taking initiative and being deferential. He knew which callers were to be obliged and passed on to Virgil, and which were to be fended off. A good cook and shopper, Lou did not mind going to the market, prepping dinner, and doing household chores. But this was not what he had been hired for, and Virgil did not take advantage of him. As Lou put it, "Virgil and I try, I think, in our working together not to ask of each other questions whose answers will very probably be no."

Over the next years, poking around Virgil's place, going through the papers, and taping interviews, I got to know the way he conducted business. It was a grave mistake for journalists or researchers to interview Virgil if they had not done their homework. Once, in red-hot fury he tossed out a filmmaker and his crew who were making a documentary about John Cage and Merce Cunningham because the interviewer asked too many "Tell me about . . ." questions. However, when Carol Oja, a musicologist from Brooklyn College who was studying Virgil's Harvard years, came by, he was impressed by her questions and voluble with his answers. Carol had examined his transcripts at Harvard and asked precise questions about courses and professors. After her visit Virgil wrote to me, "I suggest you make her acquaintance and butter her up good. She can be of great use to you."[3]

Whenever people approached Virgil to request an interview for a book, film, recording, or whatever, he grilled them about money. He was not interested in vanity productions or self-funded projects. Once I overheard his half of a phone conversation, a series of withering questions and tension-filled pauses, in which he was obviously being asked to participate in a documentary film about Paul Bowles.

> Who's backing it?
> Are they really or are they trying to make you raise the money?
> You've got the money?
> How much?
> What's the distribution?
> How you gonna get it around?
> Oh, I know, I've had one.
> Who's "we"?
> What's your connection with Paul Bowles?
> Is he cooperating pretty well?
> Tell me what I know that you don't?
> I do not give music criticism verbally!

And so on. The caller turned out to be Regina Weinreich, who survived the call, won Virgil's cooperation, and made the film.

Another time a reporter from a New England newspaper called to do a phone interview. But before long it was Virgil who was asking the questions. ("Who owns your paper? Oh. I don't know him, but I knew the father. He was nice, but the wife really ran things. Does the son have a wife?") Afterward Virgil explained his technique: "I always interview them a little bit. Find out who's persecuting them. Somebody always is. The boss is always a bad guy. Has to be."

The fall of 1983 through the summer of 1984 brought Virgil high honors, deep disappointments, and a robbery. To begin with, he was selected to receive one of the 1983 Kennedy Center Honors for lifetime achievement in the arts. In the five previous rounds of awards, which started in 1978, during the Carter administration, only two composers from the classical tradition had been so honored: Aaron Copland in 1979 and Leonard Bernstein in 1980, a controversial choice and not just because he was only sixty-one. Virgil's fellow 1983 awardees were the pioneering black choreographer Katherine Dunham (from whose Harlem school Virgil and Maurice had once recruited dancers for the premiere production of *The Mother of Us All*), the director Elia Kazan, the film legend James Stewart, and the artist

Virgil was truly excited to meet ("He sings with such a beautiful legato"), Frank Sinatra.

The black-tie dinner and gala concert at the Kennedy Center took place on December 4, 1983. Prior to the dinner there was a private reception at the White House with President and Mrs. Reagan. "He has one of those pleasant Irish smiles and plays the part beautifully," was how Virgil described his host. During the portion of the gala devoted to Virgil, John Houseman paid homage to the man who had started him in the theater business, then introduced the filmed tribute and musical performances. When some weeks later the taped event was televised, Houseman's passing comment that Virgil Thomson, though not a religious man, was a composer of deeply felt religious music, was edited out of his speech. At home Virgil was blasé about the whole business. "They give you dinner at the White House and this quite ordinary medal," he would tell visitors who asked about it. But he kept that medal displayed on his piano.

On May 12, 1984, the Hartford Symphony Orchestra and the trustees of the Wadsworth Atheneum presented a concert and formal reception to commemorate the fortieth anniversary of the symphony and the fiftieth anniversary of the Atheneum, which meant it was also the fiftieth anniversary of *Four Saints*, which had opened the museum's new theater. And I never saw Virgil more hostile and bad-tempered than during this long evening tribute.

He was seething with resentment that the museum trustees had not seen fit to present a revival of *Four Saints* in honor of its anniversary. Instead, there was what Virgil thought a token concert. The program presented a selection of piano portraits performed by Nigel Cox, a fine pianist devoted to Thomson's music; a performance of his String Quartet no. 2; a sort of *Four Saints* suite for chamber orchestra arranged by Paul Reuter; and a premiere of a work supposedly written in Thomson's honor, a work for narrator and chamber orchestra by Earl Kim, a distinguished composer from the Harvard faculty who had little sympathy for Thomson's music. The most moving part of the event came when John Houseman took the stage, which he had not been on in fifty years ("I can't believe how tiny it is"), and delivered a vividly recalled memoir of the original *Four Saints*.

At the champagne reception Virgil was in a nasty mood. It was crowded and noisy; he couldn't hear anything anybody said. Hartford's cultural elite cornered him all night to offer congratulations, which only made him more angry. When he saw Scott and me standing aimlessly, he pointed to a corridor and shouted, "Get your asses down there now!" He was referring to an exhibit of memorabilia from the 1934 *Four Saints,* which he must have felt people were ignoring.

After this disappointment Virgil was eager to go that summer to Montecatini for his traditional health regimen. During his absence his flat was robbed. The burglars entered, it was determined, through the airshaft that opened into his bathroom window. An inside job was suspected, as he explained in a letter to his niece, Ruby's only daughter, Elizabeth Stouffer:

> Their looting was systematic: no pictures or clothes or hi-fi equipment were taken, but all the good silver was (nothing plated). This includes the teaspoons and tablespoons from my grandmother and my parents, also the incised ones from Aunt Lillie. These all belonged eventually to you. Unless they turn up, which flat silver seldom does, they are probably lost for good.[4]

The burglars also took Virgil's jewelry (chiefly cuff links), three Vuitton suitcases, three cases of good Bordeaux (they left the ordinary Burgundy), his address book, and, most suspicious of all, an English translation of the *Rubaiyat* of Omar Khayyám that had belonged to Gertrude Stein in her schoolgirl days and contained handwritten notes. Six detectives from the city's Major Crime Unit investigated, a large contingent. Virgil liked the detectives, though he was amused by their cultural unenlightenment. ("Lou spent a half hour trying to explain who Gertrude Stein was.")

As Virgil's ninetieth-birthday year approached, he said to anyone who asked that what he wanted more than anything was another production of *Lord Byron.* Thirteen years after its premiere, he was still convinced of the opera's worth. So plans were developed by the New York Repertory Company, a fledgling organization dedicated to presenting new and neglected operas in concert performance. Virgil cajoled both his friends with money, like Richard Flender and Theodate Johnson, and his friends without money, like Maurice and Paul, to join a Friends of Virgil Thomson Committee to solicit funds. Most of Virgil's longtime supporters responded, figuring that there would likely be few future requests. On December 7, 1985, at Alice Tully Hall, a cast and small chorus conducted by Leigh Gibbs Gore presented *Lord Byron* in a semistaged production directed by Nancy Rhodes.

Virgil had finally settled on a reason for *Lord Byron*'s poor initial reception: it was too long. When the piano-vocal score was published in 1977, whole passages were cut from it. For this revival Virgil cut more, so much that its three acts were reduced to two. But to those who admired the opera, cutting the score hurt it. One of those was Andrew Porter, the respected critic of *The New Yorker*. After a tape of the premiere performance was broadcast on WNYC in 1977, Porter reexamined this "generally underrated" opera in an article, calling it an "elegant and cultivated piece." *Lord Byron* "affords pleasures akin to those of witty, lively, precise, shapely conversation on an interesting subject."[5] Reviewing the 1985 performance, Porter was perplexed by the brutal cuts and feared that there soon would be as many confusingly different versions of *Lord Byron* as of Verdi's *Don Carlo*.

The reviews were again mixed. However, the house sold out, the audience cheered, and the affair was glittery. John Houseman and Jack Larson came from Hollywood, Jack with his good friend Debra Winger, the film star, on his arm. Since the *Lord Byron* premiere in 1972, Jack's partner James Bridges had become an important film director and screenwriter whose credits included *The Paper Chase* (which won Jim's mentor John Houseman a best-supporting-actor Oscar for his memorable portrayal of a crusty law professor), *Urban Cowboy,* and *The China Syndrome.* Jack had been tempted back into the movie business, this time as associate producer for Jim's films.

For me, this *Lord Byron* concert production inaugurated a new career. By 1985 I knew that I was going to lose my job at Emerson. Looking for something to do, I persuaded Richard Dyer at the *Boston Globe* to try me out as a reviewer. My first assignment was to report on *Lord Byron*.

When I told Virgil this news, he was excited, but curiously agitated. What bothered him, I found out, was that I was going to Jack Larson's hotel to interview him in advance of the performance. Jack, one of Hollywood's renowned storytellers, was filled with insights and anecdotes about his collaboration with Virgil. Fresh from the meeting I went to Virgil's for a late lunch. When I reported Jack's take on the opera, namely, that he felt *Lord Byron* was essentially an intimate, literate piece, like the Stein operas, not a grand spectacle for the Metropolitan Opera, Virgil erupted.

"I couldn't tell you *not* to go. He *is* the librettist. But now that you've heard it, forget it!"

"But, Virgil . . ."

"Forget it!" he shouted even louder. *Lord Byron* was indisputably a grand opera, he insisted. "There's a full chorus, a children's choir, huge ensembles, a tenor part with four high C's! You can't get more goddamn grand than that!"

Once the *Lord Byron* production was over, and Virgil's anger subsided, he became very interested in my emerging journalism career, for the *Lord Byron* article did lead the *Boston Globe* to use me as a freelancer. And Virgil became my mentor. For over a year I sent him photocopies of every review I wrote after it had appeared. Periodically, we would get together to go over his red-penciled corrections. To others he praised my progress and bragged about me. To me he was unremittingly critical. Every choice of word, every description was questioned, a tough but invaluable apprenticeship. I knew I was beginning to please him when he wrote in March 1986, "Thanks for clips. They are readable and mostly convincing. I am glad that Dyer is looking over your shoulder and that the paper seems to like your work. My suggestion is that you keep your language as plain and straightforward as possible."[6] I knew I had more or less graduated when a batch of reviews I sent him in December elicited a note card simply saying, "d. T. Reviews all thoroughly readable. Had fun. Come see. V."

Perhaps the frustration of the *Lord Byron* performance took more out of Virgil than anyone realized at the time. For as he entered his ninetieth-birthday year, he was testy and high-strung. Festivals on college campuses, celebratory performances by symphony orchestras, articles and interviews—all sorts of honors were planned. But he would be working hard this year, attending these events, playing his expected role as a curmudgeonly dean of American culture, all in an effort to keep his music alive. Yet, when he surveyed the schedule, not one event seemed truly significant. And no major company was presenting any of his operas.

In any case, the pressures brought to a crisis a long-building estrangement with Lou Rispoli. There had been an early sign of trouble ahead in late 1982, when, after three years on the job, Lou, feeling taken for granted and, at ten dollars an hour, underpaid, quit in anger.

> Virgil
> Last year my Christmas was considerably less joyous because there was no bonus. If my raise was my bonus then it was a gift I earned at an hourly rate. If you think you pay me at a high rate consider what you pay your maid. If you think I'm kidding when I write here I quit, you're dead wrong.

Enclosed, $30, should even out the petty cash money.

Please do not bother to call. I should hate to refuse to come to the phone.

I guess I just didn't want to work for you anymore anyway, and this is as easy an out as any.

Sorry,
Lou[7]

Technically, Lou was an employee. But Lou was more essential to Virgil than any other person in his life. Virgil had let the balance in this relationship tip too much in his own favor. So, with his customary tact, he corrected it that same night, sending Lou a check for $2,000 and a note:

Dear Lou,

Your bonus for this year's work is still due you. So is a substantial raise if you care to reconsider. In any case my abundant thanks.

everbest,
Virgil T.[8]

It worked. Lou's financial need at the time was great. Danyal had been sick with high doctor bills. Lou was undergoing personal confusions. This accounted, he said in his reply, for the "harsh words I'm sorry now I wrote you Christmas Eve." Lou agreed to come back. And, direct as ever, he added, "I expect I'll be a little awkward with you at first, but please let's not tip-toe around each other."

Lou's salary was doubled. From then on, their working relationship was better than ever. In 1984 Virgil asked Lou to sit for his musical portrait, and the resulting work, a barcarolle called "In a Boat," is one of Virgil's sweetest pieces. But as Lou watched Virgil manipulate and operate, he became more jaded about Virgil Thomson's renowned charm and blustery brilliance. Finally, a series of events in 1986 drove Lou away again, this time for good.

One event was the episode that began this book: the Saint Teresa incident, in which Virgil cruelly disinvited the elderly Beatrice Wayne Godfrey to the premiere of the *Four Saints* revival after Lou, with great effort, had arranged for her to attend. But this incident played against the backdrop of Maurice's deteriorating health. And Virgil's attitude toward Maurice during this period was inexplicable.

Maurice, who had turned eighty-three that year, was suffering from multiple ailments: the lingering effects of difficult prostate surgery, a weakened heart, lungs battered by old age and too much smoking. But there was another problem: Maurice was HIV infected and had developed the attendant symptoms of AIDS: MAI bacterium, atypical tuberculosis, pneumonia, Kaposi's sarcoma. All his life, Maurice had been a soft-spoken radical when it came to "queer" issues. He lived openly as a gay man decades before Stonewall. But Maurice and Paul kept his HIV infection hidden. Their relationship, though intense, was not monogamous. However, Virgil was the instigator of the silence. He persuaded Maurice that were his condition to be made public, he would be stigmatized as the oldest known person with HIV. This would completely overshadow his reputation as an artist. Maurice's instinct was to talk about it, but he caved in to Virgil's arguments. And because Maurice wanted it this way, Paul went along.

To those who suspected but did not know what was going on, Virgil acted like someone in complete denial. When I asked him once just what was wrong with Maurice, who was then in the hospital, he screamed at me, "He has the AIDS pneumonia but not AIDS!" In Maurice's presence Virgil never mentioned AIDS. But he was not exactly a source of comfort. When earlier that year Maurice was bed-ridden at St. Vincent's Hospital, Virgil visited twice and always made some wisecrack. After one visit, during which Maurice had been hazy mentally, Virgil called the next day and cheerfully asked, "Maurice! You lucid today?" Perhaps such gallows humor was a way of coping, but Paul was upset: "That's Virgil in his enfant terrible mode, almost trying to provoke you."

During his years of working for Virgil, Lou had grown very fond of Maurice and Paul. And Maurice loved Lou like a son. Virgil was jealous of this developing closeness. But he tolerated it until the late summer of 1986, when Lou started visiting Maurice at the hospital during his lunch hours. Maurice hated the hospital food and, by this point, needed help eating; but he didn't want private nurses who were strangers. And Paul, who was spending every night on a chair in Maurice's hospital room, simply had to go to work most days at the museum. So Lou would come by daily with something he had prepared for Maurice's lunch and help him eat.

One day Virgil confronted Lou sternly: "I forbid you to go to Maurice in the hospital during your lunch hour." Lou was shocked and confused. He would have thought that Virgil would welcome his kindness to Maurice. If there was anybody Virgil had truly loved in his life, Lou thought, it was Maurice. Perhaps Virgil felt guilty that he was not trying to help his old friend. Perhaps he didn't want Lou finding out about Maurice's having AIDS (which Lou already knew), talking with the doctors, looking at the charts, and coming home to tell everyone. Perhaps he was jealous. Lou would never be so devoted to Virgil, unless he was paid, which was true. Whatever Virgil's motivation, Lou was not about to be bullied. "Virgil," he told him angrily, "I do not know what the fuck you are talking about. But, in any case, what I do on my lunch hour is my business. I don't charge you extra time, you're not losing money, you're not paying for my visits. You've no right to ask such a thing."[9]

Virgil backed down. But from that point on, their relationship was strained beyond repair. They were polite, but formal. Lou decided he must find new work. In light of Virgil's behavior, the letter announcing his intention to leave was gracious. But Lou was enough of a tactician to know that a little flattery would make this maneuver easier.

> Dear Virgil,
> My resistance to you lately has to do with my having put off for more than a year now letting you know that I will be moving on to another job. I knew I was losing the knack for letting you have your way all the time, which honestly I think a man your age deserves. And you are entitled too to a secretary who can happily provide it. I was, I think, for a long time just such a one. Actually you have spoiled me. I'm sure I could never again work for someone who was not your equal in courtesy and in wisdom. And those qualities are what has made working for you such a pleasure, truly.
> . . . I dare say I don't expect your blessing. But I am hoping you will not withhold your cooperation. Actually it would embarrass me to refuse any incentives it might occur to you to offer me to stay. I want you to know this resignation is a firm decision on my part and I hope you will accept it as inevitable. Maybe once my replacement is set we can even plan a proper farewell. It would please me if such an occasion could be as satisfying as have been the long years I have served you loyally.
>
> Foreverbest,
> Lou[10]

Virgil seemed to accept it amicably. Then there was another incident that ruptured whatever good will remained between them. One day Lou was helping Virgil put together the guest list for his ninetieth-birthday dinner at Chanterelle.

An elegant French restaurant then on Grand Street in Soho, Chanterelle was owned and operated by a sweet young couple, David Waltuck, who had once studied biological oceanography but given it up to become a chef, and his wife, Karen Brown Waltuck, who managed the restaurant. David and Karen were dedicated to their work and adorably in love with each other. Chanterelle became a favorite place for Maurice and Virgil to go. Maurice, who had celebrated his seventy-fifth birthday there, painted both Waltucks' portraits. In 1981 Virgil composed their musical portrait. Only Karen sat for him; but Virgil knew that the resulting piece, "Intensely Two," a lyrical gem, was a portrait of them both because each was so present in the other. On one visit Virgil gave them a gift they treasured, two of his French cookbooks from the eighteenth and nineteenth centuries. Virgil was always an honored guest at Chanterelle. "They'll put out anybody to give me a table," he used to say.

As they had done five years earlier, David and Karen threw Virgil's private birthday party. On November 23 the restaurant would be closed to customers while forty guests, selected by Virgil, would be given a gourmet dinner, compliments of the Waltucks, an extraordinarily generous gift. Naturally Lou assumed that he and Danyal would be invited. But when Virgil handed Lou the guest list so that the formal invitations could be mailed, Lou noticed something odd: "Virgil, you forgot to put me and Danyal on your list."

Virgil answered testily: "Oh, there are already too many goddamn queer couples."

The background history of this remark was enormous, for Lou was outspoken on behalf of gay causes. He had cared for friends stricken by AIDS and felt strongly about governmental negligence and America's pervasive homophobia. It was difficult for Lou to be understanding of Virgil's hostility to openly gay people. He couldn't write it off to old age, since Maurice was thrilled by the new openness and activism. Early on in their working relationship, Lou and Virgil realized that they must agree to disagree.

But Virgil's cutting "queer couples" remark and his exclusion of Lou and Danyal from the birthday dinner seemed intentionally hostile. If the idea was to provoke Lou into quitting, it worked. This, on top of the Saint Teresa incident and Lou's visits to Maurice, was beyond the pale. Lou started preparing Virgil's friends for his departure. Norma was very upset. She wanted Lou to go to her house in Easthampton for a week, to cool off, take walks on the beach. It would help, he'd see. Virgil was ninety and ailing. He couldn't adjust to a new secretary. He needed Lou.

But Lou was sure he had to leave. Virgil accepted the decision. As a concession Lou agreed to help find his replacement and to stay as long as it took to train him. The word went out and applications arrived. Some were from aspiring composers or musicologists; a few were from persons with experience as a personal secretary. Then Virgil asked me if I knew anyone who might be good. I did.

Allan Stinson grew up in the Washington, D.C., area, where his father, an engineer, and his mother, a mathematician, did research for the Department of Defense. When Allan applied to colleges, Harvard, Yale, and MIT fought over him. He accepted Yale, where he majored in math. But his creativity and curiosity were too much to be bound by a Yale major. He acted in plays, wrote poetry in French, pledged a secret society, and sang in a rock band called the Vacant Lot. A handsome, russet-tinged black man with a string bean build, penetrating dark eyes, infectious smile, and brilliance, Allan was completely fabulous. It was impossible not to fall for him. I fell. For a time we were inseparable.

But being both black and gay at an all-male Ivy League university in the late 1960s was stultifying. Though his grades were virtually perfect, Allan dropped out midway through junior year and never came back. Then began his odyssey. He was searching for something. And when you don't know where you are going, as the Yiddish proverb goes, any road will take you there.

Somewhat arbitrarily, he went to Los Angeles, met a guy in a bar, and wound up joining a radical commune. For six weeks one summer he went to Cuba to cut sugarcane, and shook hands with Fidel. Then he threw off his radicalism, moved to San Francisco, acted again (once in a play with Divine), and got a job screening flicks in a gay film house. Eventually, he fell in love with an activist and moved to Minneapolis, where this former leftist worked for an insurance company and became captain of the company bowling team. When the relationship broke up, Allan moved to New York and took a job as a secretary at NBC. Over his desk passed highly scientific documents about cutting-edge satellite dish technology. Of course, with his background in science, Allan understood everything. So when his boss quit, Allan wound up getting his boss's job. Now he was a big-shot executive in a three-piece suit who traveled to affiliate stations explaining the new technology and persuading them to hook up.

But he was still questing for something. And it wasn't to be found in the executive offices of NBC. One day, sitting at his desk, he simply got up and walked out, never to return. He started doing temp work, which in a way was more satisfying, broke up the relationship he was in, and settled into domestic life, for good, it turned out, with a boyish artist from Oregon, Philip Zimmerman.

At the time it occurred to me that Allan and Virgil might like each other. Allan knew of Virgil Thomson only through me. But working for Virgil could not be more taxing than temp work, and would certainly be more interesting. Allan's was a late application. But my hunch was right. Virgil liked Allan immensely. He was particularly struck by Allan's resonant, articulate speaking voice. Just like the black cast members from the first production of *Four Saints,* Allan "loved using language," Virgil later told me.

On the evening of the day Allan was interviewed, he and I, dressed in tuxedos, attended the ninetieth-birthday production of *Four Saints in Three Acts,* the production that Mrs. Godfrey had been barred from. Allan, of course, had never heard the opera. The next day Lou called to tell Allan that he had gotten the job.

The party at Chanterelle went on as planned. I felt guilty attending when Lou and Danyal were not. Nor, incredibly, had Sam and Gerald, the "boys downstairs," been invited. Another "queer couple" Virgil didn't want at his posh party, it seemed. Saddest of all was Maurice's absence. Recently released from the hospital, Maurice was home, too ill to leave. People peppered me with questions about Virgil's new secretary. The Waltucks outdid themselves for the birthday dinner. One of the guests was the artist Louise Nevelson. Though not really Virgil's friend, she was close with Bill Katz. When Bill suggested bringing her along, Virgil was happy to add so illustrious a name to his guest list. Nevelson complied by designing a commemorative menu, one for each guest to keep. On one side was a Nevelson silk screen (an image of stark, dramatic black wedges); on the other was the menu for the evening, written out by hand, and the program for the postdinner performance.

Menu

Perrier Jovet Grand Brut
Wild Mushroom Ravioli with White Truffles
Roast Pheasant & Foie Gras Toast
1978 Chateau Pichon LaLande
Salad

Prune Ice Cream & Armagnac
Armagnac Marsan 1942
Coffee, Tea, & petits fours

The postdinner program began with the Suite from *The Plow That Broke the Plains,* arranged for piano and performed by Jacquelyn Helin, a New York pianist who championed Virgil's music. Following this, Joan Morris, the celebrated singer of American show music, performed two of Virgil's *William Blake* songs with William Bolcom, her pianist and composer husband. Next, Scott Wheeler and I played Scott's "Birthday Card" to Virgil—a short, four-hand piano piece that ingeniously transforms the "All My Long Life" theme from *The Mother of Us All* into a gentle rag, then mixes in tune bits from the Cello Concerto, from Virgil's whimsical musical portrait of Scott, and from his massive-chord musical portrait of me, and finally implodes into "For He's a Jolly Good Fellow."

The grand finale featured another friend of Bill Katz's not known to Virgil, the dancer and choreographer Bill T. Jones. To a suite from Virgil's Ten Etudes for Piano, played dashingly by Craig Rutenberg, Jones performed an original work in a bare-chested costume designed by Louise Nevelson and Bill Katz. He had hardly any space to work in. Yet the dance was wild. Seated on a pedestal with his back to the audience, he waved his arms and gyrated his shoulders. Gradually he turned around, moving his legs; eventually he stood up, thrashing about while virtually standing still.

After the performance, two waiters from Chanterelle brought out an enormous fallen chocolate soufflé cake with ninety candles on it. But the cake was so large and the fire from the candles so intense, that the waiters had trouble keeping hold of it. Everyone could see as it slowly started to teeter and slip from their arms, but there was nothing to be done. As a collective chorus of "Oh no-o-o-o's" resounded through the restaurant, the cake went smashing to the floor, a mass of chocolate mush and smoldering candles. ("A doubly fallen chocolate soufflé cake," David later called it.) Virgil, smiling sheepishly, said, "That's all right. I love birthday cakes so long as I don't have to eat them!"

There were drinks and toasts. Louise Nevelson, who had drunk quite a bit, struggled to her feet and, in a quavering voice, said, "This is the greatest evening of my life!" Those who had two weeks earlier attended a birthday bash for Virgil at the Harvard Club in New York thought this a curious toast. For on that occasion Louise Nevelson had also struggled to her feet, lifted her glass, and said, "This is the greatest evening of my life!" The final toast came from Virgil. He didn't stand; he didn't raise a glass. He simply surveyed the room filled with his friends—the Flenders, Craig, Morris Golde, Anne-Marie, Paul (who for once had entrusted Maurice to a night nurse instead of staying at his side), the Waltucks—and the distinguished guests, then said, "There isn't anybody here whom I don't love."

Maurice had been six weeks in the hospital, where he was always sweet-tempered, but scared. He kept saying he wanted to go home, and got very clever at finding ways to get himself out of bed at night while Paul was asleep. "He was better than Houdini," Paul said. "He'd slip out of those restraints and go walking, stark naked, in the halls."

Shortly before the birthday dinner, Maurice was allowed to return home. When he walked into his studio, he saw some unused canvases in the corner. "I've got to varnish those," he told Paul. He could hardly stand, but he varnished all six. It made him tired, but it was a "good tired," Paul said. He ate some supper, then went to bed and slept more soundly than he had for weeks.

Maurice spent three weeks at home. By mid-December he was back in the hospital, where he slipped in and out of consciousness. Sometimes when he was alert, he muttered numbers to himself. Once an honors graduate in mathematics from Harvard, Maurice was trying to work out equations in his head. As he had during the previous hospitalization, Paul slept every night in a nearby chair. He lowered the bed so that he was level with Maurice and could hold his hand.

Eventually Maurice slipped into a coma. Paul now acknowledged that Maurice would not recover. Maurice's breathing became atypical, and he was often fitful. His oxygen mask kept slipping off, so Paul was constantly having to adjust it. Early on the morning of December 22, Maurice seemed calm. Paul sat quietly next to him, just holding his hand. Only when Paul saw the lines go flat on the monitors did Paul realize that Maurice had died. It was that peaceful.

Paul called everyone with the news. Lou went in early to be with Virgil, who was badly shaken. Virgil's way of coping was to make a project of getting a proper obituary into the *New York Times*. Given that Maurice's representational painting style was not then fashionable, Virgil was afraid that Maurice's passing would be little noted. He and Lou wrote a press release, sent it to Virgil's friend Allen Hughes, the *Times* music critic, and asked him to see what he could do. Though no picture ran with the obituary, the article hewed close to Virgil and Lou's statement, calling Maurice Grosser a painter "known for his picturesque landscapes, still lifes and portraits," and citing his collaborations with Virgil and Gertrude:

> An inveterate traveler, Mr. Grosser spent long periods living and working abroad, first in Paris and then in Morocco, Spain, Greece, Israel, Turkey, Nigeria, Brazil and Canada. He painted in a style that has been characterized as "conservative realist," and his firmly structured landscapes also reflect sojourns in New England as well as the south, the southwest and California. Among his more notable portrait subjects were Alfred North Whitehead, Mary Garden, Jane Bowles and Mr. Thomson.[11]

The cause of death was reported as congestive heart failure. No mention was made of AIDS. His sister and two brothers were listed as the only survivors. Paul was not included. As the executor of the will, Paul would have to settle Maurice's affairs and decide what to do with the 150 paintings that belonged to the estate. Maurice wanted the paintings to go to museums rather than to private collectors, which would be difficult to carry out. And time was now a factor. For Paul, too, was HIV positive; and seeing Maurice through his illness until death had sapped Paul's own health.

Shortly after Maurice's death, I was in New York with Scott and his wife of less than a year, Christen Frothingham, who was then studying to become an Episcopal priest (which she has since become). Virgil was subdued. On the piano he had placed a photo of Maurice and himself on vacation in Maine, a tender snapshot of two old men standing awkwardly together. Virgil took us to lunch downstairs at El Quijote. At one point, speaking of Paul, almost shouting, he said, "Paul tended to Maurice, fed him, cleaned him, slept on a chair every night in the hospital room. Not only did he never complain, he acted as if every day was a privilege. I've never seen such devotion!"

Virgil seldom got so emotional. I thought his feelings might be intensified by a sense of guilt, given his attitude toward Lou's concern for Maurice and his own near-absence from Maurice's sickbed. But whatever Virgil's shortcomings, he had lost the one person who truly loved him, and he was suffering.

Before leaving New York, I brought Virgil some of my grandmother's homemade ravioli. Once back in Boston, I sent a letter and enclosed some recent reviews for him to red-pencil. On January 3, 1987, I received the following note, an unusually revealing one:

> d.T
> Letter lovely
> Reviews faultless.
> Memory of Brooklyn pasta to be cherished.

And so life goes on. But the absence of the presence is confusing. I keep expecting for Maurice to telephone daily, which he always did. Now Paul does, which is a comfort. Come see when you can.

Yours, V.T.[12]

28 ALL MY LONG LIFE

In the aftermath of his birthday hoopla, Virgil settled back into his quietly productive routine. He still prepared meals for friends in his cubicle of a kitchen, everything from his hardy "Missouri meatloaf" to gourmet roasted lamb cooked the "French way," blood-red rare. He worked every day, dictating letters, tending to paperwork. And he still composed, mostly musical portraits now and then, but occasionally a miniature chamber work or special piece, like the lullaby he wrote for the birth of Scott Wheeler's daughter, Margaret, in the spring of 1986. He sent it with a silver baby spoon and a note card saying, "Virgil loves you."

There to assist him and keep things orderly was his new secretary Allan Stinson. His first full day on the job, Allan was taken by Virgil through a meticulous list of dos and don'ts. After issuing a series of rules about mundane matters, Virgil suddenly said, "Next. This is what you do if you show up and I'm dead. Don't call the doctor; it will be too late. Call the lawyer. He knows what to do. Then call the locksmith to come change the locks. Then call AP, UPI, and the *New York Times*—the culture desk, *not* the obit boys."

Allan had never encountered anybody so unabashedly cantankerous; he found it sort of refreshing, at least in the beginning, as he recounted in a letter:

The new "man" in my life is sometimes tiresome, often challenging, and always engaging. Whenever he is cranky I just read something that he has written. I'll take a little 90 year old irritability sprinkled sparsely, as it is, on a mind like Virgil's anytime.

The mechanics of the job are awesome. I've worked at institutions that were just as organized but few that were as relentlessly cross-referenced. Still they are only mechanics and consistent rather than mysterious. I think that the military made a strong impression on Virgil, not to mention a "mad librarian" secretary in the past.[1]

Allan was so solid and centered that Virgil relaxed around him. When Virgil found out that, among his many job experiences, Allan had taken training as a masseur, Virgil said, "Perhaps you can give me a massage now and then." Allan agreed. So a routine developed (short-lived, it turned out) in which every day Allan would arrive to find Virgil naked ("You can't imagine a more ridiculous sight"), face down on his bed, waiting for his massage. But Allan found this silent, physical contact a calming way to begin their day together.

Of course, as a secretary this former NBC executive was singularly efficient, though it took some lobbying for Allan to win permission to use the computer. Virgil's friend Peter McWilliams, who was then writing how-to books for computer novices, could not believe that Virgil had no personal computer. Peter was so flabbergasted by the situation, that one day he just showed up with a Kaypro personal computer and printer as a gift. Virgil hardly let Lou use it; but Allan insisted. Virgil never understood the concept of word processing. He thought every letter was being typed twice: once on the computer, a second time through the printer.

Allan had to tolerate the vestiges of a plantation mentality in Virgil's attitude toward him. He winced whenever Virgil talked with a guest about being a grandchild of the Confederacy or made generalizations about "our blacks." One day, as Allan, wearing an undersized apron, was making beef barley soup in the kitchen, Virgil kept shouting orders from the den: "Allan, get me my list of works. Allan, add this to the Xerox file for your lunch break. Allan, look up when I go to Boston?" Allan kept answering, "Yes, Virgil." He thought to himself, "I might as well say, 'Yes, Massa Virgil.' If my grandmother saw me now, it would send her to the arms of Jesus." Virgil quickly grew dependent upon his new secretary; "my admirable and indispensable Allan," he called him.[2]

A few of Virgil's friends, understandably protective of him, sus-pected that I had manipulated the hiring of my old friend as Virgil's secretary so that I would have a source for the kind of intimate dope few biographers ever uncover. The idea had not occurred to me. But I did find out things from Allan that I never would have otherwise.

In January of 1988 Virgil filled out a confidential Harvard alumni health questionnaire. Allan secretly made a copy for me because it was so hilarious. In answer to one question—"Do you think a per-son of your age can do anything to prevent ill health in the future?"—Virgil checked option three: "It is largely a matter of chance," adding two handwritten words: "by now."

Then there was Allan's discovery of the most significant note card Virgil ever received. Some days work at Virgil's was hectic; other days there was little to do. So Allan found ways to look busy. He would take out correspondence, like Henry-Russell Hitchcock's wickedly gay letters, and read them for fun. One day, going through the desk af-fixed to the built-in bookcases in the living room, a desk Virgil never used, Allan found a small cardboard box filled with motley note cards and faded slips of paper: the business cards of merchants from the old days in Paris; sundry scraps of paper with decades-old addresses; formal calling cards, mostly with names that were unfamiliar to Allan. Flipping gently through them he chanced upon a business card:

Day and Night Service
BUckminster 2-2210

HERMANN COHEN
Bail Bonds

24 Snyder Avenue
Brooklyn, New York

This was obviously the bail bondsman Virgil had called on March 14, 1942, the night he was arrested at Beekman's bordello, on Pacific Street in Brooklyn. Perhaps all the tattered cards and papers had per-sonal significance for Virgil. It seemed to be a box of things he did not want officially cataloged, but did not want discarded either.

Searching more carefully, Allan found something extraordinary: the tiny envelope and formal note card that Gertrude sent to Virgil on January 21, 1931. Miss Gertrude Stein, it read, "declines further ac-quaintance with Mr. Virgil Thomson." This was the note that com-menced their long estrangement. Virgil had withheld the card from Yale; nor had he filed it with his Stein papers. Perhaps he had forgotten it was there. Allan put it back and never mentioned it.

And then, among the things I found out from Allan, there was the story of the young man from the West Coast.

Shortly after Virgil's ninetieth birthday, he received a letter from an aspiring composer, just twenty-nine, living in the Northwest. The young man had seen John Huszar's documentary, which had been reedited with some additional footage and retitled *Virgil Thomson at Ninety*. The composer, who confessed to being attracted to older men, wrote that he was irresistibly drawn to Virgil. Though living with a much older lover, he wanted to meet Virgil at least once. He enclosed a picture, which showed him to be wholesomely handsome.

Soon there was another letter from the young man, filled with excitement and anticipation. Virgil had phoned him. A day was arranged for the young man to visit. He was to come at 5:15 P.M., fifteen minutes after Allan's workday ended.

About 4:45 on the appointed afternoon, Virgil dressed in his silk bathrobe and went to wait in his armchair. Knowing what was about to happen, Allan was afraid to leave. This guy might be some weirdo, he thought. Suppose he beats up Virgil? When Allan kept working past 5:00, Virgil said nothing. The silent signal was that maybe he should stick around.

At 5:15 the young man showed up, with an eager puppy look, hardly nervous. He greeted Virgil warmly and sat on a footstool near Virgil's chair. Allan went back to his desk, but kept the door ajar so he could hear what was going on. The young man gushed over Virgil's physique. He seemed harmless enough. Then, in what Allan later described as an act of Virgilian machismo, Virgil asked him, "Am I the oldest man you've ever been attracted to?" Yes, he certainly was, the young man said. "You have to understand, there is little that I can do for you," said Virgil, meaning, little sexually. The young man understood completely. At this point, feeling that Virgil was safe and having heard all he wanted to, Allan decided to leave them alone. "Virgil, I'm going home," he said, poking his head threw the door. With an impish smile, Virgil waved so long. Allan left.

In the initial months after Allan entered the picture, Virgil was preoccupied with another book project, this one proposed by the editors at Summit Books. It was to be an annotated and edited collection of his letters. The project had begun some years earlier with an editor Virgil grew to mistrust. With the publishers' approval, he turned the project over to Tim Page, a young critic who had established his reputation at the *New York Times,* then moved to *New York Newsday,* the New York edition of the respected Long Island daily, when it started publishing in 1985. Virgil admired Tim's reviews. ("He's very knowledgeable and you can read him," Virgil told me. "He knows what words mean and they all come out in sentences.") Tim's coeditor was to be his wife, Vanessa Weeks Page, a former prodigy cellist and experienced editor. Virgil liked them both immensely. However, this hardly assured that their work would proceed smoothly.

Virgil estimated that he had written some twenty-five thousand letters; many of them were available, either in Virgil's files or at Yale. During the period when Kathleen Hoover wrote her Thomson biography and he wrote his autobiography, Virgil had made a concentrated effort to retrieve his existing letters from friends and colleagues. So Tim and Vanessa had plenty to choose from. But Virgil had his own ideas about what he wanted included in this collection.

He made clear from the start that the most personal of his letters were not to be published. "You're a newspaper man," Virgil told him. "You want to write about sex!" There were strained discussions about Virgil's letters to Briggs Buchanan. Tim and Vanessa thought they were remarkable. It was amazing to read Virgil Thomson overcome by an unrequited crush. Yet he was still Virgil: clear-headed, his arguments massed, trying his best to wear Briggs down. At first Virgil grudgingly agreed to allow the Pages to use them. Then he said that, even though the book was to be organized chronologically, the Buchanan letters would have to be put in a separate section with an introduction explaining that nothing ever happened between them. Ultimately, he ruled that only the most innocent letters to Briggs could be included.

Many letters to others were pruned of compromising references, such as those to life with Maurice, to the incident when Virgil picked up a street hustler in Paris, to the intimate lives of Virgil's friends. Even professional opinions were tampered with. Sometimes Virgil simply altered a pronouncement when he thought it immature or incorrect. In one case, a letter to a reader who had written to him at the *Herald Tribune* about a Sunday piece, Virgil spoke of Gustav Mahler's ambition: "As to Mahler, yes, I know the Second Symphony, or used to. I do think Mahler's work was more distorted by his life as a professional conductor than by his desire to storm Parnassus as a composer. He was not an ambitious man. No man of talent is."[3] When Virgil read this passage in the page proofs, with the Pages looking on, he was horrified: " '. . . not an ambitious man. . . . No man of talent is.' What rubbish!" Virgil insisted that they change it to "He was an ambitious man, of course; every man of talent is."[4] In this form it was published. For good measure he also excised the qualifier ("or used to") after the statement "I know Mahler's Second Symphony."

Yet many brilliant, colorful, penetrating, and, in their own way, revealing letters made it into the book, dating back to Virgil's report to his sister, Ruby, about field artillery school in 1917. When the book was released in the late spring of 1988, some reviewers understandably regretted the absence of truly personal letters: "either by editorial judgment or authorial choice, the letters seem to float Thomson in some vague social jello where few of his correspondents bear any clear relation to each other," Edward Rothstein wrote in the *New Republic.* "Lovers, close friends, and strangers become nearly interchangeable recipients of Thomson's prose."[5] "His wit observes the world but at the same time deflects our attention from the observer," wrote Bernard Holland in the *New York Times.*[6] Yet most critics marveled at the letters for their trenchant commentary and descriptive vitality, for his "infinite worldliness and down-home horse sense," as Richard Dyer put it in the *Boston Globe.*[7]

Far from being upset by the critics' complaints that the letters as presented portrayed a man who kept his deeper feelings to himself, Virgil was almost pugnaciously happy with the reviews. It was as if he had again pulled a fast one and kept his critics off balance, admiring but guessing.

Virgil was feeling especially feisty that fall, because earlier that year he had been hospitalized and feared he might not recover. In the weeks prior to his illness, everyone knew that something was wrong. "I don't feel well," he told me during one visit. "Ever since I turned ninety I haven't felt well. I felt perfectly fine during my eighties. Maybe you just don't feel well in your nineties."

He grew increasingly weak, dizzy, and unsteady on his feet. When one day he spat up blood, everyone—Allan, Sam, Gerald, Paul—insisted he go to the hospital. It turned out his condition had been brought on by severe dehydration. Virgil hated to drink water ("Water makes me pee!").

At the hospital he went through periods where he could not recognize anyone. On March 29 he was in very bad shape. "Do you recognize these people?" the doctor asked him, pointing to Norma and Richard, Paul, and Allan. Virgil said nothing. "Do you know where you are?" he was asked. "Yes!" Virgil said, laughing. "Do you want some Jell-O?" the nurse asked. Virgil frowned and shouted, "No!" Everyone smiled. That was a glimpse of the old Virgil. The next day he asked Allan, "Am I dying? Because if I am there are things to do."

Virgil was given intravenous fluids and plasma transfusions. He responded well. Soon he was home, feeling himself and sleeping well. Still, Paul insisted on spending the nights with Virgil. Everyone tried to persuade Paul that this was not necessary. Virgil was doing fine. Besides, Paul himself was beginning to suffer from symptoms of his HIV infection. He was in no condition to take care of anyone else. But Paul would not hear otherwise. He started to spend nights at Virgil's, sleeping on the living room sofa.

This whole drama of the blind leading the blind became a bit ridiculous. One day, when Allan walked in to start work, he saw Virgil tottering from the kitchen with a serving tray, calling out to Paul, who was sound asleep on the sofa, "Coffee woffee. Time to get up." As Paul struggled awake, Virgil pulled Allan aside and said, "I'm worried about Paul; he sleeps all the time."

By now, another young man had been added to the Thomson household: Jay Sullivan, who would become Virgil's last and closest secretary.

In some ways Jay Sullivan was an unlikely person to wind up working for Virgil. He was from an Irish Methodist family in Columbus, Georgia, an athletic young man who had broken his nose playing high school football, which rearranged his boyish features just enough to lend him a chiseled adult look that many women found irresistible.

Jay's father was an influential doctor, formerly an adviser to Governor Jimmy Carter. Jay's mother was one of those capable, attractive southern women at home in any setting. Jay had inherited his mother's courtly ways and his father's aptitude for science. When he entered St. Louis University, a demanding Jesuit college in Missouri, Jay studied philosophy and took his premed courses. But a family illness brought him back home, where he graduated with honors from Columbus College in 1983. Then, to his father's despair, Jay gave up the idea of medical school, taught high school English for a year in Columbus, and eventually headed for New York. Jay was infatuated with the arts and the artist's mystique. He wanted to write, to act, to live in the East Village and meet local characters, to mix in with New

York's hectic, wacky, diverse life. He made his living mostly doing carpentry, but threw himself into community activism.

It was at a meeting of his tenants association that Jay met Allan and his boyfriend Philip, who lived in the adjacent building. When Jay found out that Allan was working for Virgil Thomson, he was mightily impressed. "It's not so impressive, believe me," Allan said. But Jay doted on stories of Paris in the twenties. "If you ever need help, or somebody to take over when you're away," Jay told Allan, "remember me."

That's what Allan did when he decided to take time off. Virgil liked Jay, this rugged, well-mannered, impressionable southerner, then twenty-six. Jay became a part-time assistant. This was the fall of 1987. By the next summer, Virgil needed Jay's help on a more permanent basis. Allan was HIV positive; he was not entirely shocked, but he decided that he must rethink every aspect of his life.

Working for Virgil had become too stressful. Allan grew increasingly intolerant: "Our dear little Tommie Thomson gets more childlike every day with his naps, his tantrums, his unsteady walk, his peeing in his pants, and his great thirst for milk." Virgil sensed he was losing Allan's good will, but Allan had not been hired as a home health aide. Virgil would get attacks of nausea and be unable to control his bowels. Allan was expected to clean up the messes. One day Allan arrived for work with a scruffy beard (he was always growing and shaving and growing beards), dressed in black pants, a dusty flannel shirt and dingy sneakers. "Look at you!" Virgil shouted. "I don't expect you to wear a tie. But you look like the furnace man!" Allan, furious, muttered out loud, "How *should* I dress to clean up your shit?" But Virgil could not hear him.

With his changed health status, Allan needed to find fulfilling but less taxing work. He decided to return to California. A friend from San Francisco who ran the Tamalpa Institute, which used dance, movement, and ritual as therapies for healing and personal growth, offered Allan a job. He thought he should accept this offer, but was not yet ready to uproot Philip and leave New York. However, one Friday afternoon, before taking several days off, he mailed a letter to Virgil explaining his health situation and stating his wish to work less often. Virgil would receive the letter Monday morning, by which time Allan would be away.

I happened to be there when Virgil opened Allan's letter. After reading it grimly, he turned to me—he almost turned *on* me—and said, "You know about this?" I did. "Well," Virgil shouted, "I'm in danger of losing him and there's nothing I can do about it. You gave him to me," he added, testily but desperately. "Do you have another?"

Jay was the obvious choice. He wanted the work and was already devoted to Virgil. But Virgil thought Jay was not experienced enough as a secretary. This was absurd. Virgil needed a nurse more than a secretary. Soon Virgil realized that realistically he had little other choice. His friends conspired to convince Virgil that Jay was a godsend.

Jay was hired, and once again Virgil juggled two secretaries while Jay learned the ropes. At first Allan got all the white-collar jobs (writing letters, placing calls, keeping books), while Jay got the blue-collar jobs (mending things, running errands, stacking file boxes, installing new shelves). Jay got kidded about being Virgil's first "butch secretary." Virgil was impatient that summer, still miffed that people were leaving him. One sweltering day Jay worked heroically to install an enormous air conditioner that Jacquelyn Helin, Virgil's pianist friend insisted he allow her to purchase on his behalf. Allan was doing paper work trying to stay out of the way. I was scavenging through file boxes. And Jay was sweating in the living room, trying to construct a platform outside the ninth-floor window that would support this massive machine, while Virgil barked orders at him. Virgil's household tools were not sufficient. Jay would have to go home and get his own toolbox. Virgil was not pleased. "Well, hurry up and get your ass back here. Eat your lunch here. Don't go out. You've got to vacuum, make cole slaw, make iced tea, and take parts for copying."

By summer's end Virgil was calmer, partly because poor health was slowing him down. Allan wrote in November with the news.

> For the most part Thomson has been, in the words of Jay, a "baby doll" of late, but I think it's unintentional. He is losing the energy to sustain his all-out attack on life. More and more we have to be mind readers or crack detectives working with the faintest clues. "There's one of those things out there, you know what I mean, that has to go in a can" he will say without being able to tell you what the thing is or even where out there is. Or "go get me the stuff you put on your elbows" when what he wants is deodorant. Often he tells me to call someone right now and ask them something or give them a message. I listen until he begins to mumble

"comma" or "paragraph" when I realize that he is dictating a letter and I better grab a piece of paper quickly.[8]

Dealing with Virgil finally proved too much for Allan. By January of the new year, after taking Virgil through yet another hospitalization, Allan notified Virgil that he was quitting and accepted the job at the Tamalpa Institute, in Marin County. Jay would now be Virgil's sole secretary.

During that fall of 1988, while Virgil was recuperating from his hospitalization, his old friend John Houseman was home in Malibu preparing to die. For over a year he had been receiving treatment for spinal cancer, but there was no point in continuing. "Having ceased to regard death as a threat," he wrote in his last book, *Unfinished Business,* "I now accept it as the last of the many surprises of which my life is the sum."[9] As his health declined, he was attended by his wife, Joan, his two sons, and his devoted protégé James Bridges.

Jack Larson kept Virgil apprised of Houseman's state. Toward the end he was paralyzed from the chest down, but continued to give interviews, greet friends, always "freshly shaved and smiling," as Jim Bridges reported. But as he declined, he talked endlessly of Virgil. It was Virgil who had taken a gamble and selected Jack Houseman, a man who had never directed a play, let alone an opera, to preside over the premiere of *Four Saints.* "Why did he pick me?" Houseman kept asking on his deathbed. Hearing this, Virgil was genuinely moved and almost boastfully proud. "Jack talks of nothing but me," he said, with his typical propensity to exaggerate.

On Monday, October 31, John Houseman died. Virgil was gratified to see such extensive and laudatory coverage of his old friend over several days in the *New York Times.* What came through these articles was that *Four Saints* had indeed been the turning point of John Houseman's life. That much of Virgil's boast was no exaggeration.

Throughout this period of ill heath and rotating secretaries, Virgil had continued to work. On May 28, 1988, he composed a musical portrait of H. Wiley Hitchcock, a distinguished musicologist and the director of the Institute for Studies in American Music at the Brooklyn College Conservatory of Music. As Hitchcock sat for his portrait, Virgil worked effortfully for nearly two hours. When finished, he uttered a sort of

triumphant grunt. The piece, a two-part contrapuntal texture with obsessively jerky dotted-rhythm figures, was titled "Two Birds." Why?
"Well, it's two birds who don't like each other very much so they are
always pecking at each other." How this image related to Wiley Hitchcock, Virgil never explained.

When Hitchcock asked if the completed portrait might be premiered at the launching party being thrown by Macmillan Press for
the four-volume *New Grove Dictionary of American Music,* a much
anticipated scholarly work, which Hitchcock had coedited, Virgil,
ever the savvy barterer, said, "Sure, if Macmillan gives me a free
copy." This portrait would be Virgil Thomson's last completed composition.

Two weeks after composing this piece, Virgil managed to make one
last road trip. For two years, Brian Murphy, an English professor at
Oakland University in Rochester, Michigan, not far from Detroit, had
been trying to arrange for Virgil to visit. He had considerable funding at his disposal and originally proposed that Virgil make regular
visits to the campus to lecture and teach. During two years of negotiations, promises, cancellations, and illnesses, the professor's ambitious scheme was whittled down to a week-long festival, from June
12 to June 18, 1988, to be titled "Virgil Thomson in Time." Brian Murphy was an ebullient academic whose imagination was fired by making connections between the arts. He was a devotee of Paris in the
twenties and in awe of Virgil's history. Virgil was skeptical of the festival's intellectual trappings, but pleased that lots of his music would
be performed: two chamber music programs with quartets, songs, and
piano works; and a concert presenting the Warren Symphony, an amateur ensemble fortified with retirees from the Detroit Symphony, and
the college chorale in the *Symphony on a Hymn Tune,* the Concertino
for Harp, Strings, and Percussion, and Act 3 of *Four Saints.* Virgil
would attend rehearsals, give lectures, meet with student composers,
and be the featured guest at a panel of regional critics.

It all came off, though not as planned. Jay, who accompanied
Virgil for the entire trip, had worked out all the travel details in advance with Brian Murphy, everything from how far Virgil would have
to walk to get backstage at Varner Recital Hall, to the proximity of
various men's rooms. Virgil was happy to be feted, and Brian Murphy soared through the week on a nonstop, nicotine-charged intellectual high. But Virgil's bluntness ("The conductor is hopeless," he

shouted during the open rehearsal of the Warren Symphony) and his unabashed public eliminating of his bladder (he urinated outside university buildings, in the surrounding evergreen bushes, almost anywhere) took some getting used to.

On Thursday I arrived to perform some piano portraits, give a talk, and join the critics' panel. That day a near disaster occurred. While driving Virgil and me in a university car, Jay took a turn from the road outside the hotel where we were all staying and was rammed by a reckless driver speeding in the breakdown lane. The whole passenger side of the car was smashed. Jay was basically unhurt. Sitting in the back seat, I was thrown to the roof, hit my head, and grew hazy. Though jostled badly, Virgil was calm as a Buddha. His only injury seemed to be to his right hand, which turned blue-black and started to swell, but he did not resist Jay's insistence that we go to the hospital to make sure we were well. When we arrived by cab, Brian, whom I had phoned, was waiting in the lobby and looking shattered. Virgil was oddly excited by his first-ever auto accident. After being checked out, we were taken by Brian to dinner at the hotel, where Virgil, uncharacteristically, had three vodka tonics.

That weekend Virgil learned how truly efficient and concerned Jay was. When they first arrived at the university, Jay noticed that the seat belt on the passenger side of the official university car they had been lent was broken. Jay needed a screwdriver to fix it. The hotel did not have one. So Jay bugged Brian about it until he brought some tools from home. If Jay had not repaired that seat belt, Virgil might have been seriously hurt, even killed.

Walking with me the day after the accident, Virgil spoke of how much he liked Jay, how lucky he felt to have him. Then he asked a blunt question.

"Jay's not queer, is he?" Knowing that Jay and I were sharing a hotel room and were now good friends, Virgil figured that I would have gotten to the bottom of the matter.

"No, Virgil," I said. "He's not."

"Are you sure?" he asked.

"Yes, Virgil, I'm quite sure."

"That's good," he said, emphatically.

"Does it really matter to you?" I asked.

"Yes," he said. "It's better. It's much less complicated." He paused, then added, somewhat wistfully, "It's a great comfort."

Virgil was proud to have a young heterosexual secretary who was so devoted to him. Virgil's own homophobia colored his feelings about the "comfort" this gave him. But there was more to it. Virgil knew that he was failing. Jay was already caring for him, cleaning up after him, nursing him. There would be more of that, as Jay escorted Virgil through this last stage. Virgil was concerned about the public perception of this intimate relationship. It was "less complicated" that there not even be a hint of something "queer" going on.

There was one more substantial work project that Virgil was able to complete during this period. For over a year he had worked steadily on a book he had thought of writing all his life, a treatise on prosody that he eventually titled *Music with Words: A Composer's View*. He had mentioned the project to Harold Samuel at the Yale School of Music Library. Samuel brought Virgil together with the director of the Yale University Press. And if Virgil was more accommodating during the negotiations than usual, it was because he dearly wanted to write this book. He owned this subject, he felt.

Published in the summer of 1989, the book is filled with wisdom, pragmatic suggestions, and insightful analyses. But it is a slender volume of essays rather than a comprehensive presentation, not nearly the book he could have written twenty years earlier. He asked several colleagues to critique the manuscript. And he needed someone to select musical examples from the works of other composers to use as illustrations of his talking points. For this he turned to his Boston composer friend Charles Fussell, who put much time into examining scores, bringing them to Virgil for discussion, and placing them in the text. Charles had misgivings about the book and found Virgil impossibly demanding. But he revered Virgil and wanted to help.

When the manuscript was delivered to Yale, a young editor called Virgil to say that the text looked fine, everything was set to go, except for one thing: Virgil had forgotten to write an acknowledgment. "Don't you want to thank the people who helped you," she asked. "No," Virgil said. "I wrote the book." This was Virgil once again hogging credit and attention, struggling to gain recognition, even at the risk of alienating supporters. This was the sort of Virgilian behavior that Allan had found truly sorrowful.

> You must know by now that I don't think V.T. has been cheated of any recognition he was due, ignored or short-changed in any form in his life. He had a life of uncommon advantages and it is

just brattish whining to feel the world owed him more attention than he got. I do, however, have some sympathy for his music, especially the operas. They are child actresses who can't get work because no one wants to put up with their stage mother.[10]

By the end of January, Allan was off to San Francisco. He worked for the Tamalpa Institute, facilitating a dance workshop for people affected by HIV, then moved into AIDS services work. Finally, the narrative of his life, which had zigzagged from radicalism to an executive job to cooking beef barley soup for Virgil, seemed not so haphazard. Everything he had done had been preparation for the work he was now doing. He was revered within the social services network and the afflicted minority community. He spent time each summer working as a counselor at a camp for inner-city children with AIDS. He worked with fulfillment, though not without stress, and seldom thought of Virgil Thomson.

During the summer of 1989, Virgil declined steadily and Jay remained steadfast. Though hardly able to write, Virgil tried to keep composing. Earlier in the year he had accepted a commission from the International Clarinet Society, based in Anderson, Indiana, offering to compose three short musical portraits for clarinet solo. The society, "thrilled with your expedient reply to our inquiry," as the chairperson wrote to Virgil, promised a $1,500 payment. Twice that summer Virgil tried to compose a musical portrait of Jack Larson, who was passing through town. This was to be the first piece in the set. But he was unable to concentrate. As he pushed aside his manuscript paper, he told Jack, "It wouldn't be worthy of either of us." The second piece was to have been a portrait of Jay; but Virgil never even attempted it. Whom he had in mind for the third subject he never said.

The burden of seeing Virgil through his decline fell increasingly on Jay. Paul Sanfaçon could no longer help, because he too was dying. In July, Paul entered Tisch–New York University Hospital. Lou, as devoted to Paul as he had been to Maurice, was there every day. Paul was annoyed that Lou and Virgil were not speaking. He was emotionally invested in trying to mend this rift and thought Lou had gone too far. As the far younger person, Lou should make a gesture of reconciliation. Lou thought that too many people had indulged Virgil during his life and that was the last thing he needed.

Paul asked me to visit him. I was not surprised to see the sunken cheeks, the scrawny shoulders, the bony arms and elbows. This was what it meant to die from AIDS, as I knew too well from having lost three good friends already. I was surprised by Paul's thick, gray-streaked beard. He looked like an Old Testament prophet. Paul wanted to know how Virgil was. My report saddened him, but also set him to telling stories of wonderful summer vacations with Maurice and Virgil in Maine, and joyous dinners at the Chelsea. Of course, Virgil had his mean side too. Paul had seen it often, particularly (and inexplicably) when Maurice was dying.

Paul started to cry. "I never understood Virgil's meanness. Where did it come from?" Afterward, as he walked me to the street, Lou said that Paul's crying was very strange. For the last months Lou had been almost continually with Paul. He watched as Paul's siblings and friends came to see him, basically to exchange final good-byes. Paul was always loving and grateful. Not once did he cry. Only the mystery of Virgil's meanness had elicited tears.

That was the last time I saw Paul, as we both knew it would be. He died on August 29, 1989. He was forty-nine. Louis Rispoli was designated the executor of Paul's estate. With this came the responsibility of seeing after Maurice's paintings. Lou would have to rent a second apartment in his building in Woodside to house them safely.

In November, Virgil Thomson took to the sofa in his living room and basically refused to leave it. He lay there, read there, slept there, received guests there, rarely moved from that spot. After nearly dying twice in hospitals, he would have no more of them, and his doctor relented. So Virgil set up operations in the vicinity of his sofa. Everything was orderly. On a tray table within reach were a brass bell to ring when he needed assistance, tissues, glasses, hearing aids—all of which had to be in a specific place. He had an armchair moved next to the couch so that he could rest his elbow on it, propped up by a black cushion that had to be arranged just so. By this point he needed round-the-clock attention. So Jay hired three aides, all young men, to help him, and also a night nurse.

Virgil knew he was dying and no longer fought it. His end was not unlike that of his sister, Ruby. At the time, answering a note of condolence, Virgil wrote of Ruby, "At nearly 94 she was certainly entitled to die, and I am happy she did not suffer. She merely faded away, largely stopped eating, then one night she didn't breathe anymore."[11]

Jay was torn with worry. A long-planned and overdue vacation trip with his family was scheduled for ten days in September. His father wanted the family to trace the roots of the Irish Sullivans. Jay could not bear to miss it, but neither could he bear to leave Virgil. However, it was possible that Virgil could linger like this for weeks, the doctor said. "What if something happens to you when I'm gone," Jay asked Virgil. "No, no. I'll wait," Virgil answered. So Jay went on his family trip with Virgil's blessing.

I last saw Virgil two days before his death. By then he was slipping in and out of lucidity. There were many things wrong. His liver was ceasing to function. He had stopped eating completely ("I know what I'm doing," he told Jay, just six days back from his trip) and barely accepted fluids. But in the end Virgil was dying from the same condition that he listed on the Harvard health questionnaire as his mother's cause of death: "General Failure."

Virgil sat up on his sofa to visit with me. But he did not want to chat; he wanted to work on "the book," he wanted me to interview him. "Ask me questions," he said. So I went through the motions of asking him things. We talked about Briggs. "Oh, Briggs was very attached to me," Virgil said, brightening. He tried to talk about Harvard, but made no sense. "Oh," he said sadly, "I'm trying to explain the world." By having me interview him, Virgil felt productive. But the work tired him. He kept slipping away. "Call Tony," he said. "Get Tony on the phone." I smiled. "Virgil, I'm Tony." When he realized what I was saying, he laughed, almost soundlessly, then drifted off to sleep.

In the meantime other visitors arrived. Norma and Dick Flender, Tim Page, and Betty Allen. As Virgil slept, we sat with Jay in the dining room and talked, mostly of Virgil, waiting for him to wake up. Eventually he did, and Norma went in to him for a visit. As usual, she looked elegant, her jet-black hair gleaming. She was calm and affectionate. Virgil was basically unable to answer questions, so Norma talked of what she had been up to. Then Virgil blurted out an order: "Tell me about the show!"

Norma was confused. What did he mean? She had just performed in a private chamber music concert. Was that the show Virgil was asking about? Then she understood. It was with Norma and Dick that Virgil had discussed the plans for his funeral. ("Do you want to be buried or cremated?" Dick had asked one day. "Cremated," Virgil said. "Easier to ship.") They had also discussed his memorial service. This was the "show" Virgil wanted to organize. However, except for asking that it be held at the Cathedral of St. John the Divine (Virgil used to call it "St. John the Too-Too Divine"), he had not been able to suggest anything about it. Now it was too late. Norma told him that the cathedral had already been tentatively approached and that holding the memorial there, when the time came, would be no problem. She promised to make the service grand and memorable.

"Oh, Virgil," she said, wistfully. "I so loved all our trips together. I wish we could take just one more."

"We will," Virgil said. "To Kansas City." Norma had agreed to take Virgil's remains back to Missouri to be buried in the family plot.

By then two more visitors had arrived, Caroline and Gregg Glaser. Caroline was Virgil's grandniece. His sister, Ruby, had had only one child, Elizabeth. But "Betty," as everyone called her, had four daughters. Caroline was the only one who understood Virgil's life and work and kept in touch. She and her husband were puppeteers who lived in Connecticut and supported themselves doing parties for children. "Don't you look cute," Virgil said, when he recognized Caroline's smiling face. Then, one by one, each of us took time with Virgil to say good-bye.

The next day, Virgil slept restlessly for most of the afternoon. When awake he was barely lucid. But he did accept one visitor, Craig Rutenberg, who took a break from a busy day coaching singers at the Metropolitan Opera to come by. Virgil was hardly able to talk. But they sat together quietly; and this seemed to make Virgil happy.

Late that evening as Jay gave instructions to the night nurse, he figured that Virgil would not last long; but he did not think Virgil's death was imminent. Jay slept poorly. Around 5 A.M. on Saturday, September 30, 1989, the night nurse called. Virgil had died, peacefully, it appeared. For when she went to check his pulse, thinking he was still asleep, she realized he was dead. Jay rushed right over, his heart pounding. He held Virgil's hand, cried a little, and then began the long list of protocols as Virgil had stipulated: he called the lawyer, UPI, AP, and the *New York Times*. Then, after 8 A.M. or so, he started calling Virgil's friends, who called each other. When later in the day, I talked to Lou Rispoli, he said something that seemed a telling reflection on Virgil's personal life: "I feel like I should send condolences to someone. But I don't know whom to write to." It was true. There were no real survivors, other than his niece, who hardly knew him, and his one close grandniece. He had survived Maurice and all his other old friends. Truly, Virgil's closest survivor was Jay. After some time had passed, we started referring to him as "the widow."

Virgil's lengthy *Times* obituary by John Rockwell began with a lead-in photo on page one. So Virgil Thomson died just the way he had hoped he would: at home, in his sleep, and in time to make all editions of the Sunday *New York Times*.

Rockwell's obituary was insightful and affectionate, but contained one self-described "tribute," which provoked controversy within the Thomson circle. Leonard Bernstein had asked his press agent Margaret Carson to phone critics and news agencies with a statement, which read,

> The death of Virgil T. is like the death of an American city: it is intolerable. But perhaps it was almost as hard to live with him as without him. Virgil was loving and harsh, generous and mordant, simple but cynical, son of the hymnal yet highly sophisticated. We all loved his music and rarely performed it. Most of us preferred his unpredictable, provocative prose. But he will always remain rightly alive in the history of music, if only for the extraordinary influence his witty and simplistic music had on his colleagues, especially on Aaron Copland, and through them on most of American music in our century. I know that I am one twig on that tree and I will always cherish and revere Virgil, the source.[12]

Some of Virgil's admirers and friends thought the statement a fair assessment of the truth. His music was loved and not performed. It was as hard to live with him as to live without him. And Bernstein was virtually calling Virgil "the source" of American music in our century. But others thought the statement represented Bernstein's self-interested attempt to protect his still-living mentor Aaron Copland. Bernstein acknowledged that Thomson's simplicity had influenced Copland to shift the stylistic direction of his own compositions. But he did not want anyone to conclude, therefore, that Thomson was greater than, or as great as, or as influential as Copland. Hence his careful wording that Thomson's influence on American music had been "through" his colleagues and Copland. Jack Larson was angered by Bernstein's unsolicited pronouncement. "You just don't go calling up newspapers and issuing a statement no one's asked for," Jack said. "It's disrespectful and manipulative." But it was also news, which is why Bernstein's words made it into almost every obituary.

But there were tributes in the press that would have caused Virgil (who had said, "When I'm in a room where nobody knows me I know I'm in the real world") to feel that his true gifts and contributions were, after all, understood. Richard Dyer in the *Boston Globe* was particularly eloquent:

Virgil Thomson, bless him, has gone. Let's hope when he got to the other side he was greeted by harmonium and choir in anthem and in tango, and that heaven is as nice a place as everybody made it out to be in "Four Saints in Three Acts," the great opera he created with Gertrude Stein.

He's likely to shake the place up a little. "There can be no peace on earth with calm," observes St. Teresa of Avila in that opera, and that's something Thomson knew, and for sure.

. . . Thomson is certainly the most quoted music critic of our century, the most important in our country, probably because he broke all the rules. He wasn't objective, he played politics like crazy, and he had an agenda.

. . . Thomson wrote a lot of music over a very long career, and there are hundreds of pieces that still smile, kick and bawl; works that offend and reward; works that leave us thinking about who we are and how we got that way and what we ought to be doing about it.

. . . Only the great American composers of popular song rival Thomson in the precision of his wordsetting, and no one in the world of American concert music; none of his music has extra notes in it—it says what's on its mind and then it stops. It is music utterly without sentimentality, plain-spoken yet also elusive and suggestive.[13]

The *New Criterion* used the lead entry of its "Notes and Comments" section to observe that with the death of Virgil Thomson, only Aaron Copland remains from that first generation of American composers, a "living reminder that once upon a time an exciting future for a serious American music seemed to be waiting only for its discovery."[14]

For someone so meticulous, Virgil left his affairs in some disorder. His will, last updated on July 19, 1989, carefully stipulated his wishes. To his niece and his four grandnieces he left $300,000 to be divided equally. Though not especially close to his family, with the exception of Caroline Glaser, Virgil was a person to whom propriety was important. And taking care of one's family was the proper thing to do. To Jay Sullivan he left $10,000. He had originally intended to leave $5,000 each to Jay and to Allan Stinson, but later changed his mind. His relationship with Allan had ended too unpleasantly. Jay was overwhelmed by the gift. But when he found out that Virgil had left nothing to his long-serving Portuguese cleaning lady, Paula Fantao, he gave her $2,000 of his inheritance and told her it was from Virgil. Propriety was important to Jay, too.

The rest of Virgil's estate, which, with stock dividends and other holdings, totaled approximately $1.3 million dollars, was to go to the Virgil Thomson Foundation. Virgil's Foundation had existed for some ten years; every year the trustees, headed by Richard Flender and Virgil's lawyer Ellis J. Freedman, met to award small gifts to applicants, usually musical ensembles (which were friendly to Virgil) or schools (where Virgil's music was performed) or sometimes individual composers. Now that Virgil had died, the primary functions of the foundation would be the promotion, distribution, and performance of Virgil Thomson's works. This was all standard procedure for relatively modest estates such as Virgil's.

But on January 18, 1989, six months before the final updating of his will, Virgil had written an open letter to his "Dear friends Norma and Richard Flender" asking them to distribute specified souvenirs and mementos after his death. This letter was filled with bequests that either contradicted the will or inaccurately represented the ownership of certain items. For example, he wrote that Maurice's portrait of Beatrice Wayne Godfrey, the original Saint Teresa I, which "belongs to her" but had hung for years in Virgil's living room, should be returned. However, Mrs. Godfrey, who had no place in her nursing home room for the painting, had sold it to Peter McWilliams, who agreed to allow Virgil to keep it so long as he lived. So the portrait was not Virgil's to give away, which was something he knew. Also, many of the gifts were terribly vague. What did it mean that Craig Rutenberg should be given "a book by Gertrude Stein"? A signed book? A first edition? A reissue that Virgil had simply owned?

This letter caused some ill feelings among Virgil's friends. Professional friends seemed favored over personal friends. Jacquelyn Helin, the pianist who, with considerable expense to herself, had released several recordings of Virgil's piano music, was given an exquisite Baccarat carafe and twelve Baccarat claret glasses. But Sam Byers, one of the "boys downstairs" who had cooked for him and cared for him and looked after his apartment, was left merely Virgil's old cooking utensils and kitchenware, including the clunky refrigerator and the impossibly small stove, and his antique vacuum cleaner, none of which Sam wanted.

Virgil also stipulated, in concordance with his official will, that all of his artworks, furniture, photographs, and valuable books should go to the foundation, which would auction them. Those auctions, held at Sotheby's a year later, would bring in over $900,000, two-thirds of that coming from just four items: Duchamp's portrait of Florine Stet-theimer ($18,000); Stettheimer's portrait of Duchamp ($100,000); a small painted plaster sculpture by Jean Arp, a work Virgil had kept for years in the hallway storeroom ($22,000), and the Arp painted wood relief sculpture, a work Virgil had loved ($460,000). This would lift the foundation's assets to over $2 million.

But all such concerns were for the future. The issue at hand after Virgil's death was his memorial concert, announced for November 25, 1989, at St. John the Divine, which would have been Virgil's ninety-third birthday. Jay started getting calls from musicians everywhere, in-cluding some major figures, who offered to take part. This would be a high-visibility event. However, Virgil had asked Norma Flender to plan it, so she took charge; and no one who really cared about Vir-gil objected. Norma convened a group of people to help her, who met at the apartment within a week of Virgil's death. Since the Thom-son Foundation would be funding the event, it was important to in-clude Ellis Freedman, Virgil's lawyer and a foundation executive. Of course Jay was there. And Craig Rutenberg, who, with his Metropol-itan Opera connections, would be able to tap some quality singers. Tim Page was invited, since Norma thought that writings of Virgil's should be read as well. And I was also asked to join the group.

Ideas quickly fell into place. James Holmes, the organist and Ned Rorem's partner, was asked to perform Satie and Thomson organ works for the prelude and recessional. Jacquelyn Helin would play excerpts from *The Plough That Broke the Plains;* the Harvard Glee Club, which offered to come, would sing *Cantates eamus,* which Vir-gil had composed for its 125th anniversary, in 1982. Scott Wheeler would accompany the tenor Kim Scown in one of Virgil's most per-fect songs, "A Prayer to Saint Catherine," to Kenneth Koch's en-chanting poem. Rodney Lister would accompany a young Boston baritone, Paul Houghtaling, in "Remember the Poet We Knew with Our Heart," from *Lord Byron.* Norma and Craig agreed to play the fractured *Synthetic Waltzes* for piano four hands. I would play the first movement of Virgil's Piano Sonata no. 2, his musical "self-portrait." Craig Rutenberg arranged for William Warfield to sing *Pigeons on the Grass Alas,* and for Neil Shicoff, by then a reigning tenor at the Met-ropolitan Opera, who had sung a small role in the first production of *Lord Byron,* to sing one of Virgil's *Shakespeare Songs.* A string quar-tet would accompany the soprano Carmen Pelton in Virgil's *Stabat Mater;* and, with the composer Francis Thorne at the piano, Miss Pelton would perform the only music that could possibly conclude the program, Susan B.'s final soliloquy from *The Mother of Us All:* "All my long life, all my life, we do not retrace our steps, all my long life, but."

We also asked two grand singers, both essentially retired, if they would perform. Betty Allen, much as she wanted to, said no. ("I just don't sing any more, I'm afraid.") So we decided to play a recording that she had made with Virgil playing piano, "Before Sleeping," the children's bedtime prayer from *Praises and Prayers.* I called Phyllis Curtin from our meeting to ask if she would, with Ned Rorem at the piano, sing a shockingly bare song Virgil had written to a hermetic Frank O'Hara text, "From *Sneden's Landing Variations.*" Phyllis and Ned had performed its premiere in a 1972 memorial concert for O'Hara. Phyllis agreed on condition that she be allowed to sing something less grim as well, the giddy "Le Berceau de Gertrude Stein," to a text by Georges Hugnet, which she and Ned had played for years for concerts and parties to Virgil's delight. This was a lovely idea.

We decided—and there was no disagreement—that there would be no speeches or spoken tributes. Instead we would play brief tape recordings of Virgil speaking about his own life, excerpts from interviews and from John Huszar's film. This was to be Virgil's day; so there would be only Virgil's music and Virgil's talking. There would be late entries onto the program, for one, Doriot Anthony Dwyer, the principal flutist with the Boston Symphony Orchestra. However, on that day, pleased with our plans, our memorial committee wrapped up the meeting, leaving the arrangements to Jay, who was still being paid through the foundation.

Jay encountered only one problem in planning the service: the Very Reverend James P. Morton, dean of the Cathedral of St. John the Divine. The Reverend Morton assumed that he would be invited to speak. Summoning all his southern courtesy, Jay explained that we wanted there to be no spoken tributes; only Virgil's voice would be heard; although words from his eminence would otherwise be an honor, it would negate the concept of the entire memorial. But Dean Morton, who could not disguise his annoyance, virtually insisted that he would at the very least have to welcome the guests to what was, after all, his parish. Jay relented, asking that the reverend truly keep his remarks to a few moments of welcome.

On the day of the memorial, the brisk autumn sky was clear. But the cathedral, filled to capacity, was cold and damp, making it very difficult for pianists' fingers and singers' vocal cords to stay warm. At three the performers marched down the aisle as the audience sang Virgil's arrangement of "Praise Him Who Makes Us Happy" to the strains of James Holmes's robust organ playing.

When everyone was seated, Dean Morton mounted the ornate pulpit to offer his "Words of Welcome." What this turned out to be was a lengthy, pompous, and inaccurate tribute to Virgil Thomson, whom he barely knew. Basic facts of Virgil's life were incorrect, such as the years of his tenure at the *Herald Tribune,* inaccuracies that would have driven Virgil crazy. Worst of all, he stated that "every detail of this memorial was planned by Virgil Thomson himself," so as to make sure that no one "loused it up." How he came to this conclusion we could not fathom. Jay had told him that Virgil asked for the service to be held at the cathedral. But Virgil was too ill by then to make any decisions. Moreover, although Virgil was never loath to promote himself, planning his own memorial was one thing he would not have done. Clearly, only some close colleagues were going to be able to participate, and Virgil would have been uncomfortable choosing among his champions. Of course, coming from such an authoritative source, the newspaper reporters in attendance accepted it. So this misinformation wound up in almost every account of the memorial concert, including those in the *New York Times* and the *Washington Post.* Jay was outraged. We all were.

However, the memorial itself was consoling. William Warfield's voice had unraveled over the years, but it didn't matter. His unjaded, articulate singing of *Pigeons on the Grass Alas* was a reminder of why Virgil was moved to cast his opera with black singers. Neil Shicoff filled the enormous space of the cathedral with clarion tenor tones in "Was This Fair Face the Cause?" Hearing Virgil's high-pitched speaking voice brought tears and smiles to many. And Carmen Pelton sang "All My Long Life" with affecting simplicity.

Afterward there was a reception for some two hundred guests at the Century Association, near Times Square, sponsored by the American Society of Composers, Authors and Publishers (ASCAP), which recognized Virgil as a pioneer in the effort to make composers professionals. By mid-evening, a bunch of us—Vic Cardell, who had come from Los Angeles, Jay, Lou, Danyal, and I—piled into a cab and headed to Lou and Danyal's apartment, where we ate gourmet leftovers, drank lots of wine, and made fun of the Very Reverend James P. Morton.

Three weeks prior to the memorial, Norma and Virgil took the one last trip together that Virgil had talked about. Virgil's remains were taken home for burial. Of course Jay went along. And, courtesy of the Thomson Foundation, so did I. We left New York on November 3, five weeks after Virgil's death. At La Guardia Airport we nearly missed our plane. The gilded container that contained Virgil's ashes set off the metal detector. But it was sealed and could not be opened. Talking to a skeptical security guard, Jay, in hushed tones, kept referring to the container as "our friend," which just made matters more confusing. Eventually a senior officer believed him and waved us through.

In Kansas City we stayed at a comfortable old downtown hotel. There we were met by Charles Fussell, the Boston composer who served on the foundation's board. Friday night, along with some dozen friends and relatives of Virgil's, we were the guests of Sheila Kemper Dietrich and her husband, Walter, for a dinner at the downtown University Club. Sheila was the daughter of one of Virgil's old Kansas City friends, Cynthia Warrick Kemper, a woman he once affectionately described as "a mother, a hostess, and something of a *grande dame*." Cynthia had died two years earlier. Had she not, she would have hosted this dinner, her daughter Sheila told us. So she decided to do it in her mother's place. The dinner was served in the club's wood-paneled library, with a fire roaring in the marbled fireplace. Virgil would have loved the meal: squash soup; medallions of beef, chicken, and sweetbreads; excellent wines. Sheila was charming and interesting; she had served in the Peace Corps in Africa. In her dinner toast she dedicated the evening to Virgil's memory and, "if you will allow me, to my mother also."

Virgil was to be buried not in his birthplace, Kansas City, but in the town of his parents and grandparents, Slater, population 2,492, in Saline County, some of the richest farmland in Missouri—soybean, corn, and wheat country. Early the next morning, Saturday, November 4, Jay, Norma, Charles, and I made the two-hour drive through rolling countryside where we saw barns and sheds roofed with thatch, and fields lined with hedge apple trees.

Slater was a one-street town where most of the stores had been shut down except for a hardware shop, a pharmacy, an old-fashioned five-and-dime, a florist, from which we bought a floral arrangement for Virgil's grave, and a well-stocked video store. A luncheon, paid for by the foundation but organized by Jay, was held at the only place in town to eat, the Rotary Club, in which there was a restaurant, owned by Marvin Odell, the Donald Trump of Saline County, who seemed to own everything. When we entered, over twenty of Virgil's family and friends were milling about: the McDaniels, direct descendants of Virgil's pioneer great-grandfather Reuben Ellis McDaniel; the Garnetts; the Duncans; his cousin Mary Margaret Lupberger, who was the granddaughter of his aunt Leone; Sheila and Walter, who had come from Kansas City; and Betty Stouffer, Virgil's only niece, then sixty-nine, tiny, grayed, stoop-shouldered, and endearing. She was dressed in white slacks and a lime green vinyl coat. With her was Rosemary, the only daughter still living at home in Winter Springs, Florida.

The dining room was wood-paneled and dingy. In one corner stood two tables of trophies, a testimony to Marvin Odell's success as a trainer of derby hounds. Stuffed pheasant and foxes watched us from the walls; vases of plastic flowers adorned the dining tables. Before lunch, grace was said by the Reverend Donald Reed from the First Baptist Church, which maintained the cemetery. Then hearty waitresses served us fried chicken, Missouri ham, bean salad, deviled eggs, applesauce, Jell-O, and ice cream.

It was a short drive to Rehoboth Cemetery, atop a slopping hill overlooking farmfields and grazing cows. The cemetery was sparsely filled, just a few rows well kept by the church. Lining the cemetery near the road were sweet gum and ash trees. It was impossible not to think of Virgil's music: *Wheat Fields at Noon, The Plow That Broke the Plains*. In the distance you could see the Slater Town Cemetery, where, as Kirk McDaniel, the senior McDaniel and family historian, explained, "the Methodists are buried." Bordering the Baptist cemetery was a white fence, with more graves on the other side, many of them unmarked. "That's the colored cemetery," Kirk told us, where the McDaniels and Thomsons and Garnetts used to bury their slaves. It continued as a segregated cemetery until the early 1950s.

Virgil was to be buried in the Thomson family plot, next to his parents, Quincy and May, his grandparents, Quincy Adams and Flora Elizabeth, and his sister Hazel, who died in infancy. There was a space for Ruby, but Ruby had moved away, was married away and buried away, in Pittsburgh. Virgil, whose life, in some ways, was about leaving Kansas City and escaping his past, romanticized his roots. When it came time, there was no question in his mind that he belonged back home.

A tent had been set up around Virgil's grave site, which was help-ful, for it was a breezy day. A narrow, deep hole had been dug, cov-ered temporarily by a piece of artificial turf. On top of it was the container of ashes and the just-purchased floral arrangement. There were a few folding chairs for the elderly relatives, but most people stood. Norma began the service by reading Virgil's plainspoken state-ment about himself, which he used whenever a biography for a pro-gram book was requested. Then she spoke personally, recalling Virgil as a wonderful, generous, but stern man. Mary Margaret Lupberger spoke of the service as a celebration of a life well lived. "It is never a sad occasion when all the family gathers. Virgil never forgot his Mis-souri background. And I want to thank Jay for bringing us together."

Then Pastor Reed, a trim and vigorous man, spoke. "Virgil's par-ents were Baptists through and through. Virgil was read to from the Bible." Choosing his words carefully, it seemed, he added, "Virgil was raised a Baptist, and that was important." Then the pastor read from the Bible, two Psalms of David, a chapter from Revelations, and a pas-sage from John ("And I saw a new man and a new earth.") With the service concluded, there was a sense of the celebration Mary Margaret had spoken of. People were relaxed and chatty. Then, out of nowhere, up the little-traveled road that ran past the cemetery came a strange-looking woman dressed in tattered clothes and pushing a shopping cart full of plastic trash bags stuffed with rags, it seemed, and assorted junk. She was like the bag lady of Slater. Yet she was cheerful and very curious about what was going on.

"Who died?" she called out eagerly.

"Virgil Thomson," Charles shouted back, smiling like the pleas-ant southern gentleman he is.

The lady paused. Then said, "Never knew him."

For the remainder of the afternoon, we were taken by Virgil's rel-atives to the nearby town of Bethel to see the church built in 1851 by Reuben Ellis McDaniel, clearly a hero to his descendants. We walked through the adjacent cemetery where the McDaniel ancestors were buried.

Finally, we made our farewells. It was sunset. But before we left for Kansas City we took one more short drive to the Slater cemetery, now deserted. Virgil's ashes had been buried, the flowers had been placed in a sunken container, the tent and chairs had been taken away. With the sun setting and the eerie quiet, it was very moving. Jay wanted his picture taken at Virgil's grave. For Jay this was another responsibility fulfilled. He had planned everything and, as usual, every-thing had gone according to plan. Norma looked off in the distance to the closest farmhouse, where, suddenly, a light in a window went on. "They don't even know," she said; "they don't realize who is here."

NOTES

Although in preparing this book I interviewed over sixty people, the bulk of my research focused on original manuscripts and documents, most of them unpublished. Some of these papers were lent to me directly by Virgil Thomson. Other individuals entrusted me with very personal family letters and documents, for example, Briggs Buchanan, Jr. In almost all cases I have indicated in a footnote the current owner (if it is an individual) or permanent location (if it is a research library) of the document I cite.

Abbreviations

AT	Anthony Tommasini
GS	Gertrude Stein
Letters	*Selected Letters of Virgil Thomson,* ed. Tim Page and Vanessa Weeks Page (New York: Summit Books, 1988)
NYHT	*New York Herald Tribune*
NYT	*New York Times*
VT, *Thomson*	Virgil Thomson, *Virgil Thomson* (New York: Alfred A. Knopf, 1966)
VT	Virgil Thomson
VT Coll.	Virgil Thomson Collection, Beinecke Rare Book Room and Manuscript Library, Yale University

Chapter 1: THE SAINT THERESA INCIDENT

1. Andrew Porter, in *The New Yorker,* June 18, 1984.
2. John Rockwell, in *NYT,* November 14, 1986.
3. Philip Glass interview, in *Boston Sunday Globe,* May 15, 1988.
4. Richard Dyer, in *Boston Globe,* November 14, 1986.
5. Andrew Porter, in *The New Yorker,* December 15, 1986.

Chapter 2: THIS BUSINESS OF BEING BAPTISTS

1. VT, *Thomson,* 5.
2. Reuben E. McDaniel, letter to Delia Richerson McDaniel, April 28, 1838, VT Coll.
3. Reuben McDaniel, letter to Delia Richerson McDaniel, April 1, 1839, VT Coll.

4. VT, *Thomson,* 8–9.
5. Reuben McDaniel, letter to Delia Richerson McDaniel, January 1, 1835, VT Coll.
6. VT, *Thomson,* 7.
7. Ibid., 8.
8. Ibid.
9. Ibid., 9.
10. VT, interview with AT, June 22, 1987.
11. Ibid.
12. VT, *Thomson,* 3–4
13. David McCullough, *Truman* (New York: Simon and Schuster, 1992), 50.
14. Edward Dahlberg, *Because I Was Flesh* (New York: New Directions, 1964), 11.
15. VT, "Kansas City in Double View," *Kansas City Star,* December 18, 1961.
16. McCullough, *Truman,* 71.
17. VT, *Thomson,* 13.
18. VT interview.
19. Ibid.

20. VT, *Thomson,* 11.
21. Ibid., 12.
22. Wilfrid Mellers, review of VT, *Virgil Thomson,* in *Musical Times,* August 1967.
23. VT, *Thomson,* 15.

Chapter 3: VIRGIL ACQUIRES A MENTOR

1. VT, *Thomson,* 12.
2. Ibid., 14.
3. VT, interview with AT, June 22, 1987.
4. VT, interview with AT, August 18, 1988.
5. VT, *Thomson,* 28.
6. VT interview, August 18, 1988.
7. VT, *Thomson,* 20–21
8. VT, interview with AT, June 6, 1987.
9. Letter from Gladys Blakely Bush to Mrs. Kathleen Hoover, May 17, 1949, VT Coll.
10. VT, *Thomson,* 27.
11. VT interview, June 22, 1987.
12. VT, *Thomson,* 29.
13. Kathleen Hoover and John Cage, *Virgil Thomson: His Life and Music* (New York: Thomas Yoseloff, 1959), 18.
14. VT, *Thomson,* 29.

Chapter 4: THE PANSOPHIST

1. VT, *The State of Music* (New York: William Morrow, 1939), 55.
2. VT, *Thomson,* 17.
3. Ibid., 24.
4. Ibid., 25.
5. Ibid., 24.
6. Ibid.
7. VT, letter to Alice Smith, October 25, 1918, *Letters,* 34, VT Coll.
8. VT, *Thomson,* 29.
9. Ibid.
10. Letter from Alice (Smith) Edwards to Kathleen Hoover, June 28, 1951.
11. VT, *Thomson,* 30–31.
12. Memoir of Alice (Smith) Edwards, 1949–50, VT Coll.
13. Alice (Smith) Edwards, letter to VT, July 16, 1949, VT Coll.
14. VT, letter to Alice (Smith) Edwards, August 20, 1949, VT Coll.
15. VT, letter to Alice (Smith) Edwards, August 23, 1917, VT Coll.
16. Excerpts from Pans quoted in Kathleen Hoover and John Cage, *Virgil Thomson: His Life and Music* (New York: Thomas Yoseloff, 1959), 23.
17. VT, *Thomson,* 30.
18. Edgar Lee Masters, *Spoon River Anthology: An Annotated Edition* (Urbana: University of Illinois Press, 1992), 108.
19. Ibid., 134.
20. Donald Bush, letter to Kathleen Hoover, May 17, 1949, VT Coll.

21. VT, letter to Alice Smith Edwards, January 12, 1968, VT Coll.
22. VT, letter to Alice Smith Edwards, December 23, 1968, VT Coll.
23. VT, letter to Alice Smith Edwards, March 7, 1969, VT Coll.

Chapter 5: A LOVELY WAR

1. VT, *Thomson,* 33.
2. Ibid., 31.
3. Howard Zinn, *A People's History of the United States* (New York: Harper and Row, 1980), 360.
4. VT, *Thomson,* 33.
5. Ibid., 35.
6. VT, letter to Alice Smith, December 10, 1917, VT Coll.
7. VT, letter to Alice Smith, December 30, 1917, and January 1, 1918, VT Coll.
8. VT, letter to Alice Smith, March 21, 1918, VT Coll.
9. Ibid.
10. Ibid.
11. VT, letter to Alice Smith, May 21, 1918, VT Coll.
12. Ibid.
13. Ibid.
14. George Phillips, letter to VT, May 7, 1918, VT Coll.
15. Dr. Frederick Madison Smith, letter to VT, June 2, 1918, VT Coll.
16. VT, *Thomson,* 39.
17. Ibid.
18. VT, letter to Alice Smith, October 25, 1918, VT Coll.
19. George Phillips, letter to VT, August 1918, VT Coll.
20. George Phillips, letter to VT, November 27, 1918, VT Coll.

Chapter 6: I DIDN'T WANT TO BE QUEER

1. Richard Ellmann, *Oscar Wilde* (New York: Alfred A. Knopf, 1988), 183.
2. Quoted ibid.
3. *NYT,* April 7, 1895, 9.
4. VT, *Thomson,* 3.
5. Journal of Public Morals Committee of the Church Federation of Greater Kansas City, Fall 1913.
6. *Kansas City Times,* October 20, 1913.
7. Oscar Wilde, *De Profundis* (New York: G. P. Putnam, 1905), 5.
8. Ibid., 14.
9. Ibid., 9.
10. Ibid., 29.
11. Ibid., 105.
12. Ibid., 120–21.
13. VT, interview with AT, May 12, 1988.

14. VT, letter to Leland Poole, November 6, 1918, VT Coll.
15. VT, letter to Leland Poole, November 15, 1918, VT Coll.
16. VT, letter to Leland Poole, March 16, 1919, VT Coll.
17. VT, letter to Leland Poole, July 21, 1919, VT Coll.
18. VT, letter to Leland Poole, August 27, 1919, VT Coll.

Chapter 7: LONELINESS IN PLEASURE AT HARVARD

1. Edgar Lee Masters, "Archibald Higbie," in *Spoon River Anthology: An Annotated Edition* (Urbana: University of Illinois Press, 1992), 267.
2. VT, letter to Leland Poole, July 21, 1919, VT Coll.
3. VT, *Thomson,* 43.
4. VT, letter to Leland Poole, March 16, 1919, VT Coll.
5. VT, letter to Dr. Frederick Madison Smith, August 15, 1919, VT Coll.
6. VT, letter to Leland Poole, August 27, 1919, VT Coll.
7. Elliott Carter, interview with AT, February 23, 1994.
8. VT, *Thomson,* 51.
9. Ibid., 45.
10. Daniel Gregory Mason, preface to *Harvard University Glee Club Collection* (New York: G. Schirmer, 1922).
11. VT, letter to Ruby Thomson Gleason, October 8, 1919, VT Coll.
12. VT, *Thomson,* 45.
13. Edward Burlingame Hill, letter to VT, December 5, 1925, VT Coll.
14. Edward Burlingame Hill, "The Future of the American Composer," *Harvard Musical Review,* May 1915, 17.
15. Carter interview.
16. VT, letter to Dana Hill, July 22, 1960, VT Coll.
17. VT, *Thomson,* 46.
18. Malcolm Cowley, "S. Foster Damon: The New England Voice," in *William Blake: Essays for S. Foster Damon* (Providence: Brown University Press, 1969).
19. VT, *Thomson,* 46.
20. Ibid.
21. Frederick M. Smith, *The Higher Powers of Man* (Lamoni, Iowa: Herald Publishing House, 1918), 19.
22. Ibid., 98.
23. VT, *Thomson,* 42.
24. Ibid., 43.
25. Ibid., 47.
26. VT, letter to Leland Poole, August 27, 1919, VT Coll.

27. VT, letter to Leland Poole, October 24, 1919, VT Coll.
28. VT, letter to Leland Poole, December 31, 1919, VT Coll.
29. VT, interview with AT, November 14, 1988.
30. VT, letter to Leland Poole, April 6, 1920, VT Coll.
31. VT, letter to Ruby Thomson Gleason, August 26, 1920, in *Letters,* 40.
32. VT, letter to Leland Poole, July 20, 1920. VT Coll.
33. VT, *Thomson,* 49.
34. VT, letter to Leland Poole, November 27, 1920. VT Coll.
35. VT, interview with AT, May 12, 1988.

Chapter 8: VIRGY THOMSON IN PARIS

1. Anonymous diary, Harvard Glee Club archives.
2. VT, letter to Ruby Thomson Gleason, June 11, 1921, in *Letters,* 44.
3. VT, diary from Harvard Glee Club tour, Columbia University Rare Book and Manuscript Library.
4. *Boston Evening Transcript,* September 9, 1921.
5. VT, *Thomson,* 53.
6. Ibid.
7. VT, letter to Leland Poole, August 1921, in *Letters,* 48.
8. VT, letter to Ruby Thomson Gleason, August 21, 1921, in *Letters,* 44.
9. Ibid., 45.
10. Ibid., 46.
11. VT, *Thomson,* 54.
12. Nadia Boulanger, letter to Kathleen O. Hoover, April 18, 1949, VT Coll.
13. Elliott Carter, interview with AT, February 23, 1994.
14. VT, letter to Aaron Copland, November 26, 1931, VT Coll.
15. VT, *Thomson,* 54.
16. VT, letter to Leland Poole, April 21, 1922, VT Coll.; also in *Letters,* 48.
17. VT, *Thomson,* 66.
18. Ibid.
19. Ibid., 64.
20. VT, letter to Leland Poole, April 21, 1922, in *Letters,* 53.
21. H. T. Parker, "Opera Here and There," *Boston Evening Transcript,* April 5, 1922.
22. VT, *Thomson,* 60.
23. VT, letter to Ruby Thomson Gleason, February 3, 1922, in *Letters,* 50.
24. VT, letter to Leland Poole, June 22, 1922, VT Coll.
25. VT, *Thomson,* 61.
26. Richard C. Cabot, letter to VT, September 23, 1922, VT Coll.

27. VT, letter to Leland Poole, June 22, 1922, VT Coll.
28. VT, letter to Leland Poole, September 28, 1922, VT Coll.
29. Maurice Grosser, unpublished memoir from 1986, property of Louis Rispoli.
30. VT, *Thomson*, 65.
31. Eugene McCown, letter to VT, January 11, 1923, VT Coll.
32. VT, *Thomson*, 67.
33. Walter Spalding to VT, May 31, 1923, VT Coll.
34. Ibid.

Chapter 9: THE MAN WHO WOULD NOT FIGHT

1. Briggs Buchanan, letter to VT, October 25, 1923, VT Coll.
2. Briggs Buchanan, letter to VT, July 15, 1923, VT Coll.
3. VT, *Thomson*, 69.
4. Briggs Buchanan, letter to VT, September 22, 1923, VT Coll.
5. VT, letter to Briggs Buchanan, September 1923, VT Coll.
6. VT, *Thomson*, 67.
7. Eugene McCown, letter to VT, October 1923. VT Coll.
8. VT, letter to Briggs Buchanan, October 26 [1923], property of Briggs Buchanan, Jr.
9. Briggs Buchanan, letter to VT, October 25, 1923, VT Coll.
10. VT, letter to Briggs Buchanan, n.d. [December 1923?], property of Briggs Buchanan, Jr.
11. VT, letters to Briggs Buchanan, n.d. [Summer 1924?], property of Briggs Buchanan, Jr.
12. VT, letter to Briggs Buchanan, July 3, 1925, in *Letters*, 61.
13. Briggs Buchanan, letter to VT, August 1, 1925, VT Coll.
14. VT, letter to Briggs Buchanan, August 4, 1925, in *Letters*, 62.
15. VT, "Maxims of a Modernist" (draft), Columbia University Rare Book and Manuscript Library.
16. Briggs Buchanan, letter to VT, January 9, 1926, property of Briggs Buchanan, Jr.
17. Ibid.
18. Briggs Buchanan, letter to VT, April 28, 1926, property of Briggs Buchanan, Jr.
19. VT, interview with AT, August 18, 1988.

Chapter 10: SHERRY, GEORGE, GERTRUDE, ALICE, AND SUSIE

1. VT, postcard to Mrs. Carole Lawrence, University of Tulsa, March 17, 1973, in *Letters*, 339.
2. VT, *Thomson*, 74.

3. VT, letter to Briggs Buchanan, n.d. [probably Summer 1925], VT Coll.
4. GS, *Paris France* (1940; reprint, New York: Liveright, 1970), 55.
5. Alan M. Wald, *The Revolutionary Imagination: The Poetry and Politics of John Wheelwright and Sherry Mangan* (Chapel Hill: University of North Carolina Press, 1983), 70.
6. Sherry Mangan, letter to VT, August 28, 1929, VT Coll.
7. Sherry Mangan, letter to VT, dated 1927, VT Coll.
8. Mary Ellen Jordan Haight, *Walks in Gertrude Stein's Paris* (Salt Lake City: Peregrine Smith Books, 1988), 64.
9. VT, Thomson, 83.
10. Ibid., 78.
11. Ibid., 75.
12. VT, letter to Briggs Buchanan, n.d. [probably 1926], in *Letters*, 72.
13. Robert Offergeld, liner notes, recording from Composers Recordings, Inc. (CRI SRD 207).
14. VT, letter to Briggs Buchanan, n.d. [probably 1926], VT Coll.
15. Ibid.
16. Ibid.
17. Kathleen Hoover and John Cage, *Virgil Thomson: His Life and Music* (New York: Thomas Yoseloff, 1959), 55.
18. VT, *Thomson*, 81.
19. Ibid.
20. Ibid., 82.
21. Ibid., 89.
22. *Virgil Thomson at 90*, a film produced and directed by John Huszar (Film America, 1991).
23. Ibid.
24. *VT, Thomson*, 90.
25. Ibid.
26. VT, letter to Briggs Buchanan, n.d. [probably 1926], VT Coll.

Chapter 11: MAURICE

1. VT, *Thomson*, 92.
2. Ibid., 109.
3. GS, *Selected Writings of Gertrude Stein* (New York: Random House, 1962), 212–13.
4. Maurice Grosser, unpublished memoir, chap. 7, p. 7, property of Louis Rispoli.
5. Stein, *Selected Writings*, 215.
6. Ibid., 214.
7. VT, *Thomson*, 85.
8. Ibid., 87.
9. Kathleen Hoover and John Cage, *Virgil Thomson: His Life and Music* (New York: Thomas Yoseloff, 1959), 69–70.
10. Robert H. Byington, personal communication to AT.

11. Ibid., 72.
12. Grosser, memoir, chap. 2, pp. 1–2.
13. Ibid., chap. 3, p. 7.
14. Ibid., 11.
15. Ibid., 5–6.
16. Ibid., chap. 4, p. 2.
17. Ibid., 3.
18. VT, *Thomson,* 75.
19. Grosser, memoir, chap. 5, p. 10.
20. Ibid., 13.
21. Ibid., chap. 7, p. 4.
22. Ibid., 5–6.
23. Maurice Grosser, "Visiting Gertrude and Alice," *New York Review of Books,* November 6, 1986, 37.

Chapter 12: FOUR SAINTS ARE NEVER THREE

1. Kathleen Hoover and John Cage, *Virgil Thomson: His Life and Music* (New York: Thomas Yoseloff, 1959), 50–51.
2. Ibid.
3. Ibid., 142.
4. Richard Buell, " 'An American Celebration' That Really Was," *Boston Globe,* November 6, 1986.
5. VT, introd. to *Capital Capitals* (New York: Boosey and Hawkes, 1968).
6. VT, letter to Briggs Buchanan, July 17, 1927, in *Letters,* 82.
7. Ibid.
8. Hoover and Cage, *Virgil Thomson,* 62.
9. GS, *The Autobiography of Alice B. Toklas,* in *Selected Writings of Gertrude Stein,* ed. Carl Van Vechten (New York: Vintage Books, 1972), 214.
10. VT, *Thomson,* 90–91.
11. GS, letter to VT, August 3, 1928, VT Coll.
12. GS, letter to VT, March 26, 1927, VT Coll.
13. James R. Mellow, *Charmed Circle: Gertrude Stein and Company* (New York: Praeger, 1974), 307.
14. GS, *Lectures in America* (Boston: Beacon Press, 1985), 131.
15. Donald Sutherland, *Gertrude Stein: A Biography of Her Work* (New Haven: Yale University Press, 1951), 124.
16. GS, letter to VT, March 30, 1927, VT Coll.
17. GS, letter to VT, April 27, 1927, VT Coll.
18. Mary Ellen Jordan Haight, *Walks in Gertrude Stein's Paris* (Salt Lake City: Peregrine Smith Books, 1988), 19.
19. VT, *Thomson,* 128.
20. VT, letter to Briggs Buchanan, March 15, 1927, VT Coll.
21. VT, letter to Briggs Buchanan, December 27, [1926?], in *Letters,* 75–76.
22. VT, letter to Briggs Buchanan, July 17, 1927, in *Letters,* 81–82.
23. VT, *Thomson,* 100.

24. Ibid., 101.
25. Ibid., 105.
26. Ibid., 104.
27. VT, letter to Ruby Gleason, n.d. [almost certainly from January 1928], in *Letters,* 85–86.
28. GS, *The Letters of Gertrude Stein and Carl Van Vechten,* ed. Edward Burns, vol. 1 (New York: Columbia University Press, 1986), 159.
29. VT, *Thomson,* 104–5.
30. Ibid., 107.

Chapter 13: AMERICAN MUSIC AGITATORS

1. GS, letter to VT, March 11, 1929, VT Coll.
2. GS, letter to VT, July 2, 1927, VT Coll.
3. GS, letter to VT, August 4, 1927, VT Coll.
4. GS, letter to VT, September 24, 1927, VT Coll.
5. VT, *Thomson,* 109.
6. Ibid., 115.
7. Ibid., 116.
8. Charles Jones, interview with AT, August 16, 1990.
9. VT, *Thomson,* 116.
10. Ibid., 108–9.
11. Ibid., 109.
12. Ibid.
13. Hildegard Watson, letter to VT, May 2, 1928.
14. VT, *Thomson,* 123.
15. Ibid., 124.
16. Aaron Copland, *Our New Music* (New York: Whittlesey House, McGraw-Hill, 1941), 219.
17. VT, *Thomson,* 117.
18. Ibid., 118–19.
19. Louise Varèse, *Varèse: A Looking-Glass Diary* (New York: W. W. Norton, 1972), 166–67.
20. Claire R. Reis, *Composers, Conductors, and Critics* (New York: Oxford University Press, 1955), 7.
21. Minna Lederman, *The Life and Death of a Small Magazine (Modern Music, 1924–1946)* (Brooklyn: Institute for Studies in American Music, 1983), 6.
22. Ibid., 4.
23. Marion Bauer and Claire R. Reis, "Twenty-five Years with the League of Composers," *Musical Quarterly* 34 (1948): 2.
24. VT, *Thomson,* 71.
25. Lederman, *Life and Death,* 21.
26. Aaron Copland, "America's Young Men of Promise," *Modern Music,* 3, no. 3 (March–April 1926): 18–20.
27. Aaron Copland, "Playing Safe in Zurich," *Modern Music* 4, no. 1 (November–December 1926): 29.

28. Roger Sessions, "An American Evening Abroad," *Modern Music* 4, no. 1 (November–December 1926): 35.

29. Aaron Copland, letter to Roger Sessions, n.d. [March 1928], in *The Correspondence of Roger Sessions,* ed. Andrea Olmstead (Boston: Northeastern University Press, 1992), 91.

30. Roger Sessions, letter to Aaron Copland, August 24, 1926, ibid., 66.

31. Olin Downes, review in *New York Times,* April 23, 1928.

Chapter 14: THE FLOWERS OF FRIENDSHIP

1. VT, *Thomson,* 131.

2. VT, letter to GS, December 29, 1928, in *Letters,* 92.

3. GS, letter to VT, January 14, 1929, VT Coll.

4. GS, letter to VT, September 27, 1929, VT Coll.

5. GS, letter to VT, January 14, 1929, VT Coll.; also in VT, *Thomson,* 131.

6. GS, *Portraits and Prayers* (New York: Random House, 1934), 198.

7. VT, letter to AT, April 20, 1983.

8. VT, letter to Alice B. Toklas, January 16 [1929], in *Letters,* 93.

9. Ibid., 94.

10. VT, *Thomson,* 134.

11. Carl Van Vechten, letter to GS, February 13, 1929, in *The Letters of Gertrude Stein and Carl Van Vechten,* ed. Edward Burns, vol. 1 (New York: Columbia University Press, 1986), 190–91.

12. Review in *NYHT,* February 25, 1929.

13. Review in *New York Sun,* February 25, 1929.

14. Charles D. Isaacson, review in *New York Morning Telegraph,* February 25, 1929.

15. Review in *New York Evening Post,* February 25, 1929.

16. Review in *New York World,* February 25, 1929.

17. Roger Sessions, letter to Aaron Copland, March 22, 1929, in *The Correspondence of Roger Sessions,* ed. Andrea Olmstead (Boston: Northeastern University Press, 1992), 138–39.

18. VT, *Thomson,* 140.

19. Ibid., 141.

20. Elliott Carter, interview with AT, February 23, 1994.

21. VT, *Thomson,* 138.

22. Ibid., 162.

23. Ibid., 182.

24. GS, letter to VT, May 18, 1929, VT Coll.

25. GS, letter to VT, May 22, 1929, VT Coll.

26. GS, letter to VT, November 18, 1929, VT Coll.

27. Maurice Grosser, Scenario, *Four Saints in Three Acts* (New York: G. Schirmer, 1948).

28. GS, *Everybody's Autobiography* (New York: Random House, 1937).

29. GS, letter to VT, March 6, 1930, VT Coll.[30] GS, letter to VT, September 27, 1929, VT Coll.

31. GS, letter to VT, December 1928, VT Coll.

32. GS, letter to VT, January 14, 1929, VT Coll.

33. GS, letter to VT, April 16, 1930, VT Coll.

34. GS, letter to VT, July 12, 1930, VT Coll.

35. GS, letter to Georges Hugnet, quoted in VT, *Thomson,* 186.

36. Georges Hugnet, letter to GS, quoted in James R. Mellow, *Charmed Circle: Gertrude Stein and Company* (New York: Praeger, 1974), 341.

37. VT, letter to GS, n.d. [1930], VT Coll.

38. GS, letter to VT, October 6, 1930, VT Coll.

39. Carl Van Vechten, letter to VT, December 1, 1930, VT Coll.

40. GS, letter to VT, October 21, 1930, VT Coll.

41. GS, letter to VT, December 9, 1930, VT Coll.

42. GS, letter to VT, December 1930, in VT, *Thomson,* 194.

43. VT, *Thomson,* 195.

44. GS, letter to Carl Van Vechten, January 17, 1931, in *Letters of Gertrude Stein and Carl Van Vechten,* 1:233.

45. Carl Van Vechten, letter to VT, February 24, 1931, VT Coll.

Chapter 15: CONTACTS AND CONTRACTS

1. VT, *Thomson,* 215.

2. John Houseman, *Run-Through: A Memoir* (New York: Simon and Schuster, 1972), 99.

3. VT, *Thomson,* 219.

4. Ibid., 135.

5. Franz Schulze, *Philip Johnson* (New York: Alfred A. Knopf, 1994), 94.

6. VT, *Thomson,* 220.

7. William Aspenwall Bradley, letter to GS, May 6, 1933, GS Collection, Beinecke Rare Book and Manuscript Library, Yale University.

8. William Aspenwall Bradley, letter to VT, May 15, 1933, GS Collection.

9. VT, letter to GS, May 30, 1933, VT Coll.; also in *Letters,* 106–7., and VT, *Thomson,* 229–31 (excerpted).

10. William Aspenwall Bradley, letter to GS, May 20, 1933, GS Collection.

11. GS, letter to VT, June 6, 1933, GS Collection; also in VT, *Thomson,* 231 (excepted).

12. VT, letter to GS, June 9, 1933, in VT, *Thomson,* 232–32, and *Letters,* 108–9.
16. Lincoln Kirstein, interview with Anthony Tommasini, October 8, 1990.
17. Lincoln Kirstein, published diaries in *The New York City Ballet* (New York: Alfred A. Knopf, 1973), 18.
18. Lincoln Kirstein, letter to A. Everett Austin, Jr., July 16, 1933, in *Avery Wadsworth Atheneum: The First Modern Museum,* ed. Eugene Gaddis (Hartford: Wadsworth Atheneum, 1984).
19. Lincoln Kirstein, *By With To & From* (New York: Farrar, Straus & Giroux, 1991), 153.

Chapter 16: A KNOCKOUT AND A WOW

1. John Houseman, *Run-Through: A Memoir* (New York: Simon and Schuster, 1972), 95.
2. Ibid., 99.
3. Ibid., 100.
4. Ibid., 101.
5. VT, interview with AT, March 6, 1988.
6. Houseman, *Run-Through,* 101.
7. Ibid., 104.
8. Thomas Anderson, interview with AT, February 20, 1990.
9. Houseman, *Run-Through,* 107.
10. Anderson interview.
11. Zoë Dominic and John Selwyn Gilbert, *Frederick Ashton: A Choreographer and His Ballets* (London: George G. Harper, 1971), 25.
12. Ibid.
13. VT, letter to GS, December 6, 1933, in *Letters,* 112–13.
14. David Vaughan, *Frederick Ashton and His Ballets* (New York: Alfred A. Knopf, 1977), 97.
15. VT, *Thomson,* 239.
16. Ibid.
17. Anderson interview.
18. VT, interview with AT, March 16, 1988.
19. Joseph Alsop, in *NYHT,* January [?], 1934.
20. Houseman, *Run-Through,* 114.
21. Maurice Grosser, unpublished memoirs, chap. 10.
22. Houseman, *Run-Through,* 115.
23. VT, *Thomson,* 240.
24. Lucius Beebe, in *NYHT,* February 9, 1934.
25. Henry McBride, in *New York Sun,* February 9, 1934.
26. Lucius Beebe, in *NYHT,* February 9, 1934.
27. Ibid.
28. VT, *Thomson,* 240.
29. Wallace Stevens, letter to Harriet Monroe, February 12, 1934, in *Letters of Wallace Stevens,* sel. and ed. Holly Stevens (New York: Alfred A. Knopf, 1966), 267.
30. Carl Van Vechten, letter to GS, February 8, 1934, in *The Letters of Gertrude Stein and Carl Van Vechten,* ed. Edward Burns, vol. 1 (New York: Columbia University Press, 1986), 295.
31. Houseman, *Run-Through,* 121.
32. Henry McBride, in *New York Sun,* February 10, 1934.
33. Olin Downes, in *NYT,* February 25, 1934.
34. Houseman, *Run-Through,* 124–25.
35. GS, letter to William Aspenwall Bradley, April 21, 1934, GS Collection, Beinecke Rare Book and Manuscript Library, Yale University.
36. Thomson, quoted in *Kansas City Times,* May 1934.
37. Margot, Jr., in *Chicago Daily News,* November 7, 1934.
38. Houseman, *Run-Through,* 126.
39. Eugene Stinson, in *Chicago Daily News,* November 8, 1934.
40. VT, *Thomson,* 238.

Chapter 17: THE COMMANDO SQUAD

1. VT, *Thomson,* 243.
2. Oscar Levant, *A Smattering of Ignorance* (Garden City, N.Y.: Doubleday, 1939), 169–70.
3. Gilbert Seldes, review in *Modern Music* 11, no. 3 (March–April 1934): 138.
4. Theodore Chanler, letter to Kathleen Hoover, December 29, 1948, VT Coll.
5. Aaron Copland, letter to VT, n.d. [ca. 1931], VT Coll.
6. VT, *Thomson,* 252.
7. Quoted in John Houseman, *Run-Through: A Memoir* (New York: Simon and Schuster, 1972), 174.
8. Ibid., 144.
9. VT, letter to John Houseman, quoted ibid., 192.
10. Brooks Atkinson, in *NYT,* April 15, 1936.
11. Percy Hammond, in *NYHT,* April 15, 1936.
12. Pare Lorentz, *Lorentz on Film* (New York: Hopkinson and Blake, 1975).
13. VT, *Thomson,* 259.
14. Ibid., 268.
15. Ibid., 269.
16. Garrett D. Byrnes, in *Providence Journal,* February 4, 1938.
17. VT, *Thomson,* 275.
18. Ibid., 276.
19. Ibid., 275.
20. Edwin Denby, review in *Modern Music* 15, no. 3 (March–April 1938): 186.

21. VT, letter to GS, July 16, 1938, VT Coll.; also in *Letters*, 122.
22. VT, *Thomson*, 206.
23. Harry Dunham, letter to VT, January 1, 1937, VT Coll.
24. Sherry Mangan, letter to VT, August 1936, VT Coll.
25. VT, *Thomson*, 283.

Chapter 18: WHO DOES WHAT TO WHOM AND WHO GETS PAID

1. VT, unpublished article, 1925, VT Coll.
2. H. L. Mencken, letter to VT, October 23, 1924, VT Coll.
3. Minna Lederman, *The Life and Death of a Small Magazine (Modern Music, 1924–1946)* (Brooklyn: Institute for Studies in American Music, 1983), 22.
4. VT, "Aaron Copland," *Modern Music* 9, no. 2 (January–February 1932): 67–72.
5. Aaron Copland, letter to VT, January 27, 1932, VT Coll.
6. VT, "George Gershwin," *Modern Music* 13, no. 1 (November–December 1935): 13–19.
7. Samuel Chotzinoff, in *New York Post*, October 31, 1934.
8. VT, *Thomson*, 297.
9. VT, letter to Thayer Hobson, October 4, 1938, in *Letters*, 123–24.
10. VT, *The State of Music* (New York: William Morrow, 1939), 3–4.
11. Ibid., 16–17.
12. Ibid., 81.
13. Ibid., 109–11.
14. Ibid., 104–5.
15. Ibid., 211–12.
16. Ibid., 125–26.
17. VT, letter to Aaron Copland, March 20, 1939.
18. Aaron Copland, letter to VT, May 1, 1939, VT Coll.
19. Aaron Copland, "Thomson's Musical State," *Modern Music* 17, no. 1 (October–November 1940): 63.
20. VT, letter to Briggs Buchanan, January 13, 1940, in *Letters*, 132.
21. Maurice Grosser, unpublished memoirs, chap. 11, property of Louis Rispoli.
22. VT, *Thomson*, 298.
23. GS, letter to VT, September 17, 1939, VT Coll.
24. VT, letter to Briggs Buchanan, January 13, 1940, in *Letters*, 132–33.
25. VT, letter to Maurice Grosser, February 21, 1940, VT Coll.
26. Ibid.
27. VT, *Thomson*, 315.
28. VT, letter to Maurice Grosser, April 16, 1940, in *Letters*, 135.

Chapter 19: THE TRIB

1. William Zinsser, "Virgil Thomson, Writer," *The Sewanee Review* 95, no. 2 (Spring, 1987): 340
2. Richard Kluger, *The Paper: The Life and Death of the New York Herald Tribune* (New York: Alfred A. Knopf, 1986), 265–66.
3. Zinsser, 340.
4. VT, *Thomson*, 331.
5. Ibid., 321.
6. Ibid., 332.
7. Leland Poole, letter to VT, December 30, 1940, VT Coll.
8. Leland Poole, letters to VT, August 5, 1945, and April 14, 1946, VT Coll.
9. Jean Nathan, "Within the Walls of the Chelsea," *NYT*, February 7, 1993.
10. VT, "Age without Honor," *NYHT*, October 11, 1940.
11. VT, "Sonorous Splendors," *NYHT*, October 12, 1940.
12. Geoffrey Parsons, letter to VT, October 14, 1940, VT Coll.; also in John Vinton, "The Art of Gentlemanly Discourse," in *Essays after a Dictionary* (Lewisburg: Bucknell University Press, 1977), 35–38.
13. VT, *Thomson*, 333.
14. Ibid., 327–28.
15. Joseph Horowitz, *Understanding Toscanini* (New York: Alfred A. Knopf, 1987), 10.
16. VT, "Velvet Paws," *NYHT*, October 16, 1940.
17. VT, "Music from Chicago," *NYHT*, November 21, 1940.
18. Geoffrey Parsons, letter to VT, November 29, 1940, VT Coll.; also in Vinton, "Art," 43–44.
19. Carl Van Vechten, letter to GS, December 11, 1940, in *The Letters of Gertrude Stein and Carl Van Vechten*, ed. Edward Burns, vol. 2 (New York: Columbia University Press, 1986), 692.
20. VT, "The Toscanini Case," *NYHT*, May 17, 1942.
21. VT, *Thomson*, 333.
22. Geoffrey Parsons, letter to VT, May 2, 1941, VT Coll.; also in Vinton, "Art," 57–58.
23. Geoffrey Parsons, letter to VT, November 25, 1942, VT Coll.; also in "Art," 70–71.
24. Allen Hughes, interview with AT, August 13, 1990.
25. Olin Downes, in *NYT*, November 26, 1941.
26. Unidentified writer, in *NYHT*, June 19, 1941.
27. VT, "Ambitious Vocalism," *NYT*, October 24, 1940.

28. VT, *Thomson*, 325.
29. VT, in *NYHT*, October 4, 1944.
30. VT, in *NYHT*, April 21, 1941.
31. VT, in *NYHT*, December 15, 1944.
32. Paul Bowles, in *NYHT*, December 28, 1942.
33. Louis Biancolli, in *New York World Telegram*, January 6, 1943.
34. Goddard Lieberson, in *NYHT*, May 16, 1942.
35. VT, *Thomson*, 331.

Chapter 20: 329 PACIFIC STREET

1. Maurice Grosser, unpublished memoir, chap. 12, property of Louis Rispoli.
2. Lawrence R. Murphy, "The House on Pacific Street: Homosexuality, Intrigue, and Politics during World War II," *Journal of Homosexuality* 12, no. 1 (Fall 1985): 32.
3. C. A. Tripp, *The Homosexual Matrix* (New York: McGraw-Hill, 1975), 225.
4. Murphy, "House on Pacific Street," 40.
5. Walter Winchell, "On Broadway," *Daily Mirror*, May 14, 1942.
6. Dorothy G. Waxman, *David I. Walsh: Citizen-Patriot* (Milwaukee: Bruce, 1952), 351.
7. Geoffrey Parsons, letter to VT, November 25, 1942, VT Coll.; also in Vinton, "The Art of Gentlemanly Discourse," *Essays after a Dictionary* (Lewisburg: Bucknell University Press, 1977), 72.
8. VT, *Thomson*, 356.
9. VT, in *NYHT*, April 4, 1943.
10. VT, in *NYHT*, March 18, 1945.
11. John Cage, letter to VT, March 15, 1939, VT Coll.
12. VT, *Thomson*, 353.
13. Ibid.
14. *Life* magazine, March 14, 1943.
15. Noel Straus, in NYT, February 8, 1943.
16. Paul Bowles, in *NYHT*, February 8, 1943.
17. VT, in *NYHT*, January 22, 1945.
18. VT, *Thomson*, 353.
19. Lou Harrison, interview with AT, November 6, 1991.
20. Ned Rorem, *Knowing When to Stop: A Memoir* (New York: Simon and Schuster, 1994), 161.
21. Ibid., 193.
22. Ibid., 164–65.
23. Ibid., 197.
24. Ibid., 213.
25. Ibid.
26. Ibid., 211.
27. Ibid., 212–13.
28. Ned Rorem, letter to VT, August 31, 1944.
29. Rorem, *Knowing When to Stop*, 220–21.
30. Ned Rorem, letter to VT, June 17, 1946.
31. Olin Downes, in *NYT*, February 23, 1945.

32. Oscar Thompson, in *New York Sun*, February 23, 1945.
33. Paul Bowles, in *NYHT*, February 23, 1945.
34. VT, letter to Maurice Grosser, August 26, 1945, VT Coll.

Chapter 21: WHAT IS THE QUESTION?

1. James R. Mellow, *Charmed Circle: Gertrude Stein and Company* (New York: Praeger, 1974), 466.
2. Joseph Barry, letter to *Harper's Magazine*, December 29, 1947.
3. GS, letter to Carl Van Vechten, June 12, 1945, in *The Letters of Gertrude Stein and Carl Van Vechten*, ed. Edward Burns, vol. 2 (New York: Columbia University Press, 1986), 777.
4. VT, interview with AT, November 14, 1988.
5. VT, *Thomson*, 366.
6. GS, letter to VT, September 12, 1945.
7. GS, letter to VT, September 24, 1945.
8. GS, letter to VT, October 8, 1945.
9. Bruce Kellner, ed., *A Gertrude Stein Companion* (Westport, Conn.: Greenwood Press, 1988), 193.
10. GS, letter to VT, March 20, 1946, VT Coll.
11. VT, letter to Gertrude Stein, April 15, 1946, VT Coll.
12. Carl Van Vechten, letter to GS, April 17, 1946, in *Letters of Gertrude Stein and Carl Van Vechten*, 818–19.
13. GS, letter to Carl Van Vechten, June 14, 1946, ibid., 823.
14. VT, *Thomson*, 366.
15. Alice B. Toklas, letter to Carl Van Vechten, July 31, 1946, in *Letters of Gertrude Stein and Carl Van Vechten*, 835.
16. Excerpt from GS's will, in Diana Souhami, *Gertrude and Alice* (London: Pandora, 1991), 248.
17. Alice B. Toklas, *What Is Remembered?* (New York: Holt, Rinehart and Winston, 1963), 173.
18. Alice B. Toklas, letter to Carl Van Vechten, July 31, 1946, in *Letters of Gertrude Stein and Carl Van Vechten*, 835.
19. Bernard Faÿ, letter to Alice B. Toklas, August 1, 1946, in *The Flowers of Friendship*, ed. Donald Gallup (New York: Alfred A. Knopf, 1953), 402.
20. VT, *Thomson*, 377.
21. Ibid., 383.
22. VT, letter to Alice B. Toklas, April 11, 1947, VT Coll.
23. Otto Luening, *The Odyssey of an American Composer: The Autobiography of Otto Luening* (New York: Scribner's, 1980), 463.

24. Ibid.

25. Robert A. Simon, in *New Yorker,* May 17, 1947.

26. Richard Watts, Jr., in *New York Post,* May 17, 1947.

27. Irving Kolodin, in *New York Sun,* May 8, 1947.

28. *Variety,* May 1947.

29. Francis D. Perkins, in *NYHT,* May 8, 1947.

30. Olin Downes, in *NYT,* May 8, 1947.

Chapter 22: POLITICS AND PRIZES

1. VT, *Thomson,* 335.

2. Paul Bowles, letter to George Antheil, August 3, 1946, in *In Touch: The Letters of Paul Bowles,* ed. Jeffrey Miller (New York: Farrar, Straus and Giroux, 1994), 174.

3. VT, "A War's End," *NYHT,* January 12, 1947.

4. Minna Lederman, *The Life and Death of a Small Magazine (Modern Music, 1924–1946)* (Brooklyn: Institute for Studies in American Music, 1983), 199.

5. VT, *The State of Music* (New York: William Morrow, 1939), 102.

6. VT, *Thomson,* 375.

7. VT, in *NYHT,* March 17, 1947.

8. VT, letter to a reader, March 21, 1947, in *Letters,* 210–11.

9. *Time,* February 17, 1947.

10. VT, "The Philharmonic Crisis," *NYHT,* February 9, 1947.

11. Ernst Bacon, letter to VT, February 11, 1947, VT Coll.

12. Ermine Kahn, letter to VT, February 9, 1947, VT Coll.

13. Arthur Rodzinski, letter to VT, February 10, 1947. VT Coll.

14. Arthur Rodzinski, letter to VT, May 17, 1947, VT Coll.

15. Erik Barnouw, *Documentary: A History of the Non-Fiction Film* (New York: Oxford University Press, 1974), 42.

16. Bosley Crowther, in *NYT,* September 29, 1948.

17. Unidentified review in VT Coll.

18. Edwin Denby, *Dance Writings* (New York: Alfred A. Knopf, 1986), 420.

19. John Briggs, in *New York Post Home News,* December 1, 1948.

20. VT, letter to Aaron Copland, April 13, 1950, VT Coll.

21. VT, letter to Alice B. Toklas, December 31, 1947, in *Letters,* 219.

22. Kathleen Hoover and John Cage, *Virgil Thomson: His Life and Music* (New York: Thomas Yoseloff, 1959), 108.

23. Brooks Atkinson, in *NYT,* April 17, 1952.

24. VT, *Thomson,* 408–9.

25. VT, in *NYHT,* October 9, 1953, in *Music Reviewed: 1940–1954* (New York: Random House, 1967), 376.

26. VT, "Spokesman for the Met," *NYHT,* December 30, 1951.

27. *NYT,* January 18, 1953.

28. Ibid.

29. VT, letter to Ernst Bacon, February 24, 1953, in *Letters,* 266.

30. VT, *Thomson,* 411.

31. VT, letter to Maurice Grosser, February 18, 1954, VT Coll.

32. Aaron Copland, letter to VT, February 18, 1954, VT Coll.

33. *Time,* August 2, 1954.

34. VT, *Thomson,* 344.

Chapter 23: ROGER

1. VT, letter to Maurice Grosser, April 19, 1954, in *Letters,* 275.

2. VT, letter to Maurice Grosser, July 14, 1954, in *Letters,* 276.

3. Maurice Grosser, letter to VT, from Tangier, n.d., VT Coll.

4. Stuart Preston, in *NYT,* October 27, 1954.

5. Paul Henry Lang, in *NYHT,* April 20, 1956.

6. Brooks Atkinson, in *NYT,* August 8, 1957.

7. VT, *Thomson,* 405.

8. Ibid.

9. Roger Baker, letter to VT, August 8, 1956, VT Coll.

10. VT, letter to Ingram Merrill Foundation, October 10, 1970, VT Coll.

11. John Cage, interview with AT, March 3, 1991.

12. Ibid.

13. John Cage, unpublished manuscript, March 1956, pp. 111–12.

14. VT, letter to Alice Smith Edwards, August 20, 1949, VT Coll.

15. Kathleen O'Donnell Hoover, letter to VT, May 27, 1955, VT Coll.

16. John Cage, letter to VT, March 28, 1956, VT Coll.

17. VT, letter to Maurice Grosser, August 2, 1956, VT Coll.

18. John Cage, unpublished manuscript, March 1956, p. 28.

19. VT, letter to Kathleen O'Donnell Hoover, June 2, 1955, VT Coll.

20. Arnold Weissberger, letter to VT, February 5, 1958.

21. VT, letter to Maurice Grosser, June 29, 1958, VT Coll.

22. Kathleen Hoover and John Cage, *Virgil Thomson: His Life and Music* (New York: Thomas Yoseloff, 1959), 29.

23. Ibid., 69.

24. Ibid., 225.

25. Ibid., 246.

26. John Cage, unpublished manuscript, March 1956, p. 176.
27. Oliver Daniel, in *Saturday Review,* May 30, 1959.
28. *Times Literary Supplement,* September 25, 1959.
29. VT, interview with AT, May 12, 1988.
30. *A Virgil Thomson Reader* (Boston: Houghton Mifflin, 1981), 486, originally published in *New York Review of Books,* April 23, 1970.
31. Dale Burr, interview with AT, August 15, 1990.

Chapter 24: IT'S A SOFT EGG, BABY!

1. VT, letter to S. Foster Damon, February 14, 1952, VT Coll.
2. VT, letter to Francis Ferguson, February 27, 1952, VT Coll.
3. Kenneth Koch, "Angelica" (unpublished), Act 2.
4. Kenneth Koch, interview with AT, October 1, 1991.
5. Kenneth Koch, *Selected Poems* (New York: Vintage Books, 1985), 24.
6. Kenneth Koch, "Love Song," in *Thank You and Other Poems* (New York: Grove Press, 1962).
7. Kenneth Koch, letter to VT, July 9, 1959, VT Coll.
8. Kenneth Koch, letter to VT, July 26, 1959, VT Coll.
9. VT, letter to Kenneth Koch, August 14, 1959, VT Coll.
10. VT, letter to Kenneth Koch, August 24, 1959, VT Coll.
11. Koch interview.
12. Ibid.
13. VT, *Thomson,* 416.
14. Betty Allen, interview with AT, September 28, 1989.
15. John Gruen, in NYHT, October 25, 1963.
16. VT, *Thomson,* 415.
17. Maurice Grosser, *The Critic's Eye* (Indianapolis and New York: Bobbs-Merrill, 1962), 27.
18. VT, letter to Manuel Rosenthal, November 16, 1943, in *Letters,* 284.
19. VT, letter to Maurice Grosser, November 8, 1961, in *Letters,* 304.
20. Carol Truax, *Father Was a Gourmet* (New York: Doubleday, 1960), 17.
21. Frank O'Hara, in *HiFi/Stereo Review,* March 1965, 65.
22. Frank O'Hara, letter to Larry Rivers, in Larry Rivers, *What Did I Do? The Unauthorized Biography* (New York: HarperCollins, 1992), 387.
23. J. J. Mitchell, "The Death of Frank O'Hara," in *Homage to Frank O'Hara,* ed.

Bill Berkson and Joe LeSueur (Bolinas, Calif.: Big Sky [privately printed], 1978), 144.
24. Ibid., 145.
25. VT, letter to Maurice Grosser, July 25, 1966, in *Letters,* 324.
26. Herbert Weinstock, letter to VT, September 10, 1964, VT Coll.
27. VT, unpublished draft, Columbia University Rare Book and Manuscript Library.
28. VT, letter to Alfred A. Knopf, n.d. [1966], VT Coll.
29. VT, *Thomson,* 424.

Chapter 25: A LORD, A GENIUS, A MILLIONAIRE, AND A BEAUTY

1. Jack Larson, letter to VT, September 8, 1962, VT Coll.
2. VT, letter to Jack Larson, November 19, 1962, VT Coll.
3. GS, letter to Carl Van Vechten, December 22, 1935, in *The Letters of Gertrude Stein and Carl Van Vechten,* ed. Edward Burns, vol. 1 (New York: Columbia University Press, 1986), 468.
4. John Gruen, "Virgil Sings of 'Lord Byron,' " *NYT,* April 9, 1972.
5. VT, unpublished book chapter, VT Coll.
6. Jack Larson, letter to VT, November 24, 1962, VT Coll.
7. Ibid.
8. Jack Larson, "The Word on Byron," *Parnassus,* Spring/Summer 1977, 522.
9. VT, postcard to Jack Larson, n.d. [March 1965], VT Coll.
10. Jack Larson, letter to VT, January 19, 1965, VT Coll.
11. Jack Larson, letter to VT, June 10, 1965, VT Coll.
12. Jack Larson, "The Keeper of the Rose," *Canto,* Spring 1978.
13. VT, *Thomson,* 378.
14. Larson, "Keeper of the Rose," 100.
15. Ibid., 102.
16. Ibid., 103.
17. Larson, "Word on Byron," 523.
18. Margaret Harford, in *Los Angeles Times,* Feb. 12, 1966.
19. Clyde Leech, in *Los Angeles Herald-Examiner,* Feb. 14, 1966.
20. VT, letter to Jack Larson, March 5, 1966.
21. Larson, "Word on Byron," 523.
22. VT, letter to Jack Larson, August 12, 1966, VT Coll.
23. VT, unpublished book chapter, VT Coll.
24. VT, letter to Jack Larson, June 16, 1967, VT Coll.
25. VT, letter to the Rockefeller Foundation, May 18, 1968, VT Coll.

26. VT, unpublished book chapter, VT Coll.
27. Rudolf Bing, letter to VT, April 14, 1969, VT Coll.
28. VT, letter to Maurice Grosser, March 14, 1969, in *Letters,* 328.
29. Sir Rudolf Bing, *5000 Nights at the Opera* (New York: Doubleday, 1972), 212.
30. VT, unpublished book chapter, VT Coll.
31. John Houseman, *Final Dress* (New York: Simon and Schuster, 1983), 467.
32. Ibid., 466.
33. John Houseman, interview with AT, November 23, 1987.
34. Ibid.
35. Houseman, *Final Dress,* 468.
36. Harold Schonberg, in NYT, April 22, 1972.
37 Herbert Kupferberg, in *National Observer,* May 6, 1972.
38. Alan Rich, in *New York,* May 8, 1972.
39. Robert Commanday, in *San Francisco Chronicle,* April 25, 1972.
40. Harold Schonberg, in *NYT,* April 22, 1972.
41. Patrick J. Smith, in *HiFi/Musical America,* July 1972.
42. Ned Rorem, *The Final Diary* (New York: Holt, Rinehart and Winston, 1974), 383.
43. Ned Rorem, "Lord Byron in Kansas City," *New Republic,* May 6, 1972.
44. Rorem, Final Diary, 421.
45. Ibid., 421.
46. Ibid.

Chapter 26: MAKING YOUNG FRIENDS

1. VT, letter to Leonard Bernstein, March 14, 1974, in *Letters,* 343–44.
2. George Glint, in *NYT,* February 15, 1973.
3. Harold C. Schonberg, in *NYT,* February 23, 1973.
4. VT, letter to Arnold Weissberger, April 7, 1973, VT Coll.
5. VT, letter to Maurice Grosser, January 20, 1970, VT Coll.
6. VT, letter to Paul Bowles, June 2, 1973, in *Letters,* 340.
7. VT, letter to Jere Abbott, September 12, 1977, in *Letters,* 362.
8. VT, letter to Maurice Grosser, June 8, 1978, in *Letters,* 366.
9. VT, unpublished memoir, VT Coll.
10. VT, letter to Andrew Raeburn, November 16, 1976, in *Letters,* 357.
11. VT, letter to Maurice Grosser, August 1, 1981, VT Coll.
12. Betty Freeman, unpublished memoir of VT.

13. VT, letter to the Robert Flaherty Estate, May 6, 1977, in *Letters,* 360.
14. VT, letter to Paul Bowles, December 23, 1979, in *Letters,* 376.

Chapter 27: THE ABSENCE OF THE PRESENCE

1. John Rockwell, introd. to *A Virgil Thomson Reader* (Boston: Houghton Mifflin, 1981), x.
2. Andrew Porter, in *The New Yorker,* October 19, 1981.
3. VT, letter to AT, February 5, 1988.
4. VT, letter to Elizabeth Stouffer, August 28, 1984, in *Letters,* 399–400.
5. Andrew Porter, in *The New Yorker,* January 17, 1977.
6. VT, letter to AT, March 16, 1986.
7. Louis Rispoli, letter to VT, December 24, 1982, VT Coll.
8. VT, letter to Louis Rispoli, December 24, 1982.
9. Louis Rispoli, interview with AT, August 16, 1990.
10. Louis Rispoli, letter to VT, October 22, 1986, VT Coll.
11. Grace Glueck, obituary of Maurice Grosser, in *NYT,* December 23, 1986.
12. VT, letter to AT, January 3, 1987.

Chapter 28: ALL MY LONG LIFE

1. Allan Stinson, letter to AT, December 12, 1986.
2. VT, letter to AT, September 21, 1987.
3. VT, letter to a correspondent, February 6, 1942, VT Coll.
4. VT, letter to a correspondent, February 6, 1942, in *Letters,* 158.
5. Edward Rothstein, in *New Republic,* June 20, 1988.
6. Bernard Holland, in *NYT,* July 30, 1988.
7. Richard Dyer, in *Boston Globe,* August 7, 1988.
8. Allan Stinson, letter to AT, November 9, 1988.
9. John Houseman, quoted in *NYT,* November 5, 1988.
10. Allan Stinson, letter to AT, January 1, 1989.
11. VT, letter to J. Lewis Blackburn, June 19, 1979, in *Letters,* 372.
12. Leonard Bernstein, statement dictated to AT by Margaret Carson, October 1, 1989.
13. Richard Dyer, in *Boston Globe,* October 2, 1989.
14. "Notes and Comments," *New Criterion,* December 1989.

INDEX

Abdul (witch doctor), 277, 279
Acadian Songs and Dances (Thomson), 414
Action Française, 95
Adams, John, 519
Adventures of Superman, The, 477–78, 483, 500
AIDS, 536–38, 539, 552, 553, 559–60
Ailey, Alvin, 496, 507–9
Air from Racine's "Phèdre' (Thomson), 213, 346–47
Air Services Aeronautics Corps, U.S., 55, 60–62, 71
Albee, Edward, 469
Allen, Betty, 70, 421, 461–63, 508, 527, 561, 567
"All My Long Life" (Thomson), 568
Alsop, Joseph, 253
Aluminum Corporation of America (ALCOA), 223
Amelia Goes to the Ball (Menotti), 380
American Ambulance Service, 58
American Ballet, 239, 288
American Composers Alliance, 272–73, 349
American Composers Guild, 443
American Conservatory, 95
American Creed (Harris), 338–39
American Grand Opera Company, 380
American Guild of Musical Artists, 272
American Guild of Organists, 34
American Mercury, 297–98
American Music Since 1910 (Thomson), 270, 493*n*
American National Theater and Academy (ANTA), 420
American Newspaper Guild, 322
American Opera Center, 494
American Opera Society, 264
American Orchestral Association, 111
American Shakespeare Festival, 435, 436, 498

American Society of Composers, Authors and Publishers (ASCAP), 272, 568
"America's Young Men of Promise" (Copland), 190
Ames, Thaddeus H., 186
Anderson, Marian, 247, 345
Anderson, Tommy, 246, 247, 251, 252, 278
Angel Flight (Larson), 483
"Angelica" (Koch), 454–60, 461, 483
Angels (Ruggles), 186
Anons, 51–52
Antheil, George, 128–36, 152, 153, 164, 190, 192, 282, 366, 402, 523
Antheil and the Treatise on Harmony (Pound), 129
Anti-Vice Society, 66–67
Antony and Cleopatra (Barber), 486
Antony and Cleopatra (Shakespeare), 288
Anything Goes, 225
Apel, Willi, 78
Appalachian Spring (Copland), 416, 425, 427
Appleton Chapel, 77
architecture, modern, 219, 221, 222–23
Ariosto, Ludovico, 455
Arp, Jean, 156, 165, 166, 317, 566
Arrow Music Press, 273, 349
Ashbery, John, 485, 491
Ashcroft, Edward, 158
Ashton, Frederick, 9, 249–50, 251, 252, 253, 255, 256, 258, 259, 260, 420, 495–96, 497, 508–9
Askew, Constance Atwood, 219, 220, 223, 230
Askew, R. Kirk, Jr., 218–20, 223, 225, 228, 230, 238, 240, 244, 246, 250, 258, 263, 304
Aspen Music Festival, 465
Assetto, Franco, 520–22
Association of Teachers of Singing, 10
Atkinson, Brooks, 279, 421, 435

Atlantic Monthly, 235
Auden, W. H., 1, 239, 379, 431, 432, 439
Austin, A. Everett "Chick," Jr., 218, 219,
    221–22, 225, 230, 234, 236, 238, 254–55,
    258, 263, 281, 289
Austin, Helen, 221, 258
Autobiography of Alice B. Toklas, The (Stein),
    151, 159, 235, 253
Avery, Samuel, 221
Azan, Colonel, 94

Bach, Johann Sebastian, 33, 79, 103
Bach, Karl Philip Emmanuel, 103–4
Bachardy, Don, 469, 482, 483
Bacon, Ernst, 408–9, 426
Baker, Harry Claybourne, 430
Baker, Roger, 179, 430–34, 437–40, 452, 464
Balanchine, George, 237, 238, 288, 414, 431,
    438, 518
Baldwin, Maurice, 26
ballet, 220, 236–39, 288–90
Ballet Caravan, 239, 288–90, 291, 293
Ballet mécanique (Antheil), 132–33
Bankhead, Tallulah, 288
Barber, Samuel, 111, 362, 427, 432, 486
Barbirolli, John, 328, 329, 333, 335, 336,
    406–7
Barkley, Alben W., 359–61
Barnes, Howard, 413
Barney, Natalie, 163
Barr, Alfred, Jr., 219, 220, 222–23, 237
Barry, Joseph, 381–82, 385, 389, 400, 484
Barrymore, Ethel, 60, 477
Bartók, Béla, 127, 130, 187, 379
Barzin, Leon, 356, 397
Basket (Stein's dog), 140, 167, 210
Battle Zone, 477
Bavoux, Maurice, 297
Bayou, 414
Beach, Christopher, 517
Beach, Sylvia, 128, 131, 134, 135–36
Beard, Mark, 517–18
Beauty and the Beast, 141
Beebe, Lucius, 257, 258, 322, 353
Beecham, Thomas, 256, 346, 372, 377, 420
Beekman, Gustave, 355–56, 360–61, 548
Beeson, Jack, 380, 394, 396, 399
Beethoven, Ludwig van, 31, 33, 104, 107,
    127, 182, 328, 329–32, 335–36, 352, 362,
    374, 404, 419, 496, 502
"Before Sleeping" (Thomson), 462, 567
"Before the Flowers of Friendship Faded
    Friendship Faded" (Stein), 217
Benedict XV, Pope, 96
Bérard, Christian, 141, 150, 166–67, 175, 209,
    241, 314, 434, 474
"Berceau de Gertrude Stein, Le" (Thomson),
    567

Berceau de Gertrude Stein, Le (Hugnet),
    212–13, 567
Berger, Arthur, 267, 402, 424, 427, 448
Berlin, Irving, 183
Berlioz, Hector, 185, 312, 348, 404
Berman, Eugene, 140, 150, 197
Berman, Leonid, 140, 150, 432, 434
Bernstein, Leonard, 80, 120, 301, 370, 497,
    531
    as composer, 421
    as conductor, 410
    Norton lectures given by, 505–6
    Thomson's music as viewed by, 6, 563
    Thomson's relationship with, 1, 8, 77
Beyer, Johanna, 363
Bhatia, Vanraj, 466, 467
Biancolli, Louis, 348–49
Bias, Claude, 297
Biddle, Francis, 359
Billy the Kid (Copland), 291, 310, 425, 443
Bing, Rudolf, 423–24, 486, 491–94, 507
Bird, Bonny, 368
"Birthday Card" (Wheeler), 542
Blackburn, Lewis (cousin), 25, 328
Blackett, Joy, 11
Blake, William, 81, 90
Bleeck, John, 321–22
Bleeck's, 321–22, 324, 353
Blitzstein, Marc, 137, 273, 426, 486, 493–94
Bloch, Ernest, 191
Bogart, Humphrey, 477
Boguslawski, Moses, 33, 35
Bohm, Jerome D., 324, 346, 347, 353, 424–25
Bolcom, William, 542
Bonner, Embry, 246, 256–57
Boosey & Hawkes, 272, 273
Boothe, Clare, 257
Booth Ferris Foundation, 516
Boris Godunov (Mussorgsky), 102
Borlin, Jean, 102
Bornstein, Beth, 525
Bossuet, Jacques, 167, 203–4, 213
Boston Evening Transcript, 79, 91, 96, 102,
    105, 152, 297
Boston Flute Players Club, 201
Boston Globe, 11, 156, 360, 534, 535, 563
Boston Herald, 323
Boston School of Architecture, 145
Boston Symphony, 79, 80, 100, 103, 152,
    195, 196, 270, 323, 330–32, 335–36, 567
Boudreaux, Joseph, 411
Boulanger, Nadia, 87, 91, 148, 174, 402, 466
    Bowles as student of, 99–100, 292
    Copland as student of, 95, 98, 99–100,
        181, 188, 195
    Thomson as student of, 98–100, 104, 116,
        126, 129–30, 152, 153, 189, 191–92, 445,
        474, 523
Boulez, Pierre, 405, 520

Bourgeois, Stephen, 186
Boutin, Jimmy, 526
Bower, Antoinette, 482
Bowles, Jane Auer, 293, 353–54, 512, 544
Bowles, Paul:
    as Boulanger's student, 99–100, 292
    as composer, 137, 272, 290, 292, 293, 294,
        340
    as critic, 348, 353–54, 365–66, 372, 375–76,
        402, 428, 448
    Stein and, 292–93
    in Tangier, 509
    Thomson's relationship with, 291–93, 348,
        372, 503, 512, 531
Bradley, Jennie, 384, 391
Bradley, William Aspenwall, 231–35, 263,
    266, 386
Brahms, Johannes, 95, 127, 182, 183, 303,
    351, 525
Brander Matthews Theater, 378–79, 391–400
Branlière, Alice Woodfin, 132
Brant, Henry, 282
Brewsie and Willie (Stein), 381, 389
Bridgeport, University of, 506
Bridges, James, 477, 479, 482, 484, 485, 487,
    494, 534, 555
Briggs, John, 414–15
Britten, Benjamin, 379, 394
Broadmore International Theater, 465
Brooklyn Eagle, 358
Broom, 106
Brown, Mrs. (landlady), 77, 91
Brown Brothers & Co., 109, 115, 118
Bryan, William Jennings, 22, 116
Buchanan, Briggs Wheeler, 108–20, 122,
    125–26, 151, 152, 158, 191, 195, 202,
    241, 312, 314, 317, 325, 372, 432, 512,
    550, 561
Buchanan, Florence Reynaud, 119, 120
Buchanan, George Briggs, 109–10, 115,
    118
Buchanan, Henry Lush, 109–10, 115, 119
H. L. Buchanan Securities, 109
Bucher, Jeanne, 211, 214
Buell, Richard, 156
"Bugles and Birds" (Thomson), 317
Bureau of Naval Intelligence, U.S., 355–56
Burlesque (Strauss), 77
Burr, Dale, 394, 395, 450–52
Burroughs, Eric, 276
Busbey, Fred E., 425
Busby, Gerald, 517, 541
Bush, Donald, 52–53
Busoni, Ferruccio, 32, 33
Butts, Mary, 142–44, 152, 158, 164, 166, 209,
    447
Byers, Sam, 517, 541, 565
Byington, Robert H., 143
Byrnes, Garrett D., 287

Byron, George Gordon, Lord, 480
Byron a Play (Stein), 480

Cadmus, Paul, 289
Cage, John, 1, 130, 520
    background of, 362–64
    as composer, 364, 365, 441
    as critic, 368, 448
    Harrison and, 368, 369
    Thomson as viewed by, 440–41
    Thomson biography and, 440–49, 473
    Thomson's music as viewed by, 154, 442,
        443, 444, 445, 447–48
    Thomson's relationship with, 368, 373,
        440–50, 530
Cage, Xenia, 365
"Cage and the Collage of Noises"
    (Thomson), 449–50
Calvary Baptist Church, 30, 34
Calvert, Louis, 60
Camp Doniphan, 58–59
Candide (Bernstein), 8
Candied House, The (Larson), 479, 487–88
Canons for Dorothy Thompson (Thomson),
    350
Cantates eamus (Thomson), 566
"Canticle of the Sun" (Thomson), 462
Capital Capitals (Thomson), 157–59, 174,
    195, 199–201, 213, 395
Capote, Truman, 454
Cardell, Victor, 514–15, 568
Carlson, Lenus, 497
Carson, Margaret, 563
Carter, Elliott, 8, 78, 80, 99, 190, 201, 291,
    520
Carter, Jack, 276
Carter, Jimmy, 552
Casals, Pablo, 79, 463, 500
Cat and the Mouse, The (Copland), 184
Cathedral of St. John the Divine, 561–62,
    566, 567–68
Catton, Bruce, 426
Cello Concerto (Thomson), 419–20, 427, 542
cellophane, 11, 243, 254, 255, 260, 262, 264,
    420
Censored: The Private Life of the Movies
    (Lorentz and Ernst), 280
Central High School, 40–41, 42, 43
Central Luminary, 41
Century Association, 568
Cézanne, Paul, 135, 146, 149, 150
Chadwick, George Whitefield, 183
Chalmers, Thomas, 287
Chanler, Theodore, 130, 137, 148, 152, 192,
    194, 268–69, 323
Chapin, Schuyler, 507
Chase, Marian, 293, 294
Chávez, Carlos, 179, 194, 433

Chayefsky, Paddy, 452
Cherry, Larry, Sandy, Doris, Jean, Paul
    (Larson), 494
Chicago Daily News, 264
Chicago fire (1871), 29
Chicago Opera, 67
Chicago Symphony Orchestra, 407–9
Chichester Psalms (Bernstein), 505
Choice Cuts, 484
Chomsky, Noam, 505
Chopin, Frédéric, 30, 128
Chorale, Tango, and Fugue (Thomson),
    116
Chotzinoff, Samuel, 303, 311
Christensen, Lew, 289, 290
Citkowitz, Israel, 137, 272
City Center of Music and Drama, 428
Civil War, U.S., 57
Claflin, Avery, 93, 113
Clarke, Isaiah, 394, 395
Clemenceau, Georges, 383
Clift, Montgomery, 478
Clifton, Chalmers, 111, 415, 416, 417
Cliquet-Pleyel, Henri, 176, 284
Cobb, Ty, 67
Cocteau, Jean, 100, 101, 102, 141, 158, 174,
    175, 284, 314
Collected Poems (Koch), 456–57, 460
Collet, Henri, 101
Columbia Broadcasting System (CBS),
    343
Columbia Concerts Corporation, 272, 343,
    345, 406
Columbia Opera Workshop, 394
Columbia Records, 344, 350, 418
Columbia University, 55, 60, 71, 89, 378–79,
    506, 513, 514
Commanday, Robert, 501
"commando squad," 270–71, 415
Composer's Showcase Concert, 527
Concertino (Stravinsky), 102
Concertino for Harp, Strings and Percussion
    (Thomson), 556
Concerto for Flute, Strings, Harp and
    Percussion (Thomson), 433–34, 435
Concerto for Orchestra (Piston), 270
Concerts Koussevitzky, 103, 181
Connick, Charles, 147
Conservatory of Music (Kansas City), 33
Cooper Union, 185
Copland, Aaron, 220, 370, 432, 531
    Academy Award received by, 417
    as author, 204, 309–12
    background of, 180–81
    ballet scores by, 290–91, 310, 416, 425,
        443
    as Boulanger's student, 95, 98, 99–100,
        181, 188, 195
    Bowles and, 292

communist associations alleged against,
    425–27
as composer, 80, 100, 130, 137, 152, 156,
    181, 183–84, 188–89, 190, 192, 195, 270,
    298–301, 349–50, 380, 400, 416, 425,
    443, 448, 522
as conductor, 427–28
film scores by, 281, 417
Jewish background of, 180, 299, 300–301,
    443
modern music supported by, 184, 190–95,
    202, 270, 271–72, 364, 402, 415, 443,
    504
Pulitzer Prize awarded to, 416
serialism used by, 505
Sessions and, 191–95, 200–201
Thomson as viewed by, 204, 310, 311–12,
    367
Thomson compared with, 8, 180, 230, 276,
    443, 522, 563, 564
Thomson's relationship with, 1, 99,
    199–200, 202, 267, 270, 271–72, 349,
    364, 474, 506, 527
Thomson's views on, 189, 230, 298–301,
    309–10
Copland, Harris, 180
Copland, Sarah, 180
Copland-Sessions Concerts of Contemporary
    Music, 192–95, 199–201, 272
Cornell, Katharine, 275
Cornish School, 363, 368
Cortot, Alfred, 86
Cos Cob Press, 137, 272, 273
Couperin, François, 177
Covarrubias, Miguel, 158
Cowell, Henry, 190, 357, 363, 364, 366, 367,
    416, 417
Cowley, Malcolm, 81
Cox, Christopher, 517, 528
Cox, Nigel, 532
Crabb, George, 40
Craft, Robert, 506
Crane, Emily Chadbourne, 173–74, 209
Crane, Louise, 514
Crane, Stephen, 82
Crane Foundation, 515
Crashaw, Richard, 462
CRI, 462
Critic's Eye, The (Grosser), 463
Crosby, Floyd, 285
Crowther, Bosley, 278, 413
cubism, 129, 134
cummings, e. e., 81, 128, 137, 220, 345
Cunard, Nancy, 42
Cunningham, Merce, 365, 530
Curtin, Phyllis, 567
Curtis Institute of Music, 363, 370, 371,
    373
Cuthbertson, Hannah, 42

Dada, 153–54, 156
Dahlberg, Edward, 22–23
Daily Telegraph (London), 249
Dale, Clamma, 508
Dali, Salvador, 314
d'Amboise, Jacques, 427
Damon, S. Foster, 81–82, 84–85, 90, 237, 453–54
Damrosch, Leopold, 182–83
Damrosch, Walter, 130, 188–89, 330
Daniel, Mell, 355
Daniel, Oliver, 448
Daniels, Jimmy, 226
Dante Alighieri, 96
Dark Valley (Auden), 439
"Darling Nelly Grey," 29
Darrow, Clarence, 117
Davidovsky, Mario, 506
Davison, Archibald T., 78–79, 80, 88, 89, 90–91, 93, 95, 96, 105, 106, 115, 155
Day-Lewis, Cecil, 490
"Death, 'tis a Melancholy Day," 419
Death of a Salesman (Miller), 417
Debussy, Claude, 31, 91, 95, 153, 348, 374
de Casa Fuerte, Yvonne, 317
de Gramont, Elizabeth, 158
de Havilland, Olivia, 417
de Kooning, Willem, 472
de la Grange, Henri-Louis, 432
de Massot, Pierre, 213
Democratic National Convention (1900), 22
Denby, Edwin, 290, 414
Denton, Grace, 264
De Paur, Leonard, 417–18
De Paur Infantry Chorus, 418
Depression, 119, 124, 221, 225, 242, 246, 273–74, 466
De Profundis (Thomson), 90
De Profundis (Wilde), 68–69, 90
Deux soeurs qui ne sont pas soeurs (*Two Sisters Who Are Not Sisters*) (Stein), 210, 212, 213
Devil and Daniel Webster, The (Moore), 378
Diaghilev, Sergei, 237
Dial, 106, 164
Diamond, David, 339
Diamond, Milton, 272–73
Dietrich, Sheila Kemper, 569, 570
Dietrich, Walter, 569, 570
Ditson, Alice M., 379
Ditson, Oliver, 379
Ditson Fund, 379, 380
Dix Portraits (Stein), 210
Doctor Faustus Lights the Lights (Stein), 453
Doe, Doris, 346
Dollar, William, 420
Don Giovanni (Mozart), 337

Dorne, Wendell, 468
Dorsey, Abner, 246, 418
Douglas, Alfred, 65, 68
Dow, Dorothy, 395, 396, 397, 400
"Down at the Docks" (Thomson), 457
Downes, Olin, 194, 261–62, 329, 335, 336, 342, 343, 348, 371, 375, 399, 401
"downtown composers," 506
Drake, Alfred, 435
"Drink to Me Only with Thine Eyes," 29
Drucker, Eugene, 499
Dubal, David, 513
Duchamp, Marcel, 229, 474, 566
Duchess of Malfi, The (Webster), 297
Dukas, Paul, 99
Duke, Vernon, 200
du Maurier, George, 64
Dunham, Henry, 291–94
Dunham, Katherine, 394, 450, 531
Dunkel, Paul, 11
Dunn, Mignon, 518–19
DuPont, Paul, 397
Durant, Will, 36
Durlacher Brothers, 219
Dwyer, Doriot Anthony, 567
Dyer, Richard, 11, 525, 526, 534, 551, 563–64

Eaton, Lola, 40
Editions de la Montagne, 209, 212
Edwards, Frank, 45
Egmont Overture (Beethoven), 104, 328, 329–30, 335
Einstein, Albert, 454
Eisenhower, Dwight D., 385, 425, 450
Elgar, Edward, 177, 329, 335
Eliot, T. S., 82, 237, 239
Elise, Madame (concierge), 167
Ellis, Havelock, 83
Ellmann, Richard, 64
Elmslie, Kenward, 469
Elwell, Herbert, 130, 192
Elwood, Janice, 457
Emerson College, ix, 524–26, 534
Emily Dickinson songs (Copland), 400
Empire Theater, 262
Enfances (Hugnet), 210–17
Engel, Lehman, 272, 273
Engel, Paul, 353, 424
Engelking, L. L., 321
English Players, 380
English Synonymes (Crabb), 40
Enigma Variations (Elgar), 177, 329, 335
Erasmus, Desiderius, 116, 123
Ericson, Raymond, 463
Ernst, Morris, 280
Essay for Orchestra No. 1 (Barber), 362
Esty, Alice, 431

Fable de La Fontaine (Thomson), 213
Fantao, Paula, 564
Father Was a Gourmet (Truax), 465
Fauré, Gabriel, 130
Faÿ, Bernard, 101, 112, 113, 237, 388–89, 390
Faÿ, Emmanuel, 101, 112–15, 203–4, 241, 304
Feder, Abe, 255, 260, 276
Federal Music Project, 290
Federal Theater Project, 274, 276, 284
Ferguson, Francis, 454
Fifth Symphony (Beethoven), 104, 107, 330, 331–32, 362
Fighter Squadron, 477
Filling Station (Thomson), 288–90, 291, 347–48, 427
Film Service, U.S., 288
Fine, Vivian, 272
Finnegans Wake (Joyce), 139
First Symphony (Brahms), 183
Fiske, Minnie Maddern, 60
Five Orchestra Pieces (Schoenberg), 80
Five Phrases from the Song of Solomon (Thomson), 132, 164, 174, 194, 303, 363
Five Songs from William Blake (Thomson), 419, 542
Fizdale, Robert, 431
Flaherty, Frances, 413
Flaherty, Robert, 410–13, 523
Robert Flaherty Foundation, 523
Flanagan, Hallie, 274, 275
Fleishman Yeast Hour, 278
Flender, Charles, 468
Flender, Norma, 465–68, 511, 528, 539–40, 543, 561–62, 565, 566, 569, 571, 572
Flender, Richard, 465, 466, 467, 468, 528, 533, 543, 561, 565
Flender, Sylvia, 468
Ford, Ford Madox, 128, 133
Ford, John, 119
Ford Foundation, 461, 486, 493
"For He's a Jolly Good Fellow," 29, 155, 542
Forrest, Wilbur, 321
Forty-Fourth Street Theater, 259–62
Forum Theater, 507–8
Foster, Kate, 294
Fournier, Pierre, 420
Four Saints in Three Acts (Thomson), 159–72, 218–70
    Act 1 of, 161, 169–71, 206–7
    Act 2 of, 207
    Act 3 of, 207, 556
    Act 4 of, 207
    all-black cast of, 2, 10, 11, 12, 226–27, 231, 232–33, 240, 243–49, 251–52, 253, 254, 255, 258, 259, 276, 527
    auditions for, 245–49
    Broadway production of, 253–54, 259–63, 267, 380, 420–22

    Carnegie Hall concert version of, 527
    cast photographs for, 252
    cellophane used in, 11, 243, 254, 255, 260, 262, 264, 420
    Chicago production of, 216, 264–65, 325, 374, 387
    choreography of, 11, 239, 249–50, 253, 256, 259, 260, 420, 495, 507–9
    chorus for, 169, 172, 207, 243, 244–46, 253, 265, 418, 524
    Commère in, 11, 168, 169, 172, 207, 208, 246, 392, 418, 420, 508, 527
    Compère in, 168, 172, 207, 208, 246, 386, 392, 418
    conductors for, 227–28, 234, 254, 255, 256, 257, 262, 422, 527
    contract for, 231–35, 236, 263, 391
    costumes for, 228, 229, 231, 232–33, 236, 243, 255, 259, 420, 421
    diction in, 226–27, 418, 469
    finances for, 231–35, 236, 245–46, 252, 254–55, 260, 262, 263
    fortieth anniversary celebration for, 532–33
    Grosser's scenario for, 151, 172, 206–9, 251–52, 391, 417, 420
    hermeticism of, 161, 162, 227
    Houseman as director of, 9, 240–43, 246, 248, 249, 251, 252, 254, 255, 256, 257, 258, 260, 262–63, 264, 498, 532, 555
    intermezzo of, 207
    as "landscape," 162
    leads for, 246–49
    Mini-Met production of, 507–9
    Mother compared with, 383, 384, 386–87, 392, 393, 394, 395
    as opera, 227, 261–62
    Opera Ensemble production of, 1–12, 536, 539, 541
    Paris production of, 421–22, 426
    premiere of, 257–59, 322
    press coverage of, 252–53, 257–58, 322
    procession in, 162, 163, 172, 206, 249, 250
    Prologue of, 161, 170–71
    prompt book for, 508–9
    publication of, 212, 267
    radio broadcast of, 495
    recordings of, 417–18, 420, 479, 527
    rehearsals for, 250–57, 422
    religious subject of, 160–62, 249
    reviews of, 7, 11–12, 261–62, 265–66, 268–69, 421, 422, 508
    revivals of, 1–12, 291, 420–22, 461, 527–28
    Saint Cecilia in, 420–21, 422
    Saint Chavez in, 5, 162, 207, 246, 256–57
    Saint Ferdinand in, 256, 257
    Saint Ignatius in, 5, 11, 160, 161–62, 163, 172, 206–7, 246, 257, 418, 420
    Saint Settlement in, 162, 206, 508

Saint Teresa roles in, 1–12, 160–63, 168–69, 172, 206–7, 208, 246–49, 258, 265, 376, 383, 384, 418, 420, 421, 459, 508, 536, 539, 541, 564
set designs for, 11, 199, 228, 229, 236, 243, 249, 252, 254, 255, 259, 260, 264, 420, 421
stage directions for, 161, 172, 206
Stein's libretto for, 3, 11, 12, 151–63, 168, 172, 173, 199, 202, 205–6, 208–9, 227, 251–52, 253, 257, 258, 259, 261, 262, 264, 276, 376, 421, 422, 507
Stein's views on, 171–72, 205–6, 208–9, 230–36, 263, 390
success of, 37, 139, 173, 258–63, 267–68, 279, 453, 480
Thomson's direction of, 240–70
Thomson's music for, 3, 11, 154, 168–72, 173, 174, 176, 198–99, 201, 202, 206, 251, 255–57, 261, 264, 268–69, 288, 293, 380, 414, 447, 508
Thomson's one-man renditions of, 170–72, 198–99, 201, 220–21, 228, 242, 523
Toklas and, 171–72, 422
University of Bridgeport production of, 506
"unreasonably withheld" clause for, 233–35
Wadsworth Atheneum production of, 10, 172, 217, 218–59, 263, 421, 532
Four Songs to Poems of Thomas Campion (Thomson), 419
Fox, Ellen, 40
Francis of Assisi, Saint, 462
Franklin, Benjamin, 158
Franklyn, Leonard, 256–57
Frazer, James, 56
Freedman, Ellis J., 565
Freeman, Betty, 519–22
"Free Wheeling" (Thomson), 528
Friends and Enemies of Modern Music, 221, 239, 254–55
Friends of Virgil Thomson Committee, 533
"From *Sneden's Landing Variations*" (Thomson), 567
Frosch, Aaron, 515
Frost, Carolyn, 467
Frost, Hunter, 467
Frothingham, Christen, 544
Fuchs, Joseph, 111
Fuchs, Lillian, 111
Fuller, Buckminster, 221, 257
Fuller, Donald, 343
Fussell, Charles, 558, 569, 571

Gable, James, 42–43
Gagnon, Roland, 508

Gaines, Benjamin Watts (grandfather), 18, 198
Gaines, Beulah (aunt), 25, 28
Gaines, Cecil (uncle), 25
Gaines, Edward (cousin), 28
Galantière, Lewis, 240, 241–42
Gallup, Donald, 385–88, 400, 516
Gam, David, 13
Gannett, Lewis, 311
Garden, Mary, 32, 67, 91, 212, 387, 544
Garland, Charles, 147
Garland, Marie, 147
Garnett, Cecil (cousin), 28
Garnett, Charlie (uncle), 20, 24–25
Garnett, Lela (cousin), 25, 28, 29, 153
Garnett, Lulu (aunt), 20
Gebhard, Heinrich, 77
Genet, Jean, 431
Gentele, Goeran, 507
Geography and Plays (Stein), 136, 212
Gershwin, George, 181, 183, 226, 260, 262, 265, 267, 276, 301–2, 422, 461
Gide, André, 126
Gill, Jim, 482
Gilman, Lawrence, 318, 324, 334
Glanville-Hicks, Peggy, 428–29
Glaser, Caroline (grandniece), 562, 564
Glaser, Gregg, 562
Glass, Philip, 7, 8, 506
Gleason, Margaret Elizabeth "Betty" (niece), 88, 533, 562, 570
Gleason, Roy, 87, 436, 467
Gleason, Ruby Thomson (sister), 19, 20, 25, 28, 29–30, 79, 87–88, 327, 436, 466–67, 512–13, 551, 560, 562, 570
Goddess, The, 452
Godfrey, Beatrice Wayne, 1–12, 247–49, 256–57, 262, 265, 418, 420, 536, 541, 565
Godfrey, Samuel A., 9
Gold, Arthur, 431
Golde, Morris, 301, 371, 372, 375, 470, 528, 543
Golden Bough, The (Frazer), 56
Goldmark, Rubin, 181
Golschmann, Vladimir, 132
Good Day, 525
Good Natured Man, The, 40
Goodrich, Wallace, 77, 106
Gore, Leigh Gibbs, 533
Grace Episcopal Church, 34, 35
Gratto, Christine, 525
Graves, Thomas, 14
Green, Carl Preston, 510
Grieg, Edvard, 48, 462
Griffis, Theodora, 293, 294
Gross, Mrs. Christian, 131–33, 138, 141
Grosser, Edward, 145

Grosser, Maurice:
  as critic, 463–64
  death of, 560
  final illness of, 3, 4–5, 8, 536–38, 539, 541,
    543–45
  in *Four Saints* production, 3, 5, 255, 256,
    257, 258, 263, 293
  Four Saints scenario written by, 151, 172,
    206–9, 251–52, 291, 417, 420
  generosity of, 451
  at Harvard, 145–47
  homosexuality of, 144–45, 313, 433, 509,
    511–12, 537
  Mother scenario written by, 151, 391–92,
    433
  obituary of, 544
  paintings by, 120, 145–46, 149–50, 295,
    297, 313, 451–52, 463–64, 511, 537, 539,
    544, 560, 565
  Thomson as viewed by, 19, 441, 470–71
  Thomson's relationship with, 26, 107,
    144–51, 152, 202, 206, 209, 215–16, 234,
    241, 250, 286, 296, 301, 303, 313, 315,
    354, 373, 433, 464, 509, 537–38,
    543–45
Gruen, John, 462
Guggenheim, Peggy, 317, 372, 450
Guggenheim Fellowship, 190, 191, 432, 441
Gutman, John, 486, 492

Hackney, Bill, 467
Hackney, Doris, 466–67
Haggin, B. H., 421
Haieff, Alexei, 432
Haines, Julia, 350–52, 354
Hale, Dorothy, 257
Hallelujah, 244
Hamid, Sufi Abdul, 225–26
Hamlet (Shakespeare), 279–80
Hammond, Percy, 279
Hanson, Howard, 416
Harcourt, Alfred, 235
Harford, Betty, 482
Harford, Margaret, 487–88
Harlem Renaissance, 223–26
Harper's Bazaar, 406
Harrell, Mack, 419
Harris, Hilda, 508
Harris, Roy, 174, 190, 200, 270–71, 281,
    338–39
Harrison, Lou, 362–63, 364, 367–69, 372,
    416, 448
Hartford Symphony Orchestra, 532
Harvard Club, 2, 543
Harvard Glee Club, 78–79, 87, 89, 91, 92,
    93–97, 102, 105, 123, 198, 205, 269, 566
Harvard Musical Club, 201
Harvard Musical Review, 81

Harvard University:
  music faculty of, 78–82
  Thomson as student at, 6, 34, 37, 63, 69,
    71, 73, 74–92, 105–8, 135, 153, 154, 269,
    474, 530
  Thomson as teaching assistant at, 88,
    90–91, 122, 164, 189
  Harvard University Glee Club Collection
    (Davison, ed.), 79
Haussmann, Georges Eugène, 454–55, 456,
    459, 460
Hawkins, Erick, 289, 290, 513
Haydn, Franz Joseph, 404
Hayes, Helen, 500
Haywood, Alba, III, 438
  Donald Haywood Choir, 248
Hearst, William Randolph, 280
Hear Ye, Hear Ye! (Copland), 290
Heifetz, Jascha, 79, 339, 500
Heine, Heinrich, 404
Heiress, The, 417
Helin, Jacquelyn, 542, 554, 565, 566
Hellman, Lillian, 1, 426, 460
Hemingway, Ernest, 121, 128, 167, 168
Hemingway, Pauline, 168
Hendl, Walter, 414
Hendricks, Barbara, 497, 508
Henggeler, Ron, 518
Henriette-Marie de France, Queen of
    England, 167, 203–4, 213
Henry V, King of England, 13
Hepburn, Katharine, 253, 435
Hermann, Bernard, 272
Higher Powers of Man, The (Smith), 83
Hill, Edward Burlingame, 79–81, 88, 89, 90,
    91, 105, 111, 115, 183
Hillyer, Robert, 84
Hilton, Ruth, 515
Hines, Altonell, 246, 418, 420
Hiroshima bombing, 369, 376
Hirschmann, Ira, 345
Hirst, Grayson, 491, 497
Histoire du soldat (Stravinsky), 527
Historical Anthology of Music (Davison and
    Apel, eds.), 78
Hitchcock, Henry-Russell, 107, 140, 171,
    220–21, 222, 223, 225, 226, 258, 328,
    548
Hitchcock, H. Wiley, 555–56
Hitler, Adolf, 269, 284, 292
Hobson, Thayer, 297, 304
Hockney, David, 495–96, 519
Holden, Alan, 106
Holden Fellowship, 147
Holland, Bernard, 551
Holmes, James, 503, 566, 568
Homme et son désir, L' (Milhaud), 102
Honegger, Arthur, 101, 104
Hoover, J. Edgar, 359

Hoover, Kathleen O'Donnell, ix–xi, 36, 45–46, 53, 98, 132, 143–44, 153, 154, 268–69, 441–46, 473, 550
Hopkins, Harry, 274
Hopkins, Olive, 247
Horace Victorieux (Honegger), 104
Horne, William, 394
Horowitz, Joseph, 335
Horowitz, Vladimir, 339–40
Horse Eats Hat, 293
Horszowski, Mieczyslaw, 463
Horton, Asadata Dafora, 277
Horton, Lester, 368
Horvath, John, 525, 526
Houghtaling, Paul, 566
Hound and Horn, 237
Houseman, Joan, 555
Houseman, John, 2, 220, 387, 394, 479
  background of, 241
  death of, 555
  as *Four Saints* director, 9, 240–43, 246, 248, 249, 251, 254, 255, 256, 257, 258, 260, 262–63, 264, 498, 532, 555
  as *Lord Byron* director, 481, 487, 488, 494, 496, 497–98, 499, 500–501
  in *Paper Chase,* 534
  Thomson's relationship with, 242–43, 269–70, 281, 284, 301, 413, 435, 474, 497–98, 532, 555
  Welles's collaboration with, 275–79
Houseman, Zita Johann, 241
Howard, Bruce, 246, 248
Howland, Alice, 394, 400
"How Firm a Foundation," 29, 155, 156, 286
"How Modern Music Gets That Way" (Thomson), 127
HPSCHD (Cage), 449
Huckleberry Finn (Twain), 454
Hudson, Rock, 477
Hughes, Allen, 342, 485, 544
Hughes, Langston, 454
Hugnet, Georges, 171, 209–17, 276, 284, 567
Hugnet, Pierre, 209, 212, 214
Hume, Paul, 426
Hunt, James, 394–95
Huntington Hartford Foundation, 478
Hurwitz, Leo, 281
Huston, John, 477
Huszar, John, 523, 549, 567

Imaginary Landscape no. 3 (Cage), 366
"In a Boat" (Thomson), 536
Inaugural Concert Committee, 425
Indiana, Robert, 518, 523
"Intensely Two" (Thomson), 539
International Clarinet Society, 559
International Composers' Guild, 185, 186

International Educational Exchange program, 434–35
International Society for Contemporary Music, 271
Ionian Quartet, 199–200
Irving Grammar School, 39–40
Isaacs, Betty, 448
Isaacs, Julius, 448
Isherwood, Christopher, 469, 473, 482
Island God, The (Menotti), 380
Ives, Charles, 357, 369, 402, 416

Jackson, Brooks, 431
Jackson, George Pullen, 285–86
James, Henry, 485
James, Philip, 416
James, William, 177
Jarboro, Caterina, 247
jazz, 80, 100, 116, 182, 297, 299
Jeanne, Madame (concierge), 167
Jeltzs, J. E., 8
Jeremiah Symphony (Bernstein), 421
Jessye, Eva, 244–46, 265
Eva Jessye Choir, 244–46, 265
William Jewell College, 16, 18
"Jimmie's got a goil" (Blitzstein), 137
Johnny Trouble, 478
Johnson, Andrew, 382, 383, 385
Johnson, Edward, 397
Johnson, Philip, 8, 222–23, 230, 231, 241, 396, 464
Johnson, Theodate, 230, 295, 303, 313, 315–16, 317, 354, 396, 402, 464, 533
Hall Johnson Choir, 244, 245
Jones, Bill T., 542
Joyce, James, 128, 130, 135–36, 139, 159, 167, 304, 380
Judson, Arthur, 343–45, 347–48, 375, 406–10
Juilliard School, 374, 494–503, 514, 534
Juilliard Theater, 495
Juilliard Trust, 108

Kahn, Ermine, 409
Kansas City Polytechnic Institute, 43–45, 49–52, 89
Kansas City Star, 64, 65, 67
Kansas City Symphony, 419
Kansas City Times, 64, 65, 67
Kastendieck, Miles, 343, 421
Katz, Bill, 518, 528, 541, 542
Kay, Hershy, 496
Kazan, Elia, 531
Kemper, Cynthia Warrick, 569
Kennedy, John F., 426–27, 463
Kern, Jerome, 349
Key Largo, 477
Kiang, Lindsay, 528

Kim, Earl, 532
King, Rudolf, 33, 35
King's Chapel (Boston), 105–6, 107
Kirkpatrick, John, 156
Kirkpatrick, Ralph, 348
Kirstein, Lincoln, 8, 107, 220, 236–39, 241, 288–91, 393, 431, 483
Klaw Theater, 186
Kloman, Tony, 464
Kluger, Richard, 321
Alfred A. Knopf, 376, 472, 473, 474, 475
Knopf, Blanche, 198, 472
"Ko" (Koch), 455
Koch, Katherine, 457
Koch, Kenneth, 454–60, 461, 472, 483, 566
Kohon String Quartet, 462
Kolodin, Irving, 398, 421
Koop, C. Everett, 69
Kostelanetz, André, 349, 350
Koussevitzky, Olga, 323
Koussevitzky, Serge, 80, 100, 103, 152, 181, 195, 196–97, 201, 230, 270, 291, 323, 330, 331–32, 397, 406
Koussevitzky Foundation, 487
Kupferberg, Herbert, 501
Kurtz, Efrem, 414

La Guardia, Fiorello, 320, 350
Laloy, Louis, 102
Lambert, Gavin, 482
Landowska, Wanda, 375
Lang, Paul Henry, 379, 428, 435, 441
Lange, Louis, 297
Langlois, Louise, 141–42, 165, 209, 216, 237
Lanner, Joseph, 277
Larned, Emily, 264
Larson, Jack, 555, 559, 563
   background of, 476–80
   Lord Byron libretto of, 475, 479–83, 487, 488–90, 496, 500, 501, 503, 534
   plays by, 477, 478, 479, 483, 487–88, 494
   in *Superman* series, 477–78, 483, 500
   Toklas visited by, 484–85
Larson, Roy, 113
Lasell, Chester Whitin, 164, 196
Lasell, Hildegard, 164, 165, 176, 198
Lasell, Jessie, 164, 165, 167, 170, 174, 178, 180, 240, 304
Lasell, Josiah, 171
Lasell, Philip, 164–65, 171, 198
Latouche, John, 293, 294
Law Enforcement Association, 67
Lawrence, D. H., 461–62
Lawrence, Robert, 324
Lawson, Danyal, 530, 536, 539, 541
Lawson, Kate Drain, 243, 252, 254, 260
Leacock, Richard, 411

League of Composers, 184, 186–87, 190, 192–93, 201, 230, 271, 301, 349, 364, 403, 425, 443
Leana (Thomson's cook), 372
LeClercq, Tanaquil, 438–39
Lectures in America (Stein), 476
Lederman, Minna, 19, 186, 187–90, 268, 298–99, 300, 301, 355, 356–57, 368, 402–3, 445, 449
Lee, Canada, 276
Lee, Edward, 461
Leech, Clyde, 488
"Left to Right" (Stein), 235–36
Léger, Fernand, 132–33
Leibowitz, Samuel S., 358
Lemon, Brendan, 10
Lenya, Lotte, 1, 460
Leppard, Raymond, 518, 519
Leschetizky, Theodor, 77, 441
LeSueur, Joe, 469, 470
"Let's Take a Walk" (Thomson), 457
Levant, Oscar, 267–68, 340, 372
Levy, Julien, 258, 313
Levy, Martin David, 486
Lewis, Anthony, 490
Lewis, Rosa, 170
Lhevinne, Josef, 336–37
Liberace, 65, 465
Liberal Club, 106–7, 108, 110, 140, 144, 146
Liberator, 274–75
Lichtenwalter, Geneve, 35–37, 51, 62, 91
Lieberson, Goddard, 350
Life, 124, 365
Lincoln, Abraham, 349–50, 382, 425, 426
Lincoln Portrait (Copland), 349–50, 425
Lippmann, Walter, 184
Lipsky, Alexander, 200
Lister, Rodney, 566
Liszt, Franz, 7, 30, 33, 128, 352, 404
Littell, Robert, 278
Lodge, Henry Cabot, Jr., 360
Lohengrin (Wagner), 30
Lomax, Alan, 412
London Symphony (Vaughan Williams), 330, 331
Lord Byron (Thomson), 475, 479–503
   auditions for, 496, 497
   ballet in, 496, 501, 507
   broadcast of, 534
   Byron in, 480–83, 491, 496, 501
   choreography of, 495, 496, 507
   conductors for, 495, 535
   contract for, 487
   dialogue in, 492, 493
   dress rehearsal of, 501
   as grand opera, 487, 491, 496, 501, 534–35
   Houseman as director of, 481, 487, 488, 494, 496, 497–98, 499, 500–501
   Juilliard production of, 494–503, 534

Larson's libretto for, 475, 479–83, 487, 488–90, 496, 500, 501, 503, 534
Metropolitan Opera commission for, 485–94, 496, 498, 499, 507
New York Repertory Company production of, 533–35
Poet's Corner in, 481, 482, 490, 498–99
premier of, 500–503
press coverage of, 485, 490
reading of, 482
"Remember the Poet We Knew with Our Heart" in, 489–90, 566
reviews of, 499, 501–3, 534
set designs for, 495, 498–99
stage directions for, 482
tape recording of, 491, 493, 519, 534
Thomson's music for, 475, 482, 483, 485, 488–94, 496, 499–503, 504, 506, 533–35
Tom Moore in, 488–90
tryout of, 490–94
Lorentz, Pare, 280–88, 411, 474
Loring, Eugene, 289, 290, 291
"lost generation," 121–22
Lost Generation Journal, 121
Louisiana Story, 6, 29, 410–17, 427, 523
"Love Farm," 147
"Love Song" (Thomson), 457
Lowell, Abbott Lawrence, 88
Lowell, Amy, 82, 90
Lowell, Robert, 454, 480
Luce, Henry, 124
Luening, Ethel, 381
Luening, Otto, 379, 380–81, 393, 394, 395, 396–97, 415–16, 442, 444, 506
Luhan, Mabel Dodge, 198, 199, 227
Lupberger, Mary Margaret, 570, 571
Lynes, George Platt, 252

Ma, Yo-Yo, 499
Maar, Dora, 179
Macbeth (Shakespeare), 276–79, 418
McBride, Henry, 258, 259, 261
McBride, Robert, 290
McCarthy, Joseph, 426
McCown, Eugene, 42, 58, 100, 104, 107, 113
McCue, Lillian, 465
McCullough, David, 21, 23
McDaniel, Delia (great-grandmother), 14–16
McDaniel, Kirk, 570
McDaniel, Reuben Ellis (great-grandfather), 14–17, 18, 437, 570, 571
MacDowell, Edward, 31, 36, 48
MacDowell Colony, 488
McKinley, William, 22
Maclanahan, Mrs., 35
MacLeish, Archibald, 258, 275
McLendon, Rose, 275
McWilliams, Peter, 2–3, 4, 10, 547, 565

Mahler, Gustav, 432, 550–51
Mahoney, James, 146, 150
Major Bowes Family Radio Hour, 244
Makers of Opera (Hoover), 441
Making of Americans, The (Stein), 209–10, 235
Malle, Louis, 484
Mangan, John Joseph, 123
Mangan, John Joseph Sherry, 123–25, 143, 211, 294, 303–4, 310, 312, 313–14, 316, 317
Mangan, Marguerite Landin, 294, 303, 304, 313, 316
Mannes, Leopold, 86
Mariés de la Tour Eiffel, Les (Cocteau), 102
Marinoff, Fania, 158
Markus, Boski, 128, 131
Marriage of Figaro, The (Mozart), 340
Marthe-Marthine, Madame, 174, 176, 178
Martin, John, 261
Mason, Daniel Gregory, 79, 183
Massenet, Jules, 67
Massine, Leonide, 139
Masters, Edgar Lee, 51–52, 74–75
Mata Hari, 163
Matthews, Edward, 246, 257, 418, 420
Matthews, Inez, 420, 422
"Maurice Bavoux: Young and Alone" (Thomson), 297
"Maxims of a Modernist" (Thomson), 117–18, 123, 300, 467, 482
Mayer, Arthur, 283
Mayner, Dorothy, 344–45
Mayor La Guardia Waltzes (Thomson), 350
Meadow Park Nursing Home, 3–4
Measure for Measure (Shakespeare), 435, 479
"Meditations of Saint Augustine" (Thomson), 462
Medium, The (Menotti), 380
Meistersinger, Die (Wagner), 166
Mellers, Wilfrid, 25–26
Mellow, James R., 162
Melville, Herman, 82
Mencken, H. L., 66, 181, 297–98
Mendelssohn, Felix, 30
Mennin, Peter, 494–96
Menotti, Gian Carlo, 111, 379–80, 432
Merman, Ethel, 225
Ingram Merrill Foundation, 439
Messiaen, Olivier, 7
Metropolitan Museum of Art, 389, 461, 462
Metropolitan Opera, 60, 183, 340, 352, 395, 400, 423–24, 428, 485–94, 496, 498, 499, 507
Metropolitan Opera Guild, 312
Metropolitan Opera Studio, 486, 490
Milhaud, Darius, 101, 102, 174, 175, 187, 402
Miller, Arthur, 327, 417

Millet, Jean-François, 41, 66
Milnes, Sherrill, 486
Missa pro defunctis (Thomson), 461
"Miss Gertrude Stein as a Young Girl"
    (Thomson), 178
Missouri National Guard, 55, 57–58
"Missouri plainchant," 3
Mitchell, David, 498
Mitchell, J. J., 469, 470–71
Mitchell, William J., 444
Mitropoulos, Dimitri, 397, 410, 423, 435
Mock, Alice, 174
Modern Music, 187–90, 191, 192, 268–69,
    298–303, 318, 333, 368, 402–5
Moe, Henry Allen, 193
Mondrian, Piet, 463–64
Monroe, Marilyn, 452
Monteux, Pierre, 79, 103, 417
Moody, William Vaughan, 199
Moore, Douglas, 378, 379, 380, 391, 393
Moore, Edward C., 93
Mormons, 44, 48, 53, 75–76, 82–83
Morris, Joan, 542
Morrison, Paul, 420
William Morrow, 303, 310
Morton, James P., 567, 568
Moses, Harry, 253–54, 259, 260, 262, 263
Mostly about Love (Thomson), 457, 460
Mother of Us All, The (Thomson), 378–400
    Act 1 of, 391–92
    "All My Long Life" theme from, 542
    Andrew Johnson in, 385
    Angel Moore in, 391
    Anne in, 384, 392
    Anthony Comstock in, 385
    auditions for, 393–95
    black dancers for, 394–95
    Brander Matthews production of, 378–79,
        391–400
    broadcast of, 397
    Broadway production of, 398, 399
    choreography for, 393, 450, 531
    chorus for, 393
    Chris the Citizen in, 385, 386, 391, 392–93,
        397
    conductor for, 396–97
    Constance Fletcher in, 385, 393, 394
    contract for, 386, 387, 391, 399
    costumes for, 397
    Daniel Webster in, 384–85, 391, 394, 450
    diction in, 396, 398, 469, 526
    directors for, 393, 525
    Emerson College production of, ix, 525–26
    epilogue of, 391–92
    Four Saints compared with, 383, 384,
        386–87, 392, 393, 394, 395
    Gertrude S. in, 392
    Grosser's scenario for, 151, 391–92, 433
    Henrietta M. in, 397
    Indiana Elliot in, 385
    Interlude of, 392
    John Adams in, 385, 393, 397
    Jo the Loiterer in, 385, 391, 392–93, 394,
        397, 526
    Lillian Russell in, 385, 450
    open reading of, 506
    political rhetoric in, 382
    premier of, 397–400
    publication of, 395, 396, 417
    recordings of, 397–98, 518–19
    rehearsals for, 395–97, 525–26
    reviews of, 7, 398–99
    Santa Fe Opera production of, 518–19
    set designs for, 397, 518
    Stein's libretto for, 16, 151, 377, 380,
        382–87, 391–93, 395, 396, 398, 399, 456
    Stein's views on, 384
    success of, 453, 502
    Susan B. Anthony in, 383–84, 386, 391,
        392, 394, 395, 397, 400, 450, 459,
        518–19, 525, 567
    Thaddeus Stevens in, 385
    Thomson's music for, 16, 380, 387, 391,
        395, 398, 399, 402, 414
    title of, 384
    Toklas and, 391, 392, 395
    Ulysses S. Grant in, 385, 392
    Virgil T. in, 386, 387, 391, 392, 526
Mourning Becomes Electra (Levy), 486
Mozart, Wolfgang Amadeus, 96–97, 316, 323,
    337, 340, 404, 502
"Mozart's Leftism" (Thomson), 337
"Mrs. Chester Whitin Lasell" (Thomson), 178
Much Ado About Nothing (Shakespeare), 435
Muck, Karl, 80
Munch, Charles, 417
Murphy, Brian, 556, 557
Murray, Francis, 31
Murray, Jane James, 31
Murray, Robert Leigh, 42
    homosexuality of, 32, 38, 43, 68
    Thomson's relationship with, 30–38, 62,
        68, 91
Murrow, Edward R., 278–79
Museum of Modern Art, 219, 222, 223, 312,
    364–66, 428
music:
    "academic," 307
    African American, 182
    American, 98, 133, 175, 182–95, 269,
        270–73, 289, 349, 406, 415, 425, 440,
        518, 563, 564
    appreciation of, 309–10
    atonal, 504–5
    complex vs. simple, 81, 405–6, 504–6
    early, 78–79
    elitism in, 184
    financial aspect of, 304, 306–7

French, 80, 91, 101, 175, 183, 376, 505
Germanic tradition in, 78, 81, 91, 181–83, 192, 324, 351, 505
international style in, 189, 307–8, 311, 404, 405
minimalism in, 506
modern, 175, 181, 182, 183–95, 202, 221, 269, 270–73, 304, 337–39, 340, 364, 366–67, 402–6, 415, 423–24, 441, 443, 447, 449–50, 486, 504–6
popular, 79, 182, 299
post-modern, 526–27
program-note, 133
prosody for, 137, 156, 170, 226–27, 396, 398, 418, 469, 513, 524, 526, 558–59, 564
Russian, 81, 183
serialism in, 504–5, 506
South American, 182
Musical America, 464
Musical Scene, The (Thomson), 376
Music Critics Circle of New York, 342–43, 399
"Music for the Modern World" (Thomson), 263
Music for the Theater (Copland), 80
"Music in Our Changing Society," 370
Music Right and Left (Thomson), 472
Music with Words: A Composer's View (Thomson), 558–59
Mussorgsky, Modest, 102, 181
My Life (Wagner), 37
"My Master Hath a Garden" (Thomson), 462

Nabokov, Nicolas, 258, 427, 432, 493
Nagasaki bombing, 369
Nanook of the North, 410–11
National Book Critics Circle Award, 527
National Symphony, 356, 425, 427
Nazis, 356, 358, 359
Negro Chamber of Commerce, 255, 258
Negro Theater Project, 274–79, 394, 418, 498
Neo-Romantics, 140
Neue Zürcher Zeitung, 501
Nevelson, Louise, 541, 542, 543
"Never Alone" (Thomson), 517
New Criterion, 564
New Deal, 263, 281, 283, 284, 287, 320
Newell, Gertrude, 317
New England Conservatory, 183
New Friends of Music, 345
New Grove Dictionary of American Music, 556
New Jersey Symphony Orchestra, 347
New School for Social Research, 366–67
"New Standard for Glee Clubs, A" (Davison), 78
New World Records, 518

New York City Ballet, 239, 427, 431
New York City Opera, 10
New York *Daily Mirror,* 360
New York *Daily News,* 319
New Yorker, 200
New York Evening Post, 200
New York Herald Tribune, 188, 200, 257, 267, 283
  music division of, 322–25, 350, 353–54, 424–25
  as newspaper, 319–22
  Thomson's criticism in, 318, 323–429, 430, 432, 568
New York *Journal-American,* 319
New York *Mirror,* 319
New York Morning Telegraph, 200
New York Philharmonic, 60, 156, 230, 328–30, 332–33, 335, 340, 344, 346, 347–48, 362, 375, 406–10, 423, 435
New York Post, 319, 358, 359, 360
New York Repertory Company, 533–35
New York Sun, 200, 319
New York Symphony Society, 183, 188–89
New York Times, 8, 65, 130, 188, 199, 278, 319–20, 360, 411, 416, 462–63, 485, 507, 544, 546, 550, 555, 562–63, 568
New York University, 514–15
New York World, 200
New York *World-Telegram,* 319
Nietzsche, Friedrich, 37, 50, 51, 56
Nine O'Clock Opera Company, 340
North Easton Church, 87, 89, 92
Novaës, Guiomar, 435
Nude Descending a Staircase (Duchamp), 229

Occult Review, 84
Odell, Marvin, 570
Ohana, Maurice, 507
O'Hara, Frank, 454, 469–72, 477, 483, 567
Oja, Carol, 530–31
Olefsky, Paul, 419
Olivier, Fernande, 151
Olivieri, Anthony, 439–40
Olivieri, Phyllis, 439–40
129th Artillery Division, U.S., 58, 60, 61, 62
opera, 227, 261–62, 487, 491, 496, 501, 534–35
Opera Ensemble of New York, 1–12, 536, 539, 541
Oraison funèbre de Henriette-Marie de France reine de la Grande-Bretagne (Thomson), 167, 203–4, 213
Orators, The (Auden), 239
Orchestra of Our Time, 527
Orlando Furioso (Ariosto), 454
Ormandy, Eugene, 336, 346, 376, 397, 408, 413, 414, 419

Oud, J.J.P., 222
Our New Music (Copland), 204
Overseas Press Club, 462–63

Paderewski, Ignace, 32, 33, 36, 41, 66, 67
Paepcke, Walter, 465
Pagany, 143, 211
Page, Ruth, 290
Page, Tim, 549–51, 561, 566
Page, Vanessa Weeks, 550
Paine, John Knowles, 91
Painter's Eye, The (Grosser), 463
Painting in Public (Grosser), 463
Paley, William, 343
Panic (MacLeish), 275
Pans, 49–50
Pansophists, 49–52, 89
Paper Chase, The, 534
Paramount Studios, 287
Paris Diary, The (Rorem), 475
Parker, Dorothy, 260
Parker, Henry Taylor, 102, 103, 265–66
Parker, Horatio, 191
Parsifal (Wagner), 30
Parsons, Geoffrey, 318, 323, 324, 325, 328,
    348, 351, 356, 357, 427, 428
  Thomson's criticism as viewed by, 329,
    332–34, 338–39, 341–42, 344, 361
Parson Weems and the Cherry Tree
    (Thomson), 513
Passacaglia (Copland), 184
Joseph Patelson's, 425
Paul Bunyan (Britten), 379
Payne, Oliver, 92
Pazmor, Radiana, 194
Peabody Conservatory, 513
Peanuts (Schulz), 177
Pelléas et Mélisande (Debussy), 95
Pelton, Carmen, 566–67, 568
Pendergast, James, 66
Pendergast, Tom, 66, 67
People's Music League, 184–85
Perkins, Francis D., 322, 324, 346–47, 350,
    354, 368, 398–99, 401
Perkins, Helvetia, 354
Perkins, Minnie, 45, 47
Perry, Edward, 243, 244, 245, 246, 247, 250
Pershing, John J., 58
Pétain, Henri Philippe, 388
Peter Grimes (Britten), 379, 394
Peters, Roberta, 450
Petit Parisien, 95
Petrides, Frédérique, 339
Petrov, Basil, 432
Philadelphia Orchestra, 255, 336, 343, 344,
    346, 376, 413, 414, 419
Phillips, George, 42, 58, 59, 61, 62, 116
Phillips, Montague, 36

Piano Sonata no. 1 (Thomson), 202–3
Piano Sonata no. 6, in F major (Beethoven),
    419
Piano Sonata no. 2 (Sessions), 405–6
Piano Sonata no. 2 (Thomson), 203, 566
Picasso, Pablo, 44, 134, 135, 139, 151, 159,
    165, 179, 199, 210, 221, 227, 238, 304,
    314, 317, 381, 389, 474
Pidgeon, Walter, 425
Pigeons on the Grass Alas (Thomson), 568
Pint, Anthony, 420
Piston, Walter, 80, 190
  background of, 270
  as composer, 130, 192, 194, 270, 416
  Thomson's relationship with, 86–87, 416
Plow That Broke the Plains, The, 29, 280–84,
    290, 295, 346, 347, 348–49, 542, 566, 570
Pocahontas (Carter), 291
Poems of Love and the Rain (Rorem), 478
Poiret, Paul, 148
Poole, Leland Stanford, 63, 71–73, 75, 76,
    85–86, 87, 100, 105, 106, 325–27, 474
Porgy and Bess (Gershwin), 262, 265, 276,
    301–2, 422, 461
Porter, Andrew, 7, 11–12, 527, 534
Porter, Cole, 225
Porter, Katherine Anne, 381
Porter, Quincy, 415
"Portrait of Señorita Juanita de Medina
    Accompanied by Her Mother"
    (Thomson), 178
Post, Lillie (aunt), 29
Poulenc, Francis, 96, 101, 474
Pound, Ezra, 128, 129, 133, 231, 237
Powell, Adam Clayton, Jr., 226
Powell, William, 40
"Praise Him Who Makes Us Happy," 568
Praises and Prayers (Thomson), 462–63, 567
"Prayer to St. Catherine, A" (Thomson), 457,
    566
Prayer to Venus, A (Thomson), 522
"Preciosilla" (Thomson), 156, 476
Prelude for Piano (Thomson), 101
"prepared piano," 366, 367
Preston, Roger, 434
Price, Leontyne, 420–21, 422, 486
Price Greenleaf Aid, 88
Prohibition, 77, 220, 321
Pryor, Arthur, 30
Psycho, 272
Purcell, Henry, 507

Quintet for Wind Instruments (Schoenberg),
    191

Racine, Jean Baptiste, 213, 346–47
radio, 313, 330, 397, 513

Radio City Music Hall, 428
Rainsburg, Ross, 57
Rake's Progress, The (Stravinsky), 424
Rathbone, Basil, 275
Ravel, Maurice, 80, 91, 95, 127, 130, 352, 462
Ray, Man, 317
Reagan, Ronald, 532
Red Pony, The (Copland), 417
Reed, Donald, 570, 571
Reedy's Mirror, 51
Reese, Gustave, 512
Reeves, George, 478
Refice, Licinio, 7
Rehoboth Cemetery, 570–72
Reid, Elizabeth Mills, 320
Reid, Helen Rogers, 320, 324–25, 351, 428
Reid, Ogden, 320, 321, 351
Reid, Whitelaw, 320
Reiner, Ethel Linder, 420
Reiner, Fritz, 420
Reis, Arthur M., 184
Reis, Claire Raphael, 184–90, 192–93
Rendezvous, Les, 249
"rent parties," 225
Requiem (Berlioz), 185
Resettlement Administration, U.S., 280, 284
Restaurant Michaud, 167
Reuter, Paul, 532
Reynolds, Debbie, 477
Rheingold, Das (Wagner), 491
Rhenish Symphony (Schumann), 423
Rhodes, Nancy, 533
Rhodes Scholarship, 88–90
Rhodes, Willard, 393
Ribicoff, Abraham, 120
Rich, Alan, 501, 519
Richter, Jean-Paul, 404
Riefenstahl, Leni, 288
Rispoli, Louis, 1–6, 10, 530, 533, 535–40, 541, 544, 545, 547, 559, 560, 562
Rite of Spring, The (Stravinsky), 259, 373
River, The, 284–88, 290
Rivers, Larry, 454, 469, 472
Robbins, Jerome, 291
Rockefeller Foundation, 490, 518
Rockwell, John, 7, 8, 506, 526–27, 562–63
Rodakiewicz, Henwar, 119, 146–47
Rodzinski, Arthur, 346, 406–10
Romeo and Juliet (Shakespeare), 275
Roosevelt, Eleanor, 350
Roosevelt, Franklin D., 263, 273–74, 280, 283, 284, 285, 288, 320, 359, 376
Roosevelt, Theodore, 22, 56–57
Roosevelt Year: 1933, The (Lorentz), 280
Rorem, C. Rufus, 370, 371, 373–74
Rorem, Gladys, 370
Rorem, Ned, 8, 70–71, 120, 370, 454, 460, 469, 475, 478, 479, 497, 520, 567

background of, 363
Thomson as viewed by, 149, 371, 372, 373, 374, 502–3, 516
as Thomson's copyist, 370, 371–72, 373, 374, 375
Thomson's music as viewed by, 502–3
Thomson's relationship with, 370–75, 475, 502–3
Rosenfeld, Paul, 184, 185
Rosenthal, Manuel, 464
Ross, Robert, 68
Rothstein, Edward, 551
Rowe, Bertram, 394, 396
Rubenstein, Anton, 177
Ruffo, Tito, 67
Ruggles, Carl, 186
Run-Through (Houseman), 498
Rutenberg, Craig, 517, 528, 542, 543, 562, 565, 566
Ryan, John, 491, 493
Ryle, Herbert E., 490

Sacco and Vanzetti (Blitzstein), 486, 493–94
Sachs, Paul, 219, 220, 240
St. Philip's Church, 247, 253
"Saints Procession" (Thomson), 198
Salle d'Orgue, 174
Salomé (Wilde), 60
Salón México, El (Copland), 291
Salzedo, Carlos, 185
Samuel, Gerhard, 495, 499, 500, 519
Samuel, Harold, 516, 558
Sanfaçon, Paul, 4, 5, 8, 509–12, 537, 543–44, 545, 552, 559–60
Santa Fe Opera, 518–19
Sartain, Geraldine, 253
Sartre, Jean Paul, 139
Satie, Erik, 81, 82, 101, 116, 127, 153, 158, 159, 175, 204, 205, 210, 368, 372–73, 508, 566
Sauguet, Henri, 175, 176, 178, 311, 314
"Sauguet: From Life" (Thomson), 178
Scalero, Rosario, 111, 370
Schippers, Thomas, 432
Schneider, Alexander, 463
Schoenberg, Arnold, 80, 82, 127, 130, 182, 187, 191, 364, 366–67, 368, 474, 505
Schoettle, Gustav, 33
Schonberg, Harold C., 499, 501, 502, 508
School of American Ballet, 239
School of Military Aeronautics, 55, 59–60
Schopenhauer, Arthur, 50
Schubert, Franz, 31, 36, 48, 428, 462
Schultz, Jennie, 34
Schulz, Charles M., 177
Schuman, William, 415
Schumann, Robert, 177, 348, 351, 374, 404, 423

Schweitzer, Albert, 96
Scown, Kim, 566
"Sea Coast" (Thomson), 220
Sea Pieces (MacDowell), 36, 48
Sea Piece with Birds (Thomson), 419
Sears, Clarence, 34, 35
Seattle Symphony, 346
Second Symphony (Mahler), 550–51
Seine, La (Thomson), 212
Seine at Night, The (Thomson), 419
Seldes, Gilbert, 268
Sessions, Roger, 130, 137, 190
  as composer, 191, 194, 270, 271, 405–6
  Copland and, 191–95, 200–201
  Thomson as viewed by, 268–69
  Thomson's relationship with, 191–92, 338, 367, 527
  Thomson's views on, 405–6
Severns, Scott, 464
Shaffer, Elaine, 434
Shakespeare, William, 13, 275, 276–80, 288, 340, 370, 418, 435, 476, 479
Shakespeare and Company, 128–29, 135–36
Shakespeare Songs (Thomson), 566
Shaw, Anna Howard, 384
Shaw, Wallace, 166–67
Sheehan, John, 8, 11, 12
Sheridan Square Theater, 185
Sherman, Emily, 92
Shicoff, Neil, 497, 566, 568
Show Piece, 290
Sibelius, Jean, 82, 95, 329, 330, 332–33, 335, 336, 347
Silva, Luigi, 111, 419
Simon, Robert A., 398
Sinatra, Frank, 7, 532
Sitwell, Edith, 209
Six, Les, 81, 100, 101, 102, 153, 176
60 Minute Chef, The (Truax and McCue), 465
slavery, 14, 15, 18, 384, 570
Smallens, Alexander, 227–28, 234, 254, 255, 256, 257, 262, 282, 287, 316–17, 323, 324, 397, 422
Smith, Alice, 44–54, 59, 60, 63, 63, 75, 443–44, 474
Smith, Frederick Madison, 44, 48–49, 53, 61, 75–76, 82–84
Smith, Joseph, 44
Smith, Joseph, Jr., 44
Smith, Melville, 87, 91, 94, 98
Smith, Milton, 378–79, 380, 393
Smith, Patrick J., 501–2
Smith, Peter, 171
Smith College, 191, 194
Société des Droits d'Auteurs, 232
Société Musicale Indépendante, 130
Socrate (Satie), 158, 204, 205, 368, 372–73

"Something of a Beauty" (Thomson), 528
Sonata da chiesa (Thomson), 116, 130–31, 132, 153, 174, 192, 201, 269
Sonata for Violin and Piano (Thomson), 203, 271
Soullière, Anne-Marie, 516, 528, 543
Sousa, John Philip, 22, 30
South Boston School of Art, 145–46
Southern Harmony, The, 286
Sowerby, Leo, 416
Spalding, Walter R., 78, 80, 91, 107–8
spirituals, 285–86
Spoils of Poynton, The (James), 485
Spoon River Anthology (Masters), 51–52, 74–75
Stabat Mater (Thomson), 230, 272, 374, 566
Stagehands Union, 276
Standard Oil Company of New Jersey, 411–12, 436
Stanley, Kim, 452
Stanton, Elizabeth Cady, 383
Stapleton, Maureen, 497, 498
"Star-Spangled Banner, The," 329–30
State of Music, The (Thomson), 302–12, 318, 368, 374, 463
Stein, Allan, 389, 484
Stein, Gertrude:
  art as interest of, 135, 140–41
  Bowles and, 292–93
  death of, 389–90
  estate of, 389, 391
  film scenario by, 210, 212, 213
  Four Saints as viewed by, 171–72, 205–6, 208–9, 230–36, 263, 390
  Four Saints libretto of, 3, 11, 12, 151–63, 168, 172, 173, 199, 202, 205–6, 208–9, 227, 251–52, 253, 257, 258, 259, 261, 262, 264, 376, 421, 422, 507
  at Harvard, 135, 177, 199
  ill health of, 387–90
  literary portraits by, 177–78, 197, 210
  "lost generation" and, 121
  Mother as viewed by, 384
  Mother libretto of, 16, 151, 377, 380, 382–87, 391–93, 395, 396, 398, 399, 456
  papers of, 387–88, 389, 400, 516
  Paris residence of, 134–35, 381–82
  Thomson's collaboration with, 7, 82, 139, 151, 205–6, 216, 217, 230–36, 268, 377, 390, 399, 400, 406, 453, 457, 458, 480, 487
  Thomson's estrangement from, 209–17, 230–31, 235–36, 548–49
  Thomson's first meeting with, 134–38
  Thomson's musical portrait of, 178
  Thomson's relationship with, 134–38, 141, 150–51, 159, 165–66, 167, 173–74, 197, 204–17, 265, 284, 301, 314, 372, 390, 474

Thomson's settings of short pieces by, 116, 137–38, 156–59

Toklas's relationship with, 134, 135, 150–51, 158–59, 161, 199, 209, 216–17, 381–82, 388–90, 392

U.S. lecture tour of, 216, 264–65

will of, 389

as writer, 82, 135–36, 146, 157, 163, 177–78, 209–17, 235, 242, 253, 259, 266, 381, 389, 449, 454, 456, 476, 533, 565

Stein, Leo, 134

Stein, Michael, 389

Steinbeck, John, 417

Steinberg, William, 414

Stein Collection, 516

Steiner, Ralph, 280

Stettheimer, Carrie, 229

Stettheimer, Ettie, 228, 255

Stettheimer, Florine, 11, 198–99, 228–29, 231, 234, 243, 249, 252, 254, 255, 257, 259, 260, 301, 420, 566

Stettheimer, Walter, 228

Stevens, Wallace, 259

Stevenson, Adlai (grandfather), 22

Stevenson, Adlai (grandson), 426

Stewart, James, 531

Stich, Teresa, 397, 400

Charles Stieff, 76–77

Stinson, Allan, 540–41, 546–49, 551, 552, 553–55, 558–59, 564

Stokowski, Leopold, 227, 336, 407

Story, 236

Stouffer, Elizabeth (niece), 88, 533, 562, 570

Strand, Paul, 281

Stransky, Josef, 60

Straus, Noel, 365

Strauss, Richard, 77, 182, 228, 347, 441, 502

Stravinsky, Igor, 1, 80, 91, 102, 116, 126, 127, 129, 130, 140, 153, 181, 187, 189, 192, 259, 352, 373, 402, 424, 502, 504–5, 527

Stream of History, The (Parsons), 323

String Quartet no. 2 (Thomson), 203, 230, 372, 496, 532

Suite from *Louisiana Story* (Thomson), 414–17, 427

Suite from *The Plow That Broke the Plains* (Thomson), 542

Sullivan, Jay, 552–55, 557–58, 560–61, 562, 564, 566, 567, 568, 569, 571–72

Sullivan Auditorium, 264–65

Summit Books, 549

"Sun Flower" (Thomson), 90

surrealism, 126, 221

"Susie Asado" (Thomson), 136–38, 156, 272

Sutherland, Donald, 162, 484

Symphony for Organ and Orchestra (Copland), 188–89, 193

Symphony Hall, 79

Symphony no. 1 (Harris), 270

Symphony no. 2 (Sibelius), 329, 330, 335, 336

Symphony no. 2 (Thomson), 202–3, 342, 346, 347, 423

Symphony no. 3 (Piston), 416

Symphony no. 3 ('The Camp Meeting') (Ives), 416

Symphony no. 3 (Thomson), 203

Symphony on a Hymn Tune (Thomson), 7, 29, 154, 155–56, 176, 195, 196–97, 201, 202, 203, 286, 291, 375–76, 408, 414, 416, 556

Synchronisms no. 6 for Piano and Elecronic Sound (Davidovsky), 506

Synthetic Waltzes (Thomson), 116, 566

Szell, George, 362, 417

Tamalpa Institute, 553, 555, 559

Tannhäuser (Wagner), 30, 400

Tanning, Dorothea, 414

Taras, John, 393, 394, 395

Taubman, Howard, 311, 426

Taylor, Alfred, 65

Tchaikovsky, Piotr Ilyich, 7

Tchelitcheff, Choura, 204

Tchelitcheff, Pavel, 140–41, 150, 204–5, 431, 438

Tender Buttons (Stein), 82, 136, 456

Ten Etudes for Piano (Thomson), 542

Tenor Lead (Madrigal) (Thomson), 29

Ter-Arutunian, Rouben, 11, 12

Terry, Walter, 322

Texaco Opera Quiz, 7

Thomas, Edna, 244, 276

Thome, Joel, 527

Thompson, Dorothy, 350

Thompson, Oscar, 343, 375

Thompson, Randall, 80, 86, 190

Thomson, Asa (great-great-grandfather), 13

Thomson, Clara May Gaines (mother), 18–21, 23, 24, 25, 29, 32, 33, 91–92, 264, 367, 436–37, 561, 570

Thomson, Flora Elizabeth (grandmother), 17–18, 24, 76, 570

Thomson, Hazel Louise (sister), 20, 570

Thomson, Leona (aunt), 18, 21, 34, 570

Thomson, Quincy Adams (grandfather), 17, 570

Thomson, Quincy Alfred (father), 17, 18–21, 23, 24, 32–33, 57, 62, 91–92, 127, 264, 325, 361–62, 437, 570

Thomson, Reuben (uncle), 18

Thomson, Reuben Yancey (great-grandfather), 18

Thomson, Ruby Richerson (sister), 19, 20, 25, 28, 29–30, 79, 87–88, 327, 436, 466–67, 512–13, 551, 560, 562, 570

Thomson, Samuel, 13–14

Thomson, Virgil Garnett:
  acting by, 40, 482–83
  ancestry of, 13–21, 570, 571
  anti-Semitism accusation against, 46,
    300–301, 302
  apolitical nature of, 191, 283, 304, 313–15,
    362, 425–27, 463
  arrest of, 356–57, 548
  art owned by, 165, 166–67, 566
  author's meetings with, ix–xi, 524–26,
    528–35, 542, 548–49, 557
  in auto accident, 557
  autobiography of, 21, 25–27, 57, 70, 76,
    143, 144, 265, 436, 472–75, 478–79, 483,
    485, 550
  Baptist background of, 14, 19, 30, 34–35,
    155, 297–98, 570, 571
  biography of, ix–xi, 36, 45–46, 53, 98, 132,
    143–44, 153, 154, 268–69, 441–46, 473,
    550
  David Bispham Medal awarded to, 264
  Chanterelle dinner for, 538–39, 541–43
  Chelsea Hotel apartment of, x, 1, 6, 25, 41,
    141, 156, 327–28, 468, 513–14, 515, 517,
    533
  childhood of, 23–27, 39–40
  as choir director, 87, 89, 92
  clothing of, 79, 167
  composers as viewed by, 305–7, 311,
    352
  as conductor, 96, 108, 111, 262, 346, 401,
    408, 422, 427–28, 432, 434
  conductors as viewed by, 307, 308,
    331–32, 340, 406–10, 423
  in Corfu, 520–22
  correspondence of, 37–38, 58–60, 111–18,
    124–25, 142, 151, 351–52, 514, 515, 516,
    546, 549–51, 555
  counterpoint studied by, 98, 99, 100, 107,
    108, 153
  creativity of, 179–80
  culinary skills of, 48, 451
  death of, 546, 560–62
  debating by, 51
  depressions of, 125–26
  diary of, 94, 96
  documentary film about, 523, 549, 567
  education of, 6, 24, 32, 39–54, 74–92
  egotism of, 4–6, 8, 47–48, 430, 440–41
  estate of, 564–65
  as expatriate, 121–22, 269, 284
  financial situation of, 75–76, 79, 88, 106,
    126, 127, 138, 152, 164, 173–74, 176,
    204, 222, 223, 317, 325, 326, 372, 436,
    437, 565
  as Francophile, 105, 324, 340, 402
  French spoken by, 77, 94, 110, 251
  friendships of, 70, 123, 139–44, 202, 209,
    291–95, 543, 561–62

  "frustration grippe" of, 213–14, 216
  funeral of, 561, 569–72
  generosity of, 9, 326–27, 451, 484
  in Germany, 96
  gravesite of, 562, 569, 571–72
  harmony studied by, 33, 78, 98, 107, 111,
    153
  hearing problems of, 471, 496–97, 513,
    517, 519
  homosexuality of, x, xi, 42, 47, 64–73, 86,
    110–12, 120, 143, 144, 146, 148–49, 151,
    225, 229–30, 231, 294, 315, 353–62,
    432–33, 452, 467–69, 470, 474–75, 509,
    517–18, 528, 549, 557–58
  honorary degrees of, 513
  ill health of, 551–52, 554–55, 560–61
  insecurity of, 24, 27, 73, 85
  as intellectual, 27, 35, 36, 45, 47–53, 85,
    123, 149, 192, 202, 230
  interviews of, 523, 525, 530, 531, 561
  investments of, 436, 565
  isolation of, 122–23, 452
  in Italy, 96, 98, 520, 521
  Kansas City as hometown of, 6, 21–23,
    33, 64–67, 69, 74–75, 122, 226, 473,
    474
  Kansas City visited by, 198, 263
  at Kennedy Center Honors, 7, 531–32
  in Lamoura, 297
  lecturing by, 434–35, 513
  literary efforts of, 40–41, 54
  in London, 376, 377
  memorial service for, 561–62, 566–68
  military service of, 48, 54, 55–63, 71–73,
    89, 92, 362, 446–47, 547
  Missouri background of, 2, 3, 6, 21–23, 75,
    571
  at Montecatini, 520, 521
  in Moumour, 317
  name of, 20, 36
  in New York, 60–62, 71–72, 92, 198–201,
    223, 240, 269–70, 291, 317–77,
    391–562
  nickname of, 60
  obituaries of, 546, 562–64
  orchestration studied by, 81, 374, 419,
    496
  as organist, 34–35, 37, 57, 63, 77, 87, 89,
    92, 105–6, 107, 164, 497
  at Oxford, 97
  in Pacific Street raid, 355–61, 548
  painters as viewed by, 306–7, 314
  papers of, 513–16, 530, 548–51
  Paris residence of, 6, 26, 37, 70, 71, 75, 91,
    92, 93–105, 107, 115, 116, 118, 121–95,
    202–23, 264, 269, 283–84, 291, 295,
    296–318, 376–91, 432, 509
  patrons of, 131–33, 165–66, 173–74, 209,
    212, 237–38, 304, 308, 519–20

personality of, x, 6, 149, 241, 530, 545, 546–47, 553, 560

personal philosophy of, 49–51, 56, 117–18, 123, 300, 467, 482

peyote taken by, 82–84

physical appearance of, 23–24, 104, 303, 327

as pianist, 24, 25, 28–30, 31, 33–37, 39, 40, 57, 76–77, 98–100, 125, 316, 323, 462–63, 497

Pulitzer Prize awarded to, 6, 280, 415–17

quai Voltaire apartment of, 165–68, 223, 269, 296–97, 303, 317, 377, 432, 509, 520

"queer couples" as viewed by, 225, 293–94, 354–55, 539, 541

racism accusation against, 76, 226, 227, 251, 344, 547

radio broadcasts by, 513

reputation of, 6–8, 267, 356–57, 371, 425, 558–59

rue de Berne room of, 100, 126, 152

rue Jacob room of, 163

St. Cloud apartment of, 147–48, 152, 377

scholarships awarded to, 75–76, 88, 100, 108, 111, 269

secretaries of, 1–6, 514–15, 535–41, 546–49, 551, 552–55, 557–58, 560–61, 562, 564

as singer, 31, 79, 87, 89, 91, 92, 93–97, 102, 105, 123

as Southerner, 14, 15, 19, 21

spinal disc injury of, 518

Stettheimer's portrait of, 229

in Switzerland, 97–98

teaching residencies of, 506–7

U.S. visited by, 180, 195, 196–202, 223–30, 240–64, 295, 315–77

vegetarianism of, 48

will of, 564, 565

women friends of, 70, 92, 141–44, 315–16, 354–57, 447, 464–68, 474–75, 512, 528

work habits of, 150, 179, 329, 523, 546

Thomson, Virgil Garnett, criticism by:

breadth of, 339–40, 352

collections of, 376, 472, 473, 526–27

conflict of interest in, xi, 323–24, 345–49, 406, 412

debut column of, 328–34

early efforts in, 102–4, 110, 125, 126–27, 134, 152, 297–312

in *Herald Tribune*, 318, 323–429, 430, 432, 568

influence of, xi, 6, 98, 134, 156, 175, 311–12, 339, 343, 345–49, 352, 368, 371, 372, 376, 381, 393–94, 401–2, 422, 423, 425, 427, 429, 434, 442, 472, 503, 564

"island home" concept in, 305–6

in *Modern Music*, 298–303, 318, 404

modern music supported in, 184, 190, 304, 337–39, 340, 366–67, 402–6, 423–24, 441, 449–50

Parson's views on, 329, 332–34, 338–39, 341–42, 344, 361

partisanship in, 324, 345–49

performances reviewed in, xi, 328–46, 379, 380

praise in, 339, 352

promoters attacked in, 339–40, 341, 343–45, 347–48, 406–10, 423–24, 486

reader response to, 342, 351–52

slang used in, 341–42, 345, 361

style of, 27, 104, 324, 329, 332–36, 423

Thomson, Virgil Garnett, works of:

ballet scores in, 288–90

choral works in, 90, 101

commissions for, 34, 201, 349–50, 380–81, 418–19, 485–94, 559

early efforts in, 37, 48, 54, 74, 90, 101–2, 111, 116, 122, 192

film scores in, 6, 29, 180, 280–88, 295, 410–17, 418, 452, 460

influence of, 7, 290, 506, 527, 563, 564

influences on, 28–33, 35, 153–54, 155

musical landscapes in, 419

musical portraits in, ix, 29, 139, 176–80, 210, 220, 297, 316–17, 348, 349–50, 376, 433–34, 435, 513, 517, 522, 528–30, 532, 536, 539, 542, 546, 555–56, 559, 566

organ works in, 34, 101–2, 154–55, 566, 568

performances of, 130–31, 174–76, 191–92, 204, 230, 303, 345–49, 363, 375, 408, 414, 417, 419–20, 423, 427, 434, 435, 461–63, 506–7, 516, 542, 556–57, 563, 565, 566–67, 568

piano pieces in, 101, 179, 202–3, 565, 566

prosody in, 156, 170, 513, 524, 558, 564

publication of, 212–13, 272, 395

recordings of, 376, 413, 419, 463, 565, 567

reviews of, 6, 130, 156, 174–75, 191–92, 194, 200, 201–2, 267–69, 271, 342, 345–49, 350, 375–76, 398–99, 413, 414–17, 419, 435, 462–63, 473

simplicity of, 6, 11, 175, 290, 311, 350, 398, 405–6, 453, 502, 504–6, 563

songs in, 6–7, 90, 291, 380–81, 419, 447, 457, 460, 461–63, 566, 568

style of, 6, 11, 152–54, 301

tangos in, 99, 101, 116

theater music in, 180, 275–80, 297, 435, 436, 460, 479

vocal works in, 90, 101, 212–13, 214, 461–63

see also individual works

Thomson, Will (uncle), 24

Thomson, William, 13

Virgil Thomson Collection, 37, 375, 514–17

Virgil Thomson Foundation, 565–66, 567, 569, 570
Virgil Thomson Room, 515
Thorne, Francis, 566
"Those Endearing Young Charms," 489
Thoughts at Sunset, 244
Three Pictures for Orchestra (Thomson), 419, 427
Time, 124, 200, 287, 303, 304, 407, 428
Times Literary Supplement, 448–49
Toklas, Alice B.:
  Bowles and, 292–93
  death of, 485
  Four Saints and, 171–72, 422
  Larson's visit with, 484–85
  Mother and, 391, 392, 395
  Stein's relationship with, 134, 135, 150–51, 158–59, 161, 199, 209, 216–17, 381–82, 388–90, 392
  Thomson's relationship with, 204–17, 265, 284, 372, 460, 474, 483–85
Tonny, Kristians, 140, 150, 217
"Tony Tommasini: A Study in Chords" (Thomson), 529
Toscanini, Arturo, 260, 312, 314, 329, 340, 343, 352, 400, 406, 407
Edith Totten Theater, 194
Touraine, La, 93–94
transition, 205
Tremont Street Methodist Church, 77
Tristan und Isolde (Wagner), x
Trotsky, Leon, 304
Truax, Carol, 464–65, 466, 511–12
Truax, Charles Henry, 464, 465
Truman, Harry S., 22, 28, 56, 58, 376
Truman, John, 22
Tuesday in November, 418
Tugwell, Rexford Guy, 280, 284–85
Twain, Mark, 349, 454
Twelfth Night (Shakespeare), 340
twelve-tone system, 504–5, 506
Twentieth Century Exposition of the Arts, 421–22
"Two Birds" (Thomson), 555–56
Tzara, Tristan, 171

Ulanowski, Paul, 462
Ulysses (Joyce), 128, 136
Unfinished Business (Houseman), 555

Valse grégorienne (Hugnet), 213
Van Dutton, Vernon, 394–95
Van Dyke, Willard, 285
Vanessa (Barber), 486
Vanity Fair, 126–27, 297
Van Vechten, Carl, 9, 158, 171, 198, 199, 209, 212, 217, 220, 221, 225, 227, 228, 231, 243–44, 255, 259, 265, 339, 382, 387, 389, 390, 480
Varèse, Edgar, 185–86, 366
Variations and Fugues on American Hymns (Thomson), 174
Variations on Sunday School Tunes (Thomson), 154–55
Variety, 398, 399
Vaughan Williams, Ralph, 330, 331
"Velvet Paws" (Thomson), 336
Venice Film Festival, 287
Verdi, Giuseppe, 30, 67, 495, 498, 534
"Vernal Equinox" (Thomson), 90
Vidal, Gore, 469, 480
Vidor, King, 244
Villon, François, 128
"Virgil Thomson" (Stein), 197, 210
Virgil Thomson (Thomson), 21, 25–27, 57, 70, 76, 143, 144, 265, 436, 472–75, 478–79, 483, 485, 550
Virgil Thomson: His Life and Music (Hoover and Cage), ix–xi, 36, 45–46, 53, 98, 132, 143–44, 153, 154, 268–69, 441–45, 473, 550
Virgil Thomson at Ninety, 523, 549, 567
"Virgil Thomson in Time," 556–57
Virgil Thomson Reader, A (Rockwell, ed.), 526–27
Voice of Firestone, 450

Wadsworth Atheneum, 10, 172, 217, 218–59, 263, 421, 532
Wagner, Richard, x, 30, 37, 166, 183, 330, 400, 404, 491, 493
Walküre, Die (Wagner), 493
Wallenstein, Alfred, 397, 415, 495
Walsh, David Ignatius, 358–61
Walsh, Raoul, 477
Walter, Bruno, 410
Waltuck, David, 539, 541, 542, 543
Waltuck, Karen Brown, 539, 541, 543
Warburg, Edward, 240
Warfield, William, 466, 568
Warner Brothers, 477
Warren, Robert Penn, 480
Warren Symphony, 556–57
Warrior's Husband, The, 253
"War's End, A" (Thomson), 403–5
Washington, George, 160, 349, 382, 513
Waste Land, The (Eliot), 239
"Was This Fair Face the Cause" (Thomson), 568
Watson, Sibley, 164, 168
Watts, Richard, 398
Wayne, Beatrice Robinson, 1–12, 247–49, 256–57, 262, 265, 418, 420, 536, 541, 565
Wayne, Ivanhoe, 8–9, 247

Webb, Chick, 247
Webb School, 144, 145
Weber, Karl Maria von, 347, 404
Webster, Beveridge, 417
Webster, John, 297
Weinreich, Regina, 531
Weinstock, Herbert, 356–57, 445, 473, 474
Weissberger, Arnold, 391, 446, 487, 497, 508–9
Welles, Orson, 275–79, 297, 474
Wertheim, Alma, 137, 186, 198, 199
What to Listen for in Music (Copland),
    309–12
Wheat Field at Noon (Thomson), 419, 570
Wheeler, Margaret, 546
Wheeler, Scott, 524, 528, 532–33, 542, 544,
    546
Wheelwright, Louise, 84–85
White Spirituals in the Southern Uplands
    (Pullen), 286
Whitfield, Irene Therese, 412
Whitman, Walt, 349
Whitney, John Hay, 320
"Wide-Awake" (Thomson), 528
Wilde, Oscar, 41, 42, 51, 60, 64–66, 68–69,
    71, 90, 117, 166, 385
William Blake: His Philosophy and Symbols
    (Damon), 81
Williams, Tennessee, 432
Willkie, Wendell, 328
Wilson, Robert, 7, 10, 527–28
Wilson, Woodrow, 55

Wincenc, Carol, 499
Winchell, Walter, 319, 360
Windham, Olivia, 244
Winger, Debra, 534
WNCN, 513
WNYC, 397, 534
Wolfe, Thomas, 168
Works Progress Administration (WPA), 274,,
    275, 279, 290
World War I, 43–44, 48, 54, 55–63, 71–73, 91,
    92, 135, 204, 362
World War II, 362, 376–77, 382, 416
Wright, John, 522
Wright, Richard, 276, 387
Wummer, John, 435

Yaddo artist colony, 272
Yale University, 119–20, 387–88, 389, 507,
    516, 548, 550
Yankee Clipper (Bowles), 290, 291
"Yes, Jesus Loves Me," 29, 155, 286
Yoseloff, Thomas, 446
Young, Brigham, 44
Young Composers' Concerts, 188
Young Composers Group, 272, 402

Zatkin, Nathan, 252–53
Zimmerman, Philip, 541
Zinsser, William, xi, 321, 322